28	FRANCIS BACON	43	HEGEL	56	POINCARÉ
	DESCARTES		KIERKEGAARD		PLANCK
	SPINOZA		NIETZSCHE		WHITEHEAD
					EINSTEIN
29	MILTON	44	TOCQUEVILLE		EDDINGTON
					BOHR
30	PASCAL	45	GOETHE		HARDY
			BALZAC		HEISENBERG
31	MOLIÈRE				SCHRÖDINGER
	RACINE	46	AUSTEN		DOBZHANSKY
			GEORGE ELIOT		WADDINGTON
32	NEWTON				
	HUYGENS	47	DICKENS	57	VEBLEN
					TAWNEY
33	LOCKE	48	MELVILLE		KEYNES
	BERKELEY		TWAIN		
	HUME			58	FRAZER
		49	DARW...		WEBER
34	SWIFT				HUIZINGA
	VOLTAIRE				LÉVI-STRAUSS
	DIDEROT				
				59	HENRY JAMES
35	MONTESQUIE...		...STOEVSKY		SHAW
	ROUSSEAU		IBSEN		CONRAD
					CHEKHOV
36	ADAM SMITH				PIRANDELLO
		53	WILLIAM JAMES		PROUST
37	GIBBON I				CATHER
		54	FREUD		MANN
38	GIBBON II				JOYCE
39	KANT	55	WILLIAM JAMES	60	WOOLF
			BERGSON		KAFKA
40	AMERICAN STATE		DEWEY		LAWRENCE
	PAPERS		WHITEHEAD		T. S. ELIOT
	THE FEDERALIST		RUSSELL		O'NEILL
	J. S. MILL		HEIDEGGER		FITZGERALD
			WITTGENSTEIN		FAULKNER
41	BOSWELL		BARTH		BRECHT
					HEMINGWAY
42	LAVOISIER				ORWELL
	FARADAY				BECKETT

A statue of Buddha, mid-12th century, in Polonnaruwa, Sri Lanka. Standing 23 feet
(7 meters) high, it is one of four sculptures of Buddha, carved from a single granite wall,
that comprise the Gal Vihara ("rock shrine").

The
Great Ideas
Today

1992

Encyclopædia Britannica, Inc.

CHICAGO
AUCKLAND • GENEVA • LONDON • MADRID • MANILA • PARIS
ROME • SEOUL • SYDNEY • TOKYO • TORONTO

Photographs in "The Evolution of *Homo sapiens*" are used
with permission of the author.

Lines quoted from "The Great Explosion," by Robinson Jeffers,
in "Kepler's Anguish and Hawking's Queries: Reflections on
Natural Theology" are used with permission of Random House, Inc.

Monkey: Folk Novel of China, translated by Arthur Waley,
is reprinted (in part) with permission of Grove Weidenfeld and
Unwin Hyman of HarperCollins Publishers Limited.

"Rediscovering Natural Law" is reprinted with permission of
Douglas Buchanan.

Library of Congress Number: 61-65561
International Standard Book Number: 0-85229-569-3
International Standard Serial Number: 0072-7288

A NOTE ON REFERENCE STYLE

In the following pages, passages in *Great Books of the Western World* are referred to by the initials "*GBWW*," followed by a roman numeral (indicating the first edition of 1952 [I] or the second edition of 1990 [II]) with volume and page number. Thus, "*GBWW* I: 5, 100; II: 4, 112" refers to a passage from Sophocles' *Oedipus the King*, which is on page 100 in Volume 5 of the first edition, and on page 112 in Volume 4 of the second edition. Sometimes only one reference will be given, since the contents of the first and second editions differ. Also note that passages quoted in an article may differ from the translation of that passage in either the first or second edition, since newer translations of some works are included in the second edition.

Gateway to the Great Books is referred to by the initials "*GGB*," followed by volume and page number. Thus, "*GGB* 10, 39–57" refers to pages 39 through 57 of Volume 10 of *Gateway to the Great Books,* which is James's essay, "The Will to Believe."

The Great Ideas Today is referred to by the initials "*GIT*," followed by the year and page number. Thus, "*GIT* 1968, 210" refers to page 210 of the 1968 edition of *The Great Ideas Today.*

Contents

Preface

Our volume this year is arranged in customary fashion. That is, it contains discussions of the arts and sciences followed, first, by essays on the *Great Books* and the Great Ideas themselves, second, by what we call "Special Features," devoted to topics of particular interest not otherwise classified, and last, by "Additions to the Great Books Library," wherein we publish reprints of worthwhile books and essays for the convenience of readers who would like to have them in their personal libraries.

Attention is for the first time directed to Latin America, specifically to the literature which that region has produced in the twentieth century, much of it so recently translated that our contributor on the subject, René de Costa, calls the phenomenon a "boom," meaning that it has appeared with a kind of explosion in North America (and indeed elsewhere round the world) only in the past twenty-five years or so. This, although the poetry and fiction chiefly comprehended reach back two or three generations, as do many of the authors we now celebrate. And we do celebrate them. The literature of our age is no longer thinkable without the names of Borges, Octavio Paz, and Neruda; of García Márquez, Vargas Llosa, and Julio Cortázar—to name only a few that come immediately to mind.

Of course these writers and their works, novel as they are in certain ways, are not wholly encompassable by the "Great Conversation" of our *Great Books.* But they are not wholly alien to it, either. It is, after all, *Latin* America from which they come, and the word implies the influence of Europe not only in language but in religion and in politics: the constitutions of a number of the Latin-American republics were designed originally by Jeremy Bentham, an Englishman. If it comes to that, the education of Jorge Luis Borges, Argentinian though he was, was in English literature, as anyone who reads his critical writings can see—and the Latin-American poets show the influence of European and North American figures who were making a literary revolution of their own at about the same time.

Professor de Costa's account of all this is in two parts, of which the second will appear next year. Meanwhile, we must say something of another essay in this part of the volume devoted to a very different subject, that of human origins, where the issue of the moment is whether we are all as human beings descended from a single ancestor who lived in Africa some 200,000 years ago, or not. The evidence that we are, if evidence it really is, is not paleontological, a matter of fossil finds; or rather, it is based not upon bones but on samples of molecules of DNA that can now be recovered from bones. Strange, indeed, that anything like biological signs can be found in such a source. How can fossils of such great age have anything of the stuff of life left in them? It happens, however, that DNA is quite an inert molecule, not subject to deterioration; that studies, though as yet far from complete, are being made of what can be recovered from fossil remains; and that among the principal researchers in the field is Christopher B. Stringer, who contributes a discussion of the whole matter to this year's *The Great Ideas Today*. His focus here *is* on fossils, it should be said at once, rather than on this esoteric aspect of them, and he brings us very usefully up-to-date on the state of paleontological studies at present. But he introduces us, at least, to the possibility of a common ancestor for all of humankind.

Among our "Reconsiderations of Great Books and Ideas" this year, our regular contributor Thomas K. Simpson takes up the subject of Isaac Newton and his *Principia Mathematica* (*GBWW* I: 34; II: 32). This is given an unusual reading, yet one that we are inclined to suppose is the right one. For Mr. Simpson does not think we do Newton justice by regarding him only as the great mechanist of cosmological theory— thinks we must take with greatest seriousness his interest in alchemy (well known to scholars, but ignored in traditional histories of science), as well as his conviction that the universe demonstrates the existence of an immanent God. This makes the *Principia* a stranger book than we have been led to believe it is, while at the same time it appears as deeply human—not mechanical, finally, at all.

Following that, in Part Two of this year's *The Great Ideas Today*, will be found a discussion of happiness—that is, of the idea of happiness— by Professor Deal W. Hudson, of Fordham University, who, though himself a philosopher, takes us through the mostly psychological literature the idea has inspired since the seventeenth century and which now chiefly claims it. Happiness, this is to say, has become the concern of the social scientists, not the philosophers or the theologians, who in earlier times would have thought it their province. (Professor Hudson has recently completed a book of his own on happiness, it should be noted, which reasserts philosophical rights.)

Of the "Special Features" in this year's volume, one is on Buddhism by George Anastaplo, who completes a series of essays he has contributed to us on non-Western religions. Another is an essay on romanticism by Maurice Cranston of London University, which briefly and elegantly summarizes the thought of the chief figures in the development of that idea. Professor Cranston is writing a biography—

clearly *the* biography, we can already see from the first two published volumes—of Rousseau, who began the romantic movement and is still arguably its greatest figure.

Three further "Special Features" this year could be better listed, perhaps, as one. That is because the first of them, by Professor Owen Gingerich (himself a former contributor to *The Great Ideas Today*), which addresses the age-old question whether the universe is a matter of chance or design, inspired the second, in which Mortimer J. Adler, the editor of *The Great Ideas Today,* considers the possible answers and points out that only one of them (the least obvious one) is consistent with our supposition of the existence of God. Professor Gingerich, who had not anticipated any such debate, was then allowed space for a brief response, after which the subject was regarded as closed—for the time being.

Our "Additions to the Great Books Library" this year are greatly different in tone and substance. The first is a portion of one of the great folk stories of China, here called *Monkey* and consisting, after this introduction, of the fabulous adventures of a monk who set out for India in search of the founding articles of Buddhism. That is followed by Kate Chopin's novel *The Awakening,* a classic of feminism written a hundred years ago and dealing with a woman's discovery of her own sexuality. And after it, to a very different purpose, will be found an essay by Scott Buchanan on natural law, which is a subject often considered by the authors of the *Great Books.* And perhaps this does have something to do, after all, with what concerned Kate Chopin, as in turn Buddhism reflects a response of its own, quite opposite, to what is natural in us— which suggests that these three "Additions to the Great Books Library" have more to say to one another, perhaps, than we imagined.

Current Developments in the Arts and Sciences

Latin-American Literature Today
Part One: Background to the "Boom"

René de Costa

René de Costa is an American of Greek descent who, after graduating from Rutgers in 1964, taught mathematics in Colombia, South America. It was there, at the beginning of the "boom" referred to in the following article, that his interest in literature was kindled, and he returned to the United States to do a doctorate in Spanish-American literature at Washington University in Saint Louis. He has been at the University of Chicago since 1970 and has served as the director of its Center for Latin American Studies (1979–84).

Author of numerous studies in Spanish on diverse aspects of twentieth-century art and literature, Professor de Costa is best known in the United States for two books in English: *The Poetry of Pablo Neruda* (Harvard, 1979) and *Vincente Huidobro: The Careers of a Poet* (Oxford, 1984). He has traveled extensively in Europe and Latin America, and he is currently preparing a book on the Spanish painter Juan Gris called *Juan Gris and the Poetics of Cubism*.

In recent years, Latin-American literature—once considered exotic and local, even by Latin Americans—has suddenly become international. Writers like Pablo Neruda, Jorge Luis Borges, Gabriel García Márquez, and Julio Cortázar have emerged on the world scene, making the literary tradition from which they sprang an object of inquiry for contemporary readers. This essay—in two parts—will discuss the merits of their work, and that of other twentieth-century Latin-American writers, in an effort to highlight their uniqueness as well as their universal appeal.

Where and how did it all begin? Histories and anthologies of "New World" literature from North and South America would have us believe that everything started with the arrival of the Europeans. And to a certain extent this is true. The "literaturization" of reality, of a new experience, begins with a new experience—whether real or imagined—and for Europe the mediator was Christopher Columbus, that Genovese navigator of uncertain birth who sailed to the West for Spain. Long before sighting land, his imagination began to transform everything he saw, or thought he saw. The manatee, a kind of sea lion, became a mermaid, and when he touched land he heard nightingales singing. Everything was renamed, Europeanized. As he sailed from island to island in the Caribbean, he imposed a new order, a European order, on whatever he saw, giving new names to everything:

> To the first island which I found I gave the name *Sant Salvador,* in remembrance of His Heavenly Majesty, who marvelously hath given all this; the Indians call it *Guanahani.* To the second I gave the name *Isla de Santa María de Concepción;* to the third, *Ferrandina;* to the fourth, *La Isla Bella;* to the fifth, *La Isla Juana;* and so *to each one I gave a new name.* [emphasis mine] [1]

What Columbus did not see, he invented, and in a straightforward matter-of-fact tone he described the gold he expected to find not too far from "two provinces where *I have not been,* one of which they call *Auau,* and there the people are born with tails," giving rise to what a contemporary Latin American, the Mexican historian Edmundo

3

O'Gorman, has called *The Invention of America* (1958).* What Columbus began was continued by others in this "new" world where everything seemed possible. Thus, one hundred years later, in 1646, when a native-born Chilean, the learned Jesuit Alonso de Ovalle, published in Rome his *Histórica relación del reino de Chile* (Historical Account of the Kingdom of Chile), he included an illustrated map of his country, where among other curiosities—people who clothe themselves with dried mud—we find a sketch of a man with a tail. Not surprisingly, a contemporary writer, Colombia's García Márquez, in his justly famous *One Hundred Years of Solitude* (1967), builds on this tradition of the marvelous, relating the extraordinary as though it were an everyday occurrence. When two cousins (Ursula and José Arcadio) announce their intention to get married, their relatives try to stop it:

> They were afraid that those two healthy products of two races that had interbred over the centuries would suffer the shame of breeding iguanas. There had already been a horrible precedent. An aunt of Ursula's, married to an uncle of José Arcadio Buendía, had a son who went through life wearing loose, baggy trousers and who bled to death after having lived forty-two years in the purest state of virginity, for he had been born and had grown up with a cartilaginous tail in the shape of a corkscrew and with a small tuft of hair on the tip. A pig's tail that was never allowed to be seen by any woman and that cost him his life when a butcher friend did him the favor of chopping it off with his cleaver. José Arcadio Buendía, with the whimsy of his nineteen years, resolved the problem with a single phrase: "I don't care if I have piglets as long as they can talk."

This particular narrative mode, which is characteristic of much recent Latin-American fiction, has come to be called "magic realism" [2] and has influenced contemporary English-language writers as diverse as E. L. Doctorow and Salman Rushdie, with *Ragtime* (1975) and *Shame* (1983) being perhaps the most popular examples of this freewheeling blend of the real and the marvelous.

Things were not always this way. In the heyday of the colonial period, writers went out of their way to conform to the stylistic and thematic norms of the metropolis, the so-called mother culture. Sor Juana Inés de la Cruz, a seventeenth-century Mexican nun and self-proclaimed "Tenth Muse, Lately Sprung Up in America," published her collected

---

*When referring to works which have already been translated into English, I will first give the English-language title, followed however by the date of first publication in the original language. Conversely, works which have yet to be translated into English—or whose titles have been radically altered—will be cited with their original titles, followed by a literal translation into English. Since translations are always approximations, and since this essay is based on a reading of the originals, I have sometimes found it necessary to retranslate certain passages. A complete bibliographic description of all works mentioned, both in the original language and translation, is provided in the endnotes.

works in Madrid, just as her Boston counterpart, Anne Bradstreet, published her poems in London. The yardstick of success was Europe, and colonial literature by and large was just that, "colonial," subject to the aesthetic standards of the dominant power center.

Political independence from Europe, which coincided with Romanticism and its revolutionary notion of originality, brought to the literature of the Americas innovations of a topical and lexical nature—William Cullen Bryant's New York-inspired "To a Waterfowl" (there are no nightingales in America), the expatriated Cuban poet José María Heredia's "Ode to Niagara"—and little else. It was only in the latter part of the nineteenth century that truly original voices began to emerge in both North and South America, such as Walt Whitman in the United States and Nicaragua's Rubén Darío. Their success, both in the so-called New World and the Old, legitimated a kind of bastard eclecticism, a syncretic melding of diverse and sometimes conflicting literary modes to create something totally untraditional, totally original.

In Latin America, however, this creative license went on to spawn a most unusual new kind of writing, a writing which has changed the parameters of literature for our time, moving the power center from the Old World to the New. So far-reaching was this change that by the 1960s critics were analyzing what they called the "new novel" and its lyric counterpart, "antipoetry," a new breed of literature lacking the traditional markings of these venerable genres. Many writers—and many sociocultural factors—contributed to this change, making its manifestations known and appreciated, read and imitated.

Columbus penned his memo to the king; and de Ovalle geared his history to a small circle of Jesuits in Rome; García Márquez, though, directed his first major novel not just to his readers in Colombia but to the larger Spanish-speaking world—and that world is large, comprising over twenty nations with a combined population of more than 500 million people. An understanding of *how* that came to pass is necessary for an appreciation of *what* came to pass.

Up until the mid-twentieth century, most Latin-American writers directed themselves to a local reader. The literature of Argentina, for example, was exotic and unknown for, say, a Mexican; and the literature of Mexico was equally foreign to an Argentine or a Spaniard. This provincialization of literature was not necessarily detrimental to its production or its quality; it simply kept it relatively unknown, and in a sense nonexistent—outside of the local circle of cognoscenti, the national arbiters of fame but not fortune. Borges, for example, who had published his landmark collection of *Fictions* in Buenos Aires in 1944 with a probable print run of less than 2,000, was still a minor figure in the Spanish-speaking world a decade later, in 1954, when the first book on him appeared in his native Argentina. This book, *Borges y la nueva generación* (Borges and the New Generation) by Adolfo Prieto, did not

5

praise Borges but rather faulted him for being too cosmopolitan, for not being sufficiently local, sufficiently "Argentine."

And, some ten years later, when Mario Vargas Llosa published his first novel, *The Time of the Hero* (1963), a riveting exposé of the ritual of repression in a military academy, the authorities of his native Peru had the book confiscated and burned, finding it to be a bit too local, a bit too close to home. Yet the novel went on to enjoy an international success, becoming, along with *One Hundred Years of Solitude*, one of the cornerstones of the "new novel." By that time—thanks in part to the Formentor Prize, shared in 1961 with Samuel Beckett—Borges had become a household word, and even nonliterary people would talk of something arcane or intricate as being "Borgesian," much as people use the adjective "Kafkaesque." What had happened in the interim? How did Latin-American literature liberate itself from the suffocating provincialism of the local power centers, becoming suddenly international?

Its quality of course assured its success in the wider marketplace, but this marketplace, some ten years before—when Prieto smugly dismissed Borges—simply did not exist. It was both created and discovered by chance and circumstance. By the 1950s, a century of protective import tariffs designed to foment and protect local industries—among them the publishing business—had divided Latin America into a maze of mini-markets. New printing methods, based on photo-offset, now made it possible to produce the same layout on several presses without the necessity of mechanical typesetting. Major publishing houses from Argentina, Mexico, and Spain saw the potential of an international Spanish-language market based on low-cost simultaneous editions with a local imprint. In the mid-1960s, *Mundo Nuevo* (New World), a Paris-based magazine modeled on the British *Encounter* and distributed throughout the Americas, under the astute direction of the late Emir Rodríguez Monegal, had drawn to its pages the best new writers from all over the Spanish-speaking world, as well as Brazil. And, of course, the sudden awareness and concern with things Latin American generated by the Cuban revolution helped bind the continent together culturally—while further dividing it politically. All these things coincided to "internationalize" Latin America, breaking up its provincial cultural coteries, thrusting it and its literature onto the world scene.

Older, major writers like Borges (1899–1986) and Neruda (1904–73) began to enjoy mass printings of their works; and newer, younger writers like Vargas Llosa, García Márquez, and Cortázar were catapulted to best-seller status. Translations soon followed, and they and their works became known in the United States, Western Europe, and elsewhere. Brazilian writers like Clarice Lispector and Jorge Amado became international figures, and Brazilian readers demanded and got translations of Spanish-American writers. Spain and Portugal joined in, and Barcelona became the mecca for writers and their agents. (All this, to be sure, would not have been possible had there not existed a product to sell, a first-class product that could not only satisfy the varied tastes of this broad spectrum of readers but shape and promote them as well.)

This internationalization is a phenomenon of the 1960s, retrospectively known as the "boom." The writers who made it possible, and those who were its beneficiaries, are the subject of this two-part essay. In chronological order we have the pioneers, Borges and Neruda, two extraordinarily different men, each of whom blazed new trails, transforming the language of poetry and prose, making the local and autochthonous into something universal. The next trailblazers, Octavio Paz and Nicanor Parra, emerged to prominence in the 1950s. Parra, a professor of theoretical physics, introduced the antipoem; and Paz, an accomplished poet, the lyric essay, a genre which persuades through seduction. Both legitimated the local as the proper point of departure for arriving at universal truths. The 1960s saw the triumph of the great narrators, the incomparable storytellers: Vargas Llosa, Carlos Fuentes, García Márquez, Cortázar, and Amado. In recent years, Latin-American literature has witnessed yet another seismic shift, the emergence of major female writers: Isabel Allende, Rosario Castellanos, and Clarice Lispector. These twelve figures, and their work—much of which has been successfully translated into English—will be the focus of what follows. They are not alone, and I will of necessity discuss other major writers whose work is equally important and influential, but these twelve are central to the panorama of Latin-American literature today. The essay consists of two parts; the first, dealing with the background to the "boom," highlights the work of Borges, Neruda, Paz, Parra, and Amado. Next year the focus will be on their successors, the more contemporary writers of the "boom," and its aftermath.

Borges

Born into an upper middle-class family in turn-of-the-century Buenos Aires (1899), Jorge Luis Borges might perhaps have developed into a typical dilettante like his father (author of a minor novel, *El Caudillo*, 1921), had not circumstances altered his literary formation. It began simply enough. Almost too simply, with his learning English at an early age from his paternal grandmother, Fanny Haslam, and reading widely in his father's library. His parents, especially his mother, encouraged his literary interests, and his first story, "El rey de la selva" (The King of the Jungle), in the style of Kipling, was published in a local magazine when he was just thirteen. In the summer of 1914, his father, losing his eyesight—a family affliction Borges was to inherit—decided to take his wife and children (Borges and his younger sister, Norah) off to Europe, to make the grand tour. The war broke out shortly afterward, and

Jorge Luis Borges

fearing the danger of an ocean voyage back home, the family decided to wait things out in Switzerland. There Borges learned French and German and became familiar with the early manifestations of Dada and Expressionism. This direct contact with the European avant-garde was decisive, and in 1919, after the armistice, when the family took up residence in Spain, Borges quickly became involved with the nascent Spanish avant-garde movement, Ultraism, whose goal was to revolutionize literature, giving primordial importance to the metaphor—bold and daring imagery designed to surprise the reader by confronting him with something new, something startling.

In his early Ultraist poetry, published in the literary magazines of Spain in 1920–21, an otherwise simple seascape with a sailboat on the horizon on a moonlit night is described as: "La media luna se ha enroscado a un mástil" (The half moon got snagged in a mast); while the profile of a cathedral against the night sky becomes: "La catedral colgada de un lucero" (The cathedral hanging by a star). And a poetic subject as traditional as the rising sun is transformed into a veritable kaleidoscope of dazzling imagery:

> Ebrio como una hélice
> el sol toca la diana sobre las azoteas
> el sol con sus espuelas desgarra los espejos
> Como un naipe mi sombra
> > ha caído de bruces sobre la carretera. . . . [3]

[Blazing drunk like a spinning propeller / the sun hits the target of the rooftops / the sun with its spurs rips into the mirrors / Like a playing card my shadow / falls face down on the road. . . .]

What Borges and other proponents of the avant-garde were trying to do in the 1920s was to transform artistic reality, to create an entirely new aesthetic experience where the reader is not passive but rather an active participant in the construction of the literary artifact, in the intellection of its meaning.

Returning to Buenos Aires toward the middle of 1921, he founded an Argentine branch of Ultraism and assiduously began to propagate its views. This too he did in a most unusual way, with the creation of a "revista mural," a wall-magazine, a broadside the size of a poster, on which was imprinted a manifesto and a showcase of the new writing. According to Borges, he and his Ultraist companions "sallied forth at night . . . , armed with pastepots and brushes provided by my mother, and, walking miles on end slapped them up along . . . [the] streets." [4] Later, he would say that not even the walls read them.

All of this at the time, though, made Borges into an important local figure, and he used this newly gained authority to write scathing critical essays ridiculing some of the sacred cows of high Spanish literature (such as Luis de Góngora y Argote and Juan Ramón Jiménez), while praising the creative genius of local writers and the gaucho tradition. In this same spirit of rebellion, his first book of poems, *Fervor de Buenos Aires* (Fervor for Buenos Aires), published in 1923, did not celebrate the burgeoning metropolis but its outskirts, peopled by poor immigrants from abroad and rural migrants from the Argentine great plains. His next book of poetry, *Luna de enfrente* (The Moon Across the Way), published in 1925, imitated their speech patterns; and an impassioned essay of 1928, actually a book, *El idioma de los argentinos* (The Language of the Argentines), defended the creative originality of the local variety of Spanish.

Thus it is not surprising that Borges's first important short story, "Hombre de la esquina rosada," which dates from 1933 and has been variously translated as "Streetcorner Man" and "Man from the Slums," was written in a kind of dialect, the language of a tough braggart who relates an important moment in his life, the moment when he becomes a man, killing a rival in a knife fight. It begins in this straightforward way, with a street-smart tough addressing someone who is obviously more refined:

9

Fancy your coming out and asking me, of all people, about that stiff Francisco Real. Sure, I knew him, even though he wasn't from around here. He was a big shot on the Northside—that whole stretch from the Guadalupe pond to the old Artillery Barracks. I never laid eyes on the guy above three times and these three times were all on the same night. But nights like that you don't forget. It was when La Lujanera got it in her head to come around to my shack and bed down with me, and Rosendo Juárez took off from the Maldonado for good. Of course, you're not the kind that would mean much to. [5]

This story was first published in a breezy tabloid in 1933, where it appeared under a pseudonym, "F. Bustos," not so much to hide Borges's identity as author but as a kind of authenticating device to support the "as told to" structure of the piece. Borges, or some city slicker named Borges, is the listener. After the killing takes place, the speaker confides:

Nice and easy, I walked the two or three blocks back to my shack. A candle was burning in the window, then all at once it went out. Let me tell you, I hurried when I saw that. Then, Borges, I put my hand inside my vest—here by the left armpit where I always carry it— and took my knife out again . . . , you couldn't see the slightest trace of blood on it.

The way the narrator talks, and what he says (and doesn't say), is what permits the reader at story's end to conclude that the braggart is really a coward, one who knifed his rival in the back. And this is precisely what makes the tale so intriguing, prompting our complicity to read between the lines.

What Borges had originally learned as an avant-garde poet—the implication of the reader in the intellection of the poem—is now applied to a story by the skillful use of a dramatized narrator. The reader is never informed of exactly what transpired that fateful night but is enabled, indeed prompted, to surmise what must have happened as he inevitably begins to question the reliability of the low-life narrator.

A similar manipulation of reader expectations was employed in another piece, from 1935, "The Approach to al-Mu'tasim," a seemingly erudite critique of a nonexistent novel, published—for greater authenticity—in the guise of a book review. For Borges, literature was a game, a game of chance. In the Dada-like manifesto of *Prisma* (Prism), the 1922 wall-magazine, he said:

Shuffling a deck of cards it is possible to come up with a more or less decent lineup of values. Of course the possible combinations are limited and of no transcendent interest. But, if instead of shuffling cards, we were to deal with words, potent words, words with torchlights and haloes, then we would really have something!

And, in the 1923 prologue to *Fervor de Buenos Aires,* he closed with this Dada-like conceit:

> Should the following pages contain some good verses, the reader will
> have to excuse the boldness of my having written them down first. We
> are all someone; our individual thoughts are not very much different
> from one another, and circumstances influence us all so much that
> it is only mere chance that you are the reader and I am the writer
> of these poems.

The idea of authorship is even more directly questioned in Borges's next important piece, "Pierre Menard, Author of the *Quixote,*" a not so subtle spoof of Paul Valéry and the stuffy conservatism of the French literary tradition. For this story, disguised as a necrology and published with the dateline "Nîmes," in the May 1939 issue of *SUR*—a now historic high-powered literary journal founded by Victoria Ocampo, the Virginia Woolf of Argentine literature—Borges creates another dramatized narrator. He is an effete and bigoted snob who sings the praises of one Pierre Menard, lately deceased, whose greatest accomplishment was to have rewritten *Don Quixote,* word for word, in the seventeenth-century Spanish of Cervantes—a twentieth-century feat which far surpasses that of the novel's original author, for whom everything was supposedly easy by comparison: it's a cinch to write like Cervantes if you are Cervantes! That this is a spoof is evident from the outset, by the way in which the "author" of the necrology, a wildly militant Catholic, begins the piece:

> The *visible* work left by this novelist is easily and briefly enumerated.
> Impardonable, therefore, are the omissions and additions perpetrated by
> Madame Henri Bachelier in a fallacious catalogue which a certain daily,
> whose Protestant tendency is no secret, has had the inconsideration to
> inflict upon its deplorable readers—though these be few and Calvinist, if
> not Masonic and circumcised.

In this piece, Borges really gets carried away with the ironic portrayal of his dramatized narrator, having him superciliously boast of his "high" social connections (among the hungry aristocracy of the French Riviera):

> I am certain that it would be easy to challenge my meager authority.
> I hope, nevertheless, that I will not be prevented from mentioning two
> important testimonials. The Baroness de Bacourt (at whose unforgettable
> *vendredis* I had the honor of becoming acquainted with the late lamented
> poet) has seen fit to approve these lines. The Countess de Bagnoregio,
> one of the most refined minds in the principality of Monaco (and now of
> Pittsburgh, Pennsylvania, since her recent marriage to the international
> philanthropist Simon Kautsch). . . .

A year later, in the May 1940 issue of the same magazine, *SUR,* Borges would further exploit the fictional possibilities of the dramatized narrator with a metaphysical tale, "Tlön Uqbar, Orbis Tertius," in which the narrative "I" is none other than Borges himself. Disguised as an essay, as a personal account of a disquieting experience, all the referents are real and would be recognized as such by Borges's original Argentine reader. It begins this way:

> I owe the discovery of Uqbar to the conjunction of a mirror and an encyclopedia. The unnerving mirror hung at the end of a corridor in a villa on Calle Goana, in Ramos Mejía; the misleading encyclopedia goes by the name of *The Anglo-American Cyclopaedia* (New York, 1917), and is a literal if inadequate reprint of the 1902 *Encyclopædia Britannica.* The whole affair happened some five years ago. Bioy Casares had dined with me that night and talked at length about a great scheme for writing a novel in the first person, using a narrator who omitted or corrupted what happened and who ran into various contradictions, so that only a handful of readers, a very small handful, would be able to decipher the horrible or banal reality behind the novel. From the far end of the corridor, the mirror was watching us; and we discovered, with the inevitability of discoveries made late at night, that mirrors have something grotesque about them. Then Bioy Casares recalled that one of the heresiarchs of Uqbar had stated that mirrors and copulation are abominable, since they both multiply the numbers of man. I asked him the source of that memorable sentence, and he replied that it was recorded in the *Anglo-American Cyclopaedia,* in its article on Uqbar. It so happened that the villa (which we had rented furnished) possessed a copy of that work. In the final pages of volume XLVI, we ran across an article on Upsala; in the beginning of volume XLVII, we found one on Ural-Altaic languages; but not one word on Uqbar. A little put out, Bioy consulted the index volumes. In vain he tried every possible spelling— Ukbar, Ucbar, Ooqbar, Ookbar, Oukbahr. . . .

Back in Buenos Aires the next day, Bioy Casares checks his copy of the encyclopedia to find that the reference does indeed exist there exactly as he had remembered it. Further investigation determines that his copy of the encyclopedia is unique, containing some additional pages with the entry on "Uqbar." What follows is a detailed account of a series of "finds" which leads Borges as narrator to conjecture that a secret society had decided to invent a planet, seeding the world with clues to its existence. As the account progresses and the details accumulate, the invented planet turns out to have an uncanny resemblance to our own world. It is at this point that Borges gives his narrative an additional twist, revealing to the reader—even the not so alert reader—that this is just a fiction, an entirely made-up story. The device is a postscript, an otherwise standard authenticating stratagem. Borges's use of the postscript, though, obliges the reader to reflect on what he is reading.

The story, when it was first published in 1940, carried a postscript dated 1947, a calculated anachronism. And, to prevent the May 1940 reader of the green-covered *SUR* from dismissing it as a typo, Borges drives the point home:

> *Postscript, 1947:* I reproduce the preceding article just as it appeared in the May 1940 issue of *SUR,* #68, green covers, with no omission other than that of a few metaphors and a kind of sarcastic summary which now seems frivolous. So many things have happened since then. . . . I shall do no more than recall them here. In March of 1941. . . .

Originality for Borges obviously does not depend simply on *what* is being told but rather on *how* it is told and, most importantly, *how* it is being read. The closing paragraph of "Pierre Menard, Author of the *Quixote*" offers a surprisingly modern, *avant* post-structuralist lesson on what is today called the "phenomenology of reading":

> Menard (perhaps without wishing to) has enriched, by means of a new technique, the hesitant and rudimentary art of reading: the technique is one of deliberate anachronism and erroneous attributions.

This technique is of course that of Borges himself in the postscript to "Tlön." The idea is to surprise the reader, to force a reflection on what is being read, and in so doing to generate another, closer reading of the piece. Significantly, when Borges collected his narratives in 1944, he called the volume *Ficciones,* "fictions," to stress their invented quality.

This early volume, now his most famous, marks an important break with standard narrative practice, which was traditionally concerned with realism, with authenticating the veracity of what is being told. Borges of course uses realism, or at least the tricks of realistic narrative, to create his unique variety of the fantastic. For Borges, reality is a product of the imagination. Things are real as long as one thinks they are, as long as one thinks about them as being real. Borges was fascinated by the ideas of Berkeley, an Anglo-Irish philosopher, author of *An Essay Towards a New Theory of Vision* (1709), who held that things exist only in the mind: "esse est percipii." For Berkeley, the world exists in the mind of God. And for Borges, the world (and God) exists in the mind of man. This idea, and its consequences, informs a clever *Fervor* poem of 1923, "Daybreak." Returning home in the early morning hours, Borges realizes he is the only person on the streets; all of Buenos Aires is asleep. Thanks to him, the city is saved:

> Under the spell of the refreshing darkness
> and intimidated by the threat of dawn,
> I felt again that tremendous conjecture

of Schopenhauer and Berkeley
which declares the world
an activity of the mind,

. . . .
If all things are devoid of matter
and if this populous Buenos Aires
is no more than a dream
arrived at in magic by souls working together,
there's a moment
in which the city's existence is at the brink of danger
and that is the trembling moment of dawn
when those who are dreaming the world are few
and only a handful of night owls preserve
ashen and sketchy
a vision of the streets
which they will afterwards define for others.
. . . .
But once more the world comes to its own rescue.
The light streaks in inventing dirty colors
and with a tremor of remorse
for my complicity in the daily rebirth
I seek my house,
while a songbird holds the silence back
and the spent night
lives on in the eyes of the blind. [6]

This same conceit would see many variations in Borges's later writings. In "The Circular Ruins" (*Fictions*), a man dreams the invention of another man, his son. Each night he progressively dreams more and more of this slow creation of his mind—his arms, his legs, his hair—until he finally gives him life:

Within a year he had come to the skeleton and the eyelids. The innumerable hair was perhaps the most difficult task. He dreamed an entire man—a young man, but who did not sit up or talk, who was unable to open his eyes. Night after night the man dreamt him asleep. . . . Gradually, he began accustoming him to reality.

The story closes with his son being put to the test of fire. At this point, as our dreamer rushes into the fire to save his son, he feels the heat and realizes—too late—that he too is being dreamed by someone else. Not surprisingly, this very same idea was in one of the poems of *Fervor*, "Afterglow," which speculates on the setting sun:

How hard holding on to that light, so tautly drawn, . . .
that hallucination which the human fear of the dark
imposes on space
and which ceases at once

> the moment we realize its falsity,
> the way *a dream is broken*
> *the moment the sleeper knows he is dreaming.*
>
> [emphasis mine] [7]

Fictions was followed by several other collections, comprising a total corpus of less than a hundred stories, all of which are characterized by the author's constant desire to play with the reader's expectations and beliefs. The single overriding characteristic of this writing, the characteristic which was to be so influential for subsequent generations of writers, prompting Fuentes to call Borges the "founding father" of the "new novel" of Latin America, the novel of "magic realism"—was the reality not of life but of words and literature. Borges does not copy from reality but creates another kind of reality through his writing—an imagined reality. For him, a writer does not invent anything new, he simply weaves and reweaves the already invented realities of others; he is a remaker of the literary tradition. In his mature years, when owing to his blindness his prose took on a more conversational style, Borges began to rework his own tradition. In *Doctor Brodie's Report* (1970), there is "Rosendo's Tale," a delightful retelling of "Street-corner Man," this time by a minor character, Rosendo Juárez, the tough who originally walked away from the knife fight in the 1933 version. Significantly, the narrative frame is identical: a now older Borges walks into a café and is recognized by another older man, who invites him for a drink:

> You don't know me except maybe by reputation, but I know who
> you are. I'm Rosendo Juárez . . . , I'm going to tell you exactly what
> happened that night. The night the Butcher got killed. You put all that
> down in a storybook, which I'm not equipped to pass judgement on, but
> I want you to know the truth about all that trumped-up stuff.

From beginning to end, from the beginning of his career as a poet to his triumphant emergence as a master storyteller, Borges used literature to invent reality—and reality to make literature. Even about himself. Realizing that he had become an institution, a literary monster called "Borges," he wrote a self-reflective piece called "Borges and Myself," in which he gives us a split image of himself, the writer and the man:

> It's to the other man, to Borges, that things happen. I walk along the
> streets of Buenos Aires, stopping now and then—perhaps out of habit—
> to look at the arch of an old entranceway or a grillwork gate; of Borges
> I get news through the mail and glimpse his name among a committee of
> professors or in a dictionary of biography. I have a taste for hourglasses,
> maps, eighteenth-century typography, the roots of words, the smell of
> coffee, and Stevenson's prose; the other man shares these likes, but
> in a showy way that turns them into stagy mannerisms. It would be

an exaggeration to say that we are on bad terms; I live, I let myself live, so that Borges can weave his tales and poems, and those tales and poems are my justification. It is not hard for me to admit that he has managed to write a few worthwhile pages, but these pages cannot save me, perhaps because what is good no longer belongs to anyone—not even the other man—but rather to speech or tradition. In any case, I am fated to become lost once and for all, and only some moment of myself will survive in the other man. Little by little, I have been surrendering everything to him, even though I have evidence of his stubborn habit of falsification and exaggerating. Spinoza held that all things try to keep on being themselves; a stone wants to be a stone and the tiger, a tiger. I shall remain in Borges, not in myself (if it is so that I am someone), but I recognize myself less in his books than in those of others or than in the laborious tuning of a guitar. Years ago, I tried ridding myself of him and I went from myths of the outlying slums of the city to games with time and infinity, but those games are now part of Borges and I will have to turn to other things. And so, my life is a running away, and I lose everything and everything is left to oblivion or to the other man.
  Which of us is writing this page I don't know.

Prose is continuous, a steady flow of words. Borges uses this to create a seamless sequence, leading us word by word into the labyrinth of his thought. At various points, difficult to determine, the speaker shifts voices, from Borges the man to Borges the writer, and shifts back again, and again. At the end, we, like the speaker, cannot be sure about which of these personae is writing the piece. And that is its charm.

Borges—the man and the writer—made meaningful literature out of literature and out of everyday experience. After the assassination of President Kennedy in 1963, he wrote a kind of necrology, "In Memoriam J.F.K.," which succinctly demonstrates the creative power of his imagination, his talent for fusing people and objects, time and space, into a movingly coherent narrative discourse on the cyclic nature of human events and the power of things over people, in this case a weapon whose function is to kill:

> This bullet is ancient.
> In 1897, Arredondo, a young man from Montevideo shot it at the President of Uruguay, after spending a long time in hiding, so that no one would suspect him of having any accomplices. Thirty years before, the same projectile killed Lincoln, through the criminal or magic act of an actor, whom the words of Shakespeare had made into Brutus, the assassin of Caesar. In the middle of the 17th century, vengeance made use of it to kill Gustave Adolphe of Sweden, in the midst of the public hecatomb of a military battle.
> Before, the bullet was other things, because Pythagoric transmigration is not only for humans. It was the silken cord that the visirs get in the Orient, it was the cannon fusillade and the bayonets which destroyed the defenders of the Alamo, it was the triangular blade that chopped

off the head of a queen, it was the dark nails that penetrated the flesh of the Redeemer and the wood of his cross, it was the poison which the Carthaginian general kept in his ring of iron, it was the serene cup from which Socrates drank one evening.

At the dawn of time it was the stone which Cain threw at Abel, and it will go on to become many things that today we can not even imagine, and which may one day do away with all men and their prodigious and fragile destiny. [8]

Borges liberated narrative from the straitjacket of the real and made it somehow more real. Another writer of his same generation, from a vastly different background and temperament, did much the same for poetry, bringing it to the lips of the people: Neruda.

Neruda

Born into a working-class family in the frontier town of Parral, in the south of Chile in 1904, Pablo Neruda hardly seemed destined for fame. Yet, thanks to a government scholarship which brought him to a teacher's college in the nation's capital, Santiago, and thanks even more to his unbridled talent, he became a celebrated national poet while still nineteen with the publication of his *Twenty Love Poems and a Song of Despair* in 1924. A decade later he was an international figure, hailed in Europe as "one of the most authentic realities of poetry in the Spanish language." In 1934, at a public recital in Madrid, he was introduced by none other than García Lorca:

You are about to hear an authentic poet. One of those whose senses are trained to a world that is not ours and that few people perceive. A poet closer to death than to philosophy, closer to pain than to insight, closer to blood than to ink. A poet filled with mysterious voices that fortunately not even he knows how to decipher. . . . This is poetry that is not ashamed to break with tradition, that is not afraid of ridicule, and that can suddenly break out sobbing in the middle of the street. [9]

Neruda was never ashamed to break with tradition, even his own, and this constant innovation and renovation is what turned him into the Picasso of poetry, inaugurating, anticipating, and assimilating all the major changes in poetic diction until his untimely death in September of 1973, just a few weeks after the bloody military coup in Chile which ushered in the long reign of terror of Augusto Pinochet Ugarte. Fifty years of poetry, a full half-century of literary ascendancy crowned with a Nobel Prize in 1971, is an extraordinary feat for someone of such simple origins.

Borges, who read English as a child and was initiated into the subtleties of French and German in the Switzerland of Dada, broke

Pablo Neruda

the rules of literature in a conscious effort to create something new; Neruda broke the rules and created something new out of ignorance, the innocent ignorance of the culturally deprived. Unaware of the European avant-garde, indeed, unfamiliar with his own literary tradition, Neruda started out by creating his own rules with a self-assurance bordering on arrogance. His first important book, for example, *Twenty Love Poems,* was initially rejected by the publisher for being too erotic and too explicit, in a word, too pornographic. The problem was that Neruda celebrated not love but passion; not the usual lyricism of unrequited love for one ideal woman but lust for women in general. The book's first poem, explicitly titled "Body of Woman," begins in this unabashed way:

> Body of woman, white hills, white thighs,
> you're like the world, lying in surrender.
> My rough peasant's body digs in you
> and makes a child sprout from the depths of the earth.

Love poetry has traditionally equated woman with nature, but Neruda makes her into a veritable force of the universe with the proposition that she is, like the world, bounteously available, and he is the earthy cultivator of that plenitude. Neruda's metaphor is more powerful than the hackneyed simile on which it is based because it is the reader who imaginatively supplies the link between the two things being related: woman's body and the world. The idea, when stated directly, as I have just done, is a preposterous hyperbole. Neruda uncannily makes it persuasive, almost "natural," by a simple, seemingly ingenuous repetition of the adjective *white* which serves syntactically to relate thighs to hills and forces the reader to mentally complete the metaphor, an imagistic transference which is, in truth, based not on the stated similarity of the color white but on an implied similarity of shape. Neruda, almost artlessly, short-circuits words and meanings in order to create a highly charged *stil nuovo* (new style) in these modern poems of carnal love.

The sequence is progressive, and by Poem XIII it is the discontinuous and irregular lines of free verse which pace the frenzy of lovemaking:

> I have gone along marking with crosses of fire
> the white atlas of your body.
> My mouth was a spider that would move about hiding itself.
> In you, behind you, timid, thirsty.

Again, it is the special and strategic use of an ordinary word, the adjective *white,* which serves to place this composition's imagery of action in the same cosmic dimension as the volume's opening poem, "Body of Woman."

The Chilean reader of 1924 was both shocked and titillated by this bold display of passion. The North American reader of today, sensitized by the women's movement, while appreciating the book's literary merits, will be shocked by its dated sexism. The Latin-American reader, on the other hand, will identify with this language, to the book's enduring popularity—millions and millions of copies have been sold, and continue to sell—will recognize this as the language of love. The fact is that Neruda's *Twenty Love Poems* have been not only read but assimilated, transmuted by generation after generation of enamored adolescents into the standard discourse of *amor* in late twentieth-century Spanish. So much so, that in Allende's celebrated novel, *The House of the Spirits* (1982), whole sections appear—without quotes—in the mouths of its lovers. And Neruda, who is a character in the novel, is never referred to by name; he is simply "the Poet."

A book which is so instantly successful can have an adverse effect on an author, causing him to repeat himself and become fossilized. Some authors never have a second best-seller. In the case of Neruda, the effect was just the opposite: success gave him the authority and confidence to change, to set the love poetry behind him and move on to other modes of expression. In the early 1930s he championed a kind of metaphysical hermeticism—this is the poetry of "mysterious voices" so admired by García Lorca. But then came the jolt of reality of the Spanish Civil War, which cost García Lorca his life, and which prompted Neruda to shift to a more direct, politically committed mode of expression. He, like Picasso, knew he was changing and knew too that change was essential not only to his art but to life itself. In a book of 1937, *Spain in My Heart,* there is a long narrative section called "I Explain a Few Things." There, he speaks directly to the reader of his literary transformation; the shifting pronouns (*his > I;* emphasis mine) demonstrate this change of persona:

> You will ask: And where are the lilacs?
> And the metaphysics covered with poppies?
> And the rain that often would beat down
> on *his* words filling them with holes and birds?
>
> *I'm* going to tell you everything that happened to me.
>
> *I* used to live in a part
> of Madrid. . . .

The poet is now a protagonist in his own story, the real story of his personal quest for meaning and of the different literary stages which marked his progress. Having passed beyond the lyricism of his love poetry, beyond the meditative mode of his metaphysical stage, he now speaks directly of what he, Pablo Neruda, has witnessed in Spain. His new role is that of a chronicler, a modern-day jongleur, and the discursive situation is openly conversational:

> I used to live in a part
> of Madrid, with bells,
> with church clocks, with trees.
>
> From there one could see
> the dried-out face of Castille
> like an ocean of leather.
>   My house was called
> the house of flowers, because everywhere
> there burst forth geraniums: it was
> a beautiful house
> with dogs and children.
>   *Raúl,* do you remember?
> Do you remember, *Rafael?*
>   *Federico,* do you remember
> from under the earth,
> do you remember my house with balconies where
> the light of June would smother flowers in your mouth?
>   [emphasis mine]

In lyric poetry the problem is to convince the reader of the sentiment expressed. Here, the problem is to persuade the reader of the truth, the factuality of what is being narrated. Neruda employs an interesting authenticating device. The poem is addressed to us; and we readers are made to feel part of a much larger group; we are included in the literary circle of the poet and his friends: *Federico* (García Lorca), *Raúl* (González Tuñón), and *Rafael* (Alberti) are all victims of the war, either dead or in exile. Neruda's personal story is thus made part of a larger community of interests. No longer unique, it is universal. The poet's experience is made to stand for that of Spain; his radicalization is that of the Spanish people.

The purpose of *Spain in My Heart* was twofold: to chronicle the author's experience and to persuade his readers to share the interpretation of that experience. Fundamental to the rhetoric of persuasion is the device of repetition. For this reason, "I Explain a Few Things" closes with a variation of the rhetorical question with which it began:

> You will ask why does his poetry
> not speak to us of dreams, of the leaves,
> of the great volcanoes of his native land?
>
> Come and see the blood in the streets.
> Come and see
> the blood in the streets,
> come and see the blood
> in the streets!

This is poetry in the grand oratorical style, and the repeated lines, variously cut, indicate the extent of Neruda's transition—from the written soliloquial mode of the love poems ("I could *write* the saddest verses," Poem XX) to the present declamatory style: "I'm going to *tell* you." And tell he does.

Neruda eventually joins the Communist party (in 1945) and by 1950 is both a victim and a hero of the cold war—a victim in the sense that he is forced into exile when the party is outlawed in Chile, and a hero with the publication in Mexico of *Canto general* (General Song, 1950), a long epic-narrative poem which offers a revisionist view of history, the history of the vanquished. Its protagonists are the underdogs, the defeated, what Ralph Ellison at the same point in time, and referring to the black man in this country, called the *Invisible Man* (1952).

Canto general is one of the earliest manifestations of a third-world consciousness. By mid-century, Neruda's poetry had permeated every aspect of Latin-American life, not only how and in what language people made love, but how and in what way they articulated the world around them and their place in it. Significantly enough, at the zenith of his poetic career, realizing that poetry is a powerful medium, Neruda also realizes that it is a restricted medium, not read by everyone, and he makes yet another radical change writing poetry for what was then popularly called "the masses," and what Neruda preferred to call "the man in the street." This new poetry, the *Elemental Odes* (1954), was first published not in book form but in the sports and financial pages of *El Nacional,* a Caracas daily newspaper; hence its typographical distribution—a long and narrow column of verses winding their way down the page. He wrote odes to ordinary, "elementary" things like onions, socks, and fish stew. Hundreds and hundreds of them on every imaginable subject—most of course, not the traditional subjects of poetry. But perhaps the most significant poem of the series was one of the first, "Invisible Man," a poem which registers yet another change of skin: (*I > they*), the transformation of the poet from the legion of seers to someone ordinary, to everyman:

> I laugh,
> I smile
> at the old poets,
>
> . . . . . .
>
> they're always saying "I,"
> with each step
> something happens to them,
> it's always "I,"
>
> . . . . .
>
> no one suffers,
> no one loves,
> only my poor brother,
> the poet,
> everything
> happens to him, . . .

Once Neruda learned how to stand back from the literary tradition, his own literary tradition, he moved into a totally new area of exploration, that of the "antipoem," a genre invented by his younger compatriot, Nicanor Parra, but a genre which Neruda rapidly assimilated, making it his own. In this new vein, Neruda went on to make fun of himself, of what he had become. In a poem called "Fear," from *Extravagario* (1958), he was derisive:

> Everyone picks at my poetry
> with invincible forks
> looking, no doubt, for a fly.
> I am afraid.
>
> I am afraid of everyone,
> of cold water, of death.
> I am like all mortals,
> undelayable.

Therefore in these short days
I'm not going to pay any attention to them,
I'm going to open myself up and close myself in
with my most perfidious enemy,
Pablo Neruda.

Here is fear, not of himself but of the institution he had become. A little like Borges in his haunting monologue "Borges and I."

Neruda dominated Latin-American poetry from the 1920s through and beyond the 1950s, liberating lyric language from refined aestheticism and ponderous conceits, demonstrating in the process that poetry, although an art form for the few, was also a way of giving voice to the voiceless. What is more, the universal popularity of his work had the effect of legitimating the Latin-American variety of Spanish, changing it from a quaint variant of Castilian into a respected literary language.

It is this language which Paz and other younger writers used to articulate the new concerns of Latin America. Borges showed that a Latin American could beat the Europeans at their own game of sophistication, and Neruda showed that Latin Americans could invent new rules for the same game. Between the two of them, Borges and Neruda, Latin America came of age. One of the first writers to realize this was the then young Paz, who in 1950—the same year as Neruda's revisionist *Canto general*—published a landmark book, a long meditative essay on Mexico and Latin America which reads like a poem: *The Labyrinth of Solitude*. His point of departure was the other, the "pachuco," the zoot-suited chicano of Southern California. Significantly, the book's final chapter, "The Present Day," closed with these words: "For the first time in our history, we [Latin Americans] are contemporaries of all mankind." [10]

Paz

Octavio Paz, who was awarded the Nobel Prize for Literature in 1990, was born in Mexico City in 1914 to a typical middle-class mestizo family, Spanish on one side and Indian on the other. While studying to become a lawyer, he became involved in student politics and the bohemian world of literature. His first book of poems, *Luna silvestre* (Wild Moon, 1933) reached Neruda in 1937 while plans were being made for the International Congress of Anti-Fascist Writers in support of the Spanish Republic. Neruda recalls his role in bringing Paz to Spain:

Along with the Norwegians, the Italians, the Argentines, the poet Octavio Paz arrived from Mexico, after a thousand adventures and misadventures. I was proud of having brought him. He had published just one book, which I had received two months before and which seemed to contain genuine promise. No one knew him yet. [11]

Octavio Paz

Paz, only twenty-three at the time, the youngest person at the Congress, which took place in Madrid, Barcelona, and Valencia, [12] hobnobbed with the principal writers of the left: César Vallejo, Vicente Huidobro, Alejo Carpentier, Antonio Machado, Rafael Alberti, Tristan Tzara, Louis Aragon, Stephen Spender—all supporters of the Spanish cause. He stayed on in Spain for a year, before going briefly to Paris. Back in Mexico in 1938, he repaid the favor, reviewing *Spain in My Heart* in an essay titled "Pablo Neruda en el corazón" (Neruda in My Heart), [13] praising the Chilean for having introduced "reality" into the stilted language of poetry. Partisan politics would later drive them apart, but it is interesting to note how at the beginning there was a meeting of minds, indeed of "hearts."

The young Paz was an active promoter of literature in his native Mexico, publishing his own poetry and that of others in various literary reviews and anthologies, but it was not until 1949, at the height of the cold war, when he brought out a rigorous selection of his verse under the politically charged title *Libertad bajo palabra* (Liberty on Parole), that he made a real impact on the international literary scene. This volume put him on the map. One of its poems, simply titled "Words," synthesizes a tough new attitude toward the words of poetic language:

> stomp on them, tough guy,
> wring their necks, cook,
> pluck them,
> rip their guts out, bull,
> drag them down, bullock,
> make them, poet,
> make them eat their own words. [14]

Words here are not mere ornaments; poetry is not the result of midnight inspiration or a flight of the refined imagination. Poetry is a creative act; words must be disciplined, made to perform.

Cortázar reviewed this book of 1949 in *SUR,* [15] the influential Argentine literary review which had earlier launched Borges's career. Cortázar (then young too; he was born in 1914, the same year as Paz) was dazzled by some of the poems, and in particular by a verse from "Cuerpo a la vista" (Body on View): "Siempre hay abejas en tu pelo" (There are always bees in your hair). Through the simple device of understatement, Paz manages to invoke literary tradition (*bees > flowers > honey*), making the hair of the beloved into a magnet of attraction, without resorting to cliché. This is what the new "realism" of poetry was all about: to be immediately, almost viscerally, communicative.

Paz, meanwhile, after a Guggenheim fellowship brought him to New York in 1944, had joined the Mexican Foreign Service, and one of his first postwar assignments was to Paris. Seeing war-torn Europe must have made him realize that things there were worse than in his own country, or in any case it may have helped him to see his own country in a new light—not as a bastard spin-off of Spain but as an integral part of the larger world. One of the poems from *Libertad bajo palabra,* "Hymn Among the Ruins," datelined Naples, 1948, is written in various voices shifting from the Old World to the New, and back again. The result is a compression of the multilayered levels of civilization into a single composite image of contemporaneity; or, as Paz was soon to declare in *The Labyrinth of Solitude,* the idea that "we are contemporaries of all mankind." The fragment cited below shifts geographically between Mexico and the Mediterranean, and on to a wider, or should we say smaller, world:

> Eyes see, hands touch.
> Here a few things suffice:
> prickly pear, coral and thorny planet,
> the hooded figs,

> grapes that taste of the resurrection,
> clams, stubborn maidenheads,
> salt, cheese, wine, the sun's bread.
> An island girl looks on me from the height of her duskiness,
> a slim cathedral clothed in light.
> A tower of salt, against the green pines of the shore,
> the white sails of the boats arise.
> Light builds temples on the sea. [16]

As circumstances change, as the world changes, Paz changes; and his lucid writing forcefully changes our way of thinking about these circumstances. A single example will suffice. In 1970, some twenty years after *Labyrinth,* Paz brought out a sequel, an update, significantly titled *Posdata* (Postscript), like the "P.S." one adds to a letter. At that time the student movement in the United States was at its zenith, and De Gaulle was coping in France with the unrest that had come to a head in May 1968. Mexico that year had suffered its "night of Tlatelolco," when protesting students were gunned down by riot police in the Plaza of Three Cultures. Looking at these phenomena from a wider perspective, Paz sees a common denominator and his *Posdata* opens with this sweeping poetic vision:

> 1968 was a pivotal year: protests, disturbances, and riots in Prague, Chicago, Paris, Tokyo, Belgrade, Rome, Mexico, Santiago. . . . Just as the plagues of the Middle Ages respected neither religious borders nor social hierarchies, so the rebellions of the young annulled ideological classifications. . . . [17]

Paz goes on to analyze what he now sees as a single phenomenon from an international perspective. Noting the absence of the so-called revolutionary class—the "proletariat"—he finds that students all over the world constitute a singular group: "the youth of the developed nations are part of an international sub-culture, product in turn of an equally international technology."

Posdata was an update to *Labyrinth.* The singularity of the earlier book was its break with tradition, the tradition of nationalistic introspection. Throughout the nineteenth century, New World nations under the spell of Romanticism and its exaltation of individual uniqueness sought to define the peculiarities of being an Argentine, a Bolivian, or a Mexican based on deterministic sociogeographic principles. Because Argentina had the great plains, reasoned Domingo Faustino Sarmiento in *Facundo* (1845), its gauchos had the fierce independence of Arabian horsemen; because the United States had the frontier, reasoned Frederick Jackson Turner (1893), its inhabitants were sturdy pioneers. In the early twentieth century this dreamy determinism of how things should be shifted to a brooding psychological diagnostic of national maladies. Books like Martínez Estrada's *X-Ray of the Pampas* (1933) and Samuel

Ramos's *Profile of Man and Culture in Mexico* (1934), like Franklin D. Roosevelt's "Good Neighbor Policy," are typical of this prescriptive approach.

Octavio Paz's *Labyrinth* made a radical break with this tradition, viewing Mexico and being Mexican as something both distinct from and similar to other Latin-American nations and the world. Paz did this not through simple assertion—his book does not begin with its conclusion, the idea of "contemporaneity"—but rather with the idea of otherness. Furthermore, his idea of otherness is taken from a poet, Antonio Machado, a twentieth-century transplanted Andalusian who became enamored of Castille; Paz is a transplanted Mexican who became a world citizen. *Labyrinth* begins with this epigraph from Machado:

> The *other* does not exist: this is rational faith, the incurable belief of
> human reason. Identity = reality, as if, in the end, everything must
> necessarily and absolutely be *one and the same*. But the *other* refuses to
> disappear; it subsists, it persists; it is the hard bone on which reason
> breaks its teeth. Abel Martin, with a poetic faith as human as rational
> faith, believed *in the other*, in "the essential Heterogeneity of being,"
> in what might be called the incurable *otherness* from which *oneness*
> must always suffer.

Paz is led into the labyrinth by the "pachuco," the unassimilated chicano outsider who is neither Mexican nor American and yet is paradoxically both, a kind of outsize caricature of both cultures. Paz sees the chicano as a key to understanding the hybrid culture of Mexico, itself an amalgam of Hispanic and indigenous elements. From this insight he goes on to understand—always with the leaping intuition of a poet—the other hybrid amalgamated peoples of the Americas, and of the world itself. In the twentieth century there is no "pure" culture, we are all aliens:

> We Mexicans have always lived on the periphery of history. Now the
> center or nucleus of world society has disintegrated and everyone—
> including the European and the North American—is a peripheral
> being. We are all living on the margin because there is no longer
> any center. . . .
>
> Ever since World War II we have been aware that the self-creation
> demanded of us by our national realities is no different from that which
> similar realities are demanding of others. The past has left us orphans, as
> it has the rest of the planet, and we must join together in inventing our
> common future. World history has become everyone's task, and our own
> labyrinth is the labyrinth of all mankind. [18]

These quotes are from the book's penultimate chapter, expressing ideas which were revolutionary for their time, though now they have the confirmation of history. What made them persuasive forty years ago, back in 1950, was Paz's unique ability to communicate what was then not so obvious—the intangible feeling, or intuition, of how things really are. Paz is heir to the Rimbaudian idea of the poet as *voyant,* a "seer."

In the opening chapter of *Labyrinth,* "The Pachuco and Other Extremes," setting things up for his "vision," Paz recounts, memoirlike, the pedestrian details of his arrival in Los Angeles. This passage, which gradually moves from the prosaic to the poetic, is as good an example as any of how Paz transports the reader through words, in a flight of the imagination, taking us from a distanced postcard impression of the vaguely Hispanic "air" of Southern California, to the magic intimacy of the palpably intangible experience of its "Mexican-ness":

> This Mexicanism—delight in decorations, carelessness and pomp, negligence, passion and reserve—floats in the air. I say "floats" because it never mixes or unites with the other world, the North American world based on precision and efficiency. It floats, without offering any opposition; it hovers, blown here and there by the wind, sometimes breaking up like a cloud, sometimes standing erect like a rising skyrocket. It creeps, it wrinkles, it expands and contracts; it sleeps or dreams; it is ragged but beautiful. It floats, never quite coming into its own, never quite going away. [19]

Paz is first and foremost a poet and uses the rhetoric of poetry to make his prose persuasive. As a poet, he went on to bolder experiments in verse, becoming part of the neo-avant-garde with the visual pyrotechnics of *Blanco* (1967) and *Discos Visuales* (Visual Disks, 1968). As an essayist, he brought his lucidity to a wide range of cultural subjects, from Sor Juana to Marcel Duchamp to Lévi-Strauss, exciting admiration with the clarity and vivacity of his insight. All this, coupled with his steadfast commitment to liberal democracy, is what earned him the Nobel Prize.

In his long and brilliant career as a thinker and poet-essayist, Paz always took the high road, the well-traveled road of high culture. Others, like Chile's Nicanor Parra and Nicaragua's Ernesto Cardenal, picked up where Neruda left off, finding their inspiration in the byways, in ordinary things. They made a new and different kind of poetry out of the commonplace.

Parra

There is a famous passage in García Márquez's *One Hundred Years of Solitude* where José Arcadio Buendía takes his children to the gypsy carnival so that they can experience the wonders of the world. There they all come to know ice and marvel over it as "the greatest invention

Nicanor Parra

of our time." Nicanor Parra, some twenty years before, adopted the same attitude of childlike innocence to make poetry out of a real-life experience. When his father took him down to the coast from their inland town so that he might see the ocean,

> We descended from the train amidst flags
> And a solemn fiesta of church bells
> When my father took me by the arm
> And . . . , as someone intoning a prayer
> Said in a voice which is still in my ear:
> "This, my son, is the sea." *The serene sea,*
> The sea *which bathes with crystal the shores of our nation.*
> [emphasis mine] [20]

The poem is from 1942. The emphasized line is a quote from the Chilean national anthem.

At this time, poets everywhere were talking about the idea of bringing poetry to the people, of making it conversational. Even an older, established figure like Huidobro, who back in the 1920s had almost single-handedly implanted the aesthetic ideals of the Parisian avant-garde in Spain and Latin America, by the 1940s was feeling the need for something different, a new voice for a new age: "a new kind of writing, without a literary tone, a writing that would use the language of conversation, not the language of song, but the language of speech." [21] Paz, too, retrospectively spoke of his own awareness back then of the need for "a conversational language, a colloquial language." [22] Needs notwithstanding, Parra was the first to actually *use* ready-made speech in texts which began to appear in magazines and anthologies during the late 1940s, and which were later collected in a watershed volume: *Poems and Antipoems* (1954), a book which created a dividing line, a "before and after" era in twentieth-century poetry in Spanish.

How this came to pass is an interesting story in its own right, for Parra was not primarily a poet but a mathematician. Born in 1914 to a talented and bohemian family in San Fabián, a village near Chillán in the south of Chile, he holds advanced degrees in theoretical physics from Brown and Oxford. His first attempts at poetry while a young academic in Chile were, by his own admission, derivative, modeled after García Lorca. Dissatisfied with his first book, *Cancionero sin nombre* (Nameless Songbook, 1937), Parra surreptitiously tried his hand at other kinds of writing, keeping these experiments to himself and only publishing an occasional poem or two at the insistence of friends. One of these was "The Viper," a 1948 text which gives a new twist to a standard theme: the speaker as a slave to his beloved:

> For many years I was condemned to adore a despicable woman,
> Sacrifice myself for her, suffer countless humiliations and affronts,
> Work day and night to clothe her and feed her
> Undertake deceits, commit petty crimes
> Steal a bit *in the light of the moon.*
>
> [emphasis mine] [23]

In this otherwise corrosive discourse, Parra surprises the reader with the insertion of a tried-and-true cliché: "in the light of the moon," a lyrically resonant hand-me-down from the classical tradition. And as the speaker goes on, we are jolted by yet another variant of the same procedure:

> Then I had to go out in the street and live off public charity,
> Sleep on park benches,
> Where many times I was found half-dead by the police
> Amidst *the first leaves of autumn.*
>
> [emphasis mine]

Ready-made images such as these, charged with "poetry" but situated in an unlikely contextual frame, are a calculated part of the author's strategy to detune, or retune, the chords of our received literary sensibility. With the publication of this text, Parra knew he was onto something new, for while he was away at Oxford in 1949 he urged a soul mate back in Chile to read it and join the "crusade" against what he felt was wrong with the literature of the time:

> The egocentric poetry of our predecessors in which they try to show the reader how wonderful is man, how intelligent and sensitive they are, how admirable are the objects of this world must move over and make way for a more objective writing. . . . These romantics are like opera singers, good, bad, and excellent sometimes, even brilliant like our friend Neruda, but they have a narrow and outdated notion of what art is. The solemnity and dogmatic weightiness of the nineteenth century lives on in them. . . . A poem ought to be a kind of cross-section of man in which we can see all the nerves and fibers, the bones and arteries, the thoughts and associations, etc. etc. etc. It's not a question of whipping up something easy to swallow. I'm convinced that the poet has no right to interpret, only to describe. . . . [24]

Parra gave himself over completely to writing in this new objective mode, a mode which he later came to call "antipoetry." Collecting this work in 1954 under the title *Poems and Antipoems,* he placed a "Warning to the Reader," alerting us to what was different:

> The author is not responsible for the discomforts these writings may
> cause
> Although he may not like it
> The reader will always have to make do with whatever he gets. . . .

What it contains and what it does not contain: "real" things displacing the idealizations of traditional literature, a matter-of-fact recognition of the world instead of the sanctimonious posturing of the "doctors of poetry." All of this sardonically justified by a nursery-rhyme closure: "Because in my view, the sky is falling."

This new authorial voice—singular and multiple, leaping back and forth between frankness and irony, between wisdom and puerility— would soon become the public voice of Parra himself in his unexpectedly official role of "antipoet" as the book went on to become a runaway best-seller just a week after its publication. Instant fame draws detractors, and the author, suddenly the darling of many, became for others detestable. A former poet-friend, the Maoist Pablo de Rokha, would try to cut Parra down to size, likening him to "a piece of gum on Vallejo's shoe"; a populist Spanish priest, Father Salvatierra, condemned the author and his "antipoems," likening both to "a can of garbage." [25] To all of this Parra arrogantly replied in his second book, *Versos de salón* (Drawing-Room Poetry, 1962): "For half a century now/Poetry has been/The paradise of the solemn fool. . . ."

In this collection of verses, he handled head-on the now inevitable interview question of what is and is not "poetry" and/or "antipoetry":

TEST

What is antipoetry:
A tempest in a teapot?
A stain of snow on a rock?
A serving tray of human waste
As Father Salvatierra believes?

.   .   .   .

A jet-propelled coffin?
One that runs on kerosene?
A wake without the corpse?

Check off
The definition you consider correct.

What Parra accomplished in 1954 with his *Poems and Antipoems*—and what Neruda that same year had not been able to do in his *Elemental Odes,* despite the congenial change of focus in "Invisible Man" where he complacently laughed at the omnipresent "I" of the *other* poets—was to poke fun at himself. Parra's "Self-Portrait" took an ironic look at Parra:

Just think, kids:
I'm a professor in this obscure school.
I've lost my voice giving classes.
(After all, I teach forty hours a week).
What do you make of my beaten face?
Doesn't it make you sorry just looking at me?
And what do you say about this nose clotted up
By the degrading chalk dust. . . .

The idea is not to inspire pity, but to get a self-conscious laugh, along the lines of Woody Allen, highlighting through black humor an underlying truth: work is degrading. The speaker of this poem goes on listing his misfortunes, progressively worse, until he suddenly does an about-face, and concludes with an absurdity: the forty hours a week becoming five hundred:

Look at these hands
And these cadaverous white cheeks,
These few hairs left on my head.
These dark wrinkles!
Nevertheless, I was once like you,
Young, full of beautiful ideals,
I dreamt about smelting copper,
and polishing the faces of diamonds:
Here you have me

Behind this uncomfortable desk
Brutalized by the singsong monotony
of five-hundred hours a week.

There are multiple voices in Parra's poems. The speaker is not one but several, shifting voices like a circus barker to draw attention, not to himself, but through himself to the subject at hand. Parra is not simply trying to be entertaining but seeks to disarm the reader, eliciting our complicity in the reading. In this way, the literary artifact is not something distant and above us but part of our common experience, our own disillusion with the banality of life in the "no-exit" mid-twentieth century. The speaker in these texts doesn't pretend to have any special knowledge of the world, no panacea for life's problems. Things are tough, and there is nothing we can do about them; but life goes on. In this typically 1950s existentialist view it makes no sense to poetize; therefore says Parra—almost in resignation—we must somehow "de-poetize" the world.

In a later text, collected in *Versos de salón,* in a composition titled "Women," even this sacrosanct theme is made "antipoetic":

All of these Valkyries
All these respectable matrons
With their major and minor lips
Will end up driving me out of my tree.

This text, quite naturally, provoked a feminist reply, by none other than Erica Jong of *Fear of Flying* fame. Jong employs the same technique, a composite parody called "Men," with the same jolting finale:

All these Adonises
All these respectable gents
Those descended
& those undescended
will drive me out of my skull sooner or later. [26]

Literature is a composite, a palimpsest of texts which have a dialogue with one another. Parra with his "antipoems" struck an antiliterary stance and ended up reinventing the language of poetry for our time. It is a language that is as poetic as it is "anti," for today's readers identify with these texts and make them their own, much as previous generations of lovers adopted the erotic language of Neruda.

Nicaragua's Ernesto Cardenal, a contemporary of Parra (born in 1925) and a priest who was minister of culture in the recent Sandinista government, called his particular brand of this kind of writing "exteriorism" and did much the same thing, with a slight variant: distancing himself by putting words into the mouths of others. The speaker in his variant is not necessarily the poet, and is often an *other*, a true-to-life character—real or invented—not unlike Borges's "Rosendo Juárez" or "Pierre Menard." Cardenal did this fictionalization with himself as priest, rewriting the Psalms and even interceding for Marilyn Monroe ("Prayer for Marilyn Monroe"), and too with Anastasio Somoza, the self-aggrandizing ex-dictator of Nicaragua, in a poem called "Somoza Unveils the Statue of Somoza in Somoza Stadium":

> It's not that I think the people put up this statue to me,
> because I know better than you, that I ordered it myself.
> Nor that I have any illusions about passing with it into posterity
> because I know the people will one day tear it down.
> Nor that I wished to erect to myself in life
> the monument you'll not erect to me in death:
> I put up this statue because I know you'll hate it. [27]

The diction is that of public oratory. The text reads as though it were a transcript, and we can easily characterize the dramatized narrator, an

" 'USA, where liberty is a statue,' This particular artifact became so popular that it was translated to another medium, to the illuminated newsboard on Times Square."

arrogant tyrant, who gloats in the knowledge that his power base is fear. The power of this kind of poetry comes from its anonymity; it seems to be as public as graffiti, an art form that we all know how to read—and whose reading is not complicated by the interference of authorial voice.

Parra made use of this too in later poems inventing another speaker, a crazy evangelist, the Christ of Elqui, [28] whose sermons and homilies comment on all aspects of contemporary life, from the sexual revolution to the pope's recent visit to the Chile of Pinochet, and earlier in a box of printed postcards, called *Artefactos* (Artifacts, 1972), adding or modifying a verbal cliché to a well-known graphic image and creating a special kind of "artifact," something whose meaning is instantly recognized: "USA, where liberty is a statue." This particular artifact became so popular that it was translated to another medium, to the illuminated newsboard on Times Square. In the spring of 1987, Parra's daughter Catalina (who is a New York artist), transferred this to a Spectacolor presentation.

Parra has achieved the kind of popularity, the kind of mass readership for poetry in Spanish, that Neruda once had, and that—until our time—was usually the exclusive province of the novel. And, in truth, it was the novelists in the early 1960s who became the new divas, the stars of Latin-American literature for an international audience, a world readership. Foremost among these was a Brazilian, Amado.

Amado

Brazil is a country so vast and so populous, with an internal market so large, that its art and literature need not look for reception beyond its borders. But its artistic production is so dynamic that it cannot be contained, and on occasion—as with *cinema nôvo,* the *samba,* or more recently the *lambada*—is discovered by the international community. This is what happened to Jorge Amado. Born to a sharecropping family in the northeast of Brazil in 1912, he was already the author of ten novels, several books of poems, biographies, and stage plays, before he was "discovered" in 1958 with the publication of *Gabriela, Clove and Cinnamon.* This book—subsequently translated into over thirty languages, made into a movie, and serialized for television as an immensely popular open-ended saga on the order of *Dallas*—has made its author an international celebrity. He repeated this success with *Dona Flor and Her Two Husbands* (1966) and to this day continues producing blockbuster best-sellers every two or three years.

Amado's earlier work, admired and respected in Brazil, was in the realistic vein, the literature of social realism. *Gabriela* broke with that tradition and introduced an element of fantasy which has come to be hailed as the hallmark of the "new novel" in Latin America: "magic

35

Jorge Amado

realism." It is significant that in that same year, 1958, Fuentes published his first important novel, *Where the Air Is Clear*. Vargas Llosa and García Márquez were soon to follow with their best-sellers: *The Time of the Hero* and *One Hundred Years of Solitude*.

What set *Gabriela* apart, both from Amado's own previous work and most of Latin-American fiction up to the mid-1950s, was its creative appropriation of the folkloric, transforming the purely local from something quaint into something universal. Borges transported his readers from the plane of reality into the fantastic; his successors found the marvelous to be part and parcel of the everyday reality of Latin America. The Cuban novelist Alejo Carpentier (1904–80), after a long sojourn in Paris as a practicing Surrealist, openly stated this proposition in the prologue to *The Kingdom of This World* (1949), a historical novel dealing with the slave rebellion which brought Haiti to independence:

> Because of the dramatic singularity of its events, because of the fantastic stature of its characters who at a certain point in time came together in

the magic crossroad of Cap Haitien, everything seems to belong to the realm of the marvelous in a history that would be impossible to situate in Europe, and which is nevertheless as real as any of those exalted—for pedagogical edification—in the textbooks. But what is the history of America, if not a chronicle of the marvelously real? [29]

Not surprisingly, the extraordinary story of *Gabriela* is presented in the style of a chronicle. In fact, the original Brazilian edition carries a subtitle, "Crônica de uma cidade de interior" (Chronicle of an Interior Town)—inexplicably dropped from the English version—which helps to couch the narrative as a kind of antiquated colonial "Account of Discovery and Exploration," much like de Ovalle's seventeenth-century *Historical Account of the Kingdom of Chile*. Even its chapter summaries read like a book of old, part fact, part fantasy, all extraordinary:

> Part One: Adventures and Misadventures of a Good Brazilian (Born in Syria), All in the Town of Ilhéus in 1925, When Cacao Flourished and Progress Reigned, With Love Affairs, Murders, Banquets, Crèches, Divers Stories for All Tastes, A Remote and Glorious Past of Proud Seigneurs and Rogues, a More Recent Past of Rich Plantation Owners and Notorious Assassins, With Loneliness and Sighs, Desire, Hatred, Vengeance, With Rain and Sun and Moonlight, Inflexible Laws, Political Maneuvers, Controversy about a Sandbar, With a Miracle, a Danceress, a Prestidigitator, and Other Wonders,
> or,
> A Brazilian From the Arabies. [30]

The narrative is fast-paced. Several intersecting plot lines, with numerous major characters, give an epic sweep to this saga of sex and sentiment, power and politics, in the changing social world of a Brazilian boomtown of the mid-1920s. The struggle is between the old order and the new, feudal power politics versus modern methods of social organization among the plantation owners—all self-styled "colonels" in the tradition of the Old South—between an archaic code of social and sexual deportment for their wives, daughters, and mistresses, and real-life behavior characterized by female self-assertion and independence. The romance of Gabriela, a beautifully sensuous mulatto cook, and Nacib, the Syrian-Brazilian owner of a bar-cum-restaurant which also doubles as the town's social center, is the glue which holds the various plot lines and sociopolitical themes together. Progress, in the form of "changing times," is the driving force which keeps everything moving. What keeps the reader interested, besides the author's considerable dexterity in manipulating extraordinary turns of character and event, is his talent for making it all somehow believable. The trick is in the technique of "chaotic enumeration," a poetic device much employed in Surrealism, whereby a seemingly random series of enunciations is

37

suddenly factored into sense by a unique common denominator. In the following example, taken from the opening lines of the first chapter, we can see the process at work:

> In that year of 1925, when the idyll of the mulatto girl Gabriela and
> Nacib the Arab began, the rains continued long and beyond the proper
> and necessary season. . . . The crop gave promise of being the biggest
> in history. With cacao prices constantly rising, this would mean greater
> wealth, prosperity, abundance. It would mean the most expensive
> schools in the big cities for the colonels' sons, homes in the town's new
> residential sections, luxurious furniture from Rio, grand pianos for the
> parlors, more and better stocked stores, a business boom, liquor flowing
> in the cabarets, more women arriving in the ships, lots of gambling in
> the bars and hotels—in short, progress, more of the civilization everyone
> was talking about. (5)

Through this technique, what might otherwise seem preposterous (the arrival of new prostitutes as a sign of progress = civilization) is made credible, indeed becomes the very element which brings outside authenticity to the account.

Brazil is an immigrant country like the United States. The complex process of Brazilianization is vividly rendered in an equally extraordinary summary paragraph. Here, it is the criminal act of "killing people" which is inserted into the narrative sequence as an absolute proof of total assimilation into the national character:

> They arrived, and soon they were true Brazilians, breaking through
> the forest, planting cacao trees, setting up stores, opening roads, killing
> people, gambling in the cabarets, drinking in the bars, founding villages,
> making and losing money, feeling as close to the land as the oldest
> natives, sons of the families of pre-cacao days. (35)

In this way, through these sweeping enumerations, Amado creates a total ambience, understandable not only to Brazilians but also to that larger reading public which brought him international success.

In *Dona Flor and Her Two Husbands,* a mélange of creole recipes and a Brazilian version of voodoo (*candomblé*) help make a plausible concoction out of the truly fantastic. The central character, Dona Flor, who runs a cooking school, is married to a classic rake, Vadinho, from "a poor wrong-side-of-the blanket branch of an important family." [31] This outsize character, an inveterate gambler, womanizer, and drunkard, suddenly drops dead on the street after a night of heavy carousing with his buddies during Carnival. The widow, after an appropriate period of mourning and sexual longing for her dead husband, finally remarries with the most eligible bachelor in town, a respectful and respectable druggist. One night, when she is longing for the sexual acrobatics of her dead husband, he reappears to claim his rightful place

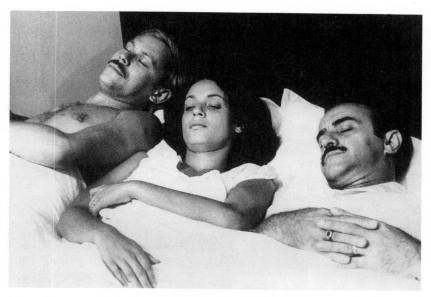

A scene from the film adaptation of "Dona Flor and Her Two Husbands." Dona Flor (Sonia Braga) is shown snoozing with the ghost of her first husband (Jose Wilker) on the left. On the right is her second husband (Maura Mendoca).

in her marital bed. What ensues is a ribald comedy of contrasts between the dutiful servicing of Dona Flor by her pajamaed druggist ("every Wednesday with the possibility of an encore on Saturdays"; pp. 335, 426ff.) and the unmitigated lustiness of the naked Vadinho. In short, Dona Flor has the best of both worlds, sex and security. The novel ends on a serendipitous note, with Dona Flor on a ritual Sunday stroll with her respectable husband—and the ghost of Vadinho in tow:

> On the arm of that lucky dog of a husband, Dona Flor smiled gently.
> Oh, that mania of Vadinho's for feeling her breasts and buttocks on
> the street, fluttering about her like the morning breeze. That clear,
> rain-washed Sunday morning, with Dona Flor strolling along, happy with
> her life, satisfied with her two loves. (518)

The authorial voice in these novels is that of a popular storyteller, not the classic "impartial observer" of realist fiction but the chatty know-it-all tone of a good village gossip. Telling stories from within, in the local language of the people, is what gives a special ring of truth to the fiction of Amado. And to that of other writers of the "boom," who at the same point in time, in Mexico, Buenos Aires, Bogotá, São Paolo . . . , from exile in Europe and the United States, were attempting an equally ambitious retelling of the saga of their people. Next year, in the second part of this essay, we shall turn to the work of Fuentes, Cor-

tázar, García Márquez, Vargas Llosa, Allende, Lispector, Castellanos—
the major Latin-American writers of our time who speak to us with a
special urgency today.

1. *A New and Fresh Translation of the Letter of Columbus Announcing the Discovery of America*, trans. Samuel Eliot Morison (Madrid: Yagués, 1959), p. 7.

2. A much used and often abused term in Latin-American literary criticism, it refers to a combination of the "real" and the "marvelous," a combination which many writers and critics hold to be innate to the American experience. First formulated as a critical term by Angel Flores ("Magical Realism in Spanish American Fiction," *Hispania*, 38 [1955], 187–192), it derives from the concept of "lo real maravilloso" (the marvelously real), expounded by Cuban novelist Alejo Carpentier in the prologue to *The Kingdom of This World* (1949), a historical novel situated in Haiti: "But what is the history of America, if not a chronicle of the marvelously real?" (in his *Obras completas* [México: Siglo XXI, 1983], vol. 2, p. 18). In 1975 a major convention was devoted to this theme, with more than fifty scholars inconclusively debating the legitimacy or illegitimacy of the term(s): *Fantasía y realismo mágico en Iberoamérica* (Michigan State University, 1975).

3. The examples cited are from "Singladura" (Day's Run), "Catedral" (Cathedral), and "Mañana" (Morning), poems originally published in 1921 in the Spanish magazines *Baleares* and *ULTRA*, and now collected by Carlos Meneses in his *Poesía juvenil de Jorge Luis Borges* (Barcelona: Olañeta, 1978).

4. In his "Autobiographical Essay," a text prepared directly in English with the assistance of Norman Thomas di Giovanni; it was first published as a *New Yorker* "Profile" (Sept. 19, 1970) and was subsequently included in the translation of *The Aleph and Other Stories* (New York: Dutton, 1970).

5. Originally published in *Crítica* (1933); first collected in *Historia universal de la infamia* (1935), and translated as *A Universal History of Infamy* (New York: Dutton, 1972).

6. *Selected Poems: 1923–1967* (New York: Dell, 1972), pp. 21–23.

7. *Ibid.*, p. 19.

8. Included in later editions of *El hacedor* (1960), partially translated as *Dreamtigers* (Austin: University of Texas, 1964); the text cited is my translation from the 6th edition in Spanish (Buenos Aires: Emecé, 1969).

9. "Presentación de Pablo Neruda" (Madrid: Dec. 6, 1934), Federico García Lorca, *Obras completas* (Madrid: Aguilar, 1964), p. 148.

10. *The Labyrinth of Solitude* (New York: Grove, 1961), p. 194.

11. *Memoirs* (New York: Farrar, Straus, 1977), p. 131.

12. In 1987, when the Socialist government of Spain decided to commemorate the fiftieth anniversary of the Congress, bringing the principal intellectuals of our time to discuss in Valencia the prospects for democracy in the next century, Octavio Paz was invited as president.

13. *Ruta* (Mexico), 4 (Sept. 15, 1938).

14. *Early Poems: 1935–1955* (New York: New Directions, 1973), pp. 58–59.

15. "Octavio Paz: *Libertad bajo palabra,*" *SUR* (Buenos Aires), 182 (December 1949), 93–95.

16. *Early Poems*, pp. 94–99.

17. *The Other Mexico: Critique of the Pyramid* (New York: Grove, 1972). Despite the title, this *is* a translation of *Posdata*. Old habits die hard; publishers traditionally take abusive liberties with translated works. Here, Octavio Paz's internationalist view is "Mexicanized"; the same thing happened to *The Labyrinth of Solitude* with the addition of a descriptive subtitle which is *not* in the original: "Life and Thought in Mexico."

18. *Labyrinth*, pp. 170–73.

19. *Ibid.*, pp. 12–13.

20. A translation, *Poems and Antipoems,* was first published by Ferlinghetti and Ginsberg in City Lights (1960); it was modified and reissued under the same title by New Directions in 1967 and has been more recently updated and republished as *Antipoems: New and Selected* (New York: New Directions, 1985). These editions are complemented by *Emergency Poems* (New York: New Directions, 1972) and *Sermons and Homilies of the Christ of Elqui* (Columbia: University of Missouri, 1984).

21. In a letter to Spanish poet Juan Larrea (Santiago: Aug. 8, 1941); reproduced in a monographic issue of *Poesía* dedicated to Huidobro (Madrid), pp. 30–32 (1989).

22. "Los pasos contados," *Camp de l'arpa* (Barcelona), IV, 74 (April 1980), 55.

23. First published in *13 poetas chilenos* (Valaparaíso: Imprenta Roma, 1948), pp. 84–86; later collected in *Poems and Antipoems*.

24. Unpublished letter to Tomás Lago (Oxford: Nov. 30, 1949), reproduced in facsimile in the text of my critical edition of *Poemas y antipoemas* (Madrid: Cátedra, 1988), p. 91.

25. Newspaper articles from Santiago de Chile, cited more extensively in the prologue to the 1988 edition of *Poemas y antipoemas* (*see* previous note).

26. *Half-Lives* (New York: Holt, 1973), p. 24.

27. *Apocalypse, and Other Poems* (New York: New Directions, 1977), p. 14.

28. *See* note 20.

29. In his *Obras completas* (México: Siglo XXI, 1983), vol. 2, p. 18.

30. *Gabriela, Clove and Cinnamon* (New York: Knopf, 1962); I cite from the most recent Avon printing (1988), p. 3, and henceforth will indicate page numbers parenthetically in the text.

31. *Dona Flor and Her Two Husbands* (New York: Knopf, 1969); I cite from the most recent Avon printing (1988), p. 15.

The Evolution of *Homo sapiens*

Christopher B. Stringer

Christopher B. Stringer is head of the Human Origins Group at the Natural History Museum, London, where he has worked since 1973. He was also a visiting lecturer at Harvard in 1979. He graduated in anthropology from University College, London, in 1969 and studied for his doctorate in Pleistocene hominids at Bristol (awarded 1974). His major research interest centers on the evolutionary relationship of Neanderthals and modern humans, but he also has published studies on *Homo habilis* and *Homo erectus* fossils, as well as taking a wider interest in the origin of modern *Homo sapiens*. In particular he has been involved in the development of the "Out of Africa" theory of modern human origins, now supported by an extensive body of genetic data. As part of more general studies of the Miocene and Pleistocene he has excavated sites in England, Wales, Gibraltar, and Turkey.

Dr. Stringer has authored or coauthored over ninety papers on the subject of human evolution and is completing a book called *The Neanderthal World* for Thames and Hudson.

Introduction

Over two hundred years ago, when Carolus Linnaeus, the great Swedish naturalist, first named the human species *Homo sapiens* ("man the wise"), there was no conception of our evolutionary history, let alone the recognition of a fossil and archaeological record which might document such a history. However, in the last one hundred and fifty years, many early representatives of the genus *Homo* have been discovered, as well as even earlier forms of hominid (our zoological family, usually taken to include all forms which are more closely related to us than are the African apes, the gorilla and chimpanzees). [1]

Much scientific effort in the earlier years of this century went into reconstructing the evolution of *Homo sapiens,* [2] but subsequently this area of study underwent a period of relative neglect. This was partly because of damaging misuse and misinterpretation of the fossil and biological data to support theories of racial superiority and inferiority. [3] It was also because of an increasing focus on our more ancient origins, as the earlier human fossil record began to grow. However, there has been a great resurgence of interest in the evolution of our species in the last decade, fueled by new fossils and interpretations, better dating techniques, and, especially, the new attention of geneticists to reconstructing the course of recent human evolution.

Prior to this, most of the scientific and public attention of the last thirty years of hominid evolutionary studies had been concentrated on the spectacular discoveries which had been made in East Africa, particularly in the countries of Tanzania (e.g., the footprint site of Laetoli, the long sequence of Olduvai Gorge), Kenya (e.g., the fossil-rich sites of East and West Turkana), and Ethiopia (e.g., the Hadar site of "Lucy's" skeleton). These discoveries told us a great deal about human evolution between 1.5 and 4 myr (million years) ago, and in particular they indicated that early human evolution was not the straightforward process of one species giving rise to another in an inexorable progression toward *Homo sapiens.* [1,4,5]

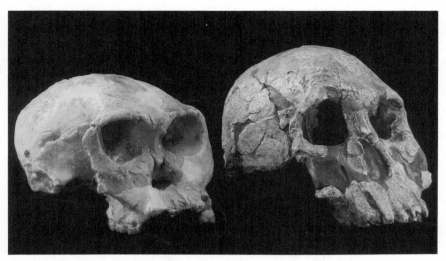

Figure 1. Two fossils attributed to *Homo habilis:* (left) Olduvai Hominid 24 and (right) KNM-ER 1470 from East Turkana, Kenya. Note the size difference, usually explained as the variation between males and females of the species.

   Instead we have learned that early human evolution was more like a bush of complex radiations and extinctions, rather than a single stem leading gradually to modern humans at the tip. The earlier, in some ways more apelike, genus *Australopithecus* ("southern ape") existed in at least five different forms across southern and eastern Africa, and it is unclear which of these forms (with perhaps even more to be discovered) was closest to our origins, which are coincident with the origin of our zoological genus *Homo.* However, the first recognizable human being had evolved from australopithecine forebears by two million years ago. The brain sizes of certain fossil specimens show a noticeable increase beyond that found in apes and *Australopithecus;* the skeleton looks more human, there are changes in the face, jaws, and teeth, and stone tools appear in the archaeological record. To what extent all these developments were connected to form a chain of cause and effect is unclear, but the African fossils that show these changes are generally regarded as representing the earliest human species, *Homo habilis* ("handy man"). [6,7]

   With *Homo habilis,* a transition was apparently taking place from the essentially apelike adaptations of *Australopithecus* to the more human features which followed in the species *Homo erectus* and *Homo sapiens* (*see* below). However, the *habilis* fossils show a confusing array of characteristics which have led to much recent argument about their affinities and classification. Some specimens (e.g., KNM-ER 1470 from East Turkana) are large-brained but have wide projecting faces reminiscent of *Australopithecus* (fig. 1). Although no reasonably com-

44

plete associated skeletons are known, the body of such large *habilis* individuals is believed to have been quite human in proportions and structure. There are also small-brained fossils (e.g., KNM-ER 1813 from East Turkana and Olduvai Hominid 13) that have faces and jaws which look more human. A recent discovery of a partial skeleton from Olduvai (Olduvai Hominid 62) indicates that some small *habilis* individuals were far more like *Australopithecus* and apes in their body form (e.g., in the much shorter legs relative to the arms and trunk). While it would be simplest to ascribe this degree of variation to the differences normally found within a species (e.g., between males and females), [6,7,8] several workers consider it goes far beyond such a level of distinction. In which case, even the beginnings of our genus *Homo* may continue the earlier pattern of complex radiations, so that there are in fact at least two kinds of early human now confused together in the species *Homo habilis*. From brain and body size data, the larger type of *habilis* might be considered the best candidate for the ancestry of later humans, but there is no simple solution to this problem at the moment.

The next stage of human evolution, that of *Homo erectus*, was first recognized over one hundred years ago with the discovery of the skullcap of *Pithecanthropus* ("ape man") in Java (Indonesia). [1,9] These were the first widespread early humans, although areas of northern Europe, Asia, the Americas, and Australia were not colonized until long after the time of *Homo erectus*.

Until recently it was Chinese material, fossils of "Peking man" from Zhoukoudian cave, which provided the main information on the species. This large sample of fossils was found prior to World War II but disappeared during that conflict and is still missing. These Chinese specimens were relatively young in age (about 250–450 kyr [thousand years] old). The most spectacular discoveries attributed to *Homo erectus* have come from African deposits more than one million years older.

Richard Leakey's team at East Turkana in northern Kenya has recovered numerous fossils of a very early form of *Homo erectus* dated at 1.7 myr ago. These fossils are much less robust than their Chinese counterparts, lacking the thick walls and bony ridges which characterize the skulls of *Homo erectus* from China and Java. They also had only about 80 percent of the brain size of the Asian specimens and only about 60 percent of the modern average. [7]

These important Kenyan discoveries have in turn been followed by the discovery in 1984 of an almost complete *Homo erectus* skeleton at the site of Nariokotome, on the opposite site of Lake Turkana (West Turkana). Identical datable volcanic deposits are present on both sides of the lake, so the new fossil can be dated at about 1.6 myr ago. It is a very impressive skeleton of a boy aged about eleven years who was already nearly 170 cm (5 ft 7 in) tall, with some growing still to do. When this discovery has been studied in detail, it may be possible to answer many questions about the entire body of *Homo erectus* for the first time. It will also provide more information about the growth rate of *Homo erectus* children and could well indicate a surprising speed of maturity compared to children of today.

The species *Homo erectus* was characterized by great robusticity in the sense that there is a great deal of dense, compact bone in the skeleton, suggesting that bones, especially in the hip and limbs, were being subjected to much greater stress and strain through physical activity than is the case in modern populations. This suggestion is reinforced by the degree of muscularity which can be inferred from the depth and extent of muscle markings on the bones. The robusticity extends to the head, since there is a thick-walled braincase and a heavy lower jaw, the former having bony reinforcements such as keeling (additional ridges on the top of the skull) and an occipital torus (a ridge across the back of the skull; fig. 2). The whole skull is long, low, and angular, with little forehead development and a massive browridge across the front, above the eye sockets. The face projects outward toward the jaws but is rather flat and broad, with a broad nose. The lower jaw lacks a chin at the front and is usually receding in profile. Brain size in *Homo erectus* ranged between just over 50 percent and over 90 percent of the modern average (which is about 1,400 ml), but large samples of *Homo erectus* and *Homo sapiens* reveal a clear overlap in this feature, which is therefore not definitive.

While it is generally accepted that *Homo erectus* gave rise to *Homo sapiens,* the details of this evolutionary transformation are not at all agreed upon (fig. 3). *Homo erectus* certainly developed local geographic variation, and there was also variation through time. The extent and direction of the variation through time is disputed, with some workers arguing for evolutionary stasis and a negligible approach to a modern human morphology through time, while others see a gradual progression in each *erectus* population toward *Homo sapiens*. In this latter view, the geographic variation of *Homo erectus* also foreshadows modern "racial" variation, which is seen to have begun its evolution in local *erectus* populations. [3,10] The intervening fossil samples generally assigned to "archaic *Homo sapiens*" are crucial to a resolution of the origin of modern *Homo sapiens* and its regional variation. We will therefore review the fossils assigned to "archaic *Homo sapiens*" in some detail. First, though, we will briefly discuss how the fossil record is dated, and we will look at what is meant by *Homo sapiens*. We will also discuss the two dominant theoretical models of our origins. Finally, at the end of the article, when we have reviewed the fossil evidence, we will combine the fossil and genetic data to summarize the present state of knowledge concerning our origins.

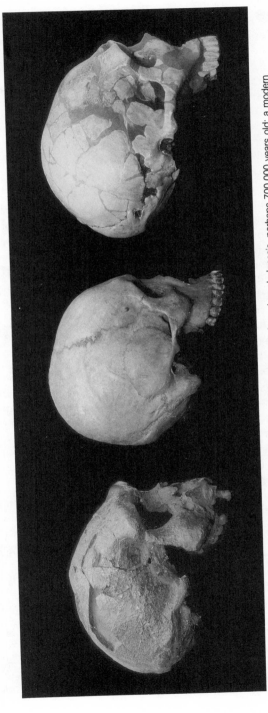

Figure 2. A comparison of skulls of (from left to right) *Homo erectus* (Sangiran 17) from Java, Indonesia, perhaps 700,000 years old; a modern human male from Southeast Asia; and a Neanderthal male (La Ferrassie 1) from France, dated at about 50,000 years old. The *Homo erectus* skull clearly shows the low, flattened angular braincase and strong ridges of bone at the back (occipital torus) and front (browridge or supraorbital torus). The modern skull shows a typical high, rounded braincase, with face tucked in. The Neanderthal skull shows the large but relatively low braincase and the projecting midface and nose.

Dating recent human evolution

In the early years of human evolutionary studies, assessing the actual antiquity of a fossil hominid could be no more than guesswork. [1,2] However, where a fossil is stratified (i.e., incorporated into a sequence of deposits such as in a river terrace, or cave), it is often possible now to date the specimen by reference to its surrounding materials (e.g., geologic features, mammal bones, artifacts). This technique of "relative dating" allows a fossil to be fixed in relation to some other datum point (e.g., earlier than a volcanic ash, later than an occupation by cave bears, the same age as the deposition of a stalagmite). Through extrapolations from one site to another, it is possible to correlate fossils with each other. Thus a number of Neanderthal fossils from Europe have been correlated through mutual association with cold-adapted mammals such as the reindeer and mammoth, indicating that they all probably date from the last major ice advance of the Pleistocene epoch, which itself spans the last two million years.

The Pleistocene epoch has in turn been subdivided into early, middle, and late stages, each one characterized by successive global alternations of colder/drier (glacial) and warmer/moister (interglacial) conditions. There were corresponding changes in ice caps, deserts, and sea levels. The earth's climate has periodically oscillated between these extremes by virtue of changes in the orbit and orientation of the planet, and these oscillations have become especially marked during the last 700 kyr, an interval that covers the whole time period of the evolution of *Homo sapiens*. So-called absolute dating methods generally use natural radioactive decay to estimate ages in years; hence this is called radiometric dating. Such methods (some of which are discussed below) have dated the boundaries of the Pleistocene epoch as running from about 1.6 myr to 10 kyr ago, and the internal boundaries at about 730 kyr (early–middle Pleistocene transition) and 130 kyr ago (middle–late Pleistocene transition). [5]

The best-known radiometric dating technique [11] is radiocarbon dating, which estimates the age of a specimen from the quantity of radioactive carbon-14 (^{14}C) remaining within it, since this is known to decay at a constant rate from the levels found in living organisms (it has a half-life of about 5,700 years, which means that half of the ^{14}C in any sample will decay over that time period). Unfortunately, because the half-life is so short, material such as fossil human bone will have only very small amounts of measurable ^{14}C remaining at an antiquity of more than, say, 40,000 years. This sets a practical limit on accurate radiocarbon dating, which means that it is a very useful technique for recent prehistory but cannot reach back to the origins of *Homo sapiens*.

Three other radiometric techniques which can fill the void left by the limitations of radiocarbon dating are Uranium Series (U-S),

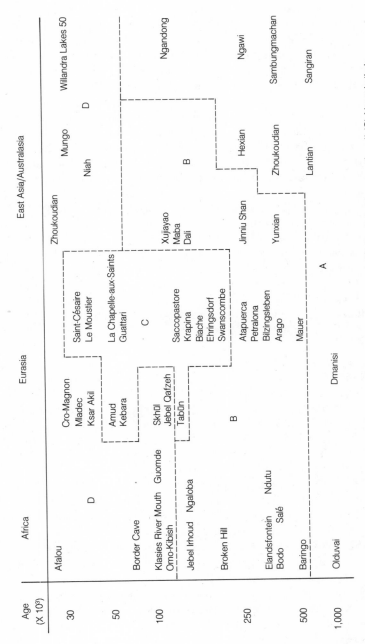

Figure 3. A chart of important fossil human remains assigned to (A) *Homo erectus,* (B) "archaic *Homo sapiens,*" (C) Neanderthals, and (D) anatomically modern *Homo sapiens.* The dating of some sites is uncertain.

Thermoluminescence (TL), and Electron Spin Resonance (ESR). The first method uses the decay of the ^{234}U and ^{238}U isotopes to estimate the length of time since decay began. As long as there is a closed system, the ratios of "parent" and "daughter" isotopes can be reliably determined to give the age. But the technique is complicated where isotopes are gained or lost, for example, by crystallization or the action of water. The method has been used on shells, bones, and tooth enamel but is perhaps most effective in dating natural deposits of carbonates such as cave stalagmites.

TL and ESR are related techniques which measure accumulated damage to crystalline substances from natural radioactivity in the environment (e.g., from uranium in cave deposits). TL can be used on materials such as pottery in the recent past, and flint tools in earlier prehistory, where ancient heating (e.g., burning in a fire) has set the TL radioactivity signal back to zero. ESR can be used on a wider range of materials, such as coral or stalagmite, but has proved especially valuable when applied to the tooth enamel of animals such as the mammoth, rhinoceros, and horse. These animals are commonly associated with human fossils and provide much scope for ESR dating work. However, both TL and ESR require accurate estimation of radiation exposure through the whole history of the specimen to be dated, whether it is a burnt flint artifact or an antelope tooth, and since this has to be reconstructed from present-day data, it gives rise to one of the major areas of uncertainty in such age estimates. [12]

Homo sapiens

Until quite recently it was common for workers who studied new fossil hominids to create new species or even genus names for virtually every new find, even where the specimen was clearly similar to previous finds. [2,13] The first such example was when the Neanderthal discovery of 1856 was made the type of a new species of the genus *Homo,* called *Homo neanderthalensis.* This was repeated by workers for various other Neanderthal finds, such as those from Spy, Belgium (*Homo spyensis*), Le Moustier, France (*Homo transprimigenius mousteriensis*), and La Chapelle-aux-Saints, France (*Homo chapellensis*). Similarly, outside Europe the Broken Hill cranium from Zambia was assigned to *Homo rhodesiensis* and later to *Cyphanthropus rhodesiensis,* and the Skhūl remains from Israel to *Palaeoanthropus palestinus.*

During the middle years of this century a number of influential papers reexamined basic concepts of hominid classification from the perspectives of more general paleontology and from the developing field of population genetics. It was argued that, since living *Homo sapiens* represented a polytypic species (i.e., a species with considerable physical variation), so did humans at any one time level in the past. Central to these discussions was the status of the Zhoukoudian remains of Peking man (then commonly attributed to *Sinanthropus pekinensis*) and the Mount Carmel (Skhūl and Tabūn) remains (then commonly attributed to the single nonmodern species mentioned above, *Palaeoanthropus palestinus*). Several workers suggested that the Zhoukoudian remains in fact represented merely one subspecies of an earlier human species, *Homo erectus* (so-called because the species name *erectus*, previously applied to *Pithecanthropus*, took priority). [9] Interpretations of the Mount Carmel fossils as representing a highly variable single population also led to the suggestion that the taxonomic boundary between Neanderthals and modern *Homo sapiens* had been broken down. The Mount Carmel "population" could be interpreted as a group in the process of evolving from a Neanderthal to a modern form or as a hybrid population between two closely related forms.

Thus reassessments of the fossil material suggested that only one human species had existed at any one time in the past, as in the present, and that *Homo erectus* (including such geographic variants as Java man and Peking man) and *Homo sapiens* (including such variants as Neanderthals and modern humans) were polytypic species. This viewpoint was formalized in the 1960s, when it was proposed that the species *Homo sapiens* of Linnaeus should be subdivided into the following living or fossil subspecies: *sapiens* (modern humans), *neanderthalensis*, *steinheimensis* (for the Steinheim skull from Germany), *rhodesiensis*, and *soloensis* (for the Ngandong remains from Java). [14] This scheme has been widely adopted, and a number of previous and new fossil discoveries have been incorporated under one or other subspecific categories. In the 1970s it became common to differentiate the anatomically modern form of *Homo sapiens* (*Homo sapiens sapiens*) from the other forms of the species by the additional epithets "modern" or "archaic" *Homo sapiens*, and thus "archaic *Homo sapiens*" includes middle or late Pleistocene hominids that are distinct from, but supposedly closely related to, modern humans. [10]

Modern Homo sapiens

Anatomically modern *Homo sapiens* can be characterized by a number of skeletal features found in all living human populations, many of which are related to an overall gracility of the skeleton compared with earlier humans. Although present *Homo sapiens* around the world display a remarkable variation in stature, physique, and weight (much of which can be attributed to environmental adaptations and nutritional factors), most living humans are relatively large-bodied but have slenderly constructed bones and a less heavy musculature than was the case in archaic humans such as *Homo erectus* and "archaic *Homo sapiens*." This could be an indication of the extent to which sophisticated behaviors

51

found in living humans have taken the selective weight off the skeleton through an emphasis on economy of effort rather than high activity and muscle power as the basic behavioral adaptation of the species. In other words, modern humans emphasize brain rather than brawn in problem solving.

Compared with archaic humans, modern *Homo sapiens* display large brains (also found in Neanderthals), with an average volume exceeding 1,300 ml (but varying somewhat according to sex and body size). To contain this large brain there is a highly distinctive and derived cranial shape in modern humans (*see* fig. 2). The vault is relatively short (front to back) and high, with a domed forehead and well-arched (rather than flattened) sides to the skull (the parietal bones). The base of the skull is narrow, as is the back, and this bone (the occipital bone) is rounded in profile, lacking the transverse bony ridge and heavy neck muscles inferred for many archaic forms, as well as the distinctive shape found in Neanderthals. As in Neanderthals, but to an even greater extent, the walls of the skull are relatively thin, and this lack of robusticity is also reflected in the small or nonexistent browridge and the more delicate face and jaws with small teeth. The lower jaw is not thickened and has a bony chin on its outside. The degree of flatness of the face and the shape of the nose varies among different populations, but in none of them is there the large and projecting nasal region found in Neanderthals. The whole skeleton is lightly built with thin walls to the limb bones and only moderate muscularity. The shoulder blade (scapula) has less muscle attachment on the back edge, and the hipbone is not as strongly constructed, while also lacking the unusual features found in Neanderthals (*see* later).

The behavioral evolution of *Homo sapiens*

Although beyond the scope of this article, and well covered in other sources, [4,5] a brief discussion of distinctive human behavioral features would be useful. Modern humans differ from all other animals in the complexity of behavior and the degree of behavioral differences (manifested as cultures and customs) evident among different populations. Thus, although there are basic shared gestures and expressions (e.g., the smile), populations inhabiting single large islands (e.g., New Guinea) may be mutually incomprehensible to each other because of linguistic differences. Their social and religious systems may also differ greatly. Nevertheless, the features which humans share behaviorally do unite us as a species and are, potentially at least, discernible in prehistory through the archaeological record.

The transmission of information and learned behavior between generations forms the basis of culture and presupposes the existence of a

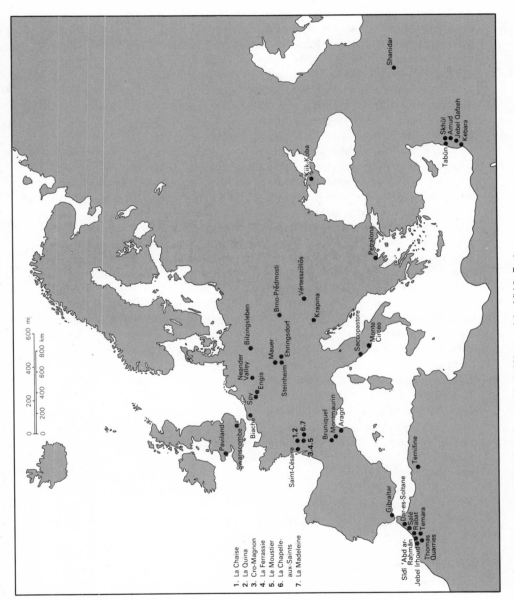

Major sites of hominid fossil finds in Europe, North Africa, and the Middle East.

Sites labeled on map: Shanidar, Skhūl, Amud, Jebel Qafzeh, Kebara, Tabūn, Kiik-Koba, Petralona, Brno-Předmosti, Vértesszöllös, Krapina, Neander Valley, Bilzingsleben, Spy, Engis, Mauer, Steinheim, Ehringsdorf, Saccopastore, Monte Circeo, Paviland, Swanscombe, Biache, Bruniquel, Montgaudin, Arago, Saint-Césaire, 1,2, 6,7, 3,4,5, Gibraltar, Termifine, Dar-es-Soltane, Salé, Rabat, Temara, Sidi 'Abd ar-Rahmān, Jebel Irhoud, Thomas Quarries

Scale: 0 200 400 600 800 km / 0 200 400 600 mi

stable social system for teaching children, a long period of childhood for learning, and most importantly, an enhanced memory and language. Much of the information may be encoded in symbols—art, rituals, and myths—linked to complex religious systems, which can be seen as both the medium for transmitting such information and a powerful device for social unification (at least in non-plural societies, unlike our own, where competing religions or ideologies may, in contrast, be divisive instead of cohesive).

Toolmaking was once regarded as a unique human attribute and defining characteristic. Human adaptation is assisted by toolmaking and tool using, not just of obvious items such as digging sticks and hunting weapons, but also of things such as jewelry, clothes, and houses. Although there is now unequivocal evidence of such abilities in our closest relatives, the African apes, by comparison with any recent hunter-gatherers (the term generally used for the universal human method of subsistence prior to the introduction of agriculture, pastoralism, and industrialization), the use of tools by chimpanzees remains rudimentary. Modern humans use their technology in association with planning depth—that is, the ability of human societies to map their environment and anticipate the future, not just one day ahead, but provisioning for future seasons and even years. This allows a more intensive and efficient use of natural resources, and the possibility of more stable occupation patterns. It is such human behavioral characteristics which have allowed our species to colonize, and adapt to, nearly every terrestrial environment and space on our planet.

Examining the archaeological record for signs of the first development of aspects of modern human behavior is fraught with difficulties. Much of the evidence would have been mental, vocal, or otherwise perishable, and even that which survives to be excavated by archaeologists today has probably been seriously disturbed by various natural processes and only selectively preserved. Excavating a cave deposit containing ancient hearths and stone tools is a long way from examining the original habitation site as it existed on one particular day in the past, and even that last unrealistic possibility would provide few clues as to the whole cultural milieu of which the habitation site was a tiny transitory reflection. Nevertheless, archaeologists have made much progress toward extracting the maximum information available from ancient sites.

The old ideas of a uniform progression toward modern human behavior have now been abandoned. The three stages of the Paleolithic (Old Stone Age) were named when it was believed that these categories really represented successive stages of human evolution. The Lower Paleolithic (now stretching back to the beginnings of stone toolmaking over 2 myr ago, probably at the evolutionary grade of *Australopithecus* rather than *Homo habilis*) was the era of "simple" stone tools, from

Major sites of hominid fossil finds in sub-Saharan Africa.

pebble chopping tools and unspecialized flake tools to hand axes, while the Middle Paleolithic added to this more specialized flake tools and better control of the final product. Finally the Upper Paleolithic saw the dominance of narrow stone blade blanks which could be struck off in well-controlled quantities from blade cores and could then be modified into specialized tools such as scrapers, knives, and chisels. The Upper Paleolithic brought with it extensive utilization of previously neglected resources such as bone, antler, and ivory for artifact production. With the presence of art, symbolism, and complex burial patterns, the Upper

Paleolithic has been seen as a watershed in human behavioral evolution, certainly recording the presence of modern *Homo sapiens* and the behavioral repertoire found in recent hunter-gatherers. [4,5,15]

However, it is clear that the divisions of the Paleolithic have only a loose correlation with the physical evolution of humans. The Lower Paleolithic was probably the product of *Australopithecus, Homo habilis, Homo erectus,* and "archaic *Homo sapiens,*" while the Middle Paleolithic is now known to have been produced by "archaic *Homo sapiens,*" the Neanderthals, and early modern *Homo sapiens.* As we shall see, even the most cherished correlation, that of the Upper Paleolithic and modern humans, has been contradicted recently by the association of a Neanderthal skeleton with early Upper Paleolithic stone tools in France. There has thus been a decoupling of supposed cultural evolutionary stages from the physical evolution of humans, and a realization that these divisions of the Paleolithic are of only limited value. The possibility that modern human behavior has gradually and steadily developed to its present form through the whole of the Pleistocene now seems less probable than that behavioral evolution occurred in fits and starts, with long periods of relative stagnation. On this reading of the archaeological evidence, many of the features of modern human behavior (such as language and planning depth) only reached their present levels of complexity in the later Pleistocene, near the time of the arrival of a modern human anatomy. Whether even the Neanderthals and the first modern-looking humans were fully human in a behavioral sense is now a hotly disputed topic.

Theories of *Homo sapiens* origins

Two extreme models have been produced recently to account for the origin of modern-looking people, with other workers adopting various intermediate positions between the extremes. [16,17] One view proposes that modern humans evolved locally in different parts of the world from dissimilar archaic ancestors at the *Homo erectus* and "archaic *Homo sapiens*" stages. [18] This multiregional model of local continuity is sometimes called the Neanderthal phase model, since it postulates hominids of comparable evolutionary grade to the European Neanderthals giving rise to local descendant modern populations through parallel evolution worldwide. Thus in Europe a direct unilinear evolutionary sequence might exist between ancient European populations, represented by the Mauer jaw, and modern Europeans, via such intermediates as the Neanderthals and Cro-Magnons. Similarly, in the Far East the Zhoukoudian *Homo erectus* specimens could represent ancient ancestors for modern Asian peoples, via such intermediates as the Jinniu Shan and Dali material. And in Indonesia, *Homo erectus* fossils could represent populations that eventually gave rise to modern Australian peoples, via such intermediates as the Ngandong (Solo) and Willandra Lakes fossils.

In this model, regional "racial" variation is very ancient, with local features persisting between ancient and modern populations over periods longer than half a million years. Most proponents also allow for significant gene flow to have occurred between the local lineages, so that speciation did not occur and so that the fundamentally similar anatomy of all modern peoples could have evolved everywhere. In the "centre and edge" version, for example, the great variation found in recent and Pleistocene Australians is explained as a result of local evolution (from Javanese *Homo erectus*) combined with migration or gene flow from the Asian mainland (e.g., as represented by the Mungo fossils). [19]

In stark contrast with the local continuity model, the Noah's Ark model postulates that all modern humans derived from a single recent common ancestral population. From this model it follows that population movement or expansion rather than local evolution was the primary determinant of the spread of modern human characteristics during the last 50 kyr. In this proposal, the dispersal of modern humans was at the expense of the resident "archaic *Homo sapiens*" populations (such as the Neanderthals in Europe), who became extinct without evolving into modern humans. Local "racial" features evolved after the anatomic features that are shared by all living *Homo sapiens*, whereas in the local continuity model, "racial" features were the more ancient. [20]

The exact geographic location of such a source population for all living humans was previously uncertain, but most proponents of the Noah's Ark model now favor Africa or Southwest Asia as the likely area(s). [21] The model is often termed "Out of Africa." The evidence for the earliest occurrence of anatomically modern fossils in these areas will be discussed later, but there is support for the model that is independent of the fossil evidence, from considerations of recent human skeletal variation and recent genetic analyses (*see* below). Geographically and physically distinct human populations show a fundamental similarity in anatomy, and it is difficult to believe that such a large number of characters in common could have evolved independently under very different environmental or cultural conditions in various parts of the world, or that the process of gene flow alone could account for their ubiquitous nature. Features which distinguish modern humans from each other are relatively minor and thus could have been superimposed on a fundamental modern anatomic blueprint inherited from a recent common ancestor.

As mentioned above, there are various intermediate scientific viewpoints which lie between the extremes of multiregional evolution and the Noah's Ark/Out of Africa model. Thus one could envisage an area like Africa as first providing more of the novel characteristics of modern *Homo sapiens,* which were then spread by interbreeding and selection through "archaic *Homo sapiens*" populations. [17] These local populations thus gradually changed in situ into modern humans. There would thus be an assimilation of modern features, rather than a complete replacement by them. One further possibility is that there were distinct centers of modern human evolution in different continents, e.g., one in Africa and one in, say, China. "Archaic *Homo sapiens*" in both areas could have evolved modern features, which then spread and mixed through the world. On this model, people like the Neanderthals might still have been replaced in Europe. [22,23]

"Archaic *Homo sapiens*"

The Neanderthals are usually regarded as a type of "archaic *Homo sapiens*" by most workers, but since we know so much more about them, and they have their own special characters, they will be discussed separately later. Determining which specimens actually belong in "archaic *Homo sapiens*," rather than in the earlier and also temporally overlapping species, *Homo erectus,* is not always easy, as many fossils from the middle Pleistocene display mixed features from the two species which may reflect the gradual nature of the evolutionary transition or transitions between the two groups. The fact that fossils with such mixed and apparently intermediate characteristics have been preserved in the meager fossil sample so far available suggests that the evolution of "archaic *Homo sapiens*" was not a punctuational event. [9,10,24]

Characteristics of "archaic Homo sapiens"

It is possible to list a series of characteristics which typify (but do not occur universally or exclusively in) the various fossil specimens from Europe, Asia, and Africa which are generally grouped in "archaic *Homo sapiens*" (excluding the Neanderthals, as we have mentioned). [9,10,25] Endocranial capacity (equivalent to maximum brain volume) ranges between about 1,000 and 1,400 ml, with the lowest figure similar to the mean of *Homo erectus* and the maximum figure close to the means of Neanderthal and modern samples. In the face there is a reduction in total prognathism (i.e., the face juts out less from the cranial vault) compared to *Homo erectus* specimens, and it thus approximates the form of Neanderthal and modern skulls. The upper face retains the breadth found in *Homo erectus,* including the area between the orbits, but there is a greater degree of midfacial projection, similar to the mean level found in modern *Homo sapiens* and in some cases even matching that of Neanderthals. On the base of the skull the tympanic bone of the ear region is not greatly thickened and is nearly aligned with the adjoining petrous bone. These features are found in Neanderthal and modern humans, while in *Homo erectus* the tympanic is more robust and orientated more like that of earlier hominids. [9,25] The temporal bone is relatively short with an evenly curved upper edge, as in later humans, but unlike that of *Homo erectus*. Undoubtedly this feature is correlated in some way with the increase in brain size and cranial height compared with most *Homo erectus*, as are a number of other changes in the shape and proportions of the braincase. The cranial vault remains relatively long and low, as in *Homo erectus*. Nevertheless, the parietal bones tend to be somewhat longer and more arched, and the shape of the skull from behind does not show the upward convergence found in *Homo erectus* specimens. Instead the parietal bones are usually nearly vertical, with some expansion and rounding in their upper regions, where *Homo erectus* skulls are poorly filled or flattened. At the rear of the braincase, the occipital bone is higher and often less sharply angled, while the transverse occipital torus is usually reduced, especially at the sides. The nuchal (neck) musculature may still be strongly developed in both extent and depth of muscular impressions on the bones, but the nuchal area faces downward rather than backward.

A number of features of the cranium of "archaic *Homo sapiens*" show a reduced robusticity or thickness compared with those of *Homo erectus*, and although the extent of this is very variable, the reduced occipital torus development, the usually less thickened vault, and the reduced extent of midline "keeling" and overall "buttressing" (e.g., the less common occurrence of a bony protuberance at the back of the parietal, known as the angular torus) all reflect this. In general the browridges are still strongly developed, but there may be a more curved shape, and internally there is often a considerable lightening through the presence of large air cavities (sinuses), which are still of uncertain significance.

Not much is yet known of the rest of the skeleton of "archaic *Homo sapiens*" specimens, although a number of isolated finds have been made. Until the considerable collection of material from Atapuerca [26] and the Jinniu Shan skeleton from China [27] have been fully published, there is little to compare with the more complete material available for *Homo erectus*, Neanderthals, and, of course, modern *Homo sapiens*. Nevertheless, for the few parts which are known or published, there is an overall robusticity (in features such as limb bone shaft thickness) like that found in *Homo erectus* and Neanderthals, and of the three pelvic specimens so far described which have been assigned to "archaic *Homo sapiens*," two (Arago 44, Broken Hill) show the presence of the strong vertical thickening above the hip joint (the iliac pillar), which is known from early *Homo* hipbones. [28] Despite this, there are, in some specimens, hints of a closer approach to the modern morphology in details such as thighbone (femur) shape.

"Archaic Homo sapiens" *in Europe*

Europe and Africa still have the best records of "archaic *Homo sapiens*" material, although significant finds continue to be made in Asia. [29] The European specimens include incomplete fossils such as those from Mauer, Vértesszőllős, and Bilzingsleben, which some workers classify as actually representing *Homo erectus,* and it is true that from their preserved parts it is difficult or impossible to resolve their taxonomic status. [8,30,31]

The Mauer mandible was discovered during quarrying in a sand and gravel pit at Mauer near Heidelberg, Germany, in 1907. The associated fossil mammals suggest a middle Pleistocene age estimated at about 500 kyr. Apart from the Georgian find of the Dmanisi mandible, [32] this jaw is probably still the oldest European fossil hominid yet discovered. Although it has been claimed that stone and bone artifacts have also been found at Mauer, there remains considerable doubt about this. The jaw has a thick body and a very broad ascending ramus. There is no chin development, but the teeth are quite small, leading to the suggestion that this could represent a female individual. Although there is no development of a space behind the molar teeth found in Neanderthal jaws, the specimen is long, indicating that the associated face was probably quite projecting. Originally classified as the type of a new species, *Homo heidelbergensis,* most workers now regard the jaw as representing a European form of *Homo erectus* or an "archaic *Homo sapiens.*"

The travertine of Vértesszőllős, near Budapest in Hungary, produced two hominid specimens between 1964 and 1965. The site is generally dated to a warm stage within the Mindel glaciation of continental Europe, and uranium series dates originally suggested an age of >300 kyr. However, recent dating by U-S suggests an age of only 200 kyr for the hominid levels. The hominid specimens comprise some teeth of a child and the occipital bone (the back part of the skull) of an adult. The latter specimen has been the subject of much dispute regarding its affinities. Although thick and fairly angulated, with a centrally developed bony ridge—the occipital torus—the specimen is also large and relatively rounded. The brain size was probably more than 1,300 ml, leading some to suggest that it is "archaic *Homo sapiens,*" but others, pointing to its disputed age, its thickness and shape, classify it as *Homo erectus.*

Where more complete material of comparable age is known from Europe, it is apparent that referral to *Homo erectus* is not the most appropriate option. [31] One cranium is a particularly fine example of such a fossil, and it is a pity that dispute about its age has clouded its significance. It was found in 1960 deep in a cave near the village of Petralona in northeastern Greece. Although it has been claimed that a whole skeleton was originally present, this seems unlikely. Because the original location was not studied carefully at the time of the discovery,

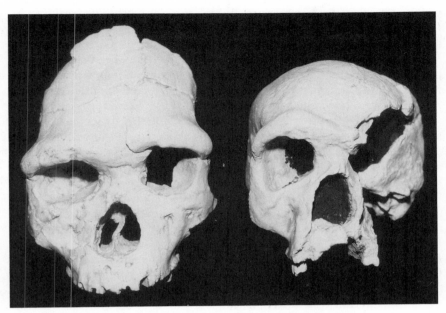

Figure 4. A comparison of two European fossils from the middle Pleistocene: (left) Arago 21, from France, and (right) Steinheim, from Germany. Both show very strong browridges, but Steinheim is considerably smaller and thinner boned, with a flatter face and signs of a hollowed cheek region.

many uncertainties about the associations and age of the skull can never be resolved. Absolute dating by U-S, TL, and ESR suggests that the cranium may be as young as 200 kyr, or older than 350 kyr. Study of fossil mammals found elsewhere in the cave supports the more ancient age estimates, but claims for an antiquity of more than 700 kyr are extremely unlikely. The cranium does show *Homo erectus*-like characters in its uniformly thick browridge, its broad upper face, palate, and base, its centrally strong occipital torus, and its thickened braincase. Brain capacity is about 1,220 ml, overlapping the *Homo erectus* and late *Homo sapiens* ranges, while the endocranial cast of the brain cavity is rather less flattened than in typical *Homo erectus* specimens. However, there are also advanced (derived) characters which are shared with later Pleistocene (especially Neanderthal) crania. These include a lesser degree of total facial prognathism, but increased midfacial projection, a double curvature of the browridge, prominent nasal bones, and an occipital torus that is lower in position and reduced laterally.

The extensive sample of fossil human material from the Arago Cave has been classified as *Homo erectus* by some workers, mainly on the basis of primitive characteristics and the supposedly high antiquity of the specimens [31] (fig. 4). This cave, near Tautavel in the French Pyrenees, has been under excavation since 1964. The Arago specimens, which include a face, jawbones, a hipbone, and other fragments, in fact compare well with European fossils that are generally accepted as representing "archaic *Homo sapiens,*" such as the Petralona, Steinheim, and Atapuerca materials. It is even conceivable that the Arago sample, like these, derives from a population that ultimately gave rise to the Neanderthals, and characters of the Arago 21 face and the Arago 2 mandible have been cited in support of this view. [24,37]

Even more difficult than the classification of the Arago material is an appropriate assignment for the Bilzingsleben cranial fragments. The travertine site of Bilzingsleben in eastern Germany has been known as a paleontological site for many years, but it is only since 1973 that its importance has been recognized through large-scale and productive excavations. Abundant faunal and archaeological remains dated to about 350 kyr have been found in hominid occupation levels which apparently include extensive butchery debris and possibly even remains of hut structures. [30] The cranial fragments are certainly the most *Homo erectus*-like of all the European cranial specimens in the strong browridge and occipital torus development, and in the proportions and angulation of the back of the skull. Yet this material lacks the areas which appear most advanced in the Petralona skull, and the missing areas of the parietal region may well have been less primitive. Even considering the *Homo erectus*-like occipital region, it is less robust than that of any of the Zhoukoudian (Peking man, *Homo erectus*) adults and is similar in proportions to that of the African Elandsfontein cranium, which is usually referred to African "archaic *Homo sapiens.*"

The Steinheim skull was found in a quarry near Stuttgart, Germany, in 1933. [10,25,31] It is a nearly complete cranium but is badly distorted (*see* fig. 4). Brain size is small (less than 1,200 ml) and the cranial walls are thin, but the browridges are strongly developed. The back of the vault is evenly curved, and in its present state of preservation the position of maximum breadth of the skull is quite high. The damaged face is relatively small, broad, and flat, with a large nasal opening and apparently rather delicate cheekbones with a canine fossa. However, the cheekbones may also be distorted. It is a puzzling specimen, small brained and relatively large browed, yet in other respects it shows advanced characteristics in the thin vault and the occipital shape. In certain respects the back of the skull resembles that of Swanscombe and the Neanderthals (*see* below), yet the shape and proportions of the face seem distinctly primitive (and, paradoxically in this respect, also more modern). The combination of a somewhat Neanderthal-like occiput and apparently primitive face is exactly the opposite of the situation in the Petralona skull, and unless we can accept that these differences are expressions of characters which are mainly related to sexual dimorphism (i.e., differences due to sex, with Petralona as a male and Steinheim as a female), it is difficult to classify these fossils together or arrange them in an orderly morphological sequence from *Homo erectus*-like to Neanderthal-like specimens. The Steinheim skull does not fit comfortably into either the *Homo erectus* or Neanderthal groups, and by default it has remained assigned to "archaic *Homo sapiens.*" A recent suggestion has been that it could represent a distinct middle Pleistocene species. [33]

As we have seen, several other middle Pleistocene fossil hominids are difficult to assign because of incomplete or conflicting data. This is especially true of mandibular specimens such as the one from Mauer. Some of the less complete specimens do appear to show Neanderthal characteristics, but it seems premature to classify them until the large sample of hominids from Atapuerca has been published, when we should be in a much better position to assess the more fragmentary finds. The complex of caves at Atapuerca in Spain has produced a number of hominid fossils from stratified and unstratified contexts. [26] Believed to be of middle Pleistocene antiquity, perhaps 200,000–300,000 years old, the main specimens from the Sima de los Huesos include most parts of the skeleton from perhaps twenty individuals. Although highly fragmented, it is anticipated that much more complete cranial and postcranial bones will be reconstructed from the fragments. They are already reported to show a considerable mixture of archaic and Neanderthal characteristics.

By the later middle Pleistocene, Europe was certainly populated by peoples who were closely related to the Neanderthals. The Swanscombe skull probably belongs in this group, along with the Biache, Fontéchevade, and the more ancient of the La Chaise fossils. As we will discuss, it may be more appropriate to refer these specimens to the species *Homo neanderthalensis* than to the "archaic *Homo sapiens*" grade.

"*Archaic* Homo sapiens" *in Africa*

A number of North African fossil hominids from the middle Pleistocene have been referred to *Homo erectus* on the basis of primitive characteristics, such as the Salé partial skull, with its cranial capacity of only 900 ml, and the specimens from the Thomas Quarries. [9,34]

The Salé skull was found in a quarry in Morocco in 1971. It probably approximates the Thomas Quarries specimens in age, with a possible antiquity of about 400 kyr. It is small, but the vault is long, low, and relatively thick walled. Muscle markings are only slightly developed, suggesting derivation from a female individual. While most of the characters already mentioned would suggest assignment of the Salé skull to *Homo erectus,* there are also some more advanced characters which are found in "archaic *Homo sapiens*" specimens. These include the basicranial proportions, an expanded parietal region, and a rounded back to the skull, with minimal development of an occipital torus. However, the back is quite abnormal in its proportions, suggesting the presence of disease. Because of its mixed characteristics, the classification of the Salé fossil is not generally agreed upon.

Three quarries near Casablanca in Morocco have produced Pleistocene faunal material, and hominid specimens were found at the Thomas 1 Quarry in 1969 (a mandible) and Thomas 3 Quarry in 1972 (cranial fragments). The sites are of approximately the same middle Pleistocene age as each other and Salé. The Thomas 1 jaw is rather similar to those attributed to *Homo erectus* from Ternifine, especially Ternifine 3, but is robust with large teeth, although the third molar is reduced in size. The Thomas 3 cranial fragments have not yet been published in detail, but they include frontal, facial, and dental parts of a small individual, probably comparable to the Salé specimen in size. The associated teeth, like those of Salé, are large and heavily worn, yet the associated face is rather delicately built. These fossils also bear a general resemblance to European material discussed above under the category of "archaic *Homo sapiens*," and further study may establish their relationships on firmer grounds.

Certainly, from evidence elsewhere in Africa, there are strong reasons to link African and European hominids of the middle Pleistocene in at least a general way to differentiate them from Asian *Homo erectus* fossils. In particular there are definite similarities in overall cranial form and in certain anatomic details between the Broken Hill, Bodo, and Petralona crania. However, the Bodo specimen, while probably having the largest brain size, was also the most *Homo erectus*-like in features such as cranial thickness, keeling on the top of the skull, and facial projection. So there is a real problem involved in determining whether these fundamentally similar specimens should be grouped together in a category like "archaic *Homo sapiens*" or *Homo heidelbergensis,* or whether the Bodo skull should be separated off as representing *Homo erectus.* [9,25,33]

One additional aspect of interest here is the postcranial material which may be associated with the Broken Hill skull and other bones. [28] These were discovered during mining operations in what is now Zambia between 1921 and 1925. They derived from a cave which was subsequently destroyed. The main discovery was the well-preserved cranium of an adult which became the holotype of the species *Homo rhodesiensis,* and which is now sometimes assigned to *Homo sapiens rhodesiensis.* The skull shows evidence of disease, e.g., dental decay and abscessing, and perhaps also a tumor in the temporal bone. The cranium shows a mixture of characteristics, with a quite large cranial capacity of about 1,280 ml, a moderately thick, long, and flattened vault, and a massive and pneumatized browridge. There is a well-developed occipital torus centrally like those of *Homo erectus* skulls, but the cranium is high with parallel walls. The remainder of the Broken Hill human material cannot be directly related to the cranium because of the uncontrolled manner in which it was excavated, but a rather modern-looking shinbone (tibia) was closely associated. The only significant additional cranial material recovered was an upper jaw fragment like the one from Ngaloba (*see* below). However, postcranial remains of at least three individuals appear to be present, represented by fragments of femurs, humeri, and hipbones, as well as the tibia. In general the postcranial bones, although robust, appear somewhat more modern in shape than those of the Neanderthals, despite the presence of a strong buttress (iliac pillar) on one of the hipbones.

For other African middle Pleistocene specimens such as Ndutu and Elandsfontein, there are fewer problems about assignment to "archaic *Homo sapiens*." [5,9,22,35] The Tanzanian Ndutu skull, believed to date to about 400 kyr ago, is a specimen which combines a small face and rather rounded cranial vault with large brows, rather reminiscent of the Steinheim and Salé/Thomas Quarry fossils. The middle Pleistocene site of Elandsfontein, also known as Saldanha, near Hopefield in South Africa, has produced extensive faunal remains and hand axes. A partial human cranium lacking the face and base was discovered there in 1953, and a mandible and skull fragment that may be associated were found some distance away. The skull resembles the Broken Hill cranium in its general shape, although it is less robust, with a smaller browridge and an estimated brain size of about 1,225 ml. It may represent a female individual of the same kind of population, although the Elandsfontein specimen is probably more ancient, of the order of 300 kyr ago.

In the absence of more advanced Neanderthal or modern features, the term "archaic *Homo sapiens*" is usually extended to include later African fossils such as those from Eliye Springs (Kenya), Florisbad (South Africa), Jebel Irhoud (Morocco), and Ngaloba (Tanzania). [22,35] The latter skull (Ngaloba Laetoli Hominid 18) was discovered in late middle–early late Pleistocene deposits in 1976 (fig. 5). Middle Stone Age (Middle Paleolithic) artifacts were reportedly associated with the discovery, which can be dated to about 120 kyr ago by correlation with a dated volcanic deposit at nearby Olduvai Gorge. The fossil comprises most of the cranial vault and the lower part of the face, which unfortunately cannot be directly fitted together because of damage. Browridge development is archaic but not strong, the frontal bone is long, low, and receding, but the back is rounded. In this respect and in details of the ear region, the specimen is rather Neanderthal-like. Brain size was originally quoted as only about 1,200 ml, but a higher figure (about 1,350 ml) has also been measured. Although generally regarded as an "archaic *Homo sapiens*" fossil, it is believed by some workers to have nearly a modern human morphology.

The Florisbad partial skull was discovered in 1932 from the lowest peat level at this South African site near Bloemfontein. The skull has recently been reconstructed more accurately, and its broad frontal bone is now accompanied by a broader face and palate. The vault is thick, the forehead moderately low, and browridge development is strong by modern standards, although less than in crania such as Elandsfontein and Broken Hill. Radiocarbon dates from a Middle Stone Age occupation site higher in the sequence suggests an age for this level of more than 43 kyr, and new absolute dates for the skull layer suggest an antiquity of more than 100 kyr. The Florisbad hominid is thus probably of late middle or early late Pleistocene age, and it may provide a link between the archaic southern African hominids associated with hand axes (e.g., Elandsfontein) and early modern humans associated with the succeeding Middle Stone Age (e.g., Klasies River Mouth).

The Moroccan cave of Jebel Irhoud has produced a number of fossil hominid specimens, along with Middle Paleolithic artifacts, since 1960. The most complete are an adult skull with face, the braincase of another adult, and a child's lower jaw. There are also fragments of a child's arm bone, and of a hipbone. The child's jaw has quite a small body but very large teeth, and it shows signs of a developing chin. The adult skulls are rather long and low, as in Neanderthals, but skull 1 has a broad flat face, with a rather small nose and modern-looking cheekbones, while skull 2 has smaller brows and a high forehead. The child's arm bone is strongly built, similar in the parts preserved to a Neanderthal. The age of these finds has been uncertain until recently, but ESR dating suggests

Figure 5. An "archaic *Homo sapiens*" skull from Africa (Laetoli Hominid 18 from Ngaloba, Tanzania). Sometimes regarded as anatomically modern, this specimen combines a flattened forehead and parietal region with a more modern-looking face and rear of the braincase. It is believed to date from about 130,000 years ago.

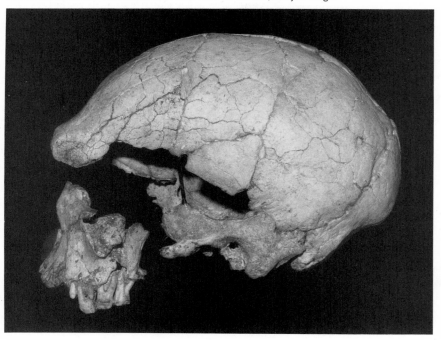

an antiquity of between 100 and 200 kyr. [12] When we arrive at the terminal middle and late Pleistocene, shared features of modern *Homo sapiens* begin to appear in specimens such as Omo-Kibish 2 (Ethiopia) and Jebel Irhoud 2, and this marks the point at which the term "archaic *Homo sapiens*" loses whatever validity it might possess.

"Archaic Homo sapiens*" in Asia*

Apart from a few uninformative fragments, the only probable pre-modern and pre-Neanderthal fossil in the Middle East is from Israel. The cave site of Mugharet-el-Zuttiyeh was excavated between 1925 and 1926, and it produced the first archaic fossil hominid recovered in western Asia. [36] The frontal bone and part of the upper face of this fossil human was derived from a low level at the site, which is believed to date from the late middle Pleistocene, perhaps 150 kyr ago. The specimen therefore appears to predate Neanderthals such as those from Tabūn, Amud, and Kebara. The Zuttiyeh specimen must have had a relatively small brain size, and the browridge is quite straight and strongly developed laterally. The upper face is flat, in contrast with that of later Neanderthals, and this has led to debate about the affinities of the fossil. Some scientists believe that the Zuttiyeh specimen represents a primitive ancestral Neanderthal, in which midfacial projection had not yet evolved, while others believe that it is more closely related to the ancestry of the modern people represented at the sites of Jebel Qafzeh and Skhūl about 100 kyr ago. Further to the East, the recently discovered skulls from Yunxian in China [37] and Narmada in India [38] are possible candidates for assignment to "archaic *Homo sapiens*" although they have alternatively been referred to *Homo erectus*. While the Narmada specimen does appear to have a poorly filled and keeled vault, it is also very high, with a rather rounded back. The Yunxian crania, found in 1990, are badly distorted but are very large. Although apparently robust in features such as cranial thickness, dental size, and the structure of the ear region (as in many *Homo erectus*), they also display a lack of buttressing features, a less-projecting face, and large brains (as in "archaic *Homo sapiens*"). They are provisionally dated to about 400 kyr ago.

More probable examples of "archaic *Homo sapiens*" are known from China, at sites such as Maba, Dali, and Jinniu Shan. [39] The latter two specimens are the most complete, although still not published in any detail, and the Jinniu Shan specimen in fact consists of a partial skull and much of the postcranial skeleton. [27] It is remarkable for its rather advanced characters, despite large brows and an absolute age determination of ca. 280 kyr, in that the vault is thin and well expanded (capacity more than 1,300 ml), and the face is not very massive. This might have been considered as a female individual of the Dali group but for the fact that it is sexed as male from the associated skeleton and has a considerably larger estimated brain size than Dali. If the Jinniu Shan skeleton is correctly dated, it has a number of important implications for human evolution in the Far East, particularly in the difficulty involved in deriving it from the apparently approximately contemporaneous *Homo erectus* populations known from Zhoukoudian (Peking man) and Hexian. The new Yunxian material may instead be more closely related to the ancestry of Jinniu Shan and Dali. [37]

The Dali skull was found in late middle Pleistocene loess (windblown) deposits in Shaanxi province in 1978. It is a well-preserved cranium with an estimated brain size of less than 1,200 ml, a large browridge, but a rather gracile and flat face. It is usually classified as a Chinese "archaic *Homo sapiens*."

In Southeast Asia, the only plausible claimants for "archaic *Homo sapiens*" status are those from Ngandong (Solo) on the Indonesian island of Java. However, many of the apparent *Homo sapiens*-like characteristics may be merely reflections of an increase in brain size achieved in parallel with that of middle Pleistocene specimens in Europe and Africa, for in the majority of features the Ngandong crania closely resemble their *Homo erectus* antecedents, with whom they are most reasonably classified. [9,35,39] Recent dating work suggests that they could be as young as 100,000 years in age. [40]

The Neanderthals

The Neanderthals are usually considered as late Pleistocene European hominids of the early part of the last glaciation (ca. 100–35 kyr ago), yet they undoubtedly had a much wider distribution in time and space than this. [5] The term *Neanderthal* has sometimes also been used in multiregional models in a very wide sense to indicate fossils which are considered to represent their grade equivalents throughout various parts of the world (including the Far East and Africa), [2,10] although this usage has declined recently, as the special characters of the European specimens have been increasingly appreciated. However, the wider use of the term *Homo neanderthalensis* could, perhaps, be justified, as we will discuss below. As yet there is no evidence that Neanderthals in the strict sense ever extended into Africa, but they were certainly present in western Asia, as known from occurrences in Israel, Iraq, and almost as far as Afghanistan with the Uzbekistan site of Teshik-Tash. Their western limits reached as far as Portugal, Spain, Gibraltar, and the British Isles. To the north, they extended at least as far as northern Germany and Poland. There is increasing evidence that the Neanderthals were cold adapted, as is indicated by their body proportions, and perhaps also by their facial shape, although in fact they never lived in true Arctic environments. However, they did inhabit a variety of temperate as well as boreal environments, including Mediterranean interglacial as well as northern glacial conditions.

The first recognized Neanderthal discovery was made at the Feldhofer Cave in the Neander Valley, Germany, in 1856. [1,2,31] This find was the first one of a fossil human type which was clearly distinct from living humans. William King in 1864 actually named a new human species *Homo neanderthalensis* for the remains, and that was the first time this had been done. Unfortunately, associated faunal or archaeological materials were not recovered, so the precise age of the specimen remains uncertain. The skull has a strong, curved browridge, is flattened and elongated, and has a projecting rear (*see* fig. 2). Brain size is about 1,400 ml, which is lower than average for a late Neanderthal individual, sexed as male from the hipbone. The skeleton is robust, with long bones which are thick walled and bowed (which led to erroneous suggestions that rickets was responsible). However, the skeleton shows a pathology of the elbow joint, probably caused by a fracture.

Earlier unrecognized finds of the same type had been made at the Engis Cave, Belgium, between 1829 and 1830 and at a cave in Forbes Quarry, Gibraltar, in 1848. [1,2,31] Initial informed and uninformed disputations about the significance of the unusual appearance morphology of the Neander Valley partial skeleton were gradually settled by further fossil discoveries during the next sixty years. These showed a comparable skeletal form, e.g., such as the Belgian finds from La Naulette and Spy, and in particular, the French finds from La Chapelle-aux-Saints, La Ferrassie, and La Quina. Important material of numerous but fragmentary Neanderthals from Krapina in Croatia received less scientific attention at the turn of the century but in fact represented a very informative source of data about the group. [42] By this time also, two very different interpretations of the evolutionary position of the Neanderthals were emerging. Some workers believed that they were the direct ancestors of living Europeans, while others believed that they represented a lineage of primitive hominids which had become totally extinct. As the sample size increased and morphological variation was noted in the fossils, further intermediate viewpoints developed. [2]

The characteristics of the Neanderthals

Many observations made on the relatively small sample of Neanderthals known by the beginning of this century have been confirmed by further study, while others have been shown to be misconceptions based on incomplete knowledge or preconceived ideas about the course of human evolution. [5,43] Some Neanderthal features previously regarded as primitive are known from wider study to be present in at least some modern populations (for example, details of the neck vertebrae), while others appear to be rather specialized (for example, the shape and size of the nose). Some supposedly aberrant features are in fact primitive for

69

hominids and can be recognized in recent discoveries representing more archaic groups. Some examples are the long, low cranial vault with a flattened top to the skull, and a short parietal arch (*see* fig. 2, fig. 6). There is a primitive (for humans in general) well-developed browridge which is stronger centrally, a relatively large face with a broad nasal opening, fairly large teeth (especially the front teeth, the incisors), and a lower jaw (mandible) which in most cases lacks a bony chin. The base of the skull is quite broad and in some Neanderthals, at least, is flattened out rather than well flexed. The rest of the skeleton shares a whole suite of characters with those of earlier humans, through an emphasis on strong musculature and thickened shafts to the bones. [42]

Advanced (derived) characters which the Neanderthals appear to share with living humans include the lateral reduction of the browridge, the reduced development of the occipital torus, the relatively rounder profile at the back of the skull, the large brain (mean value above the present mean of about 1,400 ml), reduced total facial projection, and the lack of a vertical ridge of bone (the iliac pillar) above the hip joint (acetabulum) of the pelvis.

The Neanderthals also have their own special characteristics, present in most or all specimens but rarely found outside the group. These features, which appear to be specializations, include the spherical profile of the cranial vault in rear view, and the posterior position of the (usually very large) maximum breadth of the skull, giving almost a teardrop shape when viewed from above. At the back there is a central depression at the upper limit of the neck musculature (called a suprainiac fossa) and a prominent ridge along the lower edges of the occipital bone. In the face there are a number of features associated with the phenomenon of midfacial projection, where the enormous nose stands out from the swept-back and convex cheekbones, and the tooth rows are also positioned far forward. This positioning of the teeth leads to the presence of a space behind the wisdom teeth—the third molars (called a retromolar space). On the inside of the rear of the lower jaw there is often an unusual form to the mandibular foramen or hole, which is probably related to the strong musculature of the jaws in Neanderthals, particularly those used to clamp the jaws together.

In the rest of the skeleton there are other features which could be specializations in Neanderthals, although because of limited information about these areas in earlier hominids we cannot always be sure. One concerns the body proportions of Neanderthals, which, as we shall see, may have been the result of cold adaptation. Another concerns the shoulder blade (scapula), which has on its back edge a well-developed groove for a muscle that runs forward to the upper arm. And at the front of the hipbone, the bone in the pubic region (the superior pubic ramus) is usually long and flattened in all Neanderthals (males, females, and even children), where this part has been preserved. [42] This latter

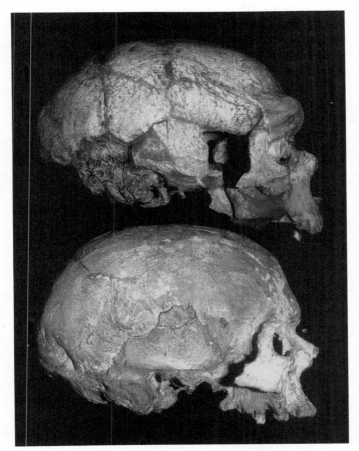

Figure 6. A comparison of (top) a French Neanderthal (La Chapelle-aux-Saints) and (bottom) an early modern (Cro-Magnon 1). Although separated by only some 20,000 years, the two skulls contrast markedly in the shape of the braincase and face.

feature has been linked with the birth of large-headed infants in Neanderthal women, or has been regarded as an effect of their peculiarly large-brained, large-headed, but short and stocky physiques. However, the discovery of a very complete Neanderthal skeleton in the Kebara Cave, Israel, [43] has led to the suggestion that the unusual pubic bone form is part of a hip structure which was still rather primitive. [44] This would have meant that the Neanderthals walked more forcefully than modern humans, with a greater side-to-side tilt.

Neanderthals were certainly large bodied by the standards of modern hunter-gatherers, and by various methods it is possible to estimate their body weight as about 65–70 kg (over 140 lb) in males and perhaps 50–60 kg (somewhat over 110 lb) in females. These weights would have been for lean and heavily muscled bodies, without the surplus weight that many of us carry around. Since many Neanderthals lived in relatively cold environments, it is not surprising, considering Bergman's biological "rule" of increasing body mass in colder environments, that they were heavily built. Similarly, following Allen's "rule," it would be expected that body extremities would be shortened if Neanderthals were cold-adapted, as this would tend to reduce heat loss from the extremities. This also appears to be the case in Neanderthals. As in present-day cold-adapted peoples such as the Lapps and Eskimos, their forearms (radius and ulna) and shinbones (tibia, plus the adjoining fibula) were proportionately shorter compared with the upper arm and leg bones. This effect was somewhat less marked in the Neanderthals of Iraq and Israel. [42,45]

As well as being stockily built (especially so in the massive trunk of the Kebara man), the Neanderthals were fairly short in stature. Estimates from the long bones of their skeletons suggest that males averaged about 169 cm (5 ft 6 in), while females averaged about 160 cm (5 ft 3 in) in height. As already mentioned, the Neanderthals were large brained, and their known average brain capacity is larger than the modern figure (over 1,450 ml). However, in common with *Homo erectus* and "archaic *Homo sapiens*," the brains of Neanderthals were low and broadest near the base, with small frontal lobes and large, projecting occipital lobes at the back. The significance for Neanderthal intellectual capabilities of the large size and unusual shape of their brains is unclear. Part of their larger brain size compared with modern humans might simply be related to their larger muscle masses, rather than a sign of great intelligence. In addition, it has been noted that modern populations nearer the poles tend to have larger brain sizes as well as body sizes, and this would again apply to the Neanderthals.

The early evolution of the Neanderthals

The ancestors of the Neanderthals are thought to have been the middle Pleistocene hominids of Europe (and perhaps also of western Asia, although little is known of them), which we have discussed above under the term "archaic *Homo sapiens*." However, the extent and significance of Neanderthal characters in such fossils is a matter of some dispute, as we have seen. Early European fossils such as those from Mauer and Bilzingsleben are not complete enough to be conclusively classified, but they are rather primitive in the characters they do display. A limited number of Neanderthal features are present in fossils such as those from Arago, Petralona, Vértesszőllős, and Atapuerca. Despite this, it is difficult to justify assigning any of these specimens to the Neanderthal group proper, and it is not until we reach the later middle Pleistocene that Neanderthal-derived characters begin to predominate over more primitive ones. [24,30,31]

Three parts of the back of a human skull associated with flint hand axes were discovered in a gravel pit at Swanscombe, near the River Thames, in England. [31] The occipital bone was discovered in the upper Middle Gravels in 1935, followed by the left parietal a year later, and the right parietal in 1955. The bones are thick by modern standards, but the occipital torus is only slightly developed, as are the muscle markings, leading to the suggestion that the skull belonged to a female individual. The brain size of the Swanscombe woman was probably about 1,300 ml, and the overall cranial shape is rather modern, without the characteristic angulation and torus development found at the back in earlier hominids, or the bulging back found in many Neanderthals. However, the curvature of the parietal is slight, and it is short, while the base is broad as in many archaic hominids. Three features particularly point to Neanderthal affinities. These are the slight, double-arched occipital torus surmounted by a central depression (the suprainiac fossa) and the suggestion at the occipital margins that there was a developed crest of bone. Overall it seems probable that the Swanscombe woman was a member of an early Neanderthal population that lived in Europe over 200 kyr ago.

Neanderthal affinities are even more obvious in the Biache partial cranium. [31] This site in northwestern France was exposed during commercial excavations in a river terrace. Hominid occupation occurred during relatively warm phases at a time of climatic fluctuation, probably during the penultimate (Saalian or Rissian) glaciation, since the site has been dated by TL to about 170,000 years. Archaeological material from the site consists mainly of flint flake tools rather than hand axes, and there are also a number of Middle Paleolithic tool types. The Biache hominid consists of the back part of a skull and parts of the upper jaw and dentition; it is probable that the whole skull was originally fossilized, but the remaining parts were not recovered. The partial vault is thin, but it does derive from a subadult individual. Brain size was fairly small, with an indicated capacity of about 1,200 ml. The overall cranial form is certainly Neanderthal-like, with a spherical shape when viewed from behind and a protruding back, very like the form of the later La Quina Neanderthal skull. In addition there is a prominent crest at the edges of the occipital and a suprainiac fossa. There seems little doubt that the specimen represents a member of an early Neanderthal population, and it provides an evolutionary link between earlier specimens such as Swanscombe and the later Neanderthals. The Fontéchevade specimens which, like Swanscombe, were once directly linked in an evolutionary scheme with modern humans in the supposed "presapiens" lineage, are now generally also regarded as representing early Neanderthals.

Further probable early Neanderthals from the period between 100 and 220 kyr ago include the specimens from La Chaise (Abri Suard and Bourgeois-Delaunay) in France, Ehringsdorf (Germany), and Saccopastore (Italy), [31] as well as a recently announced partial skull from Reilingen, Germany, which closely resembles the Swanscombe fossil. Saccopastore produced an interesting association of two early Neanderthal crania with fauna such as elephant and hippopotamus, and these specimens differ from later specimens primarily in their smaller size and somewhat less developed midfacial projection and the flattening of the skull base. They date from the last interglacial, about 120 kyr ago.

The Ehringsdorf hominids were recovered during both commercial and controlled excavations between 1908 and 1925 from travertine (spring carbonate) deposits in eastern Germany. The most significant specimens are an adult braincase, an adult lower jaw, a child's lower jaw, and various remains of the rest of the child's skeleton. Found in association with artifacts of Middle Paleolithic type, the fossils appear to represent early Neanderthals, and from U-S and ESR techniques they date from more than 200 kyr ago. The La Chaise material, which includes very Neanderthal-like jaw and occipital specimens, mostly dates from the period 100–150 kyr ago.

The large collection of early Neanderthals from the Croatian site of Krapina has been the subject of many different interpretations since its discovery at the turn of the century. [2,41] Some workers, noting the fragmentary condition and apparent variation displayed by the human fossils, believed that they resulted from a battle between Neanderthal and early modern populations which was followed by a cannibalistic feast. Others thought that the specimens were related to so-called generalized Neanderthals from western Asia (that is, the Zuttiyeh, Tabūn, and Skhūl fossils, when these were regarded as representing a single late Pleistocene population which was thought to be ancestral to both Neanderthals and modern people). However, further study of the Krapina specimens has shown that they actually represent rather robust early Neanderthals, with large teeth and strong brows in some specimens. Where shoulder blades, hipbone, hand and limb bones are preserved, these seem to display the typical Neanderthal pattern. The large sample of teeth is especially important, since it derives from at least fifteen individuals, many of which were children, and the condition of taurodontism (unseparated roots in the molars, with expanded pulp cavities) is especially developed. The real factors that lie behind the fragmentary condition of the Krapina sample are still uncertain, but ancient human interference seems to be at least partly responsible. Actual cannibalism by Neanderthals may have occurred, or skeletons may have been defleshed and broken up for ritual reburial, as still happens in some parts of the world today.

One cave that was believed to be a late Neanderthal site has recently been shown by TL and ESR dating to contain early Neanderthals. This is the cave of Tabūn on Mount Carmel, Israel, which was originally excavated between 1929 and 1934 by the same team that investigated the nearby early modern site of Skhūl. [36] Middle Paleolithic stone tools were recovered from levels C and D at the site, which also produced two hominid fossils—a skeleton of a female (Tabūn 1) and a lower jaw, probably of a male (Tabūn 2). Recent research at the site suggests a possible age of about 120 kyr for level C. [12,46] Tabūn 1 is a reasonably complete skeleton of an adult female with a relatively small skull (brain volume about 1,300 ml) and body. Brow development is strong, and although the occipital region is rather rounded, the specimen has some Neanderthal features. The skeleton was the first one in which the unusual Neanderthal morphology of the front of the hipbone was recognized. The separate lower jaw of Tabūn 2 is large, but it shows a slight chin and only small spaces behind the third molars. Its affinities are less clear than that of Tabūn 1.

The late Neanderthals

The best-known Neanderthals are those from the period between 50 and 70 kyr ago in western Asia and between 35 and 70 kyr ago in Europe. [5,31,41] The western European specimens in this time range probably include the original Neander Valley partial skeleton that gave its name to the whole group (although its date cannot now be established accurately), the Spy Neanderthals from Belgium, the Devil's Tower and (perhaps) the Forbes Quarry partial skulls from Gibraltar, the Guattari Cave (Monte Circeo) skull and lower jaws from Italy, and the La Quina, La Chapelle-aux-Saints (*see* fig. 6), La Ferrassie, and Saint-Césaire partial skeletons from France. The latter specimens are particularly significant, as the La Ferrassie assemblage comprises several late Neanderthal skeletons which could even have derived from a family cemetery of an adult male, female, and young children, while the Saint-Césaire skeleton is the youngest fairly complete specimen in age (associated with early Upper Paleolithic Châtelpérronian stone tools dated to about 36 kyr by TL). Combined with the established contemporaneity of the Châtelpérronian and the Aurignacian, which appears to be the exclusive product of early modern people, this demonstrates with a fair degree of certainty the contemporaneity of late Neanderthals and modern populations in Europe between 30 and 40 kyr ago. [5,31]

Until this 1979 discovery at the rock shelter near Saint-Césaire, the nature of the population responsible for the manufacture of early Upper Paleolithic Châtelpérronian stone tools remained an enigma. [31] While the tools appeared to represent a local development for the earlier local Middle Paleolithic, only the Neanderthal-like teeth from Arcy-sur-Cure and the modern-looking (but apparently wrongly associated) skeleton from Combe Capelle provided clues as to the nature of the manufacturers. However, the Saint-Césaire skeleton is from the higher of the two Châtelpérronian levels at the site and is assumed to represent a contemporaneous human population dating from about 36 kyr ago. The main skull parts consist of the right side of the front with the face and right half of the lower jaw. The frontal bone, brows, face, and jaws are Neanderthal, although the nose and teeth are relatively small. The rest of the skeleton is fragmentary but Neanderthal-like in its robusticity.

The central and eastern European material consists of less complete fossils but does include a lower jaw and other specimens from Subalyuk (Hungary), an upper jaw and other fragments from Kulna (Czechoslovakia), and various specimens from Vindija (Croatia). [41] This cave in Croatia has produced a number of fragmentary late Pleistocene fossil hominids from a sequence containing Middle and Upper Paleolithic tools. [47] The earlier specimens are definitely Neanderthal-like, while the later specimens are modern in morphology, but there are specimens in an intermediate position in the cave deposits which are said to show a transitional morphology and which are claimed to be associated with Aurignacian tools. However, the specimens in question are very fragmentary, and this exceptional archaeological association of Aurignacian and "Neanderthals" remains very uncertain. Some scientists [10,18,41] consider that certain of central eastern European fossils show evolutionary trends that indicate a gradual approach toward a modern morphology, and the Vindija specimens certainly appear less robust than the earlier Krapina hominids. However, no European specimens have yet been discovered which display an undoubted transitional morphology between Neanderthals and early modern humans, and therefore there is no proof of regional continuity.

The Neanderthals of western Asia differed in certain respects from their European counterparts. [36,42] Variation in size, robusticity, and morphology is apparent when comparing the Shanidar Neanderthals from Iraq with each other, or with the Neanderthals from the Israeli sites of Amud and Kebara. Yet these fossils and others from sites such as Kiik-Koba and Teshik-Tash (both in the former Soviet Union) share major similarities in derived characteristics with European Neanderthals. In 1938–39 the incomplete skeleton of a Neanderthal boy about eight years old was found in the Teshik-Tash cave in Uzbekistan. The child was apparently buried surrounded by an arrangement of goat skulls. The cranium is particularly well preserved and shows clear Neanderthal features in the face, lower jaw, and braincase. The brain size was already very large (over 1,500 ml) and must have been close to its adult value. The antiquity of the specimen is unclear, although it is often assigned to the last glaciation.

The large Shanidar sample is especially important, probably spanning many millennia prior to 50 kyr ago, consisting of nine individuals of both sexes and various ages. [42] These include a man who had suffered extensive injuries some time before he died (Shanidar 1) and one of the most massive but characteristic Neanderthal faces ever discovered (Shanidar 5). There was also a skeleton (Shanidar 4) claimed to represent a burial with flowers, although the evidence has been disputed. The Amud and Kebara skeletons from Israel show further variation, since the Kebara male had a very massive lower jaw and skeleton, while the Amud man was the largest brained (about 1,740 ml volume) and tallest (about 179 cm (5 ft 10 in) stature) Neanderthal so far discovered. The cave of Kebara first produced fossil hominid specimens in 1931 and has recently been further excavated. Earlier work produced the remains of a child from Middle Paleolithic levels, but the more extensive recent work has recovered the most complete body skeleton of a Neanderthal yet found. [43] This presumed burial had no skull preserved, but it did have the massive lower jaw and skeleton of the entire upper part of the body of an adult male. The well-preserved shoulder blades and hipbones show characteristic Neanderthal features.

Amud was first excavated in 1961 [36] and produced the important partial skeleton of an adult male Neanderthal. Despite his large size, he had relatively small teeth and a lower jaw with a slight chin development. Recent work at Amud has revealed further finds, including the skeleton of a baby, and ESR dating suggests a relatively young age for the Neanderthals—about 50 kyr. [12] As with the central and eastern European specimens, some workers discern signs of evolution toward a modern morphology in the Neanderthals of Asia, but the dating of the specimens is not precise enough to construct valid evolutionary trends for the whole sample. Nevertheless, the Asian Neanderthals do seem less extreme than their European relatives in some respects when both are compared with modern humans. However, new dating work has revolutionized our oversimplified picture of recent human evolution in the Middle East by showing that Neanderthals such as Kebara and Amud could not have been ancestral to the first modern people there, since the early moderns apparently *preceded* them by a considerable period!

Early fossil evidence of modern *Homo sapiens*

If we take the suite of skeletal characteristics given earlier to describe modern *Homo sapiens* and make that suite of features the basis for recognizing whether a particular fossil falls within the overall range of modern *Homo sapiens,* then there is no reliable evidence of this complex of features prior to 150 kyr ago. At less than 100 kyr ago there were areas of the world where hominids still fell outside this range: Europe and the Middle East with Neanderthals, and (perhaps) Java with the Ngandong fossils commonly assigned to *Homo erectus.* For China the evidence is too poor for definitive statements about the first appearance of the modern anatomic pattern. However, two areas do contain more convincing evidence for a modern human presence at around 100 kyr ago. These areas are Africa and the Middle East. [5,16]

The African evidence for early modern humans

The African record of early moderns consists of specimens from the South African sites of Klasies River Mouth and Border Cave, the North African site of Dar-es-Soltane, and the East African sites of Guomde (Kenya) and Omo-Kibish (Ethiopia). [22,23,35] Florisbad (South Africa), Jebel Irhoud (Morocco), and Ngaloba (Tanzania) have already been discussed; they contained fossils which some workers include in the early modern category, although that is not a view which I share. Because some of the specimens are derived from dubious contexts, or ones where absolute dating has not been a practical proposition until now, some workers have not accepted any as representing genuinely early records of a modern morphology from Africa. [18]

The material from the Klasies River Mouth complex of caves (South Africa) is fragmentary and shows clear variation in size and shape. The specimens are believed by their excavators to be more than 70 kyr old, and they are all associated with Middle Stone Age (Middle Paleolithic) artifacts. [48] Doubt had been expressed about the reliability of correlations used to date the Klasies material to the early late Pleistocene, but the results of recent excavations and absolute dating have supported the proposed antiquity of the hominid specimens and have produced new upper jaw fragments that can be dated at more than 100 kyr ago. [12,48,49]

The Middle Paleolithic-associated material from Klasies consists of cranial, maxillary, mandibular, dental, and skeletal fragments. [49] The cranial pieces include one (adult?) fragment of forehead that displays a small, modern type of browridge and other fragments that suggest a rounded but perhaps low braincase. The jaw fragments are generally modern looking, with small teeth, but there is variation in size and robusticity and chin development. The few limb bone fragments recovered suggest a gracile and modern body form. Although the specimens are so fragmentary, they are certainly close to or actually represent the modern skeletal pattern at around 100 kyr in age. Even more fragmentary evidence of probable Middle Paleolithic-associated early modern material has recently come from other South African sites such as the Die Kelders and Equus caves.

While there might be some doubts about the assignment of all the Klasies material to modern *Homo sapiens,* the modernity of the Middle Paleolithic-associated fossil hominids from Border Cave (South Africa) is unequivocal for most experts. [22,35,50] The specimens consist of a partial skull and limb bones of an adult, the partial skeleton of an infant, and two lower jaws. All fall into the overall range of modern humans, with only the moderately strong browridge development of the skull indicating any possible archaic character. However, the skull and limb bones and one of the lower jaws were not excavated in a con-

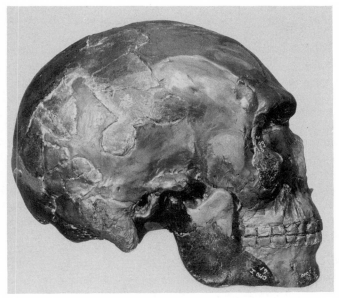

Figure 7. A reconstruction of the skull and lower jaw of Omo 1 (Ethiopia) by the author and Professor Michael Day. This specimen could represent the oldest known modern human skeleton.

trolled manner (they were exposed by a farmer looking for fertilizer). The infant's skeleton and the other jaw were excavated from Middle Paleolithic levels; nevertheless, doubts have been expressed about claims that they are all more than 70 kyr in age. Further work at the site is needed to resolve some of these questions, but ESR dating supports ages of about 60 kyr for one of the jaws and more than 70 kyr for the child's skeleton. [51]

The site of Omo-Kibish in southern Ethiopia has produced two fossil hominids that may represent early moderns as well as a third skull of nonmodern type. [22,35,52,53] The more complete early modern specimen is a partial skeleton which was found in a layer that considerably predates 40 kyr ago, based on radiocarbon dates from higher levels. According to U-S dates on shells, it could be as old as 130 kyr, making it the oldest modern *Homo sapiens* yet discovered. The skeleton indicates a heavily built but modern individual, and the same can be said for the associated skull. This has a long and broad frontal bone with fairly strong brows, but the rear of the skull and lower jaw appear entirely modern (fig. 7). The Omo skeleton seemingly documents the presence of essentially modern humans in northeastern Africa in the early late Pleistocene.

Elsewhere in Africa are specimens of fossil hominids that, while certainly more than 35 kyr in age, are difficult to classify as early moderns because they show a predominance of archaic characters and specimens that, while certainly representing modern humans, are not certainly more than 35 kyr old. Examples of the former category are the fossils from Ngaloba (Laetoli Hominid 18) and Irhoud, discussed above; examples of the latter category are the fossil cranial fragments from Kanjera (Kenya) and Springbok Flats (South Africa).

There is one more African sample that probably represents early modern *Homo sapiens:* the material from Dar-es-Soltane in Morocco. [15,23] Mostly unpublished, these fossils include a robust but modern front of a skull and lower jaw associated with the Middle Paleolithic Aterian industry. It probably predates 40 kyr ago. After this date, North Africa was populated by robust modern humans associated with Upper Paleolithic stone tools at sites like Nazlet Khater (Egypt), Afalou (Algeria), and Taforalt (Morocco). These populations resemble contemporaneous early modern people in Europe (the Cro-Magnons— *see* later), with whom they probably shared a recent ancestry.

The Middle East

This area has rich samples of early modern skeletons from the Israeli sites of Skhūl (Mount Carmel) and Jebel Qafzeh, many of which appar-

Figure 8. The skull of Qafzeh 6 (Israel). Materials from an equivalent level of this cave site been dated by TL and ESR to about 80,000 to 120,000 years ago.

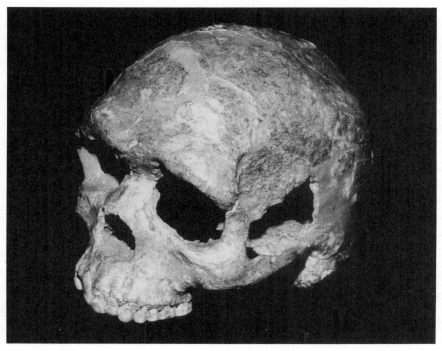

ently originate from intentional burials. [5,36] The extensive material from the former site was at first mistakenly linked with the Neanderthal material from the adjacent cave of Tabūn but is now believed from ESR and TL age estimates to date from about 100 kyr ago. [12] The antiquity of the even larger Qafzeh sample of partial skeletons has also recently been established from TL and ESR dating to about 90–120 kyr ago. Thus the Skhūl and Qafzeh material actually antedate many Neanderthal fossils, as well as other unequivocally modern humans from all other areas except Africa.

The fossil humans from Skhūl and Qafzeh consist of partial skeletons of adult males and females, as well as children and subadults. The adult crania have, by modern standards, large and quite prominent faces with large teeth, well-developed browridges, and large brain sizes (fig. 8). These features have been used to link the specimens to the Neanderthals, [10,18] but they are not specifically Neanderthal-like, and details of the shape of the face and nose contrast strongly with those of Neanderthals. Similarly, in the rest of the skeleton there is little of the robusticity and muscularity so typical of the Neanderthals and earlier humans, and details of hipbone structure are like those of recent humans. [36,44] Additionally, limb and body proportions for the Skhūl and Qafzeh skeletons are unlike those of Neanderthals and instead resemble those of present-day tropical or subtropical peoples. [45] Overall the appearance of these Israeli early moderns can be characterized as modern, but with some primitive features retained from middle Pleistocene ancestors. Those ancestors, to judge from certain details of the fossils, may have been African contemporaries of the early Neanderthals, such as Irhoud or Florisbad.

Early moderns from other areas

Claims for the occurrence of modern human skeletal materials that date from more than 35 kyr ago outside of Africa and the Middle East are rare and controversial. In Asia, early moderns possibly occur at Darra-i-Kur (Afghanistan), while in Europe possible examples are found at such sites as Krapina (a child's skull labeled "A"), Starosel'e (Ukraine), and Bacho Kiro (Bulgaria). [41] While the presence of modern humans in Europe is not clearly established prior to 35 kyr ago, they were probably widespread in Europe soon after this, to judge by the appearance of the Upper Paleolithic industry called the Aurignacian as far west as Spain and France by that time.

In all cases where a fossil human association with the Aurignacian is definite, the hominid is always anatomically modern *Homo sapiens,* and the European populations of these early modern people are collectively known as "Cro-Magnons," after a discovery made in the last century. [31] Several partial skeletons were recovered from the Cro-Magnon rock shelter near Les Eyzies in France in 1868 (*see* fig. 6).

They derive from late Aurignacian burials and gave their name to the whole Upper Paleolithic "race." Although strongly built and large headed, they contrast markedly with the Neanderthals in their anatomy and inferred physique. The term became synonymous with the term *Upper Paleolithic humans,* covering the period from ca. 35 to 10 kyr ago in Europe, but the discovery of a Neanderthal associated with early Upper Paleolithic Châtelpérronian stone tools at Saint-Césaire (France) has meant a change of usage. The term *Cro-Magnon* now covers a wide range of fossil material associated with different "cultures," such as the Aurignacian, Gravettian, Solutrean, and Magdalenian, but the extent to which it is really legitimate to group this range of material is debatable.

While no one doubts that the Cro-Magnons represent anatomically modern humans, they were undoubtedly different in several respects from Europeans of today. In some aspects it is possible to see retained primitive characters, such as relatively large teeth and brows, but attempts to recognize these as retained from ancestral Neanderthals are generally unconvincing. In some respects it is the Neanderthals who seem more specialized in their characters. For example, the bodies of the Cro-Magnons were quite distinct from those of the Neanderthals, since the lower portions of their arms and legs were elongated compared with the upper parts and with trunk height, whereas in the Neanderthals they were relatively shortened. In modern humans this physique is characteristic of warm-adapted populations, and it may therefore be a Cro-Magnon retention from African ancestors. [45] Similar retentions may be observed in certain indices of facial shape (such as in possessing a shorter, flatter, and relatively broader face, with low orbits and short nose), since such features were present in middle Pleistocene African specimens but not in Neanderthals.

Another feature that distinguishes Neanderthals from Cro-Magnons is the estimated greater stature of the latter, despite their overall similarity in estimated body weight, probably comparable with that of living Europeans. The Cro-Magnons probably averaged a stature of more than 180 cm (over 6 ft) in men and around 167 cm (5 ft 6 in) in women, a significant increase over typical European Neanderthals (men about 167 cm and women about 160 cm [5 ft 3 in]). [42] The tall and narrow-hipped physique of the Cro-Magnons certainly more closely resembled that of the Skhūl and Qafzeh fossils than that of Neanderthals, since average height in the European and Israeli early moderns was virtually identical. There is some uncertainty about the ancestral African pattern, but from the Nariokotome *Homo erectus* skeleton and the Broken Hill leg bones it seems to have been like the European and Asian earliest moderns, rather than like the Neanderthals.

However, some early Cro-Magnon specimens from eastern Europe do not fit so readily into such a definite Neanderthal/Cro-Magnon dichotomy. [41] One such sample is from the Mladec Caves in Czechoslovakia. Skeletal remains of several adults and a child were recovered from a blocked cavity which also contained Aurignacian stone, and bone, tools. Several of the skulls were very robust and have been regarded as Neanderthal-like. Unfortunately, most were destroyed in a fire in 1945, but replicas have survived, as well as the most complete skull, stored in Vienna. Some skulls show bulging backs reminiscent of Neanderthals, while another skull from Czechoslovakia, Prĕdmosti 3, even shows some Neanderthal-like features in facial shape. This suggests the possibility that some intermixture did occur between late Neanderthal and early modern humans in Europe during a probable period of coexistence between at least 40 and 33 kyr ago. If such hybridization did occur, it must have been on a limited scale, and there is no certainty that such hybrids contributed to the ancestry of later Europeans. [54]

From the inadequate evidence available from central Asia, certain populations of the late Pleistocene in the region seem to have been physically and culturally related to those of the European Upper Paleolithic. However, further east there is evidence of populations that could be related to modern aboriginal populations of the Far East and the Americas (which were apparently not colonized until less than 30 kyr ago, although the date of arrival is hotly disputed). [5,56] Several partial skeletons from the Upper Cave at Zhoukoudian (China), dated by radiocarbon to about 25 kyr ago, may represent a population ancestral to Oriental or Native American groups, but they show little sign of racial differentiation and rather resemble the contemporaneous Cro-Magnons [57] (fig. 9). Interestingly, they were associated with Upper Paleolithic-style artifacts.

In Southeast Asia there is evidence from a skeleton at the cave site of Niah (in the Malaysian part of Borneo) that modern humans were present there by 40 kyr ago, but this controversial date needs independent confirmation. [56] Farther south there is archaeological evidence that modern humans had used boats to reach Australasia by 50 kyr ago, but the nature of the original colonists, and whether they represented a single population or multiple migrations from different source areas, is still disputed in the absence of early fossil evidence. [18,19,54] However, the later Mungo (Willandra Lakes) skeletons from southern Australia are dated at 24–32 kyr ago, and the most complete specimens seem quite lightly built by the standards of many early moderns from elsewhere in the world, or even in comparison with some peoples alive today. The contrast is all the more marked because the same region of Australia was also populated by much more robust peoples at the end of the Pleistocene, as represented by the Willandra Lakes 50, Cohuna, and Kow Swamp samples. Publications concerning the latter (now sadly lost to science by reburial at the insistence of aboriginal activists) have tended to emphasize the specimens' robusticity (certainly very evident), but the sample also includes Mungo-like cranial and postcranial material.

One model postulates that two founder populations originally entered Australia, the first derived from Indonesian ancestors (such as Javanese *Homo erectus,* including the Ngandong material) and represented later on by specimens like Willandra Lakes 50, Kow Swamp, and Cohuna, while another migrated into the region from the Asian mainland, as represented by the Mungo and Keilor fossils. These two groups somehow coexisted through the later Pleistocene and eventually gave rise to native Australian populations by hybridization. An alternative proposal is that there was only one ancestral Australian population from either Indonesia or farther afield and that much of the variation developed within Australia as this huge unpopulated continent gradually became colonized. This variation may also have been exaggerated by disease and local customs such as head binding, which was certainly responsible for some of the peculiarities in skull shape among the Kow Swamp sample.

By 10 kyr ago, humans had reached most of the regions which are currently inhabited, including the Americas down to the southernmost regions and some of the Mediterranean islands. [55] Other more remote areas such as New Zealand and Madagascar remained uncolonized until much more recent times. The processes that drove human colonization were probably centered on population growth and a growing ability to adapt to new environments through behavior rather than just physiology. So, having reached the point where humans had established themselves over most of the earth's land surface, it is time for us to

Figure 9. (Left) A skull from Czechoslovakia (Předmosti 3) compared with (right) one from Upper Cave at Zhoukoudian, China. In a number of respects these near contemporaries, both dated 20,000 to 30,000 years ago, resemble each other more than they resemble their recent, and possibly descendant, local successors.

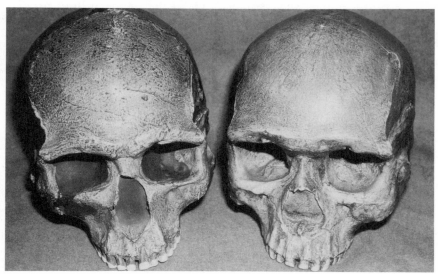

look at genetic variation in these dispersed populations and what it can tell us about the relationships and the origins among them.

Genetic reconstructions of recent human evolution

We all hold within our body cells information on our origins. The material of inheritance—DNA (deoxyribonucleic acid)—is organized into *genes,* the fundamental units of heredity, and it is the genes that determine features such as our blood groups and our skin, hair, and eye colors. [4] Our genes also set limits on our physical makeup, such as bone shapes, height, and body proportions, subject to additional factors such as nutrition and health. Our genes directly link us with our immediate ancestors, in particular our parents, who each pass on half of their genes to make up the new gene sets of their children. This last statement is, in fact, not the whole story of inheritance, because we actually all have two sets of genes in our body cells. One set is in the chromosomes of the cell nucleus (made up of *nuclear* DNA), and the other much smaller set is in the structures called mitochondria, which supply energy to the cell and lie outside the nucleus. Each mitochondrion has its own DNA, and this mitochondrial DNA (mtDNA) is inherited largely or entirely through females. So while a man has inherited nuclear genes from his mother *and* father in equal quantities, he has in all probability only inherited the mitochondrial genes of his mother. In turn, he would pass on half his nuclear DNA to a son or daughter, but none of his mtDNA.

Going further back in time, an individual's nuclear genes are linked with an increasing number of ancestors of both sexes, while mtDNA genes are largely or totally linked with a lineage of female "mothers." These separate genetic lines may or may not track the same evolutionary history when we move from a consideration of individuals to the larger groups (populations and species) they make up. The genes of populations will show considerable internal variation, since even similar-looking people will differ in the many thousands of genes which govern their body structure. The differences are reflections of polymorphisms—that is, genes may exist in several different forms, such as one coding for brown eyes and one for blue. In some populations there may be a fixation of particular genes, with no variation present—for example, some African populations appear to have a fixation for brown eye color. But even here there may be exceptions that either represent infrequent genes which only occasionally surface in the population or may represent a newly created variation produced by *mutation.* Such a mutation is the result of a copying mistake in DNA transfer between individuals (i.e., parents to children) or within an individual as cells replicate.

A mutation may be damaging to the individual carrying it, in which case it will be removed by selection over one or more generations; it may be "neutral"—that is, not conferring any special advantage or disadvantage; or it may be beneficial and thus likely to build up in frequency in the population through time. Some areas of the DNA seem to be more prone to mutation than others, and this seems to be so for mtDNA, which accumulates mutations at about ten times the average rate of nuclear DNA and appears to be largely selectively neutral. While rates of change for particular genes vary greatly, the evolutionary rate for large numbers of nuclear genes combined is believed to be approximately constant, while that for mtDNA is believed to change at about one part in 33 (3 parts per 100) every million years. Particularly with mtDNA, it has been possible to estimate the date of the last common ancestral gene pattern for all living humans studied so far. [57,58]

No one has yet succeeded in extracting useful DNA from fossil human bones in order to reconstruct our genetic evolution directly. However, techniques are now available which may allow such an exciting development in the near future. This would then permit a direct comparison between portions of the DNA of, say, a Neanderthal and a modern European, to test the likelihood that the former was closely related to, perhaps even ancestral to, the latter. Until that is achieved, we are dependent on reconstructions from modern individuals or populations, working backward from the present to hypothetical ancient ancestral individuals or populations.

For mtDNA, modern humans show close relationships to each other, whatever their geographic or "racial" origins. All human mtDNA variation today could have been produced in about 200 kyr, based on the 3 percent rate of mutation for mtDNA given earlier. Such a date is well after the dispersal and differentiation of *Homo erectus* and is within the time span of "archaic *Homo sapiens*" and the Neanderthals. Moreover, it appears that mtDNA variation is not spread evenly across the world. African populations show a greater degree of diversification compared with those of other continents, and this would suggest that they have had a longer time to build up that diversity compared with the populations of Europe, Asia, Australasia, and the Americas. [57,58]

Computer-generated evolutionary trees have also been used to reconstruct the pathways of mtDNA changes leading to recent human mtDNA variation. Many of these have shown a clear separation of African individuals from other groups analyzed, and this has been used to support the concept of a recent African ancestry for human mtDNA variation. However, recent reanalysis of these data have led to doubts about the accuracy of the evolutionary trees and the conclusions drawn from them. Some of the conclusions about recent human evolution drawn from such mtDNA analyses must therefore be viewed with caution until further research has been performed.

Analyses of patterns of human variation in nuclear DNA or its products, such as blood groups, have been in use for much longer than those for mtDNA. Initial results provided no clear-cut pattern of population relationships. More recently, analyses of nuclear DNA and its products have yielded much clearer results, giving a basic African/non-African split in human gene patterns. [59,60] The non-African populations usually split into a European + Oriental/native Australian subgroup, and a Southeast Asian + Australian subgroup. Within Africa, populations such as Khoisan ("Bushman") and Pygmies are often quite distinct from each other. While the nuclear DNA patterns are consistent with an African origin, setting a date on such an origin is much more difficult.

Given that the two non-African subgroups are about equally diverse, and there is evidence from archaeology that the Australian group may have begun to differentiate after settlement in Australia about 50 kyr ago, the African–non-African split could have occurred at about 75 kyr ago, and the whole human origin at about 100 kyr ago. Some analyses of human language diversity also show comparable patterns of clustering to those described above from genetic studies. This has led to speculation that languages have differentiated in parallel with populations, and to the inference that if there *was* a single African ancestral population that gave rise to modern human genetic diversity, that same population could also have given rise to modern human language diversity. [59] Speculating even further, perhaps that ancestral population was the one in which true human language first developed, which was why the population that possessed it was successful enough to give rise to all living humanity.

Not all geneticists believe that the evidence points to a recent African ancestry for modern *Homo sapiens*. Some feel that the evidence is still insufficient for firm conclusions; others feel that there are too many uncertainties about important factors such as past population sizes and gene flow (hybridization and intermixture) between groups; while yet others believe that areas such as Asia have an equal or greater claim for our evolutionary homeland. Still others believe that the observed geographic patterns are accurate but reflect a more ancient "Out of Africa" migration—that of *Homo erectus,* which we discussed at the beginning of this article. This would then be consistent with multiregional models of human evolution. [18] Such questions will only be resolved to general satisfaction by further genetic analyses and by comparisons with the fossil and archaeological records of the last million years. The next decade will see such work undertaken along with the exciting prospect of direct genetic analyses from the fossils themselves. Having discussed the importance of genetic analyses to the debate about modern human origins, we will now attempt to provide an overview of all the data discussed so far.

Overview and concluding remarks: The origin of modern *Homo sapiens*

There seems little doubt that "archaic *Homo sapiens*" evolved from some form of *Homo erectus,* although it is unclear in which region(s) this transition occurred (*see* fig. 3). The presence of fossils with mosaic characteristics in Europe and Africa, at least, suggests that the transition was not restricted to one region and was not rapid. It had occurred by 400 kyr ago in Europe and Africa, and perhaps also in China (Yunxian), but there is evidence in the Far East that *Homo erectus* survived for much of the middle Pleistocene (late Zhoukoudian and Hexian fossils), and perhaps even into the late Pleistocene (less than 130 kyr ago in Ngandong, Java). There are only two later major developments which can be clearly identified from the fossil record. One is the origin and continuation of Neanderthals in Europe and western Asia. The transition from "archaic *Homo sapiens*" to Neanderthals occurred between about 200 and 300 kyr ago in Europe and is recorded in fossils such as Swanscombe, Atapuerca, and Ehringsdorf. Unfortunately, there is no comparable fossil record for western Asia. The second evolutionary development was the origin of anatomically modern *Homo sapiens,* occurring in both Africa (e.g., Klasies, Omo-Kibish) and the Middle East (Skhūl, Qafzeh) by about 100 kyr ago, and reaching Europe (Cro-Magnons) and the Far East (e.g., Zhoukoudian Upper Cave, Niah, Mungo) by 30–40 kyr ago.

The fossil record is not adequate to determine the exact time and place of origin of the first modern humans, with a dearth of fossils from certain regions and a lack of complete skeletons, but African fossils between 100 and 200 kyr in age (e.g., Ngaloba, Jebel Irhoud) are the most plausible ancestral forms known in terms of their cranial characters and shape. The next most plausible ancestral forms known are Chinese specimens such as Dali, and the least plausible ancestors are the Neanderthals and the Ngandong specimens, because of their much greater cranial differences from modern humans. In the case of the Neanderthals, this is due to specialized features; in Ngandong it is due to a retention of the primitive features of *Homo erectus.* Under the multiregional hypothesis, all of these groups would be regarded as equally plausible ancestors for modern *Homo sapiens* and in fact would have been ancestors for modern Africans, Orientals plus Native Americans, Europeans, and native Australians respectively. Yet when analyzed comparatively they show no special approach to their regional successors. For example, if we compare Neanderthal crania with a range of modern ones from around the world, there is no special relationship between Neanderthal and European crania—the Neanderthals are equally distinct and distant from all modern groups. In the case of the Dali skull the distances are somewhat less, but again there is no special relationship between Dali and the crania of modern regional counterparts such as Japanese, or related forms such as Native Americans. Even the later African "archaic *Homo sapiens*" specimens show no special relationship to any living human groups.

This lack of special "archaic *Homo sapiens*"–modern *Homo sapiens* connections seems to indicate that modern regional differentiation occurred separately from the origin of modern *Homo sapiens* itself, and rather than preceding that origin (multiregional model), it succeeded it (Noah's Ark/Out of Africa models). This would be consistent with the fact that early modern specimens in each region are rather undifferentiated in terms of resembling their modern counterparts, e.g., early modern *Homo sapiens* in Europe have faces and body proportions unlike modern Europeans. If they are, nevertheless, ancestral to recent Europeans, such regional features must have developed over the last 30 kyr, rather than deriving from Neanderthal ancestors. [54]

The status of "archaic Homo sapiens" *and the Neanderthals*

We have seen how the transition to "archaic *Homo sapiens*" in Europe was followed by the origin and evolution of Neanderthals, but not, apparently, of modern *Homo sapiens*. In fact it is difficult to justify the present common taxonomic practice of uniting the various archaic groups (including the Neanderthals) with us as *Homo sapiens*. If modern *Homo sapiens* is as distinct a form skeletally (and perhaps behaviorally) as appears at present, the main link appears to be between "archaic *Homo sapiens*" and the Neanderthals. If this were recognized specifically, the species name *Homo neanderthalensis* would be the most appropriate for this group. However, should this term be applied more widely than just in Europe and Southwest Asia? Such usage would be close to the "Neanderthal phase" concept to which we referred in our discussion of *Homo sapiens* origins. Any decision would have to be based on a consideration of the extent of separation of the Neanderthal lineage from contemporaneous groups elsewhere, and there is evidence both for and against such a proposition. Neanderthals did show distinctive cranial (e.g., facial and nasal shape) and body (e.g., limb and body proportions) features, but were these distinctions any greater in scale between Neanderthals and their contemporaries than is shown in modern regional variation? For facial form the answer is, perhaps, yes, while for body form, on the limited evidence available, probably no. In addition, there is the evidence of a shared skeletal robusticity and archaic cranial shape partly, at least, retained from middle Pleistocene ancestors and lost in modern *Homo sapiens*.

We can thus propose a new evolutionary scenario for later evolution within the genus *Homo*. During the middle Pleistocene, an evolutionary split occurred in the species *Homo erectus*. In some regions, a new species evolved and spread, *Homo neanderthalensis* (formerly "archaic *Homo sapiens*"). This evolutionary transition had occurred in Europe and Africa by about 400 kyr ago, and the new species may even have reached China, based on preliminary age estimates for the Yunxian crania. However, in the east, *Homo erectus* continued in China until perhaps 250 kyr ago, and in Java (Ngandong) until as recently as 100 kyr ago. *Homo neanderthalensis* developed regional variation and, in the northwest parts of the species range, under the influence of temperate and cold climates, evolved physical specializations leading by 100 kyr ago to the most specialized and terminal (and, ironically, the best known) Neanderthal populations of Europe and western Asia. In both Africa and China (perhaps also India [Narmada] and Israel [Zuttiyeh]), *Homo neanderthalensis* remained less specialized facially and cranially, while continuing to evolve a larger brain size in parallel (or from gene flow) with the European and western Asian populations. In Africa, at least, these populations retained a tropically adapted physique from their ancient *Homo erectus* ancestors, which was lost in more northerly populations (e.g., Eurasian Neanderthals and, perhaps, Jinniu Shan).

Behavioral changes in late middle Pleistocene African populations led to a gracilization of the skeleton through the development of more efficient subsistence techniques, perhaps including the production of the first complex language systems. By 100,000 years ago, populations showing modern skeletal features existed in southern and eastern Africa, and Southwest Asia (Israel), and this date represents the known minimum origin date for *Homo sapiens* as more narrowly described in our introduction to the species. Omo-Kibish may indicate an even earlier origin for the species (>130 kyr ago?), with support from the mosaic morphology of the (probably) even earlier Jebel Irhoud material for an African late middle Pleistocene transition. The western Asian populations of early *Homo sapiens* may have migrated directly eastward through subtropical regions to begin the colonization of Australia by 50 kyr ago, still at a Middle Paleolithic technological stage.

However, these early modern *Homo sapiens* populations apparently did not penetrate northward and westward from Southwest Asia, which suggests that they were not yet capable of competing with their *Homo neanderthalensis* predecessors in these areas. Indeed, Neanderthals seem to have reestablished themselves in Southwest Asia (e.g., Kebara, Amud). The situation must have changed with the development and spread of Upper Paleolithic technologies after about 45 kyr ago, because these behavioral novelties (accompanied by their anatomically modern makers?) appear in eastern Europe soon after this and reach parts of western Europe by 40 kyr ago. Even then, there was a long phase of coexistence before *Homo neanderthalensis* finally became extinct by about 30 kyr ago. Upper Paleolithic technology seems to have been part of a general and very successful behavioral system of fully modern type, which initiated a remarkable phase of artistic creativity in Europe, and colonization events in many other parts of the world. The Neanderthals, to judge from Saint-Césaire and the Châtelpérronian, were not entirely divorced from this remarkable phase of human evolution, but their part in it was small.

Homo sapiens inherited the earth, for better or worse, and in doing so may have caused the extinction of the ancestral species *Homo neanderthalensis* (in Europe and mainland Asia) and *Homo erectus* (in Java). However, their replacement was a result of economic competition rather than a Pleistocene holocaust caused by modern humans. Some gene flow may have occurred in this process of replacement, but the main physical and genetic variations in people today exist because of local evolution within *Homo sapiens* populations, rather than any differential impact of the genes of *Homo neanderthalensis* and *Homo erectus*. Our species is very young in geologic terms but has shown both stability (in certain skeletal features) and change (in such features as body proportions, skin color, behavior, linguistic and genetic evolution) over its known brief existence of about 100 kyr. The sorts of major challenges which lie immediately ahead of us (e.g., changes in climate, overpopulation, and shortage of resources) have been successfully met in our past, or we would not be here today, but the scale of the challenges facing us now are enormous and global. We can only hope that the brain and behavioral system which has (only recently) made us such a successful species will be adequate for the great challenges still to come.

Acknowledgments

I would like to thank the staff of the many Institutes who have given me access to fossil human material for study or photography. I would also like to thank Professor Michael Day for the print of Omo 1, and the Photographic Unit of the Natural History Museum for producing most of the figures. Mrs. Irene Baxter helped greatly with the production of the typescript.

1. John Reader, *Missing Links: The Hunt for Earliest Man* (London: Penguin, 1988). This book, written by a popular science writer, is beautifully illustrated by the author's own photographs.

2. Frank Spencer, "The Neanderthals and Their Evolutionary Significance: A Brief Historical Survey," in Fred H. Smith and Frank Spencer, eds., *The Origins of Modern Humans: A World Survey of the Fossil Evidence* (New York: A. R. Liss, 1984), pp. 1–49. This scholarly review is by one of the foremost historians of anthropology.

3. Carleton Stevens Coon, *The Origin of Races* (New York: Knopf, 1962). Unfortunately, in this book Coon argued that modern "races" were at different evolutionary levels.

4. Roger Lewin, *Human Evolution: An Illustrated Introduction,* 3d ed. (Boston: Blackwell, in press). A well-illustrated introductory text.

5. Richard Klein, *The Human Career: Human Biological and Cultural Origins* (Chicago: University of Chicago Press, 1989). A detailed and scholarly textbook.

6. Phillip V. Tobias, *The Skulls, Endocasts, and Teeth of Homo habilis* (Cambridge: Cambridge University Press, 1991). A detailed two-volume descriptive monograph of the Olduvai fossils.

7. Bernard Wood, *Hominid Cranial Remains—Koobi Fora Research Project,* vol. 4 (Oxford: Clarendon Press, 1991). An up-to-date and detailed study of important Kenyan fossils assigned to *Homo habilis* and *Homo erectus.*

8. Christopher B. Stringer, "The Credibility of *Homo habilis,*" in Bernard Wood, Lawrence Martin, and Peter Andrews, eds., *Major Topics in Primate and Human Evolution* (Cambridge: Cambridge University Press, 1986), pp. 266–94. An early attempt to "split" *Homo habilis* into two species.

9. G. Philip Rightmire, *The Evolution of Homo erectus* (Cambridge: Cambridge University Press, 1990). A scholarly review of this early human species.

10. Milford H. Wolpoff, *Paleoanthropology* (New York: Knopf, 1980). A good general text, written by the leading proponent of multiregional evolution.

11. M. J. Aitken, *Science-based Dating in Archaeology* (London: Longman, 1990). The author is one of the major figures involved in the development of thermoluminescence dating.

12. Rainer Grün and Christopher B. Stringer, "ESR Dating and the Evolution of Modern Humans," *Archaeometry* 33 (1991): 153–99. An up-to-date review of a fast-moving area of research.

13. Bernard Campbell, "The Nomenclature of the Hominidae" (Royal Anthropological Institute Occasional Paper no. 22, 1965). An important review of the confusing plethora of names proposed for hominid species.

14. Bernard Campbell, "Quantitative Taxonomy and Human Evolution," in Sherwood L. Washburn, ed., *Classification and Human Evolution* (London: Methuen, 1963), pp. 50–74. Campbell's influential attempt to reorganize the naming of fossil human species.

15. Paul Mellars and Christopher B. Stringer, *The Human Revolution: Behavioural and Biological Perspectives on the Origins of Modern Humans* (Edinburgh: Edinburgh University Press, 1989). Papers from an important conference in 1987.

16. Christopher B. Stringer, "The Emergence of Modern Humans," *Scientific American* 263, no. 6 (1990): 98–104. An introductory review article.

17. Fred H. Smith, Anthony B. Falsetti, and Steven M. Donnelly, "Modern Human Origins," *Yearbook of Physical Anthropology* 32 (1989): 35–68. A good review, favoring an assimilation model of recent human evolution.

18. Milford H. Wolpoff, "Multiregional Evolution: The Fossil Alternative to Eden," in Mellars and Stringer, eds., *The Human Revolution,* vol. 1, pp. 62–108. A strong critique of the recent African origin model.

19. Milford H. Wolpoff, X. Z. Wu, and A. Thorne, "Modern *Homo sapiens* Origins: A General Theory of Hominid Evolution Involving the Fossil Evidence from East Asia," in Smith and Spencer, eds., *The Origins of Modern Humans,* pp. 411–83. This influential paper marked a period of renewal for the model of multiregional evolution.

20. W. W. Howells, "Explaining Modern Man: Evolutionists Versus Migrationists," *Journal of Human Evolution* 5 (1976): 477–95. A clear and prescient discussion prior to the rise of the recent African origin model.

21. Christopher B. Stringer and Peter Andrews, "Genetic and Fossil Evidence for the Origin of Modern Humans," *Science* 239 (1988): 1263–68. A controversial assessment of evolutionary models, favoring a recent African origin.

22. Günter Bräuer, "A Craniological Approach to the Origin of Anatomically Modern *Homo sapiens* in Africa and Implications for the Appearance of Modern Europeans," in Smith and Spencer, eds., *The Origins of Modern Humans,* pp. 327–410. Paper by a leading proponent of an African gene flow-hybridization model.

23. Günter Bräuer, "Africa's Place in the Evolution of *Homo sapiens,*" in Günter Bräuer and Fred H. Smith, eds., *Continuity or Replacement: Controversies in Homo sapiens Evolution* (Rotterdam: Balkema, 1992), pp. 83–98. A critique of multiregional evolution, and especially the work of Milford H. Wolpoff.

24. Christopher B. Stringer, "Middle Pleistocene Hominid Variability and the Origin of Late Pleistocene Humans," in Eric Delson, ed., *Ancestors: The Hard Evidence* (New York: A. R. Liss, 1985), pp. 289–95. An early paper in the development of the recent African origin model.

25. Christopher B. Stringer, "The Definition of *Homo erectus* and the Existence of the Species in Africa and Europe," *Courier Forschungs Institut Senckenberg* 69 (1984): 131–43. A study of variation in *Homo erectus.*

26. Rosine Orban, ed., *Hominid Remains—An Up-date: Spain*, vol. 4 (Université Libre de Bruxelles, Belgium, 1991). This volume lists part of the enormous sample of fossil human material recently recovered at Atapuerca.

27. X. Z. Lu, "La découverte de l'homme fossile de Jing-Niu-Shan, Première étude," *L'Anthropologie* 94 (1990): 899–902. This short paper has pictures of the Jinniu Shan material at the time of discovery.

28. Christopher B. Stringer, "An Archaic Character in the Broken Hill Innominate E.719," *American Journal of Physical Anthropology* 71 (1986): 115–20. A discussion of the rather neglected skeletal material from Broken Hill.

29. Christopher B. Stringer, "The Asian Connection," *New Scientist* 1743 (1990): 33–37. A look at Far Eastern evidence from a recent African origin perspective.

30. Jill Cook, Christopher B. Stringer, Andrew Currant, Henry P. Schwarcz, and Ann Wintle, "A Review of the Chronology of the European Middle Pleistocene Hominid Record," *Yearbook of Physical Anthropology* 25 (1982): 19–65. A detailed review of the fossils and their dating.

31. Christopher B. Stringer, Jean-Jacques Hublin, and Bernard Vandermeersch, "The Origin of Anatomically Modern Humans in Western Europe," in Smith and Spencer, eds., *The Origins of Modern Humans*, pp. 51–135. This paper concentrates on the evolution of Neanderthals and concludes that they were not modern human ancestors.

32. Patricia Shipman, "Human Ancestor's Early Steps out of Africa," *New Scientist* 1806 (1992): 24. A short news report on the important Dmanisi *Homo erectus* jawbone discovery from Georgia.

33. Ian Tattersall, "Species Recognition in Human Palaeontology," *Journal of Human Evolution* 15 (1986): 165–75. An argument for recognizing more species in human evolution.

34. Jean-Jacques Hublin, "Human Fossils from the North African Middle Pleistocene and the Origin of *Homo sapiens*," in Delson, ed., *Ancestors*, pp. 283–88. A study favoring evolutionary continuity in North Africa.

35. G. Philip Rightmire, "*Homo sapiens* in Sub-Saharan Africa," in Smith and Spencer, eds., *The Origins of Modern Humans*, pp. 295–325. A cautious assessment of the fossil material, prior to the rise of the recent African origin model.

36. Erik Trinkaus, "Western Asia," in Smith and Spencer, eds., *The Origins of Modern Humans*, pp. 251–93. A review of the material before the impact of the redating of Qafzeh and Skhūl.

37. Li Tianyuan and Dennis Etler, "New Middle Pleistocene Hominid Crania from Yunxian, China," *Nature* (in press). A first report in English on this important new material.

38. Kenneth A. R. Kennedy, Arun Sonakia, John Chiment, and K. Verma, "Is the Narmada Hominid an Indian *Homo erectus?*" *American Journal of Physical Anthropology* 86 (1991): 475–96. This paper argues that Narmada represents "archaic *Homo sapiens*."

39. Albert Santa Luca, *The Ngandong Fossil Hominids* (Yale University Publications in Anthropology) 78 (1980): 1–175. A detailed study which firmly attributes this material to *Homo erectus*.

40. Gert-Jan Bartstra, Santosa Soegondho, and Albert van der Wijk, "Ngandong Man: Age and Artifacts," *Journal of Human Evolution* 17 (1988): 325–37. Although uranium series dating on bone is very difficult, this paper proposes a very young age (less than 100,000 years) for the Ngandong *Homo erectus* fossils.

41. Fred H. Smith, "Fossil Hominids from the Upper Pleistocene of Central Europe and the Origin of Modern Europeans," in Smith and Spencer, eds., *The Origins of Modern Humans*, pp. 137–209. This study covers comparable ground to [31] but comes to quite different conclusions about the Neanderthals.

42. Erik Trinkaus, *The Shanidar Neanderthals* (New York: Academic Press, 1983). A monographic study of these important fossils.

43. Ofer Bar-Yosef, Henri Laville, Liliane Meignen, Anne-Marie Tillier, Bernard Vandermeersch, Baruch Arensburg, A. Belfer-Cohen, Paul Goldberg, Yoel Rak, and Eitan Tchernov, "Le sépulture néandertalienne de Kébara (unité XII)," in Marcel Otte, ed., *L'Homme de Neanderthal*, vol. 5 (Liège: La Pensée, ERAUL, 1988), pp. 17–24. A description of the Kebara burial site.

44. Yoel Rak, "On the Differences Between Two Pelvises of Mousterian Context

from the Qafzeh and Kebara Caves, Israel," *American Journal of Physical Anthropology* 81 (1990): 323–32. This paper stresses the contrast between the Qafzeh (modern) and Kebara (Neanderthal) hipbones.

45. Erik Trinkaus, "Neanderthal Limb Proportions and Cold Adaptation," in Christopher B. Stringer, ed., *Aspects of Human Evolution* (London: Taylor and Francis, 1981), pp. 187–224. This paper presents good evidence that Neanderthals were cold adapted.

46. Rainer Grün, Christopher B. Stringer, and Henry P. Schwarcz, "ESR Dating of Teeth from Garrod's Tabun Cave Collection," *Journal of Human Evolution* 20 (1991): 231–48. A controversial redating of a key archaeological site, now supported by other techniques.

47. Milford H. Wolpoff, Frank Smith, Mirko Malez, Jakov Radovcić, and Darko Rukavina, "Upper Pleistocene Hominid Remains from Vindija Cave, Croatia, Yugoslavia," *American Journal of Physical Anthropology* 54 (1981): 499–545. A study which describes these fossils and attempts to demonstrate their intermediate nature between Neanderthals and modern humans.

48. H. J. Deacon, "Late Pleistocene Palaeoecology and Archaeology in the Southern Cape, South Africa," in Mellars and Stringer, eds., *The Human Revolution*, vol. 1, pp. 547–64. A summary of the new excavations at Klasies and the dating of the sequence.

49. G. Philip Rightmire and H. J. Deacon, "Comparative Studies of Late Pleistocene Human Remains from Klasies River Mouth, South Africa," *Journal of Human Evolution* 20 (1991): 131–56. This study stresses the modern anatomy of most of the Klasies fossils.

50. Peter Beaumont, Hertha De Villiers, and John Vogel, "Modern Man in Sub-Saharan Africa Prior to 49000 years BP: A Review and Evaluation with Particular Reference to Border Cave," *South African Journal of Science* 74 (1978): 409–19. A paper favoring the great age of the Border Cave human fossils.

51. Rainer Grün, Peter Beaumont, and Christopher B. Stringer, "ESR Dating Evidence for Early Modern Humans at Border Cave in South Africa," *Nature* 344 (1990a): 537–39. This paper provides dating of the cave sequence but cannot resolve the uncertainties concerning Border Cave 1 and 2.

52. Michael Day and Christopher B. Stringer, "Les restes crâniens d'Omo-Kibish et leur classification à l'intérieur du genre *Homo*" (The Omo-Kibish cranial remains and classification within the genus *Homo*), *L'Anthropologie* 95 (1991): 573–94. A comparative study of Omo-Kibish 1 and 2 and a controversial attempt to define the species *Homo sapiens*.

53. Michael Day, Mark Twist, and Suzanne Ward, "Les vestiges post-crâniens d'Omo I (Kibish)" (The Omo 1 (Kibish) post-cranial remains), *L'Anthropologie* 95 (1991):595–610. The first detailed comparative study of this important material.

54. Christopher B. Stringer, "Replacement, Continuity, and the Origin of *Homo sapiens*," in Bräuer and Smith, eds., *Continuity or Replacement*. A critique of the multiregional model.

55. John Putman, "In Search of Modern Humans," *National Geographic Magazine* 174 (1988): 438–47. A popularly written but beautifully illustrated article.

56. Kenneth A. R. Kennedy, "The Deep Skull of Niah: An Assessment of Twenty Years of Speculation Concerning Its Evolutionary Significance," *Asian Perspectives* 20 (1979): 32–50. A review of the evidence favoring the great antiquity claimed for the Niah fossil.

57. Rebecca Cann, Mark Stoneking, and Allan C. Wilson, "Mitochondrial DNA and Human Evolution," *Nature* 325 (1987): 31–36. A very controversial paper. Some of its methods and conclusions have been seriously questioned.

58. Linda Vigilant, Mark Stoneking, Henry Harpending, Kristen Hawkes, and Allan C. Wilson, "African Populations and the Evolution of Human Mitochondrial DNA," *Science* 253 (1991): 1503–7. A paper which dealt with some of the criticisms aimed at the previous study, but which has now also been challenged in its conclusions.

59. Luigi Luca Cavalli-Sforza, "Genes, Peoples and Languages," *Scientific American* 265, no. 5 (1991): 71–78. An African-origin presentation which synthesizes nuclear DNA analyses with language patterns.

60. Anne M. Bowcock, Judith R. Kidd, Joanne L. Mountain, Joan M. Herbert, Luciano Carotenuto, Kenneth K. Kidd, and Luigi Luca Cavalli-Sforza, "Drift, Admixture and Selection in Human Evolution: A Study with DNA Polymorphisms," *Proceedings of the National Academy of Sciences, U.S.A.* 88 (1991): 839–43. An article which presents some of the complexities involved in analyzing the genetic data.

PART TWO

Reconsiderations of Great Books and Ideas

Science as Mystery:
A Speculative Reading
of Newton's *Principia*

Thomas K. Simpson

Thomas K. Simpson, born in Brooklyn and pictured here standing on its famous bridge, is a frequent contributor to *The Great Ideas Today*. Until 1990,
when he retired, he was a tutor at St. John's College in Annapolis, Maryland,
and Santa Fe, New Mexico. Under a grant from the National Endowment for
the Humanities, he worked recently on an edition of papers on the electromagnetic field by James Clerk Maxwell, designed to make Maxwell's text
accessible to readers without special training in mathematics and sciences.
In addition, he has been a consultant with the Museum of History and Technology at the Smithsonian Institution, the Franklin Institute, and the Science
Museum of Minnesota. Other projects include a study of Leon Trotsky's *History of the Russian Revolution* and a computer investigation of a claim by
Henri Poincaré that nothing in principle prevents consistent intuitions of non-
Euclidean geometry, including those with dimensionality greater than three.

Mr. Simpson's education was at the Virginia Polytechnic Institute, at St.
John's College, at Wesleyan University, and at Johns Hopkins University,
where he earned a doctorate in the history of science and technology.

Is it possible that the workings of certain human minds are so ceaseless and boundless that they eventuate in books too big to be read? Something of this sort seems to be the case with Newton's *Principia*—more fully, the *Philosophiae Naturalis Principia Mathematica* (*Mathematical Principles of Natural Philosophy* [GBWW I: 34, 1–372; II: 32, 1–372]). Not merely the daunting task of mastering its mathematical demonstrations, but the challenge of incorporating into one's own thought its hierarchy of stacked purposes and multiple lines of implication has over the years perplexed even the best-equipped minds. Those with the technical ability to deal with the mathematics have tended to be pressed to other tasks or have missed the metaphysics, while most readers have been able to get only limited distances into the text. Within the work itself, though rather late in the game, Newton acknowledges the difficulty; at the beginning of Book III, he roundly advises against having read Book II and prescribes a road map for Book I which unfortunately would stop well short of some of the most essential material. [1] Such maps have disserved readers over the years; but even stalwarts who make their way to the end of the first book normally leave the second book unopened and thus get only a very partial sense of the terrain as a whole.

The result is that it has been the habit of scholars and general readers alike to assume a common understanding of what the book was about. It has been recognized as a portal through which Western society entered upon its modern era—a portal rather too confidently characterized as the "Scientific Revolution." Newton, it has been thought, set in the book a magnificent example of something we call the "scientific method," and he sealed the world's faith in it by exhibiting its ability to compute and predict the motions of the heavenly bodies. Its basic terms, *mass* and *force*—even *time* and *space*—have become so current among us that, encrusted as verbal and mental habits, they have become almost impenetrable to critical reflection.

Just now, however, we may be in possession of a historical opportunity to make a new start at these matters. We have reached a point in our relation with the sciences at which a combination of the unsettling of fundamental concepts, on the one hand, and disenchantment with practical outcomes, on the other, is causing us to wonder about the sciences and to question the concept of progress with which they for so long lured us. This is a moment, then, at which it is timely to reconsider our understanding of the idea of science itself. Concurrently, new evidence has been coming in that we may have been misunderstanding the *Principia,* our presumed guidebook to the modern sciences, as well. Newton certainly did think he was precipitating a revolution in thought, but his vision of the nature of that revolution may not have been much like that which we have imputed to him.

Close reading of even a limited assignment in the text has always suggested that we and Newton might be looking at things differently. There are strong indications within the text that he was on the track of *science* in something closer to Aristotle's own meaning of that term, as the theory of things true, and known with the greatest certainty: systematic induction was for Newton, his text suggests, a refined method for making sure of absolute truth. We, on the other hand, positivists all in these matters, had in effect to read his intentions out of the text in order to take it in our own mode as a primer for our own understanding of scientific method, essentially a method for evading the really interesting questions. The general excuse for this performance was that Newton, one foot in the future but one equally somehow stuck in the past, wrought better than he knew. History had kindly edited his text to make it say what future generations needed to derive from it.

Now, however, revelations of current scholarship make certain of Newton's own intentions inescapable and may rightly send us back to the *Principia* to give it a less cavalier, more speculative reading. Quantities of Newtonian manuscripts are coming to light and receiving competent scholarly interpretation, which begin to take fuller measure of his work as a passionate theologian, an obsessive historian, and above all, for our present purposes, as a magnificent alchemist. [2] These disturbing truths about our author are not indeed altogether new. Dark reports had always had it that Newton engaged in covert projects in alchemy, and it was always suspected that he had a twisted bent for synoptic history, theology, and the interpretation of Scripture, especially of the prophecies of Daniel and John. Indeed, it has long been known that he had indulged in alchemy, though the cover story was that he had only copied and recopied, presumably in fits of nervous compulsion, the manuscripts of others. Now a deluge of his hidden and despised manuscripts has burst upon the scholarly world, by way of what must be one of the more embarrassing archival misdemeanors of modern times—an auction at Sotheby's in which a wealth of Newton manuscript materials was dispersed to the winds of the marketplace, with only the Sotheby catalog left to document their existence for posterity. [3] Most of these have since been tracked down, and enough have been read and reported to dispel any notion that

Newton was simply mad, or a part-timer in these exotic fields. No; it is now quite clear that the same brilliant and relentless operations of mind which had generated the *Principia* and the *Optics* (*GBWW* I: 34, 377; II: 32, 377) went at least equally and concurrently into what we can only call the most earnest commitment to alchemy, and an immense, disciplined study of history and theology as well, the latter based upon a critical evaluation of scriptural text which anticipates in method and concern our modern biblical textual criticism. Prospero himself has emerged before our astonished eyes, with the *Principia* his magic book.

To take the hardest point first: we must face squarely the fact that Newton was a full-scale professional alchemist. One scholar in a position to make an estimate suggests that never before or since has there been such a master of alchemy—both of the intricate texts and of the solemn and exacting practices at the furnace. Suddenly, a sense of mystery falls over the *Principia*, once the very key to the liberation of the modern world from all such dark suggestions. Thus, I propose that at this point, at which we have reason in any case to reconsider the nature of the sciences themselves as the foundation of our dubious modern era, we take occasion as well to return to Newton's text and embark upon a more speculative reading, with the Newtonian alchemy in mind as a leading thread. The *Principia* is a deeply dialectical work, meant to advance one thesis and to dispel another. Given that terms such as *Newtonian mechanism* are so often encountered today in summaries written at a second remove, it may be surprising to discover that the *Principia* is thoroughly organized as a polemic *against* mechanism. In its place, Newton invites, I believe, a legitimate sense of science as mystery. Newton's term *force*, a surrogate for the alchemist's *spirit*, is essential to the operations of nature once clockwork mechanisms have been dispersed. It is meant to invoke a mystery, to make way for agencies in the cosmos which are not material, and so to leave room for the divine. Newton's theology is thus by no means incidental to the rest of his work: it is even possible that Newton understands the *Principia* to hold a crucial position in the prophetic succession, as a new and decisive revelation of God's work, and that thus a divine voice animates its propositions. [4] Of what philosophy, then, is the *Principia* the "principles"? What does "natural philosophy" include in Newton's mind? This is Christian natural philosophy, equivalent neither to the philosophy of the ancients nor to the pragmatic enterprise we call "science" in our time. "Nature" is for Newton, I suspect, the field of God's working among us; the *Principia* is a tormented, mystic work, shaped to open the way to this vision. Let us experiment in any case with reading it from this point of view, taking in the present essay what can be no more than a very brief walking tour through certain halls and chambers of an immense and in some way magic work.

The Newtonian alchemy

Let us begin by attempting to characterize certain features of the Newtonian alchemy which will serve as guides to this reading of the *Principia*. It is not possible here to embark on an account of the alchemy itself, a field far too complex and still for most of us too obscure to summarize readily. Newton was in some way, we may say, embarked on a systematic and disciplined and, we must add, perfectly rational search for real principles hidden behind the appearances of ordinary materials. For example, the "opening" of common mercury would yield a real, or philosophical mercury. Once achieved, mastery of such true substances would make possible not only a new order of knowledge of nature but the ability to command practical outcomes which indeed included transmutations. Newton believed that Robert Boyle had accomplished the transmutation of water into earth.

Here, we can only list certain of the attributes of alchemy, a list which will be deliberately selective—chosen with an eye to those features which most tend to shape Newton's understanding of the task of what we now call mathematical physics. For the *Principia* is conceived as instrumental, as mathematical servant to a greater project. And that greater project, natural philosophy, evidently takes its own shape in Newton's searching mind in the context of the vast work which he was deriving from the alchemic tradition. As we have suggested, the result is something which is on the face of it very far from what we have been taught to think of as "scientific method"—yet perhaps not so far from the project in fact under way in the laboratories of the modern world when considered from this alternative point of view. About this last question we must reserve judgment until we have come to terms with the *Principia* in this new context.

What "science" is

It is regularly said that the Scientific Revolution freed men's minds from shackles of an encrusted tradition, characterized as the weary reiteration of principles drawn from the philosophy and logic of Aristotle. In the figure of Simplicio in Galileo's *Dialogues,* we see well enough the kind of complacent common sense to which this reproach applies. Flying under other flags, the type is familiar in any age. But we should be careful not to underestimate the influence, and possible truth, of principles articulated by Aristotle and conveyed in Newton's time by better men than Simplicio. However true it is that Newton as a student at Cambridge turned to the new "mechanical philosophy" and left blank the pages in his personal notebooks reserved for the traditional topics, certain understandings concerning the role of mind

Archetype of the alchemist, the upper register of a "Ripley Scroll," a classic alchemical document. The wisdom of the domain which he surveys, coextensive with the Creation itself, incorporates the most powerful organic and theological symbols. The processes of alchemy, culminating in this ultimate flask, mirror the mystery of passage through death and resurrection. The forces it invokes are those associated with soul—animal and vegetative spirit—not those now supposed to belong to the realm of "physics."

and the nature of the sciences may have been more deeply implanted. What we turn from in our youths we tend not to leave altogether behind but rather incorporate in new structures. Such is the dialectic of learning, and Newton at Cambridge was engaging in intense dialectical maneuvers. Alchemy in certain fundamental features borrows concepts of Aristotelian science, and so, I would suggest, does the *Principia*.

Aristotle defines the term *science* in that culminating section of his logic known to tradition as the *Posterior Analytics*. [5] The essential point is that "science" concerns that which we know best: knowledge which is scientific is certain, and not hypothetical. The exemplar is our knowledge of mathematics—arithmetic or geometry. The sum of two and two is four: that is not a contingent or hypothetical statement. The principles on which a science such as geometry is founded are correspondingly evident: to see them is to grant them. They are of the sort Descartes calls "clear and distinct." But in human practice, we have to learn even these mathematical sciences through experience, first encountering individual instances, and only gradually coming to perceive in them the universal principles which they illustrate. That coming-to-see of principles which are ultimately evident is what Aristotle calls "induction." There is nothing probabilistic or insecure about such induction, and its culmination is not in a statement which is tentative or (in the terms of modern technicians of these matters) "corrigible." Therefore it is not much like what is called "induction" in our talk about the experimental sciences, in which induction is understood to yield principles which are more-or-less likely, and which stand only until they are tested and corrected or revised by experiment. They are never certain, and even the most widely supported of them are ultimately contingent and subject to the next major revision of our scientific paradigms. We have seen too many revolutions in the foundations of even the most secure sciences to take any current offering as final; to think otherwise is seen as dogmatism, closure of the mind to the prospect of new and unexpected empirical evidence. Whether we are simply right in this, or whether Aristotle has something yet to teach us, we need not resolve at this point. It is enough to note that Newton and the alchemic tradition stand in this respect on the side of the ancients: for both, disciplined induction can lead to absolute truth.

Alchemy fundamentally extends the Aristotelian assumption to include nature as a whole; in principle, the whole body of nature becomes knowable as only the mathematical sciences had once been. Underlying the shifting phenomena are constant factors, principles which in their hidden operations generate the world as we perceive it. These principles, obscured as they are beneath the veil of appearances, can become objects of knowledge. Fetching the true and philosophical reality out of the confusion of common appearances requires high art, art which in the traditions of alchemy, for reasons not necessarily misguided, was passed on in secrecy and mystery. Such knowledge, the great goal of alchemy, would be not contingent but as certain as any object of an Aristotelian science.

Before going further, it is important to distinguish more carefully: Aristotle was no alchemist! Alchemy, as an alternative tradition, extended to all things the certainty which in Aristotle belongs only to the objects of intellect. At the root of the distinction between alchemy and Aristotelian science lies the obscure concept of matter, or more generally, the character of the material world. For Aristotle, matter is a shifting and in itself unknowable principle, which in its mingling makes of the world a problematic realm. Matter as the "principle of individuation" brings the universal to bear at a place or at a time, and with such individuation comes an inherent obscurity. Scientific knowledge therefore is not of individuals but of the forms which give shape. Alchemy proposes by contrast that hidden beneath this flux are knowable principles embodied in real and philosophical entities. Material substances, characterized in such terms as the *philosophical mercury* or the *philosophical sulfur* are real entities which would be knowable if they could be fetched out. To know them would in turn be to gain power over phenomena, to secure at once knowledge and command of the realm of nature. As we shall see in more detail shortly, Newton thus speaks as an alchemist throughout the *Principia,* as he frames his arguments and his experiments to find out the true and philosophical behind the complications of common appearances.

Evidently, the watershed which divides alchemy from the philosophy of either Plato or Aristotle is the Judeo-Christian God, and the account of Creation. That "matter" which for Aristotle blurs being in time or place is no blur when it is made by God: with the idea of Creation, we may say, the fact takes primacy over the universal. And that is a leading thread we may borrow from alchemy in our reading of the *Principia:* for Newton as well, fact has primacy over universality. In this, a theorem of the *Principia* is not at all like a theorem in Euclid. A proposition of the *Elements* (*GBWW* I: 11; II: 10) is a truth, to be known, contemplated, and prized as such. A comparable proposition in the *Principia* is instrumental. It is universally true, but it is interesting primarily as a means of finding out truth of another kind, truth which exists in this world as philosophical and knowable Being. The *Principia* is essentially a Judeo-Christian work. The truth, the "philosophy," to which its theorems are instrumental is the truth of God's concrete work in the world. We see, then, that here alchemy, theology, and history belong comfortably together; they are facets of what Newton calls "philosophy."

We are on the track, I believe, of the Newtonian alchemy. "Natural philosophy" thus understood becomes science—not in the sense of our modern convention, according to which "science" is contingent theory entrained to ever-evolving empirical evidence, nor simply, either, in the sense of the *Posterior Analytics,* in which "science" means knowledge as universal—but in a third and new sense, close in its certainty to Aristotle, but giving primacy to truth as fact in the spirit of a created cosmos. We know now that Newton pored over the alchemic tradition, mastering enormous bodies of esoteric literature, comparing and cataloging terms, revising treatises, imbibing the powerful symbolism Carl Jung would later come to recognize among the archetypes. As he did so, Newton felt himself to be on the track of a science in this new sense. And it is such science—science as certain as classical geometry and arithmetic, but now directed to objects incarnate in matter—for which the *Principia* is designed to serve as instrument. The term *incarnate* is appropriate in this context, no less so for its theological overtones; for indeed, with the entrance of God's truth into the world of flesh, Christ becomes the paradigm. Alchemic symbolism is appropriately suggestive of Christian iconography.

Truth in the classical sense is called mathesis: strictly formal and teachable knowledge. If we are to find such truth in the alchemist's laboratory, then it will not be out of order to envision "mathematical principles" of alchemy, and indeed we see that that is just what has happened with the *Principia.* Newton has given alchemy its mathematical principles, in good theoretical form. What we shall try to show is that in the *Principia* the mathematics is ordered and shaped to point back to the Creation, the universal thus servant to the fact of God's work in the world.

The rhetoric of interpretation

We today are imbued with the spirit of "progress," however our sense of this may have been lately eroded by concerns about global warming and the problem of closure of our proliferation of technological waste and pollution. We have looked to Newton, and the Scientific Revolution so closely associated in our minds with him, as the very models of the possibility of progress in human history. But the sense of these matters is very different in alchemy, and I believe Newton understood the *Principia* in the alchemic sense. On the whole, the long Western tradition has thought of the course of history rather as decline than as progress. Much of the excitement of Renaissance thought, as the term implies, concerned the recovery of something which had been lost: there had been a better time, when people knew more. The Renaissance was encouraged in this by passages in the Greek texts it was finding, which themselves looked back mythically to a Golden Age. Alchemy tends to make this assumption in terms of the Hermetic tradition of an earlier learning, a *prisca scientia,* and Newton accepted this view, not without complication, but ultimately perhaps without real question. It was perfectly plausible for him to accept the conviction of the alchemists that they were bearers of precious texts, the meaning of whose symbols had to be retrieved, embodying wisdom once known but now lost and recoverable only through intense and resourceful study of documents which had come down from ancient times.

Newton works with a sometimes feverish sense of discovery, and it may be that things he came to know he believed had never been known in the form in which he was articulating them—yet all of this is in the context of a sense of human time which relates back to earlier wisdom. It is not a ridiculous point of view, certainly, for the paradigm is the Scriptures themselves. Many of the most respected minds of all Judeo-Christian epochs have devoted themselves to the interpretation of Scripture, with the conviction that no higher learning could be achieved than the fullest realization of the wisdom contained there.

As has now been fully demonstrated, Newton spent a very large portion of his most rational energies in just this work: long, exacting labors at the alchemic furnace, matched by imaginative, almost furious efforts to extract the meaning of a very large body of alchemic texts—some published, many circulated only in manuscript form; some ancient, others still being produced in his own time. Since such *interpretation* is part of the work of classical rhetoric, what this means, especially for our reading of the *Principia,* is that Newton's work belongs to a branch of the art of rhetoric—and again, we are reminded of Aristotle and the university tradition.

Classical rhetoric distinguishes two branches of its art, the composition of new works and the interpretation of the works of others. For the classical rhetorician, it is clear that the art of composition held the highest place—the Orator was the exemplar of the man of virtue in society. But with the advent of the Judeo-Christian faith, sacred text took priority, and the bias within the art of rhetoric shifted from composition to interpretation. Augustine in *De Doctrina Christiana (On Christian Doctrine)* sets the new mode, and Newton's work is to be understood as falling within this aspect of the rhetorical tradition. [6] A very great part of Newton's labors thus went into the highly artful interpretation of texts. As we shall see, he elaborated his own new interpretations of certain Judeo-Christian texts, and he labored endlessly over the interpretation of the texts of alchemy. In the *Principia* two great classical streams thus flow together: it is a mathematical work, but as interpretive, it employs mathematics in the service of the art of interpretation—thus, mathematics in the service of rhetoric. We shall see as we examine the methods of the *Principia* just what this mathematical rhetoric will look like.

The texts in question—both those of the sacred tradition, and those of alchemy—involve a special task not met by the classic rhetoricians, and again, we may take Augustine as guide to the new challenges involved.

Saturn, or *Mercurius senex* ("mature mercury"), being prepared through
heating until spirit, symbolized by the white dove, emerges. In alchemy,
"mercury" signifies, not the specific element, but a true or philosophical
metallic principle of much broader significance. Heat is not effecting a
mechanical separation, but works as a transforming principle; Newton
in his own alchemical program followed the way called "maturation by
heat." Spirit is the essentially active agent principle. The problematic
relation between the two elemental principles seen as emergent here, a
material principle and pure agency in the form of spirit, may constitute the
question which the *Principia* attempts to answer, for matter in that work
is passive, while agency is infused through the cosmos in the universal
presence of "force."

For classic rhetoric was addressed to the expression of objects to which the human mind was inherently adapted, while both the sacred and the alchemic texts addressed objects intrinsically hidden. Words, signs, and metaphors in Aristotle have major roles, but these are functions which are somehow bearable. Even Aeschylus, speaking the unspeakable, finds metaphors which contrive to bear their burdens. But no metaphor is adequate to the God of the Jews and the Christians; God does not admit comparison with other objects of thought. In place of metaphor, which as the Greek word it is derived from suggests "bears thought across" by comparing object with like object, we meet symbol which must be understood in another, mystic sense. Interpretation cannot in this case take the direct path but becomes in itself the art of elaboration of interpretive structures, the penetration of mystery to break through to hidden meanings.

Thus Newton was comfortable operating with the mythic symbolism of the alchemists, and he did not think it unscientific to meet the alchemic authors on their own grounds. The symbols of the lion, the dragon, allusions to the constellations, Leo and the star Regulus, were not out of order where the objects were of the sort Newton understood alchemy to address—hidden powers, active spirits, male and female, principles of growth and decay. For alchemy, the paradigms are first of all organic, the symbols are borrowed from life processes, and this again I think we can assume did not strike Newton as unscientific. As we shall see, these organic and psychological processes are just the matters he was concerned to bring within the scope of his physics. Freud and Jung are close in principle to the heart of his project: Newton's regular symbols are, as we have suggested, among Jung's archetypes, while the energies he is concerned to manage—the prototypes of the Newtonian "forces" of the *Principia*—are close kin to the energies Freud recognizes as surging in the psyche. We tend to think of the *Principia* as laying the foundation of *physics* in the modern sense of the term, but if we are correct in the present claim, the customary view of Newton's work is far too limited. Rather, Newton is most concerned with questions of biology and the psyche, with vital principles at the foundation of organic process and the functions of the psyche. Application to the motions of the planets was only the first and most available application of his principles; all of nature and the mind of man lay ahead.

The mathematical rhetoric of the *Principia*

Let us turn now to Newton's text, beginning with his "Preface to the Reader." On the whole, Newton writes with a grammatical and rhetorical precision which rewards careful reading. We might note that the standards, or rules, for his own writing may be understood as the inverse of the rules he formulates for the interpretation of a text: everywhere the arts of language and its uses—the arts which tradition calls those of the trivium—have these two faces. As arts of composition, of the making of discourse, they are guides to speaking or writing; while as arts of interpretation, they are guides to listening or reading. For Plato and Aristotle, as we have suggested, emphasis was on the arts of making; with Augustine and the Judeo-Christian tradition, a transformation takes place by which, in the presence of sacred text, the art of interpretation necessarily takes first place and becomes greatly and subtly elaborated. Newton is working in this latter tradition. For him, human learning is a question of the interpretation of immense bodies of text. These are first of all two, sacred Scripture and the phenomena of nature; the Bible, and the Book of Nature. Beyond them lie, as we have seen, the texts of deep traditions from earlier learnings, original *prisca theologia* and *prisca scientia,* gathered as the classics of theological interpretation and, of special interest to us here, of alchemy.

Readings of Scripture take us first to moral law and theological truth, while readings of the phenomena of nature take us to laws of nature and the understandings we call philosophy—but the two reflect fundamentally and intricately on each other. What we may call the Newtonian project is shaped to the conviction that Truth is one. Thus it is not surprising that when Newton formulates rules of procedure for the new adventure of mind on which he is embarking, the rules for the interpretation of Scripture, the *regulae interpretandi,* and those for the interpretation of the Book of Nature, the *regulae philosophandi,* mirror one another. Among the vast number of documents which Newton left unfinished or unpublished are two which set forth these new guides for the working of reason in the two faces of its interpretive mode. [7] At the beginning of one work, on the interpretation of prophecy, he set out what were denoted explicitly "rules of interpretation"; and at the outset of the third book of the *Principia,* called "The System of the World," he set out the other set of rules which, though they are called "rules of doing philosophy," are really rules of interpretation as well.

Our mathematical physics is thus legitimate heir to the long and rich tradition of the art of rhetoric, in its aspect as the art of interpretation. Francis Bacon had seen this clearly—the crucial experiment, the *experimentum crucis,* lies at the crossroads between alternative interpretive paths, highways of thought we now call "paradigms" of scientific theory. These rules of interpretation interweave as well with rules of composition: the *Principia* is at once a careful and exact composition on Newton's part, and the outcome of a new interpretation of nature. It is a composition which formulates a new method of interpretation, using mathematics to unveil realities not before seen. In this sense Newton's intention is to forge a new kind of instrument to serve the needs of a new understanding of philosophy, a philosophy in accord with what we are calling "the Newtonian alchemy." He designs the *Principia* to articulate this new way and thus to effect a turning, a dialectical reversal in the liberal arts. The *Principia,* as we are seeing, looks both ways: in its propositions the arts of the past and the arts of an envisioned future are suspended in extreme tension. We now call this state of intellectual and social tension the "Scientific Revolution." Perhaps a reading of Newton's subtle text in this rhetorical aspect helps, as we have suggested, to throw renewed light on that complex revolution, to which we are the uncertain heirs.

Newton's "Preface to the Reader"

In the "Preface to the Reader," which he wrote for the first edition of the *Principia,* Newton gives a very tight account of the revolution he intends to launch upon the world. The first sentence already carefully, if very schematically, locates the *Principia* in the history of natural philosophy. Newton first characterizes the ancient investigation of nature as culminating in a certain understanding of "mechanics"—he means most of all the mathematics of Archimedes (*GBWW* I: 11, 401–592; II: 10, 401–592). He then alludes in a phrase to a long middle period in which the trivium had displaced the quadrivium, the arts of language displacing those of mathematics. Mathematics was set aside and other terms of analysis were substituted, "substantial forms," he says, and "occult qualities." The third, modern period, he sees as a restoration of the old—literally, a recalling of natural philosophy to its mathematical mode, yet in a new guise of what he calls mathematical "laws." We should take note of that term, for it bespeaks the passage we are embarking on. Mathematics in its first instantiation had spoken by way of theorems, universal statements addressed to the contemplative mind; now its utterances will be laws addressed not in the first instance to mind but in the form of commands to action, directed to an obedient nature. This history—the whole intellectual history of Western man in relation to the study of nature—has been set out in a single dependent clause: we may think of it as the "whereas" clause of Newton's own proclamation. Let us try restating it in the form of a manifesto:

> WHEREAS the ancients . . . most of all prized mechanics in the investigation of nature . . . and those of more recent times, having discarded substantial forms and occult properties, have undertaken to recall the phenomena of nature to mathematical laws, . . .
>   IT IS PROPOSED in this treatise to cultivate mathesis insofar as it looks to philosophy. (Cf. *GBWW* I: 34, 1; II: 32, 1.)

This is the very form of a declaration, a manifesto launching a new intellectual endeavor. Others, Newton says, have gone far: but they have failed to achieve the full union of mathesis and philosophy, and it is this which the *Principia* will teach mankind to do. The first word of the Latin title is *philosophy*.

We should notice that his three-part account of history is in the precise form of the dialectical process, as we meet it first in Socrates, but ultimately in Hegel and Marx. There is first the affirmation in the mode of innocence—here, the initial, brilliant thrusts of the ancients, Euclid and Archimedes. These gave us universal propositions, addressed to timeless mind. Then there is the medieval negation in the name of spiritual aims and an omnipotent, omniscient God, mysteries which dispelled such ambitions of the merely natural intellect. Now at last there is to be Newton's synthesis in a new mode. As we shall see, this will empower anew mathesis and the old intellect but will incorporate spirit and mystery, to go beyond mere universal mind to address all things in a nature recognized as a Creation infused with the operations of divine agency.

Newton uses the Greek term *mathēsis* in his declaration, to suggest the scope of the enterprise: he means demonstrative argument and the cultivation of intellectual intuition in a new sense, and in a new application. Though he embraces Euclid, Apollonius, and Archimedes as teachers, we shall see that he boldly extends the bounds of their geometry to become something he will call "universal mathematics"; and though his argument in the *Principia* will on the whole be in the form of demonstration, his intention is to transform altogether the concept of a mathematical treatise. Rather than a theoretical composition such as Euclid's *Elements,* setting forth what is known and unknown for the ultimate benefit of an understanding mind, learning as an end in itself, Newton's work is designed as instrumental. Offering its propositions as instruments of an interpretive inquiry of an altogether new kind, it is to transform the nature of both mathematics and philosophical investigation. Its mathesis is to open anew all studies, studies directed to a Creation which is throughout, mathesis incarnate.

The "opening question" of the *Principia,* then, must be this puzzle: "How can mathesis bear upon (or 'look to') philosophy?" In contemporary terms, we might tentatively put it this way: "How can a broad philosophy of the Creation find its principles in, or through, mathematical physics?" In terms of our present intellectual scene, we may wonder, "How can the mathematical sciences and their corollary, a technological society, be brought back into the circle of philosophy—of human purpose, and the understanding of ultimate things?" Common wisdom today assumes that it can't be done—that our science or mathesis is of one sort of thing, which we may in some sense come to know, while the larger circle of philosophy and theology escapes mathesis, and hence deals with things about which we may have opinions or beliefs but cannot resolve as matters of knowledge. We see how far we may

An idealized image of an alchemist's study, symbolizing the depth of the relation in alchemy between the Creation and its Creator. On the right is the laboratory, with vials of the sort recognizable from the Ripley Scroll on the shelves above; on the left, the alchemist kneels before an altar. Invocation of the divine is intrinsic to the work.

be, or suppose ourselves to be, from the endowment Newton meant for us. We seem in some way to have missed Newton's intention.

Having in his opening declaration given this epitome of the problem he has set for himself and the world, Newton now takes some time to consider what the extended and inclusive mathesis of the *Principia* will be like. To achieve it, Newton must first bring about a revolution within mathematics itself; thinking in terms of the traditional seven liberal arts (the four mathematical arts of the quadrivium, together with the three linguistic arts of the trivium), we might say that Newton, in order to bring the quadrivium into an effective new relation with the trivium— to get mathesis actually to serve philosophy—must first perform a revolution within the quadrivium itself. The pivotal term for Newton at this point is *mechanics*. The ancients, even when they brought the full power of their mathematics to bear upon what they thought of as mechanics, considered it under the paradigm which ultimately Homer had given them, and us, when he called Odysseus *polymechanos*—a general-purpose mechanic, or a man of many "devices" (*GBWW* I: 4, 183–322; II: 3, 307–541). In this sense, Newton says mechanics was for the ancients a realm of human forces. When Archimedes, as the ultimate mathematical Odysseus, proposes to use the lever to move the world, the lever is a machine—one of the five classic "machines" (the lever, the screw, the inclined plane, the wheel, the pulley)—but the force upon it is the beast of labor or the hand of man. Newton sets up his own view in dialectical opposition to Archimedes in this way:

> This part of mechanics was cultivated by the ancients, with an eye to manual arts, in terms of the five powers, and they considered gravity—since it is not a manual power—hardly otherwise than in respect to moving heavy bodies by those powers.
>   We, however—consulting not arts but philosophy, and hence writing not of manual but natural powers—treat most of all of those which look to gravity, levity, elastic force, the resistance of fluids, and forces of this kind. (Cf. *GBWW* I: 34, 1; II: 32, 1.)

Mechanics, then, had been seen as belonging to human arts and the realm of human *praxis,* the lower realms, we might say, of that divided line according to which Plato organizes the hierarchy of human functions in *The Republic* (*GBWW* I: 7, 295–441; II: 6, 295–441). Newton proposes to transform mechanics to much higher philosophical status, by recognizing in nature—that is, in a domain which is not of man's contriving—"forces" or powers which we can understand by a sweeping analogy to those human arts and powers of Odysseus and Archimedes. Here for Newton nature imitates art, in the sense that we move from the classical mechanics of human machines to a new, philosophical mechanics of natural powers, in which nature—or some agent which moves in and through nature—is the artificer. What were human arts are to be seen now as divine workmanship: God is the new artificer.

We see, then, the prospect of a philosophical mechanics. To relate this to the classical quadrivium of arithmetic, geometry, music, and astronomy, however, we must back up to look at an earlier section of Newton's Preface. Newton has made the following claim:

> Geometry is founded therefore in mechanical praxis, and it is nothing other than that part of universal mechanics which exactly proposes and demonstrates the art of measuring. (Cf. *GBWW* I: 34, 1; II: 32, 1.)

Here Newton is joining issue with Euclid and arguing that what Euclid takes for granted—demands, or "postulates," in the language of the *Elements*—or asks the beginner in his art to grant, in fact derives from another science: namely, the de-scription, the scribing-out, of the circle and the straight line. For Newton, this small distinction is not a quibble but a fundamental clue. These two operations upon which geometry must be built he here calls *praxis,* again perhaps using the Greek term in order to open a concept anew. *Praxis,* from the Greek verb *prattein,* means a "making" or "doing," but this geometric scribing is not the kind of doing which belongs to the artificers at the bottom of Plato's line. It must be a making which is higher in the intellectual hierarchy than geometry itself—that is, it must be as clear to the mind as the propositions of Euclid themselves, and prior in the order of understanding. If it were not, geometry would be founded on a clouded insight. Newton is thus proposing that there is a *praxis* which is a higher mathesis, and that by confusing this with ordinary mechanics the ancients overlooked a fundamental possibility. He says:

> However, the errors are not of the art, but of the artisan. Whoever works less accurately, is a less perfect mechanic, and if anyone were able to work most accurately, he would be the most perfect mechanic of all (*mechanicus omnium perfectissimus*). (Cf. *GBWW* I: 34, 1; II: 32, 1.)

Clearly, Newton has a candidate for this post of *mechanicus omnium perfectissimus,* who will bridge the erstwhile abyss between the accuracy of even the best human workmanship and the exactness and intellectual clarity of mathematical demonstration. It is God Himself, God the Creator whose word has entered upon the human scene between the time of Archimedes and the time of Newton. This concept of the omnipotent Creator as divine craftsman makes it possible for Newton to pass from imperfect mechanics to a *praxis* so exact that it becomes mathesis. The God of Genesis transforms the quadrivium and clears mechanics of its confusion. We must recognize, above geometry in the hierarchy of the liberal arts, a new, dominant member of the former quadrivium: universal mechanics. Within this new structuring of the quadrivium, motion is primary; the mechanics of powers or forces will be one branch, while pure geometry, as art of measurement devoid of the question of force, will be another. We might say now that universal mechanics is the "real geometry," of which Euclid's is one limited aspect. The other part Newton goes on to term "rational mechanics," and this is the part concerning powers, or forces,

> In which sense rational mechanics will be the science of motions which result from any forces whatever, and of the forces which are required for any motion whatever, exactly enunciated and demonstrated. (Cf. *GBWW* I: 34, 1; II: 32, 1.)

Here, in this brief definition, we see a link forged between the new mathesis and philosophy. Essentially, I believe, Newton agrees with Aristotle in one aspect of his understanding of natural philosophy: namely, that the object of natural philosophy is motion—those motions which

113

occur in the natural order, regularly and without man's assistance. The object of the natural philosopher is to discover the true causes of these motions. In implementing the new program for the conversion of natural philosophy, the initial difficulty must be to pin down a concept of motion at the level of strict mathematics; the next will be to come to an agreement about "cause."

It would seem, as indeed it seemed to the ancients, that the concept of motion inherently resists any effort to achieve intellectual clarity. If an object of thought is to be clear, it must first come to rest before the mind—but motion is exactly that which never rests. Mathesis would seem essentially addressed to stasis; kinesis would seem to be by its nature to defy strict knowing. Aristotle led the ancients to a solution of this problem in his *Physics* by means of a brilliant grammatical artifice. He captures the concept of motion—not mathematically, it is true, but adequately for a philosophy of nature committed to operating in a less mathematical cosmos—by means of a double predication of being: to be potentially, and to be in actuality. The motion of the growing tree is caught by seeing double: once *in potentia,* as acorn, once again in actuality, as the mature oak. This is no small triumph of the ancients, this old way, for it has the power of showing us the motion in its wholeness, and it applies across the board—to falling bodies, or in the *Poetics,* to falling kings. It was the old way, to grasp the concept of motion through the instrumentality of the trivium. Ptolemy, you might object, did more through the concept of uniform motion, the ratios of elapsed times and interpolation in tables—but always he is dealing with the relations between finished motions, not with the planet in the process of the motion itself; he tells a story but does not claim a cause. Newton is intent on going directly to motion itself, not such results of elapsed intervals, as the primary object. How he achieves this we shall see shortly, when we turn to what he calls his "lemmas," but first we must consider Newton's treatment of the question of "cause."

In the domain of cause, Aristotle's *Physics* distinguishes four modes of answer to our question, "Why?" [8] The response may come in terms of the matter, the agent, the form or definition of the thing itself, or the end or goal of the motion. Aristotle's Greek is always simpler than our English: these are, respectively, the *in-what,* the *by-what,* the *what,* and the *that-for-the-sake-of-which.* Again, Aristotle is using the instruments of the trivium, projecting nature into language by means of crucial and indeed highly effective distinctions of grammatical structure. And again, in a world which is the workshop of a different God, Newton carries the question into the realm of the quadrivium, in this case by locating the issue in a single concept of cause, in Latin *vis,* meaning "power" or "force," and claiming that the relation of motion to its cause—of motion to force—is a problem for solution by mathesis, exact enunciation and demonstration. For Aristotle, the relation of cause to

The Greene Lyon devouring the Sun, paradigm of Newton's own alchemic investigations. The lion is the pure antimony (the ore), while the Sun is the universal spirit, invoked in alchemic mystery. The death is also a birth; the blood, a vivified mercury.

effect in nature (and nature is the source of all action for Aristotle, organic, inorganic, vital, or mental) is orderly, but blurry, for matter, that principle of confusion, dispels precision. For Newton, nature in effect snaps to attention, precisely because behind all action is that divine agency which imposed law upon its Creation.

While we are still speaking of Newton's purposes, and before we turn to look at the new mathematics which will be the key to his method, we might well pause to look ahead to the actual structure of the *Principia*. The *Principia* is organized in three books. The first two contain the body of basic propositions which constitute what Newton calls the "mathematical principles of natural philosophy"—strictly, perhaps, these two books are the *principia,* the "principles." The third book, called "The System of the World," is then appended to the work as an illustration, or one might say, an initial realization. Where the first two books, as the books of the new mathesis, only await their application in philosophy, the third book is a brilliant example of that new philosophy itself. The first two books are thus books of mathematics in the new mode; the third book is an exemplary book of philosophy. As such, the third book is the first step on a way which is ultimately, I think, intended by Newton to yield a total replacement for Aristotle's *Physics* in its full range. Newton aims to be forging here a mathesis adequate to the one truth of a created world.

The sample in the third book deals with only one of those natural forces Newton has alluded to, namely gravity, and addresses the cosmos only in its aspect as a gravitational system. It conspicuously does not, for example, deal with the optical or chemical systems of the world, nor with the causes of the vital motions of nature, those which alchemy calls "vegetable" and "animal" and is primarily interested in mastering. We recall that "physics" no more denotes to Newton than it does to Aristotle that "inorganic" realm which we now call physics and distinguish from biology and psychology. Newton clearly intends a mathematical physics of all natural things, including most especially all those which live, grow, move, and feel. The gravitational system unfolded in the third book is a brilliant but relatively easy initial step into the new philosophy. The cosmos is only the beginning. The real third book, which it was not possible for Newton to compose, would be the Book of Alchemy. There is evidence that Newton was trying hard to bring his alchemy into shape in time for inclusion in a more complete picture of The System of the World, balancing the macrocosm of the planets with the microcosm of a mathematical alchemy. Newton was not able to write the *Principia* he intended. One clue to his ambitions is found in the great "Queries" appended to his *Optics,* in which he did his best to pass his vision on to future generations. It is a vision of alchemy realized.

We have seen that Newton proposes to bring the investigation of physics in this broadest sense into intimate relation with a transformed version of the quadrivium, the arts of mathematics. We have seen the aim, but not a method by which it might be brought about. The key term will be *force,* for Newton is shaping

> . . . the science of the motions which result from any forces . . . and of the forces which are required for any motion. . . . (Cf. *GBWW* I: 34, 1; II: 32, 1.)

If "forces"—we will reflect later on the possible meanings of this most mysterious term—are causes, we see that the science of mechanics will proceed by two great modes of argument. In one, we proceed from motions to find out the forces—from effect to cause; the other will be the reverse, passing from forces to resulting states—from cause to effect. The first moves in the direction of induction—from the phenomena to find out the underlying principle. The second moves in the direction of construction from the principles well known, to demonstrate the effects. In the rhetorical terms we have employed earlier, the first corresponds to the rhetoric of interpretation—interpreting the appearances to find out what lies beneath; while the second belongs to the rhetoric of composition. Both are now to be conducted by means of mathematical demonstration. Newton goes on to formulate this plan in a larger way:

> Every difficulty of philosophy is seen to turn upon this: as from the phenomena of motion we investigate the forces of nature, so thereafter from these forces we demonstrate the remaining phenomena. (Cf. *GBWW* I: 34, 1; II: 32, 1.)

When we see that the "motions" in question are to include all the phenomena with which nature presents us, and that the passage from the motions to the forces is the intellectual progress from effects to their causes, we recognize in other terms that Newton is referring here to that progression from result to cause which Aristotle calls *analysis*— that is, the direction of inquiry in physics. The reversed process, the passage from the causes, now known, to their consequences, is the direct motion of philosophical argument, the building of a system of consequences from a few first principles which are themselves best known. This is *synthesis*. Euclid's text is a work of nearly pure synthesis, and in the tradition of the *Elements,* we normally think that progression, from elements to outcomes, is the appropriate mode for demonstration. But what Newton is proposing is that both of these two great motions in philosophy—the order of inquiry and the order of knowing—be carried out by demonstration in the new mathesis. He is not however the first pioneer to cross this dramatic watershed, for he is very much the student of Descartes.

There are as well certain occasions when the ancient geometers proceed the other way: they start with the unknown and reason toward the known. How can that be done? The formula is, in effect, to "assume the thing done"—that is, take the unknown as if known. In the case, for example, of a geometric construction, suppose the figure which is sought actually to have been constructed; then, on this assumption, reason to those necessary consequences which would follow—reason in the subjunctive mode—until you arrive at some consequence which you know in fact is true. From this basis as terra firma, if the steps of the argument will admit of reversal, the demonstration can be stood on its head and, run backward, turned into a synthesis. At the end of it all, the unknown is arrived at again, now as a necessary consequence of what is indeed known to be true.

All this is familiar to the ancients, though on the whole they use strict analysis very seldom. Since that was widely believed to be the method by which they had hit upon many of their synthetic propositions, it was thought of as the method of discovery, and scholarly rumor held over the ages that the ancients had been in possession of such a systematic art of discovery which they had kept secret, disdaining to pass it on to posterity. It was perhaps the principal mathematical component of the tradition of a lost *prisca scientia*. Descartes speaks of it in these terms and proposes at the outset of his *Discourse on Method* to recover this presumed ancient art of discovery though in a new form, more powerful than anything the ancients had possessed: a universal method of reasoning from the unknown to the known. [9] In the broadest terms, his *Discourse on Method* sets forth the new universal analysis in the guise of the method of "doubt." In its mathematical implementation in relation to problems from Euclid and Apollonius, he calls it analytic geometry and appends it, as an illustration, to the *Discourse*.

Now the idea of a systematic mathematical analysis, by which to move by precise demonstration from unknown to known, is the very methodological backbone of the *Principia*. In this, Newton is altogether a disciple of Descartes. Yet what Newton gives us is not the expected algebraic analysis but a *geometric* analysis of his own devising, and this represents from the outset a significant, and very deliberate, turning away from Descartes. Newton is a master of Descartes's algebra and uses it whenever he must; he knows well what vast new powers it opens in mathematics. But he knows too that those symbols, letters representing the unknown or representing nothing, mere symbols, reduce science to an obscurity and move by way of automatic processes which bring no light to the mind. It is for this reason that there is a minimum of algebra in the *Principia,* and in its place a maximum of appeal to the eye of the mind through the artful use of what we might call a rhetoric of geometric forms. This is a true battle of the arts: from Newton's point of view, a battle against the new, illiberal art of algebra, and an effort to reinstate the geometry of the ancients, though now as the vehicle of a powerful and precise analysis as well as a synthesis.

We shall see that the *Principia* is in one most important aspect a work of polemic, against a view of the world which Newton regards as deeply pernicious. The enemy, to whose refutation Book II is chiefly dedicated, is at once Descartes and that view of the world, based on Descartes's work, known and widely prized as the "mechanical philosophy." Given our modern carelessness in the use of terms, and the fact as well that Newton is founding the *Principia* on a mathematics which he is calling a "universal mechanics," it may seem strange to paint him now as the enemy of the mechanical philosophy. The crux of the mechanical philosophy is that it reduces the workings of nature to those of a machine in the sense of a clockwork, connected throughout by linkages and gears, and actuated always by parts in direct contact. Now, algebra is such a machine in the domain of the mind. The processes of algebra turn like the gears of a clock and thus proceed without dependence on or reference to any meaning of the symbols involved, which are in their algebraic role mere blind counters. Algebra is, then, the appropriate projection of the mechanical philosophy into mathematics: and as such,

Newton excludes it from the *Principia,* not as an incidental tactical decision, but as a deep rhetorical principle. The *Principia* is aimed not at problem solving, however our modern world may have adopted it in only that sense. It is meant as a philosophical instrument, and as such, it must be an instrument composed in symbols which illuminate and clarify, as the artfully devised figures of Newton's geometric analysis will in fact do. This is for Newton a decision of deep interest, and it already points toward the largest significance of the *Principia.* It is directed in its substance against the mechanical philosophy, and in its form it defies the algebra of the *Geometrie Analytique.* These are decisions made on theological grounds, for the mechanical philosophy and its mathematical corollary are what Newton in his theological discussions calls "dead works." Turning his *Principia* against them is for Newton a most intensely motivated move in the service of God, and in defiance of Satan. These are to be the mathematical principles of a knowledge of God's works. Both substance and style of the work must therefore be appropriate to the service of God, as the mechanical philosophy and its algebraic mathematics are not.

Newton agrees with Descartes that the world is a mathematical object—an appropriate object for mathesis—to be approached by methods of mathematical analysis; to this extent, Newton and Descartes concur. But for Descartes, this means that the domain of nature is a simple object, clear and distinct in the mind's eye. "Matter is extension," Descartes tells us. Descartes means by "extension" precisely that magnitude, *megethos,* which is the subject of Book V of Euclid's *Elements.* [10] It is a mathematical object of which one can indeed, in some sense, form the kind of "clear and distinct" idea, which is the proclaimed object of the Cartesian science. It might seem, indeed, the perfect candidate for a mathematical interpretation of the concept of "matter," since magnitude is in itself at the same time quantitatively precise, and utterly without form or definition of its own. But for Descartes, this extension in motion constitutes the totality of the natural world. All bodies are configurations of this one matter, all motions are its motions, in the form of flows and vortices of every kind. This is indeed the world of the mechanical philosophy—empty in Newton's view however much it is full, "dead" however much it moves. It invites the arrogance of the calculative mind which can track its every possible complication and freely devise a hypothesis to account for any possible phenomenon. Newton's Christian mathesis of the world must therefore be in some way the opposite of Descartes's.

In place of this blind and dead clockwork of Descartes, Newton unfolds a world which is a proper object of *nous,* intellectual intuition, full of intelligible causes and evidences of purpose, plan, and drama. These are objects which are of the highest importance to comprehend. The philosophical vision which Newton's geometric analysis is shaped

The star regulus of antimony, a true alchemical icon. When after long labor he had achieved a purified antimony sign with this "star," Newton appears to have believed that he possessed an agent of special virtue on his way to the philosophical mercury. The name suggests an astronomical relation to the star Regulus, "heart" of the constellation Leo.

to achieve shows the mind the way to true causes, which will be at once both material and spiritual. In this sense, the real model for that mathematical analysis which Newton has in mind is the Christian rhetoric of interpretation, by which the Creation is to be read as our evidence of the presence and working of the Creator. Any such reading of the Book of Nature, meant to entail a transforming passage from flesh to spirit, requires art and sensitivity and does not proceed by smooth stages but rather goes through a succession of crises in the construction and interpretation of signs. It is Newton's task in the *Principia* to construct geometric signs matched to the signatures with which the Creator has signed the phenomena. Newton's project is to show that even such an interpretation may be carried out by mathematical analysis when that is couched in geometric hieroglyphs of the right contrivance. The crises of interpretation may take the form of crucial experiments in which nature is put to the test in the laboratory, or crucial observations in which the crisis is transposed to the heavens. The world becomes a mathematical problem in an interesting sense, whose solution is, ultimately, God.

This is the analysis which the third book of the *Principia* will illustrate in what it is not unreasonable to call its "revelation" of the operation of universal gravitation throughout the frame of nature: every body throughout the cosmos, Newton will demonstrate, attracts every other body with a force of a single genus called "gravity," ruled by an exact, intelligible mathematical law. Without high art and the methods of disciplined experiment, the intellect unaided could never have uncovered such a mystery, though it operates everywhere in our very midst. Its discovery is a dramatic peripety in human history, a breakthrough in man's understanding of the divine plan. As a first step in a new era of natural philosophy, it is a sure sign for Newton that time is running out on the Creation, and man is drawing closer to his God. It has, as Newton's account of the System of the World unfolds, many corollaries concerning our human history, and God's plan for the world.

Time

Between Newton and the classic understanding of reason and the work of mind—between the Lord God, on the one hand, and *o theos,* the god of Aristotle's *Physics,* on the other—lies the idea of the reality of time. Roughly speaking, we may say that Aristotle denies the existence of time. When he argues that "time is the measure of motion"— and no more—he tells us that substances exist, and they exist most when they are most in act, that is, most in motion. Time is only our count of the cycles of these motions. That is all it is: nothing in itself, only a reckoning of something else, which is. There is no past, there is no future, what is is always present, most present when it is in passage. We live in the midst of memory and expectation, indeed, but memory cannot be of anything essentially different, nor can there be expectation of anything essentially new. For ultimately there is always and only the utter constancy of the unmoved mover, whose necessary existence and invariant act guarantee the integrity of the cosmos from moment to moment and are in the fullest sense the unchanging cause of all its motions. It is a mere corollary of this denial of time that Aristotle denies as well either a creation or a terminus of existence— either a beginning or an end of things. Motion stretches in its potential infinity forever backward, forever forward, but such "forevers" hold nothing in prospect or retrospect. Broadly speaking, Plato, Homer, and the Greek tragedians share this understanding that there are cycles of natural motion and human action, but that time is nothing other than the count of their repetitions: there is no stretch of history, from a time to a time.

By contrast, time for Newton is very, very real—as it is for the modern world. Time is not for him or us a mere measure of what exists; it in some way preexists, and other things measure it, more or less accurately. We presuppose that things happen "in" it. This has consequences in every direction of our activities and our thoughts:

theologically, for Newton, the world is stretched under high tension between the Creation and the Final Judgment; every event—not least, his own composition of the *Principia*—has its place on that divine time line, and its principal significance in relation to this ultimate historical framework. Human records are no longer a complication of tragic cycles but a tracing of developments through a succession of epochs in which the conditions of existence essentially change. The past is irreconcilable with the demands of the present, and a future which is likely to be very different is loaded with threat or promise.

Finally, or perhaps in the context of our present discussion, first of all, the art of mathematics is transformed by the idea of time. When Newton claims, in the Preface, that mechanics precedes geometry, he means that time is prior to Euclid's *Elements;* for the description of the line and the circle are processes in time, and mechanics, as the mathematics of motion, takes time as a primary mathematical object. Like the cosmos of Genesis, the mathematical objects which Euclid took as timeless are to be understood in their essence as products of a creation.

We shall see how Newton uses this new resource in shaping elementary propositions of his universal mechanics, when we turn in a moment to the mathematical lemmas with which he prefaces the *Principia*. For the moment, we may simply note the fact that the *Principia* will not only build its propositions on the presupposition of mathematical time as its material, but the work itself addresses and belongs to history. Newton is acutely aware of the place of his work in history—as we have seen, it is embedded in a sense of the Christian eschatology, marking as it does for Newton a stage of the revelation of truth to mankind which must be hard upon the threshold of the end of the world and the Second Coming. The fact that he can know what he has here come to know, and convey this to us in this work which tells us what it tells, is for Newton itself a mystery, an awe-inspiring development in our relation to God. It is an event: for Newton, God reveals himself historically in the course of these pages. And it will be equally in accord with this understanding to say that what the *Principia* teaches is finally a set of truths about history, and its method becomes a method for keeping time over the centuries and interpreting the evidences of the past, and thus an instrument for doing history. Thus, the work is wrapped in time: its propositions are made out of time, their unfolding is itself a crucial event in time, and their consequences teach us about time and history, on every scale. The mathesis of natural philosophy and, with it, of theology and history, is founded on the original mathesis of time.

What is this mathematical time which has thus taken central place in our minds? Newton is generous in stepping out his text in reflective excursions he calls "scholia," to discuss with us the strange developments which he and we are witnessing together. He has these words of reflection on time:

Absolute, true, and mathematical time, of itself, and from its own
nature, flows equably without relation to anything external, and by
another name is called duration: relative, apparent, and common time,
is some sensible and external (whether accurate or unequable) measure
of duration by the means of motion, which is commonly used instead of
true time; such as an hour, a day, a month, a year. (*GBWW* I: 34, 8; II:
32, 8)

We note the formal reversal: Aristotle had said that time was the
measure of motion; now Newton says, time exists in its own right, and
motions become measures of it. Newton speaks here with the voice
of authentic alchemy: it is exactly the alchemist's quest to find the
true and philosophical existence beneath the common and deceiving
appearances. The true mercury has something to do with appearances,
but it does not normally manifest itself in the world of sensation and
qualities—only by strategies of high art can it be induced to emerge,
and when it does, we see evidences, but the unskilled eye does not
see the underlying philosophical substance. True being is manifested in
hieroglyphs, signatures which it is the work of philosophy to read. Newton is here doing with time exactly what as alchemist he was doing with
mercury—and we see that in this way, he is laying the mathematical
foundation for mechanics as rational alchemy.

Indeed, we see, as the discussion in this scholium unfolds, deep
alchemy at work—and if we feel that the "time" Newton speaks of is
the time of our modern laboratories, satellites, and stock markets, we
may sense some working kinship with this Newtonian alchemy and, even
in our jaded era, shudder in awe at the presence of mystery. Our clocks
now derive their times from the motions of atoms, ranged from the
immediacy of our laboratories to the edge of the cosmos. What do we
imagine it is which coordinates the motions of myriad atoms throughout
the stretch of nature? Our particle physicists speak earnestly of events
in the first seconds of the creation of the world of the particles we
know now: what coordinates those "seconds" with today's "seconds"?
Evidently, we, the true heirs of Newton, believe in a time, flowing
equably in itself, as an unbroken foundation of being. Newtonian time
is the first clue to our modern alchemy!

Space

From time, Newton turns in this same scholium to space, about which
he finds a great deal more to say. His opening statement is, however, a
parallel assertion of the existence of an "absolute":

Absolute space, in its own nature, without relation to anything
external, remains always similar and immovable. Relative space is some

movable dimension or measure of the absolute spaces; which our senses determine by its position to bodies; and which is commonly taken for immovable space. . . . (Ibid.)

In each of these statements, Newton's use of the term *nature* is important, for it dispels any thought that these are mere numbers, measures, or, in some nominalist sense, mere "concepts." No, it is clear, for Newton they are existent substances, something very real at the root of the Creation. This is, again, alchemy. We are not asked whether we wish (as the saying goes) to "believe" in it, or whether we wish to "assume" or "suppose" it. These dimensions are affirmed as beings, and the entire work is built on the assumption of their reality. Nothing, large or small, can move except in absolute space:

All things are placed in time as to order of succession; and in space as to order of situation. It is from their essence or nature that they are places; and that the primary places of things should be movable, is absurd. (*GBWW* I: 34, 10; II: 32, 10)

I take it that both time and space are understood by Newton to be true objects of intellectual intuition. That means, simply, that if we clear our minds of distractions, we can think about duration itself, and think about extension itself:

. . . in philosophical disquisitions, we ought to abstract from our senses, and consider things themselves, distinct from what are only sensible measures of them. For it may be that there is no body really at rest, to which the places and motions of others may be referred. (Ibid.)

Is it not clear that in entering upon the *Principia* we are embarking on a work of *science* in the sense that we are occupying ourselves with matters which are knowable to mind and in no way contingent on empirical outcomes? Kant, it is true, will save the Newtonian enterprise in another sense, by claiming that these absolutes of time and space are no other than the modes of operation of our own minds, our ways of seeing the world (of *Anschauung*). Modern readers may be more comfortable with Kant's evasion than with Newton's clarity. But if we join Newton on his own terms, we see that time and space are now objects upon which certain knowledge can be built, as confidently as Euclid built on the intellectual intuition of a point, which could be alluded to but never constructed or presented to the senses in a drawing. The note of despair, suggested in the phrase "it may be that there is no body really at rest," reflects the heavy burden of the alchemist, who may never see emerge from the furnace secure evidence of the true philosophical mercury. But the faith of the alchemist appears in this scholium as well: "But we may distinguish," Newton immediately goes on to say, "rest and motion, absolute and relative, one from the other by their

In this engraving of the Main Gate of Trinity College, Newton's quarters were to the right of the gate. In contrast to the grandeur of the alchemist's study in our earlier illustration, scholars have identified a modest wooden building at the chapel end of the garden as the likely site of his alchemical laboratory and his long hours of work at the furnace.

properties, causes, and effects." And with this begins a strategy for the extrication of truth from appearance which constitutes the balance of this long scholium and, in a larger sense, the work of the *Principia* as a whole. Just as he labored to refine the tangled mythology of traditional alchemy, Newton insists here on care in the use of terms, always with the aim of keeping reference honed to the underlying Being which is his unvarying object.

> . . . those violate the accuracy of language, which ought to be kept precise, who interpret these words for the measured quantities. Nor do those less defile the purity of mathematical and philosophical truths, who confound real quantities with their relations and sensible measures. (*GBWW* I: 34, 12; II: 32, 12)

The fierce ethical tone of these lines speaks to the nobility of Newton's art and resonates with the romance of the alchemic quest: nothing less than truth and reality is to be its object. And we see alchemic practice at work in the method Newton adduces as the sure sign of absolute rotational motion—and hence, as well, of absolute rotational rest. He has found a procedure, a very alchemy, for the revelation of absolute rotational rest. In an ingenious experiment with an object which is no more than a rotating bucket of water, Newton finds in the curvature of the surface of the revolving water a signature of absolute rotational motion. What Newton is looking for is a sure sign in the realm of phenomena of our relation to something which is real, present, and knowable—though in the common course of the world, unseen and invisible. This surface curvature, like a telling color change in alchemy, becomes a revelation. As extended later in the scholium to the measure of tension in the "cord" connecting "globes," the same test bears on the absolute motion of planets, for the cord becomes the force of gravity; the globes, two heavenly bodies. By knowing the force between them, might we not, Newton is proposing, determine their absolute rotation and thereby detect the rotational posture of true and philosophical space? That would be the cosmic alchemy, to which Newton is devoting this work.

As we shall come to see, motions and forces are intimately related, true forces to true motions. Unless we can find our way to absolute space itself, the program of philosophy may be blocked. The purpose of Newton's philosophy, the Newtonian alchemy, is not simply to *know* what is true as theory but to *find out* true Being in the world. For Newton, theory is instrumental. The real and philosophical is to be sought in the world.

> And therefore as it is possible, that in the remote regions of the fixed stars, or perhaps far beyond them, there may be some body absolutely at rest; but impossible to know, from the position of bodies to one another

in our regions, whether any of these do keep the same position to that remote body, it follows that absolute rest cannot be determined from the position of bodies in our regions. (*GBWW* I: 34, 10; II: 32, 10)

Yet the project of the *Principia* does not founder on this somber conclusion. For the real and true Newton will most want to discover is not time or space in themselves but an entity of far greater interest: that agency in the world he will introduce as "force." To reveal force, as we shall see, it is not necessary to find out absolute force directly.

The lemmas

We have claimed that the style of the *Principia* is artfully matched to its purpose, and we have tried to give some anticipatory sense of what that purpose will be. Its aim, we have said in effect, is an intellectual intuition of true forms existent in the world. Nature is everywhere to accept and reward mathesis, while the *Principia* is to be shaped as the intellectual instrument which will make this new kind of seeing possible. That is the sense in which it is to provide the mathematical principles of a new philosophy. To get started on this sweeping project, Newton must first prepare certain appropriate mathematical methods. These are the new mathematics of motion, housed in the new absolute space and time. They have developed into the art we now call the "calculus," and which Newton, conceiving the project in terms of the mathematization of flowing or fluent quantities, called "fluxions."

Two Newtonian problems

Problem 1: To find an instantaneous rate of change [11]

If we were to construct a Euclidean figure—let us say, a simple right triangle PDB (fig. 1a)—and then bring it into the Newtonian world, what world change might it undergo? From the purely relational figure of Euclid, existing timelessly and nowhere—for its own sake and according only to its own definition—it must now enter Newton's new conceptual time and space. Even as it sits quietly in the illustration, mathematical time is running, and the triangle is beginning, as Newton has said, to "endure." If we wish to, we can as well let it begin to alter in a regular way. We may for example let point B begin to move to the right at a regular rate. The triangle will begin to undergo what seems a Protean, fluent change, not only of place, but of shape. Newton's alchemy of motion demands that behind this confusion of appearances he must reveal clarity and constancy, ground on which to reason mathematically about such a blurred result.

In figure 1b, this motion has begun. Some interval of time has elapsed, and point B has moved to the right to a new position *b*. For that interesting moment at which the point was in its original position and the motion was just beginning, Newton coins a new and revealing term: he says the motion is "nascent"—in birth, just beginning. It is significant that Newton chooses the Latin verb (*nasci*, "to be born") which underlies the word *nature*, for this is the first step in the mathematization of what was not before mathematical, and it suggests the scope of the new mathematics. Nature is the domain of all things which undergo birth and death, beginnings and endings—to a first approximation, *nature* is simply Latin for Aristotle's term *physics;* the Greek *physis* is the realm of all that grows and fails, waxes and wanes. Both terms, Aristotelian physics and Newtonian nature, have in view the organic before the inorganic, and the motions of the psyche most of all. Such are the ambitions of this Newtonian triangle, the beginning as it is of the mathesis of all nature. Only in our own time, with advances such as those of psychoanalysis, neurophysiology, and information theory, are we beginning to glimpse the implications of this Newtonian mathematization of all nature.

As a consequence of the uniform growth of the base DB, the hypotenuse, of course, grows as well. Newton calls both DB and PB "fluent" quantities. The characteristic question for this new geometry—Euclid's *Elements* set into motion—is, "What is the *rate of growth* of PB?" If we suppose that DB grows at a uniform rate, its length represents or measures time—it becomes a true and absolute clock in Newton's sense—and the rate of growth of PB can in turn be measured by comparing it with an increment B*b* of the uniform motion of the base. We have not at all solved our problem, however, for evidently this "rate" is as ever-changing, or fluent, as the two quantities of which it is composed. If at a later moment, depicted in figure 1c, we look at the triangle again, we see that the stretched-out hypotenuse P*b'* will be growing at a faster rate than it was earlier, as P*b*. How can Newton bring precision to discourse about a figure as intricately fluent as this?

The crucial problem before us, in specifying this rate, is to compare two changing quantities with one another. In this case, we want to compare the increments of the hypotenuse P*b* and the base D*b*. The little triangle B*cb* (fig. 1d) will serve to relate these two interesting increments. Here, *cb* is the increment of the hypotenuse, while B*b* is the increment of the base. To measure the fluxion, or rate of change, of the hypotenuse, we need the ratio of *cb* to B*b*. However, as that ratio is itself fluent, we have not by this device as yet escaped the morass. We need, it seems, to find its exact value at some precise moment—yet of course at any one moment, the little triangle, which is composed of *increments,* has no size, and we have nothing to look at or compare.

Newton solves the problem—and opens the door to a new world—in the following way. We may think of the motion as reversed, and let the increment B*b* shrink back to zero—this will be what Newton calls the *evanescent* motion, the image of the *nascent* in a mirror of time (fig. 1e). The required fluxion will be the ratio of the two quantities, *cb* and B*b*, just as they are vanishing—their ratio as they disappear. This would hardly seem to help, but Newton's method of following the behavior of these two disappearing magnitudes is characteristic of a method which will prove triumphant as the *Principia* unfolds. For he finds a way to keep these quantities visible to the eye, and to the eye of the mind, even as they vanish. He shows that the shaded triangle B*cb* is similar to the whole triangle PD*b;* this similarity is more evident if we redraw the little triangle right side up, as the small figure has done. Then as B*b* and the shaded triangle utterly vanish, the large triangle PD*b* will always make the shape of the vanishing triangle manifest to us. And finally, at the very point of vanishing, the shape of the disappearing triangle reveals itself as nothing but *the shape of the original triangle itself!* And the fluxion, namely, the ultimate ratio of *cb*:B*b* with which those quantities vanish, is the same as the ratio of the base to the hypotenuse of the original triangle. That is Newton's theorem, and the foundation stone of the new mathesis of all things that live and grow:

> There is a limit which the velocity at the end of the motion may attain,
> but not exceed. This is the ultimate velocity. And there is the like
> limit in all quantities and proportions that begin and cease to be. And
> since such limits are certain and definite, to determine the same is a
> problem strictly geometrical. But whatever is geometrical we may use in
> determining and demonstrating any other thing that is also geometrical.
> (*GBWW* I: 34, 31–32; II: 32, 31–32)

Those who have learned their calculus in modern courses, in the analytic mode by way of Descartes's algebraic symbols and the accompanying formal arguments, may appreciate the difference marked by Newton's intuitive diagrams and concrete representation of magnitudes as geometric figures. We should recognize, on the other hand, the universality of this method: the geometric lines may represent magnitudes from any domain of nature. In every case, the clue to Newton's method is insight: to substitute, for the mechanical operations of algebraic symbols, the invitation to intellectual vision embodied in a geometrical figure. And once again, Newton steps from behind the work to discuss with us a problem which has evidently occupied his own thoughts. We are speaking of the limiting ratio, as the quantities disappear. Should we admit that either the quantities have vanished, in which case there is nothing of which to take a ratio, or speak instead of very small infinitesimals and confess that we are not in fact taking the ratio as we had claimed, but taking a ratio of very small quantities just *before*

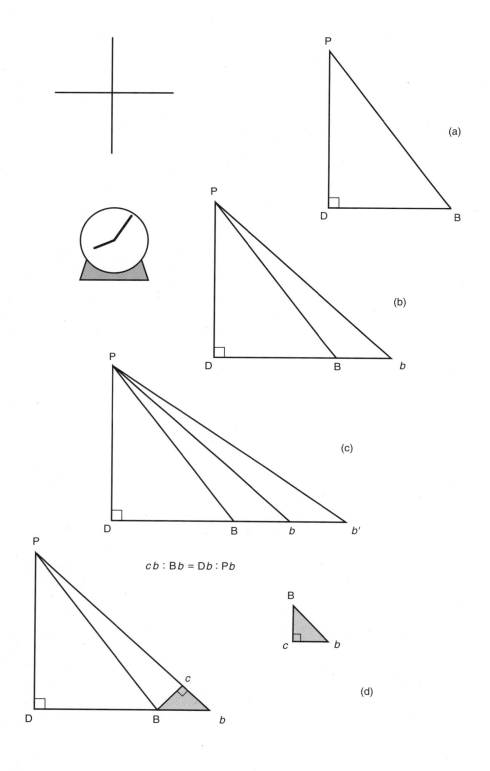

(a)

(b)

(c)

$cb : Bb = Db : Pb$

(d)

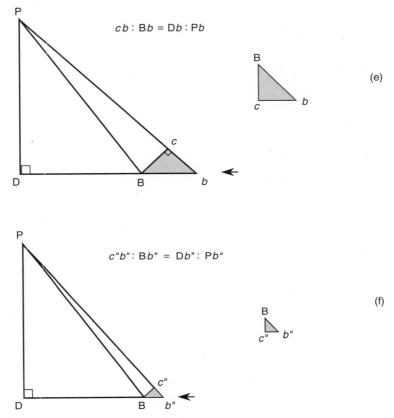

$$cb : Bb = Db : Pb$$

(e)

$$c''b'' : Bb'' = Db'' : Pb''$$

(f)

Figure 1. In this series, we watch the changing form of a Newtonian triangle, one which exists in both absolute time and space, as expressed in our icons of the coordinate system and the clock. At (a) we may say it is not so much "at rest" as "beginning to grow," and our problem is to formulate this concept with mathematical accuracy. Here the base D*b* is understood to be increasing uniformly, so that between the images (b) and (c) precisely equal intervals of absolute time have elapsed. At (d) the problem is approached by constructing the little triangle B*cb,* composed of the differences generated as the motion progresses. As expressed in the proportion, this small triangle is always similar to the whole. At (e) and (f) our strategy is reversed by watching the vanishing, or "evanescent"—rather than the "nascent"—triangle. Again, its shape is always that of the triangle PD*b.* Since that fact remains true even of the vanishing triangle B*c''b'',* it is true as well in the limit. Since the evanescent motion must be the mirror image of the nascent, the analysis has returned to the point at which it began. We have achieved a mathematical statement of the nascent motion of the triangle at (a).

they disappeared? To yield in either direction will mean abandonment of the enterprise. We must take the leap into complete continuity, the continuity of the line (and hence now, of motion on the line) assured by Euclid in Book X of the *Elements*.

> It may also be objected, that if the ultimate ratios of evanescent quantities are given, their ultimate magnitudes will be also given: and so all quantities will consist of indivisibles, which is contrary to what Euclid has demonstrated concerning incommensurables, in the tenth book of his *Elements*. But this objection is founded on a false supposition. For those ultimate ratios with which quantities vanish are not truly the ratios of ultimate quantities, but limits towards which the ratios of quantities decreasing without limit do always converge; and to which they approach nearer than by any given difference, but never go beyond, nor in effect attain to, till the quantities are diminished *in infinitum*. (*GBWW* I: 34, 32; II: 32, 32)

We see that the entrance into the new world of the *Principia* is by way of a wholly new insight concerning mathematics. We might say that at the root of this passage there lies a new view of the world itself, one in which time and space have become real, absolute, or mathematical in a wholly new way. As a consequence, motion has been transformed from what is inherently a blur, to be framed for thought only through the ingenuity of an Aristotelian philology, into a concept as precise and mathematical as Euclid's point, circle, or line.

Problem 2: Newton's microscope [12]

If we are to implement a thoroughgoing mathesis of natural processes, we cannot be content to work with figures composed of straight lines. Everywhere we will be confronted with motions along arcs of curves, whether circular, elliptical, hyperbolic, or, within bounds, of arbitrary shape.

In figure 2a, we may think of point B moving along the arc B*c*A toward A. How can we prepare a mathesis adequate to its motion? To establish a ratio which will be of value in the study of motion along such curves, Newton draws the chord of that arc, AB, and then asks the ratio of the length of the arc A*c*B to that of its chord AB. To get a further ratio, a second measure of the same motion, Newton next draws the line RD in any arbitrary direction, so that it cuts off a definite length along the tangent drawn to the arc at A. We are invited to watch the evolution of these ratios as B moves toward A.

As B moves to *b,* and the arc thus shortens, the line *rd* is always to be drawn parallel to its original position, so that a definite rule is established for cutting off the length along the tangent (fig. 2b). We are now tracking the evanescent motion to get *two* fluxions: the ratio of the arc to its chord, and at the same time the ratio of the arc to its tangent. The fluxions in question will be the ultimate ratios as b' finally reaches A, and once again all the quantities we are interested in frustratingly vanish. Again, Newton will rescue the situation by using a brilliant rhetorical device to make the vanishing ratios remain visible to the eyes of our minds.

Returning to the first position of arc, chord, and tangent, Newton now sets up what is known to tradition as his "microscope"—an enlarged figure, with arc Amk, which is similar to the one in which we are interested (fig. 2c). The arcs Acb and Amk have exactly the same shape, and differ only in size—exactly as if Acb had been magnified in a photographic enlarger.

In figure 2d the arc, which we may now designate Ab', has become very small, and in figure 2e, as Ab'', one may think of it as evanescent, on the verge of vanishing. Yet Newton has contrived to keep it fully visible: the shapes and relative sizes of arc, chord, and tangent are precisely exhibited to the eye and the mind in their enlarged counterparts, the power of the rhetorical microscope having increased in just such proportion as always to keep the size of the enlarged figure constant, though at the same time it takes the changing shape of the vanishing arc segment. Since there is presumably no limit to the power of a conceptual microscope, we see clearly the theorem Newton is placing before us. In figure 2e, as the arc, its chord, and its tangent all vanish like a trio of Cheshire cats, their magnified images will be preserved and will come to coincidence in the limit. The large arc A$m''k''$, its chord Ak'', and the tangent AD *coalesce* as the arc Ab'' vanishes. In figure 2e we glimpse them as they disappear over the conceptual horizon, at once vanishing from view and becoming fully manifest in their true relationship as nascent quantities.

Once again, the question of fluxions has been answered: the ultimate ratio of the evanescent arc to its chord is that of equality, and so likewise is the ratio of the arc to its tangent. This amazing fact licenses much of the work which must be done in the *Principia,* where arcs of trajectories and orbits are to be our constant fare. Within the limits of reasonable curvatures with which Newton will be working, curvilinear is thus universally reduced to rectilinear. No transmutation could be more potent in this new alchemy of all nature.

Definitions: Matter and force

We have seen instruments prepared by which the world of phenomena is to be revealed in a new order of clarity as a mathematical system. Newton has a distinct vision of the structure of this system, the groundwork for which is firmly laid in a set of Definitions and Laws of Motion at the outset of the work.

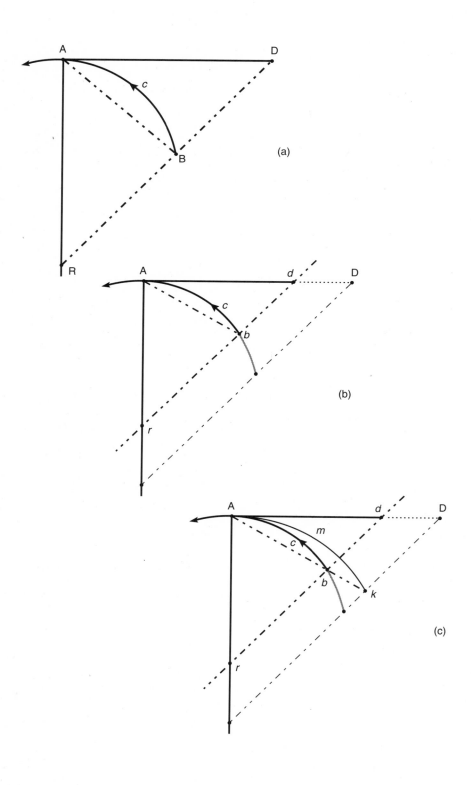

(a)

(b)

(c)

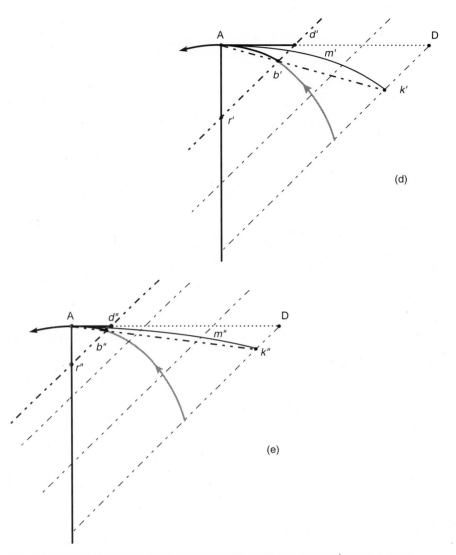

Figure 2. Here the techniques of Newton's geometrical calculus are brought to bear on the problem of motion in a curved path, the case most universal in nature. We choose any point A, and watch as point B approaches, seeking to understand with mathematical precision the state of affairs exactly as the point in its motion reaches A. To examine this limiting position, Newton invokes a strategy known to tradition as his "microscope," magnifying the trajectory as shown in (c), where the curve A*mk* reproduces A*cb* as it would be seen in a photographic enlarger. As *b* moves on, in (d) and (e), the magnifier, with ever-increasing power, tracks its progress. At the limit, as the point reaches A, the curve and its tangent are clearly seen to coincide. From this point on, Newton is licensed to reason freely about curved lines, in the limit, as if they were straight.

Matter

Underlying the entire natural world is something Newton calls "matter." He does not in fact define it, but rather, in accord with the concept of the *Principia* as the mathematical principles of the world, defines the *quantity* of matter. But the form of this definition reveals what he has in mind:

> The quantity [mass] of matter is the measure of the same, arising from its density and bulk conjointly. (*GBWW* I: 34, 5; II: 32, 5)

This seems innocent enough, but in fact it bears careful reflection. By the "mass" of matter he means the amount or volume of it. By the density, he means in effect the fraction of space occupied by matter. Thus the product "density and bulk conjointly" means "percent of space occupied by matter times the total space = volume [amount, or *mass*] of matter." What is presupposed is that matter is utterly simple, compact, and one. There are no kinds of matter: it is not that copper is one kind of matter (with one density) and lead another (with a greater density). This is the ultimate matter of the alchemists, which might have been fetched out, had Newton felt a need to discuss the question, as the *true and philosophical* matter, the analogue of the true and philosophical time and space. This is the alchemist's vision he is invoking, seeing through to that ultimate and invisible matter which finally underlies all commonplace distinctions. This ultimate matter has no properties—no color, no flavor; it is not magnetic or gravitational. Its character is that it is absolutely passive. It does not belong to the idea of matter to be hard; Newton has in fact come to believe that the matter of the world is organized in totally hard, permanent particles—atoms—but he equally admits as an idea conformable to these first principles a matter which, though otherwise identical to atomic matter and equally dense, is perfectly fluid. A great deal of the *Principia,* its second book, is devoted to serious discussion of that possible fluid matter.

This Newtonian matter has one, single principle of motion and rest. That principle, called *inertia* (literally, lacking any art or skill), expresses precisely the passivity of matter and gives rise in interactions with other bodies to something called the *vis inertiae,* the power or force of inertia. Newton calls this a *passive force.* We cannot look to Newtonian matter to initiate any motion in the cosmos: the agent in any action must always be sought elsewhere.

This is the whole story of Newtonian matter. If there were no other principle in the natural world than matter, we would have to derive the reconstituted mathematical cosmos from this concept alone: matter moving in space and time, reacting to chance encounters with other matter, but with no agent principle in the world at all. It would not be a cosmos: it would be a dark and dead world, perhaps that of Lucretius, if the matter were fixed in atoms, or that of Descartes, if the matter were continuous and fluid. The proposition that the world is of this sort is what Newton calls materialism, and the *Principia* can best be understood as a dialectical work designed to refute the idea that the world is of this sort, and to reveal and demonstrate the richer alternative. Again, we see the power of the Newtonian alchemy: by insisting on the purity of the idea of matter, as absolutely inert and without life, Newton sharpens the idea of its opposite, which the alchemists call *spirit*. That is, his vision of God as totally governing and the cause of all act demands as counterpart the idea of matter which contributes nothing. In that sense, the concept of matter as undifferentiated and inert is the other face of the idea of God.

Who is the antagonist in Newton's dialectical enterprise? Not Lucretius, for Lucretius has not brought matter into the domain of mathematics, and materialism becomes threatening only when it becomes mathematical and invites the mind. The mathematical Lucretius, and hence the serious adversary, is Descartes, who fills the natural world with a continuous and totally intelligible fluid matter. As we have seen, Newton has learned the very conception of natural philosophy as mathematical analysis from Descartes. A wave of enthusiasm among thinking persons has greeted Descartes's *mechanical philosophy,* for it admits the possibility of explanation—thoroughgoing mechanical explanation, in mathematically consistent terms. Perhaps the universe is nothing more than a mathematical clockwork, which could be understood in mechanical terms throughout: Newton knows well, at firsthand, the lure of that possibility. All the more urgent, then, that the distinction now be drawn sharply: Newton directs the *Principia* to the purgation of the fundamental error in Descartes's account of the physical world. The second book will take Descartes's principles, calculate the consequences, and undertake to show that the universe which would result is far from the one in which we find ourselves. Kepler's laws of planetary motion would not hold, and the heavenly bodies would dissipate their motions and halt in their courses.

Active force

The new element which Newton introduces into the world, in every way the opposite of matter, is an active principle which he calls the *vis motrix*—the "moving power," usually translated "motive force." This is Newton's counterpart in the *Principia* to the *spirit* of the alchemists. It is invisible, is intangible, freely penetrates matter, and everywhere works with vitality and sure signs of intelligence to accomplish the design of the cosmos. It does this by moving always according to perfect mathematical law—"law" which Newton understands first of all in the political sense, as God's ordinance, the established vehicle of God's will in the governance of the world. The *Principia* in the formal development of its mathematical principles does not address such philosophical issues, but it makes way for living force or agency by way of the *vis motrix*. As it turns out in the philosophy which Newton builds upon the *Principia,* there are several such active principles in the world: Newton speaks of the cause of gravity, of the force of cohesion, which causes bodies to form up and remain intact, and the inner principle of chemical, vital activity, which alchemy calls fermentation. These will be the true causes of the motions of the world we know, animate as well as inorganic. They will be the primary objects of philosophy, and the counterparts to Aristotle's *physis*. It is the goal of philosophy to find these first principles of all life and motion in their universality, and to trace the ways in which they cooperate to construct the living cosmos. They appear in the *Principia* as distinct measures of the *vis motrix*.

The laws of motion

Newton formulates three postulates which govern all motion in the world. He might have called them "principles" of motion, but he calls them "laws." It is completely consistent with his view of the world that he do so, for as we have seen, matter, as Newton has distilled the concept, has no propensity to new motion and must be commanded if it is to be moved. Action is utterly external to matter, and thus the initiation of motion comes through the externality of edict or law, which has no coloration of persuasion. This stark character of the laws of motion rightly suggests the spirit of the Old Testament: God commands and obedience is utter. Between God who is all act and matter which is inert, the mode of communication is law, and the resulting order is one of dominion.

It is possible to look at the same world in more than one way. Leibniz, operating from a different sense of the nature of things, is able to use the Aristotelian paradigm of potentiality and actuality, and to see in a material system at rest the potential for motion—potential energy which will be actualized by its own nature as living force. The difference shows itself in many ways, leaving its trace in virtually every way we speak of the phenomenal world. Mind approaches the world with mythic predispositions and finds ways to tell a story which reads in ways it needs to hear. What measures do we take of motion and force? Newton tells us that the quantity of motion is the product of the matter and motion conjointly—mass and velocity, yielding, we say, momentum. Leibniz, thinking otherwise and perhaps listening to the voice of a different god, takes as measure of motion the kinetic energy, an approach which, followed consistently, traces out an utterly different physics. All Newton's reckoning of his laws of force will be in terms of this quantity on which he has fixed his attention. The first law preserves that quantity:

> Every body continues in its state of rest, or of uniform motion in a right line, unless it is compelled to change that state by forces impressed upon it. (*GBWW* I: 34, 14; II: 32, 14)

The second demands that the force be proportional to the change of that chosen quantity:

> The change of motion is proportional to the motive force impressed; and is made in the direction of the right line in which that force is impressed. (Ibid.)

The third asserts that in interactions the exchange of quantities of motion will balance, with the result that in an interaction no change at all of the quantity of motion occurs:

> To every action there is always opposed an equal reaction: or, the mutual actions of two bodies upon each other are always equal, and directed to contrary parts. (Ibid.)

What is the significance of this quantity which has become so fundamental? Consider a chamber full of particles moving at random. For Newton, their total quantity of motion is nothing, for the vectors sum to zero. For Leibniz, the chamber is full of living force, and that becomes our understanding of the temperature of the system: thermodynamics and many of the finest insights of modern science flow from Leibniz, not from Newton. Although it is possible to find hints of kinetic and potential energy measures in the *Principia,* on the whole Newton, thinking of force in terms of the directed blow, is limited to a vector physics. The alternative insights of the scalar physics of Leibniz, in which processes of a system unfold spontaneously, from energy stores within, are closed to him. Each physics paints its own, very distinct myth of the world. Newton's laws are blinders as much as they are lights—to tell one story whole, we may have to be blind to others. Today we imagine we read and reconcile both stories, but we no doubt tell stories sealed with blinders of our own.

I have suggested that Newton's laws of motion breathe the air of the Old Testament, and I suspect that all we have just said tends to confirm that view. But this is only the beginning of Newton's tale, as the Old Testament is the beginning of Scripture and speaks of the beginning of time. Like the Scriptures themselves, the *Principia* moves by prophetic pathways through darkness toward new light, and we might sense that Newton's vivid sense of a new relation to God is at stake as that process unfolds.

The hieroglyph for force [13]

The laws of motion have taught us that if we are to read the book of nature, we must seek out the forces which are operating as the causes of all life and motion. How from the phenomena are we to find those forces—how can we penetrate the appearances, to find the true principles which lie beneath? This is the great alchemy, whether of macrocosm or microcosm, heaven or earth: to seek the true and philosophical principles which underlie the distracting and confusing surface of events. If, as it seems, it is good counsel to regard nature as a text, our task is indeed one of interpretation: we must learn to read a book written in the patterns of nature. But are these phenomena legible characters? Newton now pursues the proposal that they are, and that patterns can be found in them which are intelligible. These can be taken as signs or indices to causes, active forces, which lie hidden. He shapes a fundamental geometric instrument of a special sort, at once image of a structure in nature and index to underlying truths. Newton worked with powerful signs and symbols in his studies of alchemy, among them those in the form of hieroglyphs. I suggest that we may think of the geometric constructions of the *Principia,* combining representation with coded significance, as "hieroglyphs" in this sense. Let us see how Newton puts his new geometric method to use in this manner, to shape what we may think of as a hieroglyph for force.

According to Newton's First Law of Motion, or indeed to his very idea of matter, a body moving at point P in figure 3a with no force acting on it will follow a straight line at uniform velocity—that is, the body at P will follow the straight line PY. If a force acts upon it in the direction S, however, the body will be deflected according to the Second Law from the straight line and will as a result trace some arc such as PQ. Newton now constructs a strategic geometric instrument by which this force can be found out and measured. If the time did not have to be allowed for, the deflection itself, measured by the line RQ, would suffice as a measure of the force. In figure 3b, this deflection is mirrored in the line PZ, for in the parallelogram QRPZ, the opposite sides RQ and PZ are equal. PZ is here drawn as an arrow pointing in the direction of the center of force. This arrow drawn between an arc and its chord in the direction of a center of force and equal to the deflection caused by the force, Newton calls the *sagitta* of the arc. We recognize it as a vector, with direction and magnitude.

We face an important complication, however, for the same force acting for a longer time will produce a greater deflection. Evidently, our sagitta measuring the force must in some way be discounted according to the length of time during which it has been produced. An initial step, then, must be to get some measure, within the diagram itself, of the time which has elapsed as the arc PQ was swept out.

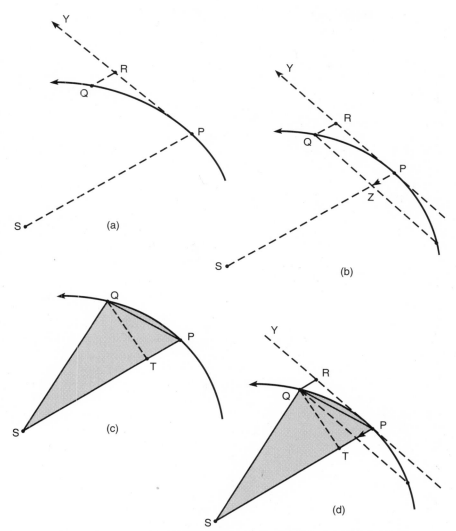

Figure 3. This figure, which we are calling Newton's "hieroglyph for force," is in effect a movable geometrical instrument, which can be used wherever needed to take the measure of a force deflecting the trajectory of a body toward a fixed center. Here S is that center of force, while P is the point whose trajectory is undergoing deflection. We may think of S and P as "sun" and "planet." In the absence of the central force, the point would move in a given time interval in a straight line toward R. Instead, however, the force toward S gives rise to the deflection QR, which thus becomes our initial measure of the force. Since the same force will give rise to greater deflections if it acts for longer times, we must contrive to take the time of action into account. As figures 4 and 5 will explain, the triangle PSQ becomes that measure.

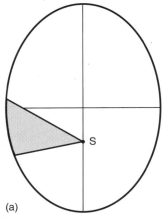
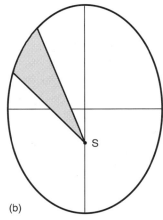

(a)   (b)

Figure 4. Kepler's Law of Areas asserts that, in the motion of a planet about the sun, equal areas are swept out in equal times. Newton's Proposition 1, Book I, has extended this to apply to any body moving under the action of a central force alone. Here the two shaded sectors are swept out by such a body in equal times, the motion speeding up at (a) to compensate for the shorter radius.

The solution to this problem is suggested by Kepler's Law of Areas: if a moving radius is drawn from a planet to the sun, that radius will in a given time sweep out equal areas in equal times (fig. 4). Cumulatively, this implies that if the times are unequal, this body will sweep out areas proportional to the times (fig. 5). If we generalize the rule from the planet and sun to any body moving under a central force, we may thus take the area swept out in the figure as geometric measure of the time.

In figure 3c, then, the area PSQ represents the time in which the body has traversed the arc PQ. In effect, we are setting up geometric figures to represent, or serve as signs for, the physical quantities in which we are interested: here, while we have proposed the sagitta as sign or measure of the force, the area PSQ becomes a figurative clock. And we may now take advantage of the license granted by our earlier investigation of fluxions and equate the arc PQ to the straight line which is its chord. We have only to focus our attention on the arc PQ in its nascent stage, zeroing in by the same token on the precise force at the very moment when the body is at point P.

To combine the sagitta measuring the deflection with the area measuring the time in one complex image (fig. 3d) will give us the ingredients of the true measure of the force. To effect this combination, Newton draws upon one further insight: with respect to its radial motion, body P is in effect falling freely toward its center S. But with that recognition, we see that we can use a theorem of Galileo's to the effect that a falling body traverses distances proportional to the squares of the elapsed times. The sagitta will in general be of a length proportional to the square of the time in which P has traced out arc PQ.

142

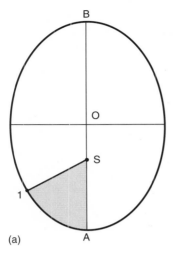

(a)

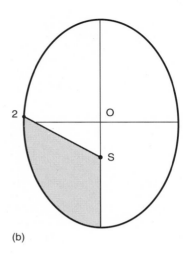

(b)

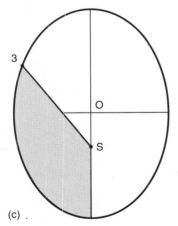

(c) .

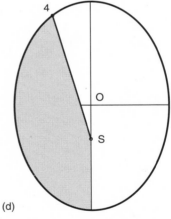

(d)

Figure 5. Since equal areas are swept out in equal times, as a body moves under a central force the sector it defines will increase in cumulative area in direct proportion to the time elapsed. Here, as the body moves in equal time intervals through positions 1, 2, 3, and 4, the area of the sector similarly increases by equal amounts. The problem of constructing an almanac of the body's position in the heavens, becomes the geometrical problem of finding the areas of these sectors.

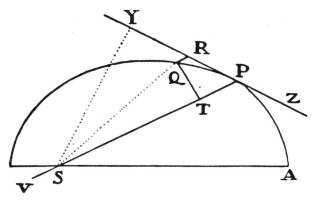

Figure 6. This figure illustrates Newton's Proposition 6, Book I, measuring the centripetal force in the case of a body which "revolves in any orbit about an immovable center, and in the least time describes any arc just then nascent." His words remind us that these relations hold only for "nascent" quantities, i.e., in the limit, at an instant.

From these ingredients arises the formula which unlocks the meaning of Newton's complex sign. The sagitta PZ equal to QR increases in proportion to the square of the time, and hence for a given force its length must be discounted by the amount of the time: we must divide the quantity QR by the square of our measure of the time. But the area PSQ measures the time, and in turn, in the limit, taking the chord PQ for the arc, this area measuring the time will be that of the triangle PSQ. If we drop the perpendicular QT, the area of that triangle will be one-half its base times its height, or proportional to (QT · SP). Finally, taking QR as measuring the deflection but discounting it in proportion to the square of the area (QT · SP), we get Newton's formula for reading his sign:

$$f \propto \frac{QR}{(QT \cdot SP)^2}$$

Figure 3d, which appears in Newton's text in the form of our figure 6, becomes a powerful sign for the interpretation of phenomena on any scale, anywhere in the universe, and for finding out forces of any kind. It is thus a universal analytic instrument for finding out causes, not merely qualitatively, but with quantitative precision. We may think of it as belonging to the rhetoric of interpretation, the alchemist's dream, converting the phenomena of nature into a readable text, and making it possible to penetrate the surface of appearances in order to find out the true and philosophical forces at work beneath them. We are reminded that rhetoric is in one sense the art by which we grasp one language in terms of another; it is thus a work of translation, here connecting appearances with their underlying and governing forces, which we can only see in this way—nature is unintelligible without interpretation.

144

Laws of force

We have already glimpsed the structure of the cosmos as Newton will depict it. Thus far, however, we have looked only at the definitions, lemmas, laws of motion, and the first of the propositions of the *Principia*. We have developed powerful instruments for the geometric analysis of the world but have not yet put those instruments to actual use. We have the tools of a new literacy, a grammar of nature, but have not yet approached the text.

To follow Newton now, we need to have a better sense of the organization of the *Principia*. As we have seen, the stance of the work is entirely instrumental: even as we now put these new mathematical instruments to work in actual analysis, the results remain hypothetical. The entire first and second books of the *Principia* are preliminary, wrapped in the syntax of conditionality: "If the phenomena are of a certain sort, then the consequence will be. . . ." It is only in the third book, "The System of the World," that Newton formally turns from what we might think of as the book of all possible worlds to the actual phenomena of the world we live in. At that point hypothesis converts to demonstration, mathematics to philosophy.

We turn to Newton's fundamental Proposition 11, which, though hypothetical, is keyed to the phenomena which will later emerge as our own:

> If a body revolves in an ellipse; it is required to find the law of the centripetal force tending to the focus of the ellipse. (*GBWW* I: 34, 42; II: 32, 42)

His drawing is reproduced as our figure 7. We see the ellipse, with one focus at S (the letter suggesting what may emerge as the sun) and a body at P (to emerge in Book III as the planet), and we recognize as well the hieroglyph, our instrument of analysis, superimposed on the figure. The force is measured by the formula we have prepared, its elements being QR, QT, and PS. To solve this problem, Newton has only to weave these elements into the geometry of the ellipse as taught by Apollonius. We will not track those steps, but the outcome is direct: "the centripetal force is inversely as . . . SP^2, that is, *inversely as the square of the distance SP*." As the body traces the circumference of the ellipse, its distance from the center of force at the focus will vary, being greatest when the body is at aphelion A and least when the body arrives at perihelion, at the opposite end of the axis AS. The force being greatest as the body approaches the center and least as it removes, it will be most attracted at perihelion and least at aphelion, in the proportion of the *squares* of the corresponding distances—i.e., very much more attracted at perihelion, and very much less at aphelion.

We may allow ourselves to anticipate the turn of the text in Book

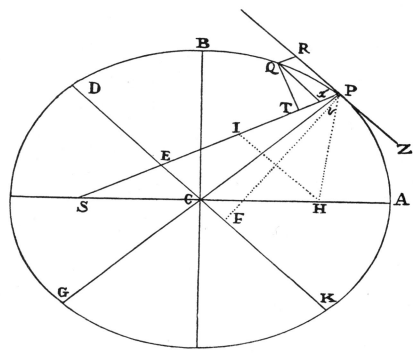

Figure 7. Newton's figure for Proposition 11, Book I, in which a body moves under the action of a force varying inversely with the square of its distance from a center. This proves to be the case when the body P moves in an ellipse about a focus S. The force is least at aphelion A and greatest at perihelion, at the opposite end of the major axis.

III and thus to recognize that here we have the phenomena of our own world. In application to the phenomena of our heavens, this analysis will reveal that the planets are bound to the sun, our moon to earth, and Jupiter's moons to Jupiter, by a force which obeys this inverse square law.

Again, Newton's account is in terms of "law," but now that concept is being applied in a somewhat different sense. The former laws, "laws of motion," applied to all matter and any motive force, by virtue we might say of the very notions Newton has arrived at of matter and force per se. But this law will apply to only certain of the forces Newton is searching out in nature, such as the one he comes to call "gravity," and it speaks of the distribution of this active principle over space. Other forces, the life-force of "fermentation" for example, or that of cohesion, or of magnetism, may be distributed according to other laws—the elastic force, for example, acting to repel rather than to attract. These are, then, laws of force in a different sense, forms of the operations of the various modes of agency. In fact, Newton goes on to generalize his analysis in this section to consider a continuous range of all possible force laws, attractive and repelling, bonding more tightly or more loosely, which might go into the making of possible universes of very different sorts.

To put this concept in terms of the theology which for Newton is its ultimate context, these forces are the modes of God's very governance of our world. What is emerging is the recognition that mathesis is God's chosen mode of action, from which it follows that God's activity is in some way intelligible to our minds. Gravity as an inverse square law holds each planet in a balanced orbit: as Newton's propositions in this book show, a tighter force law (varying inversely by a power greater than the square) would have pulled it to the center, a looser force law would have lost it to infinity. I suspect that the tone of Newton's contemplation of this intellectual order is not one of intellectual arrogance—to reduce the divine plan to the level of human strategy—but rather, immense awe at the immanent presence of a mystery. The world is revealed as a mathematical construction perfect and harmonious as the regular solids with which Euclid brings the *Elements* to conclusion. There is no *mechanism* for these divine actions: they are pure acts. Not only are they constantly and perfectly proportioned, but we can see by ranging over the options, as Newton's broad analysis permits us to do, that this proportion has been so chosen that the whole can form a lasting harmony. To watch the planets move under the guidance of such actions must have meant for Newton presence at an immanent, divine mystery. It might be so for any of us, if long habit had not made these matters seem banal, topics for textbooks.

Newton regularly exhibits a breathtaking ability to achieve an overview of a subject which it would not occur to lesser minds even to propose. That is, the Newtonian projects often exceed in their scope any reasonable level of anticipation. Such is the case with the vision he gives us in waves of propositions which follow upon the first demonstrations of motion under the action of a central force. We cannot do more, here, than note the great benchmarks of this enterprise—and then later, in due course, observe how these elements fit into Newton's still grander plan, as these still only mathematical instruments play their roles in the construction of the System of the World, in Book III. Once again, although it is crucial to Newton's design that these propositions preserve their integrity as strictly mathematical demonstrations, it is clear that they are everywhere shaped to the work to which they will be put when the time arrives, in Book III, for the turn to the phenomena and the interpretation of the world as it indeed is.

We have arrived, in Proposition 11, at that point at which Newton has analyzed the case of motion in an elliptical orbit under the action of a central force directed to one of the foci and shown that in this case the law of force will be that of the inverse square. In application to the motion of a planet, this yields a dynamic account of the first

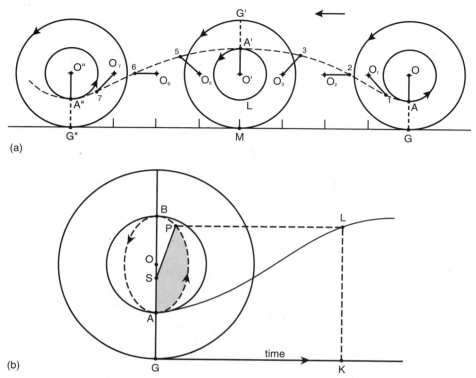

(a)

(b)

The trochoid, introduced in Proposition 31, Book I, to relate planetary positions to the calendar. As the circle rolls from right to left along GMG″, the tip of the radius OA traces the trochoid AA'A″. In (b) a planet's orbit APB, with the sun at the focus S, has been inscribed in an inner circle chosen to make OG : OA = OA : OS. Take any time GK, construct the ordinate KL, and carry the line LP back to intersect the ellipse at P. Newton shows that the shaded area will be proportional to the time GK, and thus, by the law of areas, P will be the planet's position at the chosen time. It is striking that Newton credits Sir Christopher Wren, who was Savilian professor of astronomy at Oxford before he was architect to the City of London, with the discovery of properties of this remarkable curve. The unifying concept may be design, God's and man's.

of Kepler's laws, that the geometric figure of the orbit of a planet is the ellipse. Newton had already shown in his first proposition that a planet's adherence to Kepler's Second Law, the law of areas, interprets dynamically as a sure sign that the body is moving under the influence of some central force, located at the point from which the areas are measured. What, though, of Kepler's Third Law, that the periods of the planets are to one another as the 3/2 power of the ratio of their radii? Reasoning by way of the known relations of the areas of ellipses, together with the known relation of area to time, Newton makes quick work, in Proposition 14, of this final law of Kepler's, as well. Kepler's laws, as laws of phenomena, have thus been penetrated to yield their underlying secret—that they are summarizing the phenomena under the action of an agency, centered at the focus of the ellipse, and obeying the law of the inverse square.

Newton now poses what becomes, in the later discussions, God's problem: how to launch a body in relation to a given center of force with just such a combination of position, initial direction, and speed as to insure an orbit of precisely a required size and shape? Using the combined principles of geometry and dynamics already at hand, Newton is able to solve this well in Proposition 17. In a celebrated later correspondence on the theological significance of the *Principia,* as he weighs the consequences of all the options which might be considered as possible beginnings for our solar system, Newton concludes, with an eye to this proposition especially, that the harmony of its design

> argues that Cause to be not blind and fortuitious, but very well skilled in Mechanicks and Geometry. [14]

At this point, Newton might well have rested, but far from it, he embarks now on one of his most impressive adventures of mind. He invents a sensitive hieroglyph for detecting any slight departures from the inverse square force law which he has just finished establishing; he shows that to the extent the law of force is disturbed, the axis of the ellipse will wander. Further, reversing this principle, he utilizes the moving ellipse constructively to generate his exploration of the spectrum of orbits which arises under the full range of possible algebraic force laws. This device of the moving ellipse reveals its importance, since Newton goes on to show that nowhere in the cosmos will force laws operate in isolation: the very coherence of the universe requires that all its forces be disturbed, that no ellipse rests.

The three-body problem

Newton's next major step is momentous. He begins a motion from a fictitious world of mathematical orbits computed about fixed centers to one of a very different sort, and far more realistic. What makes this inadequate is that nowhere in the cosmos is a center fixed: nowhere is there terra firma in which to anchor a central body. Newton's Third Law of Motion assures that forces are interactive, and with that recognition comes a wave of fundamental consequences: a central force is not a one-way street but in its very conception involves an interchange and a dynamic balance. Every body is both mover and moved; motions must mirror one another. If the first of the great astronomical revolutions required that the earth must move, the second, entailed as soon as the Third Law is uttered, is that the sun must move as well (fig. 8). The sun will not be the center of the solar system: it too must orbit. At the erstwhile center there will now be nothing: only the mathematical

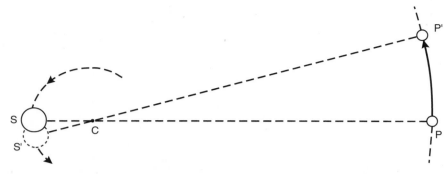

Figure 8. In earlier propositions, Newton has assumed a central body about which another revolves. Thus in Proposition 58, Book I, we find that if a body S constrains P to an orbit, S must orbit as well in reaction. All that remains fixed in space is the empty point C, the center of mass of the pair.

balancing point, the center of mass, about which all bodies of the connected system make their one, configured dance. It is this recognition, fraught as we shall see with consequence, that Newton has in view when he speaks of "system"—and names his third book, "The System of the World."

The first step into this new world is very easy; Proposition 57 (of Book I) shows us that orbits will be geometric mirrors of one another. To the earth's large ellipse about the center of force will answer another, the sun's own orbit, small in proportion as the sun's mass is great. Proposition 58 continues the inquiry, to address the question of time: the earth's year, it develops, will be lengthened by this consideration; there is a relaxation of the central force as the center now yields. In the same way, the earth yields to the moon, and the month is the longer, as the earth's hold slackens.

But the logic of this line of thought carries us beyond the interaction of two bodies to the consequence that there will always be third bodies troubling the motion of any two. The moon's motion about the earth will be affected as well by the sun's force. If the sun attracted both earth and moon alike, the two would together fall toward the sun, and their mutual motion, the monthly course, would be unaffected. It is the *difference* in the attractions, as the moon's distance from the sun becomes alternately more and less than the earth's, which affects the relation of moon to earth.

Newton addresses this ominous problem in Proposition 66, the diagram for which is adapted as our figure 9. Thinking in this way of the sun's interference with our moon's motions, Newton labels the figure S (the sun) and T (the earth), while P is the point at which the moon is located at any moment in its course. What must be reckoned is the effect of the differential force on the moon, indicated in our figure by the vector *f,* and at this point even Newton has met his match: our diagram

150

depicts the infamous "three-body" problem of mechanics, which is not solvable in closed form. That is, though approximations can be given as to the effects of the third body—of the sun on the moon's motion about the earth—no single formula exists which asserts the result in a single mathematical statement. We can readily see that when the moon is at position P in its passage toward A, it will be accelerated in its course by the disturbing force *f*, while at P′ it will be retarded. But the "orbit" is not a fixed track. It too will undergo distortion, and we see that it is not strictly true, as Kepler asserted and Newton seemed to have demonstrated, that the paths of the planets will be ellipses. For here the ellipse will be bent out of shape, bent toward the sun and away from the earth when the moon is at A, and toward the earth when the moon is at B. Everything in Newton's cosmos is bent out of shape.

We are speaking of the case of the moon's motion about the earth, and indeed that is one of the first concerns, as Newton's labeling of the figure for the proposition suggests. But it is only the beginning of the unfolding consequences. All of the orbits and times are similarly affected—every motion will affect and disturb every other. Earth in its motion about the sun will thus reflect the positions, and motions, of all the other planets, as well as the moon's motion about the earth—so that distortions and corrections must be made to the entire system. They are all in the same way, incalculable—capable, in principle, of being approximated insofar as one can find strategies for carrying out the series of arithmetic corrections necessary, but not capable of solution in good, closed form. The order and beauty of the mathematical figures and the regular times is forever destroyed. Newton spreads before us this dark revelation, in the proposition itself, whose terms become obscure: indeterminate weighings of more and less replace the precision of strict magnitude and ratio, the language has become tangled and intricate:

> If three bodies, whose forces decrease as the square of the distances,
> attract each other; and the accelerative attractions of any two towards
> the third be between themselves inversely as the squares of the distances;
> and the two least [P, S] revolve about the greatest [T]: I say, that
> the interior of the two revolving bodies [P] will, by radii drawn to
> the innermost and greatest [T], describe round that body areas more
> proportional to the times, and a figure more approaching to that of an
> ellipse having its focus in the point of intersection of the radii, if that
> great body be agitated by those attractions, than it would do if that great
> body were not attracted at all by the lesser, but remained at rest; or
> than it would do if that great body were very much more or very much
> less attracted, or very much more or very much less agitated, by the
> attractions. (*GBWW* I: 34, 118; II: 32, 118)

(Here P and S may be treated as "lesser" bodies, in the sense that, being remote, the influence of the sun, though important, is small with

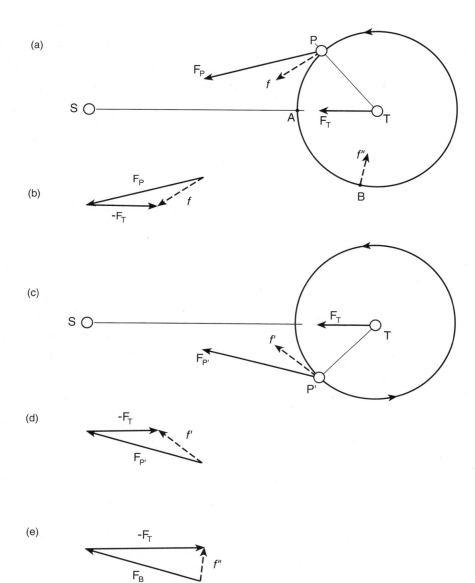

(a)

(b)

(c)

(d)

(e)

Figure 9. When a third body is introduced into the situation of figure 8, the orbits become distorted. If P is the moon and T the earth, the sun S will have a disrupting effect on the moon's orbit. The moon at P is closer than the earth to the sun, so vector F_P measuring the sun's force on it is greater than F_T measuring that of the sun on the earth. The vector triangle at (b) determines this difference as *f*, which when drawn at (a) is revealed as accelerating the moon and stretching the radius. In (c), the moon at P′ is retarded, and at B, as the vector diagram (e) reveals, the radius is shortened.

respect to the moon's motion about the earth.) The corollaries, fraught with consequence, continue in the same mode:

> COR. II. In a system of three bodies, T, P, S, if the accelerative attractions of any two of them towards a third be to each other inversely as the squares of the distances, the body P, by the radius PT, will describe its area about the body T swifter near the conjunction A and the opposition B than it will near the quadratures C and D. . . .
> COR. IV. The orbit of the body P, other things remaining the same, is more curved at the quadratures than at the conjunction and opposition.
> . . . (*GBWW* I: 34, 120; II: 32, 120)

We are mired in unpleasant discourse: here is a language of confusion, not of clarity, or of the science of which Newton has proved himself master. Yet it is not some special case, a difficulty which presents itself in certain unfortunate circumstances. It is the universal case: never does a second body orbit about a first without the interfering influence of a third body—and indeed, this sequence of complications never stops with a third, but we are confronted now with the interfering effects of every body on all bodies. The problem of perturbations is universal, endless in its implications and devastating to the project of strict scientific computation. The system of the world is not, finally, knowable: it escapes true knowing, or at least, human knowing. Newton, as we have suggested, confronts this problem bravely, but he has no recourse. There is no solution. There still, in modern science, is no solution. Computers make their ways effectively enough through the morass of complications, but they yield outcomes, not knowledge.

In classic terms, the outcome must be seen as tragic. If Newton's goal were to know in the classic sense, this would be a confrontation with sheer darkness; Plato would name it a work of "necessity" and rightly enough see it as bounding the domain of the light of knowledge with a shadow of intractable darkness. But it is not clear that it bears such tragic significance for Newton, for whom "philosophy" in this sense is not the ultimate goal of the work. That was to be the "mathematical principles of natural philosophy," and we have come to the verge: to the point at which those principles thoroughly demonstrate their own inherent limitation. Mathematics has taken its own measure. What lies beyond?

If the ultimate aim of this work is, on the other hand, to bring us closer to God, then the knowledge we seek may be of another sort, and the *Principia* may not have set out to be a work of science in the classic sense. The three-body problem has blocked our effort as theory, but if we are seeking interpretive instruments which will make it possible to read God's work in the world, we may draw a conclusion of a very different sort. The three-body problem, as Newton now shows, converts into the powerful instrument of a new order of understanding.

We have spoken at length of the role of time as an element of Newton's new mathematics: a mathematics, we said, of motion and change, for which the new method of fluxions was crucial. But time may be a dominant theme of the *Principia* in quite another way. Mathematics in its classic sense had been directed to what is timeless, to unchanging truth. Now we are on the brink of a different prospect: the truths we are after may be truths about time itself. The three-body problem is such a mathematical truth. For it demonstrates, not timeless form, but the temporal tendencies of form: with it, history becomes demonstrable knowledge. The orbits will deform, and it becomes a question for mind no longer to know the forms, as the ellipse and its elements, but the *course* of the forms, and the long effects of the perturbations.

It is this which Newton is preparing for the discussion in the third book. There, the system of the world is not a static and permanent harmony, a lasting "design," but a design which has the shape of prophetic history. The orbits are designed not for permanency but for a life of interactions, and for a lifetime which is finite and foreseeable, if not calculable, by the human mind. So, too, the planetary system is a creation which had a beginning and for which science can teach us to foretell an end. So the *Principia* takes us directly to, and itself becomes, prophetic history, and its "science" is to be understood in that context. As the mathematical principles of a science of time, the *Principia* is mathematical mirror to Scripture and prophecy. Newton is deeply committed to such interpretation and gives primacy above all to Daniel and to the Prophecy of Saint John, or the Apocalypse. [15]

Where will the *Principia*, now read as prophetic adventure, lead us? Its consequences unfold in a series of twenty-four corollaries. Apart from the deformations in shape of the orbits of the moon about the earth, and the earth about the sun, there will be tendencies for the orbit of a satellite such as our moon to increase and decrease in inclination to the plane of the ecliptic. But then Newton goes on to imagine a ring of satellites, all subject to this same tendency. First they are conceived as fluid, a great bulge of the seas about the earth's equator, while the gravitational handle of the third body upon them becomes the effect of the tides. Next, Newton goes on to imagine that ring frozen as a solid mass. The tendency which earlier drew the moon's orbit to tilt more or less with respect to the earth's ecliptic will continue, but now it will be operating on every erstwhile moon, as component of the solid mass of this frozen sea. But this mass, in turn, which was first the moon and then the seas, may now be taken as the bulge of the earth's equator; that force which earlier worked to alter the inclination of the moon's path to the ecliptic now becomes a force exerting leverage on the equatorial bulge of the earth, which will tend to tilt the axis of the earth. The earth becomes a top, precessing under the torque of the differential gravity, first of all, of the moon and the sun.

Newton has now found the force which will account for the precession of the earth's axis, long known to astronomers, a force that expresses itself in terms of the seasons of the year as the "procession of the equinoxes"—the motion of the spring point. This can also be seen in terms of the location of the pole of the earth's axis in the heavens, or the identity of the polestar. Here is the dynamic explanation of the fact that the pole wanders over the ages among the heavens—and establishes within the framework of the *Principia* a new principle of timekeeping of the utmost importance for anyone interested in prophetic history. Here is a clock, a timekeeper set by the Creator for the use of creatures who would one day come to know its use, ordered to the time scale of the Creation. For Newton it becomes the clock upon which the events of the history of the world can be ordered, as well as the clock of prophecy.

These are the new tools, then, which Newton forges out of the wreckage of the world of timeless geometry. They will serve him well, when he turns to the System of the World—a system not of an ordered harmony of balanced planets, though it bears that aspect initially, but rather more deeply and darkly understood, a "system" of complex interconnections—in an image favored by Newton, a "net"—committed throughout to the working of a divine plan through the courses of prophetic history. It bears the implications of concrete information, truth in a form we might call "existential," less like Plato or Euclid, and much more like bulletins of news. Newton is making us ready for news from God.

Book II: The refutation of mechanism

Book II of the *Principia* is a major work of great interest in its own right, in which Newton moves from the theory of central forces between bodies isolated in space to that of elastic media consisting of many bodies mutually repelling one another, or finally—with great difficulty and limited success—of continuous, fluid media. As in the case of Book I, many different themes are interwoven, and many different questions are at issue. The passage of solid bodies through elastic media, such as our air, which Newton works out extensively under ranges of assumed degrees and dispositions of density, has implications at one extreme for practical artillery, but more interestingly at the other, for the optics of refraction and diffraction. Throughout Book II, Newton is on the track of the question of the nature of light, which he believes must consist of particles moving in paths modulated by interaction with some form of medium. The greatest and overriding question of the book, however, is that of space itself. What fills the cosmos? Is it densely filled, as Descartes maintains, with a continuous medium—the plenum of the mechanical philosophy? Are the planets carried by vortices in a celestial plenum (fig. 10)? Or is the cosmos cleared of all such complications and thus a great void, through which the heavenly bodies and the particles of light may move under the mystic guidance of "force" alone? Book II thus goes to the most fundamental question, and it is essential in clearing the way for the System of the World.

As I have indicated, this second book of the *Principia* has a dialectical role: it must accomplish the refutation of Descartes and the mechanical philosophy. Yet the questions I have just put are not posed merely to be dismissed; Newton takes them very seriously and carries out an extensive, painstaking series of experiments with the pendulum in order to seek out any possible effect of a pervasive ether. Though they are little noted as such, these constitute one of the crucial experiments of classical physics, the search for an interaction between ether and ordinary matter. Newton's method is first to calibrate his experiment by determining both theoretically and practically the effect of air in damping the motion of a pendulum, and then to work with pendulum bobs in the form of containers either empty, or filled with matter in one form or another. If there is a pervasive ether, it should interact with the material of the filled pendulum and reveal its presence through the retardation of the pendulum's swing. Over many cycles, a long, slow pendulum becomes an extremely sensitive detector of any such effect. Newton's negative result, therefore, constitutes in his interpretation convincing evidence that no such effect exists. Space has been cleared for force to act without impediment.

Did Newton simply wish for this negative outcome? In his own years as a student at Cambridge he had shared the world's enthusiasm at the prospect of mechanical explanations, eager to dispel vague formulations and the assumption of occult properties. By what means does the sun move the earth? A mechanical ether offers the possibility of some intelligible answer. By refuting the hypothesis, Newton is destroying the hope of intelligible explanation, and this is a hope which he cannot himself have altogether abandoned. What is at stake is the very idea of "explanation," or the question of causality. What sort of answer do we seek when we ask the question, "Why?" Is "force" (or "spirit") an answer, or only the postponement of an answer? If "force" is mathematically ordered, according to a law of force of the sort Book I has demonstrated, does that alter the status of the question? The outcome of Book II places Newton finally in the position of asserting that a mechanical explanation is out of the question, and that force, the spirit of the alchemists, is real, operative, and causal in the world. Spirit becomes intellectually acceptable in this guise, which thoroughly admits mathesis. The result of Book II is thus at the same time acceptable to intellect and an avenue for God's presence and activity throughout the cosmos. Book II marks the death of materialism: it has never been possible again, since Newton wrote.

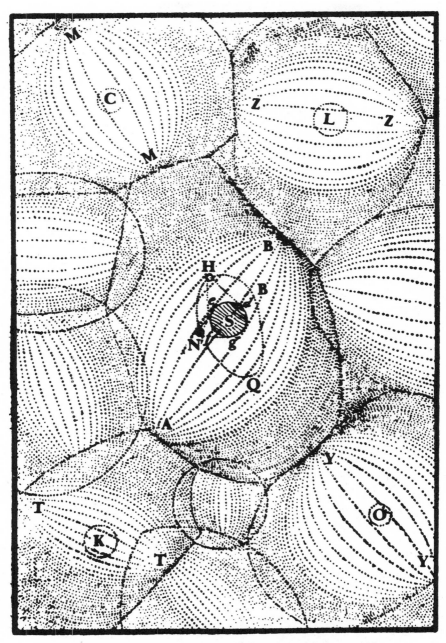

Figure 10. A figure from Descartes's *Principles of Philosophy* envisioning a world which is the dialectical alternative to that of the *Principia*. Here the cosmos is a material plenum, inviting intelligibility precisely through the absence of any further agent. Newton assigns all agency to "force," deeply related to the alchemic concept of spirit.

We leave this then, with a fundamental issue resolved. The cosmos has been cleared of any dense ether: void, empty space must take its place. Explanation by means of any intervening matter is thereby excluded; we have seen the end of materialism. Spirit or force is essential to the operation of nature and must fill the cosmos. The connection between the sun and the planets which are bound to it is confirmed as a mystery. We may add, the operation of gravity, or any other force in nature, is at least as mysterious today as it was when Newton closed Book II and turned to write his third book, "The System of the World."

The System of the World

How strange the world of shadows and lights is whose "system" we enter with Newton! He is bringing us into the very presence of God. God's signs to us are those which the first book has taught us to read: the System is a matter of reading the messages. In the General Scholium with which the *Principia* concludes, Newton draws out these theological conclusions in a way which is entirely consistent with the work as a whole. He first sets out a set of Rules of Reasoning in Philosophy which, as we have suggested, are indeed rules for the interpretation of the phenomena as text, strikingly parallel to corresponding principles for the interpretation of Scripture. In a nature which is God's creation, the phenomena become scripture. Bringing to bear the hieroglyphs which constitute the interpreter's arsenal he has spread before us in Book I, Newton is able to see through the phenomena, penetrating to the fundamental principles to which they attest. The process is the Newtonian analysis of the phenomena—"analysis" in the sense of a motion from the obscure and the complex to the simple and best known. Once completed, it secures the foundations of a corresponding constructive argument on which a synthetic science can be built, reasoning now from first principles, which are simple and best known, to consequences which are derivative and complex. What is at once the terminus of the analysis and the beginning of the synthesis is here the law of universal gravitation: the force which joins a planet to the sun joins as well every body to every other body, however small, in proportion to their masses, throughout the world.

At the point of this watershed between analysis and synthesis, Newton asserts:

> We have discoursed above on these motions from the Phenomena. Now that we know the principles on which they depend, from those principles we deduce the motions of the heavens *a priori*. (*GBWW* I: 34, 286; II: 32, 286)

The "a priori" is intended, and appropriate. This is the science at which Newton has aimed throughout, concerned with "knowledge" in a new, Newtonian sense, directed to divine act, beyond mere timeless truth. It is in this mode that Newton proceeds in the System of the World to reconstruct the cosmos he has so inexorably taken apart. As in the Creation itself, the planets and their moons appear in their turns, taking their places, each its appointed motion. We demonstrate now to the concrete fact, not to the universal conclusion.

In this constructive mode, since we know all the principles, it should be possible to compute everything we might want to know. A cornucopia of practical results is indeed ready to unfold. Yet what ought to be the great and most useful triumph of this astronomical System of the World, the calculation of the future motions of the moon in the form of a reliable almanac, Newton is not able to achieve, and it is important to us here to weigh the significance of his failure. Certainly the importance of this problem to the human management of the Creation is very great. Latitudes at sea can be determined readily by taking the height of the polestar, but longitudes must be inferred from the positions of the stars in their rotations, on the basis of known times. What is needed is an accurate timekeeper which will remain reliable in the vicissitudes of travel at sea, and in Newton's time there was no such chronometer. If the moon's motions could be predicted with precision, it would serve in effect as the long-desired chronometer of universal reference; by means of times read from the positions of the moon in conjunction with an accurate table, the positions of other bodies would yield accurate longitudes. Hooke had alluded to the importance of this problem of the longitudes in his earliest correspondence with Newton, and much later, Newton himself sat on a panel to judge entries to solve this problem of "determination of longitudes at sea." Yet after immense labors, he is forced to conclude:

> But there are yet other inequalities not observed by former
> astronomers, by which the motions of the moon are so disturbed that
> to this day we have not been able to bring them under any certain rule.
> (*GBWW* I: 34, 295; II: 32, 295)

How are we to weigh the significance for Newton of this lunar debacle? If truth were Socratic, the essential rewards for mind would stand in their universality, even if practical details could not be derived satisfactorily. In the domain of classical knowledge, facts are details. But Newton, operating in an altogether different arena, is entitled to no such satisfaction. If it is the role of the universal to serve the fact—if in a sense the universal is incarnate in the detail of the Creation—the economic and political outcome looms as large for Newton in proportion as the right positioning of the planets and the moons does for the Creator.

159

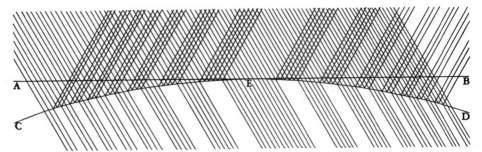

The deep relation between Newton's "physics" and his alchemy is suggested by this figure from his *Optics* (GBWW I: 34, 464–5; II: 32, 464–5). Newton had made fundamental observations on the concentric bands of color (known today as "Newton's rings") produced when a convex lens is placed on a flat glass plate, a phenomenon which he studied with great interest and accounted for by way of a theory of "fits" of easy transmission and reflection. In terms of the wave theory of light, it is recognized as a diffraction effect which arises because the distances between the surfaces are of the order of the wavelength of light. Though for compelling reasons Newton rejected the wave theory of light, he was well aware of the extremely small distances which were in this way being systematically associated with the colors of the spectrum. It was, therefore, a most interesting move on his part to relate these in turn to the colors arising in alchemy, and to explore the possibility of constructing a theory of the underlying structures of substances by way of the colors they were displaying in alchemic investigations. The fact that the center of the rings, corresponding to the least distances, is black suggested a relation to the black chaos at the foundation of the alchemic program. This was a new route for bringing quantity to bear on alchemy, perhaps an element of Newton's strategy for an ultimate, alchemic *Principia*.

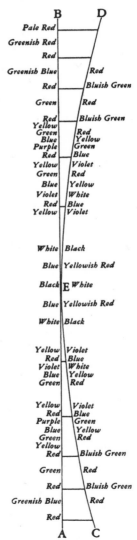

Fleets were foundering for lack of Newton's numbers. Just as we said earlier that the deterioration of the perfect orbits by the action of the three-body problem did not constitute a tragedy for Newton, though it would have for the ancients, who would have regarded elliptical orbits as imperfections, now we must acknowledge the counterpart: the failure to compute accurately to the fact, that is, the failure to bring science to bear on economic, military, and political reality, is indeed tragic in a very different sense for Newton. Good governance, by God and by man, is the new criterion for a science which man now through Newton's work comes to share more closely with God. Newton's science is genuinely humbled by its failure, in this constructive mode, to achieve an accurate computation of the moon.

The alchemy of the comets

The last of the astronomical motions considered in the Newtonian construction is that of the comets. They are of special significance because, wandering widely through the heavens, they serve as probes, marvels which put all theories to the test. Curtis Wilson has recently in these pages called our attention to their importance to Newton (*GIT* 1985, 178–229). As the *Principia* draws to a close, we literally watch Newton struggle to demonstrate what has been a crucial insight in his own experience: that the comets, too, are subject to universal gravitation, that their motions are uncluttered by any remnants of a Cartesian ether, and that therefore they move in the very trajectories demonstrated in Book I (figs. 11 and 12). We see how difficult is the practical task of fitting the orbit to observed phenomena, and how great is Newton's sense of triumph at his apparent ability to do this in the case of the comet of 1680–81, which he takes as his test.

> Hence also it is evident that the celestial spaces are void of resistance;
> for though the comets are carried in oblique paths, and sometimes
> contrary to the course of the planets, yet they move every way with the
> greatest freedom, and preserve their motions for an exceeding long
> time, even where contrary to the course of the planets. I am out in
> my judgment, if they are not a sort of planets revolving in orbits
> returning into themselves with a continual motion. (*GBWW* I: 34, 337;
> II: 32, 337)

Finally, what emerges is the sense that the comet is undergoing a form of astronomical alchemy: coming as close to the sun as Newton has computed it does, he concludes that it must have undergone immense heating, which it is nonetheless not beyond the Newtonian strategies to estimate. The comet has undergone maturation by heating at a furnace Newton could never achieve on earth:

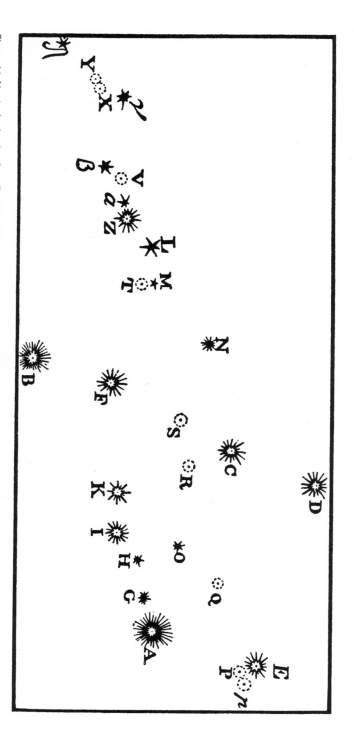

Figure 11. Newton's drawing from Book III of the progress through the heavens of the comet of 1680–81, tracked in the text on a night-by-night basis. Successive observed positions are indicated by the small circles p, P, Q, R, S, T, V, X, and Y. Newton gathered data from observers scattered over the known world, and relied heavily on the work of Edmund Halley.

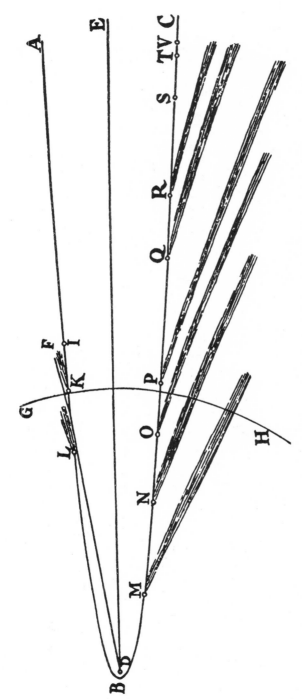

Figure 12. The trajectory Newton fits to the comet's phenomena. He carefully estimates the heat developed at perihelion in this celestial furnace. Newton shows that the comet's tail is systematically directed away from the sun, visible evidence of the distillation of spirit—the culmination at once of his alchemy and of the *Principia*. The heavens have become his laboratory.

This comet, therefore, must have received an immense heat from the sun, and retained that heat for an exceeding long time. . . .

It is further to be observed, that the comet in the month of December, just after it had been heated by the sun, did emit a much longer tail, and much more splendid, than in the month of November before, when it had not yet arrived at its perihelion; and, universally, the greatest and most fulgent tails always arise from comets immediately after their passing by the neighborhood of the sun. Therefore the heat received by the comet conduces to the greatness of the tail: from this, I think I may infer, that the tail is nothing else but a very fine vapor, which the head or nucleus of the comet emits by its heat. (*GBWW* I: 34, 354; II: 32, 354)

Newton is here recognizing that in the case of this comet, matter is being exposed to an extreme of alchemic treament quite impossible to achieve in any earthly laboratory, yet observable in its effect, and he therefore watches the vapors which result with the greatest of interest. He concludes that he is seeing in the tail of the comet the emission of that "spirit" which was always the ultimate objective of the alchemic search and is fundamentally needed in order to complete Newton's account of the true System of the World. He conceives that the vapors from such comets run a course, ultimately condensing and falling upon the planets:

. . . comets seem to be required, that, from their exhalations and vapors condensed, the wastes of the planetary fluids spent upon vegetation and putrefaction, and converted into dry earth, may be continually supplied and made up; for all vegetables entirely derive their growths from fluids, and afterwards, in great measure, are turned into dry earth by putrefaction. . . . (*GBWW* I: 34, 359; II: 32; 359)

Finally:

. . . I suspect, moreover, that it is chiefly from the comets that spirit comes, which is indeed the smallest but the most subtle and useful part of our air, and so much required to sustain the life of all things with us. (Ibid.)

Newton was not able to complete his own alchemic researches in time to balance his account of the macrocosm with a corresponding theory of the microcosm, though both belong in principle to the System of the World, but he sees by a kind of divine justice the project completed for him at a furnace in the heavens. He believes he has at last seen the spirit for which he had for so long been searching, and which bears the most important force that must be included in any full account of nature, a repelling or elastic force. He returns to the question of this spirit in the closing words of the *Principia*, as we shall see.

The General Scholium

The *Principia* closes with a frankly theological discussion, in what Newton terms the "General Scholium"—that is, the scholium to the work as a whole. This may be regarded, by those who take the *Principia* to be the first work of modern physics, as a mere commentary or afterthought, an interesting but unnecessary addendum. I think rather that for Newton it is central to the purpose and method of the entire work. It is brief and tightly written, and the reader is invited to turn directly to it. Newton first recapitulates the argument against vortices, with the result that:

> . . . all bodies will move with the greatest freedom; and the planets and comets will constantly pursue their revolutions in orbits given in kind and position, according to the laws above explained; but though these bodies may, indeed, continue in their orbits by the mere laws of gravity, yet they could by no means have at first derived the regular position of the orbits themselves from those laws.
> . . . it is not to be conceived that mere mechanical causes could give birth to so many regular motions. (*GBWW* I: 34, 369; II: 32, 369)

In discussing the concept of law earlier, we concluded that the structure of the *Principia* belongs to the spirit of the Judeo-Christian tradition. Newton now, holding this mirror to his work, reveals the sense in which that is true. Newton has shown the cosmos to be cleared of mechanisms, and thus liberated for the agency of spirit. This agency he now calls "dominion":

> And from his true dominion it follows that the true God is a living, intelligent, and powerful Being. . . . He is eternal and infinite, omnipotent and omniscient; that is, his duration reaches from eternity to eternity; his presence from infinity to infinity; he governs all things, and knows all things that are or can be done. . . . He endures forever, and is everywhere present; and, by existing always and everywhere, he constitutes duration and space. (*GBWW* I: 34, 370; II: 32, 370)

Readers must balance for themselves the elements of Newton's account. I am impressed on this reading with Newton's awe and the sense he conveys of the immediacy of mystery. What he says of his God hardly goes beyond what he has seen and demonstrated—but he has seen and demonstrated so much:

> We have ideas of his attributes, but what the real substance of anything is we know not. In bodies, we see only their figures and colors, we hear only the sounds, we touch only their outward surfaces, we smell only the smells, and taste the savors; but their inward substances are not to be known either by our senses, or by any reflex act of our minds: much

less, then, have we any idea of the substance of God. We know him only
by his most wise and excellent contrivances of things, and final causes;
we admire him for his perfections; but we reverence and adore him on
account of his dominion: for we adore him as his servants; and a god
without dominion, providence, and final causes, is nothing else but Fate
and Nature. (*GBWW* I: 34, 371; II: 32, 371)

Finally:

> And thus much concerning God; to discourse of whom from the
> appearances of things, does certainly belong to natural philosophy.
> (Ibid.)

It would be an error to think that this is all that Newton has to say
about God, and that he has in view only what we might call a "natural
religion." We know that he thought and wrote extensively on questions
of Christian faith and the interpretation of Scripture, about which he
held strong if idiosyncratic views. The *Principia* must be seen as one
aspect of this faith, essentially consistent with it. The two complement
one another, two channels of Newton's relation to his God. Probably
a stronger statement is justified: Newton could not have arrived at the
Principia without a foundation in the faith he brings to it from theology.
His concept of "law" derives ultimately from his sense of the God of
Scripture, while his faith in the simplicity of nature and the confidence
in the phenomena, on which his science is founded, rest finally on his
faith in God. Newton has spread before us a Divine Comedy; without
God, such a comedy would have no foundation. To "discourse" of
God "from the appearances of things" is appropriate for Newton. For
Newton, that study itself is only possible as God's gift.

The General Scholium, and with it, the *Principia,* close not on this
overtly theological reflection but with two questions which may seem of
a very different sort, though in truth they are not. The first concerns
the cause of gravity. To this, Newton says, he has no answer:

> And to us it is enough that gravity does really exist, and act according
> to the laws which we have explained, and abundantly serves to account
> for all the motions of the celestial bodies, and of our sea. (*GBWW* I: 34,
> 371–72; II: 32, 371–72)

Some may feel that this whole paragraph indicates that Newton is still
seeking a mechanical explanation, and it is true that he works in other
places with various notions of ethers in considering the problem of
attraction. I think, however, that the sentence above is decisive: he is
ready to rest content in the presence of mystery, and though at this
point he has only made a beginning, he does not envision a completed
natural philosophy which terminates on a note essentially different from
the one he has sounded in this General Scholium. Mystery does not
represent a failure of natural philosophy but its rightful culmination.

The final question is the most intriguing, and like the closing observation concerning the comet, takes us back to the core of his alchemic conviction. If our present reading of the *Principia* is correct, it is highly appropriate that it is on this alchemic theme that the work closes. Newton writes:

> And now we might add something concerning a certain most subtle spirit which pervades and lies hid in all gross bodies. . . . (*GBWW* I: 34, 372; II: 32, 372)

As his description of this "spirit" unfolds, we see how his thinking is running. It is to account for a very wide range of phenomena, including on the one hand the optics of diffraction and refraction, and on the other, animal spirits, the action of sense and will. Newton is inviting something like the electromagnetic ether, but something more as well, indeed the very principle of life itself. How, might we imagine, would this comport with the rest of the System of the World, if he had been able to include it?

Though it would be associated with and borne by subtle particles, we may safely assume that Newton is not speaking of a material ether; when he says "spirit," he means just that. In the alchemic context, such spirit, extracted from common air, serves to vivify inert materials and is essential to the processes of life. Spirit as an immaterial, nonmechanical vital principle is fully compatible with all we have learned from the rest of the *Principia,* and with the convictions of the Newtonian alchemy on which it rests. Newton's mathematics of nascent quantities, living and growing, is by no means coextensive with mechanism and blind determinism; we have tended to forget the possibility that mathematics may speak equally of life and mind.

It is appropriate that Newton withholds further discourse concerning this spirit, this second element of the system of his world, to which he was never able to break through. There is a note of awe in the hush which falls over the *Principia* in these closing words; God has more yet to tell mankind. The work of revelation, the prophetic tradition to which I think it is clear Newton believes the *Principia* belongs, has a further course to run. Looking ahead in this last passage, as in the final "Queries" he appended to the *Optics,* Newton seems to bring us to join him at the threshold of the temple, where it is necessary and right that silence reign.

---

1. Newton's advice comes at the outset of the book (*GBWW* I: 34, 269; II: 32, 269) in these terms:

> . . . not that I would advise anyone to the previous study of every Proposition of those books; for they abound with such as might cost too much time, even to readers of good mathematical learning.

2. Many fascinating accounts of Newton's alchemy are now appearing. The most useful general introduction is probably by Betty Jo Dobbs, who has written numerous interesting articles on this subject as well: Betty Jo Teeter Dobbs, *The Foundations of Newton's Alchemy, or "The Hunting of the Greene Lyon"* (Cambridge, Eng.: Cambridge University Press, 1975). A striking overview by David Castillejo of the weaving of the many strands of Newton's thought, based on extensive study of the new manuscripts, has been particularly valuable in the preparation of the present essay: David Castillejo, *The Expanding Force in Newton's Cosmos* (Madrid: Ediciones de arte, 1981). The first chapter of that work is devoted to a review of the alchemy.

In general, studies by Richard Westfall have led the way in much of the current scholarship. His biography of Newton, *Never at Rest* (Cambridge, Eng.: Cambridge University Press, 1980), which includes an extended bibliographic review, and his earlier work, *Force in Newton's Physics* (New York: American Elsevier, 1971), are good starting points. An earlier biography by More remains useful: Louis Trenchard More, *Isaac Newton: A Biography* (New York: Dover Publications, 1934). The classic biography is that of David Brewster, *Memoirs of the Life, Writings, and Discoveries of Sir Isaac Newton,* 2 vols. (Edinburgh: T. Constable & Co., 1855). Excellent editions of Newton's mathematical papers and of his correspondence are now available, as well as editions of his unpublished papers. These, together with a variorum edition of the *Principia* itself, provide a rich prospect for the interested reader. A number of very interesting collections of essays have appeared in recent years. Most especially, the reader is urged to refer to the essay by Curtis Wilson which appeared recently in the present series (*GIT* 1985, 178–229).

3. It was the collection of Lord Keynes which was placed on the block in 1936; as a result, it was fragmented into over one hundred auctioned lots which went to some thirty-two different buyers (Castillejo, op. cit., pp. 13, 120; Westfall, *Never at Rest,* pp. 875ff.). Over the years since, scholars have tracked down and published at least the locations of most of the components of this diaspora.

4. For reasons which will be concerns of the present essay, Newton's work on chronology, some of which was published posthumously in his *Chronology of the Ancient Kingdoms Amended,* is intimately linked with his theological studies, including his published *Observations upon the Prophecies of Daniel and the Apocalypse of St. John,* which appears in Horsley's edition of Newton's works: Samual Horsley, *Isaaci Newtoni Opera Omnia* (vol. 5, 1785). A small but most interesting collection has long been available: Herbert McLachlan, ed., *Sir Isaac Newton: Theological Manuscripts* (Liverpool: Liverpool University Press, 1950). *See* the extensive discussions in the Westfall biography, and Castillejo, op. cit., chaps. 2, 3, and 4. Frank E. Manuel has published studies of both aspects of Newton's thought: *The Religion of Isaac Newton* (Oxford: Clarendon Press, 1974), and *Isaac Newton, Historian* (Cambridge, Mass.: Harvard University Press, 1963).

5. Aristotle discusses induction and explains that scientific induction leads to the kind of knowledge which is "always true," at the close of the *Posterior Analytics* (*GBWW* I: 8, 136–37; II: 7, 136–37).

6. Augustine, *On Christian Doctrine* (*GBWW* I: 18, 621; II: 16, 701). Augustine's discussion of the rules for interpretation at the outset of this text may be compared with Newton's, referred to in the next note.

7. *See* Newton's discussion of "The Language of the Prophets," in McLachlan, *Theological Manuscripts,* pp. 119ff.

8. Aristotle discusses the possible answers to the question "Why?" in Book II of the *Physics* (*GBWW* I: 8, 275; II: 7, 275). Newton's *Principia* may perhaps best be thought of as founding a physics which is ultimately coextensive with, and an answer to, Aristotle's (i.e., closer to biology and psychology than to what we call "physics"). The world-change between the two may be thought of as the conversion of the question "Why?"

9. Descartes discusses the analytic method of the ancient mathematicians, and its relation to his own method, in the *Discourse on Method* (*GBWW* I: 31, 46–48; II: 28, 270–72). He appended his *Analytic Geometry* (*GBWW* I: 31, 295; II: 28, 523) as an illustration—perhaps much as Newton appends the astronomical "System of the World" to the *Principia,* as just one particular application. It is important to note that the method of algebra is the paradigm for the sweeping method of "doubt" of the *Discourse* and the *Meditations.*

10. Descartes's analysis to the idea of matter proceeds by way of his reflections which doubt away the qualities of a piece of wax (*Meditations; GBWW* I: 31, 80; II: 28, 306). What is left is "magnitude or extension in length, breadth or depth" (*GBWW* I: 31, 85; II:

28, 311). Euclid's general theory of magnitude, which Descartes would have particularly in view, is given in Book V of the *Elements* (*GBWW* I: 11, 81; II: 10, 81). Descartes's definition of matter is set out as one of the first principles of material things in his *Principles of Philosophy:*

> That the nature of body consists not in weight, nor in hardness, nor colour and so on, but in extension alone.

The Philosophical Works of Descartes, trans. Elizabeth S. Haldane and G. R. T. Ross (New York: Dover Publications, 1955), vol. 1, p. 255. Descartes spells out the world in terms of this plenum of extension in *Le Monde,* the book which is the system of his world: *Le Monde; ou, traité de la lumière,* trans. Michael Mahoney (New York: Abaris Books, 1979).

11. Brief summaries of Newton's mathematical work, his distinctive approach to the modern calculus, can be found in two useful collections: D. T. Whiteside, "Sources and Strengths of Newton's Early Mathematical Papers," in Robert Paleter, ed., *The Annus Mirabilis of Sir Isaac Newton 1666–1966* (Cambridge, Mass.: The M.I.T. Press, 1967), pp. 69ff.; and Jon Pepper, "Newton's Mathematical Work," in John Fauvel et al., eds., *Let Newton Be!* (New York: Oxford University Press, 1988), pp. 63ff. Serious students of the *Principia* will be much aided by a commentary which has been in use for many years at St. John's College: Robert S. Bart, *Notes to Accompany the Reading of Newton's "Principia Mathematica,"* (Annapolis, Md.: St. John's College Press, 1968), 2nd ed.

12. The technique of the "microscope" is introduced in Newton's Lemma 6.

13. According to Newton, "the language of the Prophets, being Hieroglyphical, had affinity with that of the Egyptian priests and Eastern wise men, and therefore was anciently much better understood in the East than it is now in the West" (McLachlan, *Theological Manuscripts,* p. 120).

14. The correspondence was with the theologian Richard Bentley. *See* I. B. Cohen, ed., *Isaac Newton's Papers & Letters on Natural Philosophy* (Cambridge, Mass.: Harvard University Press, 1978), 2nd ed., p. 287.

15. Castillejo, op. cit., chap. 2. *See* Frank E. Manuel, *The Religion of Isaac Newton* (London: Oxford University Press, 1974), and his biography of Newton, *A Portrait of Isaac Newton* (Cambridge, Mass.: Harvard University Press, 1968), chap. 17, "Prophecy and History." For Newton's letters to Richard Bentley on the theological implications of the *Principia* see Cohen, op. cit., pp. 271ff.

Contemporary Views of Happiness

Deal W. Hudson

Deal W. Hudson received degrees from the University of Texas at Austin
and Princeton Theological Seminary before earning his doctorate from the
Institute of the Liberal Arts at Emory University in Atlanta. He is the coeditor
of two books, *Understanding Maritain: Philosopher and Friend* and *The
Future of Thomism,* and is the author of various articles in the subjects
of happiness and contemporary Thomism. While pursuing his research,
Professor Hudson has enjoyed the support of the Earhart Foundation, the
Day Corporation, and the Association of American Colleges and Universities.
He has served as vice president of the American Maritain Association since
1985 and was recently elected to the Executive Committee of the American
Catholic Philosophical Association.

    Hudson is now an associate professor of philosophy at Fordham Univer-
sity in New York City, where he is also visiting professor of medieval and
Renaissance studies at New York University. He taught for nine years at
Mercer University in Macon, Georgia, before joining the faculty at Fordham
and being named coach of its golf team.

If it is true that the heart of man will always suffer the anguish of beatitude, it is not because man would be condemned always to stagnate here below; it is because the largest and most abounding life will always be something very small, compared with the dimensions of his heart. (Jacques Maritain, *Integral Humanism*) [1]

The distinctive mark of contemporary thinking about happiness is the ascendancy of its various psychological meanings. During the present century happiness has come to be identified with the possession of positive psychological states, from transient enjoyments to the global satisfaction of "being pleased" with one's life. This psychological conception of happiness as "well-feeling" has replaced the happiness of "well-being" and now reigns supreme without a popular rival.

Proponents of well-feeling have privatized happiness. They often assign irrefutable status to personal reports of "being happy" with one's life. Regarded in this way, the happy life can no longer represent the best life for all of us. Instead, the claim to happiness has become a subjective expression of personal preference and satisfaction.

The classical view of happiness focused on personal character and its success in meeting the challenges of circumstance through the exercise of virtue. This tradition is now referred to as eudaemonism, after the Greek word for happiness, *eudaimonia*. A eudaemonist insists that all claims to happiness, including personal satisfaction, must stand ready for moral inspection. The mere claim to satisfaction cannot be considered indisputable proof of a person's happiness.

Many issues separate these classical and contemporary conceptions of happiness, the crucial one being the relation of happiness to morality. The eudaemonist asks what ethical standards must a life meet to be called happy? The defender of well-feeling will answer that it becomes nonsensical to discuss *the* happy life at all. If the measure of well-feeling is applied, happy lives have nothing in common save their subjective reports of psychological satisfaction.

Although well-feeling reigns supreme, classical *eudaimonia* is not completely forgotten. Some recent discussions of happiness deal with the normative question: whether claims to happiness, now transposed into a psychological idiom, can be evaluated by reference to any external and objective criteria. Part of this debate has centered on the word *happiness* itself and, in particular, its suitability as the English equivalent for the Greek *eudaimonia*. Since our usage of happiness contains immediate hedonic connotations, many commentators have preferred equivalents for the Greek such as "human flourishing," "well-being," or simply "the good life." Others simply treat *eudaimonia* as untranslatable. No consensus has yet emerged solidly behind any of the alternatives.

Meanwhile, three points can be made in favor of sticking with "happiness." First, there is good reason to predict that newly minted terms such as "flourishing" will be construed as well-feeling: to flourish is to possess a desirable psychological state. Second, the word *happiness* is indebted historically to the legacy of eudaemonism; therefore, to accept a simple reduction of the meaning of happiness to well-feeling would require forgetting most of what was written about happiness between the sixteenth and nineteenth centuries. Uses of the word *happiness* have been strongly colored by eudaemonism until the present century. Third, a hedonistic conception of *eudaimonia* existed in the ancient world which treated virtue as the instrumental means to pleasure, the final good. Thus, while *eudaimonia* always includes virtue as integral to happiness, it does not necessarily rule out pleasure. [2]

Still, the twentieth century is far removed from the world which regarded *eudaimonia, beatitudo,* and *felicitas* as the summum bonum, the greatest good of human life, and which routinely sought to prescribe its catalogs of laws, virtues, and vices with happiness in mind. The idea of happiness no longer belongs exclusively to such philosophical and theological spheres of discourse. The emergence of well-feeling has enabled social scientists to investigate it, and their findings now shape popular opinion about happiness. Philosophers who still ask questions about happiness are often met with looks of bewilderment. Local bookstores now routinely place their books about happiness in the psychology or self-help section but rarely if ever on the philosophy shelf.

In spite of the changing conceptions of happiness, most commentators will agree that the human desire for happiness is unavoidable. Whether happiness is the gratification of instinctual urges as in Freud, or the greater sum of pleasures over pains as in Locke, or the intellectual vision of God as in Aquinas, the pursuit of happiness seems an intractable fact about human nature. However, shifts in meaning directly affect our moral and political expectations of other human beings. For instance, what do we expect our fellow citizens to do with their right to "the pursuit of happiness"? Is our expectation altered by the appearance of privatized well-feeling? Do we expect them to pursue the virtues, knowledge, tranquillity, freedom, money, pleasure, power, or some integrated version of these ends? Should society impose any constraints on their pursuit?

Mistakes about happiness can misdirect lives and weaken communities. Unexamined notions of happiness embedded in patterns of private and public life always need scrutiny and assessment. For example, if one of the chief mandates of a government is to provide its citizens with the necessary means to the pursuit of happiness, knowing what that happiness consists in, at least in a general way, must be a primary social concern. A privatized notion of happiness, of course, discourages political solidarity from the start.

Happiness, like love, justice, and freedom, is an idea that helped Western cultures to frame the meaning of human nature and the purpose of human institutions. As the meaning of these ideas has become unstable, people approach them in an agnostic frame of mind—"who can say what happiness is *for me?*" In the meantime, people are turning to self-help formulas of visualization and other mood-altering techniques to meet their need for happiness, which at least have the advantage of often making them feel better.

Critical surveys of opinion about happiness were once common. A catalog of false happinesses, as opposed to the true happiness of the summum bonum, was standard fare in literature from the fifth century B.C. to the eighteenth century. Philosophers have always recognized that the term *happiness* means different things to different people, even while they tried to separate the wheat from the chaff. For example, Aquinas in his catalog treats wealth, honor, fame, power, bodily goods, pleasure, knowledge, all as finite goods which people mistakenly pursue in the belief that they are happiness itself (*GBWW* I: 19, 615–22; II: 17, 615–22). In devising such a list, Aquinas stood in a long tradition of bringing moral and spiritual discriminations to bear upon claims to happiness. But the attempt to help people distinguish true from false happiness, to "correct their palates," as Locke put it, did not blind philosophers to the vagaries of pursuing happiness in everyday life. As long as the eudaemonist tradition held sway, philosophers felt free to hold people accountable for the moral and political spillover of their satisfactions.

The project of distinguishing true from false happiness is no longer generally accepted. Thus, a survey of contemporary opinions about happiness cannot be as neat and tidy as it might have been even a hundred years ago. Also, such a survey must encompass not only recent philosophical developments but the explosion of research on happiness in the social sciences. In addition, given the extent of its influence, some aspects of the popular literature on happiness must be considered. This body of literature, as we shall see, reflects both the growing importance of psychological accounts of happiness and the desire of some philosophers to regain a public audience.

Philosophers, it must be said, did not have the idea of happiness taken from them—they gave it away. In the most recent encyclopedia of philosophy, Richard Brandt writes, "The question of what conditions are necessary for happiness is manifestly a question for scientific psychology." [3] The psychologists have not dropped the ball. The story of philosophy's loss of confidence in happiness, unfolding since the time of Kant, has yet to be written. The reasons for this decline will be gleaned in part from unresolved problems in the concept of *eudaimonia* itself. Suffice it to say here that among philosophers themselves, the idea of happiness no longer commands either the attention or respect it did in earlier ages. Augustine wrote, "For man has no other reason for philosophizing than that he may be happy" (*GBWW* I: 18, 508; II: 16, 576). Even a passing acquaintance with the Greek and Roman classics, those of the High Middle Ages and the Italian Renaissance, or the European and American Enlightenment attests to this. The concept of happiness once operated like a fulcrum at the very heart of major intellectual systems and, as a consequence, of cultural self-consciousness. It was taken for granted that a society had to be clear about the nature of happiness before it could be sure of its ethics, its politics, or its religion. The right of American citizens to "the pursuit of happiness" still testifies to that foundational role.

Taking such a long view should not blind us to the fact that signs of a resurgence of interest are at hand. The intellectual currency of happiness remains low, but a new public discussion is getting under way: books and articles on the subject are multiplying—not just those of the self-help variety but also systematic treatises for specialists in philosophy and the social sciences. In the meantime, then, a survey of contemporary views of happiness can serve several purposes: (1) to provide clues to explain the relative loss of confidence in the idea of happiness, (2) to stimulate thought toward retrieving the tradition of reflection upon this "great idea," and (3) to aid in sorting through the presently competing versions of happiness, especially in evaluating the current hegemony of the psychological account.

In addition to its historical and dialectical value, an overview of the contemporary idea of happiness will have both philosophical and religious significance for those who continue to reflect upon the questions—"What is a human life for?" and "How can I live well?" The question of happiness has traditionally addressed the issues of human purpose and human goodness: they were inextricably linked within the notion of happiness. The aim of life was not considered a matter of our deliberation; it was given by the specification of our human nature. The virtues were the dispositions that enabled us to fulfill natural desire. Our choices, therefore, were about means rather than ends, especially not our final end.

For the eudaemonist, then, freedom was understood as our ability and success in seeking an unchosen end. It has been pointed out many times that this conception of freedom is too confining for contemporary tastes. The happiness of well-feeling gives people considerably more latitude in choosing ends and in maintaining self-identity. Spokesmen for modernity have applauded this new understanding of freedom and happiness. But opinion as to what it entails, and how we should seek it, has been far from unanimous.

I. The rejection of happiness

> My eyes shot glances and I salivated;
> My words came like honey and I was just.
> Soon I had the rewards of this conduct.
> Every endeavor was made to please me.
> My mind felt like a sovereign in its own weight.
>
> . . . .
>
> It may be that happiness is a sign of evil.
> (C. H. Sisson, "The Garden of Epicurus") [4]

It is ironic that a central reason for the rejection of happiness as a guide to life is the emergence of well-feeling. The earliest proponents of well-feeling were motivated in part by a concern for putting this most highly valued of all human states within the reach of everybody, not just philosophers and saints. [5] Yet, while seeming to make happiness more available, psychological happiness effectively posited a goal which turns out to be both difficult to realize and morally questionable to pursue. These objections to psychological happiness have been known for some time: a critique of it had been offered in advance of its widespread acceptance by figures as diverse as Pascal, Samuel Johnson, Voltaire, Kant, Kierkegaard, and Nietzsche. The historian Paul Hazard notes that during the eighteenth century, when this new idea of happiness was being nurtured, it was injected deeply into the political bloodstream: "The upshot was that [when] happiness became a right . . . people now gave up asking themselves whether they deserved happiness; they asked whether they were getting the happiness to which they were entitled. *The question now was not, "Am I a good man?" It was, "Am I a happy man?"* [6] The appearance of well-feeling in the political arena seriously compounded its problems. Stripped of its moral requirements, happiness became a matter of entitlement.

Both Kierkegaard and Nietzsche issued prophetic rejections of any happiness that valued placid contentment above the passionate exercise of the will. Writing out of the same existentialist tradition, Miguel de Unamuno categorically denies that the pursuit of happiness offers benefit to humankind. In *The Tragic Sense of Life* he argues that each individual inevitably faces a choice between love and happiness, between egoism and altruism, absorption in self or commitment to others. The happy person, who seeks his own uninterrupted satisfactions, is "without substance" because his central achievement in life is predicated on the avoidance of suffering. By choosing the happiness of satisfaction rather than the suffering of love, the happy man loses a life with meaning. "The satisfied, the happy ones, do not love; they fall asleep in habit, near neighbor to annihilation." [7] Unamuno calls it the "tragic formula" of the spiritual life—one either seeks love or happiness, but not both. Being in a state of happiness excludes any experience that places self-satisfaction at risk. For Unamuno, any state that excludes the suffering of love from our well-being cannot be the summum bonum. His protests against the excessive concern for complacency and the encouragement of benign isolation set the tone for this century's rejection of happiness.

The divorce between happiness and morality also troubles Aleksandr Solzhenitsyn, whose celebrated reception in the West was cooled by his criticism of its bourgeois habits. He directs his repudiation of happiness toward both the collectivism of the Soviet Union and the individualism of his adopted country. In his third novel, *Cancer Ward,* the character Shulubin dismisses happiness as "an idol of the market" and like Unamuno insists upon the choice between self-gratification and suffering love: "a wild animal gnawing at its prey is happy, but only humans can love, and love is the highest thing man can achieve." [8] Shulubin also chastises the political use of happiness by social engineers who employ well-feeling as bait: "Happiness is a mirage. . . . for happiness I burned books that contained truth. This applies even more to the so-called 'happiness of future generations.' . . . If we think only of 'happiness' and 'growth,' we shall fill up the earth senselessly and create a frightening society." [9] For Solzhenitsyn, the pursuit of happiness in both the East and the West has exacerbated the collectivism of the former and the individualism of the latter. In either case, happiness in the form of self-satisfaction represents a temptation to be resisted rather than emulated.

This disturbing vision of the role of happiness in society cannot be dismissed as belonging to reactionary writers-in-exile or gloomy existentialists preoccupied with a past centuries' angst. Their forecasts have been confirmed in a number of historical and sociological studies of American life. Nearly forty years ago Howard Mumford Jones in *The Pursuit of Happiness* disparaged the psychological transposition of happiness into "something called 'adjustment' as the social worker and eventually the psychiatrist replaced the minister as a guide to life." [10] Thomas Jefferson, he comments, would have been horrified by the governmental bureaucracy that has been generated to reap and sow the happiness of well-feeling. Jones's study was an early warning shot fired against the growing tendency to use happiness for the justification of self-centered and self-absorbed lives.

Yet the situation seems to have gone from bad to worse. A number of highly regarded authors have documented the increasing "narcissism" infecting American culture. [11] Most prominent among these studies is *Habits of the Heart,* in which Robert Bellah and his coauthors offer portraits of typical Americans, based upon personal interviews, who suffer from severe psychical and political dislocation as a result of "The Pursuit of Happiness," the title of the first chapter. For example, one subject expresses difficulty in articulating his reasons for not enjoying the demands of family life as opposed to his earlier single-minded commitment to his career. The happiness that he now experiences due to this change seems to him "arbitrary and unexamined"; it cannot be accounted for by reference to any overall purpose in his life. "Brian sees himself as consistently pursuing a utilitarian calculus—devotion to his own self-interest—except that there has been an almost inexplicable change in his personal preferences." [12] Like Brian, many of the subjects interviewed have lost their objective grounding; their most significant choices have become a matter of sheer preference. Personal satisfaction in material success may give way at a moment's notice to the delights of family life without explanation.

This kind of fragmented and inarticulate self, Bellah argues, has become a dominant type in American life and has led to increasing lack of involvement in public life and of commitment to the common good. When crucial decisions and specific actions are motivated by a privatized happiness, *reasons* for choosing one course over another are not considered.

It is significant that, as these authors stress, Americans do not report themselves as "happy" in pursuit of these satisfactions. Instead, they report feeling locked inside an isolated self of their own making. They express the desire for participation in a larger community but are seemingly stuck in an ambivalent posture of either rejecting all social expectations or accepting total conformity. In the face of these alternatives, the historic American disposition to individualism reasserts itself.

The most extreme case in Bellah's work is a young nurse named Shelia, who, it is mentioned, has received a great amount of therapy. The interviewer asks about her religious faith: "I believe in God. I'm not a religious fanatic. I can't remember the last time I went to church. My faith has carried me a long way. Its Sheliaism. Just my own little voice." [13] The findings of *Habits of the Heart* heralded perhaps the penultimate stage of the mind-cure tradition in American culture, the so-called New Age, before it became widely known through the media—an age in which happiness can mean anything a person wants it to mean. Happiness, as a result, can lend justification to any kind of life, any kind of behavior, any kind of character. No one can lay claim to any vantage point from which to challenge the authority of someone else's "own little voice." Personal preference, it seems, has become divinized.

Bellah's troubling conclusion is that the radical individualism he and his cohorts uncovered in American life has been encouraged by "modern psychological ideals" that have conceived freedom without the restraint of any received definition. To be free and happy in America, to enjoy the "good life," means to start from scratch in creating one's own identity and character, complete with a fresh set of primary commitments and values. All this must be accomplished without considering the burdensome legacy of the past and its traditions, or the social demands of conformity to a community. The problem of construing freedom negatively, as freedom from external constraint, is the loss of a common vocabulary with which people can rationally discuss their aims and cooperate in meeting them. A consistent moral vocabulary would allow them to connect their individual pursuits of satisfaction with the happiness of others and their country as a whole. Bellah and his coauthors see the fate of happiness tied closely to questions about the foundations of morality. The popular American notion of happiness through "success" epitomizes the problem, lending itself to the justification of an egoistic freedom from social restraint and a glib indifference to the common good.

This attitude toward happiness does have a provenance, however. Bellah correctly draws attention to the definition of happiness given by Hobbes, easily the most radical in the history of the concept: "Continually to be out-gone is *misery* / Continually to out-go the next before is *felicity* / And to forsake the course, is to *die*." [14] Happiness in the seventeenth century was already being reinterpreted as human nature's goad toward competition and aggression. Bellah remarks of Hobbes, "But we are beginning to see now that the race of which he speaks has no winner, and if power is our only end, the death in question may not be merely personal, but civilizational." [15] Bellah's analysis makes us aware that claims to inscrutability often mask a will-to-power. The right to pursue happiness provides the ideal opportunity for consumption and satisfaction without public challenge; right reason is not required for the privatized state of well-feeling.

Bellah's findings come as no surprise to those who had long before rejected happiness as a worthwhile aim. Freud discussed at length the supposed intrinsic cross-purposes of personal happiness and human community. Interestingly, his conception of happiness bears close affinities with that of Hobbes: both underline the aggression stemming from the happiness motive and the consequent need for some kind of social contract. This presupposition leads Freud to join those who reject happiness, while adding one more layer of commentary to the tradition of well-feeling.

Freud also accepts without question the inherited eighteenth-century notion that the universal human desire for happiness is a desire for maximum pleasure and minimal pain. But he goes a giant step further in assigning that desire a purely physiological and biological origin. In *Civilization and Its Discontents,* originally entitled "Unhappiness in Culture," he begins by identifying happiness [*Glück*] with satisfaction of instinctual drives. These drives, however, run against the grain of reality: given the "economics of the individual's libido . . . every man must find out for himself in what particular fashion he can be saved. . . . It is a question of how much real satisfaction he can expect to get from the external world, how far he is led to make himself independent of it; and, finally, how much strength he feels he has for altering the world to suit his wishes" (cf. *GBWW* I: 54, 775; II: 54, 775).

Freud recognizes a catch-22 in the human condition. The drive for instinctual gratification is destined to frustration. The external world not only fails to conform to our desires for an uninterrupted immediacy of pleasure, but the requirements of civilization also prohibit the very behavior, such as incest, polygamy, and murder, which would allow for gratification. Thus, as far as the desire for happiness goes, "there is no possibility of it being carried through. . . . One feels inclined to say that the intention that man should be 'happy' is not included in the plan of Creation" (cf. *GBWW* I: 54, 772; II: 54, 772).

Civilization demands the restriction of genital gratification for the sake of a cohesive social existence. The competition for happiness that Hobbes would limit through a social contract, Freud would stabilize through the impress of civilized laws and customs as well as the sublimation of instinct toward higher aims. The object of happiness, epitomized by the sexual orgasm and life within the womb, requires an immediacy that disallows sustained satisfaction. The sheer intensity of gratification required by the experience of happiness is incompatible with ordinary life.

Personal happiness, seen in this light, is not a rational goal. The object of psychoanalytic therapy should be "common unhappiness," Freud maintains. [16] Although the human organism finds it difficult to inhibit gratification, we can learn to mediate our pleasures and pains. Since the very thing we want cannot be possessed, Freud recommends the path of sublimation—release of these instinctual energies into higher activities such as art and work. The satisfaction of this will fall short of perfect happiness, but it will enable the patient to avoid chronic and debilitating unhappiness. Resignation enables us to cultivate lower, more realistic and socially beneficial, expectations.

In separating the moral domain from that of human desire, Freud's tone is reminiscent of Kant. Kant insisted that ethics be founded on reason rather than natural appetite. But Freud lacks Kant's religious faith that moral goodness would be rewarded with eternal happiness: a morally good will plus the satisfaction given by God equals the summum bonum. Kant and Freud both view happiness as a product of instinctual drive, not of the intellectual or psychical capacities. The higher powers only mediate the inherent dispute between the drive toward pleasure and external reality. For Freud, the only worthwhile end in sight is the common unhappiness of renunciation.

It should not be surprising that Freud's theory of happiness has been used by later psychoanalysts in rebutting some of the aspirations to well-feeling. One exception is the work of Herbert Marcuse. In *Eros and Civilization* Marcuse argues that the repression of sexual pleasure that Freud thought necessary is outmoded in a technological society. The material progress of society has created a "surplus" of repression which is no longer needed for civilization to advance. Through the liberation of sexual practices and the maximizing of genital gratification greater happiness can be secured at no cost to the social order. [17]

Marcuse's optimism stands in marked contrast to the views of Freud and of other psychoanalytic theorists. While Freud's influence insured that the hedonistic view of happiness would continue to prevail, he also injected some healthy skepticism into the attitude toward it. Freud emphasized the likelihood of false-consciousness and active self-deception in claims to happiness. This perspective casts doubts on the empirical research on happiness, since it relies on data collected from first-person reports. A Freudian might ask about the supposed benefit being derived from the correlations established by these reports? Should the data be employed by the analyst to wean the patient from the pursuit of happiness? Perhaps, but that is not the intent of the social scientists.

Freud's notion of the compulsion to repeat, implicit in the idea that human desire is fixed on pleasure, remains the basis for the psychoanalytic critique of happiness. As one analyst recently commented, "The perverted as well as the addicted would like to live in a state of unlimited narcissistic indulgence, to drift in a vast orgastic ocean, disregarding reality and decrying its limitations. . . . Can we call the resulting feeling happiness?" [18] A psychoanalyst can bring judgment to bear upon claims to happiness where contact with the given limits of reality are ignored. Adducing contentment with these limits, Isidor Silbermann suggests, is the analyst's goal for the patient. One wonders whether Freud himself would have embraced this recommendation, modest as it might seem. Psychological goals couched in positive form, such as contentment, contain their own temptations to illusory states of lasting gratification, such as that of the contented sensualist. The negative formulation of "common unhappiness" inhibits any utopian aspirations.

In Freud, sexual gratification has become the paradigm and the touchstone of happiness—"genital love" is the prototype of all happiness—although he clearly points out the futility of pursuing it in this manner. The greatest experiences of happiness are those satisfactions of sudden untamed instinctual impulses. In Freud, as derived from Kant, the biological desire for happiness belongs to the body; it arises "from below" and "dominates the mental apparatus." In the tradition of eudaemonism the desire for happiness arises from what may be said to be "above," that is, the distinguishing characteristic of the human species—rationality and its appetite for knowledge. Here in Freud the desire arises from certain drives which humans do not have in common with other species of animals. Reason is exercised not in the pursuit but in the renunciation of happiness. Our higher mental activities allow a redirection of these instinctual energies so that we may profit collectively from the benefits of a rationally orderly society.

In Freud we witness the final inversion of the classical tradition: the idea of happiness is now fundamentally at odds with what is most praiseworthy in human life. From an ideal of personal and political perfection to the primary cause and explanation of human destruction, the ideal of happiness has traveled a long way. The satisfaction that Kant rejected as a motive for a morally good action, but retained as a portion of the summum bonum, Freud regards as an inexorable human motive toward socially destructive ends.

Contemporary philosophers generally share the same suspicion of happiness; they remain reluctant to put the concept of happiness back to work. Alasdair MacIntyre, one of this generation's most influential philosophers, has consistently warned against it. He explicitly refuses to consider resuscitating the idea of happiness, in spite of his interest in virtue and the human *telos*. MacIntyre disavows happiness as a useful ethical concept, calling it "polymorphous," "morally dangerous," "a pseudo-concept," and "a conceptual fiction." The tendency since the Enlightenment, he explains, has been to understand human satisfactions as psychological preferences without reference to any external criteria. Since human beings are capable of being satisfied by "almost anything," the concept of happiness has to be kept apart from our grounds for moral choice. [19] Otherwise, people who are particularly susceptible to social conditioning will be encouraged further toward conformity by promise of happiness. Such collective aspirations can "license any enormity," for instance, the mass murder of Jews.

The modern problems of politicized happiness have been traced by Ghita Ionescu. The right to happiness has been issued like a series of "promissory notes" by governments with totalitarian intent. These promises began to be seen in the French Revolution with the rhetoric of the Jacobins, were continued forward in the utopian vision of Marx, and reached their culmination in Communist ideology. The hope for individual happiness, Ionescu argues, is inevitably smothered by the needs of mass politics under the shibboleth of public happiness. [20] The ideologies ignore the tragic side of politics, promise too much, and eventually open the door to a succession of desires as interests, each demanding their own satisfaction. They offer the promise of happiness but actually encourage a disguised struggle for power, resulting in oppression.

On a broader canvas, Eric Voegelin has analyzed this seizure of power in the name of happiness as a basic strategy of modern gnosticism. As in Ionescu's analysis of ideology, Gnostic thinkers seek to control reality and ignore its tragic limitations. They seek initially to shroud the real in a speculative system and ultimately to transform it through utopian projects. According to Voegelin, the demise of happiness as the summum bonum and the quantifying of happiness by a pleasure/pain calculus provided the perfect opportunity for this enterprise. The happiness of well-feeling allows the Gnostic to "instrumentalize" existence. The legislative "Gnostic directors of being" can ostensibly serve everyone's happiness—at the cost of their freedom. "Everybody wants to be happy, and hence everybody wants to have the power to command other people to contribute to his happiness." [21] The search for the mechanisms for acquiring the happiness to which all are entitled began, as Hazard suggested, with the political optimism of the eighteenth century. The hope of universal happiness was resounded in the millennial promises of Marx, but the darker implications of these promises were revealed in the totalitarian tactics of Lenin and Stalin's Gulag.

II. Popular views of happiness

> Anyway, there is this to be said for a volume such as Professor Phelps's *Happiness*. It is second only to a rubber duck as the ideal bathtub companion. It may be held without causing muscular fatigue or nerve strain, it may be neatly balanced back of the faucets, and it may be read through before the water has cooled. And if it slips down the drain pipe, all right, it slips down the drain pipe. (Dorothy Parker) [22]

As the concept of happiness was gradually lifted out of its traditional moral setting, a new set of problems was created for imagining a happy life. The central question was no longer, as it was among the ancients, whether happiness needed any good other than moral virtue, but whether psychological satisfaction requires ethical justification to be called true happiness. [23] Loosened from the eudaemonistic ideals of personal virtue, public citizenship, and the high calling of the *vita contemplativa,* the end represented by happiness became privatized and was transformed into a psychological and emotional state. A happy life could now be claimed by everybody on their own terms, a psychological happiness for our democratic and inclusive age. The issue of equal access to happiness is a haunting one, especially in political and economic terms, and not to be ignored.

But the solution offered by the psychological conception has, some would say, trivialized the very notion of a happy life: "Indeed, there are even philosophers who speak of happiness as if it were a *feeling.*" [24] J. S. Mill was apprehensive about this outcome when he baldly asserted it was "better to be a human being dissatisfied than a pig satisfied; better to be Socrates dissatisfied than a fool satisfied." [25] His attempt to suppress the implications of utilitarianism by assigning limits to satisfaction were, at least to most of his commentators, a failure.

Evidence for the trivialization of happiness can be found throughout the range of contemporary popular literature devoted to it. Having been identified with a subjective state, happiness is associated with practically any cause, effect, or content that is regarded as "positive." In fact, the recent entrance of this word into the language of values goes hand-in-hand with the appearance of psychological happiness. "Positivity," in its nineteenth-century meaning, represented a move away from the abstract ideals of speculative philosophy toward the concrete, the social, and the earthly plane of human action and individuality. Its mathematical connotation implies the quantitative addition of empirical and historical data to the world of thought. [26] In practice, however, the turn toward positivity has had a much greater effect than the social pragmatism envisioned by Auguste Comte. Positivity as a value has resulted in the cultivation of happiness techniques which have usurped the place once held by the moral and intellectual virtues.

These techniques offer ways of creating and maintaining mental and emotional "highs" which are free from the nagging inhibition of depression, guilt, or remorse. In his survey of the positive thinking tradition in America, a sociologist, Donald Meyer, traces the evolution of these techniques from the nineteenth-century psychology of the "mind cure," through the movements of Christian Science and Unity, to their entrance into the Protestant mainstream represented by Norman Vincent Peale and Robert Schuller. [27] Much of what Meyer discusses concerning the "psychology of auto-manipulation" and its methods of "mental photography," which is now called "visualization," is directly applicable to popular American beliefs about psychological happiness, its conditions, and its causes.

Positive thinking, as Meyer shows, encourages its adherents to turn inwardly toward the self for all the answers to their discontent; consequently, positive thinking risks denying the tragic, implacable character of much evil and suffering. It also tends to overlook the therapeutic and instrumental value of suffering. By withdrawing into the self, persons buy contentment at the cost of contact with reality, particularly the very social reality which Comte sought to elucidate. The notion of happiness generated by this tradition led toward a self insulated from the disturbances of the world. As William James writes, "Happiness like every other emotional state, has blindness and insensibility to opposing facts given it as its instinctive weapon for self-protection against disturbance." [28] One can ask whether the kind of self-deceiving figures seen in Tolstoy's *Anna Karenina* and Flaubert's *Madame Bovary* would now find themselves saved from their tragic fates by the application of mind-cure, positive-thinking, techniques. Or, perhaps, that way out has already been shown to lead toward the even greater blindness of Willy Loman in Arthur Miller's *Death of a Salesman*.

"*The classical view of happiness focused on personal character and its success in meeting the challenges of circumstance through the exercise of virtue.*" Marcus Aurelius (A.D. 121–180), a classical model of virtue, shown, in a bas-relief, receiving defeated barbarians.

"During the present century happiness has come to be identified with the possession of positive psychological states, from transient enjoyments to . . . 'being pleased' with one's life."

This confidence in a self-induced happiness through "positivity" is the common denominator in the enormous popular literature on happiness. Three of the best books in the genre, using a nonempirical approach to happiness, were written between the two world wars. They represent in its most elegant form what Meyer would call the mind-cure approach, and, it should be noted, they foreshadow the position that academic theorists would adopt in the fifties and sixties.

Bertrand Russell could certainly not plead ignorance to the classical tradition of happiness. Yet when he wrote *The Conquest of Happiness* he held that the cardinal virtue underlying happiness was not prudence, or love, or moderation but *zest*—"most universal and distinctive mark of happy men." [29] His book does not lack good advice about enjoying one's work, family, and hobbies, avoiding "Byronic unhappiness" and everyday worry, and cultivating independence of mind and high self-estimation. However, there is no hint that he regards the pursuit of happiness as either requiring a stable moral character or a moral standard as a measure. Quite the contrary, the state of happiness is a "conquest" of the energetic and independent-minded over forces of moral and spiritual gravity in the world, particularly those of organized religion and its doctrines of guilt and original sin.

More recently, Russell's attitude toward traditions of authority has been expressed once again by Paul Kurtz, who describes happiness as a "Promethean" endeavor to promote our "power" as a person. Kurtz, who is well-known as a defender of secular humanism, supports his argument with the familiar language and inflated promises of self-help: "As man enters the Space Age, the possibilities of adventure for the soaring human spirit are virtually unlimited." [30] Rhetoric of this kind, which seems to evade the tragic implications of personal limitations, misfortune, and social conditions, is typical of happiness books written for the popular market. Personal freedom allied with personal preference is writ large as the key to self-satisfaction.

Another tendency of books of this kind is to cloak their techniques in the language of magic and mysticism. The novelist John Cowper Powys was not shy about taking his philosophy of self-exaltation to a broader market. His *Art of Happiness* represents in many ways the apotheosis of the positive thinking approach. Powys encourages his reader to use "the magic of the mind" to produce the "Ichthian" and "Panergic act" of "De-incarnation" which is happiness. [31] Indeed, the very act of dissociation that Donald Meyer warned against among the prophets of the mind-cure Powys wholeheartedly recommends: "Project your soul from your troubled brain, or *pretend* to yourself that you project it." [32] Few writers in this genre are as open and consistent in pressing the logic of a self-induced happiness to its conclusion. For Powys, happiness has nothing to do with the perfection of natural capacities: happiness is artificial and can be furnished by any kind of mental trick which provides us release from painful reality. The author's level of accomplishment as a novelist in books such as *Wolf Solent* and *Weymouth Sands* is very high. Powys's recommendation of a total reliance on will and imagination at the possible cost of personal denial and social isolation cast doubts, however, upon his accomplishment as a philosopher.

The same trust in the efficacy of "mental magic" over circumstances is seen in a French contemporary of Powys and Russell, the philosopher Émile-Auguste Chartier. Under the pseudonym Alain, he wrote newspaper articles about happiness for the general public. He published ninety-three of them in a book which recommends practical techniques on how to "will one's happiness, and create it." [33] His suggestions range from better posture to wearing a constant smile to never dwelling on or even talking about one's misfortunes. Most of all, Alain insists, one should never allow sadness to detract from sociability: "Everyone seeks to live, not die; and everyone seeks out the living—by that I mean those who *say* they are happy, and who *appear* happy. What a marvelous thing human society would be if everyone put his wood on the fire instead of sniveling over the ashes!" [34] Alain's notion of encouraging happy lives, as in Powys, resembles a somewhat twisted version of Stoic tranquillity. We are directed to cultivate mental and emotional repose through close attention to mundane tasks combined with self-conscious methods of controlling thoughts, images, and moods. Tranquillity is achieved not as the concomitant of virtue, as in the Stoics, but as the result of technique.

Of course, any criticism of these books risks sounding harsh: why question the wisdom of such "positive" sounding advice? What harm can there be in managing our daily habits of thought and action in ways that result in "good cheer" about our lives? Such books, and now tapes and videos, have a devoted following and, admittedly, possess some practical solutions to problems of mood and fatigue. But the absence of any serious consideration of moral consequences implicit in their recommendations leaves a large gap between these three authors and their classical counterparts. Folk nostrums and personal prescriptions for "feeling good" reduce the human desire for happiness to a craving for subjective satisfaction. It is obvious to anyone who follows these trends that self-help techniques for momentary psychological relief raised to the level of a "philosophy of happiness" cannot satisfy that desire for happiness for very long.

Most of the kind of books I have been discussing suffer from a magnification of basic common sense. In other words, the authors take what in small doses is good advice and make too large a theory out of it—one that simply cannot do all the philosophical work required by the subject of happiness. And for those who claim these books do "help," there is the sad fact that most of them will quickly go out of print while the unhappy reader eagerly waits to consume the next one.

It has been shown that, as a consequence of its association with psychological satisfaction, the simple mention of the topic of happiness is met with either skepticism or disdain and dismissal. Some consider talk about happiness as a veiled excuse for doing whatever you feel like doing, regarding happiness as a morally unstable guide for living. They claim that the pursuit of happiness not only trivializes more sober and earnest purposes of life but also that it risks introducing an unbridled and potentially aggressive self-centeredness into our moral judgment and action. In an age when happiness is being hawked by just about everyone, it is difficult not to give some credence to these warnings. The "hucksters of happiness" promise a happy life without moral reform, a life of lasting pleasure and satisfaction resting contentedly in its own thought of itself. This seems to be precisely the message that many people want to hear and are willing to pay for.

The evidence indicates that the problems inherent in the overlapping traditions of happiness as the summum bonum and as psychological satisfaction have bequeathed an explosive conflict of meanings to the present age. What has become the unacknowledged greatest good in the public mind—subjective satisfaction—has been shown since the last half of the eighteenth century to be a questionable moral and political end. How and when happiness slipped free of its ethical moorings in classical thought and became an "Ichthian act" of "personal power" is impossible to pinpoint. It has not gone without comment, however, that some kernel of the same ambiguity was built into the American character at its foundation. Exactly what was Jefferson proposing by a right to the "pursuit of happiness"? It must be evident how radical the difference would be between his meanings if Jefferson had the eudaemonism of Aristotle clearly in mind rather than the hedonically mixed happiness of John Locke and Francis Hutcheson. [35]

The problems inherent in the psychological happiness of well-feeling are not limited to the middlebrow quality of self-help literature, or to the techniques of dissociation encouraged by positive thinkers; those problems underlie the general inarticulateness about values in private life, and they help explain the reluctance to sacrifice the energies aimed at private consumption for the sake of service to the common good. Yet, for all these issues which have been recognized since the late eighteenth century, psychological happiness nonetheless managed to receive official sanction.

III. Psychological happiness and its uses

How pregnant sometimes his replies are! a happiness that often madness hits on, which reason and sanity could not so prosperously be delivered of. (Shakespeare, *Hamlet* [*GBWW* I: 27, 42; II: 25, 42])

With the decline of eudaemonism, the idea of happiness was welcomed into the world of the social sciences. Psychological happiness, the avowed happiness of first-person reporting, has become an important subject of empirical research in both psychology and sociology. The extent of this research indicates how thoroughly the idea of happiness has been recast. The uses of psychological happiness often resemble the approaches outlined earlier in the century's popular literature, as if the call to "create your own happiness" was taken up in the name of science. But whereas objections addressed to self-help authors are unlikely to be taken to heart, those who investigate happiness scientifically are looking at the notion of well-feeling more critically.

The gradual emergence of psychological happiness fits hand-in-glove with the needs of social science research. These scholars can embrace the new conception of happiness largely because it excludes the normative and objective character of *eudaimonia*. Needing reliable empirical data from which to generate quantifiable conclusions, social scientists have the most to gain from the identification of happiness with positive subjective experiences. Classical notions of happiness which originated in larger theories of human nature and goodness create a problem of "hybridity" which compromises the purely experiential basis of reported happiness. With the moral criteria of classical happiness put aside, happiness can belong to the domain of the scientist rather than to that of the philosopher.

Social scientists correctly point out that philosophers themselves have never agreed upon the objective conditions of happiness, making the employment of objective standards in their investigation seem arbitrary. Empirical scientists simply rely on the reliability of first-person reports: if anyone says they are happy, they are. The imposition of value systems has no place in empirical research; thus, judgments about real and illusory happiness are banished.

It comes as no surprise that the scientists who study happiness have little interest in philosophical reflection on the subject. The comment of one psychologist of happiness to the effect that "little theoretical progress in understanding happiness has been made in the two millennia since the time of the Greek philosophers" was not intended as a compliment to philosophy. Even the humanistic and existential psychologists, whose theories are indebted to the earlier traditions, exhibit little interest in their philosophical precursors on happiness. [36]

One exception to this situation is Ruut Veenhoven, whose survey of the literature is the most comprehensive to date. [37] He pays close critical attention to the conceptual presuppositions and the semantic consistency of happiness research. He lists many of the vague and contradictory terms employed by researchers. Part of the problem, as he shows, is that social scientists have differing practical aims: some are interested in individual clinical results; others are concerned with advancing education or the productivity of the workplace. Some social psychologists amass "social indicators" of happiness which enable them to compare the "quality of life" between different classes, ages, genders, cities, and even nations. However, a lack of conceptual consistency, Veenhoven admits, plagues their attempts.

Although the social scientists who study happiness have found it necessary to reject any objective conditions, many of them have failed to follow any consistent or coherent definition of happiness. The description of happiness used by the psychologist Jonathan Freedman is characteristic: happiness "is a positive, enduring state that consists of positive feelings about the self and the world and that includes both peace of mind and active pleasures and joy." [38] Such rambling attempts at defining happiness stumble over the ambiguity of words like "feeling." One may ask whether he intends to include any kind of emotion as long as it is viewed as "positive"? And, again, what does "positive" mean? Does he mean to say that happy people never countenance negative or, presumably, critical feelings—that is, that they never disapprove of themselves or their world? Finally, why does Freedman need to specify "peace of mind," "active pleasures," and "joy"? Except for the notion of an "active" pleasure, his definition seems arbitrary, given the long list of qualifiers that could be subsumed under his rubric of "positive feelings."

But in spite of vague and contradictory theoretical constructs, happiness research is booming. Veenhoven collects over 2,000 studies conducted between 1912 and 1976, and other recent surveys by Michael Argyle and Ed Diener suggest that the number of studies by social scientists is multiplying at an astonishing rate. [39] Taken together, these research surveys provide an overview of the work on happiness in the social sciences.

The tools of the happiness researchers are interviews and questionnaires. The actual measuring instruments vary greatly from study to study. Approaches range from direct and indirect questions, interviews, peer-ratings, pictorial face-scales (reactions to drawings of happy and sad faces), and Rorschach inkblots. Nearly all of them rely entirely on first-person reports of "happiness," "satisfaction," "contentment," and so forth. A data base of happiness is rapidly mounting, with the "correlates," "conditions," and "indicators" of happiness being quantified as a result. Scales to measure this data have been developed: some purport only to measure specific items such as mood or positive and negative affect, others aim more broadly at measuring "subjective well-being" or "satisfaction with life." Some of the better known of the scales are Bradburn's Affect Balance Scale (1969), Andrews & Withey's Semantic Differential Happiness Scales (1976), Larsen's Affective Intensity Measure (1983), the Fordyce Happiness Measure (1972), and Kammaan and Flett's Affectometer (1983).

Studies have targeted such disparate items as "mood," "life satisfaction," "peak experiences," "well-being," "quality of life," "morale," "mental state," "adjustment," "contentment," "hedonic level," "evaluation of life," "elation," and "positive attitudes toward life." Veenhoven admits that this "babble of tongues" has made it very difficult to compare findings between the studies. Out of more than 2,000 abstracts of research, Veenhoven could accept only 156 as containing acceptable indicators of happiness. His stringent requirements stem from an attempt to organize a definition of happiness as "satisfaction with life-as-a-whole." It is notable that Veenhoven wants to go beyond measuring momentary satisfactions by factoring in Aristotle's ancient insistence that lives could be judged happy only if taken as a whole.

Most social scientists, and even some modern philosophers, base their rejection of third-person judgments on the assumption that a person's own report about his or her happiness is privileged. Each individual person is in the best, if not the only, position to know the facts of the case. Such information can only be gathered from the inside, so to speak; thus, our only access to information about happiness is to listen to what people say about themselves. For these defenders of psychological happiness, judging another person "happy" is no longer part of the general estimation of character demanded by social existence. Such appraisals of character are commonly found to be a part of making choices about people who will become significant in our lives. In fact, it can be observed that the theorists of psychological happiness deny in their theories a kind of judgment which is a daily part of social life, regardless of how tricky and inaccurate these judgments may be.

It has been asked whether or not this reliance on reported happiness will prove problematic in supporting the social indicators for quality-of-life studies. [40] Researchers admit to a number of unresolved questions about the possible bias of their findings. Beyond obvious concern about fluctuation of mood and its effect on self-reporting, there are some serious issues. First, there is the semantic problem already mentioned: when someone is asked whether they are either "satisfied," "somewhat satisfied," or "very satisfied" in their life, how is the researcher to know what the person being interviewed takes as "satisfaction" or the degrees of it being sought? Second, there is a tendency to exaggerate claims to happiness, when it is held as socially desirable. Veenhoven remarks that anonymity in interviews encourages more honest reporting. Third, the entire setting of the interview and the relationship between interviewer and respondent can strongly influence what is said. For example, how much time were people given to think about their answers? Are respondents uniformly at a good time in their lives to answer questions about life satisfaction? Last, and perhaps most problematic, can people be counted upon to give accurate accounts of their feelings, their emotions, and their satisfactions? Are we not disposed, especially in hard times, toward distortion, denial, defensiveness, and repression?

Diener mentions a number of factors that concern researchers who rely upon self-reporting: unhappy people tend to report being happy when they are not, especially when they live in a society where happiness is considered normative. Also, there is evidence that people are influenced by their moods: they tend to recall past events consonant with current affect. For Diener, however, none of these factors presents a major problem. Studies show, surprisingly, that happiness is not socially desirable to the extent that self-reporting would be compromised. Furthermore, studies employing self-report are found to correlate substantially with external criteria such as personality measures, demographic variables, facial coding such as smiling and laughing, and peer reports. Yet, Diener comments, more substantiation of self-reporting by external criteria is needed.

These problems, though recognized by some "eudologists," do not stymie their research or their confidence in their conclusions. In his *The Psychology of Happiness* Argyle expresses confidence both in research based upon self-reporting and in the conclusions he draws from it. He dismisses summarily the problems of self-reporting: "If someone says they are very satisfied with, say, their mud hut on stilts, then we must assume they *are*." [41] This laissez-faire view of happiness, as we will see, is not without philosophical support.

Argyle investigates both the happiness of global satisfaction and the happiness of transient positive emotions, organizing his data, unlike Veenhoven, with both ends in view. His conclusions are optimistic: it is possible to increase the happiness of oneself and of others. The first of his seven suggestions is as follows: "Short-term increases in positive mood can be induced by thinking about recent pleasant events, watching funny films or TV, listening to cheerful music, and to some extent by reciting positive self-statements, by smiles, jokes, small presents and hypnosis. The effects tend to be rather brief, but these activities can be engaged in regularly. The only drug which seems to be successful is alcohol, but in doses which are not too large." [42] It must give some readers pause that after the study and collation of over 300 studies the author advises us to watch "funny films or TV."

But if this advice is given to help short-term mood, the rest of his seven suggestions for long-term satisfaction fail to extend our knowledge past what seems good common sense. Argyle suggests that we can increase happiness by making a log of our most intense pleasures, which presumably would remind us to repeat them more often, by working at having good relationships, by enjoying our work and leisure, and by looking at things more positively. Given the promise of surpassing the Greeks, one can only ask how such conclusions surpass, or even approach, what the Greeks knew in the fifth century B.C. Given that a "science" of happiness is being promised, should one expect new insights or the testing of old ones?

Veenhoven's and Diener's aggregate of correlations to happiness are both more serious and a better indication of the contribution being made by researchers. Among Veenhoven's findings are the conclusions that factors such as gender, income, education, intelligence, social rank, unemployment, ascetic living, and being an only child do not affect happiness. His correlations also debunk what he calls the myth about the prevalence of unhappiness in Western society, which has been thought to result from the increasing pressures of industrialization, urbanization, and pace of life. He recognizes that such conclusions have tremendous political significance and offers careful and repeated disclaimers about both the quality of the data and the possibility of generating lawlike generalizations from that data. Nonetheless, he firmly declares his purpose is the promotion of happiness through the application of social science.

Diener organizes the research under the rubric of subjective well-being. His concern is with discovering the cognitive and affective factors influencing people who experience their lives in positive ways. Subjective well-being, as the name suggests, resides within the experience of the individual and relies upon the standards of the respondent to determine the good life. It involves a global assessment of one's life with both positive and negative measures. Like Veenhoven, Diener's happiness occupies a middle ground between normative and positive affect theories.

Contemporary happiness research really began in the 1960s when one of the first cumulative studies portrayed the happy person as a "young, healthy, well-educated, well-paid, extroverted, optimistic, worry-free, religious, married person, with high self-esteem, high job morale, modest aspirations, of either sex and of a wide range of intelligence." [43] Many of these correlations, as Diener says, have not held up under later scientific scrutiny. On the other hand, Norman Bradburn's early research into the independent relation of positive and negative affect has become a kind of cornerstone in the scientific understanding of happiness. Bradburn developed a scale to measure emotional well-being: happiness is really a global judgment people make by comparing their negative affect with their positive affect. His Affect Balance Scale works by subtracting the sum of negative items from the sum of positive ones, meaning that the absence of negative affect is not equivalent to the presence of positive affect. Thus, to enhance life one must go beyond the removal of life's irritations and supply causes of positive enjoyment.

Perhaps the most important contribution of this research is its exploration of the causes of happiness. Diener distinguishes between objective conditions and subjective conditions and raises important overall questions concerning the direction of causality. For example, among subjective factors self-esteem or self-satisfaction consistently receives the highest correlation with reports of happiness. Does this mean that self-esteem contributes to happiness or vice versa? The same is true of objective factors: do they cause happiness or does a happy person regard these factors in different ways than does an unhappy person?

This same problem of causality can be couched in terms of "top-down" vs. "bottom-up" theories of happiness. A top-down view regards happiness as a trait rather than a state, something like an attitude a person has toward himself and the world. Diener calls it a "global propensity to experience things in a positive way" which, in turn, colors a person's reading of life, its fortunes and misfortunes. The bottom-up theory is a "collection view" that considers happiness a state of summed pleasures, an accumulation of happy moments. "In the bottom-up approach, a person should develop a sunny disposition and sanguine outlook as positive experiences accumulate in the person's life." [44] The issue raised by the contrast between the two positions is a crucial one for happiness, since it raises together both the classical problem of objective success and the modern confidence in the power of mind over circumstance.

Among objective factors, the relation between income and happiness appears to be much more significant at the extreme of poverty, while the happiness of the wealthy is closely tied to their concomitant access to status and power. There is no clear correlation between age and happiness, except slightly more satisfaction among the old and positive affect among the young. Women are not happier than men but women report greater enjoyment. Blacks report more unhappiness than whites, but this data is difficult to separate from other factors, such as wealth and health. Interestingly, since the political advances of the late 1960s, blacks have reported even less happiness. Unemployment definitely harvests unhappiness, while education has little direct impact. Religious people report more positive moods, especially if they are young. Married people are happier, unless they have children.

His survey of the research leads Diener to conclude that subjective well-being will not be accounted for by a small number of variables— too many factors influence it. One interesting example of its complexity is the data regarding the intimate relation of pleasure and pain. Studies show that seeking a permanent state of fulfillment proves to be counterproductive. We are made happier by the cyclic fulfillment of "deprivation-based need" than by unremitting joy. Thus related, life's enjoyments and distresses point the way toward a more profound notion of the happy life, one that eschews the desire for pure immediacy and appreciates the role of suffering in reaching worthwhile aims.

Diener's findings suggest that avowed happiness actually may bear an eudaemonistic reading. Alan S. Waterman attempts to measure what he calls the experience of "personal expressiveness" implicit in the classical notion of *eudaimonia*. [45] Like other psychologists, he measures patterns and levels of reported satisfaction. However, Waterman distinguishes between satisfaction taken in mundane activities, offering momentary pleasures and satisfactions, and those that contribute to an overall sense of well-being and identity. His research confirms that greater satisfaction is taken in personally expressive activities—those activities in which individuals actualize their highest potentials.

To experience an activity as personally expressive, that is as eudaemonistic, the activity must "further our purposes in living, that is, those ends that are considered worth having or desiring in life." Activities will be experienced as personally expressive to the extent that they are recognized as the means for progressing toward goals that represent the most desirable kind of life. Waterman's suggestion that all such activities should be enjoyed is reminiscent of Aristotle's view that the happiest life is also the most pleasant one.

The question which naturally occurs is whether the enjoyment of any kind of goals or purposes which render a person personally expressive also renders a person happy in the classical sense. Waterman admits that he is not dealing with the normative questions of moral limits. He also acknowledges that working out of the tradition of *eudaimonia* entails greater problems in the use of self-reporting. Whereas a person can hardly be said to be wrong about reports of their own hedonic state, a person's appraisal of their own deepest potentials and the activities that realize them complicate this research.

As in some contemporary philosophers (as we will see) who seek to revive eudaemonism, certain aspects of the classical picture are employed while others are ignored. Personal ideals, human excellence, and individual responsibility are all implied by Aristotle's happy life in accordance with virtue. Waterman's contribution to research on happiness is to suggest that the subjective component of *eudaimonia* cannot be divorced from specific kinds of activities—they cannot be trivialized without loss. Greater satisfaction is found in the experiences that result from efforts "to live in accordance with one's daimon."

Another significant contribution toward a more eudaemonistic understanding of happiness is Mihaly Csikszentmihalyi's study of the phenomenon called *flow*. [46] The original data was taken from a study of rock-climbers who exemplify the experience of being so engrossed in a difficult but delightful activity that they lose consciousness of themselves. The sense of self reemerges more strongly when the activity is finished; thus, the experience of flow enhances both the activity and the person. Findings reinforce a eudaemonistic reading of happiness because flow activities are *autotelic*, that is, done for their own sake. Any thought of utility, or a "payoff," must be absent. Aristotle's analysis of pleasure once again is confirmed: pleasure is the concomitant result of activities. Aim at pleasure directly and you miss it.

195

To experience the "optimal experience" of flow, the activity must be one we can complete; it must fall within our skill range while not being too easy for us. We must be able to concentrate on the activity and to block out the anxieties of daily life. We must experience ourselves as being in control of our actions and seeking determinate goals which promise immediate feedback. Out of analysis by Csikszentmihalyi, several recommendations are generated, such as setting rational goals, cultivating concentrated attention, and seeking the ability "to control inner experience which in turn enables us to determine the quality of life." [47]

Social scientists stop short of tackling the moral question of what is good for us, but many of their findings lead back toward eudaemonism. Reflection on happiness has turned a corner. Some of the factors which were once eliminated from *eudaimonia* in order to allow for the emergence of a purely psychological happiness are reappearing and rising to the top in their findings. The well-feeling of satisfaction, we find, points outwardly toward the consideration of overall human excellence.

This development can also be seen in one of the recent uses of the research data on happiness. Starting with a definition of happiness as "justified satisfaction," Charles Murray plots a course through much of the same empirical research treated by Veenhoven and Diener and formulates some recommendations for a public policy that will support our "pursuit of happiness" better. His concern is with describing the conditions which *enable* persons to pursue their happiness with the least amount of obstruction. Governments cannot guarantee our pursuits will be successful, but they can remove unnecessary obstructions, especially those that were mistakenly put in place in the name of happiness. Murray attempts such an explanation by moving backward, as it were, from the data toward recovering a philosophy of human nature.

Much of Murray's argument amounts to the encouragement of growth in small communities—"little platoons." Good social policy consists in recognizing that people need to pursue the basic goods of life by themselves; they do not need instruction in happiness, but they do need to be freed from coercion by others. Among the obstacles to social interaction is lawlessness and the growing lack of public civility. To provide for the need of safety, governments must overcome the "rulefulness" symbolized by the *Miranda* decision which makes law enforcement appear overly complicated and inefficient. Lacking the perception that they, the police, and the courts have the power to enforce community standards of public civility, the citizenry's need for safety is unsatisfied and the bonds of community are inevitably weakened as people live in irritation and sometimes outright fear.

Another problem, Murray argues, is the established public policy of providing the basic material needs of the poor before addressing the conditions affecting happiness. The data about happiness do not support this approach. Given the basic "nutrients" of happiness, the way in which the basic material resources are provided must be considered: "The ways in which people go about achieving safety, self-respect, and self-fulfillment in their lives are inextricably bound up with each other and with the way in which people go about providing for their material well-being. We do not have the option of doing one good thing at a time." [48]

Murray uses much of the data to rethink the aims and justification of social assistance programs. If self-esteem, internality, and work are strong correlates of reported happiness, public policy must seek ways of encouraging individuals' responsibility for their lives and their possession of material goods. Murray recasts the notion of self-esteem into self-respect, since the former is so often promoted without relation to any discernible excellence in character or success in life. Unrestrained self-esteem breeds sheer narcissism. Self-respect is gained by actual achievement—we cannot have too much of it. The "enabling condition" of self-respect comes, in part, with earning one's own way in life. Long-term welfare recipients suffer the loss of self-respect because they lack a range of basic achievements crucial to being satisfied with their lives. The appeal to self-esteem, in this context, becomes the pretext for covering people's real needs with the blanket of an unjustified satisfaction, with the resulting loss of self-respect and enjoyment of life.

Murray's construal of the research data has been challenged on the basis that it ignores scholarship that would undermine his confidence in rational self-interest, in the nurturing community, and in the native ability of every person to gain access to economic opportunity. [49] Undoubtedly the issue of a "level playing field" raises serious questions for any social theorist of individual responsibility. There is also the political responsibility of making sure that access to material goods is available to anyone who makes a reasonable effort to obtain them.

Yet, in spite of restrictive social structures, one can still argue on the basis of happiness research that the pursuit of well-feeling subverts lasting happiness or *eudaimonia*. The science of happiness may be undercutting the very concept of happiness that gave it birth.

IV. Philosophers on happiness

> For it is perfectly true that the matters we are discussing are by no means trivial; rather, they are the very ones which to know is noblest and not to know is most disgraceful: the sum and substance of them is either to recognize or fail to recognize who is happy and who is not.
> (Plato, *Gorgias* [cf. *GBWW* I: 7, 265; II: 6, 265])

Most contemporary philosophers assume the primacy of psychological satisfaction in happiness. Locke and J. S. Mill, not Aristotle and Aquinas, set the parameters of the discussion. Rather than begin with the question of the best life and then proceed to question the concomitant satisfaction that accompanies it, philosophers start with satisfaction and then inquire about its possible justification. Some do not think that a justified satisfaction is necessary. Others provide reasonable criteria for evaluating happiness claims. Without undue exertion, the results can be organized into four sections—extreme subjectivism, subjectivism, moderate objectivism, and objectivism. Other typologies could be used, but this one focuses on the contrast of well-feeling with eudaemonism and the search for a justified happiness.

Before beginning the survey it would be helpful to review briefly the general characteristics of eudaemonism, so that the actual proximity of the modern accounts to the classical can be gauged. [50] Happiness is a global consideration; that is, whole lives rather than momentary states can be called happy. Happy lives are measured by a single standard, the summum bonum; the greatest or final good applies equally to everyone, based upon their human nature. That standard, however, is somewhat flexible: a person's individual capabilities, taste, luck, and social circumstances are relevant to judgments about happiness.

For the eudaemonist, final ends can be dominant or inclusive; they can specify one end, e.g., contemplation, or an aggregate of goods to be pursued in life. Either way, the moral and intellectual virtues are necessary to achieve the final end, either as instrumental to it or as constitutive of it. The requirement of virtue makes happiness a matter of character and personal responsibility—not accident, technique, or magic.

States of well-feeling, such as pleasure and satisfaction, belong to happy lives, but only as they are mediated by virtuous dispositions. What is true of pleasure is also true of the other basic goods: wealth, honor, work, etc. The presence of virtue insures that they will not be abused. The possession of any good, regardless of how highly prized, does not automatically bestow happiness. Judgments about happiness involve evaluations of character and circumstances in accordance with a norm provided by human nature.

(1) Extreme subjective theorists are at the other end of the spectrum relative to eudaemonism. While relying upon purely introspective criteria—whether pleasure, enjoyment, a satisfied state of mind—they insist upon the descriptive character of claims to happiness. The inner states that constitute happiness may be complicated by such questions as time, intensity, depth, and objects, but "being happy" is ultimately a report about how one views oneself in the world. As G. H. von Wright puts it, viewed in this way happiness is fundamentally an "attitude." Consequently, third-person judgments are dismissed as either "an expression of envy" or "a disguise for our own evaluation." [51] The sole crite-

rion for knowing whether someone is happy is his or her own report of it.

Some of the larger implications of extreme subjectivism are evident in the work of Robin Barrow, who develops a theory along the lines suggested by von Wright. He argues against any specific material or objective conditions which might be considered necessary to the happy life. "A man might be poor, yet happy; he might be sick, yet happy; he might be friendless, yet happy; he might be unpleasant, yet happy; he might even be retired to bed to pass dried peas from one saucepan to another, yet be happy." [52] Barrow dismisses the classical linkage of virtue with happiness by arguing, for instance, that there is no contradiction in the idea of a selfish person who is also happy. Furthermore, he defends the avowed happiness of the drug-induced high as well as that of the habitually self-deceived, saying that in both cases the delusion creates the happiness. Even the Orwellian specter of mass indoctrination holds the promise of genuine happiness. [53] And just so as not to leave doubt in anyone's mind about his rejection of all moral limits to happiness, he refuses to rule out the idea that Hitler may have been happy. We cannot deny a person's happiness simply because their good state of mind was caused by something we find repulsive.

Since happiness is a certain state of mind, it belongs more to the study of psychology than to that of philosophy. For Barrow, as for von Wright, the only reliable source for finding out about an individual's happiness is his or her own report of it. Barrow's argument supports the contention of social scientists that happiness can only be understood through the study of states of satisfaction and feeling to which each individual holds privileged access; the researcher has to take the subject's word for it.

However, Barrow's discussion is helpful in clarifying the extreme subjectivist position: happiness can be termed a sense of "enmeshment" with the world. Enmeshment signifies harmony. While enmeshed, a person will either not seek to withdraw from the world, nor seek relief from it, nor care to reform it. One's sense of enmeshment can rest on any rationale or belief, even those that are false or delusional, and be the product of any state of affairs. Thus, claims to happiness are limited only by the requirement that they be intelligible as reports of inner states, nothing more.

Given that happiness is the sense of enmeshment, two logical features of the concept emerge which would hold true in every instance: first, only creatures with self-consciousness can be happy, and second, being happy is fundamentally incompatible with certain negative states such as loneliness, nervousness, depression, self-doubt, low self-esteem, guilt, and remorse. In other words, being happy in the psychological sense requires self-conscious awareness of being pleased with one's state. To be in a state where one wishes that circumstances would change is incompatible with a report of "being happy." Happiness reports are intelligible to the extent that they express a favorable attitude toward one's situation in the world. To be happy means that a person does not wish the world to be different from itself. The inclination to reject one's circumstances is the only infallible symptom of unhappiness.

(2) The subjectivist argues that claims to happiness require something more than a psychological or hedonic state. Philosophers who propose subjective theories of happiness agree that individuals claiming happiness employ some criteria of self-evaluation. This stress on "internality" places subjectivism a step closer to eudaemonism. However, theorists agree that all the criteria for happiness remain in the province of personal preference.

Reasons for rejecting extreme subjectivism are given by Irwin Goldstein in his analysis of phrases like "true happiness, "real happiness," and "deep happiness." Those who insist that happiness is entirely a hedonic notion fail to recognize that people commonly employ non-hedonic criteria in talking about their happiness and others. "There seems to be enough reason to say that while being hedonic, happiness words are also non-hedonically evaluative." [54] One reason for this lies in the long-standing utopian character of happiness concepts, that is, the attempt in the classical and medieval traditions to recommend an ideal life with their notions of happiness. Goldstein points out numerous ways in which our talk about happiness remains evaluative, not just descriptive of inner satisfaction. Before we call a man happy we require that his desires be both good and commendable.

For Goldstein, philosophers who derive an extreme subjectivist theory from ordinary language actually ignore the complexity in everyday usage for the sake of simplified, uncontroversial explanation. Conversation is replete with examples that do not conform to the paradigm of inscrutable well-feeling. Claims about happiness, then, cannot be as one-dimensional as the extreme subjectivist believes them to be. Simply because people commonly express "being happy" about trivial things, such as a cool day's relief from a hot summer, does not imply that all happiness usage should be understood in hedonic ways.

It has been argued, for example, that the word *friendship* is used in a similar way, without the same consequences. The fact that we use "friend" to describe recent acquaintances does not preclude our reasonably applying it to our oldest and closest friends. [55] "Happiness" has an analogous latitude. Usage does not support its reduction to a mere description of a certain prized hedonic state, whether maximized pleasure, lasting satisfaction, peace of mind. Our talk about happiness is a complex of related factors: how one came to possess happiness, one's prospects for keeping it, and its effect on our lives. Such considerations serve both to justify actual claims to happiness and to govern its pursuit. Goldstein's analysis of ordinary language offers support to the position that both in usage and in reflection the idea of happiness recommends a way of life.

But the subjectivist stops short of recommending any external criteria in weighing claims to happiness. In what is the most widely discussed contemporary philosophical treatment of happiness, Richard Kraut rejects the extreme subjectivist position, arguing that happiness claims inevitably involve more than a report or description of a psychological state: to call oneself happy involves an *appraisal* of one's life in terms of one's standards and goals. We do in fact expect reports of happiness to arise out of some set of standards and goals, but we have no way of criticizing those standards themselves.

In other words, reports of "feeling satisfied" are contextual, as it were, in the amalgam of intentions and purposes persons have chosen for their life. "When a person is asked what his idea of happiness is, he quite naturally answers by describing the kind of life he would like to lead." [56] Thus an inquiry into a person's claim to happiness is tantamount to asking about what aims and purposes guide his life. To claim that one is satisfied implies that one is satisfied in having reached some goal or another.

For Kraut, persons are happy if they truly perceive that their major desires in life are being satisfied. Two aspects of this definition go beyond the extreme subjectivist position. First, the self-deceived are not happy—real achievement is a necessary condition. Second, he distinguishes between first-order desires for individual objects and second-order desires underlying whole sets of first-order desires. Only the satisfaction of second-order desires touches the heart of personal happiness; they express our self-identity and chosen purposes. But neither set of desires needs to be justified by an external standard. Kraut cannot accept the traditional appeals to human nature or social convention, while admitting that his relativism provides little direction in how to live our lives. Subjectivists tell us only that we should seek to possess what we value; they cannot tell us what is objectively valuable.

(3) The issue that drives the discussion toward a moderate objective theory is the justification for calling personal satisfaction "happiness." Are there standards for the happy life which exceed the internal limits espoused by subjectivists? A number of writers have offered accounts that seek to define certain external standards for judging claims to happiness. These accounts differ, however, in the specific goods and values necessary to a happy life and in the standards of personhood and rationality necessary to an acceptable "life-plan." The philosophical mainstream presently lies somewhere between this position and the subjectivist. Moderate objectivists seek a justified happiness, but they distinguish themselves from objectivists by repudiating any final good

by which all lives can be measured. They often refer to themselves as offering "minimalist" theories of happiness and evince discomfort with the kind of specificity about ideal lives that a "maximal" account would require. But they agree that something more than an individual, subjective standard is required.

For instance, the subjectivist cannot account for the complexity of our judgments about happiness. We are disinclined to accept claims based upon the satisfaction of abhorrent desires. If we despise the set of desires being satisfied, such as those of an opium addict, we do not judge the addict to be happy. On that basis, Richard Hare distinguishes between calling a person satisfied and calling him happy. Before we call someone happy, "we find it necessary to be sure, not only that *his* desires are satisfied, but also that the complete set of his desires is one which we are not very much averse to having ourselves." [57] We are in the habit of ascribing happiness to people who are, in some sense, whole and complete. For Hare, such judgments involve two kinds of criteria, one internal to another's life and the other internal to our own, yet shared with others.

Some moderate objectivists in seeking to specify these shared criteria are more minimal than others. Richard Warner, for example, emphasizes that happiness requires the satisfaction of a special class of "E-desires." Like second-order desires, these desires are integral to the realization of one's self-concept; they have objects to which we are self-consciously and freely committed. The importance of personhood informs Warner's argument for the relation of freedom to desire: one must seek to satisfy E-desires often, believe that they are being satisfied, enjoy their satisfaction, and find these desires worthy of being desired. [58]

These criteria provide Warner with grounds for rejecting the claims to happiness of those people who seek to satisfy thoughtless and random desires. However, his emphasis on self-concept as a necessary condition of happiness does not allow him to reject the claims of someone who, for example, devotes himself to counting blades of grass. For Warner, it is not necessary that all the values implicit in the realization of a person's self-concept be truly valuable: "Misspent lives need not be unhappy ones." The Counter, as Warner calls him, by virtue of his freely chosen commitment to his self-concept, is justified in claiming happiness. Warner admits that although he would like to criticize the Counter, he cannot do so given the breadth of his criteria: self-concepts cover a great deal of ground. The Counter has a freely chosen self-concept, knows what he wants, and finds it satisfying.

Other moderate objectivists maintain somewhat higher standards. Lynne McFall also applies the notion of personhood to happiness, but she finds that lives like that of the Counter are unhappy. Her overall project aims at salvaging J. S. Mill's denial of "pig-happiness." She objects to Kraut's subjectivism because it cannot support his treatment of self-deception in happiness and because it avoids altogether the issue of justifying standards. A consistent subjectivist would notice that many people in fact are willing to call happy someone who is both satisfied and deluded about having met his or her aims in life—"What if one prefers to be deceived?" [59]

She distinguishes between three conceptions of long-term happiness: satisfaction, affirmation, and justified affirmation or evaluative happiness. Satisfaction is common to each of these conceptions, but only evaluative happiness can provide an appropriate standard for judging a person's life. McFall, like other moderate objectivists, wants to provide an answer to the question that subjectivists cannot answer—"What *ought* we to care about?"

A minimum objective ideal of happy lives is proposed by employing a standard of "rationality" as it bears upon the meaning of personhood and "value-constituted" goods. McFall argues that it is always rational for persons to maximize value: as persons our values must meet this requirement of maximizing value, or we can be said to have fallen short. This is not proposed as a standard which stands independently of persons' lives, but rather as one that derives its force from the fact that it is "important to us."

Seven minimal conditions are considered necessary for the happiness of "rational affirmation": logical consistency, conformity of behavior with value, motivation by reason, conscious awareness of values, absence of regret, belief in justified values, and affirmation of one's whole life. Beliefs do not have to be true for happiness, but they must be "well-grounded." Truth sets too high a standard of justification and knowledge, one that we do not have. However, McFall adds, rational affirmation requires that one must be able to overcome the experience of learning that one's beliefs were false without sliding into dissatisfaction.

Like other minimal theorists, McFall stops short of a more "radical objectivism." The positing of values completely independent of actual beliefs is, she argues, both impossible and incoherent: "What is important *is* what is important to us. Our standards could have no further support." [60]

In spite of their rejection of happiness as an ideal final end, moderate objectivists often refer to themselves as eudaemonists. This appellation is at least partly justified, not only by their bringing moral concerns of "the good life" to bear upon claims to a happy life, but also by their emphasizing human excellence in general. John Kekes, for example, prefers to speak of eudaemonism rather than happiness, since many of the heroes and saints we admire and emulate deliberately eschewed the contentment we now identify with happiness. But Kekes's eudaemonism steers clear of a final good which gives human life the instrumental character of serving a predetermined end. [61] He considers the diversity in conceptions of good lives evidence enough for rejecting such a theory. Respect for pluralism requires that we affirm a eudaemonism that balances between morality and human individuality. The philosophical weight once allotted to human nature has shifted to the historical tradition. Many good lives are possible within the broad canvas of tradition, making it impossible to specify all their necessary conditions.

The general test of good lives is the lasting possession of external and internal goods and a satisfaction in these goods that is greater than any suffering. The subjectivist would agree and would insist that individuals must seek what goods are valuable to them; but Kekes argues that beliefs about values can be incorrect. We can make third-person objective judgments by appealing to minimal moral standards for good lives. These standards are minimal in the sense that they are both incomplete and insufficient, but they are objective in that they apply to everyone regardless of what they believe. These conditions are not infallible guides to good lives, although we can use them with certainty to predict what lives will fail.

Like Kekes, James Griffin also rejects both subjectivist accounts of happiness but stops well short of a "perfectionist" theory of happiness: there is no single ideal life by which we measure how close each of us is to happiness. Such an ideal blatantly disregards the individual variations of the human excellences that make up well-being. In its place, Griffin offers the most elaborate of moderate objectivist accounts. He declares his break with the utilitarian tradition by following the trail of informed desire as opposed to actual desires. As seen in the habits of consumerism, actual desires can be faulty—people sometimes want things that harm their well-being. Moreover, actual-desire accounts cannot explain why we desire some things over just positive states of mind. When a father wishes happiness for his children, "what he wants, what is valuable to him, is a state of the world, not a state of his mind; merely to delude him into thinking that his children flourish, therefore, does not give him what he values." [62] The fulfillment of human desire cannot be understood in just a psychological way: a desire is fulfilled when what is desired comes about.

Griffin's informed-desire account places happiness once again in the public arena. Happiness no longer depends entirely upon the makeup of individual desires: some values are "values for everyone," even while they might be in conflict in the lives of certain individuals. He develops a minimum list of objective prudential values, prudence meaning the factors that bear upon a person's self-interest. The global realization of these fundamental values holds the best chance for a happiness that is at once sensitive to the differences between individuals and in opposition to pig-happiness. These values which "contribute to making a normal human life go well" provide Griffin with more determinate content than other moderate theories of happiness: (1) accomplishment, (2) the components of human existence: autonomy, health, liberty, etc., (3) understanding, (4) enjoyment, and (5) deep personal relations. [63] His argument in support of these values is consensual, meaning almost everybody would be willing to affirm them.

While individuals will agree on these values in theory, they will realize them in differing ways. Thus, like the other moderate objectivists, Griffin cannot tell us specifically what purpose in life one ought to pursue. Yet Griffin is optimistic about the individual inclinations: persons who *want* to fulfill these basic prudential aims will find they *ought* to follow some moral standards. Prudential values and moral values to a large extent coincide. "Part of having a life of point and substance is having a life in which moral reasons take their place, along with other practical reasons, in motivation." [64] Griffin, like other moderates, can go no further than this; he is bound by his rejection of the perfectionist position to keep the moral content of his theory at the level of a formal necessity.

(4) An objectivist theory of happiness can embrace the content and the rationale of other theories. It can acknowledge the necessity of subjective satisfaction without regarding it as the only content of happiness. An objectivist can affirm the importance of freely choosing personal goals and being committed to personal values without a relativist accent on the "personal." An objectivist could no doubt stress the importance of employing a rational approach to weighing and measuring important choices within the context of an overall life-plan that embraces what are regarded consensually as the basic goods of life—as long as the weighing and measuring is done with a universal and determinate goal in mind.

The problem that arises for the objectivist when he surveys his minimalist counterpart is the question of how those basic goods are ordered and how the life-plan is chosen. Does not some single factor have to outweigh the others? Do not both practical deliberation and action require a final end without which these basic goods simply square off in incommensurable confusion? And most of all, is not the idea of happiness inextricably wed to facts about human nature and not to the results of individual deliberation? Or, are we back to square one of personal preference?

Among contemporary philosophers, Thomists have most consistently addressed the issue of happiness in line with the tradition of eudaemonism. However, their philosophical work, especially in the area of ethics, is complicated by the fact that the existence and the content of the summum bonum is anchored by Christian belief. Because of this, Maritain, a leading modern Thomist, caused some controversy fifty years ago when he proposed an outright subordination of moral philosophy to moral theology. Moral philosophy, he argued, could not provide an adequate account of our ordination to God—it needs theology to provide its revealed data.

Few Thomistic philosophers have been willing to adopt this strategy explicitly. Nonetheless, the topic of human happiness will have immediate theological implications for Thomists and will remind them of the limits of their philosophical enterprise. While some Thomists continue to affirm that the immortality of the soul and the existence of God can be established by rational means, personal encounter with God cannot. The final object of our happiness thus outstrips unaided philosophy. This places philosophers in the tradition of Aquinas, and those working in other religious traditions, in a peculiar position. On the one hand, as philosophers they are charged with seeking the truth, while on the other, they are expected not to exceed the natural and rational means put at their disposal. However, the fact that Thomists work in a tradition which, at least implicitly, relies on revelation is most likely responsible for their continued support of an objectivist position when many Aristotelians have retreated to weaker claims. [65]

But this is not to say that Thomistic thought bears no resemblance to the mainstream of the philosophical world. Apart from the obvious issue of the relationship between happiness and morality, modern Thomists have been concerned with the problem of Aristotelian intellectualism, inclusive vs. dominant-end theory, practical reasoning and canons of rationality, politics and happiness, and the role of affectivity. Yet for modern Thomists, the most important issue remains the relation of intermediate to final ends, the happiness we seek in this world and the happiness of the next. Thomists have understandably been concerned with defending the veracity of the latter while, it must be admitted, doing very little to fill out the picture of the former.

The most recent and highly visible treatment of the subject among more recent Thomists is metaphysically undecided just at the point where the well-known Thomists of a generation ago were the most insistent—the grounding of earthly happiness directly on the final end of the Beatific Vision. Germain Grisez, Joseph Boyle, and John Finnis have collaborated on a minimalistic version of Thomistic ethics and happiness founded upon eight basic goods and integral human fulfillment. They spurn the intellectualist and dominant-end theory of happiness as an outmoded Thomism which depreciates the complexity of the basic needs of the human person. [66]

Finnis, for example, affirms the formal manner of Aristotle's eudaemonism while rejecting its content—the contemplative life. The desire for happiness, he argues, is for the individual's free integration of the basic goods. These basic goods, not God, provide our reasons for acting; they answer to our natural need for fulfillment. [67] Actions are rational only when they are motivated by these goods. God cannot be the ultimate reason for our actions because, first, human happiness must be actualized by human action. "The hearts of human persons, considered precisely according to their human nature, are not made for God; rather they are made for human fulfillment." [68] Second, human actions cannot instantiate divine goodness, that is, what is a gift from God cannot be claimed through human action. These distinctions serve the purposes of preserving both the strictly philosophical approach to ethics and the distinctive character of a theology of grace and the sacraments.

The Aristotelian-Thomistic ideal of contemplation has been dominated by empiricist images of knowing, making human fulfillment entirely too simple, too isolated, and too passive, in the view of Finnis. Earthly or imperfect happiness, in their view, is a manifold of goods, each of which is a good in itself but not a final good: happiness comes about through the unifying of these goods in a life which is ordered by practical reasoning.

More traditional Thomists have been quick to object to a "plan of life" approach. Stephen Theron objects that this type of deliberated moderation for the sake of quantified satisfaction makes no room for passion or sacrifice for one great aim: "to fall in love, what havoc that would work with this plan of life!" [69] The experience of passion better suits the trajectory of Aquinas's account. His happiness is not the gathering together of various goods but a lover's vision of his beloved. When we love we quit calculating, we want nothing less than to reach the person we desire, even if the search requires suffering.

In this way, Theron defends a dominant-end theory of happiness. The object of happiness, for better or worse, is a transcendent one. This can be shown by Aquinas's account of human desire, willing, and action. What we naturally desire as a final end is not chosen; it does not fall within the scope of our freedom. Happiness stills all desire, but there is no willing in this life that results in lasting satisfaction. Experience teaches us that even the greatest of joys can be lost. Time and change always frustrate desire. To be happy, as Boethius said, one must know one will always be happy. Thus, temporal life is a chain of events, a means to an end. Only the hope of happiness, not beatitude itself, is possible in this life; patience, not calculation, is preparation for what is to come.

Theron's kind of straightforward affirmation of Aquinas's theological intellectualism was almost standard among Thomists of the mid-twentieth century. Étienne Gilson, for example, insists upon the primacy of the contemplative act, rooted philosophically in the Aristotelian view of human nature and theologically in the goal of the Beatific Vision. The natural aspirations of a rational nature can only be met by an act of the intellect, since neither the motions of the will nor those of the sensitive appetites are capable of possessing an object of knowledge. Happiness requires that all human desire be brought to rest and satisfaction be complete; this occurs only when the highest human faculty grasps its highest possible object—God. [70]

As Gilson's historical work shows, this contemplative and theological account did not pass through the Renaissance unscathed. Dante, who is so often mentioned in the same breath with Aquinas, is responsible for the most dramatic challenge to the Thomistic view. Aquinas had allowed for the possibility of an imperfect happiness on earth but kept the notion of a final end reserved for God alone. Dante posited two final ends of happiness, one belonging to the order of the natural world, the other to the order of grace and eternity. Although it was Dante's antipapal politics that encouraged this formulation, his two final ends made it possible to pursue a happy life outside of theological jurisdiction, so to speak. Although Dante considered these happinesses compatible with one another, his distinction between them signals further developments in the Italian Renaissance that would eventually make eternity irrelevant to the consideration of happiness at all. [71]

Josef Pieper, however, attempts to make Aquinas's view more plausible by writing an apologetics for contemplation itself. He maintains that the notion of contemplation is misunderstood as an arid and elitist kind of scholarly endeavor. The cognitive activity of contemplation, rather, is the "indispensable premise" of love and joy in everyday life. Pieper makes the point, often underemphasized by Thomists, that human beings differentiated from other animals by their rationality are also differentiated by this factor in all of their actions, including their emotional life. In other words, to assume that the call to contemplation somehow excludes the "passions of the soul" completely misses the role of the intellect in producing these affections. "Only the presence of what is loved makes us happy, and that presence is actualized by the power of cognition." [72] Human happiness is founded upon the possibility of seeing what is *other* than us, and possessing what we love through an act of knowledge. Our mistake is overlooking the unique rational power underlying and informing the human gaze.

Other Thomists seek to do justice to the rational character of happiness but without seeking to revive the priority of contemplation. Yves R. Simon regards accounts like those of Gilson and Pieper as discounting the importance of the active life and, especially, the role of meaningful work. He interprets the intellectualism of Aquinas in terms of the overall rationality and aim of the happy life. True happiness is the end of voluntary action and involves real achievement in satisfying the tendencies, desires, and inclinations of the whole person for the good.

What Simon regards as crucial in this pattern of satisfactions is the teleological relation in practical judgment of intermediate ends to the final end. Happiness in this life is complicated by a multiplicity of real goods which must be given their due while being ordered toward God. The dynamic character of practical reasoning ensures that some good will serve as the last end in deliberation, but it will not necessarily be God. "Within the same day of the same man the last end may be placed first in God, then in some good—say, pleasure—then in another created good—say, honor—and in God again." [73] Simon is not denying the Thomistic principle that the will unconditionally desires the *bonum universale;* but here he accounts for the manner in which God becomes the object of deliberation and choice among other real and apparent goods. Even though human beings possess a determined will, choice remains free. This allows God, who is the final end, to take the character of a means and become an object of our free choice. Yet, at the same time we are choosing God, He remains the formal cause of our choice.

Jacques Maritain concurs with both Simon and Gilson that at the heart of any Thomistic account of earthly happiness is the proper ordering of this life to the next. The central issue is not just contemplation, but where we direct our attention and our love. Do we seek only an immanent human end or an "infravalent" earthly end stretching toward a transcendent end? This contrast represents the essential difference between the Aristotelian and Thomistic accounts of happiness: for Aristotle happiness consists in realizing a human ideal, while for Aquinas human beings must possess God before they can be fully perfected in themselves. "It is impossible for Aristotelian ethics to escape from the embrace of the self. . . . And yet in the end it is just such a deliverance that we long for." [74]

Yet this ordering of the self and society toward eternity does not have the expected result of making Maritain's philosophy other-worldly. Quite the contrary: the necessity of turning outward textures his discussion of happiness with a deep appreciation of its psychological and affective aspects. The suffering and self-giving required of a temporal happiness extending beyond itself exposes the core of human subjectivity. It is here that Maritain finds an "anguish" in our pursuit of happiness, a painful longing that underlies our search through the finite goods of this life for an object which satisfies our infinite desire.

Maritain contends with the ideologies that sought to exploit this vulnerability for their own collectivist and totalitarian purposes. [75] He proposed an "integral humanism" that would seek to revivify temporal institutions by reordering them toward a spiritual end, one that would ensure that the dignity of the individual never be destroyed by a perverted notion of the common good. Governments should not interfere with a person's destiny beyond this world, least of all deprive him or her of basic rights in the name of a "just" or "happy" society. Indeed for Maritain it was this recognition of persons as having an eternal destiny that gave the political sphere its decisive importance for human happiness. The perfecting of the human person, the preparation for eternity, takes place in society. Not to recognize this fact is another symptom of the Cartesian angelism which Maritain diagnosed at the heart of modern thought. Descartes thought he had direct intuitive access to "clear and distinct" ideas; he rejected the evidence of the senses and the necessary reliance of the mind's operation upon the working of the body. In contrast, Maritain would have said, we do not pursue happiness in isolation from our bodies, whether individual or corporate.

Finally, it must be said that no contemporary writer has paid greater attention to the civic importance of happiness than Mortimer J. Adler. Properly understood, Adler maintains, happiness provides a criterion by which a just or unjust society can be recognized. The Hobbesian portrayal of happiness as a mad scramble over the bodies of others to the top of the pile may describe our age, but it distorts the philosophical tradition by trading on the old news that human beings are corruptible. Adler, like Aristotle, cannot conceive of an individual's happiness apart from the happiness of the city. Individuals aim at their happiness as citizens guided by the virtue of justice which serves the happiness of others. Whereas we are disposed by justice to consider the happiness of our friends and acquaintances, the state is mandated to serve the happiness of all. But, again, if happiness is misunderstood as well-feeling, those who govern are left without a clear picture of how to serve the common good.

Adler has consistently sought to promulgate an objective, Aristotelian view of happiness. Nothing has come to pass, he argues, since the fifth century B.C. that requires any basic modernization of the *Nicomachean Ethics*. For Adler, to call an idea unpopular is not a judgment on its truth. Yes, social life has changed, but human nature and its moral problems remain the same. Human happiness is objectively grounded in the perennial, fundamental needs of human beings for basic goods—health, wealth, pleasure, the goods of self-improvement (leisure, friendship, knowledge, etc.), and the goods of fortune. And it consists in possessing those goods over the course of a person's lifetime. Happiness is, therefore, better described as the *totum bonum,* the whole good, than the summum bonum, the highest good. The latter suggests an identification of happiness with moral perfection, whereas happiness embraces both goods of choice and goods of fortune. By seeking the possession of all the basic goods of life over one's lifetime, a person does justice to the array of human needs and avoids the top-heavy quality of detached intellectualism. The notion of contemplation itself is subsumed under leisure, which is a need of everyone.

If happiness is the possession of basic goods over a lifetime, it can never be experienced or enjoyed in the manner of well-feeling. For example, one could enjoy a friend at a given time, but happiness evades direct experience since it spans the whole of a person's life. Adler has repeatedly argued against psychological happiness. His favorite example is that of the contented miser whose contentment demonstrates that such a happiness is available to both the morally good and the morally bad. [76] Such a view of happiness not only diminishes personal life but also makes it impossible for a government to rule with an eye to promoting happiness, for such an aim becomes hopelessly conditioned by individual preferences. Adler's analysis of apparent goods, real goods, needs, and wants anticipates the current distinctions between informed and actual desires and between first- and second-order desires.

Adler refers to himself as an Aristotelian rather than as a Thomist. But in his treatment of the problem of ends he is an objectivist who leaves the door open for a supernatural version of the final end. In this world, Adler explains, the happy life is dynamic; if we are happy it can be rightly said that we are continually "becoming happy." [77] There is no state of culminating perfection because the goods of fortune can always be lost. Like Priam, we can be visited at any time by a traumatic misfortune that strips us of our happiness.

Though temporal happiness is never perfect, Adler rejects the inference, made by John Dewey, that happiness cannot be a final end. Here Adler distinguishes between a terminal end, which can be possessed, and a normative end which, while beyond possession, nonetheless retains finality. This is perfectly compatible with Aquinas's rationale for the difference between the imperfect happiness of this world and the perfect happiness of eternity. Adler's defense of normative ends upholds the plausibility of a final end beyond this world.

If there were such an eternal happiness, he maintained in an early work, it would be the only situation in which satisfaction could be considered the sole criterion for happiness. [78] Yet, as we have seen, this conception of happiness has been seriously entertained for nearly a century. That is partly because philosophers like Adler and his Thomist friend, Maritain, never succumbed to the spirit of the age. Perhaps they knew that we would soon be getting over what the historian Carl L. Becker described as the legacy of the eighteenth century to modernity: the project of transposing the Kingdom of Heaven, with its complete and unending satisfaction, into a kingdom on earth. [79] The philosophical evidence suggests that the eighteenth-century dream of sublime self-satisfaction has been exhausted.

V. A final comment

> I feel quite happy, as if happiness
> Did not consist in getting what one wanted
> Or in getting rid of what can't be gotten rid of
> But in a different vision.
> (T. S. Eliot, *The Family Reunion*) [80]

There has never been or will ever be unanimity of opinion concerning our great ideas. Arguments for and against certain interpretations of happiness at best aim to influence the broad strokes of its accepted, consensual meaning. Debates over the distinctions of the philosophers and the correlations of the social scientists rarely reach the minds of ordinary citizens. But the fundamental notions promulgated by the theorists still have their consequences. Psychologists and sociologists are regularly granted access to the public through the media. Therapists abound; their language now saturates common conversation. Philosophers still have their classrooms and occasionally write a book that appeals to a wide audience.

What can be made of the data collected here? It is not complete, of course. No one who has worked on the idea of happiness would be foolish enough to claim completeness. Yet the samples offered in this essay of the rejection of happiness, of popular and psychological views, and of current philosophical treatments, suggest a new interest in eudaemonism. This is not, as we have seen, a *eudaimonia* that specifies either a final end or determinate moral limits. This resurgent eudaemonism treads lightly around both moral pluralism and the question of human nature, now even more fragmented by considerations of gender and race. Most present-day eudaemonists reject well-feeling in the name of personhood and on the grounds of freedom and rationality, while touching on moral criteria only formally or "minimally." The objective goods approach offers little offense since, lacking a final good, people are left free to integrate these goods in their own fashion. Insofar as the concept of virtue is implied by eudaemonism, it is construed broadly, and properly, as a human excellence rather than just moral or intellectual dispositions. Judgments can once again be made about someone's claim to happiness; however, the focus is now less on meeting moral standards than on exercising a free, rational agency toward certain consensually established goods of life.

Empirical investigation has to a large extent corroborated both the centrality of such goods—friendship, self-respect, work—and also the importance of personal responsibility in acquiring them. These empirically established patterns of human satisfaction suggest that people are not so easily conditioned and duped as some imagine. As further evidence one might ask whether anyone predicted the powder keg of dissatisfaction that recently exploded and changed once again the map of Eastern Europe? Why did the Communist catechists fail to shape the satisfactions of their citizens? Were we not supposed to be at "the end of history"? These recent events may only serve to show that dissatisfactions speak more truly than satisfactions, but certainly they testify to a hunger that cannot be appeased for long. It is a hunger for a restored vision, not simply the material prosperity of the West, that seems to be working in the starved souls of dictatorship.

The idea of happiness has passed through a period of reductivism. If the bubble of well-feeling has not quite burst, it is slowly losing its air.

No doubt well-feeling is one of life's real goods, but it cannot support the weight it must bear if it is equated with happiness. Linguistic usage alone does not settle the issue. "Happiness" and "happy," like other important words, are applied analogically to things that are transient and trivial as well as to what we most deeply value. There is nothing trivial about calling a life happy—such usage carries implicit recommendations for the kind of beliefs, dispositions, and behavior we want for ourselves and others. For the most part we can distinguish easily between claims to happiness that are trivial and those that are not. At the level of public policy, it is everybody's business to demand justification for the theoretical and empirical basis of these assertions. At a personal level, only certain kinds of relationships offer the appropriate moment to challenge reports of happiness. To let all claims pass as inscrutable encourages our friends in the pursuit of self-destructive aims. The motive for these conversations need not be dismissed as judgmental. Rather, one of the great opportunities of friendship is precisely the help one receives in clarifying a sense of identity and purpose. Self-knowledge pursued in a closet seems a more dangerous alternative than that of listening to an imprudent but well-intentioned friend.

The revival of eudaemonism is welcome if only because it makes happiness once again the topic of reasonable discussion. We are no longer condemned to pursue happiness privately, at the mercy of our own devices without the help of other eyes to keep our reports honest. This eudaemonism is a long way from proposing the ideal life in accord with the summum bonum, but it has recaptured the grounds for a public standard of rationality by which pig-happiness can be revealed for what it is. With human rationality back in place, it may be that even the concept of a final end for every person sharing human nature stands a chance for another hearing. [81]

---

1. Trans. Joseph W. Evans (New York: Charles Scribner's Sons, 1986), p. 56.

2. Gregory Vlastos, "Happiness and Virtue in Socrates' Moral Theory," *Proceedings of the Cambridge Philological Society* 30 (1984), p. 183.

3. "Happiness," *Encyclopedia of Philosophy*, ed. Paul Edwards, 3 (New York: Macmillan Publishing Co., Inc., & The Free Press, reprinted 1972), p. 414.

4. C. H. Sisson, *Collected Poems, 1943–1983* (Manchester: Carcanet, 1984), p. 111.

5. Agnes Heller, *Renaissance Man*, trans. Richard E. Allen (New York: Schocken Books, 1981), chaps. 3 and 9.

6. Paul Hazard, *European Thought in the Eighteenth Century: From Montesquieu to Lessing* (London: Hollis & Carter, 1954), p. 24; emphasis added.

7. Miguel de Unamuno, *The Tragic Sense of Life in Men and Nations*, trans. Anthony Kerrigan (Princeton, N.J.: Princeton University Press, 1972), p. 225; originally published in 1913.

8. Trans. Rebecca Frank (New York: Dell Publishing Co., Inc., 1968), p. 253.

9. Ibid., p. 513.

10. (Cambridge, Mass.: Harvard University Press, 1953), p. 104.

11. Relevant works have been written by Christopher Lasch, Ernest Becker, Allan Bloom, Marion Montgomery, Tom Wolfe, and Walker Percy, among others. Lewis Mumford's comment on the growing confidence in the power of technology to improve the

quality of life is typical: " 'Happiness,' people used to say, wistfully. But did they not mean anesthesia?" In "Reflections: Prologue to Our Times," *The New Yorker*, March 10, 1975.

12. Robert N. Bellah, Richard Madsen, William M. Sullivan, Ann Swidler, and Stephen M. Tipton, *Habits of the Heart: Individualism and Commitment in American Life* (New York: Harper & Row, Publishers, 1986), p. 6.

13. Ibid., p. 221.

14. Cited in Bellah, p. 294; cf. also Hobbes, *Leviathan* 1.7 (*GBWW* I: 23, 65; II: 21, 65) and *Human Nature* 7.

15. Bellah, op. cit., p. 294.

16. Quoted in Philip Rieff, *Freud: The Mind of the Moralist* (Garden City, N.Y.: Doubleday & Company, Inc., 1961), p. 358.

17. *Eros and Civilization: A Philosophical Inquiry into Freud* (New York: Vintage Books, 1962). A critique can be found in Martin G. Kalin, *The Utopian Flight from Unhappiness: Freud against Marx on Social Progress* (Chicago: Nelson-Hall Company, Publishers, 1974), pp. 182–89, and in Alasdair MacIntyre, *Herbert Marcuse: An Exposition and a Polemic* (New York: The Viking Press, Inc., 1970), pp. 43–48.

18. Isidor Silbermann, "On Happiness," *The Psychoanalytic Study of the Child*, 40 (New Haven, Conn.: Yale University Press, 1985), p. 461.

19. *A Short History of Ethics* (New York: Macmillan Publishing Co., Inc., 1966), p. 167, and *After Virtue* (Notre Dame, Ind.: University of Notre Dame Press, 1984; 2nd ed.), p. 64. *See also* the rough treatment of happiness in Bernard Williams, *Ethics and the Limits of Philosophy* (Cambridge, Mass.: Harvard University Press, 1985).

20. *Politics and the Pursuit of Happiness* (New York: Longman, 1984), p. 105.

21. *From Enlightenment to Revolution*, ed. John J. Hallowell (Durham, N.C.: Duke University Press, 1975), p. 48.

22. Dorothy Parker, *Constant Reader* (New York: The Viking Press, 1970), p. 19. Review of *Happiness* by William Lyon Phelps (New York: E. E. Dutton, 1927), published Nov. 5, 1927, in *The New Yorker*.

23. In his recent summa of happiness Wladyslaw Tatarkiewicz, while showing an obvious affinity for both eighteenth-century hedonistic and twentieth-century psychological accounts, argues that satisfaction must nonetheless be justified; see *Analysis of Happiness*, trans. Edward Rothert and Danuta Zielinska (The Hague: Martinus Nijhoff, 1976), pp. 15–18.

24. Richard Taylor, "Ancient Wisdom and Modern Folly," *Midwest Studies in Philosophy* 13 (Notre Dame, Ind.: University of Notre Dame Press, 1988), p. 55.

25. J. S. Mill, *Utilitarianism* (Indianapolis, Ind.: The Bobbs-Merrill Company, Inc., 1957), p. 14 (*GBWW* I: 43, 449; II: 40, 449).

26. For a succinct overview of this development, *see* Abraham Edel, "Happiness and Pleasure," *Dictionary of the History of Ideas* (New York: Charles Scribner's Sons, 1973), pp. 374–87.

27. Donald Meyer, *The Positive Thinkers: Popular Religious Psychology from Mary Baker Eddy to Norman Vincent Peale and Ronald Reagan* (Middletown, Conn.: Wesleyan University Press, 1988; rev. ed.).

28. Cited in Meyer, p. 322.

29. Bertrand Russell, *The Conquest of Happiness* (New York: Horace Liveright, Inc., 1930), chap. 11.

30. Paul Kurtz, *Exuberance: An Affirmative Philosophy of Life* (Buffalo, N.Y.: Prometheus Books, 1978), p. 21.

31. John Cowper Powys, *The Art of Happiness* (New York: Simon and Schuster, Inc., 1935), pp. 69 and 95.

32. Ibid., p. 47; emphasis added.

33. Émile-Auguste Chartier, *Alain on Happiness,* trans. Robert D. and Jane E. Cottrell (New York: Frederick Ungar, 1973), p. 248; originally published in 1928 under the title *Propos sur le bonheur.*

34. Ibid., pp. 245–46; emphasis added.

35. For varying interpretations of Jefferson *see:* Gary Wills, *Inventing America: Jefferson's Declaration of Independence* (Garden City, N.Y.: Doubleday & Company, Inc., 1978); Carl Becker, *The Declaration of Independence* (New York: Vintage Books, 1922); Morton White, *The Philosophy of the American Revolution* (New York: Oxford University Press, 1978); John P. Diggs, *The Lost Soul of American Politics: Virtue, Self-Interest, and the*

Foundations of Liberalism (New York: Basic Books, 1984); and Forrest MacDonald, *Novus Ordo Seclorum: The Intellectual Origins of the Constitution* (Lawrence, Kansas: University Press of Kansas, 1985).

36. For a treatment of Abraham Harold Maslow and other self-realization theorists, cf. V. J. McGill, *The Idea of Happiness* (New York: Frederick A. Praeger, 1967), chap. 11 (*GIT* 1967, 272). This book remains the best study of happiness in English.

37. Ruut Veenhoven, *Conditions of Happiness* (Dordrecht: D. Riedel Publishing Co., 1984).

38. Jonathan Freedman, *Happy People: What Happiness Is, Who Has It, and Why* (New York: Harcourt Brace Jovanovich, 1978), p. 35.

39. Ed Diener, "Subjective Well-Being," *Psychological Bulletin* 95 (1984), pp. 542–75; Michael Argyle, *The Psychology of Happiness* (New York: Methuen, 1987). Another major source of research is a journal founded in 1974: *Social Indicators Research: An International Journal for the Study of the Indicators of Well-Being*.

40. Michael Freund, "Towards a Critical Theory of Happiness: Philosophical Background and Methodological Significance," *New Ideas in Psychology* 3 (1985), pp. 3–12.

41. Argyle, p. 3.

42. Ibid., p. 216.

43. Diener, p. 542.

44. Ibid., p. 565.

45. Alan S. Waterman, "Personal Expressiveness: Philosophical and Psychological Foundations," *Journal of Mind and Behavior* 11 (Winter 1990), pp. 47–74; cf. also "Two Conceptions of Happiness: Research on Eudaimonia and Hedonic Enjoyment," a paper delivered at the American Psychological Association, New Orleans, 1989.

46. Mihaly Csikszentmihalyi, *Flow: The Psychology of Optimal Experience* (New York: Harper & Row, 1990). There is historical warrant for this usage: *Eurhoia*, or good flow, was often used by the Stoic Epictetus to describe happiness (*Discourses* II, 19, 24 [*GBWW* I: 12, 162, 172; II: 11, 153, 162]).

47. Csikszentmihalyi, op. cit., p. 2.

48. Charles Murray, *In Pursuit of Happiness and Good Government* (New York: Simon and Schuster, 1988), p. 85.

49. *See* William Julius Wilson, "The Charge of the Little Platoons," *The New York Times Review of Books*, Oct. 23, 1988, p. 12. Diener's survey of the research, however, supports much of Murray's argument.

50. This overview is not intended to represent any particular classical school. Theories of *eudaimonia* in the Greek world were highly varied. Stoics, Epicureans, Cynics, Aristotelians, and Platonists each put their twist into its meaning.

51. G. H. von Wright, *The Varieties of Goodness* (London: Routledge & Kegan Paul, 1963), pp. 98–99.

52. Robin Barrow, *Happiness and Schooling* (New York: St. Martin's Press, 1980), p. 69.

53. A further implication of Barrow's position is seen in his defense of Plato against Karl Popper. Barrow argues that in the kind of state proposed in *The Republic* there is much more likelihood that its citizens will report happiness given the fact that its leaders will have the power to change both the expectations of every individual and the actual circumstances in which he or she lives. The open society as proposed by Popper with its liberal values of freedom and equality will lead inevitably to greater reported unhappiness due to the instability of personal expectation in relation to actual attainment. There could be no clear example of the political consequences of our theories of happiness. Robin Barrow, *Plato, Utilitarianism, and Education* (Boston: Routledge & Kegan Paul, 1975), pp. 65–74.

54. Irwin Goldstein, "Happiness: The Role of Non-Hedonic Criteria in Its Evaluation," *International Philosophical Quarterly* 13 (1973), p. 530; emphasis removed.

55. Douglas den Uyl and Tibor R. Machan, "Recent Work on the Concept of Happiness," *American Philosophical Quarterly* 20 (April 1983), p. 115. This is a helpful survey of the contemporary philosophical literature.

56. Richard Kraut, "Two Conceptions of Happiness," *The Philosophical Review* 88 (April 1979), pp. 167–97.

57. Richard Hare, *Freedom and Reason* (Oxford: The Clarendon Press, 1963), p. 128.

58. Richard Warner, *Freedom, Enjoyment, and Happiness: An Essay on Moral Psychology* (Ithaca, N.Y.: Cornell University Press, 1987), pp. 172–73.

59. Lynne McFall, *Happiness* (New York: Peter Lang, 1989), p. 30.

60. Ibid., p. 117.

61. John Kekes, *Moral Tradition and Individuality* (Princeton, N.J.: Princeton University Press, 1989), p. 115.

62. James Griffin, *Well Being: Its Meaning, Measurement, and Moral Importance* (Oxford: Clarendon Press, 1986), p. 13.

63. Ibid., p. 131.

64. Ibid., p. 132.

65. One notable exception is Henry Veatch; see *Human Rights: Fact or Fancy?* (Baton Rouge: Louisiana State University Press, 1985), chap. 2.

66. Germain Grisez, Joseph Boyle, and John Finnis, "Practical Principles, Moral Truth, and Ultimate Ends," *American Journal of Jurisprudence* 32 (1987), pp. 99–151.

67. John Finnis, "Practical Reasoning, Human Goods, and the End of Man," *Proceedings of the American Catholic Philosophical Association,* ed. Daniel O. Dalhstrom, 58 (1985), pp. 23–36. His basic goods are life, knowledge, play, aesthetic experience, sociability, practical reasonableness, and religion.

68. Grisez et al., p. 134.

69. Stephen Theron, "Happiness and Transcendent Happiness," *Religious Studies* 21 (September 1985), pp. 349–67.

70. *The Christian Philosophy of St. Thomas Aquinas,* trans. L. K. Shook, C.S.B. (New York: Random House Inc., 1956), p. 353.

71. *Dante and Philosophy,* trans. L. K. Shook, C.S.B. (New York: Random House Inc., 1956), pp. 191–201.

72. Josef Pieper, *Happiness and Contemplation,* trans. Richard and Clara Winston (New York: Pantheon Press, 1958), p. 71.

73. Yves R. Simon, *Freedom of Choice,* trans. Peter Wolff (New York: Fordham University Press, 1969), p. 59.

74. Jacques Maritain, *Moral Philosophy* (London: Geoffrey Bles, 1964), p. 49.

75. Jacques Maritain, *Integral Humanism,* trans. Joseph W. Evans (New York: Charles Scribner's Sons, 1986), chap. 2.

76. *Ten Philosophical Mistakes* (New York: Macmillan, 1985), p. 122.

77. *The Time of Our Lives: The Ethics of Common Sense* (New York: Holt, Rinehart and Winston, 1970), p. 62.

78. *The Dialectic of Morals: Towards the Foundations of Political Philosophy* (New York: Frederick Ungar Publishing Co., 1941), p. 50.

79. *The Heavenly City of the Eighteenth-Century Philosophers* (New Haven, Conn.: Yale University Press, 1932), pp. 49 and 129.

80. T. S. Eliot, *The Complete Poems and Plays, 1909–1950* (New York: Harcourt, Brace & World, Inc., 1971), p. 275.

81. The author wishes to thank Peter Pagan for his advice and the Earhart Foundation of Ann Arbor, Michigan, for its support of this research.

PART THREE

Special Features

An Introduction to Buddhist Thought

George Anastaplo

George Anastaplo and his wife, Sara Prince Anastaplo.

George Anastaplo, who has studied our legal system for many years, is himself a tutelary figure in it. His career began in 1950 when, after graduating at the top of his law school class at the University of Chicago, he was denied admission to the Illinois Bar because of his opinions about the fundamental right of revolution. These opinions had led to questions being put to him about his political affiliations, which questions he on principle refused to answer. Ever since an adverse ruling on the case (over an eloquent dissent by Justice Hugo L. Black) by the U.S. Supreme Court in 1961, appeals for his admission to the bar have been made from time to time by prominent lawyers, but he rejects the idea of making any further application.

Mr. Anastaplo is professor of law at Loyola University of Chicago and lecturer in liberal arts at the University of Chicago. Among his books are *The Constitutionalist: Notes on the First Amendment* (1971), *Human Being and Citizen: Essays on Virtue, Freedom, and the Common Good* (1975), *The Artist as Thinker: From Shakespeare to Joyce* (1983), and *The American Moralist: On Ethics, Law, and Government* (1992). He is also the author of a book-length series of lectures entitled *The Constitution of 1787*, published in 1989 by Johns Hopkins University Press. He has prepared a sequel with a series of lectures, *The Amendments to the Constitution*.

I had rather believe all the fables in the [Golden] Legend, and the
Talmud, and the Alcoran than that this universal frame is without a
mind. And therefore God never wrought miracle to convince [refute]
atheism, because his ordinary works convince it. It is true, that a little
philosophy inclineth man's mind to atheism, but depth in philosophy
bringeth men's minds about to religion. For while the mind of man
looketh upon second causes scattered, it may sometimes rest in them,
and go no further; but when it beholdeth the chain of them, confederate
and linked together, it must needs fly to Providence and Deity.

(Francis Bacon) [1]

I

What is there in the human soul that can be appealed to by radical self-abnegation, that comprehensive suppression of appetites
which goes far beyond ordinary temperance? Perhaps efforts at self-
abnegation have the appeal they sometimes do because they represent
heroic attempts to control, far more than otherwise seems possible to
most of us, the ever-changing and unpredictable tribulations that flesh
is heir to. The heroism of such efforts, characterized by both remarkable self-sacrifice and determined mastery, can attract (when it does not
happen to naturally repel) those who yearn for models of greatness.

The turning point in the life of the founder of the Buddhist movement followed his being exposed to ordinary experiences that left him
in a severe depression. He learned for the first time at age twenty-
nine what most people learn as children. His doting father, the local
ruler in a region in Nepal, had rigorously sheltered the young prince
from disagreeable things. Siddhārtha Gautama had been attractive and
sensitive from youth; he lived in exquisite ease; and he acquired at age
sixteen a lovely wife and then thirteen years later an infant son.

In any movement numbering five hundred million (as the Buddhists
do today) we can anticipate a wide variety of stories and beliefs. But
there are certain elements in the stories, especially about the life of
Gautama, who came to be recognized as the Buddha (the Enlightened
One), which seem to be generally accepted. Among the elements in
the vast Buddhist literature of hundreds of thousands of pages is the

standard account of how the Buddha's career, at least during his sixth century B.C. incarnation, got started. [2] Here is a summary of that account for the modern reader:

> One day, while out driving with his charioteer, [Gautama] saw "an aged man as bent as a roof gable, decrepit, leaning on a staff, tottering as he walked, afflicted and long past his prime." The charioteer, questioned by the Prince as to what had happened to the man, explained that he was old and that all men were subject to old age if they lived long enough. The Prince, greatly perturbed by this sight, went back to the palace and became absorbed in thought. Another day, again driving with his charioteer, he saw "a sick man, suffering and very ill, fallen and weltering in his own excreta, being lifted up by some. . . ." Because [Gautama] was perturbed, the charioteer explained, as before, that this was a sick man and that all men are subject to sickness. On a third occasion the Prince saw a dead body and again the charioteer provided the explanation. Finally, [Gautama] saw "a shaven-headed man, a wanderer who has gone forth, wearing the yellow robe." Impressed with the man's peaceful and serene demeanour, the Prince decided to leave home and go out into the world to discover the reason for such a display of serenity in the midst of misery.
>
> . . . On his way back to the palace after seeing the yellow-robed ascetic, [Gautama] received the news of the birth of his son. . . . Upon receiving this news, the Prince decided to make what is known as the great renunciation: giving up the princely life to become a wandering ascetic. . . . [3]

It should be noticed at the outset of our inquiry that physical pleasure is not dismissed by Buddhism as simply inconsequential. Rather, pleasure seems to be recognized as in a sense desirable but not truly possessable, no matter how many incarnations one has. So fleeting and otherwise illusory is physical pleasure bound to be that it is something to be avoided. [4] Centuries after Gautama's traumatic experiences, a Buddhist monk could instruct a ruler, "Whoever, great king, orders his walk aright, grasps the course of the Aggregates [all the composite things in the world, including of course human beings]. Grasping their course, he sees therein Birth, he sees therein Old Age, he sees therein Disease, he sees therein Death. He sees therein nothing that is pleasant, nothing that is agreeable; from the beginning to the middle to the end he sees nothing therein which it is possible for him to lay hold of." [5]

The prospect of his inevitable decay moved Gautama to seek release by putting a stop to the endless series of lives that human beings can expect. Inevitable decay leads to the suffering critical to life on earth and evidently elsewhere also. Gautama is celebrated as having addressed his followers in this fashion: "I teach only two things, O disciples, the fact of suffering and the possibility of escape from suffering." [6] A scholar can observe, therefore, that "the premise of Buddhism is that

Buddha, when still Prince Gautama, depicted with his charioteer, discovering age, sickness, death, and a serene spirit in the midst of them (the man in the robe, which by tradition is always yellow) as elements of human life. From a fresco found at a Buddhist temple in Chiang Mai, Thailand.

Again, a fresco from Chiang Mai, Thailand, showing Buddha (Gautama) as he bids farewell to his wife and newborn son, renouncing princely splendor for the ascetic life, by which he thinks to endure human misery.

life is suffering, that suffering arises from desires or passions, and that desires or passions arise from the erroneous conviction that the ego exists." [7] Gautama is distinguished, it seems, by the intensity of his compassion for the dreadfulness of that suffering which living things are destined to endure, suffering which is keyed to the mutability of all things. It also seems, however, that enough of our being usually endures to permit us to suffer, including that most exalted form of suffering identified as compassion.

Gautama's response to death may be usefully compared to that of Gilgamesh, the hero in the ancient Mesopotamian epic (at the other extreme, geographically, on the continent from that East Asia in which Buddhism has flourished). Gilgamesh, too, is confronted by death in a special way. Although, as an adventurous warrior, he has seen death before, it does not become "personal" for him until his beloved comrade is mortally stricken. [8]

The two heroes, Gilgamesh and Gautama, have quite different responses to their depressing discoveries. In neither case is a preoccupation with death dismissed as childish or unmanly. Rather, the audiences of these two stories are expected to accept the fact that the discovery of mortality and hence of the insubstantiality of all things is "naturally" traumatic. Gilgamesh's response is to try to grasp life more firmly: he desperately seeks immortality, or deathlessness, searching for and finding the only survivors of the Great Flood. He secures from them access to a plant which wards off death. After losing this plant on the way home, however, he is reduced to political projects and to leaving a name for his city and hence for himself. [9]

We have seen, on the other hand, that Gautama tries to secure release by a determined pursuit of selflessness. If life is the way Gautama now knows it to be, he wants no part of it: it is clear to him that it is always better not to be born (or reborn) at all. [10] Or, as Albert Schweitzer has put it, "When [Gautama was] nine-and-twenty years of age he left his wife and child, and [as an ascetic] went forth 'from home into homelessness.' The thought that all birth leads only to suffering and death, and that the succession of births is endless, had robbed him of all joy in life. He now sought deliverance from reincarnation." [11]

Gautama, like Gilgamesh before him, can also be said to have had recourse to a political project, in that he founds a great monastic order that embodies the enlightened way he has discovered for an effective renunciation of life. It can even be said that monks are the only Buddhists in the proper sense of the word. [12] Certainly Gautama's discourses are ordinarily addressed to monks. He can be considered more successful as a founder than Gilgamesh, since not only Gilgamesh but even his very name suffered oblivion for thousands of years. Gautama, in founding, or perhaps re-founding, the yellow-robed monastic order, had to experiment, as Gilgamesh did, with an alternative (of radical asceticism) to the mode into which he finally settled.

II

I attempt in this introduction to search for the core of Buddhism, particularly as it may be seen in the stories most intimately connected with Gautama himself. We can do no more than sample the vast literature that is available, literature that has no single text generally recognized as are, say, the Bible or the Koran in the West. [13]

Gautama's renunciation of household life initially takes the form evidently traditional in Hindu society: not only does he leave his family in assuming the role of the homeless monk, but he so subjects himself to the rigors of extreme asceticism that he almost starves himself to death. What finally puts a halt to these practices is his recognition that the enlightenment (Nirvana) he seeks depends on rational processes which are difficult to maintain if the body should be wrecked. "The human body, Gautama saw, was the one instrument man had through which to attain enlightenment." [14] Earlier, Gautama's father, perhaps because of some prophecies, had provided another approach for his son: he had sheltered him from all unpleasant things, offering him the best that wealth and position could provide, including a lovely wife. [15]

Gautama himself chooses a middle way between the life of pleasure and the life of asceticism. He works this out in a period of sustained contemplation (at the outset of his career, after his experimentation in radical asceticism) and is then prepared to deliver his first sermon (that at Benares). Gautama's first audience and first converts are made up of five ascetics who had been appalled by his recent abandonment of the life of asceticism. The sermon includes these observations:

> [There are] two extremes, monks, [which] are not to be practiced by one who has gone from the world. What are the two? That conjoined with the passions and luxury, low, vulgar, common, ignoble, and useless; and that conjoined with self-torture, painful, ignoble, and useless. Avoiding these two extremes the Tathagata [the Buddha] has gained the enlightenment of the Middle Path, which produces insight and knowledge, and tends to calm, to higher knowledge, enlightenment, Nirvana.
>
> And what, monks, is the Middle Path, of which the Tathagata has gained enlightenment, which produces insight and knowledge, and tends to calm, to higher knowledge, enlightenment, Nirvana? This is the noble Eightfold Way: namely, right view, right intention, right speech, right action, right livelihood, right effort, right mindfulness, right concentration. This, monks, is the Middle Path, of which the Tathagata has gained enlightenment, which produces insight and knowledge, and tends to calm, to higher knowledge, enlightenment, Nirvana. [16]

All this, Gautama explains in his inaugural sermon, is grounded in four truths:

> Now this, monks, is the noble truth of pain: birth is painful, old age is painful, sickness is painful, death is painful, sorrow, lamentation, dejection, and despair are painful. Contact with unpleasant things is painful, not getting what one wishes is painful. In short the five groups of grasping are painful.
>
> Now this, monks, is the noble truth of the cause of pain: the craving, which tends to rebirth, combined with pleasure and lust, finding pleasure here and there; namely, the craving for passion, the craving for existence, the craving for non-existence.
>
> Now this, monks, is the noble truth of the cessation of pain, the cessation without a reminder of craving, the abandonment, forsaking, release, non-attachment.
>
> Now this, monks, is the noble truth of the way that leads to the cessation of pain: this is the noble Eightfold Way; namely, right view, right intention, right speech, right action, right livelihood, right effort, right mindfulness, right concentration. [17]

The fourth noble truth leads again to an enumeration of the elements in the Eightfold Way. (Both enumeration and repetition are made much of in Buddhist accounts.) Several times in the course of this sermon Gautama can announce, "Thus, monks, among doctrines unheard before, in me sight and knowledge arose, wisdom arose, knowledge arose, light arose." [18]

The career of Gautama is reflected in how his body can both be talked about in literature and represented in art. Consider this account:

> We must now consider the Buddha in his *glorified body*. When he walked about as a human being, [Gautama] naturally looked like any other human being. But this ordinary human body of the Buddha was nothing but a kind of outer layer which both enveloped and hid his true personality, and which was quite accidental and almost negligible. It was not at all an adequate expression of the Buddha's own being. Hidden behind this outer shell was another kind of body, different in many ways from that of ordinary mortals, which could be seen only with the eye of faith. The Buddhists variously called it "the enjoyment body," "the unadulterated body," "the body which expresses the Buddha's own true nature." A list of 32 "marks of a superman," often supplemented by a list of 80 "subsidiary marks," described the most salient features of the Buddha's "glorious body." The list of the 32 marks is common to all schools, and it must be fairly old. The paintings and statues of the Buddha which we find in Buddhist art never depicted the human body visible to all, but they always try to represent the "glorious body" of the Buddha. [19]

Another scholar reports,

> The image of [Gautama], whether seated in meditation or standing (the two most common types of images), walking, or reclining in the hour of death, represents for the whole Asian world the equivalent of the Christ image for the West. Yet, interestingly enough, centuries passed after the Buddha's death before any representations of him as an actual physical being were conceived or executed. This was in keeping with an old [Buddhist] scripture that states, "The Buddha, who has gone beyond the fetters of the body, cannot be endowed by art with the likeness of a body." When an artist, in telling stories of the Master's life and teaching, found it necessary to indicate the Buddha's presence, he used only specific symbols: an empty throne, an umbrella (symbol of sovereignty), a *stupa* (mound for relics), the wheel of his first sermon, footprints. Even in such lively scenes as the future Buddha's departure from his father's palace, the horse—whose hoofs are being lifted up by divine beings to prevent all telltale sounds—departs riderless through the palace gates. [20]

The statues of the Buddha, which may be the most important things in Buddhist art, are indeed revealing, as may be seen in the pieces on display in museums such as the Art Institute of Chicago. He is usually presented in a seated position, serene, contemplative, complete, healthy, full-fleshed, in the prime of life but with no sexual energy suggested.

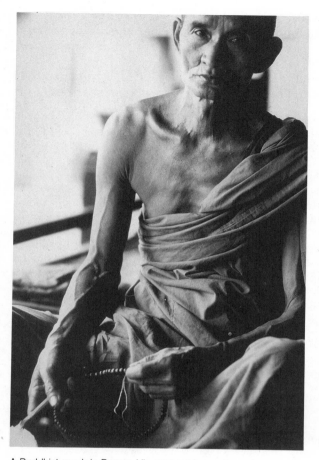

A Buddhist monk in Burma. His garment is a yellow robe, and in his right hand he holds a fan, a small indulgence with which he meets his human needs.

The representation is low-keyed, with little in the way of "action," except in the form of meditation. The faces, not only of the Buddha but also of those around him, tend to be expressionless. This can be considered relaxed, impassive, resigned, at rest—almost insistently so, if that is not a contradiction in terms. A timeless quality, not any particular time or place, is indicated: this is the way things are and should be. One occasionally encounters a graphic representation of the ascetic Gautama, reduced almost to skin and bones. Ordinarily, however, even the statues of the dying Buddha show a reclining, relaxed, full-fleshed, and anything but decrepit man, despite his eighty years.

Such statuary should be contrasted with that produced both by Hindus and Christians. Hindu statuary is replete with distorted bodies, multiheaded "people," sometimes violent actions (including intense lustful embraces), contorted features, and even monstrosities. It is easy to see the calmer Buddhist approach as a determined reaction to Hindu excesses. [21]

Then, of course, there is the characteristic Christian portrayal of the agonized body on a cross, something quite foreign to typical Buddhist representations. The Christian can find the stoic detachment of the Buddhist troublesome, as Albert Schweitzer, for one, did:

> For the Buddha's monks there can be no question of active love, if for no other reason, because it assumes that one loves something in the world and so in some way gives one's heart to it. But this would mean a limitation of freedom from earthly cares. How pathetic is the Buddha's saying: "Those who love nothing in the world are rich in joy and free from pain." To a father who has lost his little boy, he knows nothing better to say than: "What one loves brings woe and lamentation."
>
> He draws the ideal of monastic perfection with hard lines in the saying: "He who cares not for others, who has no relations, who controls himself, who is firmly fixed in the heart of truth, in whom the fundamental evils are extinguished, who has thrown hatred from him: him I call a Brahmin." [22]

A Buddhist priest in Japan saying morning prayers at his small private house shrine. Many stages of public and private life are marked by religious ceremony, of which the aim is to purify the mind and cultivate sympathy for all forms of life.

Schweitzer goes on to say:

> . . . Jesus and the Buddha have this in common, that their form of ethics, because it is under the influence of world and life negation, is not an ethic of action but an ethic of inner perfection. But in both the ethic of inner perfection is governed by the principle of love. It therefore carries within it the tendency to express itself in action and in this way has a certain affinity with world and life affirmation. With Jesus the ethic of the perfecting of the self commands active love: with the Buddha it does not get so far.
>
> It must be noted that the world and life negation of Jesus is in origin and in essence quite different from that of the Buddha. It does not rest on the distinction between material and immaterial Being, but abandons the natural world as evil, in the expectation that it will be transformed into a world that is supernatural and good. The world and life negation of Jesus is conditioned by ethics. [23]

The agonies of Jesus can be seen as expressive of that love for all mankind which Schweitzer finds lacking in the Buddhist approach. Consider what more can be said about that approach by someone such as Schweitzer with his dedication to "reverence for life":

> The Buddha says nothing about the question of the redemption of the world. Really we should expect him to voice the hope that in time all living creatures will enter Nirvana and that in this way the sorrowful process of coming and going will some day quite come to an end. But he takes into account the difficulty of imagining the world-Nirvana if, in accordance with the hypothesis of the doctrine of reincarnation, all being can only attain redemption by the circuitous route of a human existence capable of the highest knowledge.
>
> According to the Buddha, it already borders on the impossible that a human being who, as a result of evildoing, enters into a non-human form of existence should later be born again in human form, "because in the low forms of existence there is mutual murder and no good action." If a yoke with one opening be thrown into the sea and in the sea there is a one-eyed turtle which only rises to the surface once in every hundred years, there is much more probability, according to a parable of the Buddha, that this turtle will one day put its neck into this yoke than that the fool who has once sunk to low forms of existence will again attain to human existence.
>
> The fact that the Buddha, the preacher of compassion, makes man only occupied with his own redemption, not with that of all living creatures, is a weakness of his teaching. [24]

Whether Schweitzer is correct about the lack of concern among the Buddhists for all living creatures, would not Gautama (who could even eat meat on occasion, if the animal had not been killed for him) have been inclined to criticize the Schweitzer approach as hardly an adherence to the Middle Way?

III

Both Hindus and Christians consider themselves guided, in their concerns for a desirable resolution of their existence, by conformity to the will of the divine. Hindus must cope with a system in which one's life (or soul?) is inevitably repeated in one form or another again and again; Christians must cope with the condition of the immortal soul with a view to its perpetual existence after its single manifestation on earth.

Buddhists, on the other hand, make far less of a godhead or the divine. A man can be freed from his fetters by a rational system of thought and the way of life he determines to be appropriate for liberation, something which Gautama considered himself particularly adept at doing. [25] Buddhists also make far less, certainly less than do Christians, of their individuality: it can and should be overcome. Thus it has been reported,

> The Buddhists also preserved few names, because it was, in the best
> periods, bad form for a monk to make a name for himself by literary
> work. It did not matter to them *who* said something, but whether it was
> true, helpful and in keeping with tradition. Originality and innovation
> were not encouraged, and anonymity was a concomitant of sanctity. [26]

One is able, if properly disciplined, to release oneself from the cycle of deaths and rebirths: the prospect of an immortal life, as ordinarily understood, is not treasured; the chain of rebirth should and can be broken. Gautama himself is considered to have been able to grasp his lives past and (in compassionate interest in mankind) his lives yet to come on earth. Is it not assumed that if a man is fully and hence truly to control his life now, and to insure what is to happen to him ever after (as well as to be able to offer guidance to others), then he must know everything about himself, which includes knowing all that has happened and that is yet to happen? [27] This ability to take control over one's "life" in the most decisive manner includes control over when and how one dies during any particular reincarnation. [28]

All this should be contrasted to the Hindu teaching that Arjuna confronts in the *Bhagavad Gītā:* his natural compassion must be subordinated to his duty. [29] The Buddhist may deny that there is any substantial thing (a permanent ego) transmitted from one life to the next. But is there not a consciousness or "identity" to "collect" one's *karma,* that compendium of things fated to happen to someone? [30] The self-denying Gautama has "succeeded" in maintaining something of himself permanently, if only in the imaginations of his followers, for millennia now.

There are various Buddhist doctrines and practices that serve the end of liberation, of total self-control, which culminates in Nirvana, a condition of complete self-abnegation which is nevertheless (or because of this) blissful beyond description. The effort must be made, therefore, to overcome the demands of one's body and the allure of other bodies. If "one" does succeed in controlling one's body, one's individuality is suppressed, so much so that there would be nothing around to "enjoy" any heavenly benefits. This means, among other things, that the status even here on earth of marriage and of the family has to be radically depreciated, however much those institutions have permitted the production of the men and women who become monks and nuns.

One may wonder what confidence there can be that the condition a man gets himself into here on earth will forever determine his eternal career, even to the extent of total extinction. It seems that the control he exercises over his passions extends to the development of confidence that he is indeed on the right path, the path out of the universe, so to speak. [31] What routine control of one's passions can mean is suggested by an anecdote from Zen Buddhism:

> Two monks, one old, one young, came to a muddy ford where a
> beautiful girl was deliberating whether to cross. The elder monk
> grabbed her and, without a word, carried her across. As they continued
> on their way the younger, astonished at the sight of his companion
> touching a woman, kept chattering about it, until at last the elder monk
> exclaimed, "What! Are you still carrying that girl? I put her down as
> soon as we crossed the ford." [32]

IV

At the core of the Buddhist position is the denial of any considerable goodness of human life on earth (or of any life anywhere?), so long as *life* does mean change, disintegration, and death (and, perhaps also, the awareness of those gloomy prospects for others as well). Gautama did not depend on revelation, it seems, in arriving at this assessment of human life, however much he relied upon the revelations of the Hindus for various assumptions and doctrines (if not experiences), as about reincarnation. In principle, it can be said, others could figure out (perhaps many had already figured out, but not publicly?) what Gautama did. [33] This is not to deny that the teachings that reason suffices to establish for a few might need (for the sake of the many) considerable embellishment by tales of miracles and of a saintly life. [34] The many may even require stories about the physical torments of hell. [35] What is to be made of the fierce punishments depicted for those souls in hell? Is that sort of thing consistent with the assumptions about the insubstantiality of the ego? What does such fierceness itself reveal, whether among Buddhists or among Christians? Is it "politically" necessary for so rational a religion as Buddhism? [36] The common sense of Buddhism is suggested by another Zen Buddhist anecdote:

Women turning prayer wheels during a religious ritual in Kāthmāndu, Nepal. The wheel is a hollow metal cylinder mounted on a rod and containing a consecrated mantra. The act of turning it is equivalent to reciting the mantra, a sacred syllable or verse.

Ex-Emperor: Gudo, what happens to the man of enlightenment and the man of illusion after death?

Gudo: How should I know, sir?

Ex-Emperor: Why, because you're a master!

Gudo: Yes, sir, but no dead one! [37]

The Buddhist reservations about earthly life may be contrasted with the affirmation of life found among such peoples as the Jews, an affirmation which reflects the goodness that God Himself sees in the Creation depicted in Genesis. Does not philosophy back up this finding of revelation? Consider, for example, the Aristotelian recognition of the sweetness of existence. [38] True, Socrates, for one, had no over-powering desire to live. But he could see life among the dead, if one did survive death, as not unpleasant, especially if one could continue inquiring and learning. [39]

Is there not something unnatural in the insistence upon suffering as decisive to human life on earth? To insist upon that is to suggest that the only happiness we can reasonably hope for is a release from all life. That there is something to this may be indicated by the old saying, made more of by some than by others, that philosophy prepares one for dying. The Buddhist approach to what life is truly like is suggested by this account:

> Most of us are inclined by nature to live in a fool's paradise, to look on
> the brighter side of life, and to minimize its unpleasant sides. To dwell
> on suffering runs normally counter to our inclinations. Usually, we
> cover up suffering with all kinds of "emotional curtains." For most of
> us life would be intolerable if we could see it as it is, and if our mental
> perspective would emphasize its distasteful features as much as its
> gratifying ones. We like to keep distressing facts out of sight. [40]

The natural grasp of the goodness of existence, in the fashion of
Aristotle, is questioned. It is seen as self-deception, sometimes even as
deliberate self-deception. And yet, can it be truly said that Aristotle was
deceived—that he did not know the realities of life which Buddhists,
like the rest of us, know well? Did he not see life—as we know it with its
mortality, pains, failures, and disappointments—as permitting growth,
maturation, challenge, and accomplishment?

Does this Aristotelian approach depend on taking nature seriously,
something that may be impossible to do if routine reincarnations is
made much of? If nature is not taken seriously, bizarre results can come
to be accepted by quite intelligent people. For example, a Buddha is
commended for having given up his life in order that a starving tigress
and her litter might live. [41] Or a nun plucks out an eye to discourage
a persistent suitor drawn to her by the beauty of her eyes. [42] Then
there is this story:

> In order that [a monk] should have no attachment to food, he is bidden
> to eat everything and anything which is thrown into his bowl; and the
> Venerable Pindola has been held up to the reverence of posterity for
> calmly eating a leper's thumb which had fallen into his bowl [upon
> "begging" his food the way monks do]. Monastic discipline would be
> undermined if monks would start to pick and choose their food. [43]

The acceptance of reincarnation on earth as routine undermines in
various ways any reliance upon nature—that nature which points to
the goodness of a life keyed to our natural faculties. When one's "life"
is seen as aeons long, it must be difficult to grasp as a whole: control
is difficult—as is any reliable knowledge and hence the possibility of
genuine satisfaction with what one has done. The only effective control
we can hope to exercise may be seen as the result of efforts to eliminate
once and for all the sequence of lives in which we are enmeshed.

Without a proper grasp of nature, philosophy itself is not possible,
however much is made by modern scholars and others of Buddhists as
philosophers. [44] The ancient dialogue *The Questions of Milinda* (which
exhibits Greek influences) is often regarded as philosophical; but it is
much more a kind of rhetoric, if not even sophistry, which reflects
the cleverness and subtlety repeatedly evident in Buddhism. The difference that nature, or rather its absence, makes is suggested by this
exchange:

[Said the king:] Reverend Nagasena, you Buddhists say: "Far hotter than any ordinary fire is the Fire of Hell. A tiny stone, cast into any ordinary fire, will smoke for a whole day and not crumble. But a rock as big as a pagoda, cast into the Fire of Hell, will crumble in an instant." But on the other hand you also say this: "As for the living beings that are reborn in Hell, no matter how many thousands of years they are tormented therein, they go not to destruction." That is something I do not believe.

[Said the Elder:] . . . What do you think about this, great king? Do not the delicate princesses of the Greeks and of the Warriors and of the Brahmans and of the householders eat pieces of meat that are hard and tough?

Yes, Reverend Sir, they do.

Now these hard substances, once inside of their abdomen, once in their belly, go to destruction; do they not?

Yes, Reverend Sir, they do.

But does the embryo in their belly also go to destruction?

No, indeed, Reverend Sir.

For what reason?

I suppose, Reverend Sir, it is because of the Power of Kamma [Karma] that it does not go to destruction.

Precisely so, great king, because of the Power of Kamma, the denizens of Hell, no matter how many thousands of years they are tormented in Hell, go not to destruction. Right there are they born, right there do they grow up, right there do they die. Moreover, great king, this was said by the Exalted One: "He shall not die so long as that Evil Kamma is not yet exhausted."

You are a clever man, Reverend Nagasena!" [45]

It is obvious, at least to us, that the physiology relied upon here is mistaken: an embryo that is swallowed would be digested as any other meat would be. Another way of putting it is to say that the womb is far different from the stomach. The physiological error is not the interesting point here, but rather the fact that the author and his readers are prepared to believe that there *could* be diverse consequences routinely following upon the activity of the same agent (in this case, the stomach). Thus flesh is digested ordinarily, but not in the case of the embryo. This means that there can be, routinely, diverse effects resulting from the same cause: critical to the way things are ordered is the role of kamma (or karma), which affects much if not all of what happens to us. Nature is thereby circumvented or ignored, a circumvention anticipated perhaps by what Gautama's father had attempted to do in shielding his son from exposure to evidences of human mortality.

One consequence of the lack of dependence on nature is that simple understanding, or understanding for its own sake, is not made much of in Buddhism. Again and again one can see in Buddhist thought an emphasis upon inquiry for the sake of the practical; theoretical inquiry is disparaged. [46]

We can again see why compassion rather than reason is the human attribute ultimately to be prized. If reason is given the second place, and nature little or no place at all, then prudence, as well as political philosophy, is not likely to be taken seriously. Are not grave political problems apt to emerge when the best in the community systematically neglect a concern for this world? It must be a concern for community-minded citizens when celibacy is encouraged and expected, on a large scale, for the true believers and hence for the most virtuous. This may be made even more acute when those who do separate themselves from worldly concerns live by "begging," appearing daily among the others for this purpose in quite conspicuous garments. [47]

One result of all this seems to be the promotion of gentleness, making Buddhism perhaps the least violent in practice of the great religions known to us. [48] But to promote gentleness is to discourage spiritedness—and this raises, in still another way, the question of whether a proper political ordering is possible on Buddhist terms. Are not both justice and courage likely to be neglected in this case? Is not spiritedness as much a part of the natural whole as gentleness? [49]

One may ask as well what the status of beauty is when the things of this world, and the appearances of things, are systematically disparaged. Nothing, it would seem, can be taken at face value. This implies that common sense, which respects the surface of things, may not mean much. Still, is it not natural and wholesome to give beauty its due, whatever the chattering monk at the river ford (to say nothing of his elder companion) may have believed? Appearances *can* be deceiving—but we would not be moved to notice this if "appearance" and "reality" did not match to a considerable extent in the everyday world. [50]

V

I have attempted to work out some implications of the Buddhist approach to life and death. Why did Gautama take the way he did? Is not this one major way "out," considering the prevailing opinions and conditions of his time? Those prevailing opinions include, we have seen, what seem to have been fixed, deeply held convictions about the prospects of repeated reincarnations. [51]

Among the Hindus from whom Gautama emerged, it can be said, the prospect of a soul's repeatedly waging vital battles, generation after generation, appears to have led to resignation if not despair. This is dramatized in the *Bhagavad Gītā,* where Arjuna receives critical instruction from his charioteer. (Is there not an echo of this ancient encounter in Gautama's learning decisively about life and death from *his* charioteer at age twenty-nine?) According to the sources drawn upon in the *Gītā,* one's divinely required duty may call for battle and extreme violence;

A Zen Buddhist monk collecting alms in Japan. His reading of a book at the same time testifies to the fact that whatever the monk must do to live, and rigorous as his rituals may be, his chief business is the life of the mind: thought.

one has a destiny to fulfill; one cannot simply take charge of one's life. [52] Gautama, on the other hand, figures out (almost in a parody anticipating the *Gītā*) that gentleness is called for, that one *can* take charge of one's life, that Arjuna's suppressed effort to do so in the name of compassion had been, after all, a move in the right direction, a move that Gautama was able to see to its proper conclusion.

Perhaps, also, the prevalence and unavoidability of suffering in Gautama's day, reinforced by the violence and mutual exploitation implicit in a Hindu caste system that had become more and more rigid, stimulated a man naturally inclined toward compassion and gentleness to assert himself. [53] Is a new, more humane, political order, or at least a more humane set of social relations, reflected in the Brotherhood promoted by Gautama?

However much of an innovator Gautama was, he may well have recognized the limits of innovation. We have noticed that much of Hindu thought, including its cosmology, is taken for granted by Gautama, or at least by his followers. The critical difference is that Gautama pointed the way to a deliberate self-annihilation which permits one to avoid, if not to overcome, the hopelessness that the Hindu belief in reincarnation can degenerate into. Even if Gautama did not take this Hindu view seriously himself, was he not obliged to take seriously its temporal consequences?

To suggest how desperate things might have become in Gautama's time is to approach these matters with both the advantages and the limitations of an outsider, somewhat as an anthropologist would. This approach may even consider Gautama to have been something of an anthropologist himself. Or, alternatively if not additionally, Gautama can be approached for psychological study: was he a man whose character traits or psychic makeup required a total withdrawal from physical struggle, if not even from life itself? So intense may such a withdrawal be that one can, in the name of self-denial, exercise a powerful hold upon others.

VI

The questions of the anthropologist and the psychologist must be ultimately subordinated to the question whether Gautama's way has hold of the truth about human things, to say nothing of divine things. That is, a proper study of Buddhism must consider whether the ideas Gautama developed are sound.

One place to begin in any such assessment is with the Buddhist—and before it the Hindu—belief in routine reincarnations. What *is* the evidence for all this? Is it not evidence which should, if valid, be available as well to us in the West? What experiences do we have, what things do we know, that point to, or away from, earthly reincarnations? What does nature, and one's natural grasp of things, say about a belief in routine reincarnations? That so many intensely believe in reincarnation cannot suffice to establish it, even though such extensive testimony does oblige us to consider it with care. Is it not significant that routine reincarnations rarely occur to us in the West as something to be taken seriously? We can suspect why so many could come to believe in it, if it is *not* so. But can we understand how so many who have heard again and again of reincarnation could fail to take it at all seriously, if it *is* so? [54]

Much is made in Buddhism of meditation. This is related to the oft-stated opinion that Buddhism is a rational religion, however pious (in the ordinary sense) its people at large may be. Although meditation is not simply philosophy, it can include sustained thinking that permits one to work things out somewhat as philosophers do. Does not modern cosmology, with its vast time and space and perhaps with its notions about how life can emerge anywhere in the universe, lend support to the Hindu-Buddhist approach to things? We are still left with the question of how good the understanding of modern science, or of any cosmology, can be without a sound, if not even continually examined, grasp of nature. Is there something artificial or hypothetical, however salutary, about what modern scientists and perhaps ancient Buddhists do?

The thinking we see in Buddhism may be more that of the artist than that of the philosopher. Consider the significance of so many apt images and engaging stories in Buddhism. This is related to the status of the particulars of which artists make so much. How self-conscious is Gautama about these matters, deliberately relying on particulars, in the form of stories and in the form of his own life, in order to spread his message? Was Gautama then an artist who was counter-Homeric in his inclinations, a poet who made peace and self-abnegation, not war and self-assertion, the stuff of his "Iliad"? [55] Did Gautama believe all that he said when he talked about the whole? Considerable common sense and a grasp of the natural order are exhibited in his approach to things, not least in the way he turned away from his original asceticism and then organized his monastic order. [56]

What will happen to Buddhism in an age when modern science does even more hereafter than it already has done with its own immense (perhaps incomprehensible) cosmological scope, and when image-making is already practiced so extensively all around us? The answer to this question might depend, in part at least, on whether conventional Buddhism is to be accounted for primarily in anthropological-political-psychological terms or is to be accounted for as itself a significant grasp of the truth. [57]

VII

We must wonder what the significance is of the tradition of esotericism in Buddhism, something which is referred to even in what Gautama is reported to have said as he was about to die, "What, then, Ananda, does the order [of monks] expect of me? I have preached the truth without making any distinction between exoteric and esoteric doctrine; for in respect of the truth, Ananda, the Tathagata has no such thing as the closed fist of a teacher who keeps some things back." [58] Although Gautama and his immediate adherents disavowed esotericism, the many indications of and references to it oblige us to wonder what was truly going on among them.

Esotericism presupposes that, for one reason or another, a few can understand and hence are taught what the many are not able to understand. What did Gautama himself really believe about the matters which he discussed? If we assume he was as intelligent as he is generally

Buddha's footprints in Bodh Gayā, India. The footprints (buddhapāda), carved in stone, are regarded as symbolic of the Buddha's presence. Some examples are over a yard long and covered with signs of good omen that are supposed to have been imprinted on Buddha's feet.

reputed to have been, we must reconsider what he said in the light of what we ourselves can see from the evidence, or lack of evidence, that was available to him. [59]

Did Gautama, in his extended meditation into the nature of things, see an abyss confronting the thinking man? Was he terrified, or exhilarated, or at least challenged about the prospect of groundlessness? We must wonder whether Gautama anticipated in certain respects the view of things that Friedrich Nietzsche, for one, developed in our own time. [60] But Gautama, we have seen, sought to rise above or dispense with the eternal return, whereas Nietzsche asserted the eternal return and evidently clung to it as his salvation, closer in a sense to the spirit of Gilgamesh in this respect than to that of Gautama. Both Gautama and Nietzsche try to take control of their lives with an exercise of the will (bordering, it can seem to the outsider, on madness) that extends to the past as well as to the future, perhaps even to the extent of inventing (or is it discerning?) both one's predecessors and one's successors in the chain of births and deaths. In neither case, perhaps, is philosophy taken fully seriously or on its own terms, especially insofar as philosophy presupposes both the eternity of the universe and the temporary appearances on earth of individual souls. These souls can reasonably aim at happiness here and can look back at their lives on earth as on net good. In short, the philosopher can contemplate a natural wholeness in things: it would be considered odd by him to regard complete personal annihilation as perfection, however temporary particular lives may naturally be. [61]

Gautama, whatever he may have believed, was obliged to take certain "givens" seriously in prescribing for his community. Did he succeed in reshaping what had been a violent community? Or was it that Buddhism had to move on, in the centuries after its founding among the Hindus, to more receptive regions in Asia, thereby reaffirming elsewhere, rather than creating, a peaceful way of life?

We are left, then, with the puzzle of what Gautama truly believed and did, as well as of what the status of nature and of the desire to understand may be in his thought. Whatever esotericism he may have resorted to permitted him a very long life, a career evidently pursued without serious conflict or persecution. His "religion" could even be suspected in some quarters (and repeatedly across the millennia) of "atheism," without turning him and his followers into outcasts, perhaps in part because of the trappings of religion and self-sacrifice with which the activities of the conspicuous Buddhist monks are invested. In any event, Gautama's life *can* be presented without miracles; very little is said about the divine, except negatively perhaps in the form of a devil. What there is said about the supernatural tends to treat it as "natural." The human being, moreover, should not expect help from the divine but must work out his own salvation. [62]

Both conventional religion and traditional philosophy can be expected to exhibit one trait which Gautama very much exhibited as well: a determined pursuit of perfection. Whether the ordinary religious spirit or the familiar philosophical temper can properly accept the form of perfection Gautama seemed to settle upon—the perfection of complete personal annihilation or nothingness—is a question to be left for further consideration on another occasion. With this question we remind ourselves that there is probably much left to be learned by all of us about the very nature of things. [63]

---

1. Francis Bacon, *The Essayes or Counsels, Civill and Morall* (1625), Essay no. XVI, "Of Atheism." Consider also Essay no. XVII, "Of Superstition," which includes these sentiments:

> It were better to have no opinion of God at all than such an opinion as is unworthy of him. For the one is unbelief, the other is contumely, and certainly superstition is the reproach of the Deity. . . . And as the contumely is greater towards God, so the danger is greater towards men. Atheism leaves a man to sense, to philosophy, to natural piety, to laws, to reputation, all which may be guides to an outward moral virtue, though religion were not, but superstition dismounts all these, and erecteth an absolute monarchy in the minds of men. Therefore atheism did never perturb states, for it makes men wary of themselves, as looking no further, and we see the times inclined to atheism (as the time of Augustus Caesar) were civil times. . . . There is a superstition in avoiding superstition, when men think to do best if they go furthest from the superstition formerly received; therefore care would be had that (as it fareth

in ill purgings) the good be not taken away with the bad, which commonly is done when the people is the reformer.

Consider as well note 62 below.

I have found very helpful the criticism of this article by Mahinda Deegalle, a Buddhist monk from Sri Lanka doing research at the University of Chicago. *See* M. Deegalle, *Nirvana saha sadacaraya* (Sri Lankal: Dipani Piakasapa, 1986), pp. 90–92 (bibliography).

2. The Hindu doctrine of reincarnations, which figures prominently in Buddhist thought, is repeatedly drawn upon in this article. *See* Anastaplo, "An Introduction to Hindu Thought: The *Bhagavad Gītā*" (*GIT* 1985, 258–85). *See also* notes 51, 54, and 59 below.

The Hindu-Buddhist doctrine of Nirvana, as a state of extinction of desire and individual consciousness and as freedom from rebirth, is also drawn upon in this article. *See* W. Theodore de Bary, ed., *The Buddhist Tradition in India, China and Japan* (New York: Vintage Books, 1969), pp. 9, 11–12, 21, 30; Albert Schweitzer, *Indian Thought and Its Development* (Boston: Beacon Press, 1956), pp. 99–106; Nancy Wilson Ross, *Three Ways of Indian Wisdom* (New York: Simon and Schuster, 1966), pp. 90, 113–14.

"Buddha" is not the name of a person but designates a type. " 'Buddha' is Sanskrit for someone who is 'fully enlightened' about the nature and meaning of life. Numerous 'Buddhas' appear successively at suitable intervals. Buddhism sees itself not as the record of the sayings of one man who lived in Northern India about 500 B.C. His teachings are represented as the uniform results of an often repeated irruption of spiritual reality into this world" (Edward Conze, ed., *Buddhist Scriptures* [Penguin Books, 1959], p. 19). *See also* note 51 below. On Buddhism, *see* Ross, p. 79:

> Buddhism, the religion of reason and meditation and the faith of approximately one fifth of humanity, was founded by the so-called "historic" Buddha, Siddhartha Gautama, a unique spiritual genius born in northeastern India at a date generally accepted as 563 B.C. Although in the land of its origin Buddhism was in time reabsorbed into the all-embracing Hinduism from which it sprang, it was destined to become and remain the dominant influence in vast sections of Asia, including Ceylon, Burma, Cambodia, Thailand, Vietnam, Laos, as well as Nepal, Sikkim, Tibet, Mongolia, China, Korea, and Japan.

Buddhism is said to be the major religious denomination of our fiftieth state, Hawaii (ibid., p. 134).

3. *Encyclopædia Britannica*, 15th ed., s.v. "Buddhism." "Gautama" is the Sanskrit spelling of a name spelled "Gotoma" in Pāli, the other principal language of the earliest Buddhist literature. *See also* the accounts of Gautama's career in Conze, *Buddhist Scriptures*, pp. 39–40, 43; de Bary, pp. 6–7; Ross, pp. 84–87; and E. A. Burtt, *The Teachings of the Compassionate Buddha* (New York: Mentor Book, North American Library, 1982), pp. 20–21. It should be noticed that the institution of monks in yellow robes preceded Gautama, just as monasteries preceded Saint Augustine, a key figure in the development of monastic life in Christendom. It should also be noticed that for the first five hundred years after the career of Gautama the Buddhist "Scriptures" may have been orally transmitted (Conze, *Buddhist Scriptures,* p. 11). "Buddhists possess nothing that corresponds to the 'New Testament.' The 'continuing tradition' is all that is clearly attested" (ibid., p. 11).

Parallels to the development of Christianity are suggested in this account of the early career of Buddhism:

> A first Buddhist council was summoned in the reign of [Emperor] Ashoka—about 240 B.C.—with a view to the settlement of sectarian disputes. It is clear that heresies had already arisen, for certain of Ashoka's edicts are concerned with the unfrocking of schismatics; and, indeed, we know that heresies were promulgated even during the life of the Buddha himself. In course of time we find that a large number of sects developed, all equally claiming to be followers of the true doctrine, just as has been the case with Christianity and every other great faith. The Buddhist sects are divided into two main groups: those of the Hinayana ("The Little Raft") and the Mahayana ("The Great Raft"). The former, whose scriptures are preserved in Pali, claim to represent

the pure original teaching of Gautama, and do in the main preserve its rationalistic, monastic and puritanical features to a marked extent: the latter, whose scriptures are in Sanskrit, interpret the doctrine in another way, with a development that is mystical, theological and devotional. The Hinayana had maintained its supremacy mainly in the South, particularly in Ceylon and Burma; the Mahayana mainly in the North, in Nepal and China. But it is misleading to speak of the two schools as definitely Southern and Northern.

Let us recall that according to the orthodox Hinayana, Gautama was regarded as a man like other men, and differed from others only in his intuitive penetration of the secret of life and sorrow, in his perception of things as they really are, as an eternal Becoming; with that knowledge he attained Nibbana [Nirvana], and for him the causes of birth [that is, reincarnation] were extinguished. (Ananda K. Coomaraswamy, *Buddha and the Gospel of Buddhism* [New York: Harper Torchbooks, Harper & Row, 1964], pp. 222–23)

See note 56 below. Compare note 59 below.
See, on Gautama's charioteer, the text at note 52 below.
4. *See* Conze, *Buddhist Scriptures*, pp. 222–24.
5. From *Questions of Milinda,* in Lucien Stryk, ed., *World of the Buddha: A Reader* (Garden City, N.Y.: Anchor Books, Doubleday & Company, 1969), p. 120. *See,* on *Questions of Milinda,* note 45 below. Had the anticipated birth of his child triggered Gautama's anxiety about disease, old age, and death?
How deeply rooted was Gautama's anxiety in the languages and way of life in which he and Buddhism were nurtured? *See* Guy Richard Welbon, *The Buddhist Nirvana and Its Western Interpreters* (Chicago: University of Chicago Press, 1968), pp. vii–viii:

According to the Buddhists, a man's lot in this life is characterized by suffering (Sanskrit: *duhkha;* Pali: *dukkha*). The texts make it clear that suffering is linked to ignorance. Indeed, in the Buddhist view, suffering and ignorance are invariably associated. The one is never found without the other. Most poignant and consequential among the aspects of ignorance, say the Buddhists, is man's failure to comprehend the basic truth about the phenomenal universe: no phenomenon is permanent—nothing abides. Ignorant of that truth, his proclivities (habitual thirst—*trsna, tanha*—for objects and experiences) nurtured accordingly, a man lives out of harmony with himself, his fellows, his world. He suffers.

The Buddha is the compassionate physician, his pronouncements prescriptions. The Way of the Buddha is, in a manner of speaking, the way from disease to health. But of what does "health" in the Buddhist sense consist? To be sure, it is deliverance (*moksa, mokkha*) from suffering. It is described variously, most commonly as *nirvana* (*nibbana*).

Nirvana is the absence—the destruction—of suffering (*duhkhanirodha*). It involves the eradication of ignorance through the acquisition of wisdom (*sambodhi*)—knowledge, conceived classically in India not merely as intellection but as operational and effective knowledge. Yet, more specifically, more positively than the absence of debilities, what is nirvana? The ultimate aspiration of all Buddhists, their *summum bonum,* what is its "essential" nature? What does attainment to it involve for the existence of the previously suffering individual? One of the oldest in the history of ideas, that question, in its various modes, has been debated furiously by Buddhists and non-Buddhists alike.

See also note 32 below. In 1863 a French scholar announced,

Today, as in 1856, I am convinced that it is morally impossible that in Magadha in the sixth century before our era the son of Mayadevi [Gautama] preached the absolute annihilation of virtuous souls until six hundred years later in Galilee the son of Mary could come to preach the Gospel of their eternal beatitude. (Ibid., p. 81)

See notes 47 and 57 below. Does Buddhism, seen in this way, mean that ours is a universe from which the very best are systematically removed? *See* the text at note 24 below.
6. *See* Ross, p. 81. *See also* the quotation under the photograph of the Buddha statue

facing the title page of A. L. Herman, *An Introduction to Buddhist Thought: A Philosophical History of Indian Buddhism* (Lanham, Md.: University Press of America, 1982).

7. Laurence G. Thompson, *Chinese Religion, An Introduction* (Encino, Calif.: Dickerson Publishing Company, 1975; 2d ed.), p. 95.

8. *See,* for the text of the *Gilgamesh* epic, *GIT* 1986, 318–47.

9. *See* Anastaplo, "An Introduction to Mesopotamian Thought: The *Gilgamesh* Epic" (*GIT* 1986, 288–313).

10. *See* Edward Conze, *Buddhism, Its Essence and Development* (New York: Harper Torchbooks, 1959), p. 63. *See also* note 61 below.

11. Schweitzer, p. 89.

12. *See* Conze, *Buddhism,* p. 53; Conze, *Buddhist Scriptures,* p. 70; Richard A. Gard, ed., *Buddhism* (New York: George Braziller, 1962), p. 52.

13. *See,* for a useful account of Gautama's career, Conze, *Buddhist Scriptures,* pp. 19–66.

14. Ross, p. 88. See also *Encyclopædia Britannica,* s.v. "Buddhism"; Conze, *Buddhist Scriptures,* pp. 45f.; Schweitzer, pp. 92–93.

15. Is this a mild form of the sensuality of the boisterous Gilgamesh? *See* notes 8 and 9 above.

16. Burtt, pp. 29–30. The Tathāgata is "he who has fully arrived," that is, the Perfect One (and hence *completely gone?*). This is a title of the Buddha. See also *Encyclopædia Britannica,* s.v. "Buddhism"; de Bary, pp. 15–17.

17. Burtt, p. 30. *See,* on the significance of numbers, Anastaplo, "An Introduction to Hindu Thought," notes 30, 33, and 34. *See also* note 57 below.

18. Burtt, p. 30; *see also* pp. 28, 65.

19. Conze, *Buddhism, Its Essence and Development,* p. 36.

20. Ross, p. 125; *see also* p. 95. There was a similar delay "before any representations of [Jesus] as an actual physical being were conceived or executed." Compare the concern from the outset of Moses Maimonides' *The Guide of the Perplexed.*

21. Compare the four-headed statue in Bangkok, which is the center of attraction to worshipers and which is evidently widely known in Southeast Asia as the "four-headed" Buddha. See *India News,* Aug. 19, 1985, pp. 4, 5. See also Ezekiel, chap. 1. The Buddha has been assimilated into Hindu worship in various places.

Compare also Islām with its vigorous abjuration of human portraits, especially of sacred personages. *See* Anastaplo, "An Introduction to Islamic Thought: The Koran" (*GIT* 1989, 234–82). One can be reminded by the more "glorious" Buddhist statuary of the statues of Greek gods. Consider as well how Socrates was portrayed—not as an athlete but full-bodied, sturdy, self-possessed. *See* further, on Buddhist statuary, Ross, pp. 125–27.

22. Schweitzer, pp. 109–10.

23. Ibid., p. 113.

24. Ibid. *See* note 5 above.

25. See *Encyclopædia Britannica,* s.v. "Buddhism"; de Bary, pp. 10–11; Conze, *Buddhist Scriptures,* pp. 52–54, 229f.

26. Conze, *Buddhism, Its Essence and Development,* p. 30.

27. *See* Conze, *Buddhist Scriptures,* pp. 25–26, 31, 53f. *See also* pp. 237–42, 258f., on the eventual coming to earth of the last Buddha, Maitraya. *See also* note 33 below.

28. *See* Conze, *Buddhist Scriptures,* pp. 58f. *See also* Burtt, p. 48.

29. This is similar to what desperate defenders of the Jewish law said to the first Christians with respect to such matters as healing on the Sabbath. *See* the discussions of the trial of Jesus in Anastaplo, "On Trial: Explorations," 22 *Loyola University of Chicago Law Journal* 539 (1991). *See also* the discussions therein of the trial of Adam and Eve and of the Binding of Isaac.

30. *See* Thompson, pp. 83f. *See also* Anastaplo, *The American Moralist: On Law, Ethics and Government* (Athens, Ohio: Ohio University Press, 1992), pp. 10–11.

31. *See,* on the certainty of having attained liberation, Conze, *Buddhist Scriptures,* p. 31.

32. Stryk, pp. 388–89. Zen Buddhism has been described as "a unique blend of Indian mysticism and Chinese naturalism sieved through the rather special mesh of the Japanese character" (Ross, p. 139).

Compare, as a reminder of not only the immediate appeal of certain urges but also of the transcendent significance of the naturally erotic, William Butler Yeats's poem "Politics." *See* Anastaplo, *The American Moralist,* p. 497. *See also* notes 47 and 50 below. *See,* on nature, Anastaplo, *Human Being and Citizen: Essays on Virtue, Freedom and the Common Good* (Athens, Ohio: Swallow Press/Ohio University Press, 1975), Essays no. 2, 4, 6, and 16; Anastaplo, *The American Moralist*, p. 616; sections IV and VI below, note 62 below.

It seems to have been easier for the older monk than it was for the younger monk not to grasp the girl as girl. Another Buddhist elder was asked (perhaps by a young man?), "Reverend Sir, have you seen a woman pass this way?" The elder responded, "Was it a woman, or a man that passed this way? I cannot tell. But this I know, a set of bones is travelling upon this road" (Coomaraswamy, p. 159). Compare note 47 below (the world as "cemetery").

We are apt to regard as healthier the reminiscence of the repentant Augustine: he recalls that, as a young man, he had prayed, "Give me chastity and continence, but not yet" (*Confessions,* VII, 7). *See* note 58 below. Gautama's efforts at renunciation seem in some ways more desperate than those of someone such as Augustine. The Buddhist's fundamental problem is with life itself, while the Christian's is with life in one's earthly body, something which should be easier to deal with than any thorough repudiation of existence itself. Socrates and Plato could also address, without being crippled by, the problem of the fetters of the body. *See,* on the sweetness of existence for the philosophers, the text at note 38 below. *See also* the text at note 1 above. *See* as well note 57 below.

Augustine may have been moderated somewhat in his heroic attempts at self-abnegation by the philosophical tradition which Christianity inherited, in however diluted and altered a form, along with the language of the New Testament. *See,* on how the Church was obliged to take more than it wanted of classical antiquity with the Latin language, Machiavelli, *Discourses,* II, 5. *See,* on the significance of Shakespeare for modern republicanism, Anastaplo, *The Constitution of 1787: A Commentary* (Baltimore: Johns Hopkins University Press, 1989), pp. 1, 74–88. *See also* note 5 above.

The Christian reliance upon an elevated individuality can be instructively contrasted with the Buddhist yearning for complete personal annihilation. *See* note 5 above. The student of great religious movements must wonder what can be accounted for, in each case, by the chance circumstances and the natural talents of inspired mortals. We cannot help but wonder, upon reflecting on the celebrated lives of Gautama and Augustine, what the good was that was truly being sought by each of them and whether it was indeed secured. We take as our point of departure here the observation by Aristotle, "All human beings have by their nature an appetite for knowing" (*Metaphysics,* I, i, trans. Eva T. H. Brann).

33. Compare Conze, *Buddhist Scriptures,* pp. 126f. Gautama, it should again be noticed, is not said to be either the first or the last Buddha to appear on earth. *See* pp. 19–20, 30–33, 35–36, 49; Ross, p. 124. *See also* note 27 above. Is he, at least for human beings, central to all the Buddhas that will ever appear?

34. *See* Conze, *Buddhist Scriptures,* p. 57.

35. *See* ibid., pp. 221, 224f.

36. *See* the concluding section of Plato's *Gorgias* (*GBWW* I: 7, 252; II: 6, 252). *See also* the text at note 48 below. *See,* on the political services rendered by organized religion, Anastaplo, "Church and State: Explorations," 19 *Loyola University of Chicago Law Journal* p. 61 (1987). *See also* note 56 below.

Is biblical-style revelation such as not to leave sufficient room for the reason, or the will, of the Buddha? Compare God's appearances to Moses and Jesus' appearance to Saul on the road to Damascus. Gautama, on the other hand, considers himself to have figured out the way to his distinctive doctrines. *See* de Bary, p. 360. Consider also the text at note 1 above. Do we move away from the spirit of Gautama if we assume that this Buddha was destined to appear, that the divine had provided for the enlightenment of mankind in due time? Is it to misconceive the fundamental claim of Gautama to a rational approach to consider as a problem, as is done in *Questions of Milinda* (note 45 below), whether the Buddha (meaning Gautama) ever lived?

37. Stryk, p. 399. Gudo's dates are A.D. 1579–1661.

38. *See* Aristotle, *Politics* 1278b25–29 (*GBWW* I: 9, 476; II: 8, 476); Anastaplo, *The American Moralist,* p. 600. The Confucian teaching seems far closer to Aristotle than to Buddhism with respect to these matters. *See* Anastaplo, "An Introduction to Confucian Thought," (*GIT* 1984, 124–70). *See,* on Chinese Taoism here, Thompson, p. 85. *See also* note 32 above, note 47 below.

39. *See* Anastaplo, *Human Being and Citizen,* Essay no. 2. Consider (in Homer's *Odyssey*) the condition in which Odysseus found Achilles among the dead: Achilles' interests and limitations (unlike, say, those of Socrates) were such as to require bodies (his and those of others) for his personal fulfillment. Consider, also, the Confucian respect for old age. *See,* on Confucius, note 38 above.

40. Conze, *Buddhism, Its Essence and Development,* p. 44.

41. *See* Conze, *Buddhist Scriptures,* pp. 24–26; Schweitzer, p. 104; Ross, pp. 91–92.

42. *See* Burtt, pp. 80–83. *See also* Matthew 5:29. *See,* on some offending eyelids, Ross, p. 152.

43. Conze, *Buddhism, Its Essence and Development,* p. 62. There is a tradition that Gautama died, in his eighties, of a tainted meal. Then there is the apt explanation by Sam Houston upon spitting out, at a formal dinner, the very hot food he had inadvertently taken into his mouth, "A damned fool would have swallowed that!" *See,* on nature, note 32 above.

44. *See,* e.g., Burtt, pp. 22, 25; Gard, p. 14; de Bary, p. xvi.

45. Stryk, pp. 107–08. A variation upon this exchange uses, instead of delicate princesses, "female sharks and crocodiles and tortoises and peacocks and pigeons [that] swallow hard stones and gravel" (ibid., p. 107). *See also* Ross, p. 115. *See,* on *Questions of Milinda,* Stryk, p. 89:

> The non-canonical Pali work *Milindapannha* (*Questions of Milinda*) . . . is a collection of imaginary dialogues between Menander, Greek king of Bactria, 125–95 B.C. (there is some divergence of opinion regarding these dates), and the sage Nagasena, whose expositions of Buddhist teaching on the non-existence of the soul and Nibbana (Nirvana) are of significance to all interested in Buddhist philosophy.

However questionable Nagasena's handling of nature and natural processes may be, there *is* something commonsensical (and hence Aristotelian) about a common refrain, "That man might say whatever he would, but all the same . . . " in the following passage taken from *Questions of Milinda* where Nagasena explains to the king the continuity of the soul that is manifested in successive reincarnations:

> Great king, it is precisely as if some man or other were to take a lamp and were to climb to the attic of a thatched house and were to eat, and the lamp as it burned were to set fire to the thatch, and the thatch as it burned were to set fire to the house, and the house as it burned were to set fire to the village, and the village-folk were to catch that man and were to say, "Why, Master man, did you set fire to the village?" and the man were to say, "Friends, I didn't set fire to the village; the fire of the lamp by whose light I ate is one thing, but the fire that burned the village is another." Suppose they carried the dispute to you. Whose side, great king, would you take?
> The side of the village-folk, Reverend Sir.
> Why?
> That man might say whatever he would, but all the same, that last fire came straight from the first.
> Great king, it is precisely as if some man or other were to choose a young girl to be his wife and were to pay the purchase-money and were to go his way, and after a time that young girl were to become a grown woman, were to attain her majority, and then a second man were to pay the purchase-money and were to marry her, and the first man were to come and say, "But why, Master man, are you carrying off my wife?" and the second man were to say, "I am not carrying off your wife; that young girl of tender years whom you chose to be your wife and for whom you paid the purchase-money is one person; this grown woman who has attained her majority, whom I chose to be my wife and for whom I paid the purchase-money, is another person." Suppose they carried the dispute to you. Whose side, great king, would you take?
> The side of the first man, Reverend Sir.
> Why?
> That man might say whatever he would, but all the same, that grown woman came straight from that young girl. . . . (Stryk, pp. 98–99)

Zeno-like paradoxes can be dealt with thus.

46. *See,* e.g., Burtt, pp. 32f.; de Bary, p. 18n.; Ross, p. 113; Conze, *Buddhism, Its Essence and Development,* p. 19; Schweitzer, pp. 96–97. Compare Burtt, pp. 70–71.

47. *See* de Bary, pp. 27n., 32, 46–47, 72, 258; Schweitzer, p. 112. *See also* Pliny, *Natural History,* V, xv, 73 (on "the remarkable tribe" of celibate Essenes). Compare the Chinese concern about childlessness. *See* de Bary, pp. 133–34, 243, 247–51. The Buddhist repudiation of earthly existence is reflected in someone's regarding "the world of men [to be] no better than a cemetery, as being under the sway of old age and death, and as being always in distress" (Conze, *Buddhist Scriptures,* p. 224). *See* note 32 above ("a set of bones"). Although the better thinkers of antiquity in the West recognized the fragility of human life on earth along with the fragility of the earth itself, they could still take political life and prudence more seriously than Buddhism seems to. *See* Anastaplo, *The American Moralist,* pp. 100–102.

Is the use today of Buddhist monks as social workers and teachers a concession to modernity or to Western ways? Consider this summary of the European Enlightenment attitude toward Buddhism during the seventeenth and eighteenth centuries:

> Buddhism always appears simply as a "monstrous religion," as an "abominable sect" founded by a "very wicked man." It is a "plague," a "gangrene." Chinese philosophers and statesmen have had reason to combat it not only as a "ridiculous doctrine" but as a "moral monster and the destruction of civil society." (Welbon, p. 20)

See notes 5 and 38 above.

The future Buddha can be presented, as in an ancient statue in the Art Institute of Chicago, seated in a regal throne: he is ruling. This does suggest an opening to the political in traditional Buddhism. *See* note 56 below.

48. *See,* e.g., Burtt, p. 39. *See also* pp. 40f., on the virtues which are promoted. *See* as well Schweitzer, pp. 100f., 115–16, 119. Compare the text at note 36 above.

49. *See* the discussion of conscientious objectors in Anastaplo, "Church and State: Explorations." *See* the discussion of the Vietnam War in Anastaplo, "Freedom of Speech and the First Amendment: Explorations," 21 *Texas Tech Law Review* 1941 (1990); Anastaplo, *The American Moralist,* pp. 108–21, 225–44. *See,* on the Gulf War, ibid., pp. xvi–xix, xxii, 225n.

50. *See,* on the beauty of Gautama, Conze, *Buddhist Scriptures,* pp. 35–36, 125, 129, 132. Consider this observation in Augustine's *The City of God* (X, 14):

> The Platonist Plotinus discourses concerning providence and, from the beauty of flowers and foliage, proves that from the supreme God, whose beauty is unseen and ineffable, providence reaches down even to these earthly things here below; and he argues that all these frail and perishing things could not have so exquisite and elaborate a beauty were they not fashioned by Him Whose unseen and unchangeable beauty continually pervades all things. (*GBWW* I: 18, 307; II: 16, 358)

See also Matthew 6:23–30. Compare Augustine, *Confessions,* IV, 13. *See* "A Primer on the Good, the True, and the Beautiful," in Anastaplo, *The Artist as Thinker: From Shakespeare to Joyce* (Athens, Ohio: Swallow Press/Ohio University Press, 1983), p. 275. *See also* note 32 above.

51. *See* note 2 above, note 59 below. Did not Gautama welcome that kind of reincarnation that for him took the form of the institutionalizing his spirit in the Buddhist monastery movement?

Compare the Socratic recourses to reincarnation in Plato's *Meno* and *Phaedo* (but *not* at the end of Plato's *Apology,* where Socrates reviews the alternatives available to him upon his immediately impending death). Do not the conventional Platonic recourses to reincarnation seem, much more than do the conventional Hindu-Buddhist recourses, to be tentative stories which are enlisted in the service of philosophy? One does see in the Platonic dialogues an insistence upon the necessity, for philosophy (if not for the virtues generally), of rising decisively above the appetites of the body.

52. *See,* for the text of the *Bhagavad Gītā, GIT* 1985, 290–337. *See also* note 2 above. I am assuming here that although the *Bhagavad Gītā* was composed in about 300 B.C. (and hence after the career of Gautama, which was two or more centuries earlier), something of the story about the relation between Arjuna and his charioteer was known long before

the composition of the *Gītā*. If I am mistaken here, the *Gītā* may be seen as an echo of the career of Gautama.

53. It has been suggested, "On the metaphysical side, Buddhism is not fundamentally different from Hinduism. It stands in the same relation to Hinduism as Christianity to Judaism" (Paul Thomas, *Epics, Myths and Legends of India* [Bombay: D. B. Taraporevala Sons, 1960; 5th ed.], p. 110). It has also been suggested that Gautama is like Martin Luther. *See* Schweitzer, p. 91; *see also* pp. 134–37.

54. *See,* on reason, revelation, and nature in the *Bhagavad Gītā,* Anastaplo, "Church and State: Explorations," pp. 183–90.

The doctrine of reincarnations does not keep many (most?) of the faithful from taking death much as we do in the West, as may be seen in the famous mustard-seed parable. *See* Burtt, pp. 43–46; Ross, pp. 122, 133. *See,* on reincarnation experiences, Ian Stevenson, *Cases of the Reincarnation Type* (Charlottesville: University of Virginia Press, 1975, 1977).

55. But Homer could also have an *Odyssey.* Did Gautama, too, develop a companion piece, one which made much more of political considerations than radical self-abnegation would suggest? Is this seen perhaps in the rules devised for his Brotherhood?

56. Does not any long-established institution, especially if large numbers of people are recruited and trained, have to respond to and respect (in practice, if not in "theory") the dictates of nature? *See* note 52 above. Consider also the significance of the sometimes-passionate Augustine's three decades of highly practical service as the Bishop of Hippo. *See* note 36 above, note 57 below.

See, on the importance of the Emperor Ashoka for the success of Buddhism, de Bary, pp. 7–8; Ross, pp. 125, 127; note 3 above. *See also* Machiavelli, *The Prince,* chap. VI: "Whence it comes to pass that all armed prophets conquer and the unarmed ones are ruined" (trans. Leo Paul S. de Alvarez: *GBWW* I: 23, 9; II: 21, 9).

57. A key question of fact for Buddhists could well be, Has Gautama ever returned "personally"? The significance of the "personality" (or "consciousness" or "identity"), or lack of it, has been noticed with respect to Buddhist thought, and in such a way as to throw light on such Christian works of apparent self-abnegation as Augustine's *Confessions:*

> The denial of the ego or self is undoubtedly one of the Buddha's original tenets. From the viewpoint of Western mysticism, it seems to strike hard at what Underhill called a fundamental principle: the existence of a self capable of communion with God. (Richard Woods, "Buddhism and Mysticism," *Mysterion, A Thomas More Newsletter,* no. 16, p. 3)

Augustine, in the central chapter of the central book of his *Confessions,* suggests (in a chapter which is, appropriately enough because of its subject matter, remarkably short),

> Also I considered all the other things that are of a lower order than yourself [God], and I saw that they have not absolute being in themselves, nor are they entirely without being. They are real insofar as they have their being from you, but unreal in the sense that they are not what you are. For it is only that which remains in being without change that truly is. (*Confessions,* VII, 11; *GBWW* I: 18, 49; II: 16, 61)

See note 5 above. *See,* on the significance of the number seven, Augustine, *The City of God,* XVII, 4 (*GBWW* I: 18, 451–55; II: 16, 514–18). *See also* note 17 above.

58. Burtt, pp. 48–49. *See* de Bary, pp. 28–29, 282, 287, 295; *Encyclopedia of Religion* (New York: Macmillan Publishing Company, 1987), vol. 2, pp. 172–81, 481, 526–27. *See also* chapter 2 of Wu Ch'êng-ên's *Monkey* tale for a critical reading by the Monkey King of significant esoteric signals ("Additions to the Great Books Library," *GIT* 1992). *See* as well Welbon, pp. 139–41, 168. *See* further ibid., pp. 299–300:

> The Buddha was not a philosopher. . . . Obviously, the Buddha was a genius as a soteriological tactician. Depending on the context and in particular the needs of the individual(s) to whom he spoke, his emphasis varied. To those full of self, his message was expressed negatively. To those full of fear, the message expressed confidence. To those full of suffering, the message expressed hope.

Was not Augustine, too, a master rhetorician? *See* note 32 above.

59. Many among the Buddhists tend to see Gautama as a divinity. Compare note 3 above. Certainly, he can seem to us as very thoughtful. What lessons, we may well consider, would be included among the esoteric teachings of Gautama? Our prime candidate is likely to be with respect to the widely accepted doctrine of reincarnations, the belief in which was a massive fact that had to be reckoned with by any would-be leader of Gautama's time and place. *See* notes 2 and 51 above. If there really is no reincarnation of human souls, and if Gautama believed there are reincarnations, what do we make of any reports he might have made about having recollected his past (to say nothing of his future) existences?

60. *See*, on Nietzsche, Welbon, pp. 184–93; Anastaplo, *The American Moralist*, pp. 125–34. Does it matter whether the world is eternal and whether we know whether it is eternal? Consider this passage in Ross, p. 113:

> The Buddha's characteristic attitude toward those who overindulged themselves in speculating, theorizing and debating comes through most effectively in the story of a follower named Malunkyaputta. This monk, who had a restless, overactive mind, announced to the Buddha on one occasion that if he did not get some specific straightforward answers to his inquiries about First Causes, and in particular as to whether life was eternal or not eternal, he intended to give up the Sangha [the order of Buddhist monks] for good. The Buddha replied that such an attitude reminded him strongly of a man who, having been struck by a poisoned arrow, refuses to accept the services of a physician, or even to have the arrow removed, until he has made a lengthy detailed inquiry about who shot the arrow and how and why; or again, of a man in a burning house who refuses to put out the blaze, or even to leave the doomed edifice, until he has discovered who started the conflagration.
>
> "Whether the dogma obtains, Malunkyaputta, that the world is eternal, or that the world is not eternal, there still remain birth, old age, death, sorrow, lamentations, misery, grief and despair—all the grim facts of human existence—for the extinction of which in the present life I am prescribing."

61. *See* Anastaplo, *The American Moralist*, pp. 5–6. *See also* the text at note 10 above.

62. *See*, on Buddhism and "atheism," Welbon, p. 312. Consider, on working out one's own salvation, the following counsel:

> An ant is a wise creature for itself, but it is a shrewd [mischievous] thing in an orchard or garden. And certainly men that are great lovers of themselves waste the public. Divide with reason between self-love and society; and be so true to thyself as thou be not false to others, specially to thy king and country. It is a poor centre of a man's action, *himself*. It is [exactly like the earth]. For that only stands fast upon his own centre, whereas all things that have affinity with the heavens move upon the centre of another, which they benefit. The referring of all to a man's self is more tolerable in a sovereign prince, because themselves are not only themselves, but their good and evil is at the peril of the public fortune. But it is a desperate evil in a servant to a prince, or a citizen in a republic. (Francis Bacon, *The Essayes or Counsels, Civill and Morall* [1625], Essay no. XXIII, "Of Wisdom for a Man's Self")

Consider also Essay no. XXXVIII, "Of Nature in Men." *See*, on nature, notes 32 and 56 above. *See also* note 1 above.

63. To what extent does Gautama build *not* on nothingness but on a perhaps desperate effort to secure nothingness? Is there not something Cartesian about such determined self-centeredness, albeit in the ostensible service of complete personal annihilation? *See* note 57 above. *See*, on Descartes and modern science, Anastaplo, *The American Moralist*, pp. 83–102. *See*, on modern science, Anastaplo, *The Artist as Thinker*, pp. 250–53, 339–42, 496. *See also* the text at note 1 above.

The Romantic Imagination

Maurice Cranston

Maurice Cranston has taught political science at the London School of
Economics since 1959. He was seconded to the European University in
Florence, Italy, from 1978 to 1981 and at the same time served as president
of the Institut International de Philosophie Politique. His many publications
include award-winning biographies of Locke and Rousseau, together with
essays on freedom and human rights. As a historian of ideas, he has
specialized in French thought of the eighteenth century, and his books in
this subject include *Philosophers and Pamphleteers: Political Theorists of
the Enlightenment*. His most recent book is a short history of *The Romantic
Movement*. He contributed articles to *The Great Ideas Today* in 1975,
1985, and 1986.

Professor Cranston is an honorary fellow of St. Catherine's College,
Oxford, and the London School of Economics, and visiting professor of
political science at the University of California, San Diego. In 1988 he was
appointed Commandeur de l'Ordre des Palmes Academiques in Paris.

Beginning in France

Literary criticism in the twentieth century has been generally hostile to romanticism. *Rousseau and Romanticism,* published in 1919 by the eminent Harvard professor of French and comparative literature Irving Babbitt, is perhaps the most famous of many attacks on a movement in art which the nineteenth century had held in high esteem. Various forms of "neo-humanism"—all antipathetic to romanticism—became fashionable after World War I. Defenders of romanticism were few in number: Jacques Barzun [1] in America and Sir Herbert Read [2] in England were solitary, dissenting voices until after World War II, when their teaching helped to bring about a revaluation of romanticism.

Critics and champions of romanticism are agreed about one thing: Rousseau is the first of the Romantics. In 1761 he published the original romantic novel *La nouvelle Héloïse,* and even earlier he had set down, in a controversy about music with the composer Jean-Philippe Rameau, a statement of what we now call "romantic" aesthetics against Rameau's rationalism (Maurice Cranston, *GIT* 1986, 268–87). Rameau argued that the essential element in music was harmony, which incorporated the same mathematical principles as physics; harmony in music provided, as he put it, a "double confirmation" of the order which astronomy discovered in the movements of the spheres; harmony united art with science. Against this theory Rousseau claimed that the essential element in music was melody, for it was melody which expressed human thoughts and feelings and enabled music to depict the world of nature.

Rousseau and Rameau agreed that art must be true to reality, but whereas reality for Rameau was that of the Newtonian universe, accessible to reason, reality for Rousseau was that of personal observation and experience, known through the senses. While Rameau demanded unity, Rousseau rejoiced in variety; where Rameau looked for fixed rules in music and other arts, Rousseau argued that artistic styles must be as diverse as nature itself and reflect the multiplicity of individual perceptions of the world.

Although Rameau was a better musician than Rousseau, their debate was more philosophical than technical, and Rousseau proved himself the more effective advocate. Moreover, he went on from expounding the theory of romanticism to producing a model of romantic art—his novel *La nouvelle Héloïse*. Its publication in 1761 transformed Rousseau from a literary celebrity into the object of a cult. His novel was devoured by readers and altered their ways of thinking and feeling. Rousseau's message was seen as a liberating one: that the imagination need no longer be the slave of reason, that emotions should not be denied in the name of decorum, that the laws of society were not the laws of nature, and that if only one could strip away the falseness and pretense by which social relations were dominated, the human heart would be found to be good.

The form Rousseau chose for his novel was one which Samuel Richardson and others had made popular in the eighteenth century—a *roman épistolaire,* a series of letters through which fiction could be given the appearance of fact. However contrived the method, the aim was to achieve the effect of authenticity; Rousseau's fiction was dressed up as fact to serve, like melody in music, to be the true voice of feeling, to communicate an understanding of life in all its immediacy and intensity.

Rousseau also intended *La nouvelle Héloïse* to be read as a moral tale, although it does not preach conventional morality as does, for example, Richardson's *Pamela*. In that English novel, the heroine cherishes her virginity as a capital which she will exchange for nothing less than a marriage contract—a bargain she triumphantly achieves after many trials and temptations. *La nouvelle Héloïse* has a more complex moral dimension. The central conflict is not between passion and reason, for it is one of the principles of the romanticism which Rousseau introduced that human beings are not governed by reason; the conflict is between one passion and another.

Julie, the heroine of *La nouvelle Héloïse,* is the daughter of a Vaudois baron who employs as her tutor a young man of bourgeois birth named Saint-Preux. Saint-Preux falls in love with Julie and she with him; she encourages him to become her lover and promises to be his forever. Her father, however, forbids their marriage, telling Julie that she must marry into her own class and to a man of his own choosing, Baron de Wolmar. Julie, who adores her father and dreads the consequences of breaking his heart, asks Saint-Preux to release her from her pledge. Saint-Preux nobly consents, and Julie goes on to atone for the youthful misdemeanor of sleeping with her tutor by becoming a model Christian wife and mother in Wolmar's household. Some years later Saint-Preux returns from a lonely wandering life to Wolmar's feudal estate on the shores of Lake Geneva as tutor to his children; and there, against a backdrop of Alpine scenery and summer storms, it becomes agonizingly clear that Julie has never really ceased to love Saint-Preux, and death itself has to intervene to ensure that awakened passion is thwarted.

In correspondence with readers of the novel, Rousseau explained that his purpose had been not to show people acting as they ought to

Jean-Jacques Rousseau (1712–78).

act (in the way that Richardson, for example, set out to do) but to show people acting according to their natures, just as they would in real life. Although he did not use the word *romanticism,* what he was saying was that romanticism is concerned with truth, not fantasy; if imagination was preferred to reason, it was as a faculty for seeing into the reality of human conduct.

Rousseau's belief that human behavior is governed by passion rather than reason was not new. Pascal and the German Pietists, whose works Rousseau had read as a young man, said no less; but those were Christian writers to whom the Self was hateful. For Rousseau, and for the romanticism he inspired, the Self was an object of the highest and most enduring interest. Some years after finishing *La nouvelle Héloïse,* Rousseau wrote an autobiography of a kind unprecedented in European literature, the *Confessions,* in which he declared his purpose to be to unveil the truth about one man's experience of life as candidly and openly as no author had ever done before. Rousseau took the title of his book from Augustine, but whereas those *Confessions* (*GBWW* I: 18, 1–125; II: 16, 1–159) were addressed by a penitent to God, Rousseau's *Confessions* were without repentance, an exercise at once in self-justification and self-display. But while he asserted his individuality and uniqueness, he believed that all human beings had, at the deeper level, something in common. He once told Sophie d'Houdetot that he could learn about her soul by looking into his own. [3] He discovered the secrets of the human condition by means of introspection.

251

If Rousseau was the first philosopher of romanticism, he was not the only one to emerge from the milieu of the French Enlightenment. There was also his great contemporary, the close friend with whom he quarreled, the editor of the *Encyclopédie,* Denis Diderot. Diderot was as much a man of science as a man of letters, but the sciences which interested him were not those which informed the rationalism of Newton and Rameau—astronomy and physics, where nature was observed in its most ordered and mathematical regularity—but the biological sciences, which studied the far less readily predicable movements of living things. In Nature thus perceived, Diderot noted, "everything changes, everything passes."

The true artist for Diderot was not essentially different from the scientist; both required "a delicate awareness" of things seen, and both required intuition. He argued that science was more an activity of imagination and conjecture than of experiment and induction. The scientist, he suggested, [4] needed *"l'ésprit de divination"* in order to "sniff out" the hidden connections between things and to pursue vague ideas, hints, suspicions, and even fantasies. Where the Newtonian scientists found models of Nature's laws in the movements of the planets, Diderot urged scientists instead to study irregular phenomena, to examine, for example, "monsters" such as Siamese twins, in order to gain access to Nature's secrets. Diderot had the highest regard for what was different and original. He said it was from the ranks of *Les originaux* that men of genius sprang. He was even attracted by wicked men, so long as their deeds were daring: "I hate all those sordid little things that reveal only an abject soul, but I do not hate great crimes, first because beautiful paintings and great tragedies are made out of them, and secondly because noble and sublime deeds share with great crimes the same quality of energy." [5]

Germany

Although both Rousseau and Diderot were *philosophes* of the French Enlightenment, their romantic ideas were more eagerly received in Germany than in France. This may well be because Germany was more Protestant than Catholic, for it was from Protestantism, especially in the Pietist form, with its heavy emphasis on individualism and inwardness, that Rousseau derived the original inspiration for much of his romanticism. We cannot be surprised that the first theorist to incorporate romantic ideas into German philosophy should have been a Lutheran pastor, Johann Gottfried von Herder. After reading Rousseau's *Émile,* Herder decided that religion had no need for reason; it could be reconstructed on the basis of feeling. He developed a system in which sensibility took the place of intellectual persuasion, claiming that knowl-

Johann Gottfried von Herder (1744–1803).

edge of God could be attained through a consciousness of oneness with the whole—the whole meaning nature, history, and all the works of men as well as of the deity. Herder went on to elaborate theories of history and language which were no less important for the formation of a distinctively German form of romantic thought. [6] He depicted history as an evolutionary process in which, by stages, men struggled within their various cultures and language groups toward the ultimate development of all the potentialities of humanity. In the light of this system, Herder claimed that Germany could no longer be regarded as a loose assembly of separate autonomous principalities but must be seen and felt to be a cultural unity or "nation," with a common destiny and mission.

Herder was not satisfied with theoretical exposition; he proceeded to call on the poets and artists and scholars of Germany to participate in the creation of a new national consciousness. German authors in the eighteenth century were only just beginning to use the German language. Leibniz wrote in Latin, Frederick the Great spoke French, Gotthold Ephraim Lessing's models were Racine and Pierre Corneille. Herder insisted, however, that there was a German literature, however much neglected, and, following Rousseau, he looked for it in an old tradition of popular, demotic, or folkloric verse and, to prove his argument, he published a two-volume collection of *Volkslieder*, drawn from distant Germanic sources.

At Strasbourg in 1777 Herder acquired an unlikely convert to his Rousseauesque ideas in the person of the young Goethe—unlikely because Goethe had established his reputation as the author of lyrics in the rococo mode and of plays written in gallic alexandrines. However, Herder persuaded him that Shakespeare might be a better model than the French classical dramatists, and Goethe went on to write a historical play animated by all the fire and fury of *Macbeth,* with a sixteenth-century German knight as its protagonist, *Götz von Berlichingen.* This was a highlight of what became known as the Sturm und Drang movement in German drama, a curtain raiser to full-blooded German romanticism.

Goethe, while still under Herder's influence, produced a short novel, *The Sorrows of Young Werther,* [7] which is totally romantic, indeed totally Rousseauesque apart from an added element of violence. First published thirteen years after *La nouvelle Héloïse,* it is the same kind of epistolary novel, and it has the same cast of three: Werther, the young lover, corresponding to Rousseau's Saint-Preux; Lotte, the loved one, a somewhat paler version of Julie; and Lotte's husband, Albert, very much another Wolmar. The plot is also similar: Werther, a young man of delicate sensibility, is sent on a matter of family business to a small German town where life is simple, society patriarchal, and the country-side close at hand. Werther falls in love, first with Nature, then with a local girl named Lotte. Unfortunately Lotte is already engaged to the estimable Albert, and Werther goes away hoping to banish his love of Lotte from his heart. He fails, and returns to find Lotte married to Albert. However, Lotte encourages Werther to flirt with her, and he spends hours in her company reading poetry. His sense of hopelessness intensifies with his love, and in the end, he borrows a pair of pistols from Albert and shoots himself.

Like *La nouvelle Héloïse,* Goethe's novel enjoyed an immense success; indeed rather too much so for the author's peace of mind, for numerous lovesick young men imitated Werther and shot themselves. Goethe became almost embarrassed by the book, feeling he had put too much of himself into it. He decided that romanticism needed to be corrected by a measure of classicism, and he held aloof from the other young German poets and critics who went forward from *Werther* to create what they called *die romantische Schüle,* or Romantic School.

Several of these young men gathered at the University of Jena, where Johann Gottlieb Fichte became professor of philosophy at the age of thirty-two. Fichte was not a Romantic himself, but he provided the German Romantics with what they demanded: a theory. [8] This theory was a variation of Kant's thesis that the mind can have no knowledge of things in themselves, but whereas Kant had stressed the rational nature of the categories the mind had to impose on the world in order to make it intelligible, Fichte asserted the independence, the isolation of each man's mind, and maintained that the world is the product of the individual observer. On the one side, here am I, the Ego or Self; out there is the universe created by my imagination.

The writers and artists of German romanticism found in Fichte's theory a justification for the interest they took in their own egos. The narcissism of Saint-Preux and Werther became respectable, even noble. For while Fichte seemed to deny any access to objective truth, he recognized man's yearning for the Absolute, if only because it energized the striving which was a necessary part of the creation of reality by the ego. This "impulse towards something entirely unknown which reveals itself only in the sense of need for it," said Fichte, was what united the poet and the philosopher.

At Jena, Fichte's students started a literary review called *Die Athenaeum*, which introduced to the world the poets and critics who became famous as the exponents of German romanticism. The Schlegel brothers, Friedrich and Wilhelm, were the leaders, and they drew toward them such writers as Novalis, Johann Ludwig Tieck, Wilhelm Heinrich Wackenroder, and, more distantly, Johann Christian Friedrich Hölderlin. Friedrich Schlegel's importance was largely that of a literary critic. He provided *die romantische Schüle* with its aesthetics. [9] In his earliest publications, Schlegel had reiterated classical principles: the law of unities and all the other rules laid down by Aristotle for the judgment of a literary genre. However, in the light of Fichte's repudiation of objective universals, he concluded that there could be no fixed laws of beauty and that aesthetic judgments could be neither demonstrated nor proved.

Classical aesthetics, Schlegel decided, must be abandoned in favor of a new kind of romantic aesthetics, which must be given its own principles of judgment. What should these be? Schlegel suggested that in the absence of universal standards, each individual work of art must be judged by the principles it incorporated in itself. It was the function of the critic, he argued, to investigate the work of art to ascertain what ideal it sought to achieve and then to judge how far it satisfied that ideal.

Schlegel admitted that such judgments could not be demonstrated, but he claimed that they could be justified. Romantic judgments could not be allowed to be merely subjective; they must be given authority. "We cannot prove our judgments, but we can vindicate our right to make them." The critic could vindicate that right by acquiring a profound and extensive knowledge of the field—whether literature, art, or music. In a word, the critic must be a scholar.

Friedrich Schlegel himself was a formidable scholar—deeply versed in the literature and philosophy of several cultures. His brother Wilhelm was a better poet—indeed his translations of Shakespeare achieved such perfection that Shakespeare came to be read as much as a German as an English dramatist, as German as Goethe himself. Friedrich Schlegel did, however, make at least one memorable contribution to creative literature, a novel in the style of *La nouvelle Héloïse* and *Werther,* but designed to press romanticism beyond the limits that Rousseau and Goethe had imposed on themselves. *Lucinde* is about a love affair between a young writer, Julius, and a married woman, the Lucinde of the title. There is not much of a plot, but the message is unmistakable. Whereas both *La nouvelle Héloïse* and *Werther* record the triumph of conventional marriage over romantic love, Schlegel's novel presents the triumph of romantic love over conventional marriage. It introduces a new and significant figure into literature: the liberated woman. Lucinde loves Julius, and she follows the promptings of her heart. She gives herself to Julius and finds love in his arms, true love being shown to be both spiritual and sensual. Moreover, Lucinde's adultery is unpunished; she finds happiness as well as love with Julius. Life "flows between them like a beautiful song."

The story has no ending, but one is hinted at: Julius and Lucinde exchange the thought that they might make their love eternal by dying together in the moment of its greatest intensity. There is both an echo here of the suicide of Werther and an intimation of the double suicide of Tristan and Isolde, which Wagner was to exploit in the form of an opera.

Goethe was as disgusted by *Lucinde* as were many of Schlegel's good Protestant readers. Goethe was a firm believer in conventional marriage, and he could see no artistic merit in a novel without plot or conflict. If passion were not pitted against reason, then passion must be pitted against passion: and in the great work on which he was then embarking, *Faust,* Goethe was to have love punished as cruelly as it is punished in any play by Racine.

Frustrated love is also dominant in the work of most of the poets of *die romantische Schüle*—and in their lives. Novalis fell in love with a girl of thirteen, who died when she was fifteen; and until his death from consumption at the age of twenty-nine, all his poetry expresses not only what Fichte had called a "striving for the Absolute" but also what Novalis himself called a yearning for "the sleep which is an eternal dream." Hölderlin's life was hardly less melancholy. Although he did not have the desire for death that Novalis expressed, his career was a series of frustrations, tragically ending with a descent into madness.

The child of a poor family, Hölderlin was disappointed in his hopes of an academic career and forced to seek work as a private tutor. Like Rousseau's Saint-Preux, he fell in love with his employer, a married woman named Susette Gontard, who proved to be another Julie or Lotte, leading him on but finally choosing to remain faithful to her husband. The end of the affair destroyed Hölderlin's mental equilibrium:

> Woe is me, when from
> A self-inflicted wound my heart is bleeding, and
> Peace is utterly lost. [10]

Heinrich von Kleist had few dealings with the members of *die romantische Schüle,* but he was a magnificent prose writer who carried romantic ideas to even greater extremes than his contemporaries: his work gives powerful expression to the alienation of the sensitive soul from bourgeois society, to a pervasive sense of anxiety and loneliness, a yearning for the unknown, or *Sehnsucht,* and a certain thirst for violence which expressed itself in the end in the undertaking of action for the sake of action. Kleist's life ended when a woman friend told him she was terminally ill and wished to die. He took her to the banks of the Wannsee, shot her, and then shot himself.

Kleist was one of many young Germans of his time who began as an admirer of Napoleon and ended by calling on all Germans to unite themselves politically so that they might never again be conquered by a foreign despot. He became a fervent nationalist: and the philosopher Fichte underwent a no less radical change in response to the defeat of Prussia. At the outset of the French Revolution in 1789, Fichte was a vigorous champion of the Rights of Man, in the sense of the rights of each individual, as one might expect in view of his theory that each ego constructs reality and that only private worlds exist. However, by the early nineteenth century, Fichte had come to believe in the existence of a public ego: the German nation with a collective soul.

Where Herder had advanced the idea of Germany as a cultural nation, Fichte now called for the creation of Germany as a political nation. The earlier doctrine of the Rights of Man was now restated as the doctrine of the Rights of the People: and notably the right of the German people to rule itself as a united, sovereign state. This alliance of romanticism with nationalism was one of the reasons why it became such a powerful force in German history, dominating German culture throughout the nineteenth century and after.

England

In England romanticism assumed both left- and right-wing ideological tendencies. Edmund Burke was a key figure in the formulation of English romantic theory. It is ironic that he should also have been one of the most savage critics of Rousseau. However, Burke's quarrel with Rousseau was political, prompted by the belief that Rousseau's writings had inspired the French Revolution of 1789, which Burke considered a disaster. It was a much younger Burke who published in 1757 his *Philosophical Enquiry into the Origin of Our Ideas of the Sublime and Beautiful,* [11] which is an attack on classical aesthetics and an early exposition of romanticism.

Against the classical view that painting is superior to poetry because of the greater clarity it achieves in representation, Burke argues that poetry is superior precisely because it can better convey obscurity and ambiguity: "It is our ignorance of things that causes all our admiration and chiefly excites our passions." Burke dismisses those classical aesthetic doctrines which define beauty in terms of proportion, fitness, and moral perfection on the grounds that such qualities appeal to the understanding, whereas art speaks to the emotions. Besides, he claims that the sublime is more important than the beautiful, and in the contemplation of the sublime, he adds, awe, even terror, is part of our delight. Terror he connects, in turn, with power, the "untamed strength that comes upon us in the gloomy forest and in the howling wilderness in the form of the lion, the tiger, the panther or rhinoceros."

Two conflicting responses to the French Revolution could equally be considered romantic. Among the English poets who were emerging in 1789 as Romantics, William Blake, William Wordsworth, Samuel Taylor Coleridge, and Robert Southey all welcomed an event which they saw as a rising of the people of France in support of freedom. On the other hand, Burke disapproved of the Revolution because he did not see it as a struggle for freedom along the lines of the American Revolution but as a rationalist endeavor, aimed at rebuilding the society and institutions of France according to the abstract ideological designs of the Enlightenment. Burke's romantic conservatism rested, like the romantic nationalism of Herder in Germany, on a belief in the primacy of history. A nation, in his view, was a living organism, held together by habit, custom, and tradition; and as such it should be cherished.

At first very few poets agreed with Burke. Blake, [12] for example, adopted virtually all Burke's ideas about art, and he often seems to be saying in verse the very things that Burke said in prose, but he rejected Burke's theory of politics. Blake's response to the Revolution in France was to call for a revolution in England: "Rouze up, O Young Men of the New Age," he wrote in 1789. [13] He looked forward to the creation of what he called "Jerusalem" in England. This entailed the casting off of conventional ideas, not only in politics but in society and the family as well; the abolition of hierarchies in church and state, the liberation of women, and the inauguration of the rule of love. The basis of such a revolution, Blake insisted, must be changes in men's inner lives and characters.

The one revolution Blake opposed was the Industrial Revolution; the "dark satanic mills" he indicted in a celebrated line represented all the industrial installations, factories, mines, and other technological developments which were taking men away from the town and the artisans' workshops to become slaves of machines. It has been argued by several historians that the triumph of romanticism in England in the early nineteenth century has to be understood as a reaction, among the numerous sensitive souls for whom Blake spoke, to the uglier aspects of the new industrialization, which was more advanced at that time in England than elsewhere.

Edmund Burke (1729–97).

Blake had philosophical ambitions. "I must create a System," he wrote, "or be enslaved by another man's." But Blake did not have the intellectual culture to create a philosophical system. Coleridge had. The son of a clergyman-scholar, and a graduate of the University of Cambridge, Coleridge possessed the mind of a philosopher as well as a poet; he became in effect the leading theorist of romanticism in nineteenth-century England.

He first achieved fame as a poet in 1798 when, together with Wordsworth, he brought out a volume of *Lyrical Ballads* (*GIT* 1968, 352–405). Unlike Blake's *Songs of Innocence* and *Songs of Experience* (*GIT* 1989, 316–53), which had been published four years previously, these poems attracted widespread attention and did more than any other single work to redirect English taste from the neoclassical to the romantic. Wordsworth once said that "every great and original writer must himself create the taste by which he is to be relished." With a well-argued Preface [14] to the *Lyrical Ballads,* Wordsworth tried to do just this. At this stage of his collaboration with Coleridge, he was the leader of the tandem. Only four poems in the collection were by Coleridge, although one of them was "The Rime of the Ancient Mariner," recognized to be the most notable contribution. It soon emerged that there were significant differences between Wordsworth's idea of romantic poetry and Coleridge's. Wordsworth was an aesthete, inspired by nature; Coleridge was a metaphysician, inspired by the unseen world. Both subscribed to the principle of the supremacy of the imagination, but each had his own conception of what that meant. Wordsworth was close to Rousseau

John Keats (1795–1821).

in his love of the visible world and his contempt for science. Coleridge believed in mind and the necessity of science, however subordinate to metaphysics.

Soon after the publication of the *Lyrical Ballads,* Coleridge persuaded Wordsworth to accompany him on a visit to Germany. His purpose was to study the philosophy of *die romantische Schüle* at the source, and he made his way to seek out the professors who had instructed the poets. [15] Wordsworth lingered in another German city. Already fluent in French, he felt no urge to study the German language, let alone the German metaphysics. The sojourn in Germany meant little to Wordsworth, but it contributed much to the formation of Coleridge both as a poet and a philosopher, although he soon ceased to acknowledge any real distinction between the two: "No man was ever yet a great poet, without being at the same time a profound philosopher."

In the early days of the French Revolution, both Wordsworth and Coleridge had welcomed the overthrow of the *ancien régime* and in their enthusiasm for liberty, equality, and fraternity had proposed to set up in Pennsylvania a little utopian community with Southey and several other fellow poets. However their enthusiasm for this project soon faltered, and Coleridge "put away" his "squeaking baby trumpet of sedition." In the end, all three of them became as conservative in their politics as Burke, if not more so.

Nevertheless, English romanticism continued to have its radical side. In March 1811, a young undergraduate at University College, Oxford, was expelled for writing a pamphlet on atheism, and he soon began to publish poetry. He was a beautiful youth, aristocratic, bold, and defiant of authority, by name Percy Bysshe Shelley. Not only did he write romantic poetry, he offered the world a model of what a romantic poet should look like and how a romantic poet should live. He swept a girl of sixteen off her feet, married her, left her for another girl of sixteen, and then died by drowning at the age of thirty.

With lyrical poems and verse dramas Shelley had already established a high reputation, but if news of his death was greeted with sorrow by every reader who had come to appreciate his poetry, it was also undoubtedly received with a certain public satisfaction. The examples of Werther, Kleist, and Novalis all served to establish the notion that the complete romantic poet should die young, [16] so that Shelley's public might have been disappointed if he had lived longer. He himself wrote in one of his verses:

> How wonderful is Death
> Death and his brother Sleep. [17]

Shelley's friend, John Keats, died at an even earlier age—twenty-six—in 1821. He was one of the purest poets in the English language, and by all accounts the most lovable of men. He gave up his studies in medicine to nurse his mother, then his brother, as they lay dying of consumption, becoming infected himself in the process. Critics were hostile toward his work, treating him as a half-educated Cockney upstart who had no business even to attempt to be a poet. Keats had little sympathy for the Coleridgian project of fusing poetry with philosophy:

> Do not all charms fly
> At the mere touch of cold philosophy? [18]

In a letter to a friend, Keats declared: "I am certain of nothing but the holiness of the heart's affection and the truth of imagination— what imagination seizes as beauty must be truth." Although his earliest inspiration as a poet was derived from visible things, Keats became increasingly responsive to the unseen world and what he called "ethereal things." Several of his finest poems were written in a few weeks of feverish activity in the year before he died. One of his last great poems, "Ode on a Grecian Urn," is a philosophical poem against philosophy:

> Thou, silent form, dost tease us out of thought
> As doth eternity. [19]

Keats is always linked in the history books with Lord Byron as well as Shelley, but while his verse has much in common with that of Shelley, it has little in common with that of Byron. Keats himself remarked on this in a letter to his brother: "You speak of Lord Byron and me—there is great difference between us. He describes what he sees. I describe what I imagine."

There is, in fact, some doubt as to whether Byron's verse should properly be considered romantic at all. His style is modeled on that of the neoclassical Alexander Pope. He had no belief in imagination; and it is wit which confers distinction on his work. Admittedly, Byron writes a great deal about love, but his voice is always one of irony and mockery.

> Think you, if Laura had been Petrarch's wife
> He would have written sonnets all his life? [20]

Difficult as it is to claim that Byron's poetry is romantic, there is no questioning his romantic *persona*. Even more than Shelley, he gave the nineteenth century its popular image of the Romantic Poet: he was handsome and dark in a brooding way; he was rich, extravagant, immoral, and the lover of many women; he was lame, a lord, and a soldier who died at the age of thirty-six in a war for the liberation of Greece. It was not, however, simply a matter of image. Byron was wholly dedicated to one supremely romantic ideal: liberty—liberty in the simple sense of the abolition of despotism:

> For I will teach, if possible, the stones
> To rise against earth's tyrants. [21]

Byron had no interest in those more rarefied notions of freedom which were cultivated by Fichte and Coleridge and other Romantics of the Right. He remained an individualist and a radical; and where other romantic poets exemplified the man of feeling as opposed to the man of reason, Byron presented himself to the world as a man of action. He provided romanticism with what it had hitherto lacked— the poet as hero.

The romantic movement in England was largely literary. There were no great English composers at the time, and although J. M. W. Turner made a seminal—and indeed sensational—contribution to romanticism in painting, he was a unique figure in the visual arts. Even in literature, it was the poets, rather than prose writers, who produced the most important work. Leading novelists such as Jane Austen and Thomas Love Peacock chose only to mock romanticism. However, in 1847 an unknown schoolmistress in Yorkshire named Emily Brontë produced, shortly before her death at the age of thirty, a single work which is a masterpiece of romantic fiction—*Wuthering Heights*. The plot is again that of *La nouvelle Héloïse* and *Werther:* a young lady, Cathy, falls in love with a rough plebeian foundling, Heathcliff, who loves her in return. She pledges undying love, but instead of marrying him she makes a suitable match with a man of her own class, Linton. Heathcliff goes away, and when he returns years later, a rich and educated man, Cathy realizes that she has always loved him, and although she remains faithful to her husband, the emotional stress of reawakened passion drives her to an early grave. Heathcliff, however, is not a stoic like Rousseau's

Emily Brontë (1818–48).

Saint-Preux; he never forgives Cathy for choosing Linton, and he takes a terrible revenge on her husband and all her middle-class relations for the humiliations inflicted on him. The sphere of class conflict is not only one degree lower than in *La nouvelle Héloïse*—proletarian *versus* bourgeois instead of bourgeois *versus* aristocratic—it is far more extreme and impassioned. And although Cathy dies halfway through the novel, it loses none of its intensity, because her spirit lives on, haunting Heathcliff as he exacts his vengeance on the world that has robbed him of her until, finally, his heart softens.

Emily Brontë explores more deeply the motivation of her characters than Rousseau does of his. She shows Heathcliff to be a monster in much of his behavior, and yet he never entirely loses the reader's sympathy. He is indeed something of a hero—a flawed hero like Byron—rather than an antihero like Saint-Preux and Werther, for where those two simply give up, Heathcliff acts, cruelly, vindictively, but determinedly, in the assertion of his rights and his pride. The strangest thing about *Wuthering Heights* is that it was written by a clergyman's spinster daughter with very little personal experiences of love or life, a triumph of the imagination—imagination of the kind which Coleridge said was possessed only by the artist, a faculty which enables the artist to see into the human soul and to impose an order on the diverse elements of experience.

The literary merits of Emily Brontë were not at first widely recognized. Public taste at the time responded more readily to another romantic novelist who wrote in English but was not English, Sir Walter Scott. Scott was to all appearances a very ordinary Edinburgh lawyer, who collected Scottish ballads as a hobby and published a set in volume form. He was one of those people who had done well out of the political union of Scotland with England and the economic prosperity which the Industrial Revolution had brought to the Lowlands. However, his interest in folklore opened his eyes to another Scotland, that of the Highland clans who had rallied to Prince Charles in 1745 and attempted by marching south against the army of George I to restore the independence of Scotland and the reign of the Scottish royal house of Stuart. It was a doomed enterprise but a colorful and passionate one. Scott tried to recapture the spirit and the glamour of it in the form of fiction. *Waverley* was the first of a series of historical novels designed, as he explained it, to bring the past to life.

The success of Scott's novels was astonishing. A more extensive public education, and cheaper methods of printing, greatly enlarged the reading public in the first quarter of the nineteenth century, and Scott captured the imagination of readers of all social classes. In Scotland his novels prompted Lowlanders to invent tartans for their families, wear kilts and listen to the bagpipes, and find all the ways they could to assert their identity as Scotsmen. But his novels did not generate a widespread desire for Scottish independence. Scottish readers were too conscious of the material advantages of the union with England to wish for secession. Scott's romanticism was essentially conservative; Scott himself felt nostalgia for the past without discontent with the present; and his British public, reading him, felt much as he did.

Continental figures

It was not the same on the Continent. In France and Italy especially, where millions of copies of his novels were sold, their impact was subversive rather than conservative. Romanticism needed a long time to take root in France. Although Rousseau and Diderot introduced the theory of romanticism as early as the 1750s, they met great resistance. Rationalism and classicism were deeply embedded in the national culture. The French Revolution rejected many traditions, but it perpetuated, and even strengthened, the cult of reason. Napoleon, who saw himself as the Caesar of the modern world, wished to reinforce adherence to the classical principles of the Roman Empire. It was only after the defeat of Napoleon in 1815 that the cultural environment of France became favorable to romanticism.

Literature had languished in France under both the Revolutionary and the Napoleonic regimes: and the writers who emerged with the Restoration of the monarchy in 1815 had assimilated, in their years of

Chateaubriand (1768–1848).

exile, cosmopolitan influences. Chateaubriand and Benjamin Constant, both romantic writers, assumed the leadership of literary society in Paris and also became active in Restoration politics. Both were as familiar with English literature as they were with French. Madame de Staël, the most influential literary critic, called on French writers to study the Germans, cast off the constraints of the French classical and Cartesian tradition, and give free reign to the creative imagination.

The romanticism these writers championed was not simply a revolt against rationalism and classicism; it was also a movement of revival. The Germans, as Madame de Staël informed her French readers, had recovered a cultural heritage which dated back to a period before the Renaissance. Chateaubriand suggested that the French had also a similar medieval heritage in the age of Christian chivalry and troubadour song which offered a better model for modernity than either classical antiquity or the Age of Reason.

Chateaubriand's most important work was one entitled *La Génie du christianisme,* in which he pleaded for Christian values against the pagan values incorporated in classicism. [22] The Christianity he evoked was that of the medieval Church, and thus a Catholic Christianity. Devotion to the Catholic Church was indeed a central feature of Chateaubriand's romanticism, and it is one of the reasons why romanticism was favored to some extent in Restoration France in preference to the classicism which had come to be identified with the overthrown Napoleonic empire.

Chateaubriand was a nobleman, and he wanted the Restoration to signal the end not only of Revolutionary turmoil but also of the royal absolutism which had dominated France from the Renaissance onward:

so there was a strong political element in his desire to revive the culture of the feudal Middle Ages and the authority of the Catholic Church which provided spiritual support for the feudal system.

Constant, on the other hand, was a Protestant and a liberal, and therefore more critical of the Restoration government than Chateaubriand. Indeed, in France, as in England, romanticism assumed both a conservative and a radical form, exciting political passions equally intense, since each side equally believed its policies were directed to the supremely romantic goal of freedom.

In the earlier years of the Restoration, the younger French Romantics were closer to Chateaubriand than to Constant. The literary group around *La Muse française,* which was both royalist and Catholic, included such celebrated poets as Alphonse de Lamartine, Alfred Victor Vigny, and Victor Hugo. In a preface to his play *Cromwell,* Hugo explained what he believed to be romanticism's debt to Christianity: the Church had taught the world about the double nature of man. In the light of the Creation and the Fall, man was revealed to be at once both good and evil, part angel and part beast. This was an insight the philosophers of classical antiquity did not have, with the result that classical aesthetics, like classical ethics, insisted on the total separation of good and evil, of beauty and ugliness, of darkness and light, of truth and falsehood. Christian theology, by contrast, opened the mind to the possibility of a synthesis of opposites, and romantic art sought to achieve, in a similar way, what Hugo called *"l'harmonie des contraires."*

The play to which Hugo wrote these words as a preface was one of many works inspired in France by the novels of Scott. For it was not only the French novelists but also the French dramatists, poets, and historians who followed Scott in exploring the romance of the past. Augustin Thierry, one of the most eminent historians of the time, said there was more "true history" in a novel of Scott than in all the work of the academic historians. In Scott's descriptions of the wars in the British Isles, Thierry saw a revealing parallel with the wars in medieval France between Franks and Gauls. Moreover, he depicted the Gauls as a conquered people who had yet to recover their rights against an earlier regime.

The most notable effect of Scott's novels in France was to stimulate a radical form of romanticism against the conservative romanticism of Chateaubriand. Hugo, who had once been conservative himself, again spoke for most of his fellow poets when in 1877 he wrote—again in a preface to a play:

Romanticism, taken as a whole, is only liberalism in literature. Literary liberalism will be no less democratic than political liberalism. Freedom in art and liberty in society are the twin goals to which all consistent and logical thinkers should march in step. [23]

The Revolution of 1830, which put the constitutional monarch Louis-Philippe on the throne of France in place of the reactionary Charles X, was largely the result of the alliance between romanticism and liberalism.

Italy

A similar alliance was forged at about the same time in Italy, and again the influence of Scott played a not inconsiderable role. Resistance to romanticism was at first very stubborn in Italy. In the birthplace of the Renaissance, the principles of classical aesthetics were cherished with almost proprietorial pride. However in 1815, Madame de Staël, who had done much to introduce romantic ideas into France, published in a new Italian literary review, the *Biblioteca Italiana,* a challenge to Italian writers and artists to renounce their slavish adherence to the dead hand of classicism and open their minds to the liberating, creative ideas of romanticism which were already reinvigorating the cultural life of Germany, England, Scotland, and France.

Madame de Staël was attacked as a foreigner attempting to impose foreign values on the Italian people, [24] but she recruited the support of the younger literary critics—Pietro Borsieri, Ludovico Di Breme, and Giovanni Berchet; and the best new poets—Ugo Foscolo, Giacomo Leopardi, and Alessandro Manzoni—were those most responsive to romantic ideas, both in philosophy and in the poetry that was being published in other languages. Manzoni was the writer most influenced by Scott: for it was in emulation of Scott that he turned from writing poetry to writing historical drama and fiction. Noting the prodigious success of Scott's novels with the general public, Manzoni decided that the only way to make an impact on history was to write in a form which could command the same universal audience.

Manzoni was a patriot; and indeed patriotism was a central element in Italian romanticism from its earliest beginnings. Foscolo's poems, for example, were filled with protests against Napoleon's despotic rule in Italy. When the Napoleonic rule was ended in 1815, only to be succeeded by Austrian despotism, romantic writers expressed the dismay of the Italian people. They were concerned, above all things, with the cause of Italian freedom. Romanticism in Italy was thus less focused than romanticism in France and England on the individual soul or the Rousseauesque adoration of the divine in nature. The freedom it sought, like that of the Romantics in Germany, was a national freedom even more than a personal freedom.

The situation of Italy, however, was different from that of Germany. Germany, as Herder had pointed out, was already a "cultural nation," united by language, customs, and historical experience: it needed only, according to Fichte, to be transformed into a political nation. Italy, however, was not such a "cultural nation." Different provinces spoke different dialects, had different customs and different historical experiences, since the peninsula had for centuries been divided into princely, republican, and papal states with separate cultural identities.

Manzoni saw the function of romanticism in Italy as the creation of a "cultural nation" in preparation for its eventual transformation into a political nation. It was with this purpose in mind that he set out to write what proved to be his masterpiece—a historical novel on the model of Scott's called *I promessi sposi* [The Betrothed]. The project plunged Manzoni into months of research—not only into history but also into language, for he was determined that his novel should afford a model of pure Italian prose. Having started to write the book in his native Lombardy, he moved to Tuscany in pursuit of a nobler model of the Italian language, and there he began months, even years, of fastidious activity, correcting and polishing the style of his writing. [25]

I promessi sposi is set in the Italy of the seventeenth century, when large areas were under Spanish occupation. The main plot concerns the adventures of two young peasants who try to get married but are thwarted at every stage by the forces which flourish under alien rule. Without being didactic, it is a profoundly patriotic book. It is also supremely well written, and it was an instant and universal success when it was first published in 1827. In Italy it became almost a sacred text, a vital force in that patriotic movement which became the Risorgimento and culminated in the establishment of Italy as a united and sovereign kingdom in 1861.

The movement as a whole

Romanticism in other parts of Europe continued to enact the ambiguous role of reinforcing either conservatism or radicalism according to the political circumstances of the place. In Poland and the Balkan countries, romantic art served largely, as in Italy, to promote revolution against imperial alien rule. In Russia and Spain, it stimulated a revival of cultural traditions felt to be national against the cosmopolitan influences of classicism. In France and England, exponents of romanticism were fairly evenly divided between the ideologies of Right and Left.

The United States was too much the creature of the Enlightenment, its culture too profoundly imbued with eighteenth-century rationalism, for romanticism to be immediately welcomed. Besides, the American commitment to the ideal of a republican society caused its citizens to respond to the austere maxims of ancient Rome rather than to the charms of feudal medieval Christendom. Ralph Waldo Emerson was able to make romanticism a significant presence in nineteenth-century

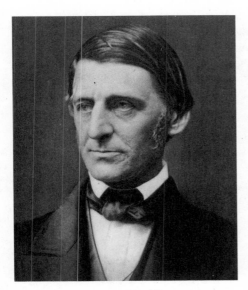

Ralph Waldo Emerson (1803–82).

American culture because he gave it the elevated form he called transcendentalism, something that could appeal to the American puritan tradition. Emerson himself started out as a Unitarian preacher, only to be impelled by religious doubts to study the then fashionable European philosophers, notably those recommended by Madame de Staël in *De l'Allemagne*. In 1836, at the age of thirty-three, he published an essay entitled *Nature*, [26] which endures as the first manifesto of American romanticism, a work of lofty eloquence which almost matches that of Rousseau himself. In these pages Emerson suggests that since God is within us, the highest purpose of life must be to explore one's own inwardness. He also claims that since there is a correspondence between the human soul and everything that exists in the universe, the study of one's soul can be an exercise in pursuit of truth.

The differences in aim and emphasis between the Romantics of different nationalities reflect differences in historical experience; and yet, for all this variety, a whole series of resemblances unites romanticism as a common movement—or "moment"—in the evolution of Western culture, as universal in its way as the Renaissance in an earlier century. Underlying the differences are certain shared themes: liberty, however variously interpreted; the contemplation of the self; love, which draws one self to another; truth, in the expression of feeling no less than of thought; nature as an object of veneration rather than of scientific curiosity or mastery; an appreciation of the sublime; a tolerance of the grotesque and irregular and of ideas not necessarily distinct or clear; a taste for the lyrical and melodic; an interest in the primitive and exotic;

269

a demand for authenticity, coupled with contempt for polite pretense; and, in general, more trust in imagination than in reason.

Romanticism, in all its manifestations, must be understood as a philosophy of life as well as a philosophy of art, and only this can explain the extent of its impact throughout the Western world.

1. *See* Barzun's *Romanticism and the Modern Ego* (Boston: Little, Brown and Co., 1941), *Berlioz and the Romantic Century* (London: Sollancz, 1950), *The Energies of Art* (London: Secker and Warbarg, 1956), and *Classic, Romantic, and Modern* (London: Secker and Warbarg, 1961).

2. *See* Read's *Art and Society* (London: Faber, 1936), *The Philosophy of Modern Art* (London: Routledge, 1952), and *The True Voice of Feeling* (London: Routledge, 1953).

3. Cited in M. Cranston, *The Noble Savage: Jean-Jacques Rousseau, 1754–1761* (Chicago: University of Chicago Press, 1991), p. 124.

4. *Pensées* No. XXX, trans. in John Lough, ed., *Diderot: Selected Philosophical Writings* (New York: Cambridge University Press, 1953), p. 45.

5. Diderot, *Salons,* ed. J. Seznec and J. Adhémar (New York: Oxford University Press, 1957–67), vol. II, p. 147.

6. *Outlines of a Philosophy of the History of Man,* 2 vols., trans. T. O. Churchill (London: Johnson, 1800); cf. F. M. Barnard, *Between Enlightenment and Romanticism* (New York: Oxford University Press, 1964).

7. Trans. by B. Q. Morgan (London: Weidenfeld and Nicolson, 1957).

8. *The Popular Works of Johann Gottlieb Fichte,* 2 vols., 4th ed., trans. William Smith (London: Turner and Co., 1889).

9. Friedrich Schlegel, *Lectures on the History of Literature,* 2 vols., trans. J. G. Lockhart (Edinburgh: Blackwood, 1818).

10. Cited in Michael Hamburger, *Contraries: Studies in German Literature* (London: Weidenfeld and Nicolson, 1970), p. 16.

11. Edited with an introduction by James T. Boulton (Oxford: Basil Blackwell, 1975).

12. G. E. Bentley, Jr., ed., *William Blake's Writings,* 2 vols. (New York: Oxford University Press, 1978).

13. Cited in John Clubbe and E. J. Lovell, *English Romanticism* (Champaign: University of Illinois Press, 1983), p. 26.

14. Reproduced in Nowell C. Smith, ed., *Wordsworth's Literary Criticism* (London: Humphrey Milford, 1926), pp. 11–46.

15. Richard Holmes, *Coleridge: Early Visions* (New York: Viking Press, 1990), pp. 205–37.

16. "Romanticism and youth belong together, so many Romanticists die young," A. Thorlby, *The Romantic Movement* (London: Longmans, 1966), p. 24.

17. *Queen Mab,* chap. II, verse i.

18. Cited by C. M. Bowra, *The Romantic Imagination* (New York: Oxford University Press, 1950), p. 288.

19. H. W. Garrod, ed., *Poetical Works of John Keats* (New York: Oxford University Press, 1958), p. 262.

20. *Don Juan,* chap. III, verse viii.

21. Cited in C. M. Bowra, op. cit. p. 170.

22. *See* Roger Fayolle in D. G. Charlton, *The French Romantics,* 2 vols. (New York: Cambridge University Press, 1984), vol. II, p. 255.

23. Cited in G. de Bertier de Savigny, *The Bourbon Restoration* (Philadelphia: Pennsylvania University Press, 1966), p. 358.

24. Grazia Aviltabile, *The Controversy on Romanticism in Italy* (New York: Vanni Inc., 1959), pp. 12–25.

25. Jean-Pierre Barricelli, *Alessandro Manzoni* (Boston: Twayne Publishing, 1976), pp. 28–33.

26. A. R. Ferguson and J. F. Carr, eds., *Collected Works of Ralph Waldo Emerson,* 3 vols. (Cambridge, Mass.: Belknap Press, 1983), vol. III, pp. 97–114.

Kepler's Anguish and Hawking's Queries: Reflections on Natural Theology

Owen Gingerich

Owen Gingerich is senior astronomer at the Smithsonian Astrophysical Observatory in Cambridge, Massachusetts, professor of astronomy and of the history of science at Harvard University, and chairman of the university's history of science department. A leading authority on both Copernicus and Kepler, he is the editor as well of modern works, among them the twentieth-century part of the International Astronomical Union's *General History of Astronomy* (1984–   ), and he has written papers offering standard models of the solar atmosphere based on his own researches.

His many publications include two collections of essays, *The Great Copernicus Chase* and *Eye of Heaven: Ptolemy, Copernicus, and Kepler,* both published this year. He is a former vice president of the American Philosophical Society. Earlier articles by him appeared in *The Great Ideas Today* in 1973, 1979, and 1983.

A remarkable fact I learned not long ago is that all the gold mined in historical times would fill a cube only fifty-five feet on each side. I can imagine it outside my window, dwarfing my neighbor's house but not larger than a modest office building. Now contrast this with iron. Six hours of steel production in the United States would fill this same cube. In other words, iron is enormously more abundant than gold.

If, sixty years ago, you had asked a physicist *why* iron is ten million times more abundant than gold, or why oxygen is twenty times more abundant than iron, he would probably have considered you a pest. It would have been like asking why the sun appears half a degree wide in the sky, or why a naked-eye supernova occurred in 1604. Kepler asked questions like that, but most people considered him a little odd.

Today if you ask a physicist why iron is ten million times more abundant than gold, or a hundred million times more abundant than uranium, he would no longer tell you to get lost. Instead, you would find an astonishing story about giant cauldrons in the interiors of stars where the elements are cooked up in an esoteric witches' brew. This modern alchemy is one of the impressive achievements of astrophysics in the past several decades.

Physicists now believe that fifteen billion years ago—give or take a few billion years—the basic building blocks of atoms were formed in the first moment of a mighty explosion called the Big Bang. From the pure energy of that initial blast came nuclear particles, including protons and electrons—the makings of hydrogen, the lightest and by far the most abundant element. Protons smashed into protons to form heavy hydrogen and helium, helium being the second heaviest and second most abundant element. But the universe expanded so quickly that before elements like carbon or oxygen could form, the incredible density of that primordial cosmic egg had abated, and the collisions became too few to produce any appreciable amounts of the higher elements—elements that are vital to life and to our being here today.

My purpose here is not to give a course in stellar evolution but to present some reflections on natural theology. But as a preamble, let me briefly sketch how stars spend their lives, in order to explain where elements like carbon and oxygen come from. Most of the time stars shine by converting hydrogen into helium. But when the available hydrogen has been exhausted, the core of the star pulls together under the irresistible tug of gravity, the temperature increases, and now the formerly inert helium becomes a fuel, fusing into carbon and later into oxygen. If the star is massive enough, a long sequence of higher elements will be generated.

Eventually, however, there comes a place in the periodic table where the atoms no longer yield up nuclear energy for powering the star, but instead, they *demand* energy. This happens when the chain has gone about a quarter of the way through the list of elements, approaching the element iron. When the star has burned the atoms to this point, it swiftly falls into bankruptcy, and the star is about to become a supernova. Gravity resumes its inexorable grasp, and within seconds the core of the star collapses, squashing the electrons and protons into a dense sphere of neutrons. On the rebound, the neutrons irradiate the lighter atoms, and in a colossal overshoot they build up the heavier elements, including the gold and uranium. From the cosmic debris come the building blocks for future stars and planets, and even for you and me. We are, in a sense, all recycled cosmic wastes, the children of supernovae.

Early in this century, after the work of Darwin, which emphasized the fitness of organisms for their various environments, the Harvard chemist L. J. Henderson wrote a fascinating book entitled *The Fitness of the Environment,* which pointed out that the organisms themselves would not exist except for certain properties of matter. He argued for the uniqueness of carbon as the chemical basis of life, and everything we have learned since then, from the nature of the hydrogen bond to the structure of DNA, reinforces his argument. But today it is possible to go still further and to probe the origin of carbon itself, through its synthesis deep inside evolving stars.

Carbon is the fourth most common atom in our galaxy, after hydrogen, helium, and oxygen. A carbon nucleus can be made by merging three helium nuclei, but a triple collision is tolerably rare. It would be easier if two helium nuclei would stick together to form beryllium, but beryllium is not very stable. Nevertheless, sometimes before the two helium nuclei can come unstuck, a third helium nucleus strikes home, and a carbon nucleus results. And here the details of the internal energy levels of the carbon nucleus become interesting: it turns out that there is precisely the right resonance within the carbon that helps this process along.

Let me digress a bit about resonance. As you tune your radio, there are certain frequencies where the circuit has just the right resonance and you lock onto a station. The internal structure of an atomic nucleus is something like that, with specific energy or resonance levels. If two nuclear fragments collide with a resulting energy that just matches a resonance level, they will tend to stick and form a stable nucleus. Behold! Cosmic alchemy will occur!

In the carbon atom, the resonance just happens to match the combined energy of the beryllium atom and a colliding helium nucleus. Without it, there would be relatively few carbon atoms. Similarly, the internal details of the oxygen nucleus play a critical role. Oxygen can be formed by combining helium and carbon nuclei, but the corresponding resonance level in the oxygen nucleus is half a percent too low for the combination to stay together easily. Had the resonance level in the carbon been 4 percent lower, there would be essentially no carbon. Had that level in the oxygen been only half a percent higher, virtually all of the carbon would have been converted to oxygen. Without that carbon abundance, neither you nor I would be here.

I am told that Fred Hoyle, who together with Willy Fowler found this remarkable nuclear arrangement, has said that nothing has shaken his atheism as much as this discovery. Occasionally Hoyle and I have sat down to discuss one or another astronomical or historical point, but I have never had enough nerve to ask him if his atheism had really been shaken by finding the nuclear resonance structure of carbon and oxygen. However, the answer came rather clearly in an issue of the Cal Tech alumni magazine, where he wrote:

> Would you not say to yourself, "Some supercalculating intellect must have designed the properties of the carbon atom, otherwise the chance of my finding such an atom through the blind forces of nature would be utterly minuscule." Of course you would. . . . A common sense interpretation of the facts suggests that a superintellect has monkeyed with physics, as well as with chemistry and biology, and that there are no blind forces worth speaking about in nature. The numbers one calculates from the facts seem to me so overwhelming as to put this conclusion almost beyond question. [1]

Now Sir Fred and I differ about lots of things, but on this we agree: the picture of the universe is far more satisfying if we accept the designing hand of a superintelligence. Hoyle might feel a little uncomfortable to be classified as a natural theologian or a modern-day William Paley, but natural theology is, in fact, the central subject of this essay—a topic that I'm slowly spiraling in on. Here I need to delve a little more deeply into this example of the age-old argument of design.

Not long ago I used the carbon and oxygen resonance in a lecture at a university in the Midwest, and in the question period I was interrogated by a philosopher who wanted to know if I could quantify the argument by Bayesian probabilities. Now I'll confess that, at the time, I hadn't a clue that Bayesian statistics meant evaluating a proposition on the basis of an original probability and new relevant evidence. But even knowing how to handle that would hardly have enabled me to perform a convincing calculation, that is, a probability so overwhelming as to be tantamount to a proof that superintelligent design was involved in the placement of the resonance levels.

Clearly my petitioner was daring me to convince him, despite the fact that I had already proclaimed that arguments from design are in the eyes of the beholder and simply can't be construed as proofs to convince skeptics. Furthermore, in posing his question he had already pointed out the quicksands of using numerology to prove the existence of divine order in the cosmos. So I hasten to dampen any notion that I intend the resonance levels in carbon and oxygen nuclei to prove the existence of God.

Even Paley, with his famous watch and his conclusion that it pointed to the existence of a watchmaker, said that "My opinion of Astronomy has always been, that it is *not* the best medium through which to prove the agency of an intelligent Creator; but that, this being proved, it shows, beyond all other sciences, the magnificence of his operations." [2]

In fact, I am personally inclined to find more impressive hints of design in the biological realm. As Walt Whitman proclaimed, "a leaf of grass is no less than the journey-work of the stars." [3] I would go still farther and assert that stellar evolution is child's play compared to the complexity of DNA in grass or mice. Whitman goes on, musing that,

> the tree-toad is a chef-d'oeuvre for the highest,
> And the running blackberry would adorn the parlors of heaven,
> And the narrowest hinge in my hand puts to scorn all machinery,
> And the cow crunching with depress'd head surpasses any statue,
> And a mouse is miracle enough to stagger sextillions of infidels.

Even Hoyle, by his allusion to the biology, seems to agree that the formation of, say, DNA, is so improbable as to require a superintelligence. Such biochemical arguments were popularized about forty years ago by Lecomte du Noüy in his book *Human Destiny*. Lecomte du Noüy estimated the probability of forming a 2,000-atom protein as something like one part in 10^{321}. He wrote, "Events which, even when we admit very numerous experiments, reactions, or shakings per second, *need an infinitely longer time than the estimated duration of the earth in order to have one chance, on an average, to manifest themselves can, it would seem, be considered as impossible in the human sense.*" [4]

Lecomte du Noüy went on to say, "To study the most interesting phenomena, namely Life and eventually Man, we are, therefore, forced to call on an anti-chance, as Eddington called it; a 'cheater' who systematically violates the laws of large numbers, the statistical laws which deny any individuality to the particles considered." [5]

There are many who place their faith in the roulette of chance, and they will find Lecomte du Noüy and Hoyle an aggravation to their fervently held assumptions about the meaninglessness of the universe. But

275

there seem to be just enough evidences of design in the universe that those who accept as their credo faith in what has recently been called the blind watchmaker have had to give the existence of these evidences a name, the anthropic principle. Ironically, the anthropic principle was invented by several Princeton physicists with just the opposite intention, to highlight some of the remarkable properties of the universe that seem so well tuned to human existence. For example, had the original energy of the Big Bang explosion been less, the universe would have fallen back onto itself long before there had been time to build the elements required for life and to produce from them intelligent, sentient beings. Had the energy been more, it's quite possible that the density would have dropped too swiftly for stars and galaxies to form. As Goldilocks said at the little bear's bowl, "This porridge is just right."

Nowadays, however, another team has taken over the anthropic principle, scientists who wish to deny the role of design. Briefly stated, they have turned the argument on its head. Rather than accepting that we are here because of a deliberate supernatural design, they claim that the universe simply must be this way *because* we are here; had the universe been otherwise, we would not be here to observe ourselves, and that is that. Such is almost precisely the view enunciated by Stephen W. Hawking in his inaugural lecture as Lucasian Professor at Cambridge University—an illustrious chair once held by Newton—and a view of nature repeated by Hawking in his best-selling *A Brief History of Time*. [6] As I said, I am doubtful that you can convert a skeptic by the argument of design, and the discussions of the anthropic principle seem to prove the point.

Although it's unlikely that natural theology can offer proofs for the existence of God, I hasten to point out that surprisingly little in science itself is accepted by "proof." Let's take Newtonian mechanics as an example. Newton had no proof that the earth moved, or that the sun was the center of the planetary system. Yet, without that assumption, his system didn't make much sense. What he had was an elaborate and highly successful scheme of both explanation and prediction, and most people had no trouble believing it, but what they were accepting as truth was a grand scheme whose validity rested on its coherency, not on any proof. Thus, when a convincing stellar parallax was measured in 1838, or when Foucault swung his famous pendulum at 2 A.M. on Wednesday morning, January 8, 1851, these supposed proofs of the revolution and of the rotation of the earth did not produce a sudden, newfound acceptance of the heliocentric cosmology. The battle had long since been won by a persuasiveness that rested not on proof but on coherency.

Indeed, in science I find the idea of "belief" somewhat curious. A few years ago I conducted a workshop for a rather diverse group of Christians, and I asked, "Can a theist believe in evolution?" Let me stop here and put in a footnote. Jehovah's Witnesses have sent me any number of copies of a book provocatively entitled *Life—How Did It Get Here? By Evolution or by Creation?* In replying to the donors, I point out that the question gives the wrong choice, and that it would be better to ask, "By chance or by design?" since it's entirely reasonable to accept *both* creation and evolution. I shall return to this point later, but first, back to the workshop question on whether a theist can believe in evolution.

I got a variety of responses, but it didn't occur to any of them to challenge what it might mean to *"believe"* in evolution. Does that mean to have faith in evolution in a religious sense? I have heard one leading paleontologist announce himself as a "devout evolutionist" when asked his faith, and I guess that is a possibility. But when pressed, most scientists would, I think, claim only that they accept evolution as a working hypothesis. In everyday, nonphilosophical usage, most people, scientists included, would say they believe in the results of science and that they believe the results of science to be true. Yet, and this is the anomalous part, most scientists would be mildly offended at the thought that their beliefs constituted an act of faith in a largely unproved but intricate system of coherencies.

Two autumns ago I heard a most extraordinary lecture about the mind and the brain viewed completely mechanistically, presented by a scientist with supreme confidence that his approach could explain everything. Afterward, on the way out, a thoughtful listener remarked to the somewhat startled speaker, "That was wonderful—in twenty years I have never met such a man of faith." She referred, of course, to his unshakable confidence that his extrapolations gave all the answers.

Now if we understand that science's great success has been in the production of a remarkably coherent view of nature rather than in an intricately dovetailed set of proofs, then I would argue that natural theology can also have a legitimate place in human understanding even if it falls short of proof. What is needed is a consistent and coherent worldview and, at least for some of us, the universe is easier to comprehend if we assume that it has both purpose and design, even if this cannot be proved with a tight logical deduction.

Nevertheless, there has been a persistent criticism that arguments from design will cause scientific investigators to give up too easily. If the resonance levels of carbon and oxygen are seen as a miracle of creation, would a Christian physicist try to understand more deeply why, from the mechanistic view of physics, the levels are that way and not in some other configuration? Might it not be potentially detrimental to the faith to explain a miracle? We must therefore surely ask, "Dare a scientist believe in design?"

There is, I shall argue, no contradiction between holding a staunch belief in supernatural design and being a creative scientist, and perhaps no one illustrates this point better than the seventeenth-century astronomer Kepler. Perhaps that is why he is one of my favorite characters in the entire history of science.

Kepler was nearly finished with the Lutheran theological curriculum at the University of Tübingen when he was more or less ordered by the duke, who had supported him with a scholarship, to become a provincial mathematics and astronomy teacher in far-off Austria. It was as if a Harvard senior, a likely candidate for a summa in philosophy, was abruptly told in November to pack up and head for a position as math teacher in a high school in Guam. Kepler left the university under protest, claiming that there was no evidence that he even had any talent for astronomy. In fact, he was a straight A student *except* in astronomy, where he got an A—.

In Graz, Kepler put his mind to the heavens and soon began asking remarkable questions about the design of the universe. Why are there just six planets? Why are they spaced the way they are? Why do they have the speeds they have? To ask why there were just six planets meant that Kepler was already a Copernican, so that he counted the earth as a planet, but not the sun and moon. The geocentrists, on the other hand, named the sun and moon as well as the five naked-eye planets to reach the mystical number of seven. One of the principal reasons Kepler was a Copernican arose from his deeply held belief that the sun-centered arrangement reflected the divine design of the cosmos: The sun at the center was the image of God, the outer surface of the star-studded heavenly sphere was the image of Christ, and the intermediate planetary space represented the Holy Spirit. These were not ephemeral notions of his student years but a constant obsession that inspired and drove him through his entire life. [7]

Writing to a favorite correspondent, Herwart von Hohenburg, he said, "Copernicus piously exclaimed, 'So vast, without any question, is the Divine handiwork of the Almighty Creator.' But wow! It's quite refreshing to consider that we ought not to feel so astonished at the huge extent of the heavens as at the smallness of us human beings. Yet we must not infer that bigness is of special importance; otherwise the crocodile or elephant would be closer to God's heart than man." [8] And to his teacher Michael Maestlin back in Tübingen he wrote, "For a long time I wanted to be a theologian; for a long time I was restless. Now, however, behold how through my effort God is being celebrated in astronomy!" [9]

But Kepler did not stay long in Graz; the Counter-Reformation swept in, and the Protestant teachers were given until sundown to leave. Then, and throughout his life, he yearned for the call to Tübingen, but it never came. His theological views were suspect; among other things, a faculty committee specifically criticized him for believing that Calvinists should be considered Christian brothers.

Instead of returning to his alma mater, Kepler turned the other direction, to Prague, where he became associated with the great observational astronomer Tycho Brahe. Their stormy direct interaction lasted only ten months, but it was a critical encounter, for it gave Kepler's work a new direction and provided him with the critical observations needed to find the elliptic path of Mars. This discovery and another, the so-called law of areas, are chronicled in his *Astronomia nova* (*GIT* 1983, 307–41), truly the New Astronomy. In its introduction he defended his Copernicanism from the point of view that the heavens declare the glory of God:

> I implore my reader [he writes] not to forget the divine goodness conferred on mankind, and which the psalmist urges him especially to consider. When he has returned from church and entered on the study of astronomy, may he praise and glorify the wisdom and greatness of the creator. . . . Let him not only extol the bounty of God in the preservation of living creatures of all kinds by the strength and stability of the Earth, but also let him acknowledge the wisdom of the creator in its motion, so abstruse, so admirable.
>
> If someone is so dumb that he cannot grasp the science of astronomy, or so weak that he cannot believe Copernicus without offending his piety, I advise him to mind his own business, to quit this worldly pursuit, to stay at home and cultivate his own garden, and when he turns his eyes toward the visible heavens (the only way he sees them), let him with his whole heart pour forth praise and gratitude to God the creator. Let him assure himself that he is serving God no less than the astronomer to whom God has granted the privilege of seeing more clearly with the eyes of the mind. (*GIT* 1983, 321–22) [10]

A detailed study of Kepler's life reveals an evolution of ideas on a number of topics, such as whether planets have "souls" that guide them. He had grown up in an age when philosophers still attributed heavenly motions in part to the individual intelligences of the planets, and in his youthful *Mysterium cosmographicum*, published while he was still in Graz, he endorsed the idea of animate souls as moving intelligences of the planets. But by the time of his mature work he could flatly state that, "I deny that the celestial movements are the work of mind" (*GBWW* I: 16, 933; II: 15, 933). However, on his views of God as a geometer and of a universe filled with God's geometric designs he was unwavering.

Kepler's life and works provide central evidence that an individual can be both a creative scientist and a believer in divine design in the universe, and that indeed the very motivation for the scientific research can stem from a desire to trace God's handiwork. As Kepler put it in his ecstatic introduction to his *Harmonice mundi* of 1619, "The die is cast—I am writing the book—to be read now or by posterity it matters not. It can wait a century for a reader, as God himself waited six thousand years for a witness." [11]

Near the end of the same book Kepler cast his credo in the form of a psalm of praise and a prayer:

> I give Thee thanks, O Lord Creator, because I have delighted in thy handiwork and I have exulted in the works of thy hands. Behold! now, I have completed the work of my profession, having used as much of the ability as Thou hast given me; I have made manifest the glory of thy works, insofar as the narrows of my mind could grasp its infinity. If I have been allured into brashness by the wonderful beauty of thy works, or if I have loved my own glory among men, while advancing in work destined for thy glory, gently and mercifully pardon me: and finally, deign graciously to cause that these demonstrations may lead to thy glory and to the salvation of souls, and nowhere be an obstacle to that. Amen. [12]

I shall return to Kepler, but for now I realize that a single sterling example may not be convincing that belief in design is always innocent in guiding a scientist. For example, critics can easily point to Newton, who felt that God was continually adjusting the planetary system to keep the gravitational perturbations from throwing it out of kilter. In Query 31 of his *Opticks,* he refers to the irregularities that arise in the motions of planets because of the disturbing influence of the other planets, and he suggests that these irregularities will increase "till this system wants a reformation" (*GBWW* I: 34, 542; II: 32, 542). Leibniz, in a biting critique, commented that according to such a doctrine, "God Almighty wants to wind up his watch from time to time; . . . he is even obliged to clean it now and then by an extraordinary concourse. . . . I hold that this is a very mean notion of the wisdom and power of God." [13]

There's an interesting sequel to this Newton-Leibniz controversy. One actor is William Herschel, the discoverer of the planet Uranus and the man whose huge telescope, and the view of the heavens through it, inspired Haydn to write "The Heavens Are Telling." Herschel explored questions such as how one kind of nebula might evolve into another over long periods of time. His ideas challenged the French mathematical astronomer Pierre Simon Laplace to think about the formation of the solar system from a swirling nebula, something Laplace called the nebular hypothesis. Eventually, in 1802, Herschel made a trip to Paris to visit Laplace, and on 8 August the two of them called on the emperor Napoleon.

Napoleon was intrigued by the nebular hypothesis but felt Laplace had left something out. "Where is God in your proposal?" Napoleon asked. "Ah," replied Laplace, "I have no need for that hypothesis." Down through the centuries this has seemed like an arrogant and atheistic remark; in fact Laplace was just doing his science, saying that his own system of the planets, unlike Newton's, did not require a divine hand to keep things in order.

Some people feel threatened by a way of looking at the universe that does not explicitly require the hand of God. But it doesn't mean the universe is actually like that, just that science generally has no other way of working, because science can't cope with miracles. Science is, by its very nature, an attempt to find automatic, mechanistic explanations of the universe. Science isn't anti-God or atheistic, it's just neutral in the way it goes about explaining things. In the context, Laplace was being a good scientist, though I can't help feeling he was pretty arrogant as well, and he actually was a militant atheist.

Was Laplace being a better scientist than Newton because he didn't need design and the hand of God in his explanation? I think there is no doubt that Laplace's science superseded Newton's, but it's debatable that Newton's acceptance of a Deity made him the poorer scientist [*see* the discussion of Newton on pp. 96–169 of this volume].

Nevertheless, chance as opposed to design has been raised to such a level of scientific orthodoxy that some of our contemporaries forget that this is just a tactic of science, an assumption, and not a guaranteed principle of reality. Few, however, have enunciated the mechanistic credo so stridently as the evolutionary biologist and historian of science William B. Provine, who has recently written,

> When [Darwin] deduced the theory of natural selection to explain the
> adaptations in which he had previously seen the handiwork of God,
> Darwin knew that he was committing cultural murder. He understood
> immediately that if natural selection explained adaptations, and evolution
> by descent were true, then the argument from design was dead and
> all that went with it, namely the existence of a personal god, free will,
> life after death, immutable moral laws, and ultimate meaning in life.
> The immediate reactions to Darwin's *On the Origin of Species* exhibit,
> in addition to favorable and admiring responses from a relatively few
> scientists, an understandable fear and disgust that has never disappeared
> from Western culture. [14]

Provine, in defending the gospel of meaninglessness, goes on to say that if modern evolutionary biology is true, then lofty desires such as divinely inspired moral laws and some kind of ultimate meaning in life are hopeless. I'm not sure why Professor Provine has such fear and loathing of design, but apparently, despite the examples of Kepler and Newton, he is still afraid that the arguments from design may block the march of science, and such a view is perhaps not totally unfounded. Let me explain.

Several years ago I participated in a remarkable conference of theists and atheists in Dallas. One session considered the origin of life, and a group of Christian biochemists argued that the historical record was nonscientific since it was impossible to perform scientific experiments on history. Furthermore, they amassed considerable evidence that the current scenarios of the chemical evolution of life were untenable. One of the atheists aligned against them, Professor Clifford Matthews from the University of Chicago, conceded that their criticisms had considerable validity. Calling their book on *The Mystery of Life's Origin* [15] brilliant, he summarized their arguments with respect to the standard picture of chemical evolution as saying, "(1) the evidence is weak, (2) the premises are wrong, and (3) the whole thing is impossible."

As someone fully convinced in the existence of a superintelligence and a Divine Creator, I soon found myself in the somewhat anomalous position that to me, the atheists' approach was much more interesting than the theists'. That particular group of Christian biochemists had concluded that ordinary science didn't work in such a historical situation, that is, with respect to the origin of life, and they attempted to delineate some alternative "origin science" in which the explicit guiding hand of God could make possible what was otherwise beyond any probability. The reason I admired the atheist biochemists so much was that they hadn't given up. They were still proposing ingenious avenues whereby catalytic effects in the chemistry made the events far more likely. "Let us not flee to a supernaturalistic explanation," they said, "let us not retreat from the laboratory."

Now it might be that the chemistry of life's origins *is* forever beyond human comprehension, but I see no way to establish that scientifically. Therefore it seems to me to be part of science to keep trying, even if ultimately there is no accessible answer.

Am I contradicting myself to say, on the one hand, that the resonance levels in carbon and oxygen point to a superintelligent design and, on the other hand, that science must continue to search for underlying reasons why the resonance levels are that way and not some other way? I think not, for even if it is shown that those levels had to be the way they are because of some fundamental, invariable reason, there is still the miracle of design that led it to be so, choice or not. Therefore, I see no reason that an appreciation of the astonishing details of design should prevent us from trying to search further into their underlying causes. Hence I'm not prepared to concede that arguments from design are necessarily contra-scientific in their nature.

Perhaps part of Provine's outrage came because he was responding to Phillip Johnson, professor of law at Berkeley, who is an articulate legal champion of the right to believe in God as Creator and a critic of an evolutionary process running entirely by chance. Earlier I mentioned the incredible odds calculated by Lecomte du Noüy against the chance formation of a protein molecule. Since we do have proteins, and since a mechanistic science has been highly successful, the overwhelming reaction has just been to ignore Lecomte du Noüy, since he is so obviously wrong. But is he? For science to overcome the odds, it is necessary for us to postulate catalysts and unknown pathways to make the formation of life from inert matter enormously easier, and it is of course precisely such pathways that are the challenge for science to find. But is not the existence of such pathways also evidence of design? And are they not inevitable? That is what materialists such as Provine do not want to hear, but as Hoyle says, the numbers one calculates put the matter beyond question.

So, while I differ from those Christian biochemists who postulate some new kind of "origin science," I do think a science totally devoid of the idea of design may be in danger of running into a blank wall. And this brings me to ask again, "Is natural theology and the idea of design a threat to science?" and I answer no, perhaps design might even be a necessary ingredient in science. In fact, I think it's the other way around—rather than natural theology being a threat to science, using design in science may be a threat to natural theology. If natural theology weds its arguments to particular scientific insights as evidences of design and arguments for a deity, it always runs the risk of having the ground cut out from under it.

Let me illustrate the danger by turning to what I call Hawking's Query. One of the great accomplishments of twentieth-century astronomy has been the explication of the expanding universe, and the idea that everything began in an indescribable explosion, the so-called Big Bang. "There is no way to express that explosion," writes the poet Robinson Jeffers.

> All that exists
> Roars into flame, the tortured fragments rush away from
>   each other into all the sky, new universes
> Jewel the black breast of night; and far off the outer nebulae
>   like charging spearmen again
> Invade emptiness. [16]

This is a thrilling scenario, and its essential framework, of everything springing forth from that blinding flash, bears a striking resonance with those succinct words of Genesis 1:3: "And God said, 'Let there be light.'" Who could have guessed even a hundred years ago, not to mention two or three thousand years ago, that a scientific picture would emerge with electromagnetic radiation as the starting point of creation!

But in fact, if we accept that moment of blazing glory as the whole work of the Creator, we are on rather thin ice. Scientific theories, especially cosmological views, are notoriously subject to change, and cosmologists have taken it as a special challenge to eliminate the singularity of the beginning zero point when space and time do not yet exist. And thus Professor Hawking, treating time as one of the dimensions of the curved space-time in that opening sequence, claims to have made a coordinate transformation that eliminates the origin. In *A Brief History of Time,* Hawking writes:

The idea that space and time may form a closed surface without boundary also has profound implications for the role of God in the affairs of the universe. With the success of scientific theories in describing events, most people have come to believe that God allows the universe to evolve according to a set of laws and does not intervene in the universe to break these laws. However, the laws do not tell us what the universe should have looked like when it started—it would still be up to God to wind up the clockwork and choose how to start it off. So long as the universe had a beginning, we could suppose it had a creator. But if the universe is really completely self-contained, having no boundary or edge, it would have neither beginning nor end: it would simply be. What place, then, for a creator? [17]

From a Christian perspective, the answer to Hawking's Query is that God is more than the omnipotence who, in some other space-time dimension, decides when to push the mighty ON switch. A few years ago I had the opportunity to discuss these ideas with Freeman Dyson, one of the most thoughtful physicists of our day. "You worry too much about Hawking," he assured me. "And actually it's rather silly to think of God's role in creation as just sitting up there on a platform and pushing the switch." Indeed, creation is a far broader concept than just the moment of the Big Bang. God is the Creator in the much larger sense of designer and intender of the universe, the powerful Creator with a plan and an intention for the existence of the entire universe. The very structures of the universe itself, the rules of its operation, its continued maintenance, these are the more important aspects of creation. Even Hawking has some notion of this, for near the end of his book he asks, "What is it that breathes fire into the equations and makes a universe for them to describe? The usual approach of science of constructing a mathematical model cannot answer the questions of why there should be a universe for the model to describe. Why does the universe go to all the bother of existing?" [18] Indeed, this is one of the most profound, and perhaps unanswerable, theological questions.

In reflecting on natural theology I have attempted to delineate a place for design both in the world of science and in the world of theology. As Kepler described astrology, the stars impel, but they do not compel. [19] There is persuasion here, but no proof. However, even in the hands of secular philosophers the modern mythologies of the heavens, the beginnings and endings implied in the Big Bang, give hints of ultimate realities beyond the universe itself. Milton Munitz, in his closely argued book, *Cosmic Understanding*, [20] declares that our cosmology leads logically to the idea of a transcendence beyond time and space, giving the lie to the notion that the cosmos is all there is, or was, or ever will be.

Yet ultimately natural theology is unsatisfying. With the eyes of faith the heavens declare the glory of God, but of what kind of God? Simply a God of very large numbers. [21] And this brings me to Kepler's query, to Kepler's Anguish. In 1613 he wrote:

> There is nothing I want to find out and long to know with greater urgency than this: can I find God, whom I can almost grasp with my own hands in looking at the universe, also in myself? [22]

Munitz, in coming to the concept of transcendence, describes it as unknowable, which is somewhat paradoxical, since if the transcendence is unknowable then we cannot know that it is unknowable. Could the unknowable have revealed itself? Logic is defied by the idea that the unknowable might have communicated to us, but coherence is not. For me, it makes sense to suppose that the superintelligence, the transcendence, the "ground of being" in Paul Tillich's formulation, has revealed itself through prophets in all ages, and supremely in the life of Jesus Christ.

As this essay draws to a close, I have obviously opened up a completely new vista that I don't have space to address: while natural theology could allow Kepler almost to grasp God with his own hands in looking at the universe, where is the equivalent to finding God within ourselves? Is it not within the moral precepts revealed in the sacrificial life of Christ? Can we be good without God? That was a question thoughtfully and provocatively raised in the *Atlantic Monthly* a few years ago, [23] and it deserves our attention. I suspect that the answer is deeply tangled with one of the most profound of Hawking's queries: Why does the universe go to all the bother of existing? Perhaps that part of the transcendence will lie forever beyond the narrows of our minds.

1. "The Universe: Past and Present Reflections," in *Engineering and Science,* November 1981, pp. 8–12, esp. p. 12.

2. William Paley, *Natural Theology or Evidences of the Existence and Attributes of the Deity* (Edinburgh, 1816), chap. 22, p. 287.

3. Walt Whitman, "Song of Myself," stanza 31, in *Leaves of Grass* (1891–92 edition).

4. *Human Destiny* (New York, 1947), p. 35.

5. Ibid., p. 38.

6. Stephen W. Hawking, *A Brief History of Time* (New York, 1988), p. 125.

7. *See,* for example, his *Epitome of Copernican Astronomy* (1618) (*GBWW* I: 16, 853–54; II: 15, 853–54).

8. Dec. 16, 1598, *Johannes Kepler Gesammelte Werke*, 13, no. 107:144–58; my translation based on the one by Carola Baumgardt, *Johannes Kepler: Life and Letters* (New York, 1951), pp. 48–49.

9. Oct. 3, 1595, *Johannes Kepler Gesammelte Werke*, 13, no. 23:256–57; from Gerald Holton, "Johannes Kepler's Universe: Its Physics and Metaphysics," *American Journal of Physics* 24 (1956): 340–51, esp. 351.

10. Slightly abridged and modified from my translation in *The Great Ideas Today* 1983.

11. Introduction to *Harmonice mundi, Johannes Kepler Gesammelte Werke*, 6, no. 290:6–9 (*GBWW* I: 16, 1010; II: 15, 1010).

12. End of book V, chapter 9, of *Harmonice mundi, Johannes Kepler Gesammelte Werke*,

6, no. 362; my translation is based on the ones by Charles Glenn Wallis (*GBWW* I: 16, 1050; II: 15, 1050) and by Eric J. Aiton, forthcoming, American Philosophical Society.

13. "Mr. Leibniz's First Paper, November, 1715," in H. G. Alexander, *The Leibniz-Clarke Correspondence* (Manchester, 1956), p. 11.

14. *First Things,* no. 6 (October 1990): 23.

15. Charles B. Thaxton, Walter L. Bradley, and Roger L. Olsen, *The Mystery of Life's Origin: Reassessing Current Theories* (New York, 1984).

16. Used by permission from Robinson Jeffers, "The Great Explosion," in *The Beginning and End* (New York, 1963), p. 3.

17. *A Brief History of Time,* pp. 140–41.

18. Ibid., p. 174.

19. Kepler elaborates this idea in book IV, chapter 7, of his *Harmonice mundi* (1619).

20. Milton K. Munitz, *Cosmic Understanding: Philosophy and Science of the Universe* (Princeton, 1986).

21. From John Turkevitch, quoted in Diogenes Allen, *Quest* (New York, 1990), p. xiv.

22. Kepler to an unidentified nobleman, Oct. 23, 1613, *Johannes Kepler Gesammelte Werke,* 17, no. 669:20–22; translation from Baumgardt, *Johannes Kepler: Life and Letters,* pp. 114–15.

23. Glenn Tinder, "Can We Be Good Without God?" *Atlantic Monthly,* December 1989, pp. 69–85.

Natural Theology, Chance, and God

Mortimer J. Adler

Mortimer J. Adler, editor of *The Great Ideas Today,* is also chairman of the board of editors of Encyclopædia Britannica, Inc., and editor in chief of the 1990 edition of *The Great Books of the Western World.* Dr. Adler received his Ph.D. from Columbia University and went on to teach for many years at the University of Chicago. In 1952 he founded the Institute for Philosophical Research, a center for the study of ideas of Western thought. Since 1953 he has been a trustee of the Aspen Institute, where he teaches each summer.

Dr. Adler's autobiography, *Philosopher at Large,* first appeared in 1977 and will be reissued in paperback to coincide with the publication of its sequel, *A Second Look in the Rearview Mirror.* Both books are scheduled for publication in the fall of 1992.

1. Introduction

The preceding excellent essay by Professor Owen Gingerich was delivered at the Center of Theological Inquiry at Princeton. Its title refers to Kepler, a sixteenth-century astronomer, and Stephen Hawking, a twentieth-century cosmologist, both of whom make copious references to God, but only one of whom was a person of Christian religious faith.

In the title Professor Gingerich gave his essay, he added: "Reflections on Natural Theology." In that essay, he set forth scientific reasons for supporting the arguments of certain Christian natural theologians against chance and in favor of design in the natural processes of cosmological development and in biological evolution.

I mention all these things because in the *first* place, I think natural theology, as it has been developed in the nineteenth century, following Bishop William Paley in modern times, is not sound philosophically. It should be regarded as Christian apologetics, which is the use of reason to defend the truths of the Christian religion and to reconcile Christian faith with scientific knowledge. The truths of Christian faith are much more clearly and competently presented in dogmatic or sacred theology, as that was formulated in the great *Summa*s of the Middle Ages.

Philosophical theology, which must never be confused, as it so often is, with natural theology, is strictly a branch of philosophy, and totally apart from any religious faith. As I have made clear in my recently republished book, entitled *How to Think About God,* it is theology written by pagans for pagans who are similarly deprived; that is, by and for persons without any religious faith. The theology in Book Lambda of Aristotle's *Metaphysics* is philosophical theology as thus defined; it is defective in its conception of God, as will be pointed out presently.*

In the *second* place, I think that the argument for design that is presented by Aquinas in his fifth argument for the existence of the God in whom Christians believe is an unsound teleological argument, unsound because it is based on Aristotle's error of attributing the operation of final causes to the processes of natural motions or actions, whereas they properly belong only in the production of human works of art. This erroneous argument is later presented in Paley's *Natural*

---

*The *Summa contra Gentiles* by Aquinas does not replicate the *Summa Theologica,* nor is it a work in philosophical theology. It is, strictly speaking, a work of Christian apologetics, written to persuade the Jews and Moors in Spain of the truth of the Christian religion.

Theology, or Evidences of the Existence and Attributes of the Deity (1816), in which the watchmaker's design of the timepiece he makes is proposed as the model in terms of which we should think of God's relation to the universe he creates. The creator is *not* an artist making an artifact; the created universe is *not* a work of art.

In the *third* place, as I have shown in *How to Think About God,* the presence of chance in the universe, both in cosmological developments and in biological evolution, lies at the heart of an indispensable premise in the only sound philosophical argument for the existence of God.

That argument, occurring in philosophical theology, not in Christian apologetics, does not prove the existence of the God in whom Christians believe, whom they worship, and to whom they pray; but most, though not all, of the properties attributed to the God that Pascal calls the God of the philosophers are identical with the properties attributed to the God of Abraham, Isaac, and Jacob and the God of the Christian religion, as well as of Islām.

This, as I pointed out above, cannot be said of the God of Aristotle's *Metaphysics,* who is a prime mover and a final cause, but not the sole creative cause, or "exnihilator," of a universe that did not come into existence with the Big Bang, but preexisted the Big Bang.

In the *fourth* place, it is necessary to point out that according to sacred, dogmatic Christian theologians, there is no incompatibility between the existence of an omnipotent and omniscient God, eternally (that is, timelessly) existing, and the presence of chance occurrences in natural process and human acts of free choice, acts which those physicists, who are both materialists and determinists, deny because they cannot explain them in terms of their understanding of the causal and statistical laws of their science.

In the *fifth* place, what has just been said requires me to call attention to Hawking's serious errors in his *A Brief History of Time,* which Professor Gingerich fails to criticize. The Lucasian professor of physics at Cambridge University, holding Newton's chair, is undoubtedly a great physicist and cosmologist, but his understanding of God and creation is woefully deficient. He is philosophically naive and theologically ignorant, both with respect to sacred theology and with respect to philosophical theology, while at the same time referring to God and to God's mind frequently in his book, a book in which, for reasons I will point out, his own principles should prevent him from ever mentioning God.

Furthermore, if the Big Bang were the exnihilation of the cosmos studied by physicists, there would be no need for proof of the existence of God. On the contrary, any philosophically sound argument for the existence of God, in order to avoid begging the question, must assume that the physical cosmos had no beginning.

Both Aquinas and Kant give philosophically sound arguments showing that neither of these two assumptions—a beginning for the cosmos and of time, on the one hand, and an everlasting cosmos without a beginning or end in time, on the other hand—can be proved. Unless we accept the second hypothesis we cannot avoid begging the question. Hence, any sound philosophical argument for the existence of God must include the assumption that time and the cosmos are everlasting, i.e., have no beginning or end.

Hawking could have avoided the error of supposing that time had a beginning with the Big Bang if he had distinguished time as it is measured by physicists from time that is not measurable by physicists.

Here let me call attention to the error made in quantum mechanics of thinking that its uncertainties with respect to subatomic motions indicate an indeterminacy in nature or reality rather than indeterminability by us, caused by the intrusive action of our measurements. This is combined with the error made by some theoretical physicists, such as Arthur Holly Compton at the University of Chicago, the error of thinking that quantum indeterminacy in reality may help to explain human free choice. This is philosophical nonsense, no worse of course than the philosophical nonsense in Hawking's popular book.

In the sections to follow, I will amplify—and in the course of doing so, undoubtedly repeat—what I have just briefly outlined: *first,* with respect to sacred theology, philosophical theology, and natural theology, or Christian apologetics; *second,* with respect to the philosophical unsoundness of the teleological argument for God's existence, and the misconception of God as an artist like the watchmaker; *third,* with respect to the reason why I say that chance in cosmological developments and in biological evolution lies at the heart of the one sound philosophical argument for the existence of God; and here also why that argument must assume everlasting time and a cosmos without beginning or end; *fourth,* why there is no incompatibility between the eternal existence of an omnipotent and omniscient God and the occurrence of chance events and human free choice in time; and *fifth,* with respect to the central error to be found in Hawking's *A Brief History of Time,* an error shared by many other great physicists in the twentieth century, the error of saying that what cannot be measured by physicists does not exist in reality.

2. The domain of theology

Theology began in Greek antiquity, in Book X of Plato's *Laws* and in Book Lambda of Aristotle's *Metaphysics.* Both Plato and Aristotle were pagan philosophers without any faith in the Olympian polytheism of Greek mythology and, of course, unenlightened by the divine revelation in which the Jews believed, and later the Christians and the Muslims.

Aristotle regarded theology as the highest grade of human knowledge, the highest level of abstraction reached by metaphysics, or what later came to be called *philosophia prima*. Let us call this discipline "philosophical theology" to avoid its confusion with what in modern times came to be miscalled "natural theology."

Aristotle's cosmology viewed the physical cosmos as a universe eternally (i.e., everlastingly) in motion. For him, the word *eternal* as applied to the world did not refer to the timeless and the immutable but to the everlasting and forever in time.

Aristotle never asked the existential question: *What caused the everlasting cosmos in motion to exist?* He asked instead: *What caused the everlasting cosmos to be forever in motion?* His answer to that question was: God, the prime mover, but not as the prime efficient cause from which the motion in the world first sprang as an effect, rather as the ultimate final cause, the object of desire which everlastingly motivated the observed changes in the cosmos.

Aristotle's philosophical theology contains an error that is also present in his physics; i.e., the error of attributing final causes to natural changes or motions. This error improperly attributes to natural processes the same teleology that is properly attributed to works of human art.

There is no doubt at all that final causes operate in human artistic production. The carpenter who makes a chair is not only its efficient cause, as the wood out of which it is made is its material cause, but the carpenter also has in his mind a formal cause (the design of the chair to be made) and a final cause—the purpose for which the chair, when made, will be used. In natural processes, there are only three causes— material, formal, and efficient—but no final cause. Teleology is not present in nature as it is in art.

The other work of purely philosophical theology in antiquity is to be found in the *Enneads* of Plotinus. It represents the flowering of neo-Platonic philosophy in the Hellenistic period. In the centuries of the Middle Ages there is one other work, written by a Christian—Anselm, the archbishop of Canterbury. The first three chapters of the *Proslogium* (*GIT* 1969, 316–43), containing an argument that has been called "the ontological argument for God's existence," does not employ any article of Christian faith. It could have been written by a pagan and it was intended for pagans—the fools that Anselm is trying to argue against when they deny God's existence. Anselm wrote other works, such as *Cur Deus homo?*, which could only have been written by a person of profound Christian faith.

I shall explain later why the so-called ontological argument fails as a proof of God's existence. It was dismissed by Aquinas and later by Kant as a flawed proof. I will give better reasons than they gave for dismissing it. But the reasoning in those first three chapters of the *Proslogium* must be retained in any well-constructed philosophical theology as an explanation of how we must think about God as the one supernatural

Supreme Being, who should be thought of as necessarily existing, i.e., as a being incapable of not existing.

With this one exception in the Christian Middle Ages, a new type of theological writing emerged with authors in the Patristic period, notably Augustine and Chrysostom, who were Platonists; and in the later Middle Ages with Albert the Great, Aquinas, and Duns Scotus, who were Aristotelians.* These were all persons of religious faith— Christian, Jewish, and Muslim. Their theology should be called "sacred dogmatic theology" because its first principles were articles of religious faith, based on interpretations of Sacred Scripture.

Strictly speaking, with the one exception aforementioned of Anselm's *Proslogium,* there was no purely philosophical theology in the centuries from the first to the seventeenth. As I have already pointed out, the *Summa contra Gentiles* written by Aquinas was not a work in sacred dogmatic theology. It reveals itself to us plainly as a work in Christian apologetics, written by Aquinas for the purpose of persuading the Jews and Moors in Spain of the truth of the Christian religion.

Purely philosophical theology does not appear in early modern times with the *Meditations* of Descartes and the *Theodicy* of Gottfried Wilhelm Leibniz. They wrote philosophically as apologists for their Christian faith. The exception is the *Ethics* of Spinoza. That is a work in purely philosophical theology. Its pantheism and its denial of a God who created the cosmos were so obviously contradictory of the Jewish faith that it was condemned by the rabbis of Amsterdam as heretical, and Spinoza himself was excommunicated.

Other works of Christian apologetics should be mentioned here. In antiquity there was a work by Boethius entitled *On the Catholic Faith.* In early modern times there were Pascal's *Pensées* and Locke's *The Reasonableness of Christianity.* In the nineteenth century there was Cardinal John Henry Newman's *Grammar of Assent.* None of these authors would have mistakenly thought of their works as being in the category of "natural theology."

So far as I know, that mistaken denomination of a work in Christian apologetics begins in the nineteenth century with Bishop Paley's book entitled *Natural Theology, or Evidences of the Existence and Attributes of the Deity* (1816). Clearly, this was not a work in philosophical theology, written by a pagan. Clearly, it was a work in Christian apologetics, and a poor one at that, as I will point out later.

Works written by Christians for Christians or for nonbelievers are clearly not works in philosophical theology, and just as clearly they are not works in sacred dogmatic theology. They do not represent faith

---

*For the sake of brevity, I will deal only with Christian authors in this period. An expanded account would, of course, include Jewish authors, such as Maimonides, and Muslim authors, such as Avicenna.

seeking understanding. Instead they represent faith offering reasons for the truth of its beliefs.

I have already suggested the epithet "Christian apologetics" as the correct denomination of such works to replace "natural theology," a term which came into use only in the nineteenth century. A very recent book written by John Polkinghorne, chaplain of Trinity Hall, Cambridge University, and entitled *Science and Creation* (1989) has an opening chapter entitled "Natural Theology." While still retaining that denomination, Polkinghorne's book is a fine work in Christian apologetics, not a work in philosophical theology. It is of great interest to us because of its explicit repudiation of the erroneous denials of chance and contingency in Bishop Paley's *Natural Theology*. I will quote the relevant passages from Polkinghorne's book in a later section of this essay.

3. The central error in modern Christian apologetics

In the domain of theology, there are only three alternative categories of work: philosophical theology, dogmatic theology, and Christian or Jewish or Muslim apologetics. What has very recently come to be called "natural theology" is not a fourth alternative, for it is nothing but Christian apologetics.

In the light of what has just been said, one exception must be noted. A great Christian theologian, Aquinas was also a brilliant Aristotelian philosopher. In the *Summa Theologica* of Aquinas there are many philosophical insights that he might not have formulated had he been merely a pagan disciple of Aristotle. However, these insights are not derived from or dependent on any article of Christian faith. For that reason, they can be regarded as contributions to philosophical theology, even though they are not the work of a pagan mind.

I wish to call attention to one such insight because it is pivotal to the proof of God's existence as that is formulated in purely philosophical theology. It is the insight that being or existence is the *proper* effort of God. The italicized word "proper" signifies that God and God alone is the cause of being or existence. In the causation of being, he is not the first cause, because there are no second or other causes. All other causes, all of them natural causes, are causes of becoming or perishing. Only what is being itself can cause existent entities to exist. Such causation is supernatural. It does not occur in nature.

When God is understood not only as the Supreme Being but also as the creator (or exnihilator) of the cosmos, he must also be understood as a supernatural being and as a supernatural cause.

This involves a philosophical analysis of causation that makes a sharp distinction between the causation of being and the causation of becoming. That goes along with the differentiation between the operation of final causes in the processes of becoming that are productions of human art and the nonoperation of such causes in the phenomena of becoming that are natural processes.

The insight about God as the sole cause of being is unlike the proposition that the perfection of God as the Supreme Being includes moral as well as ontological perfection. Anselm's purely philosophical argument is that the Supreme Being—a being than which no greater can be thought—entails all the ontological perfections. Only a person of Christian (or Jewish or Muslim) faith would add God's moral perfection. That additional affirmation is an article of religious faith in a loving and benevolent God. It is totally beyond the reach of reason or purely philosophical thought.

If we put together these two contributions to purely philosophical theology made by Anselm and Aquinas we should be able to see the radical difference between the God of Aristotle (only a prime mover and only a final cause) and the God of Anselm and Aquinas (a creator *ex nihilo* of the cosmos). Understanding that difference should help us to realize the inappropriateness of using Aristotelian arguments in the five ways advanced by Aquinas in Question 2, Article 3, of his *Summa Theologica* (*GBWW* I: 19, 12–14; II: 19, 12–14).

Any logically valid argument for the existence of God must choose one of two assumptions: either the world and time had a beginning, or they always existed and never came into being out of nothing. Neither of these two assumptions can be proved true on rational grounds, as Aquinas and later Kant argued. The first assumption is an article of Jewish, Christian, and Muslim faith. But to make that assumption in purely philosophical theology begs the question, for if we assume that the cosmos and time came into being out of nothing, we are also assuming that it was created *ex nihilo,* and that God as creator (exnihilator) exists, *which was the proposition to be proved.* Hence, to avoid begging the question, any purely philosophical proof of God's existence must assume that the world and time always existed and exists everlastingly. In other words, only if we assume that the world and time never began or came into being out of nothing, do we have a genuine problem of proving God's existence as the *preservative,* not *originative,* cause of the existence of the cosmos at every moment of its existence.

The chief error that I am concerned to expose in many works of modern Christian apologetics is the error of supposing that in order to defend Christian faith they must show that there is nothing contingent in cosmic processes and in biology and evolution; in other words, that nothing happens by chance or coincidence. Instead it is thought necessary to assert that everything happens according to a fully worked out design in the mind of God.

The underlying root of this error is an inadequate analysis of the processes of becoming. (1) If God created the cosmos, that is exnihilation—bringing the cosmos into existence out of nothing. (2) Biological procreation is a mode of becoming, one in which no cause of being operates. (3) Artistic production, or human making, is unlike both exnihilation and biological procreation.

When this threefold differentiation is fully understood, it will be seen that Bishop Paley's profound error was to regard God's creation of the cosmos as like a watchmaker's production of a timepiece. That is not only a false analogy but grossly anthropomorphic. The cosmos is not a work of art on God's part any more than it is a work of procreation.

On the contrary, the cosmos is something other than the mechanism of a clock, all of whose motions are necessitated by the design imposed upon it by its human artificer. God is not the divine artificer, and the cosmos is not a work of divine art. Moreover, if nothing happened by chance and there was nothing contingent in the cosmos, no valid proof of God's existence could be philosophically constructed. I will explain why this is so in the next section.

4. A sound a posteriori argument: from a radically contingent cosmos to an exnihilating deity

Concepts are abstracted from sense-experience. They are all empirically derived. Hence we cannot have a concept of God. But not all the notions with which the intellect operates in thinking are concepts. There are, in addition, theoretical constructs, fictions of the mind that in the Middle Ages were called *entia rationis*. As in physics black holes and neutrinos are theoretical constructs, so in theology God is a theoretical construct.

Since all concepts are empirically derived, they do not raise questions about the existence of their objects. The concept of dog or cow is abstracted from perceptual instances of dogs and cows, and so we do not ask whether what we have in mind when we use the word *dog* or *cow* actually exists.

But when we are dealing with theoretical constructs in mathematical physics or in theology, the question of existence is inescapable. Do black holes really exist? Do neutrinos? Does that which we have in mind when we use the word *God* exist in reality?

Anselm mistakenly thought that because we cannot think of God as nonexisting while thinking of him as the Supreme Being, therefore God exists. The non sequitur is obvious. Anselm has instructed us about how to formulate a theoretical construct for the proper name "God," but the question still remains whether what we have in mind with that theoretical construct is only a fiction of the mind or a really existent being—an *ens reale*, not just an *ens rationis*. On the other hand, a unicorn is a fiction of the mind that, so far as all the evidence goes, is

295

just that. There are no perceptual instances of unicorns and no proof that they exist, even if not perceived.

With respect to theoretical constructs, the rule of inference by William of Ockham operates in theology in the same way that it operates in physical science. Ockham's rule—and razor—is that unless the existence of what is signified by our theoretical constructs is indispensable to explain observed phenomena or existences, the theoretical construct being thus tested is merely a fiction of the mind. Ockham's razor cuts out all unnecessary entities. It prevents us from committing the fallacy of reification—of adding to the world of real existences by positing entities that we have no reason to think exist. Ockham's rule is a principle of parsimony.

When we have the theoretical construct of God in our mind, even a God that is thought of as necessarily existing, we have to give reasons for positing the existence of the entity named. Since we cannot affirm the existence of God a priori by saying that God's existence is self-evident because we must think of the Supreme Being as necessarily existing, only an a posteriori argument for God's existence is valid. It is reasoning from the nature of the cosmos to the existence of God. Obeying Ockham's rule, we can posit the real existence of God, of whom we have a theoretical construct in our mind, because the existence of God is necessary to explain the existence of the cosmos.

The only valid argument for the existence of God is thus the inverse of the a priori ontological argument. It is reasoning from the nature of the cosmos to God, not from the nature of God to God's existence. The crucial point in this a posteriori argument is the radical contingency of the cosmos. Let me now explain how that is different from merely superficial contingency.

We usually think of the physical entities that come into being at one time and perish at another as contingent beings. If they existed necessarily, they could not come into being at one time and perish at another. But they are only superficially contingent. They do not come into being out of nothing, and when they perish, they do not pass into nothingness.

Biological progenitors cause the becoming of their progeny. They can cease to be and cease to function as causes while their progeny continue in being. When their progeny die as the result of the counteracting causes that operate against the inertia of being that has kept them alive, their perishing is merely a transformation of their matter— dust and ashes and skeletal bones instead of a living organism. The living organism has been replaced by matter in other forms, not by sheer nothingness. In contrast to such superficial contingency, we find radical contingency in the cosmos as a whole. Unless the cosmos were caused to exist at every moment of its existence, it would be replaced by the absolute void of nothingness.

How do we know that the cosmos is radically contingent? We know that all living organisms are superficially contingent because we know that they come into being at one time and perish at another. As pointed out earlier, in order to avoid begging the question, we must assume that the cosmos has everlasting existence, without a beginning or an end in time. What reason, then, do we have for thinking that this everlasting cosmos is radically contingent and in need of a cause of its existence?

Were this everlasting cosmos a necessary rather than a radically contingent existence—if it were incapable of not existing—we would have no ground for positing the existence of an exnihilating deity as the cause of its existence. Only if the cosmos is capable, at every moment of its existence, of not existing at all, would we have to posit the existence of a cause of its being, a cause that exnihilates it or preserves it from passing into nothingness.

The three crucial premises in the valid a posteriori argument for God's existence are as follows:

(1) God and God alone causes being or existence. All natural causes are causes of becoming or perishing.

(2) What does not exist necessarily and does not have the ground of its existence in itself needs a cause of its existence in another being at every moment of its existence.

(3) Whatever is capable of being otherwise (because it involves events that happen by chance or free choice) is also capable of not being at all and so needs a cause of its existence at every moment of its existence.

In the light of Ockham's rule, we are, therefore, justified in positing (or affirming) the existence of a supernatural Supreme Being as the exnihilating cause of the existence of the cosmos, which would cease to exist if it were not thus creatively caused.

Still one question remains: What grounds do we have for thinking that the cosmos could be otherwise—that its processes involve chance or coincidence? That is a question of fact, which we will deal with in the next section. Suffice it to say here that if we find an affirmative answer to that question tenable, then the a posteriori argument is grounded in facts about the cosmos.

That school in modern Christian apologetics, which follows Bishop Paley in viewing the cosmos as if it were a work of art designed by a divine artificer, denies that anything happens by chance in the cosmos and so denies its radical contingency.

5. Creation, contingency, and chance

Whether or not contingency and chance exist in the cosmos is a question of scientifically discoverable fact. It is not a question to be answered by arguing that chance and contingency in the cosmos are incompatible with Christian faith in a morally perfect God who created the cosmos as an act of benevolent love.

Before we turn to the answer given by twentieth-century natural science, let us consider the relevance of certain questions about creation that were asked in the Middle Ages in sacred dogmatic theology. In his *Summa Theologica* Thomas Aquinas asks the question whether God could have created other universes than this particular cosmos, and even whether he could have created a better one than this. Aquinas rejects a negative answer to the first question on the ground that a negative answer would entail the denial of God's freedom in the act of creation. Creation is an act of God's free choice, not something necessitated by God's nature.

That this actual cosmos is only one of a number of possible universes is a mark of its radical contingency, if it is true that whatever can be otherwise is capable of not being at all. The truth of that proposition is not self-evident, but I think it is true beyond a reasonable doubt, if not beyond the shadow of a doubt.

The Christian faith that God created man in his own image by giving human beings immaterial intellects and, with that, also free will is a further indication that in the course of human affairs the totally unpredictable is present. The power of free choice is the power to choose otherwise at any moment, no matter how one does in fact choose at that moment; it is also the power not to choose at all. The course of human history would be quite otherwise if human beings, exercising free will, had chosen it to be so.

The paleontological discoveries of Harvard professor Stephen Jay Gould provide us with ample scientific evidence of chance at work in the course of biological evolution. Twentieth-century particle physics and its cosmology, as influenced by the general theory of relativity, provide similar evidence of chance at work in the eighteen billion years since the Big Bang; and the Big Bang itself, which is not the exnihilation of the cosmos, is itself an unpredictable event.

The doctrine of the miscalled "natural theology," beginning with Paley and coming down to our own day, represents poorly conceived Christian apologetics that has its intellectual background in Newtonian classical mechanics. It is inconsistent with the scientific facts discovered, and scientific theories formulated, in the twentieth century.

I have earlier referred to a book of Polkinghorne, *Science and Creation* (1989). It is a work of Christian apologetics, not a work in pagan philosophical theology. It is written by a person of Christian faith who is also a mathematical physicist. Polkinghorne is not alone. His book includes a bibliography of other works in twentieth-century Christian apologetics that tend to confirm the views that he himself advances.

For Polkinghorne, there is no incompatibility whatsoever between the presence of chance, randomness, and contingency in the cosmos and God's creation of it. Let me quote a few passages from his book.

> The way that an element of randomness is seen to create openness to the future assigns a more positive role to chance in the process of the world than is acknowledged by those like Monod who see its operation as destructive of all significance. . . .
>
> This chapter has portrayed a world whose processes can assemble complexity within a decaying environment and where random events can prove to be the originators of pattern. Such a world is a world of orderliness but not of clockwork regularity, of potentiality without predictability, endowed with an assurance of development but with a certain openness as to its actual form. It is inevitably a world with ragged edges, where order and disorder interlace each other and where the exploration of possibility by chance will lead not only to the evolution of systems of increasing complexity, endowed with new possibilities, but also to the evolution of systems imperfectly formed and malfunctioning. The former superior entities will earn the epithet "successful" by their survival in the competition for constituent resources; the latter inferior entities will disappear from the evolving scene. It is just such a world that we live in. . . .
>
> In other words, God chose a world in which chance has a role to play, thereby both being responsible for the consequences accruing and also accepting limitation of his power to control. . . .
>
> Yet the order and disorder which intertwine in the process of the world show that the universe upheld by the divine Word is not a clear cold cosmos whose history is the inevitable unfolding of an invulnerable plan. It is a world kept in being by the divine Juggler rather than by the divine Structural Engineer, a world whose precarious process speaks of the free gift of Love. We are accustomed to think of the vulnerability accepted by the Word in the incarnation, a vulnerability potentially present in the baby lying in the manger and realized to the full in the man hanging on the cross. What is there revealed of the divine in the human life of Jesus is also to be discerned in the cosmic story of creation.

To this I would only add that Polkinghorne explicitly rejects what he regards as the outmoded as well as erroneous Christian apologetics of Paley and the anthropomorphic image of God as analogous to a watchmaker, producing a mechanical work of art that is intelligible to an extent that the cosmos known to twentieth-century physics and biology is not.

6. Theoretical physics and philosophical theology

A few Christian apologists in the twentieth century, such as Polkinghorne, are knowledgeable in the field of twentieth-century theoretical physics. But, with the possible exception of Heisenberg, few if any twentieth-century theoretical physicists manifest any competence in philosophy and appear to be totally ignorant of philosophical theology.

One would not expect them to be persons of Christian faith or apologists for Christianity, but one would expect them to be silent about matters beyond their ken. They should at least be aware of the limitations of theoretical physics and not make unfounded remarks on the basis of their knowledge of that limited subject.

Einstein was a great theoretical physicist and great human being, but not a wise man. The possession of wisdom depends to some extent on clear philosophical thought. Einstein once said that what was not measurable by physicists was of no interest to them, or had no meaning for them; he also said (in his attack on quantum indeterminacy) that God, a being not measurable by physicists, does not throw dice. He said that he did not believe in a "personal" God, using the word *personal* as if it meant the same thing as *anthropomorphic*. Man is a person because he is in the image of God, not the reverse. In theology, the word *person* signifies a being with intellect and free will.

Hawking is a great theoretical physicist, both in quantum mechanics and in cosmology. But his philosophical naïveté and his ignorance of philosophical theology fills his *A Brief History of Time* with unfounded assertions, verging on impudence. Where Einstein had said that what is not measurable by physicists is of no interest to them, Hawking flatly asserts that what is not measurable by physicists does not exist—has no reality whatsoever.

With respect to time, that amounts to the denial of psychological time which is not measurable by physicists, and also to everlasting time— time before the Big Bang—which physics cannot measure. Hawking does not know that both Aquinas and Kant had shown that we cannot rationally establish that time is either finite or infinite. When he treats the Big Bang as if it were the beginning of time, not just the beginning of measurable time, he shows his ignorance of God as cause of being and of creation as an act of exnihilation, which the Big Bang is not.

Furthermore, Hawking's book is filled with references to God and to the mind of God, both not measurable by physicists, and so nonexistent by Hawking's own assertion about what has and what lacks reality. To discourse seriously about a nonexistent being without explicitly confessing that one is being fanciful or poetical is, in my judgment, impudence on the author's part.

Most theoretical physicists are guilty of the same fault when, in quantum theory, they fail to distinguish between a measurable indeterminacy and the epistemic indeterminability of what is in reality determinate. The indeterminacy discovered by physical measurements of subatomic phenomena simply tells us that we cannot know the definite position and velocity of an electron at one instant of time. It does not tell us that the electron, at any instant of time, does not have a definite position and velocity. They, too, convert what is not measurable by them into the unreal and the nonexistent. The definite position and velocity of the electron at any moment of time is not measurable because of the intrusive effect of the measurements themselves, though this effect may not itself be discernible.

In view of the ever-increasing specialization in all fields of learning, and therefore in higher education, we probably cannot look forward to a future in which theoretical physicists will also be persons who have sufficient grounding in philosophy and in philosophical theology, in order to avoid their making unfounded assertions about matters beyond their field of specialization. But they should at least be aware of their limited knowledge and be silent about matters beyond it.

On the other hand, we should also expect Christian apologists in the twentieth century to be aware of what has been discovered in this century about the physical cosmos and about biological evolution. Only thus will they avoid the errors of their predecessors in modern times who lived in a universe that was described by Newtonian classical mechanics, which we now realize is insufficient to describe the universe we have since been able to discern.

Response to Mortimer J. Adler

Owen Gingerich

Mortimer Adler's essay springs in part from his earlier book *How to Think About God*. I was deeply intrigued as I read his book, for it was as compelling as a medieval mystery story, tightly logical and filled with excitement as flaws in past arguments by Aquinas and Anselm were systematically exposed. Finally, after a careful exposition of God's attributes as immaterial, immutable, necessary, uncaused, and infinite, he brings forth his conclusion that such a God indeed exists.

Much as I admire Adler's tour de force, I feel obliged to point out that our essays are based on fundamentally different approaches—his on logic, mine on rhetoric. In the twelfth century, logic and rhetoric were equally esteemed components of the medieval curriculum. In some pursuits logic was more suitable, whereas in others, such as ethics, rhetoric led the way. In the following century, the time of Thomas Aquinas, logic began to gain the ascendancy. Today, common opinion places logic on a pedestal, while "mere rhetoric" is a term of opprobrium. Likewise, "apologetics" has a decidedly negative ring to it. Here I shall argue that, contrary to the popular connotations of these words, rhetoric is the more relevant.

In a none-too-subtle (and rhetorical!) tone, Adler has quickly relegated natural theology to "Christian apologetics." (He ignores the fact that the first 95 percent of my essay, while being unabashedly theistic in its grounding, is not specifically Christian at all; it could equally apply to Jewish or Muslim theism.) Trying to redefine the contemporary usage of "natural theology" is a bit like Alice's Humpty-Dumpty saying words mean just what he chooses them to mean. I would go along with physicist-priest John Polkinghorne (whose work Adler cites quite approvingly) and would define natural theology as "the search for God through the exercise of reason and the inspection of the world." Polkinghorne adds that this is "not an optional extra, for indulgence by the scientifically inclined, but rather it is an indispensable part of scientific inquiry."

Although I respect and admire Adler's severely philosophical rationale, I feel it isn't fully relevant to the question at hand. Adler's book, as well as his essay, is self-confessedly written by a pagan for pagans. The God he describes is not the God anyone would worship. Perhaps the distinguished Swiss theologian Karl Barth overstated it when he said, "This absolute and supreme being, the ultimate and most profound, this 'thing in itself,' has nothing to do with God." But neither Fred Hoyle's "superintelligence," Milton Munitz's "unknowable transcendence," nor the God of the Big Bang describes much about the God of consciousness, of conscience, or of creativity, that is, about the God of the great monotheistic religions.

While Adler has brilliantly demonstrated both the power and limitations of philosophical inquiry, logic has rather little to say about what we actually believe, whether it is in science or in theology. As Pascal said (in the closing quotation from Adler's *How to Think About God*), "the heart has its reasons that reason does not know" (*GBWW* I: 33, 222; II: 30, 222).

When Galileo began to argue for the heliocentric cosmology, it was his Ptolemaic opponent, Cardinal Bellarmino, who had logic on his side. Bellarmino could correctly point out that Galileo had no logical proof that the earth moved. What Galileo could persuasively show was a series of examples that were more coherent, and somehow more reasonably understood, if one accepted a sun-centered cosmos. His argument was rhetorical, and it won the day.

Hence one of the themes of my essay: we have no proof from nature for the existence of God, no logical demonstration, but we do have pointers in the natural world—rhetorical pointers, if you will—toward the reasonableness of God's existence. This, then, is the appropriate arena for natural theology today, and it is not all that different from our system of beliefs as to what is found in natural science itself.

When I argued in my essay that the proper question is "design or chance?" rather than "creation or evolution?" I came dangerously close to what Adler has pointed out as the chief error of modern Christian apologetics. I certainly had not intended to argue that there is nothing contingent in the evolutionary process, or that nothing happens by chance. In fact, according to Alfred North Whitehead, one of the great ideas of the Judeo-Christian heritage that provided a fertile philosophical ground for the rise of modern science was the notion of God's freedom, and hence the contingency of nature. Since God could have made the universe in many different ways, the argument runs, it behooves the scientist to undertake the experiments to find out which way in fact describes the universe. The Princeton philosopher Diogenes Allen had already drawn my attention to the distinction between design and purpose, and probably I should have given more emphasis to the latter concept. A world ordered to God's purposes could be achieved in any number of ways, not merely by one preordained design.

I suppose it is the insinuation of a causal uniqueness in design (which I did not intend) that launched Adler's attack on much modern natural theology on the grounds that it is based on Newtonian mechanics rather than on the scientific theories of the twentieth century. What I find curious is the extent to which Adler seems unwittingly to have fallen into the same error. He criticizes Stephen Hawking for treating the Big Bang "as if it were the beginning of time, not just the beginning of measurable time." But what is unmeasurable time? I suppose it is something like the unicorn, an *ens rationis*. All of Newtonian mechanics is based on the notion of an absolute, independent existence of time, even though a thinker like Augustine had long ago clearly stated that "There is no time before the world began," because "time does not exist without some movement and transition" (*GBWW* I: 18, 325; II: 16, 378). The twentieth-century theory of relativity shows clearly how the march of time depends on its measurement, and the Newtonian notion of time like an ever-flowing stream, independent of the material world, is just as antiquated as Immanuel Kant's claim concerning the natural uniqueness of Euclidean three-dimensional geometry (*GBWW* I: 42, 24–26; II: 39, 24–26).

For Adler, acceptance of the Big Bang as the beginning of the universe and the beginning of time is tantamount to saying that God exists, and hence it begs the philosophical question. Natural theology's legitimate "inspection of the world" (in Polkinghorne's definition) undercuts the uniqueness of Adler's philosophical theology, which may perhaps explain his resistance to it. If I may indulge in a speculation, I suspect that here is the Achilles' heel through which some future philosopher will dissect Mortimer Adler's carefully crafted construction.

PART FOUR

Additions
to the
Great Books Library

Monkey (in part)

Wu Ch'êng-ên

Editor's Introduction

One of the great folktales of China, what is usually called *Journey to the West,* of which a portion is reprinted here, is also a basic document of Buddhism. This faith, the religion of a fifth of the world, began of course in India but was eventually absorbed there by the pervasive Hinduism. Where it survived was in China, in Tibet, in Southeast Asia, even in Japan, and in those places a sense developed after awhile of its lost source, of a need to rediscover the authoritative scriptures. The "journey" of this tale is that imagined undertaking by a certain Tripitaka, a monk of comic description in the time of the great T'ang dynasty, i.e., the seventh century.

Tripitaka's adventures are loosely based upon the pilgrimage of Hsüan-tsang (596–664), an actual monk who actually made the long and hazardous journey to India in search of sacred writings, and who became one of the best-known and revered of Buddhist figures. He was not in fact the first such to go that way; at least fifty men beginning in the third century had made the same quest, though not all of them reached the land of their faith, and some sought only to study there. In particular, the object of Hsüan-tsang was to discover whether according to original Buddhist teachings it was possible for all men to attain Buddhahood, or only a portion of them—a question which had divided Chinese Buddhism for centuries—and whether, if not, he himself had the Buddhist nature.

How this quest became the subject of popular legend is a long story. There were several versions of the pilgrimage, some as early as the thirteenth century, before the one from which this excerpt has been taken appeared, and certain characteristic figures and episodes had been established. These include the opening chapters on the Monkey Novice-Monk who, after making himself immortal, becomes the protector and guide of Hsüan-tsang, and who in the end, on completion of the quest, receives the title of Great Sage. This is the part of the tale we provide here, translated by Arthur Waley and—altogether—given the title of *Monkey: Folk Novel of China.* Hsüan-tsang himself is introduced in a subsequent chapter, and the two are joined in time by a certain Pigsy, by Sandy, and by other characters in a story that has some qualities of a picaresque novel, a fairy tale, and a fabliau. Western readers may well think as well of *The Pilgrim's Progress* and of tall tales such as that of the legendary Ohio riverboatman, Mike Fink, who boasted that he could dive deeper, swim farther, and come up drier than any man alive. It may seem hard to credit humor of this sort in the service of a doctrine noted for its dignity, the solemn quietude of its observance, but it cannot be taken any other way.

Despite the popularity which the *Journey to the West* has enjoyed since it appeared in the latter portion of the sixteenth century, its authorship remains uncertain and may have been deliberately disguised. Not until 1923 was it pretty much settled that Wu Ch'êng-ên (1500–82—the late Ming period) was the writer. He was an otherwise undistinguished person apparently—a minor official, native to Shan-yang in the province of Kiangsu, who gained a reputation as a poet and humorist in his time. He is said by an old gazetteer to have been "a man of exceptional intelligence and many talents who read most widely." Further, he was "able to compose poetry and prose at the stroke of the brush," and "also excelled in witty and satirical writing," to which is added that "the various miscellaneous writings he produced brought him resounding fame at the time."

Wu Ch'êng-ên is also recorded to have said of himself, in the preface to a group of tales now lost, that he was very fond of strange stories when he was a child; that in his school days he used to buy popular novels and histories which he read in secret places, fearing his teachers would disapprove; that he admired other storytellers of his time and wished to be like them, but that it was not till he was well in years, when he had forgotten (so he says) most of the tales he had read and heard, that he decided to compile his own work. "Hence this Book of Monsters," he explained, and added: "I have sometimes laughingly said to myself that is not I who have found these ghosts and monsters, but they, the monstrosities themselves, which have found me!" But he maintained that his book was not confined to such inventions, that "it also records the strange things of the human world and sometimes conveys a little bit of a moral lesson." We assume he was speaking of the *Journey to the West*.

Waley did not attempt to translate the poetry which is interspersed among the prose sections of the *Journey*. Perhaps, as a capable poet himself, he felt it could not satisfactorily be done. The combination of prose and verse was, however, a standard thing in Buddhist writings, where doctrines were given first in one form and immediately afterward in the other, and Wu Ch'êng-ên, if it was he, made use of the convention. A complete version of the *Journey*, translated by Anthony C. Yu, was published in 1977 with the poetry included.

Monkey (in part)

Chapter I

There was a rock that since the creation of the world had been worked upon by the pure essences of Heaven and the fine savors of Earth, the vigor of sunshine and the grace of moonlight, till at last it became magically pregnant and one day split open, giving birth to a stone egg, about as big as a playing ball. Fructified by the wind it developed into a stone monkey, complete with every organ and limb. At once this monkey learned to climb and run; but its first act was to make a bow toward each of the four quarters. As it did so, a steely light darted from this monkey's eyes and flashed as far as the Palace of the Pole Star. This shaft of light astonished the Jade Emperor as he sat in the Cloud Palace of the Golden Gates, in the Treasure Hall of the Holy Mists, surrounded by his fairy Ministers. Seeing this strange light flashing, he ordered Thousand-League Eye and Down-the-Wind Ear to open the gate of the Southern Heaven and look out. At his bidding these two captains went out to the gate and looked so sharply and listened so well that presently they were able to report, "This steely light comes from the borders of the small country of Ao-lai, that lies to the east of the Holy Continent, from the Mountain of Flowers and Fruit. On this mountain is a magic rock, which gave birth to an egg. This egg changed into a stone monkey, and when he made his bow to the four quarters a steely light flashed from his eyes with a beam that reached the Palace of the Pole Star. But now he is taking a drink,* and the light is growing dim."

The Jade Emperor condescended to take an indulgent view. "These creatures in the world below," he said, "were compounded of the essence of Heaven and Earth, and nothing that goes on there should surprise us." That monkey walked, ran, leapt, and bounded over the hills, feeding on grasses and shrubs, drinking from streams and springs, gathering the mountain flowers, looking for fruits. Wolf, panther, and tiger were his companions, the deer and civet were his friends, gibbons and baboons his kindred. At night he lodged under cliffs of rock, by day he wandered among the peaks and caves. One very hot morning, after playing in the shade of some pine trees, he and the other monkeys went to bathe in a mountain stream. See how those waters bounce and tumble like rolling melons!

There is an old saying, "Birds have their bird language, beasts have their beast talk." The monkeys said, "We none of us know where this stream comes from. As we have nothing to do this morning, wouldn't it be fun to follow it up to its source?" With a whoop of joy, dragging their sons and carrying their daughters, calling out to younger brother and to elder brother, the whole troupe rushed along the streamside and scrambled up the steep places, till they reached the source of the stream. They found themselves standing before the curtain of a great waterfall.

All the monkeys clapped their hands and cried aloud, "Lovely water, lovely water! To think that it starts far off in some cavern below the base of the mountain, and

---

*"Taking a drink" might be "taking food and drink."

flows all the way to the Great Sea! If any of us were bold enough to pierce that curtain, get to where the water comes from, and return unharmed, we would make him our king!" Three times the call went out, when suddenly one of them leapt from among the throng and answered the challenge in a loud voice. It was the Stone Monkey. "I will go," he cried, "I will go!" Look at him! He screws up his eyes and crouches; then at one bound he jumps straight through the waterfall. When he opened his eyes and looked about him, he found that where he had landed there was no water. A great bridge stretched in front of him, shining and glinting. When he looked closely at it, he saw that it was made all of burnished iron. The water under it flowed through a hole in the rock, filling in all the space under the arch. Monkey climbed up onto the bridge and, spying as he went, saw something that looked just like a house. There were stone seats and stone couches, and tables with stone bowls and cups. He skipped back to the hump of the bridge and saw that on the cliff there was an inscription in large square writing which said, "This Cave of the Water Curtain in the blessed land of the Mountain of Flowers and Fruit leads to Heaven."* Monkey was beside himself with delight. He rushed back and again crouched, shut his eyes, and jumped through the curtain of water.

"A great stroke of luck," he cried, "A great stroke of luck!" "What is it like on the other side?" asked the monkeys, crowding round him. "Is the water very deep?" "There is no water," said the Stone Monkey. "There is an iron bridge, and at the side of it a heaven-sent place to live in." "What made you think it would do to live in?" asked the monkeys. "The water," said the Stone Monkey, "flows out of a hole in the rock, filling in the space under the bridge. At the side of the bridge are flowers and trees, and there is a chamber of stone. Inside are stone tables, stone cups, stone dishes, stone couches, stone seats. We could really be very comfortable there. There

is plenty of room for hundreds and thousands of us, young and old. Let us all go and live there; we shall be splendidly sheltered in every weather." "You go first and show us how!" cried the monkeys, in great delight. Once more he closed his eyes and was through at one bound. "Come along, all of you!" he cried. The bolder of them jumped at once; the more timid stretched out their heads and then drew them back, scratched their ears, rubbed their cheeks, and then with a great shout the whole mob leapt forward. Soon they were all seizing dishes and snatching cups, scrambling to the hearth or fighting for the beds, dragging things along or shifting them about, behaving indeed as monkeys with their mischievous nature might be expected to do, never quiet for an instant, till at last they were thoroughly worn out. The Stone Monkey took his seat at the head of them and said, "Gentlemen! 'With one whose word cannot be trusted there is nothing to be done!'† You promised that any of us who managed to get through the waterfall and back again, should be your king. I have not only come and gone and come again, but also found you a comfortable place to sleep, put you in the enviable position of being householders. Why do you not bow down to me as your king?"

Thus reminded, the monkeys all pressed together the palms of their hands and prostrated themselves, drawn up in a line according to age and standing, and bowing humbly they cried, "Great king, a thousand years!" After this the Stone Monkey discarded his old name and became king, with the title "Handsome Monkey King." He appointed various monkeys, gibbons, and baboons to be his ministers and officers. By day they wandered about the Mountain of Flowers and Fruit; at night they slept

---

*The inscription is translated by Hu Shih to read: "The Blessed Land of the Mountain of Flower and Fruit and the Heavenly Grotto of the Water Curtain Cave."

†*Analects* of Confucius, II. 22 (cf. *GIT* 1984, 236).

in the Cave of the Water Curtain. They lived in perfect sympathy and accord, not mingling with bird or beast, in perfect independence and entire happiness.

The Monkey King had enjoyed this artless existence for several hundred years when one day, at a feast in which all the monkeys took part, the king suddenly felt very sad and burst into tears. His subjects at once ranged themselves in front of him and bowed down, saying, "Why is your Majesty so sad?" "At present," said the king, "I have no cause for unhappiness. But I have a misgiving about the future, which troubles me sorely." "Your Majesty is very hard to please," said the monkeys, laughing. "Every day we have happy meetings on fairy mountains, in blessed spots, in ancient caves, on holy islands. We are not subject to the Unicorn or Phoenix, nor to the restraints of any human king. Such freedom is an immeasurable blessing. What can it be that causes you this sad misgiving?" "It is true," said the Monkey King, "that today I am not answerable to the law of any human king, nor need I fear the menace of any beast or bird. But the time will come when I shall grow old and weak. Yama, King of Death, is secretly waiting to destroy me. Is there no way by which, instead of being born again on Earth, I might live forever among the people of the sky?"

When the monkeys heard this they covered their faces with their hands and wept, each thinking of his own mortality. But look! From among the ranks there springs out one monkey commoner, who cries in a loud voice "If that is what troubles your Majesty, it shows that religion has taken hold upon your heart. There are indeed, among all creatures, three kinds that are not subject to Yama, King of Death." "And do you know which they are?" asked the Monkey King. "Buddhas, Immortals, and Sages," he said. "These three are exempt from the Turning of the Wheel, from birth and destruction. They are eternal as Heaven and Earth, as the hills and

streams." "Where are they to be found?" asked the Monkey King. "Here on the common earth," said the monkey, "in ancient caves among enchanted hills."

The king was delighted with this news. "Tomorrow," he said, "I shall say goodbye to you, go down the mountain, wander like a cloud to the corners of the sea, far away to the end of the world, till I have found these three kinds of Immortal. From them I will learn how to be young forever and escape the doom of death." This determination it was that led him to leap clear of the toils of Reincarnation and turned him at last into the Great Monkey Sage, equal of Heaven. The monkeys clapped their hands and cried aloud, "Splendid! Splendid! Tomorrow we will scour the hills for fruits and berries and hold a great farewell banquet in honor of our king."

Next day they duly went to gather peaches and rare fruits, mountain herbs, yellow-sperm, tubers, orchids, strange plants and flowers of every sort, and set out the stone tables and benches, laid out fairy meats and drinks. They put the Monkey King at the head of the table, and ranged themselves according to their age and rank. The pledge-cup passed from hand to hand; they made their offerings to him of flowers and fruit. All day long they drank, and next day their king rose early and said, "Little ones, cut some pinewood for me and make me a raft; then find a tall bamboo for a pole, and put together a few fruits and such like. I am going to start." He got onto the raft all alone and pushed off with all his might, speeding away and away, straight out to sea, till favored by a following wind he arrived at the borders of the Southern World. Fate indeed had favored him; for days on end, ever since he set foot on the raft, a strong southeast wind blew and carried him at last to the northwestern bank, which is indeed the frontier of the Southern World. He tested the water with his pole and found that it was shallow; so he left the raft and

climbed ashore. On the beach were people fishing, shooting wild geese, scooping
oysters, draining salt. He ran up to them
and for fun began to perform queer antics
which frightened them so much that they
dropped their baskets and nets and ran
for their lives. One of them, who stood
his ground, Monkey caught hold of, and
ripping off his clothes, found out how
to wear them himself, and so dressed up
went prancing through towns and cities, in
market and bazaar, imitating the people's
manners and talk. All the while his heart
was set only on finding the Immortals and
learning from them the secret of eternal
youth. But he found the men of the world
all engrossed in the quest of profit or fame;
there was not one who had any care for the
end that was in store for him. So Monkey
went looking for the way of Immortality,
but found no chance of meeting it. For
eight or nine years he went from city to
city and town to town till suddenly he came
to the Western Ocean. He was sure that
beyond this ocean there would certainly
be Immortals, and he made for himself a
raft like the one he had before. He floated
on over the Western Ocean till he came
to the Western Continent, where he went
ashore, and when he had looked about for
some time, he suddenly saw a very high
and beautiful mountain, thickly wooded at
the base. He had no fear of wolves, tigers,
or panthers, and made his way up to the
very top. He was looking about him when
he suddenly heard a man's voice coming
from deep amid the woods. He hurried
toward the spot and listened intently. It
was someone singing, and these were the
words that he caught:

I hatch no plot, I scheme no scheme;
Fame and shame are one to me,
A simple life prolongs my days.
Those I meet upon my way
Are Immortals, one and all,
Who from their quiet seats expound
The Scriptures of the Yellow Court.

When Monkey heard these words he was
very pleased. "There must then be Immortals somewhere hereabouts," he said. He
sprang deep into the forest and looking
carefully saw that the singer was a woodman, who was cutting brushwood. "Reverend Immortal," said Monkey, coming
forward, "your disciple raises his hands."
The woodman was so astonished that he
dropped his ax. "You have made a mistake," he said, turning and answering the
salutation, "I am only a shabby, hungry
woodcutter. What makes you address me
as an 'Immortal'?" "If you are not an Immortal," said Monkey, "why did you talk of
yourself as though you were one?" "What
did I say," asked the woodcutter, "that
sounded as though I were an Immortal?"
"When I came to the edge of the wood,"
said Monkey, "I heard you singing 'Those
I meet upon my way are Immortals, one
and all, who from their quiet seats expound the Scriptures of the Yellow Court.'
Those scriptures are secret, Taoist texts.
What can you be but an Immortal?" "I
won't deceive you," said the woodcutter.
"That song was indeed taught to me by an
Immortal, who lives not very far from my
hut. He saw that I have to work hard for
my living and have a lot of troubles; so he
told me when I was worried by anything
to say to myself the words of that song.
This, he said, would comfort me and get
me out of my difficulties. Just now I was
upset about something and so I was singing
that song. I had no idea that you were
listening."

"If the Immortal lives close by," said
Monkey, "how is it that you have not become his disciple? Wouldn't it have been as
well to learn from him how never to grow
old?" "I have a hard life of it," said the
woodcutter. "When I was eight or nine I
lost my father. I had no brothers and sisters, and it fell upon me alone to support
my widowed mother. There was nothing
for it but to work hard early and late. Now
my mother is old and I dare not leave

her. The garden is neglected, we have not enough either to eat or wear. The most I can do is to cut two bundles of firewood, carry them to market, and with the penny or two that I get buy a few handfuls of rice which I cook myself and serve to my aged mother. I have no time to go and learn magic." "From what you tell me," said Monkey, "I can see that you are a good and devoted son, and your piety will certainly be rewarded. All I ask of you is that you will show me where the Immortal lives; for I should very much like to visit him."

"It is quite close," said the woodcutter. "This mountain is called the Holy Terrace Mountain, and on it is a cave called the Cave of the Slanting Moon and Three Stars. In that cave lives an Immortal called the Patriarch Subodhi. In his time he has had innumerable disciples, and at this moment there are some thirty or forty of them studying with him. You have only to follow that small path southward for eight or nine leagues,* and you will come to his home." "Honored brother," said Monkey, drawing the woodcutter toward him, "come with me, and if I profit by the visit I will not forget that you guided me." "It takes a lot to make some people understand," said the woodcutter. "I've just been telling you why I can't go. If I went with you, what would become of my work? Who would give my old mother her food? I must go on cutting my wood, and you must find your way alone."

When Monkey heard this, he saw nothing for it but to say good-bye. He left the wood, found the path, went uphill for some seven or eight leagues, and sure enough found a cave-dwelling. But the door was locked. All was quiet, and there was no sign of anyone being about. Suddenly he turned his head and saw on top of the cliff a stone slab about thirty feet high and eight feet wide. On it was an inscription in large letters saying, "Cave of the Slanting Moon and Three Stars on the Moun-

tain of the Holy Terrace." "People here," said Monkey, "are certainly very truthful. There really is such a mountain, and such a cave!" He looked about for a while, but did not venture to knock at the door. Instead he jumped up into a pine tree and began eating the pine seed and playing among the branches. After a time he heard someone call; the door of the cave opened and a fairy boy of great beauty came out, in appearance utterly unlike the common lads that he had seen till now. The boy shouted, "Who is making a disturbance out there?" Monkey leapt down from his tree, and coming forward said with a bow, "Fairy boy, I am a pupil who has come to study Immortality. I should not dream of making a disturbance." "*You* a pupil!" said the boy laughing. "To be sure," said Monkey. "My master is lecturing," said the boy. "But before he gave out his theme he told me to go to the door and if anyone came asking for instruction, I was to look after him. I suppose he meant you." "Of course he meant me," said Monkey. "Follow me this way," said the boy. Monkey tidied himself and followed the boy into the cave. Huge chambers opened out before them, they went on from room to room, through lofty halls and innumerable cloisters and retreats, till they came to a platform of green jade, upon which was seated the Patriarch Subodhi, with thirty lesser Immortals assembled before him. Monkey at once prostrated himself and bumped his head three times upon the ground, murmuring, "Master, master! As pupil to teacher I pay you my humble respects." "Where do you come from?" asked the Patriarch. "First tell me your country and name, and then pay your respects again." "I am from the Water-Curtain Cave," said Monkey, "on the Mountain of Fruit and Flowers in the country of Ao-lai." "Go away!" shouted the Patriarch. "I know the people there. They're a tricky, humbugging set. It's no

---

*A league was 360 steps.

good one of them supposing he's going to achieve Enlightenment." Monkey, kowtowing violently, hastened to say, "There's no trickery about this; it's just the plain truth I'm telling you." "If you claim that you're telling the truth," said the Patriarch, "how is it that you say you came from Ao-lai? Between there and here there are two oceans and the whole of the Southern Continent. How did you get here?" "I floated over the oceans and wandered over the lands for ten years and more," said Monkey, "till at last I reached here." "Oh well," said the Patriarch, "I suppose if you came by easy stages, it's not altogether impossible. But tell me, what is your *hsing?*"* "I never show *hsing,*" said Monkey. "If I am abused, I am not at all annoyed. If I am hit, I am not angry; but on the contrary, twice more polite than before. All my life I have never shown *hsing.*"

"I don't mean that kind of *hsing,*" said the Patriarch. "I mean what was your family, what surname had they?" "I had no family," said Monkey, "neither father nor mother." "Oh indeed!" said the Patriarch. "Perhaps you grew on a tree!" "Not exactly," said Monkey. "I came out of a stone. There was a magic stone on the Mountain of Flowers and Fruit. When its time came, it burst open and I came out."

"We shall have to see about giving you a school-name," said the Patriarch. "We have twelve words that we use in these names, according to the grade of the pupil. You are in the tenth grade." "What are the twelve words?" asked Monkey. "They are Wide, Big, Wise, Clever, True, Conforming, Nature, Ocean, Lively, Aware, Perfect, and Illumined. As you belong to the tenth grade, the word Aware must come in your name. How about Aware-of-Vacuity?" "Splendid!" said Monkey, laughing. "From now onward let me be called Aware-of-Vacuity."

So that was his name in religion. And if you do not know whether in the end, equipped with this name, he managed to

obtain enlightenment or not, listen while it is explained to you in the next chapter.

Chapter II

Monkey was so pleased with his new name that he skipped up and down in front of the Patriarch, bowing to express his gratitude. Subodhi then ordered his pupils to take Monkey to the outer rooms and teach him how to sprinkle and dust, answer properly when spoken to, how to come in, go out, and go round. Then he bowed to his fellow pupils and went out into the corridor, where he made himself a sleeping place. Early next morning he and the others practiced the correct mode of speech and bearing, studied the Scriptures, discussed doctrine, practiced writing, burnt incense. And in this same way he passed day after day, spending his leisure in sweeping the floor, hoeing the garden, growing flowers and tending trees, getting firewood and lighting the fire, drawing water and carrying it in buckets. Everything he needed was provided for him. And so he lived in the cave, while time slipped by, for six or seven years. One day the Patriarch, seated in state, summoned all his pupils and began a lecture on the Great Way. Monkey was so delighted by what he heard that he tweaked his ears and rubbed his cheeks; his brow flowered and his eyes laughed. He could not stop his hands from dancing, his feet from stamping. Suddenly the Patriarch caught sight of him and shouted, "What is the use of your being here if, instead of listening to my lecture, you jump and dance like a maniac?" "I am listening with all my might," said Monkey. "But you were saying such wonderful things that I could not contain myself for joy. That is why I may, for all I know, have been hopping and jumping. Don't be angry with me." "So you recognize the profundity of what

---

*There is a pun on *hsing,* "surname," and *hsing,* "temper."

Bo tree shrine being worshiped, stone relief from Bhārhut, India, ca. 2nd century B.C. According to Buddhist tradition, it was under a bo tree (also called bodhi tree, species *Ficus religiosa*) that Buddha sat when he attained enlightenment (bodhi) at Bodh Gayā, India.

I am saying?" said the Patriarch. "How long, pray, have you been in the cave?" "It may seem rather silly," said Monkey, "but really I don't know how long. All I can remember is that when I was sent to get firewood, I went up the mountain behind the cave, and there I found a whole slope covered with peach trees. I have eaten my fill of those peaches seven times." "It is called the Hill of Bright Peach Blossom," said the Patriarch. "If you have eaten there seven times, I suppose you have been here seven years. What sort of wisdom are you now hoping to learn from me?" "I leave that to you," said Monkey. "Any sort of wisdom—it's all one to me."

"There are three hundred and sixty schools of wisdom," said the Patriarch, "and all of them lead to Self-attainment. Which school do you want to study?" "Just as you think best," said Monkey. "I am all attention." "Well, how about Art?" said the Patriarch. "Would you like me to teach you that?" "What sort of wisdom is that?" asked Monkey. "You would be able to summon fairies and ride the Phoenix," said the Patriarch, "divine by shuffling the yarrow-stalks and know how to avoid disaster and pursue good fortune." "But should I live forever?" asked Monkey. "Certainly not," said the Patriarch. "Then that's no good to me," said Monkey. "How about natural philosophy?" said the Patriarch. "What is that about?" asked Monkey. "It means the teaching of Confucius," said the Patriarch, "and of Buddha and Lao Tzu, of the Dualists and Mo Tzu and the Doctors of Medicine; reading scriptures, saying prayers, learning how to have adepts and sages at your beck and call." "But should I live forever?" asked Monkey. "If that's what you are thinking about," said the Patriarch, "I am afraid philosophy is no better than a prop in the wall." "Master," said Monkey, "I am a plain, simple man, and I don't understand that sort of patter. What do you mean by a prop in the wall?" "When men are building a room," said the Patriarch, "and want it to stand firm, they put a pillar to prop up the walls. But one day the roof falls in and the pillar rots." "That doesn't sound much like long life," said Monkey. "I'm not going to learn philosophy!" "How about Quietism?" asked the Patriarch. "What does that consist of?" asked Monkey. "Low diet," said the Patriarch, "inactivity, meditation, restraint of word and deed, yoga practiced prostrate or standing." "But should I live forever?" asked Monkey. "The results of Quietism," said the Patriarch, "are no better than unbaked clay in the kiln." "You've got a very poor memory," said Monkey. "Didn't I tell you just now that I don't understand that sort of patter? What do you mean by unbaked clay in the kiln?" "The bricks and tiles," said the Patriarch, "may be waiting, all shaped and ready, in the kiln; but if they have not yet been fired, there will come a day when heavy rain falls and they are washed away." "That does not promise well for the future," said Monkey. "I don't think I'll bother about Quietism."

"You might try exercises," said the Patriarch. "What do you mean by that," asked Monkey. "Various forms of activity," said the Patriarch, "such as the exercises called 'Gathering the Yin and patching the Yang,' 'Drawing the Bow and Treading the Catapult,' 'Rubbing the Navel to pass breath.' Then there are alchemical practices such as the Magical Explosion, Burning the Reeds and Striking the Tripod, Promoting Red Lead, Melting the Autumn Stone, and Drinking Bride's Milk." "Would these make me live forever?" asked Monkey. "To hope for that," said the Patriarch, "would be like trying to fish the moon out of the water." "There you go again!" said Monkey. "What pray do you mean by fishing the moon out of the water?" "When the moon is in the sky," said the Patriarch, "it is reflected in the water. It looks just like a real thing, but if you try to catch hold of it, you find it is only an illusion." "That does not sound much good," said Monkey;

"I shan't learn exercises." "Tut!" cried the Patriarch, and coming down from the platform, he caught hold of the knuckle-rapper and pointed it at Monkey, saying, "You wretched simian! You won't learn this and you won't learn that! I should like to know what it is you do want." And so saying he struck Monkey over the head three times. Then he folded his hands behind his back and strode off into the inner room, dismissing his audience and locking the door behind him. The pupils all turned indignantly upon Monkey. "You villainous ape," they shouted at him, "do you think that is the way to behave? The Master offers to teach you, and instead of accepting thankfully, you begin arguing with him. Now he's thoroughly offended and goodness knows when he'll come back." They were all very angry and poured abuse on him; but Monkey was not in the least upset, and merely replied by a broad grin. The truth of the matter was, he understood the language of secret signs. That was why he did not take up the quarrel or attempt to argue. He knew that the Master, by striking him three times, was giving him an appointment at the third watch; and by going off with his hands folded behind his back, meant that Monkey was to look for him in the inner apartments. The locking of the door meant that he was to come round by the back door and would then receive instruction.

The rest of the day he frolicked with the other pupils in front of the cave, impatiently awaiting the night. As soon as dusk came, like the others, he went to his sleeping place. He closed his eyes and pretended to be asleep, breathing softly and regularly. In the mountains there is no watchman to beat the watches or call the hours. The best Monkey could do was to count his incoming and outgoing breaths. When he reckoned that it must be about the hour of the Rat (11 P.M.–1 A.M.) he got up very quietly and slipped on his clothes, softly opened the front door, left his companions, and went round to the back door. Sure enough, it was only half shut. "The Master certainly means to give me instruction," said Monkey to himself. "That is why he left the door open." So he crept in and went straight to the Master's bed. Finding him curled up and lying with his face to the wall, Monkey dared not wake him, and knelt down beside the bed. Presently the Patriarch woke, stretched out his legs and murmured to himself:

Hard, very hard!
The Way is most secret.
Never handle the Golden Elixir as though it
*   were a mere toy!*
He who to unworthy ears entrusts the dark
*   truths*
To no purpose works his jaws and talks his
*   tongue dry.*

"Master, I've been kneeling here for some time," said Monkey, when he saw the Patriarch was awake. "You wretched Monkey," said Subodhi, who on recognizing his voice pulled off the bedclothes and sat up. "Why aren't you asleep in your own quarters, instead of coming round behind to mine?" "At the lecture today," said Monkey, "you ordered me to come for instruction at the third watch, by way of the back gate. That is why I ventured to come straight to your bed." The Patriarch was delighted. He thought to himself, "This fellow must really be, as he says, a natural product of Heaven and Earth. Otherwise he would never have understood my secret signs." "We are alone together," said Monkey, "there is no one to overhear us. Take pity upon me and teach me the way of Long Life. I shall never forget your kindness." "You show a disposition," said the Patriarch. "You understood my secret signs. Come close and listen carefully. I am going to reveal to you the Secret of Long Life." Monkey beat his head on the floor to show his gratitude, washed his ears, and attended closely, kneeling beside the bed. The Patriarch then recited:

*To spare and tend the vital powers, this and
   nothing else
Is sum and total of all magic, secret and
   profane.
All is comprised in these three, Spirit, Breath,
   and Soul;
Guard them closely, screen them well; let there
   be no leak.
Store them within the frame;
That is all that can be learnt, and all that
   can be taught.
I would have you mark the tortoise and snake,
   locked in tight embrace.
Locked in tight embrace, the vital powers are
   strong;
Even in the midst of fierce flames the Golden
   Lotus may be planted,
The Five Elements compounded and trans-
   posed, and put to new use.
When that is done, be which you please, Bud-
   dha or Immortal.*

By these words Monkey's whole nature was
shaken to the foundations. He carefully
committed them to memory; then humbly
thanked the Patriarch, and went out again
by the back door.

A pale light was just coming into the
eastern sky. He retraced his steps, softly
opened the front door, and returned to his
sleeping place, purposely making a rustling
noise with his bedclothes. "Get up!" he
cried. "There is light in the sky." His
fellow pupils were fast asleep, and had
no idea that Monkey had received Illumination.

Time passed swiftly, and three years
later the Patriarch again mounted his jew-
eled seat and preached to his assembled
followers. His subject was the parables and
scholastic problems of the Zen Sect, and
his theme, the integument of outer appearances. Suddenly he broke off and asked,
"Where is the disciple Aware-of-Vacuity?"
Monkey knelt down before him and answered "Here!" "What have you been
studying all this time?" asked the Patriarch.
"Recently," said Monkey, "my spiritual nature has been very much in the ascendant,

and my fundamental sources of power are
gradually strengthening." "In that case,"
said the Patriarch, "all you need learn is
how to ward off the Three Calamities."
"There must be some mistake," said Monkey in dismay. "I understood that the secrets I have learned would make me live
forever and protect me from fire, water,
and every kind of disease. What is this
about three calamities?" "What you have
learned," said the Patriarch, "will preserve
your youthful appearance and increase the
length of your life; but after five hundred years Heaven will send down lightning which will finish you off, unless you
have the sagacity to avoid it. After another
five hundred years Heaven will send down
a fire that will devour you. This fire is
of a peculiar kind. It is neither common
fire, nor celestial fire, but springs up from
within and consumes the vitals, reducing
the whole frame to ashes, and making a
vanity of all your thousand years of self-
perfection. But even should you escape
this, in another five hundred years, a wind
will come and blow upon you. Not the east
wind, the south wind, the west wind, or
the north wind; not flower wind, or willow
wind, pine wind, or bamboo wind. It blows
from below, enters the bowels, passes the
midriff, and issues at the Nine Apertures.
It melts bone and flesh, so that the whole
body dissolves. These three calamities you
must be able to avoid." When Monkey
heard this, his hair stood on end, and prostrating himself he said, "I beseech you,
have pity upon me, and teach me how to
avoid these calamities. I shall never forget
your kindness." "There would be no difficulty about that," said the Patriarch, "if
it were not for your peculiarities." "I have
a round head sticking up to Heaven and
square feet treading Earth," said Monkey.
"I have nine apertures, four limbs, five upper and six lower internal organs, just like
other people." "You are like other men in
most respects," said the Patriarch, "but you
have much less jowl." For monkeys have
hollow cheeks and pointed nozzles. Monkey

felt his face with his hand and laughed saying, "Master, I have my debits, but don't forget my assets. I have my pouch, and that must be credited to my account, as something that ordinary humans haven't got." "True enough," said the Patriarch. "There are two methods of escape. Which would you like to learn? There is the trick of the Heavenly Ladle, which involves thirty-six kinds of transformation, and the trick of the Earthly Conclusion, which involves seventy-two kinds of transformation." "Seventy-two sounds better value," said Monkey. "Come here then," said the Patriarch, "and I will teach you the formula." He then whispered a magic formula into Monkey's ear. That Monkey King was uncommonly quick at taking things in. He at once began practicing the formula, and after a little self-discipline he mastered all the seventy-two transformations, whole and complete. One day when master and disciples were in front of the cave, admiring the evening view, the Patriarch said, "Monkey, how is that business going?" "Thanks to your kindness," said Monkey, "I have been extremely successful. In addition to the transformations I can already fly." "Let's see you do it," said the Patriarch. Monkey put his feet together, leapt about sixty feet into the air, and riding the clouds for a few minutes dropped in front of the Patriarch. He did not get more than three leagues in the whole of his flight. "Master," he said, "that surely is cloud-soaring?" "I should be more inclined to call it cloud-crawling," said the Patriarch laughing. "The old saying runs, 'An Immortal wanders in the morning to the Northern Sea, and the same evening he is in Ts'ang-wu.' To take as long as you did to go a mere league or two hardly counts even as cloud-crawling." "What is meant by that saying about the Northern Sea and Ts'ang-wu?" asked Monkey. "A real cloud-soarer," said the Patriarch, "can start early in the morning from the Northern Sea, cross the Eastern Sea, the Western Sea, and the Southern Sea, and land again at Ts'ang-wu. Ts'ang-

wu means Ling-ling, in the Northern Sea. To do the round of all four seas in one day is true cloud-soaring." "It sounds very difficult," said Monkey. "Nothing in the world is difficult," said the Patriarch, "it is only our own thoughts that make things seem so." "Master," said Monkey, prostrating himself, "You may as well make a good job of me. While you're about it, do me a real kindness and teach me the art of cloud-soaring. I shall never forget how much I owe to you." "When the Immortals go cloud-soaring," said the Patriarch, "they sit cross-legged and rise straight from that position. You do nothing of the kind. I saw you just now put your feet together and jump. I must really take this opportunity of teaching you how to do it properly. You shall learn the Cloud Trapeze." He then taught him the magic formula, saying, "Make the pass, recite the spell, clench your fists, and one leap will carry you head over heels a hundred and eight thousand leagues."

When the other pupils heard this, they all tittered, saying, "Monkey is in luck. If he learns this trick, he will be able to carry dispatches, deliver letters, take round circulars—one way or another he will always be able to pick up a living!"

It was now late. Master and pupils all went to their quarters; but Monkey spent all night practicing the Cloud Trapeze, and by the time day came he had completely mastered it, and could wander through space where he would.

One summer day when the disciples had for some time been studying their tasks under a pine tree, one of them said, "Monkey, what can you have done in a former incarnation to merit that the Master should the other day have whispered in your ear the secret formula for avoiding the three calamities? Have you mastered all those transformations?" "To tell you the truth," said Monkey, "although of course I am much indebted to the Master for his instruction, I have also been working very hard day and night on my own, and

I can now do them all." "Wouldn't this be a good opportunity," said one of the pupils, "to give us a little demonstration?" When Monkey heard this, he was all on his mettle to display his powers. "Give me my subject," he said. "What am I to change into?" "How about a pine tree?" they said. He made a magic pass, recited a spell, shook himself, and changed into a pine tree.

The disciples clapped and burst into loud applause. "Bravo, Monkey, bravo," they cried. There was such a din that the Patriarch came running out with his staff trailing after him. "Who's making all this noise?" he asked. The disciples at once controlled themselves, smoothed down their dresses, and came meekly forward. Monkey changed himself back into his true form and slipped in among the crowd, saying, "Reverend Master, we are doing our lessons out here. I assure you there was no noise in particular." "You were all bawling," said the Patriarch angrily. "It didn't sound in the least like people studying. I want to know what you were doing here, shouting and laughing." "To tell the truth," said someone, "Monkey was showing us a transformation just for fun. We told him to change into a pine tree, and he did it so well that we were all applauding him. That was the noise you heard. I hope you will forgive us." "Go away, all of you!" the Patriarch shouted. "And you, Monkey, come here! What were you doing, playing with your spiritual powers, turning into—what was it? A pine tree? Did you think I taught you in order that you might show off in front of other people? If you saw someone else turn into a tree, wouldn't you at once ask how it was done? If others see you doing it, aren't they certain to ask you? If you are frightened to refuse, you will give the secret away; and if you refuse, you're very likely to be roughly handled. You're putting yourself in grave danger." "I'm terribly sorry," said Monkey. "I won't punish you," said the Patriarch, "but you can't stay here." Monkey burst into tears. "Where am I to go to?" he asked. "Back to where you came from, I should suppose," said the Patriarch. "You don't mean back to the Cave of the Water Curtain in Ao-lai!" said Monkey. "Yes," said the Patriarch, "go back as quickly as you can, if you value your life. One thing is certain in any case; you can't stay here." "May I point out," said Monkey, "that I have been away from home for twenty years and should be very glad to see my monkey-subjects once more. But I can't consent to go till I have repaid you for all your kindness." "I have no desire to be repaid," said the Patriarch. "All I ask is that if you get into trouble, you should keep my name out of it." Monkey saw that it was no use arguing. He bowed to the Patriarch, and took leave of his companions. "Wherever you go," said the Patriarch, "I'm convinced you'll come to no good. So remember, when you get into trouble, I absolutely forbid you to say that you are my disciple. If you give a hint of any such thing I shall flay you alive, break all your bones, and banish your soul to the Place of Ninefold Darkness, where it will remain for ten thousand aeons." "I certainly won't venture to say a word about you," promised Monkey. "I'll say I found it all out for myself." So saying he bade farewell, turned away, and making the magic pass rode off on his cloud trapeze, straight to the Eastern Sea. In a very little while he reached the Mountain of Flowers and Fruit, where he lowered his cloud, and was picking his way, when he heard a sound of cranes calling and monkeys crying. "Little ones," he shouted, "I have come back." At once from every cranny in the cliff, from bushes and trees, great monkeys and small leapt out with cries of "Long live our king!" Then they all pressed round Monkey, kowtowing and saying, "Great King, you're very absentminded! Why did you go away for so long, leaving us all in the lurch, panting for your return, as a starving man for food and drink? For some time past a demon has been ill-using us.

He has seized our cave, though we fought desperately, and now he has robbed us of all our possessions and carried off many of our children, so that we have to be on the watch all the time and get no sleep day or night. It's lucky you've come now, for if you had waited another year or two, you'd have found us and everything hereabouts in another's hands." "What demon can dare commit such crimes?" cried Monkey. "Tell me all about it and I will avenge you." "Your Majesty," they said, "he is called the Demon of Havoc, and he lives due north from here." "How far off?" asked Monkey. "He comes like a cloud," they said, "and goes like a mist, like wind or rain, thunder or lightning. We do not know how far away he lives." "Well, don't worry," said Monkey; "just go on playing around, while I go and look for him." Dear Monkey King! He sprang into the sky straight northward and soon saw in front of him a high and very rugged mountain. He was admiring the scenery, when he suddenly heard voices. Going a little way down the hill, he found a cave in front of which several small imps were jumping and dancing. When they saw Monkey, they ran away. "Stop!" he called, "I've got a message for you to take. Say that the master of the Water-Curtain Cave is here. The Demon of Havoc, or whatever he is called, who lives here, has been ill-treating my little ones and I have come on purpose to settle matters with him." They rushed into the cave and cried out, "Great King, a terrible thing has happened!" "What's the matter?" said the Demon. "Outside the cave," they said, "there is a monkey-headed creature who says he is the owner of the Water-Curtain Cave. He says you have been ill-using his people and he has come on purpose to settle matters with you." "Ha, ha," laughed the Demon. "I have often heard those monkeys say that their king had gone away to learn religion. This means that he's come back again. What does he look like and how is he armed?" "He carries no weapon at all," they said. "He goes bareheaded, wears a red dress, with a yellow sash, and black shoes—neither priest nor layman nor quite like a Taoist. He's waiting naked-handed outside the gate." "Bring me my whole accoutrement," cried the Demon. The small imps at once fetched his arms. The Demon put on his helmet and breastplate, grasped his sword, and going to the gate with the little imps, cried in a loud voice, "Where's the owner of the Water-Curtain Cave?" "What's the use of having such large eyes," shouted Monkey, "if you can't see old Monkey?" Catching sight of him the Demon burst out laughing. "You're not a foot high or as much as thirty years old. You have no weapon in your hand! How dare you strut about talking of settling accounts with me?" "Cursed demon," said Monkey. "After all, you have no eyes in your head! You say I am small, not seeing that I can make myself as tall as I please. You say I am unarmed, not knowing that these two hands of mine could drag the moon from the ends of Heaven. Stand your ground, and eat old Monkey's fist!" So saying he leapt into the air and aimed a blow at the Demon's face. The Demon parried the blow with his hand. "You such a pigmy and I so tall!" said the Demon. "You using your fists and I my sword—No! If I were to slay you with my sword I should make myself ridiculous. I am going to throw away my sword and use my naked fists." "Very good," said Monkey. "Now, my fine fellow, come on!" The Demon relaxed his guard and struck. Monkey closed with him, and the two of them pommeled and kicked, blow for blow. A long reach is not so firm and sure as a short one. Monkey jabbed the Demon in the lower ribs, pounded him in the chest, and gave him such a heavy drubbing that at last the Demon stood back, and picking up his great flat sword, slashed at Monkey's head. But Monkey stepped swiftly aside, and the blow missed its mark. Seeing that the Demon was becoming savage, Monkey now used the method called Body Outside the Body. He plucked out a handful of hairs, bit them into small pieces, and then spat them out into the air, crying "Change!" The fragments of hair changed into several hundred small monkeys, all pressing round in a throng. For you must know that when anyone becomes an Immortal, he can project his soul, change his shape, and perform all kinds of miracles. Monkey, since his Illumination, could change every one of the eighty-four thousand hairs of his body into whatever he chose. The little monkeys he had now created were so nimble that no sword could touch them or spear wound them. See how they leap forward and jump back, crowd round the Demon, some hugging, some pulling, some jabbing at his chest, some swarming up his legs. They kicked him, beat him, pommeled his eyes, pinched his nose, and while they were all at it, Monkey slipped up and snatched away the Demon's sword. Then pushing through the throng of small monkeys, he raised the sword and brought it down with such tremendous force upon the Demon's skull, that he clove it in twain. He and the little monkeys then rushed into the cave and made a quick end of the imps, great and small. He then said a spell, which caused the small monkeys to change back into hairs. These he put back where they had come from; but there were still some small monkeys left—those that the Demon had carried off from the Cave of the Water Curtain. "How did you get here?" he asked. There were about thirty or forty of them, and they all said with tears in their eyes, "After your Majesty went away to become an Immortal, we were pestered by this creature for two years. In the end he carried us all off, and he stole all the fittings from our cave. He took all the stone dishes and the stone cups." "Collect everything that belongs to us and bring it with you," said Monkey. They then set fire to the cave and burned everything in it. "Now follow me!" said Monkey. "When we were brought here," they said, "we only felt a

great wind rushing past, which whirled us to this place. We didn't know which way we were coming. So how are we to find the way home?" "He brought you here by magic," said Monkey. "But what matter? I am now up to all that sort of thing, and if he could do it, I can. Shut your eyes, all of you, and don't be frightened." He then recited a spell which produced a fierce wind. Suddenly it dropped, and Monkey shouted, "You may look now!" The monkeys found that they were standing on firm ground quite close to their home. In high delight they all followed a familiar path back to the door of their cave. They and those who had been left behind all pressed into the cave, and lined up according to their ranks and ages, and did homage to their king, and prepared a great banquet of welcome. When they asked how the Demon had been subdued and the monkeys rescued, he told them the whole story; upon which they burst into shouts of applause. "We little thought," they said, "that when your Majesty left us, you would learn such arts as this!" "After I parted from you," said Monkey, "I went across many oceans to the land of Jambudvipa, where I learnt human ways, and how to wear clothes and shoes. I wandered restless as a cloud for eight or nine years, but nowhere could I find Enlightenment. At last after crossing yet another ocean, I was lucky enough to meet an old Patriarch who taught me the secret of eternal life." "What an incredible piece of luck!" the monkeys said, all congratulating him. "Little ones," said Monkey, "I have another bit of good news for you. Your king has got a name-in-religion. I am called Aware-of-Vacuity." They all clapped loudly, and presently went to get date wine and grape wine and fairy flowers and fruit, which they offered to Monkey. Everyone was in the highest spirits. If you do not know what the upshot was and how he fared now that he was back in his old home, you must listen to what is related in the next chapter.

Chapter III

Monkey, having returned in triumph, after slaying the Demon of Havoc and snatching the Demon's huge cutlass, practiced swordplay every day and taught the small monkeys how to sharpen bamboos with spears, make wooden swords, and banners to carry; how to go on patrol, advance and retreat, pitch camp, build stockades, and so on. They had great fun doing this; but suddenly, sitting in a quiet place, Monkey thought to himself, "All this is only a game; but the consequences of it may be serious. Suppose some human king or king of birds or beasts should hear what we are at, he may very well think that we are hatching a conspiracy against him and bring his armies to attack us. Bamboo spears and wooden swords wouldn't help you much then. You ought to have real swords and lances and halberds. How are we to get hold of them?" "That's an excellent idea," they said, "but there's nowhere we can possibly get them from."

At this point four old monkeys came forward, two red-bottomed horse-apes and two tailless apes with plain behinds. "Great king," they said, "if you want to get weapons made, nothing could be easier." "Why do you think it so easy?" asked Monkey. "East of our mountains," they said, "there are two hundred leagues of water. That is the frontier of Ao-lai, and at the frontier there is a king whose city is full of soldiers. He must certainly have metalworks of all sorts. If you go there, you can certainly buy weapons or get them made for you. Then you can teach us to use them, and we shall be able to defend ourselves. That is the way to protect us against extinction." Monkey was delighted with this idea. "You stay here and amuse yourselves," he said, "while I go off and see what can be done."

Dear Monkey! He set out on his cloud-trapeze, and in a twinkling he had crossed those two hundred leagues of water, and on the other side there was indeed a city with walls and moat, with wards and markets, and myriad streets where men walked up and down in the happy sunshine. He thought to himself, "In such a place there are sure to be ready-made weapons. I'll go down and buy some. Or better still, I'll get some by magic." He made a magic pass, recited a spell, and drew a magic diagram on the ground. He then stood in the middle of it, drew a long breath, and expelled it with such force that sand and stones hurtled through the air. This tempest so much alarmed the king of the country and all his subjects that they locked themselves indoors. Monkey lowered his cloud, made straight for the government buildings, and soon finding the arsenal he forced open the door, and saw a vast supply of swords, lances, scimitars, halberds, axes, scythes, whips, rakes, cudgels, bows, and crossbows—every conceivable weapon. "That's rather more than I can carry," he said to himself. So, as before, he changed his hairs into thousands of small monkeys, who began snatching at the weapons. Some managed to carry six or seven, others three or four, till soon the arsenal was bare. Then a great gale of magic wind carried them back to the cave. The monkeys at home were playing in front of the cave door, when suddenly they saw a great swarm of monkeys in the sky above, which scared them so much that they all rushed into hiding. Soon Monkey lowered his cloud and turned the thousands of little monkeys into hairs. He stacked the weapons on the hillside and cried, "Little ones, all come and get your arms!" To their astonishment they found Monkey standing all alone on the ground. They rushed forward to pay homage, and Monkey explained to them what had happened. When they had congratulated him on his performance, they all began to grab at swords and cutlasses, pick up axes, scramble for spears, drag off bows and crossbows. This sport, which was a very noisy one, lasted all day.

Next day they came on parade as usual, and the roll call disclosed that they numbered forty-seven thousand in all. All the wild beasts of the mountain and demon kings of every kind, denizens of no less than seventy-two caves, came to pay homage to Monkey, and henceforward brought tribute every year and signed on once in every season. Some supplied labor and some provisions. The Mountain of Flowers and Fruit became as strong as an iron bucket or wall of bronze. The demon kings of various districts also presented bronze drums, colored banners, helmets, and coats of mail. Day after day there was a tremendous bustle of drilling and marching. Everything was going well, when suddenly one day Monkey said to his subjects, "You seem to be getting on well with your drill, but I find my sword very cumbersome, in fact not at all to my liking. What is to be done?" The four old monkeys came forward and said, "Great King, it is quite natural that you, being an Immortal, should not care to use this earthly weapon. Do you think it would be possible for you to get one from the denizens of the sea?" "Why not, pray?" said Monkey. "Since my Illumination I have mastery of seventy-two transformations; greatest wonder of all, I can ride upon the clouds. I can become invisible, I can penetrate bronze and stone. Water cannot drown me, any more than fire can burn me. What's to prevent me getting a weapon from the Powers of the Sea?" "Well, if you can manage it," they said. "The water that flows under this iron bridge comes up from the palace of the dragon of the Eastern Sea. How about going down and paying a call upon the Dragon King? If you asked him for a weapon he would no doubt be able to find you something suitable." "I'll certainly go," said Monkey. He went to the bridgehead, recited a spell to protect himself from the effects of water, and jumped in, making his way along the watercourse till he came to the bottom of the Eastern Sea. Presently he was stopped by a Yaksha who was patrolling the waters. "What deity is that," he asked, "pushing along through the water? Give me an account of yourself and I will announce your arrival." "I am the monkey king of the Mountain of Flowers and Fruit," said Monkey. "I am a near neighbor of the Dragon King, and consider that I ought to make his acquaintance." The Yaksha brought in the message, and the Dragon King rose hastily and came to the door of his palace, bringing with him his dragon children and grandchildren, his shrimp soldiers and crab generals. "Come in, High Immortal, come in," he said. They went into the palace and sat face to face on the upper seat. When they had taken tea, the Dragon asked, "How long, pray, have you been Illumined, and what magic arts have you learned?" "I have led a religious life since my infancy," said Monkey, "and am now beyond birth and destruction. Recently I have been training my subjects how to defend their home; but I myself have no suitable weapon. I am told that my honored neighbor within the shell portals of his green jade palace certainly has many magic weapons to spare." The Dragon King did not like to refuse, and ordered a trout captain to bring out a huge sword. "I'm no good with a sword," said Monkey. "Can't you find something else?" The Dragon King then told a whitebait guardsman with the help of an eel porter to bring out a nine-pronged fork. Monkey took hold of it and tried a few thrusts. "It's much too light," he said. "And it does not suit my hand. Can't you find me something else?" "I really don't know what you mean," said the Dragon King. "The fork weighs three thousand six hundred pounds." "It doesn't suit my hand," said Monkey, "it doesn't suit my hand." The Dragon King was much upset, and ordered a bream general and a carp brigadier to bring out a huge halberd, weighing seven thousand two hundred pounds. Monkey seized it and after making a few thrusts and parries tossed it away saying, "Still too light!" "It's the heaviest weapon we've got in the palace," said the Dragon King. "I have nothing else I can show you." "The proverb says 'It's no use the Dragon King pretending he's got no treasures,' " said Monkey. "Just look again, and if you succeed in finding something suitable, I'll give you a good price." "I warn you I haven't got anything else," said the Dragon King.

At this point the Dragon Mother and her daughter slipped out from the back rooms of the palace and said, "Great King, we can see that this Monkey Sage is of no common capacities. In our treasury is the magic iron with which the bed of the Milky Way was pounded flat. For several days past it has been glowing with a strange light. Was this not perhaps an omen that it should be given to the Sage who has just arrived?" "This," said the Dragon King, "is the thing that was used by the Great Yü, when he subdued the Flood, to fix the depth of the rivers and seas. It's only a piece of holy iron. What use could it be to him?" "Don't worry about whether he uses it or not," said the Dragon Mother. "Just give it to him, and if he can cope with it, let him take it away with him."

The Dragon King agreed, and told Monkey. "Bring it to me and I'll have a look at it," said Monkey. "Out of the question!" said the Dragon King. "It's too heavy to move. You'll have to go and look at it." "Where is it?" asked Monkey. "Show me the way."

The Dragon King accordingly brought him to the Sea Treasury, where he at once saw something shining with innumerable beams of golden light. "There it is," said the Dragon King. Monkey respectfully tidied himself and approached the object. It turned out to be a thick iron pillar, about twenty feet long. Monkey took one end in both hands and raised it a little. "A trifle too long and too thick!" he said. The pillar at once became several feet shorter and one layer thinner. Monkey felt it. "A little smaller still wouldn't do any harm," he said. The pillar at once shrunk again, Monkey was delighted. Taking it out into the daylight he found that at each end was a golden clasp, while in between all was black iron. On the near end was the inscription "Golden Clasped Wishing Staff. Weight, thirteen thousand five hundred pounds." "Splendid!" thought Monkey. "One couldn't wish for a better treasure than this." But as he went along, he thought to himself, fingering the staff, "If only it were a little smaller, it would be marvelous." And sure enough, by the time he got outside it was not much more than two feet long. Look at him, how he displays its magic, making sudden thrusts and passes on his way back to the palace. The Dragon King trembled at the sight, and the Dragon Princes were all in a flutter. Tortoises and turtles drew in their heads; fishes, crabs, and shrimps all hid themselves away. Monkey, with the treasure in his hand, sat down by the Dragon King. "I am deeply grateful for my honored neighbor's kindness," he said. "Pray don't mention it," said the Dragon King. "Yes, it's a useful bit of iron," said Monkey, "but there is just one more thing I should like to say." "Great Immortal," said the Dragon King, "what else have you to say?" "Before I had this iron," said Monkey, "it was another matter, but with a thing like this in my hand, I begin to feel the lack of anything suitable to wear with it. If you have got anything in that line, please let me have it. I should really be grateful." "I have nothing at all," said the Dragon King. "You know the old saying," said Monkey, " 'one guest should not trouble two hosts.' You won't get rid of me by pretending you haven't got any." "You might try another sea," said the Dragon King, "it's just possible they would be able to help you." " 'Better sit in one house than run to three,' " said Monkey. "I insist on your finding me something." "I assure you I don't possess anything of that sort," said the Dragon King. "If I did you should have it." "All right," said Monkey. "I'll try my iron on you, and we shall soon see whether you can give me one." "Steady, steady, Great Immortal," said the

325

Dragon King. "Don't strike! Just let me find out whether my brothers haven't got anything that you could have." "Where do they live?" asked Monkey. "They are the dragons of the southern, northern, and western seas," said the Dragon King. "I am not going as far as that," said Monkey. " 'Two in hand is better than three in bond.' You must find me something here and now. I don't mind where you get it from." "I never suggested that you should go," said the Dragon King. "We've got an iron drum and a bronze gong here. If anything important happens, I have them sounded, and my brothers come immediately." "Very well," said Monkey. "Look sharp and sound the drum and gong." A crocodile accordingly beat the drum and a turtle sounded the gong, and in a twinkling the three dragons arrived. "Brother," said the Dragon of the South, "what urgent business has made you beat the drum and sound the gong?" "You may well ask," said the Dragon King. "A neighbor of mine, the Sage of the Mountain of Flowers and Fruit, came to me today asking for a magic weapon. I gave him the iron with which the Milky Way was pounded. Now he says he must have clothes. We have nothing of that sort here. Couldn't one of you find me something, so that we can get rid of him?" The Dragon of the South was furious. "Brothers," he cried, "let us summon men-at-arms and arrest the rascal." "Out of the question!" said the Dragon King. "The slightest touch of that iron is deadly." "It would be better not to tamper with him," said the Dragon of the West. "We'll give him some clothes, just to get rid of him, and then we'll complain to Heaven, and Heaven will punish him." "That's a good idea," said the Dragon of the North. "I've got a pair of cloud-stepping shoes made of lotus fiber." "I've got a cap of phoenix-plume and red gold," said the Dragon of the South. "I've got a jerkin of chain mail, made of yellow gold," said the Dragon of the West. The Dragon King was delighted and brought them in to see Monkey and

offer their gifts. Monkey put the things on and, with his wishing-staff in his hand, strode out. "Dirty old sneaks," he called out to the dragons as he passed. In great indignation they consulted together about reporting him to the powers above.

The four old monkeys and all the rest were waiting for their king beside the bridge. Suddenly they saw him spring out of the waves, without a drop of water on him, all shining and golden, and run up the bridge. They all knelt down, crying "Great King, what splendors!" With the spring wind full in his face, Monkey mounted the throne and set up the iron staff in front of him. The monkeys all rushed at the treasure and tried to lift it. As well might a dragonfly try to shake an ironwood tree; they could not move it an inch. "Father," they cried, "you're the only person that could lift a thing as heavy as that." "There's nothing but has its master," said Monkey, lifting it with one hand. "This iron lay in the Sea Treasury for I don't know how many hundred thousand years, and only recently began to shine. The Dragon King thought it was nothing but black iron and said it was used to flatten out the Milky Way. None of them could lift it, and they asked me to go and take it myself. When I first saw it, it was twenty feet long. I thought that was a bit too big, so I gradually made it smaller and smaller. Now just you watch while I change it again." He cried "Smaller, smaller, smaller!" and immediately it became exactly like an embroidery needle, and could comfortably be worn behind the ear.

"Take it out and do another trick with it," the monkeys begged. He took it from behind his ear and set it upright on the palm of his hand, crying "Larger, larger!" It at once became twenty feet long, whereupon he carried it up onto the bridge, employed a cosmic magic, and bent at the waist, crying "Tall!" At which he at once became a hundred thousand feet high, his head was on a level with the highest mountains, his waist with the ridges, his eye blazed like lightning, his mouth was like a blood bowl, his teeth like sword blades. The iron staff in his hand reached up to the thirty-third Heaven, and down to the eighteenth pit of Hell. Tigers, panthers, wolves, all the evil spirits of the hill and the demons of the seventy-two caves did homage to him in awe and trembling. Presently he withdrew his cosmic manifestation, and the staff again became an embroidery needle. He put it behind his ear and came back to the cave.

One day when Monkey had been giving a great banquet to the beast monarchs of the neighborhood, after seeing them off and giving presents to the leaders great and small, he lay down under a pine tree at the side of the iron bridge, and fell asleep. In his sleep he saw two men coming toward him, bearing a document on which was his name. Without giving him time to say a word, they brought out a rope and binding Monkey's dream body, they marched him away, presently bringing him to the outskirts of a walled city. Coming to himself and looking up, he saw that on the wall of this city was an iron placard saying "Land of Darkness." "Why," said Monkey to himself, suddenly realizing with an unpleasant shock where he had got to, "that's where Yama, the King of Death, lives. How did I get here?" "Your time in the World of Life is up," said the two men, "and we were sent to arrest you." "But I have got beyond all that," said Monkey. "I am no longer compounded of the Five Elements, and do not come under Death's jurisdiction. What's all this nonsense about arresting me?" The two men took no notice, and continued to drag him along. Monkey now became very angry, snatched the needle from behind his ear, changed it to a formidable size, and pounded the two messengers into mincemeat. Then he freed himself from his bonds, and swinging his staff strode into the city. Bull-headed demons and horse-faced demons fled before him in terror. A mass of ghosts rushed to the palace, announcing that a furry-faced thunder god was advancing to the attack. In great consternation the Ten Judges of the Dead tidied themselves and came to see what was afoot. Seeing Monkey's ferocious appearance, they lined up and accosted him in a loud voice: "Your name, please!" "If you don't know who I am, why did you send two men to arrest me?" asked Monkey. "How can you accuse us of such a thing?" they said. "No doubt the messengers made a mistake." "I am the Sage from the Water-Curtain Cave," said Monkey. "Who are you?" "We are the Ten Judges of the Emperor of Death," they said. "In that case," said Monkey, "you are concerned with retribution and rewards, and ought not to let such mistakes occur. I would have you know that by my exertions I have become an Immortal and am no longer subject to your jurisdiction. Why did you order my arrest?" "There's no need to lose your temper," they said. "It's a case of mistaken identity. The world is a big place, and there are bound to be cases of several people having the same name. No doubt our officers have made a mistake." "Nonsense," said Monkey. "The proverb says 'Magistrates err, clerks err, the man with the warrant never errs.' Be quick and bring out the registers of the quick and the dead, and we'll soon see!" "Come this way, please," they said, and took him to the great hall, where they ordered the official in charge of the record to bring out his files. The official dived into a side room and came out with five or six ledgers, divided into ten files and began going through them one by one—Bald Insects, Furry Insects, Winged Insects, Scaly Insects . . . He gave up in despair and tried Monkeys. But the Monkey King, having human characteristics, was not there. Not however being subject to the unicorn, he did not come into any animal category, and as he was not subject to the phoenix, he could not be classed as a bird. But there was a separate file which Monkey insisted on examining himself, and there, under the heading "Soul 3150," he found his own name, followed by the words "Parentage: natural product. Description: Stone Monkey. Life span: 342 years. A peaceful end." "I haven't got a life span at all, said Monkey. "I'm eternal. I shall cross my name out. Give me a brush!" The official hastened to provide a brush, soaked in heavy ink, and Monkey put a stroke not only through his own name, but through those of all the monkeys named in the Monkey File. Then throwing down the ledger, "There's an end of the matter," he exclaimed. "Now at any rate you've got no hold over us!"

So saying he picked up his staff and forced his way out of the Palace of Darkness. The Ten Judges dared not protest; but all went off at once to the Kshitigarbha, Guide of the Dead, and discussed with him the advisability of laying a complaint about the matter before the Jade Emperor in Heaven. As Monkey rushed naked out of the city, his foot caught in a coil of creeper and he stumbled. He woke with a start, and found that it had all been a dream. Sitting up, he heard the four old monkeys and the others who were mounting guard over him saying, "Great King, isn't it time you woke up? You drank so heavily that you've been sleeping here all night." "I must have dozed off for a time," said Monkey, "for I dreamed that two men came to arrest me." And he told them his dream. "I crossed off all our names," he said, "so the fellows won't be able to interfere with us any more." The monkeys kowtowed and thanked him. From that time onward it has been noticed that many mountain monkeys never grow old. It is because their names were crossed out from the registers of the King of Death.

One morning when the Jade Emperor was sitting in his Golden-Doored Cloud Palace, with all his ministers civil and military, an officer announced, "Your Majesty, the Dragon of the Eastern Sea is outside, with a plea to lay before you." The Dragon was shown in and when he had paid his respects, a fairy boy presented a document, which the Jade Emperor began to read.

"This small dragon of the Eastern Sea informs your Majesty that a certain counterfeit Immortal from the Water-Curtain Cave has maltreated your servant, forcing a way into his watery home. He demanded a weapon, using gross intimidation, and forced us to give him garments, by violence and outrage. My watery kinsmen were dismayed, tortoises and turtles fled in panic. The Dragon of the South trembled, the Dragon of the West was appalled, the Dragon of the North collapsed. Your servant was obliged to part with a holy iron staff, a phoenix-plume hat, a coat of mail, and a pair of cloud-stepping shoes, before we could get rid of him. But even then he threatened us with arms and magic, and called us dirty old sneaks. We are ourselves quite unable to deal with him, and must leave the matter in your hands. We earnestly beg that you will send soldiers to control this pest and restore peace to the World Below the Waves."

Having read the document, the Jade Emperor gave judgment. "The Dragon," he said, "is to return to his sea, and I will send officers to arrest the criminal." The Dragon King bowed and retired. Whereupon another officer immediately appeared, announcing that the First Judge of the Dead, supported by Kshitigarbha, the Advocate of the Dead, had arrived with a petition. With them was a fairy girl, who presented a document which read as follows: We respectfully submit that Heaven Above is for spirits, and the Underworld is for ghosts. Darkness and Light must have their succession. Such is the way of Nature, and cannot be changed. But a counterfeit Sage from the Water-Curtain Cave has violently resisted our summons, beating to death our emissaries and menacing the Ten Judges. He made an uproar in the Palace of Death, and erased names from our books, so that in future monkeys and apes will enjoy improper longevity. We therefore appeal to your Majesty to show your authority by sending spirit soldiers to deal with this monster, restore the balance of Dark and Light and bring back peace to the Underworld.

The Jade Emperor gave judgment, "The Lords of Darkness are to return to the Underworld, and officers shall be sent to arrest this pest." The First Judge of the Dead bowed and retired.

"How long has this pernicious monkey been in existence?" the Jade Emperor asked of his ministers, "and how comes it that he acquired Illumination?" At once the Officer of the Thousand-League Eye and the Officer of the Down-the-Wind Ear stepped forward. "This monkey," they said, "was emitted three hundred years ago by a stone. At first he displayed none of his present powers; but since then he has managed somehow to perfect himself and achieve Immortality. He now subdues dragons, tames tigers, and has tampered with the Registers of Death." "Which of you deities will go down and deal with him?" asked the Jade Emperor. The Spirit of the Planet Venus came forward. "Highest and Holiest," he said, "all creatures that have nine apertures are capable of achieving Immortality. Small wonder then that this monkey, produced by the natural forces of Heaven and Earth, nurtured by the light of the sun and the moon, fed by the frost and dew, should have achieved Immortality and subdue dragons and tigers. I suggest that an indulgent course should be followed. Let us send a rescript, commanding him to appear in Heaven. We will then give him official work of some kind, so that his name will appear on our rolls, and we shall be able to keep an eye on him here. If he behaves well, he can be promoted, and if he misbehaves, he must be put under arrest. This course will save us from military operations and will add to our numbers an undoubted Immortal."

This suggestion pleased the Jade Emperor. He ordered the Spirit of the Book Star to draw up a summons and bade the Planet Venus deliver it. He went out at the southern gate of Heaven, lowered his magic cloud, and soon reached the Water-Curtain Cave, where he said to the crowd of monkeys, "I am a messenger from Heaven, bearing a command that your king is to proceed at once to the Upper Realms. Tell him of this immediately." The little monkeys outside the cave sent word to the interior that an old man had come with some writing in his hand. "He says he is a messenger from Heaven, sent to ask you to go with him." "That's very convenient," said Monkey. "I have been thinking lately of making a little trip to Heaven!"

Monkey hurriedly tidied himself and went to the door. "I am the Spirit of the Planet Venus," the messenger said, "and I bring an order from the Jade Emperor that you are to come up to Heaven and receive an Immortal appointment." "Old Star," said Monkey, "I am much obliged to you for your trouble," and he told the monkeys to prepare a banquet. "With the sacred command about me, I dare not linger," said the Star. "After your glorious ascension we shall have ample opportunity for conversation." "I will not insist," said Monkey. "It is a great honor for us that you should have paid this visit." Then he called the four old monkeys to him. "Don't forget to put the young monkeys through their paces," he said. "I'll have a look round when I get to Heaven, and if it seems all right there, I'll send for the rest of you to come and live with me." The old monkeys signified their agreement, and the Monkey King, following the Star Spirit, mounted the cloud and soared up. If you do not know what rank it was they gave him, you must listen to the next chapter.

Chapter IV

When they had mounted together for a little while, Monkey forgot all about the Star Spirit and soon left him far behind; and when he reached the southern gate of Heaven, the Spirit was out of sight. He was just going in when a number of Guardian Deities, armed with daggers, swords, and halberds, barred his path. "What an old swindler that Planet is!'' exclaimed Monkey. "Fancy letting these cutthroats hold me up like this, after inviting me to come!'' At this point the Planet arrived, quite out of breath. "You old fraud," said Monkey, confronting him, "you said you had come with an invitation from the Jade Emperor. Why are these people barring the gate?'' "Don't be angry," said the Planet. "As you haven't been to the Hall of Heaven before and haven't yet been given a name, the Guardians don't know who you are, and are quite right not to let you pass. When you have seen the Emperor and received your appointment, they'll let you go in and out as you please." "That's as may be," said Monkey, "but at the present moment I can't get in." "You can if you come with me," said the Planet, and he called in a loud voice, "Guardians of the Gate of Heaven, captains great and small, make way! This is an Immortal from Earth below, whom the Jade Emperor commissioned me to bring here." The Guardians then withdrew their weapons and retired. Monkey, his confidence in the Planet now quite restored, walked slowly by his side through the gates and on into the palace. Without waiting to be announced, they went at once into the August Presence. The Planet immediately prostrated himself, but Monkey stood erect by his side, not showing any sign of respect, but only pricking his ears to hear what the Planet would say. "I beg to report," he said, "that I have carried out your command; the pernicious Immortal is here." "Which is he?" asked the Emperor, peeping over the top of his screen-of-state. At this point Monkey bowed, saying, "It's me." The assembled ministers turned pale with horror. "This barbarous monkey!" they cried. "When brought into the Presence he did not prostrate himself, and now, without being addressed, he has ventured to say 'It's me.' Such conduct is worthy of death." "He comes from Earth below," said the Jade Emperor, "and only recently learned human ways. For the present we must not be too hard on him if he

does not know how to behave in Court.''

The celestial ministers all congratulated the Emperor on his clemency, and Monkey shouted "Bravo!" at the top of his voice. Officials were then ordered to look through the lists and see what appointments were vacant. "There is no vacancy at present in any section of any department," one of them reported. "The only chance is in the Imperial Stables, where a supervisor is wanted." "Very well then," said the Jade Emperor, "make him *Pi-ma-wên* in the stables." Accordingly he was taken to the stables and the duties of this department were explained to him. He was shown the list of the horses, of which there were a thousand, under the care of a steward, whose duty it was to provide fodder. Grooms who combed and washed the horses, chopped hay, brought them their water, and cooked their food. The superintendent and vice-superintendent helped the supervisor in the general management. All of them were on the alert night and day. In the daytime they managed to get a certain amount of fun; but at night they were on the go all the time. The horses all seemed either to go to sleep just when they ought to be fed, or to start galloping when they ought to be in their stalls. When they saw Monkey, the heavenly horses pressed round him in a surging mob, and ate the food he brought them with such appetite as they had never shown before. After a week or two the other officers of the stables gave a banquet to celebrate Monkey's appointment. When the feast was at its height, he suddenly paused, and cup in hand he asked, "What does it really mean, this word *Pi-ma-wên?*" "It's the name of the rank you hold," they said. "What class of appointment is it?" Monkey asked. "It doesn't come in any class," they said. "I suppose it's too high to count as being in any class?" said Monkey. "On the contrary," they said, "it's too low." "Too low!" exclaimed Monkey. "What do you mean?" "When an officer doesn't manage to get classed, they put him to mind the horses. There's no salary attached. The most you'll get for fattening up the horses as you've done since you were here, is a casual 'Not bad!' But if any of them had gone a bit lame or out of condition, you'd have caught it hot. And if any of them had come to real harm, you'd have been prosecuted and fined.''

Flames leapt up in Monkey's heart when he heard this. He ground his teeth and said in a great rage, ''So that's what they think of me! Don't they know that on the Mountain of Flowers and Fruit I was king and patriarch? How dared they swindle me with coming and looking after horses? If looking after horses is a job for the lowest riffraff of all, what do they want to put me into it for? I won't stand it! I'm going at once!''

With a sudden cry of rage, he pushed over the official desk, took his treasure from behind his ear and rushed out to the Southern Gate. The deities on guard, knowing that he was now an official and authorized to go in and out, did not attempt to stop him. Soon he lowered his cloud and landed on the Mountain of Flowers and Fruit. ''Little Ones,'' he cried, ''Old Monkey has come back.'' They gave him a great banquet of welcome, saying, ''As your Majesty has stayed away in the upper regions for ten years, we may surely presume that you have had a great success there?'' ''I've been away about a fortnight,'' said Monkey. ''What do you mean by ten years?'' ''In Heaven,'' they said, ''you did not notice how the time was going. One day in Heaven is a year below. Tell us, please, what rank they gave you.'' ''Don't talk of it!'' said Monkey, ''or I shall die of shame. The Jade Emperor has no idea how to make use of one. He saw what I am; but all he could do with me was to make me into something they call a *Pi-ma-wên*. I was told to look after his horses—just a menial post to which no rank attaches at all. I didn't realize this when I took the job, and didn't have a bad time playing about in the stables. But today I

asked some of the others, and discovered what sort of post it was. I was furious and gave up the job at once. So here I am!'' ''And a good thing too,'' they said. ''With an enchanted spot like this to rule over, what sense is there in going away to be a groom? Little ones, prepare a banquet, to cheer our great king.''

They were just beginning to drink, when someone announced that two one-horned demon kings were outside, asking to see the Monkey King. ''Show them in,'' said Monkey. The demons tidied themselves and hastened into the cave, prostrating themselves deeply. ''What has brought you here?'' asked Monkey. ''We have known for a long time,'' they said, ''that you appreciate good qualities, but no suitable occasion presented itself for us to pay you our respects. However, hearing that you had secured a post in Heaven and returned triumphant, we thought you would not object to receiving a little present. Here is a red and yellow rug, which we hope you will accept. And if you will deign also to take into your service such humble folk as ourselves, we are ready to perform the most menial of tasks.'' Monkey wrapped the rug round himself in high glee, and all his subjects lined up and did homage. The demon kings were made Marshals of the Vanguard, and when they expressed their gratitude, they asked what position Monkey had held in Heaven. ''The Jade Emperor,'' said Monkey, ''has no regard for talent. He made me a groom in the stables!'' ''With magic powers like yours,'' they said, ''why should you stoop to look after horses? 'The Great Sage, Equal of Heaven'—that is the title for such a one as you.'' Monkey was delighted with the sound of this, and having exclaimed ''Good, good, good!'' many times, he ordered his generals to set up a banner with ''Great Sage, Equal of Heaven'' written on it in large letters. Henceforward, he said, he was to be addressed by no other name, and instructions to this effect were to be given to all fiends that acknowledged his sway.

When the Jade Emperor held his court next day, the head of the Stable appeared kneeling on the steps of the throne, announcing that the newly appointed groom had complained that the job was not good enough for him and had returned to Earth. "Very good," said the Jade Emperor, "you may return to your duties. I will send heavenly soldiers to arrest him." At once Vaiśravana and his son Natha came forward and volunteered for this service. They were put in command of the expedition, and appointed the Mighty Magic Spirit to lead the way, the Fish-Belly general to bring up the rear, and the captain of the Yakshas to drive the troops on. Soon they were out of the southern gate of Heaven, and on their way to the Mountain of Flowers and Fruit. They then chose a piece of flat ground, where they encamped, and the Mighty Magic Spirit was chosen to provoke battle. He buckled on his armor and, brandishing his great ax, he strode toward the mouth of the Water-Curtain Cave. Outside it were gathered together a band of monsters—wolves, tigers, and so on—prancing about, flourishing spears and swords, leaping, and noisily brawling. "Accursed creatures," cried the spirit, "go quickly and tell the groom that a great commandant from Heaven has come by order of the Jade Emperor to receive his submission. Tell him to be quick about it, or you will all of you pay with your lives." The monsters came helter-skelter into the cave. "A terrible thing has happened," they announced. "What's the matter?" asked Monkey. "There's a heavenly commandant at the gate," they said, "declaring that he has been sent by the Jade Emperor to receive your submission. If you don't submit at once, he says we shall all pay for it with our lives." "Bring me my arms," cried Monkey. He put on his bronze helmet, his golden corselet, and cloud-stepping shoes, and with his magic staff in his hand, he led out his followers and arrayed them for battle.

When the Mighty Magic Spirit saw him,

"Wretched monkey," he cried, "do you know me or not?" "What scurvy deity are you?" asked Monkey. "I have never set eyes on you. Tell me your name at once." "Vile trickster!" cried he, "how dare you pretend you do not know me? I am the leader of the vanguard of Vaiśravana's heavenly host, the Mighty Magic Spirit. I come by command of the Jade Emperor to receive your submission. Disarm at once and throw yourself on Heaven's mercy, or all the denizens of this mountain will be put to the sword. Breathe so much as half of the word "No," and you will instantly be sliced to pieces." "Scurvy deity," cried Monkey, very angry, "stop your bragging. If I were to strike you dead with one blow of my staff, you could not carry my message. So I shall spare your life, that you may go back to Heaven and tell the Jade Emperor that he does not know how to use a good man when he finds one. I have innumerable arts of magic. Why should I be put to mind the horses? Look what is written on this banner. If he admits my right to this title, I will leave him in peace. But if he refuses, I will come up at once and strike such a blow at his palace as will tumble him from his dragon couch." Looking about, the Spirit saw the banner, with its inscription, and laughed aloud. "The impudence of this vile monkey!" he cried. "Call yourself 'Equal of Heaven' if you please, but first swallow a good dose of this ax of mine!" and he struck at Monkey's head. But Monkey was not ruffled, and met the blow with his staff. It was a good fight that followed. At last the Spirit could withstand no longer. Monkey aimed a smashing blow at his head, which he attempted to parry with his ax. The ax split in two, and he was obliged to run for his life. Back in the camp he went straight to Vaiśravana and kneeling before him panted out, "The groom has magic powers that are too great for us. I was unable to stand up to him and have come to plead for mercy." "This wretch," said Vaiśravana, looking contemptuously at the spirit, "has humiliated me. Take him away and cut off his head!" But his son, prince Natha, slipped forward and said, bowing profoundly, "Father, do not be angry. Spare the spirit for a while, and let me go to do battle, so that we may know how things really stand." Vaiśravana accepted this offer, and ordered the spirit to go back to his camp and await trial.

The prince, having buckled on his armor, sprang from the camp and rushed to the Cave of the Water Curtain. Monkey was just disarming himself, but now came to the gate and said, "Whose little brother are you and why have you come gate-crashing here?" "Nauseous ape," cried Natha, "why pretend you do not know me? I am Vaiśravana's third son. The Jade Emperor has sent me here to arrest you." "Little prince," laughed Monkey, "you have not yet lost your milk teeth, your womb down is not yet dry. How dare you talk so big? For the moment I'll spare your life, provided that you look at what is written on that banner, and tell the Jade Emperor that if he will give me *that* rank he need send no more armies; I will submit of my own accord. But if he will not agree, I shall come and batter down his Jewel Palace of the Magic Mists."

Natha looked up and saw the inscription: "Great Sage, Equal of Heaven." "You must think yourself a wonder-worker indeed, that you dare lay claim to such a title! Don't worry! One stroke of my sword will settle you," said Natha. "I'll stand my ground," said Monkey, "and you can break as many swords upon me as you like." "Change!" roared Natha, and he at once changed into a deity with three heads and six arms. "So this little brother," said Monkey, "knows some tricks! I'll trouble you to look at my magic." So saying, he too assumed three heads and six arms, and at the same time changed his cudgel into three cudgels, each of which he grasped with two hands. The battle that followed was one that shook the earth and rattled the hills. Truly a good fight! Each displayed his terrifying powers,

and they battled as many as thirty times. The prince turned his six weapons into a thousand thousand weapons. Monkey followed suit. The sparks fell like falling stars as they fought halfway up in the sky, and still neither gained advantage.

But Monkey was very swift of hand and eye. Just at the height of the fray, he changed back into his proper shape and, cudgel in hand, closed with Natha. In his own shape he moved with greater freedom; getting behind the prince's head, he brought down a mighty blow on his shoulder. Just as Natha was preparing a new magic, he heard the swish of Monkey's cudgel as it clove the air. He had no time to dodge, and so great was his pain that he at once took to his heels, changed into his true form, and returned ignominiously to his father's camp. Vaiśravana had been watching the battle, and was just thinking of going to his son's assistance, when Natha suddenly appeared before him and, trembling from head to foot, said: "My father and king! The groom has indeed stupendous powers. Even such magic as mine could not withstand him, and in the end he wounded my shoulder." "If a fellow has such powers as this" said Vaiśravana dismayed, "how are we to bring him to heel?" "Outside his cave," said the prince, "he has put up a banner, upon which is written 'Great Sage, Equal of Heaven.' He had the insolence to say that if you would acknowledge his right to this title he would give no more trouble. Otherwise, he will batter down the Jewel Palace of Magic Mists." "If that is so," said Vaiśravana, "we had better leave him alone for the present. I will report this to the Jade Emperor and ask for heavenly reinforcements, that we may hem him in while there is still time." "Am I to believe," said the Jade Emperor, when the situation was explained to him, "that one monkey is so powerful that reinforcements are needed to deal with him?" Natha then stepped forward. "Great One," he said, "though I know that I deserve death at your hands, I beg you to hear me.

That Monkey possesses an iron cudgel with which he first defeated the River Spirit and then wounded my shoulder." "Take the whole army," said the Emperor "and slay him immediately!" At this moment the Spirit of the Planet Venus stepped forward. "That Monkey," he said, "flings his words about recklessly, and there is no reason to suppose that he can do all he threatens to do. But if soldiers are sent to deal with him, it will mean a long and exhausting campaign. It would be better if your Majesty were to pursue a policy of mercy. Say that you desire a peaceful solution and are quite willing to let him be 'The Sage, Equal of Heaven.' There will be no harm in his having a nominal post under that title, of course without salary." "I don't think I quite understand," said the Jade Emperor, "what you are proposing that his position should be." "He could be called by that title," said the Planet, "without having any special duties or any salary. The advantage would be that living on celestial ground he would soon turn from his depravity, cease his mad tricks, and the Universe would have a chance to settle down quietly." "Agreed!" said the Emperor. And the Planet was sent to convey the peace offering.

He left Heaven by the southern gate and went straight to the Cave of the Water Curtain. Things were very different this time. The place bristled with weapons; every sort of wild ogre was on guard, and they were armed with lances, swords, staves, which they brandished fiercely, leaping this way and that. Seeing the Star Spirit, they all rushed forward. "Come chieftains," said the spirit, "I'll trouble you to tell your master that I am here. I am a heavenly messenger sent by God on High, and am come with a summons to your king." "Welcome to him," said Monkey, when he heard that a messenger had come. "It must be the Spirit of the Planet Venus, who came to fetch me before. That time, although the job I got was not worthy of me, my time in Heaven was not entirely wasted. I ran round a good deal, and got to know my way about. No doubt he has come this time to offer me something better."

And he ordered the chieftains to lead the Spirit in, with a great waving of flags and rattle of drums. Monkey received him at the mouth of the cave in full panoply surrounded by hosts of lesser apes. "Step in, old Star," he called, "and forgive me for not having come to meet you." "Your colleagues," said the Planet, "informed the Jade Emperor that you were discontented with your appointment in the Stables, and had absconded. 'Everyone has to start with something small and work his way upward,' said the Emperor. 'What has he got to complain of?' And armies were sent to subdue you. When your magic powers proved superior to theirs, and it was proposed to band together all the forces of Heaven and dispatch them against you, I put in a word, suggesting that you should be accorded the title you have assumed. This was accepted, and I have come to fetch you." "I am much obliged to you for your trouble this time and last," said Monkey. "But I don't know whether there is such a rank in Heaven as 'Great Sage, Equal of Heaven!' "My proposal was that you should have this rank," said the Planet, "and it was accepted; otherwise I should never have dared to come with the message. If anything goes wrong, I am ready to take the responsibility."

Monkey wished to detain the Planet and give a banquet in his honor. But the Planet would not stay; and they both set off together for the Southern Gate of Heaven. When the "monkey groom" was announced the Jade Emperor said, "Come forward, Monkey. I hereby proclaim you Great Sage, Equal of Heaven. The rank is a high one, and I hope we shall have no more nonsense." Monkey gave a great whoop of delight and thanked the Emperor profusely.

Heavenly carpenters were ordered to build the office of the Great Sage to the right of the Peach Garden. It had two departments, one called Peace and Quiet and the other Calm Spirit. In each were Immortal Officers who attended Monkey wherever he went. A Star Spirit was detailed to escort Monkey to his new quarters, and he was allowed a ration of two jars of Imperial wine and ten sprays of gold-leaf flowers. He was begged not to allow himself to get in any way excited or start again on his pranks.

As soon as he arrived, he opened both jars and invited everyone in his office to a feast. The Star Spirit went back to his own quarters, and Monkey, left to his own devices, lived in such perfect freedom and delight as in Earth or Heaven have never had their like.

And if you do not know what happened in the end, you must listen to what is told in the next chapter.

Chapter V

Monkey knew nothing about official matters, and it was fortunate that all he had to do was to mark his name on a list. For the rest, he and his subordinates ate their three meals, slept soundly at night, had no worries, but only perfect freedom and independence. When there was nothing else going on, he went round and made friends with the other denizens of Heaven. He was careful to address the members of the Trinity as "Venerable," and the four Emperors as "Majesty"; but all the rest, Planets, Lunar Mansions, spirits of the Hours and Days, he treated as equals. Today he wandered east, tomorrow rambled west; his goings and comings were unhampered as the passage of the clouds. One day at Court an Immortal stepped forward and made the following petition: "I submit that the Sage, Equal of Heaven, has no duties to perform. He spends all his time going round and making friends. All the stars of Heaven, high and low, are now his cronies. Trouble will come of it, unless some way is found of employing his time." The Jade Emperor accordingly sent for Monkey, who arrived in high glee,

asking, "What promotion or reward has your Majesty sent for me to announce?" "I hear," said the Emperor, "that you have nothing in particular to do, and I am going to give you a job. You are to look after the Peach Garden; I wish you to devote the greatest attention to this work."

Monkey was in wild delight, and unable to wait for a moment he rushed off to take over his new duties in the Peach Garden. Here he found a Local Spirit, who cried out to him, "Great Sage, where are you going?" "To take charge of the Peach Garden," he said. "I've been appointed by his Majesty." The Spirit bowed low, and called to Hoe-earth, Draw-water, Peach-tender and Leaf-sweeper, the strong men who worked the garden, to come forward and kowtow to Monkey.

"How many trees are there?" Monkey asked of the Local Spirit. "Three thousand six hundred," he said. "On the outer side, one thousand two hundred, with inconspicuous flowers and small fruit. They ripen once in three thousand years. Whoever eats them becomes a fairy, all-wise; his limbs are strong and his body light. In the middle of the garden are one thousand two hundred trees, with double blossom and sweet fruit. They ripen once in six thousand years. Whoever eats them can levitate at will, and never grows old. At the back of the garden are one thousand two hundred trees. The fruit has purple markings and the stones are pale yellow. They ripen once in nine thousand years. Whoever eats them outlasts Heaven and Earth, and is the compeer of sun and moon." Monkey was delighted, and began at once inspecting the trees and listing the arbors and pagodas. Henceforward he amused himself only once a month, on the day of the full moon, but otherwise saw no friends and went nowhere. One day he saw that high up on some of the trees many of the peaches were ripe, and he made up his mind to eat them before anyone else got a chance. Unfortunately he was closely watched by his followers, and to shake them off he said, "I am feeling tired and am going to take a short rest in that arbor. Go and wait for me outside the gates." When they had retired, he took off his court hat and robes, and scrambled up onto a high tree, and began to pluck the ripest and largest fruit he could see. Sitting astride a bough, he regaled himself to his heart's content, and then came down. He put on his hat and robes, and called to his followers to attend him while he returned in state to his lodging. After a few days, he did the same thing again.

One morning her Majesty the Queen of Heaven, having made up her mind to give a Peach Banquet, told the fairy maidens, Red Jacket, Blue Jacket, White Jacket, Black Jacket, Purple Jacket, Yellow Jacket, and Green Jacket to take their baskets and pick peaches in the Peach Garden. They found Monkey's followers barring the gate. "We have come," they said, "by command of her Majesty to pick peaches for a banquet." "Halt, my fairy beauties," said one of the guards. "Things have changed since last year. This garden has been put in charge of the Great Sage, Equal of Heaven, and we must get his permission, before we can let you in." "Where is he?" they asked. "He's feeling rather tired," a guardian spirit said, "and is having a nap in the arbor." "Very well then," they said, "go and look for him, for we must get to work at once." They consented to go and tell him, but found the arbor empty, save for Monkey's hat and robe. They began looking for him, but he was nowhere to be seen. The fact was that Monkey, after slipping away and eating several peaches, had changed himself into a little fellow two inches long, and was curled up asleep under a thick leaf high up on the tree. "We must carry out our orders," said the fairy maidens, "whether you find him or not. We can't go back empty-handed." "Quite right, fairy beauties," said an officer, "we must not keep you waiting. Our master has been used to going about a great deal, and probably he has gone to look up some

of his old friends. Just you go and pick your peaches, and we'll tell him when he comes back."

So they went into the garden, and first they picked three basketsful from the trees in the near part of the garden, then three from the trees in the middle. But when they came to the trees at the back, they found nothing but snapped stalks. All the peaches had been taken. However, when they had looked about for some time, they did succeed in finding one solitary peach that was not quite ripe, hanging on a southward-facing bough. Blue Jacket pulled the bough toward her and picked the peach, then let go. This was the very bough where Monkey was sleeping in his diminutive form. The jerk awoke him, and rapidly changing himself back again, he cried out, "Where have you come from, monsters, and how comes it that you have the audacity to pick my peaches?" The terrified fairy maidens with one accord fell upon their knees, crying, "Great Sage, don't be angry! We are not monsters; we are seven fairy maidens sent by the Queen of Heaven to pick peaches for her Peach Banquet. When we came to the gate, we found your officers on guard. They looked everywhere for you, but couldn't find you. We were afraid to keep her Majesty waiting, so as you could not be found we came in and began to pick. We beseech you to forgive us!" Monkey became all affability. "Rise from your knees, fairies," he said. "Tell me now, who is invited to this banquet?" "It is an official banquet," they said, "and certain deities are invited as a matter of course. The Buddha of the Western Heaven will be there, and the Bodhisattvas and Lo-hans; Kuan-yin too, and all the Immortals of the Ten Islands. Then there will be the five spirits of the Pole Star, the Emperors of the Four Quarters, the gods and immortals of the seas and hills— all of them will come to the banquet." "Shall I be asked?" inquired Monkey. "I haven't heard it suggested," one of them said. "But I am the Great Sage, Equal of

Heaven," said Monkey. "I don't see why I shouldn't be invited." "We can only tell you who is invited according to the rules," they said. "What will be done this time, we don't know." "Quite right, my dears," said Monkey. "I'm not blaming you. Just you wait here while I go off and scout round a little, to see whether I'm to be invited or not to be invited."

Dear Monkey! He recited a magic formula and cried to the maidens, "Stay, stay, stay." This was a fixing magic, and the fairies in consequence of it remained rooted to the spot where they stood. Monkey set off on his magic cloud, sailed clear of the garden, and hastened toward the Pool of Green Jade. On the way he ran straight into the Red-legged Immortal. At once he thought of a plan by which he might trick the Immortal and attend the feast himself. "Old Wisdom, where are you going?" he asked. "I have been invited to the Peach Banquet," the Immortal answered. "You probably haven't heard, . . ." said Monkey. "I've been asked by the Jade Emperor, because I get about so fast on my cloud, to go round to all the guests and tell them there's going to be a rehearsal of ceremonies first, in the Hall of Penetrating Light." The Immortal was a guileless soul, and was completely taken in. "Other years we've always had the rehearsal at the same place as the banquet," he said. "However, I'm much obliged," and turning his cloud he made toward the Hall of Penetrating Light.

Then, reciting a spell, Monkey changed himself into the exact image of the Red-legged Immortal and went straight to the Green Jade Pool. After a little while he came to the Treasure Tower, and stepped softly in. Everything was set out for the feast, but no one had yet arrived. Monkey was gazing at the scene, when suddenly a smell of brewing assaulted him. He turned round and in a gallery on the right saw a number of fairy ministrants making wine. Some were carrying the mashed grain, others bringing water. Boys were keeping up the fire, jugs were being washed and jars swept. The wine that had already been made was exhaling a delicious perfume. Monkey's mouth watered, and he would have gone and drunk some at once, had it not been for the presence of all these servants. He was obliged to employ his magic powers. Pulling out a handful of his finest down, he tossed it into his mouth and bit it into ever smaller pieces; then he spat it out, crying "Change!" and the hairs changed into so many Drowsy Insects, which flew toward the servants and settled on their cheeks. Look at them, how their hands fall to their sides and their heads sink down, their eyes close and they fall asleep.

Monkey then snatched up some of the finest viands, the daintiest dishes, ran into the gallery, seized a jug, tilted a jar, set to and drank deeply.

When he had been drinking for some time and was already pretty drunk, he thought to himself, "Bad! bad! The guests will soon be arriving, and I shall get into trouble. It's no good staying here; I'd better go and have a sleep in my own quarters." Dear Monkey! Staggering and blundering along, very much the worse for liquor, he lost his way and instead of getting home he arrived at the Tushita Palace. Suddenly he came to himself and realized where he was. "Why, this is where Lao Tzu lives," he said to himself. "How did I get here? Well, I've always wanted to meet that old man and have never had the chance. It wouldn't be a bad idea, as I *am* here, to go and have a look at him." So he tidied his clothes and went in. But there were no signs of Lao Tzu or anyone else. Actually Lao Tzu was in an upper room with Dīpankara, Buddha of the Past, expounding the Way to an audience of Immortal officers, pages, and officials.

Monkey went straight into the alchemical laboratory. There was no one there, but a brazier at one side of the hearth was burning, with five gourds arranged round it, and in these gourds was finished elixir. "This," said Monkey to himself in high glee, "is the highest treasure of the Immortals. Since my Illumination I have solved the secret of the identity of Inside and Outside, and was on the verge of producing a little elixir on my own account, when unexpectedly I came home and was busy with other things. I think I'll try a pill or two." He tilted the gourds and ate up the contents for all the world as though it had been a dish of fried beans.

After a while, full of elixir, and the effects of the wine now wearing off, he again took stock of the situation, and said to himself, "Bad! Bad! This escapade of mine is even more unfortunate than the last. If the Jade Emperor gets to hear of it, I am lost. Run! Run! Run! I was better off as a king in the world below."

He rushed out of the Tushita Palace, not going his usual way, but making for the Western Gate of Heaven. Here he used a magic that made him invisible, and lowered his cloud till he was back on the borders of the Mountain of Flowers and Fruit. A flash of banners and gleam of spears told him that his followers were practicing the arts of war. "Little ones, I am here," he cried aloud. They all flung down their weapons and fell upon their knees. "Great Sage," they said, "you're very neglectful of your subjects. Fancy going off all this while without a thought about what becomes of us!" However, they made a great banquet to welcome him, and brought him a huge stone bowl full of date wine. After drinking a mouthful, he made a very wry face, saying, "What horrible stuff! I can't drink this." Two of his generals rushed forward. "Great Sage," they said, "no doubt in the Palace of Heaven you have been drinking the wine of the Immortals, and for that reason cannot stomach this date wine. But the proverb says: 'There is no water like home water!'" "And it goes on: 'There are no folk like home folk,'" said Monkey. "When I was enjoying myself at the Pool of Green Jade I saw flagon after flagon of jade juice and ruby extract, such as you have never in your lives tasted. I'll go back

and steal some for you. Half a cup each, and you'll none of you ever grow old."

All the monkeys were delighted, and the Sage went out to the cave door, turned his somersault, made himself invisible, and returned to Heaven. He found the makers of wine, carriers of dregs and water, and lighters of fire all still snoring heavily. Taking a couple of large flagons, one under each arm, and two more, one in each hand, he turned his cloud and came back. A great assembly of monkeys was held and each got a cupful or two. There was a rapturous scene.

Meanwhile the seven fairy maidens remained spellbound a whole day. When at last they could move, they took up their flower baskets, and going back to the Queen of Heaven they told her that the Sage, Equal of Heaven, had held them back by magic, that was why they were so late. "How many peaches did you pick?" she asked. "We got two baskets of small peaches and three baskets of middling peaches. But when we came to the back of the garden we found that half the big peaches were already gone. It seems that the Great Sage has eaten them. While he was being looked for, he suddenly appeared in our midst, made a fearful scene, and asked who had been invited to the banquet. We told him about the usual arrangements for such feasts, whereupon he bound us by a spell and went off we didn't know where. We have only just managed to break the spell and come back."

The Queen of Heaven went straight to the Jade Emperor, and was telling him what had happened, when a crowd of winemakers and other celestial officials came pouring in, announcing that someone had made a mess of all the arrangements for the banquet, stolen the wine, and eaten up all the dainties. At this moment the Supreme Patriarch of Tao was announced. The Emperor and his consort went out to meet him. "I am sorry to have to report to your Majesties," said Lao Tzu, "that the Elixir which I was concocting for the next Cinnabar Banquet has been stolen." Presently one of Monkey's celestial attendants arrived, and reported that the Great Sage had been missing since the day before and no one knew what had become of him. The Jade Emperor's suspicions were now confirmed. At this point the Red-legged Immortal appeared before the Throne. "I was on my way to the banquet," he said, "in response to her Majesty's invitation, when I met the Great Sage, Equal of Heaven, who told me that he had been asked to inform all guests that they were to go first to the Hall of Penetrating Light and rehearse the ceremonies of the banquet. I did as he said. But when I got there, I saw no sign of your Majesties having arrived, and thought it better to come at once to Court." The Jade Emperor was more outraged and astounded than ever. "So the rogue counterfeits Imperial orders and deceives my ministers!" he exclaimed. "Tell the Celestial Detective to get onto his tracks at once." After an exhaustive inquiry, the Detective reported that the disturbances in Heaven had been caused by the Great Sage.

The Jade Emperor then commanded the Kings of the Four Quarters and Vaiśravana and his son to marshal the twenty-eight Lunar Mansions, the Nine Planets, the Twelve Hours, and all the Stars, together with a hundred thousand heavenly soldiers, and draw a cordon round the Mountain of Flowers and Fruit, so that Monkey should have no escape.

When this had been done, the Nine Planets were called upon to issue the challenge. Monkey and his generals were drinking wine from Heaven, and when he was told that the Planets were at the door, he refused to worry himself.

If today you have wine, get drunk today;
Pay no heed to what is at the door, be it
good or ill,

he quoted. A small imp now scurried up saying that these nine fierce deities were raging at the gate, flinging battle taunts. Monkey only laughed. "Don't pay any attention to them!" he said:

Poetry and wine are enough to make this day
glad;
High deeds must take their turn, glory can
afford to wait.

But while he was speaking, another imp rushed in. "Father," he cried, "those nine fierce deities have broken down the gates and are advancing to the attack." "Have those scoundrels no manners!" cried Monkey. "I've never interfered with them. Why should they come here worrying me?" And he ordered the One-Horned Ogre to lead out the kings of the seventy-two caves to battle, while he and his four generals came in the rear. The ogre and his followers could get no further than the Iron Bridge. Here the Planets barred their path. "Make way!" cried Monkey, and he strode through their midst, brandishing his cudgel. The Planets dared not oppose him, and beat a hasty retreat. When they had re-formed their ranks a little way back, their leader cried, "Insensate groom! What crime is there that you have not committed? You have stolen peaches and stolen wine, upset the high feast, purloined Lao Tzu's elixir, and then taken more wine for your banquet here. You have piled up sin upon sin; do you not realize what you have done?" "Quite true," said Monkey, "all quite true. What are you going to do about it?" "We have been sent by the Jade Emperor," they said, "to receive your submission. If you surrender at once, you will be spared; if not, we shall stamp on your mountain till it is flat, and smash your cave to bits." "And where are you going to get the strength from," asked Monkey, "to do that? How dare you talk such nonsense! Stand your ground and take Old Monkey's cudgel." The Planets leapt at him; but Monkey was no whit afraid. He brandished his cudgel, parrying here and thrusting there, till the Planets were quite worn out and one by one slunk away trailing their weapons after them, to seek refuge in their tents. "That Monkey King is a valiant fighter indeed," they said to Vaiśravana. "We were unable to overcome him, and have had to give up the fight." The Kings of the Four Quarters and the Twenty-Eight Lunar Mansions were then ordered to advance. But Monkey did not quail, but bade the One-Horned Ogre, the kings of the seventy-two caves, and his four valiant generals to take their stand outside the cave.

The combat began at dawn, and lasted till the sun sank behind the western hills. The One-Horned Ogre and all the kings of the seventy-two caves were captured and carried away. Only the four generals and the monkeys escaped and hid in the far recesses of the cave. But Monkey all alone, cudgel in hand, held back the Kings of the Four Quarters, Vaiśravana, and Natha, warring with them halfway up the sky. At last, seeing that dusk was at hand, he plucked a handful of his hairs, tossed them into his mouth, chewed them up small and spat them out, crying "Change!" Whereupon they changed into thousands of monkeys each armed with a metal-plated cudgel. They drove back Vaiśravana, Natha, and the four kings. Then Monkey, at last victorious, withdrew the hairs and returned to his cave. At the Iron Bridge, he was met by the four generals and all the host of monkeys. On seeing him they wailed three times, and laughed, hee-hee, ho-ho, three times. "What made you wail three times and laugh three times when you saw me?" asked Monkey. "We wailed," they said, "because the One-Horned Ogre and the seventy-two kings were defeated and captured, and because we had to fly for our lives. We laughed with joy because you have come back victorious and unharmed."

"There is always defeat in victory and victory in defeat," said Monkey. "There is an old saying 'To slay ten thousand costs three thousand.' In this case the chieftains captured were all tigers, leopards, wolves, and the like. Not one of our monkey-kind

was taken or hurt; so there is nothing to worry about. By the art of self-division I have put them to flight. But it is certain that they have encamped at the foot of our mountain. We must keep strict guard and husband our strength. Tomorrow you shall see me use my most potent magic against those divinities, and avenge the captured."

Then the four generals and all the monkeys drank a cup or two of date wine and went quietly to sleep.

After the retreat of the Kings of the Four Quarters, all the celestial warriors told of their deeds. Some had captured tigers and leopards, some deer, some wolves and foxes. But not one of them could boast that he had taken a monkey. They did indeed, as Monkey had foretold, set up a camp, surrounding it with a great palisade. Here the meritorious were rewarded, and the troops who formed the cordon round the caves were instructed to give warning by bell or cry and be ready for the great battle that would begin at dawn.

How they fared after day broke, you will hear in the next chapter.

Chapter VI

So the Great Sage quietly rested, while the hosts of Heaven encompassed him. Meanwhile the Great Compassionate Bodhisattva Kuan-yin had come at the invitation of the Queen of Heaven to attend the great feast. With her she brought her chief disciple, Hui-yen, and on arriving they were astounded to find the banqueting halls in utter desolation and confusion. The couches were broken or pushed aside, and although there were a good few Immortals, they had not attempted to take their places, but were standing about in noisy groups, protesting and disputing. After saluting the Bodhisattva they told her the whole story of what had occurred. "If there is no banquet and no drinks are going," she said, "you had better all come with me to see the Jade Emperor." On the way they met the Red-legged Immortal and others, who told them that a heavenly army had been sent to arrest the culprit, but had not yet returned. "I should like to see the Emperor," said Kuan-yin. "I must trouble you to announce my arrival." Lao Tzu was with the Emperor, and the Queen of Heaven in attendance behind the throne. "What about the Peach Banquet?" Kuan-yin asked, after the customary greetings had been exchanged. "It has always been such fun, year after year," said the Emperor. "It is terribly disappointing that this year everything has been upset by that terrible ape. I have sent 100,000 soldiers to pen him in, but the whole day has passed without news, and I don't know whether they have been successful!"

"I think you had better go down quickly to the Mountain of Flowers and Fruit," said the Bodhisattva to her disciple, Hui-yen, "and investigate the military situation. If hostilities are actually in progress, you can give a hand. In any case let us know exactly how things stand."

When he arrived, he found a close cordon many soldiers deep, with sentries on watch at every exit. The mountain was completely surrounded, and escape impossible. Day was just breaking when Hui-yen, who was the second son of Vaiśravana and had been called Prince Moksha before his conversion, was shown into his father's tent. "Where do you come from, my son?" asked Vaiśravana. "I have been sent to see how things are going on," he said. "We camped here yesterday," said Vaiśravana, "and I sent the Nine Planets as challengers, but they were unable to stand up against this rogue's magic and returned discomfited. Then I led an army myself and he marshaled his followers. We were about 100,000 men, and fought with him till dusk, when he used some magic method of self-multiplication, and we had to withdraw. On examining our booty we found we had captured a certain number of tigers, wolves, leopards, and other animals, but not a single monkey. Today the fight has not yet begun."

While they were speaking a messenger rushed in and announced that the Great Sage and all his host of monkeys were outside, shouting their battle cries. The Kings of the Four Quarters, Vaiśravana, and his son Natha had just agreed to go out and meet him, when Hui-yen said, "Father, I was sent by the Bodhisattva to obtain information. But she said that if hostilities were in progress I was to lend a hand. I confess I should like to go and have a look at this Great Sage of yours." "My son," said Vaiśravana, "you cannot have studied with the Bodhisattva for so many years without having learned some form of magic. Don't forget to put it into practice."

Dear prince! Girding up his embroidered cloak and brandishing his iron cudgel with both hands, he rushed out to the camp gate, crying in a loud voice, "Which of you is the Great Sage Equal of Heaven?" Monkey held up his wishing-staff and answered, "I am he. Who are you, that you so rashly dare inquire for me?" Hui-yen said, "I am Vaiśravana's second son, Moksha. Now I am pupil and defender of the Bodhisattva Kuan-yin, and stand before her throne. My name in religion is Hui-yen." "What then are you doing here?" asked Monkey. "I was sent," said he, "to get news of the battle. And as they are having so much trouble with you, I have come myself to arrest you." "How dare you talk so big?" said Monkey. "Stand your ground and taste Old Monkey's cudgel." Moksha was not at all afraid, but advanced flourishing his iron cudgel. Those two stood face to face at the foot of the mountain, outside the gate of the camp. It was a grand fight. They closed fifty or sixty times, till at last Hui-yen's arms and shoulders were aching, he could resist no more and fled from the battlefield. Monkey too withdrew his monkey troops, and bade them rest outside the cave.

Moksha, still gasping and panting, tottered into his father's camp. "It's only too true," he said. "That Great Sage is indeed the most formidable of magicians! I could do nothing with him and have had to come back leaving him in possession of the field." Vaiśravana was very astonished. He saw nothing for it but to write out an appeal for further help. This he entrusted to the demon-king Mahābāli and his son Moksha, who at once passed through the cordon and soared to Heaven. "How are you people down below getting on?" asked Kuan-yin. "My father told me," said Hui-yen, "that in the first day's battle they captured a number of tigers, leopards, wolves, and other animals, but not a single monkey. Soon after I arrived, the battle began again, and I closed with the Great Sage some fifty or sixty times, but could not get the better of him and was obliged to retire to the camp. My father then sent the demon-king Mahābāli and me to ask for help." The Bodhisattva Kuan-yin bowed her head and reflected.

When the Jade Emperor opened Vaiśravana's missive and saw that it contained an appeal for help, he said laughing, "This is preposterous! Am I to believe that a single monkey-spirit is so powerful that a hundred thousand heavenly troops cannot deal with him? Vaiśravana says that he must have help, but I don't know what troops he expects me to send." Before he had finished speaking, Kuan-yin pressed together the palms of her hands and said, "Your Majesty need not worry. I know of a divinity who can certainly catch this monkey." "Whom do you mean?" asked the Emperor. "Your nephew, the magician Erh-lang," she said. "He lives at the mouth of the River of Libations, and there receives the incense that is burned in the world below. In old days he once overcame six ogres. He has his brothers with him and one thousand plant-headed deities of very great magical powers. Though he would not come if ordered to, he would listen to an appeal. If you send an appeal to him for troops, with his assistance we could effect a capture."

The demon-king Mahābāli was sent as messenger, and in less than half an hour

the cloud he rode on reached Erh-lang's temple. He came out with his brothers, and after burning incense, read the appeal. "Let the heavenly messenger go back," he said, "and announce that I will help to the utmost of my power."

So he called together his brothers and said, "The Jade Emperor has just asked us to go to the Mountain of Flowers and Fruit, and receive the submission of a troublesome monkey. Let's be off!" The brothers were delighted, and they at once marshaled the divinities in their charge. The whole temple set out, falcon on wrist, or leading their dogs, bow in hand, carried by a wild magic wind. In a trice they had crossed the Eastern Ocean and reached the Mountain of Flowers and Fruit. Having announced their mission they were led through the cordon and shown into the camp. They asked how matters stood. "I shall certainly have to try a transformation," Erh-lang said. "Keep the cordon closely drawn, but don't worry about what goes on overhead. If I am getting the worst of it, do not come to my assistance; my brothers will look after me. If I conquer him, do not try to bind him, but leave that to my brothers. All I ask is that Vaiśravana should use an imp-reflecting mirror, standing with it halfway up the sky. If he tries to run away and hide, watch his reflection in the mirror, so that we don't lose sight of him." The heavenly kings then took up their places, and Erh-lang and his brothers went out to give the challenge, telling their fellows to form a circle, keeping their falcons tethered and their dogs on leash. When he reached the door of the cave, Erh-lang found a host of monkeys drawn up in coiling dragon formation. In their midst was a banner with "The Great Sage Equal of Heaven" inscribed upon it. "How dare the cursed monster call himself equal of Heaven?" snarled Erh-lang. "Don't worry about that," said the brothers, "but go and challenge him at once."

When the small monkeys at the entrance to the camp saw Erh-lang coming, they scuttled inside and made their report. Monkey seized his metal-bound cudgel, donned his golden breastplate, put on his cloud-treading shoes and golden cap, and rushed out to the gate, glaring about him. "What little captain are you and where do you hail from," shouted Monkey, "that you dare come here and challenge me to battle?" "Have you eyes with no eyeballs, that you fail to know me?" shouted Erhlang. "I am the Jade Emperor's nephew. I have come now by his Majesty's command to arrest you, rebellious groom-ape that your are! Your hour has come." "I remember," said Monkey, "that some years ago the emperor's sister fell in love with a mortal of the world below, became his consort and had a son by him, who is said to have split the Peach Mountain with his ax. Are you he? I am half minded to give you a bit of my mind, but you are not worth it. I should be sorry to strike you, for one blow of mine would be the end of you. Go back where you came from, little fellow, and tell the four kings of Heaven to come instead." Erh-lang was furious. "Keep a civil tongue in your head," he cried, "and taste my blade." Monkey dodged aside and swiftly raising his cudgel struck in his turn. They closed over three hundred times without reaching a decision. Erh-lang exerted all his magic power, shook himself hard, and changed into a giant figure a hundred thousand feet high. His two arms, each holding aloft a magic trident, were like the peaks that crown Mount Hua, his face was blue and his teeth stuck far out, the hair on his head was scarlet and his expression malignant beyond words. This terrible apparition advanced upon Monkey, aiming a blow straight down upon his head. But Monkey, also using his magic powers, changed himself into an exact counterpart of Erh-lang, save that he held above him a single gigantic cudgel, like the solitary pillar that towers above Mount K'un-lun, and with this he fended off Erh-lang's blow. But Monkey's generals were completely discomfited by the giant

apparition, and their hands began to tremble so much that they could not wave their banners. His other officers were in panic and could not use their swords. At a word from the brothers the plant-headed divinities rushed in, letting loose their falcons and dogs, and bow in hand all charged into the fray. Alas, Monkey's four generals fled and two or three thousand of the creatures they commanded were captured. The monkeys threw down their weapons and rushed screaming, some up the mountain, some into the cave. It was just as when a cat at night disturbs roosting birds and their panic fills the starry sky.

When Monkey saw his followers scatter, his heart fluttered, he abandoned his giant form and fled as fast as his feet could carry him. Erh-lang strode after him with huge steps, crying, "Where are you off to? Come back this minute, and I will spare your life." But Monkey fled faster than ever to his cave, where he ran straight into the brothers. "Wretched monkey, where are you running to?" they cried. Monkey, trembling in every limb, hastily turned his cudgel into an embroidery needle, and hiding it about his person, changed himself into a fish, and slipped into the stream. Rushing down to the bank, Erh-lang could see nothing of him. "This simian," he said, "has certainly changed himself into a fish and hidden under the water. I must change myself too if I am to catch him." So he changed himself into a cormorant and skimmed hither and thither over the stream. Monkey, looking up out of the water, suddenly saw a bird hovering above. It was like a blue kite, but its plumage was not blue. It was like a heron, but had no tuft on its head. It was like a crane, but its feet were not red. "I'll be bound that's Erh-lang looking for me. . . ." He released a few bubbles and swam swiftly away. "That fish letting bubbles," said Erh-lang to himself, "is like a carp, but its tail is not red; it is like a tench, but there are no patterns on its scales. It is like a blackfish, but there are no stars on its head; it is like a bream, but

343

there are no bristles on its gills. Why did it make off like that when it saw me? I'll be bound it's Monkey, who has changed himself into a fish." And swooping down, he opened his beak and snapped at him. Monkey whisked out of the water, and changed himself into a freckled bustard, standing all alone on the bank. Seeing that he had reached the lowest possible stage in transformation, for the freckled bustard is the lowest and most promiscuous of creatures, mating at hazard with any bird that comes its way, Erh-lang did not deign to close with him, but returned to his true form, and fetching his sling, shot a pellet that sent Monkey rolling. Taking advantage of his opportunity, Monkey rolled and rolled down the mountainside, and when he was out of sight he changed himself into a wayside shrine; his mouth wide open was the door opening, his teeth he turned into door flaps, his tongue into the guardian Bodhisattva. His two eyes were the two round windows; he didn't quite know what to do with his tail, but sticking up straight behind it looked like a flagpole. When Erh-lang arrived at the bottom of the slope, he expected to find the bustard that he had toppled over, but instead he only found a small shrine. Examining it closely he noticed the "flagpole" sticking up behind and laughed, saying "That's Monkey, that is! He's trying his tricks on me again. I have seen many shrines, but never one with a flagpole sticking up behind. No doubt about it, this animal is playing one of his games. He hopes to lure me up close to him, and then he will bite me. He won't get me that way. I'll clench my fist and bang in the windows first. Afterward I'll kick down the doors." When Monkey heard this he was horrified. "That's a bit too much," he said to himself. "The doors are my teeth and the windows are my eyes. If he kicks my teeth and bangs my eyes, that won't be nice." So saying, he made a tiger-spring and disappeared into the sky. Erh-lang was just getting tired of the vain pursuit, when his brothers arrived. "Well, have you caught the Great Sage?" they asked. "He has just been trying to dodge me," said Erh-lang. "by turning into a shrine. I was just going to hit his windows and kick down his doors, when he suddenly disappeared. It's a queer business." They all began peering helplessly about in every direction, but could find nothing. "You stay here and keep a lookout," said Erh-lang, "while I go up and search for him." He mounted the clouds, and halfway up the sky came across Vaiśravana, who was holding the magic mirror, his son at his side. "Have you seen the Monkey King?" he asked. "He has not been up here," said Vaiśravana. "I can see him in my mirror, you know." When Erh-lang had told him about the capture of the lesser monkeys and the Great Sage's repeated transformations, he added, "Then he changed into a shrine, and when I hit at him he suddenly disappeared." Vaiśravana looked in his mirror and burst out laughing. "Make haste, Erh-lang, make haste," he cried. "That monkey has made himself invisible, decamped, and made straight for your River of Libations." When Erh-lang heard this he picked up his magic lance and fled toward the River of Libations as fast as he could.

Now as soon as Monkey reached the river, he changed himself into the exact image of Erh-lang and went straight into Erh-lang's shrine. The guardian demons of the shrine could not tell the difference and bowed low as he came in. He examined the incense smoke, and was looking at the votive paintings round the walls, when someone came and announced "Another Erh-lang has arrived." The guarding deities rushed out, and could hardly believe their eyes. "Has a creature calling himself the Great Sage Equal of Heaven been here?" the real Erh-lang asked. "We've seen nothing of any Great Sage," they said, "but there's another holy Erh-lang inside, examining the incense smoke."

He rushed in, and as soon as Monkey saw him he changed into his true form and said, "Erh-lang, I don't mind telling you the surname of that shrine was Sun."*

Erh-lang raised his three-pronged, two-bladed magic lance and struck at Monkey's cheek. Monkey dodged, and the two of them, cursing and fighting, edged toward the shrine gate and out into the mists and clouds, struggling as they went, till at last Monkey was driven to the Mountain of Flowers and Fruit, where the Kings of the Four Quarters were keeping strait guard. The brothers came to meet Erh-lang and surrounded Monkey, pressing about him on every side.

Meanwhile in Heaven everyone was wondering why a whole day had passed without any news from Erh-lang. "Would your Majesty," asked Kuan-yin, "permit me and the Patriarch of Tao to go down in person and see how things are going on?" "Not a bad idea," said the Jade Emperor, and in the end he and the Queen of Heaven as well as Kuan-yin and Lao Tzu all went to the Southern Gate of Heaven and looked out. They saw the great cordon of heavenly troops, and Vaiśravana standing halfway up the sky, holding a mirror, while Erh-lang and his brothers pressed round Monkey, tussling fiercely with him. "That Erh-lang, whom I proposed, hasn't done so badly," said Kuan-yin. "He has hemmed the Great Sage in, though he has not yet taken him prisoner. With a little help, I think he could manage it." "What weapon do you propose to use, how are you going to help him?" asked Lao Tzu. "I shall throw my vase and willow spray down on to his head," said Kuan-yin. "That won't kill him; but it will make him lose his balance, and Erh-lang will easily be able to catch him." "Your vase," said Lao Tzu, "is made of porcelain. If it fell in just the right place, it might be all right. But if it misses his head and falls on his iron cudgel, it will get broken. You had better leave him to me." "Have *you* got a weapon?" asked Kuan-yin. "I certainly have," said Lao Tzu, and he produced from his sleeve a magic snare. "This," said he, "is called the Diamond Snare. In old days, when I left China, converted the barbarians of the West, and became a god, I owed my success entirely to this snare. It comes in handy for keeping off all manner of dangers. Let me throw it down onto him." Standing at the gate of Heaven, he cast his snare, and it went rippling down straight onto Monkey's head. Monkey was busy warring with Erh-lang and his brothers, and did not notice that a weapon was falling upon him out of the sky. It hit him just on the crown of the head, and toppled him over. He scrambled to his feet and fled, pursued by Erh-lang's dogs, who went for his calves, so that he stumbled again. Lying on the ground, he cursed, saying, "That has done for me! Why can't you go and trip up your own master, instead of coming and biting Old Monkey's legs?" He twisted and turned, but could not rise, for the brothers were holding him down. Soon they had bound him tightly with ropes, and severed his lute-bone with a knife, so that he could not transform himself.

Lao Tzu drew in his snare, and begged the Emperor, Kuan-yin, the Queen of Heaven, and all the Immortals to go back to the palace. On Earth below the Kings of the Four Quarters and Vaiśravana, and all the heavenly host sheathed their swords and plucked up their palisades. Then they came up to Erh-lang and congratulated him, saying, "We owe this victory to you." "Not at all," said Erh-lang. "It was entirely due to the Founder of Tao and the gallant performances of the heavenly contingent. I can claim no credit at all." "Elder brother," said the brothers of Erh-lang, "you have said enough. What we must do now is to hoist this fellow up to Heaven and get a ruling from the Jade Emperor as to how he is to be disposed of." "Brothers," said Erh-lang, "you are not on the roll of Immortals, and cannot appear before the Emperor. Heavenly troops must be told to carry him up, and Vaiśravana

---

*Monkey.

and I will go up and report. The rest of you had better search the mountain, and when you can report that all is clear, come to the River of Libations and let me know. Meanwhile I will claim the reward due for my services, and then come back to make merry with you." The brothers bowed their assent. Erh-lang mounted the clouds, chanting songs of victory, and made his way to Heaven. Here he sent in a message, saying, "The Great Sage has been captured by the hosts of Heaven, and I have come to receive your instructions." The Jade Emperor accordingly told the demon-king Mahābāli and a contingent of heavenly troops to hoist Monkey up and bring him to the executioner's block, where he was to be cut into small pieces.

If you do not know what now became of this Monkey King, listen to what is told in the next chapter.

Chapter VII

Monkey was brought to the place of execution, where heavenly soldiers bound him to a pillar and began to hew him with axes, stab him with spears, slash him with swords. But all this had no effect whatever, and presently the Southern Pole-star sent for the spirits of the Fire Stars to come and set him alight; but they were quite unable to burn him. The thunder spirits hurled thunderbolts at him; but this had even less effect. "I don't know where the Great Sage got this trick of inviolability," said Mahābāli to the Jade Emperor. "Neither weapons nor thunderbolts have the least effect on him. What are we to do?" "Yes, indeed," said the Jade Emperor, "with a fellow like that, what line *can* one take?" "It's not surprising," said Lao Tzu. "After all, he ate the peaches of Immortality, drank the wine of Heaven, and stole the Elixir of Long Life; five bowls full, some raw, some cooked, are all inside him. No doubt he has worked on them with Samadhi fire and fused them into a solid, that makes his whole body harder than

diamond, so that he is very difficult to damage. The best thing would be to bring him to me. I'll put him in my Crucible of the Eight Trigrams and smelt him with alchemic fire. In a little while he will be reduced to ashes, and I shall recover my elixir, which will be left at the bottom of the crucible." So Monkey was handed over to Lao Tzu, and Erh-lang was rewarded with a hundred golden flowers, a hundred jars of heavenly wine, a hundred grains of elixir, along with a great store of jewels, pearls, brocades, and embroideries, which he was asked to share with his brothers. He thanked the Emperor, and went back to the River of Libations.

When Lao Tzu got back to the Tushita Palace, he untied Monkey's ropes, removed the blade that was stuck through his lute-bone, pushed him into the crucible, and told his servant to blow up a good fire. Now this crucible was in eight parts, each representing one of the eight trigrams. Monkey wriggled into the part corresponding to the trigram *sun*. Now *sun* is wind, and wind blows out fire; but wind raises smoke, and Monkey's eyes smarted and became red; a condition from which he never recovered, which is why he is sometimes called Fiery Eyes. Time passed, and at last the forty-ninth day came, and Lao Tzu's alchemical processes were complete. When he came to the crucible to take off the lid, Monkey was rubbing his eyes with both hands, so hard that the tears fell. When he heard the lid being moved, he looked quickly up, and the light that came in hurt him so much that he could not bear it and jumped straight out of the crucible, uttering a piercing cry and kicking over the crucible as he jumped. He rushed out of the room pursued by Lao Tzu's servants, all of whom he tripped up, and when Lao Tzu clutched at him, he gave him such a push that he went head over heels. Then he took his cudgel from behind his ear and, armed once more, ran amok in Heaven, frightening the Nine Planets so much that they locked themselves in, and the Kings of the Four Quarters vanished from the scene. This time Monkey hit out recklessly, not caring whom he struck or what he smashed. No one could stop him, and he would have broken up the Hall of Magic Mists, had not the divinity Wang Ling-kuan rushed forward with his great metal lash. "Halt, cursed Monkey!" he cried. "See who stands before you, and cease your mad pranks!" Monkey did not deign to parley with him, but raised his cudgel and struck. Ling-kuan faced him with his whip aloft. It was a great fight that the two of them had, in front of the Hall of Magic Mists, but neither gained the advantage. At last the thirty-six thunder deities came to Ling-kuan's aid, and Monkey found himself beset on every side by swords, lances, spears, whips, axes, hooks, sickles. He thought it time to transform himself, and took on a form with three heads and six arms, and wielded six magic cudgels which he whirled like a spinning wheel, dancing in their midst. The thunder deities dared not approach him.

The noise of the combat reached the Jade Emperor who in great consternation sent two messengers to the Western Region to see if Buddha could not come and help. When they had recounted Monkey's misdeeds and explained their mission, Buddha said to the Bodhisattvas who surrounded him, "You stay quietly here in the Hall of Law, and don't relax your *yoga* postures. I've got to go and deal with this creature who is making trouble at the Taoist court." But he called on his disciples Ānanda and Kāśyapa to follow him. Arriving in Heaven, they heard a fearful din and found Monkey beset by the thirty-six deities. Buddha ordered the deities to lower arms and go back to their camp, and called Monkey to him. Monkey changed into his true form and shouted angrily, "What bonze are you that you ask for me in the middle of a battle?" "I am the Buddha of the Western Paradise. I have heard of the trouble you have been giving in Heaven. Where do you come from, and how long ago did

you get your Illumination, that you should dare behave like this?"

Born of sky and earth, Immortal magically fused,
From the Mountain of Flowers and Fruit an old monkey am I.
In the Cave of the Water-Curtain I ply my home-trade;
I found a friend and master, who taught me the Great Secret.
I made myself perfect in many arts of Immortality,
I learned transformations without bound or end.
I tired of the narrow scope afforded by the world of man,
Nothing could content me but to live in the Green Jade Heaven.
Why should Heaven's halls have always one master?
In earthly dynasties king succeeds king.
The strong to the stronger must yield precedence and place,
Hero is he alone who vies with powers supreme.

So Monkey recited; at which Buddha burst out laughing. "After all," he said, "you're only a monkey-spirit. How can you delude yourself into supposing that you can seize the Jade Emperor's throne? He has been perfecting himself for 1750 kalpas, and every kalpa is 129,000 years. Just see how long it takes to achieve such wisdom as his! How can you, an animal, who have only in this incarnation received half-human form, dare make such a boast? You exceed yourself, and will surely come to a bad end. Submit at once and talk no more of your nonsense. Otherwise I shall have to deal sharply with you, and there won't be much left of the longevity you crave." "He may have begun young," said Monkey, "but that is no reason why he should keep the throne forever. There is a proverb that says 'This year, the Jade Emperor's turn; next year, mine.' Tell him to clear out and make room for me. That is all I ask. If he won't, I shall go on like this, and they will never have any peace." "What magic have you got," asked Buddha, "that would enable you to seize the blessed realms of Heaven?" "Many," said Monkey. "Apart from my seventy-two transformations, I can somersault through the clouds a hundred and eight thousand leagues at a bound. Aren't I fit to be seated on the throne of Heaven?"

"I'll have a wager with you," said Buddha. "If you are really so clever, jump off the palm of my right hand. If you succeed, I'll tell the Jade Emperor to come and live with me in the Western Paradise, and you shall have his throne without more ado. But if you fail, you shall go back to Earth and do penance there for many a kalpa before you come to me again with your talk."

"This Buddha," Monkey thought to himself, "is a perfect fool. I can jump a hundred and eight thousand leagues, while his palm cannot be as much as eight inches across. How could I fail to jump clear of it?" "You're sure you are in a position to do this for me?" he asked. "Of course I am," said Buddha.

He stretched out his right hand, which looked about the size of a lotus leaf. Monkey put his cudgel behind his ear, and leapt with all his might. "That's all right," he said to himself. "I'm right off it now." He was whizzing so fast that he was almost invisible, and Buddha, watching him with the eye of wisdom, saw a mere whirligig shoot along.

Monkey came at last to five pink pillars, sticking up into the air. "This is the end of the World," said Monkey to himself. "All I have got to do is to go back to Buddha and claim my forfeit. The Throne is mine." "Wait a minute," he said presently, "I'd better just leave a record of some kind, in case I have trouble with Buddha." He plucked a hair and blew on it with magic breath, crying "Change!" It changed at once into a writing brush charged with heavy ink, and at the base of the central pillar he wrote, "The Great Sage Equal of

Heaven reached this place." Then to mark his disrespect, he relieved nature at the bottom of the first pillar, and somersaulted back to where he had come from. Standing on Buddha's palm, he said, "Well, I've gone and come back. You can go and tell the Jade Emperor to hand over the Palaces of Heaven." "You stinking ape," said Buddha, "you've been on the palm of my hand all the time." "You're quite mistaken," said Monkey. "I got to the end of the World, where I saw five flesh-colored pillars sticking up into the sky. I wrote something on one of them. I'll take you there and show you, if you like." "No need for that," said Buddha. "Just look down." Monkey peered down with his fiery, steely eyes, and there at the base of the middle finger of Buddha's hand he saw written the words "The Great Sage Equal of Heaven reached this place," and from the fork between the thumb and first finger came a smell of monkey's urine. It took him some time to get over his astonishment. At last he said, "Impossible, impossible! I wrote that on the pillar sticking up into the sky. How did it get on to Buddha's finger? He's practicing some magic upon me. Let me go back and look." Dear Monkey! He crouched, and was just making ready to spring again, when Buddha turned his head, and pushed Monkey out at the western gate of Heaven. As he did so, he changed his five fingers into the Five Elements, Metal, Wood, Water, Fire, and Earth. They became a five-peaked mountain, named Wu Hsing Shan (Mountain of the Five Elements) which pressed upon him heavily enough to hold him tight. The thunder spirits, Ānanda and Kāśyapa all pressed the palms of their hands together and shouted "Bravo!"

Buddha, having thus quelled the baleful monkey, called to Ānanda and Kāśyapa to come back with him to the Western Heaven. Just as they were leaving, two messengers arrived from the Hall of Magic Mists saying, "We beseech the Tathāgata to wait a minute. Our master is on his way." Buddha turned his head, and a moment later saw a chariot drawn by eight phoenixes, covered by a canopy gleaming with jewels. There was a sound of many instruments and a chanting of innumerable spirit hosts. Flower petals fell through the air, and the smell of incense belched. "I am profoundly beholden to you for dealing with that monster," said the Jade Emperor, when his equipage drew up, "and if you will consent to stay for a while, I will invite all the Immortals to join us in a feast of thanks." Buddha did not like to refuse. "I could not do otherwise than come at your Majesty's request," he said. "What small success we have had is however not my work, but is entirely due to the Founder of Tao and the other divinities."

The banquet was nearing its end when one of the heavenly detectives arrived saying "The Great Sage is sticking out his head!" "No matter," said Buddha, and he took out of his sleeve a seal on which was engraved OM MANI PADME HUM. He gave it to Ānanda and told him to stamp it on the top of the mountain. So Ānanda left Heaven, carrying the seal, and when he got to the Mountain of the Five Elements, he stamped the seal hard upon a square slab of rock that lay right on the top of the mountain. At once this mountain struck root and joined its seams. There was enough air to breathe, but not a crack through which hand or head could squeeze.

"I have sealed him down," Ānanda announced; whereupon Buddha said goodbye to the Jade Emperor and all the spirits, and with his two disciples left the gate of Heaven. But in his mercy he appointed a guardian spirit to watch over the mountain. "When he is hungry," he said, "give him an iron pill to eat. When he is thirsty, give him verdigris to drink. When the days of his penance are fulfilled, there will be one who will come to rescue him. . . ."

The Awakening

Kate Chopin

Editor's Introduction

The emergence within the past two decades or so of a feminist consciousness has brought renewed attention to books that depict women rebelling against traditional lives of marriage and domesticity, seeking freedom and fulfillment in unconventional if not adulterous relationships. Instances are *Madame Bovary* and *Anna Karenina:* great novels that depict such aspirations in a world that still regarded them as unforgivable, still punished those who had them with open scorn. Perhaps these strivings were most interesting at such a time, when they were thought to matter, to be in all respects forbidden rather than a recognized, an almost usual disorder of contemporary life—most interesting, at any rate, for literature, which could regard them with a seriousness that is now less easy to assume.

The Awakening, by Kate Chopin (1851–1904), is a minor classic in this genre, one that indeed had all but been forgotten till the present interest in its theme developed. Its author was a woman of Creole ancestry who grew up in Saint Louis after the Civil War. Married to a Creole cotton planter, with whom she moved first to New Orleans and then to a plantation in Natchitoches Parish, she returned on his death to Saint Louis, where she had the brief literary career she was able to achieve. Besides one earlier novel, she wrote short stories, many for children but others of such sophistication as to show she had read her literary masters, notably Maupassant, whom she especially admired. She also read Darwin, Huxley, and Herbert Spencer, from whom she gained advanced ideas, and seems to have been familiar with the work of Sarah Orne Jewett and Mary E. Wilkins Freeman, whose writings have some of the same qualities.

She was clearly serious herself about the suffocating constraints, as she came to think they were, of late Victorian culture, the desire of women—at least of Edna Pelletier, her protagonist in *The Awakening*—to transcend them, to live "beyond culture" through the release of female sexuality. No one can suppose the book was casually written, and what is known about Kate Chopin at the time suggests how interested she was in the "New Woman" of that period, how much she had been interested in Aubrey Beardsley, Oscar Wilde, and other fin de siècle figures. But she was not prepared, apparently, for the overwhelmingly hostile reaction *The Awakening* generated—for its being banned by local libraries, for the social ostracism she suffered on account of it. The book was said by its reviewers to "leave one sick of human nature," to be "not healthy," to be written in "language not fit for publication." Even Willa Cather, who might have sympathized and did admire Chopin's art, regretted that she had "devoted so exquisite and sensitive . . . a style to so trite and sordid a theme." The effect of this in a modest woman without great literary pretensions was discouraging, the more so when she found that a subsequent collection of stories was refused for publication. Kate Chopin wrote little afterward—a few poems, some further short stories—before her early death of a brain hemorrhage at 53.

Anyone who knows the fiction of the later twentieth century (or its first decades), reads of these provincial reactions with a shrug. Such stuff belongs to social history, we would say, not letters properly, or morals, which have long since recognized, if they have not entirely accepted, everything Kate Chopin tried to do. If it comes to that, anyone familiar with the Greek tragedies, with Chaucer, Rabelais, or Fielding, in *GBWW,* will be immune to shock of the sort that provincial Saint Louis seems to have felt at the time the book appeared. Yet it is not a trivial work, a quaint tale, a mere period piece. Kate Chopin knew what she was about—understood her own material—and it is not surprising that *The Awakening* has finally established itself. Available in paperback editions, one of which, at least, is introduced by a distinguished feminist academic, who compares it favorably with the greatest women's literature—with George Eliot, that is, and the two Brontë sisters—before offering three pages of contemporary criticism listed in learned journals, Kate Chopin's book has earned its place in letters as well as feminist regard, and its popularity has long since mooted any question of its daring, any doubt of its importance.

352

The Awakening

A green and yellow parrot, which hung in a cage outside the door, kept repeating over and over:

"*Allez vous-en!* [Go on!] *Allez vous-en! Sapristi!* [euphemism for *sacristi!* (bless me!)] That's all right!"

He could speak a little Spanish, and also a language which nobody understood, unless it was the mockingbird that hung on the other side of the door, whistling his fluty notes out upon the breeze with maddening persistence.

Mr. Pontellier, unable to read his newspaper with any degree of comfort, arose with an expression and an exclamation of disgust. He walked down the gallery and across the narrow "bridges" which connected the Lebrun cottages one with the other. He had been seated before the door of the main house. The parrot and the mockingbird were the property of Madame Lebrun, and they had the right to make all the noise they wished. Mr. Pontellier had the privilege of quitting their society when they ceased to be entertaining.

He stopped before the door of his own cottage, which was the fourth one from the main building and next to the last. Seating himself in a wicker rocker which was there, he once more applied himself to the task of reading the newspaper. The day was Sunday; the paper was a day old. The Sunday papers had not yet reached Grand Isle. He was already acquainted with the market reports, and he glanced restlessly over the editorials and bits of news which he had not had time to read before quitting New Orleans the day before.

Mr. Pontellier wore eyeglasses. He was a man of forty, of medium height and rather slender build; he stooped a little. His hair was brown and straight, parted on one side. His beard was neatly and closely trimmed.

Once in a while he withdrew his glance from the newspaper and looked about him. There was more noise than ever over at the house. The main building was called "the house," to distinguish it from the cottages. The chattering and whistling birds were still at it. Two young girls, the Farival twins, were playing a duet from "Zampa" upon the piano. Madame Lebrun was bustling in and out, giving orders in a high key to a yard-boy whenever she got inside the house, and directions in an equally high voice to a dining-room servant whenever she got outside. She was a fresh, pretty woman, clad always in white with elbow sleeves. Her starched skirts crinkled as she came and went. Farther down, before one of the cottages, a lady in black was walking demurely up and down, telling her beads. A good many persons of the *pension* [boardinghouse] had gone over to the *Chênière Caminada* in Beaudelet's lugger to hear mass. Some young people were out under the water oaks playing croquet. Mr. Pontellier's two children were there— sturdy little fellows of four and five. A quadroon nurse followed them about with a faraway, meditative air.

Mr. Pontellier finally lit a cigar and began to smoke, letting the paper drag idly from his hand. He fixed his gaze upon a white sunshade that was advancing at snail's pace from the beach. He could see it plainly between the gaunt trunks of the water oaks and across the stretch of yellow chamomile. The gulf looked far away, melting hazily into the blue of the horizon. The sunshade continued to approach slowly. Beneath its pink-lined shelter were his wife, Mrs. Pontellier, and young Robert Lebrun. When they reached the cottage, the two seated themselves with some appearance of fatigue upon the upper step of the porch, facing each other, each leaning against a supporting post.

"What folly! to bathe at such an hour in such heat!" exclaimed Mr. Pontellier. He himself had taken a plunge at daylight. That was why the morning seemed long to him.

"You are burned beyond recognition," he added, looking at his wife as one looks at a valuable piece of personal property which has suffered some damage. She held up her hands, strong, shapely hands, and surveyed them critically, drawing up her lawn sleeves above the wrists. Looking at them reminded her of her rings, which she had given to her husband before leaving for the beach. She silently reached out to him, and he, understanding, took the rings from his vest pocket and dropped them into her open palm. She slipped them upon her fingers; then clasping her knees, she looked across at Robert and began to laugh. The rings sparkled upon her fingers. He sent back an answering smile.

"What is it?" asked Pontellier, looking lazily and amused from one to the other. It was some utter nonsense; some adventure out there in the water, and they both tried to relate it at once. It did not seem half so amusing when told. They realized this, and so did Mr. Pontellier. He yawned and stretched himself. Then he got up, saying he had half a mind to go over to Klein's hotel and play a game of billiards.

"Come go along, Lebrun," he proposed to Robert. But Robert admitted quite frankly that he preferred to stay where he was and talk to Mrs. Pontellier.

"Well, send him about his business when he bores you, Edna," instructed her husband as he prepared to leave.

"Here, take the umbrella," she exclaimed, holding it out to him. He accepted the sunshade, and lifting it over his head descended the steps and walked away.

"Coming back to dinner?" his wife called after him. He halted a moment and shrugged his shoulders. He felt in his vest pocket; there was a ten-dollar bill there. He did not know; perhaps he would return for the early dinner and perhaps he would not. It all depended upon the company which he found over at Klein's and the size of "the game." He did not say this, but she understood it, and laughed, nodding good-bye to him.

Both children wanted to follow their father when they saw him starting out. He kissed them and promised to bring them back bonbons and peanuts.

II

Mrs. Pontellier's eyes were quick and bright; they were a yellowish brown, about the color of her hair. She had a way of turning them swiftly upon an object and holding them there as if lost in some inward maze of contemplation or thought.

Her eyebrows were a shade darker than her hair. They were thick and almost horizontal, emphasizing the depth of her eyes. She was rather handsome than beautiful. Her face was captivating by reason of a certain frankness of expression and a contradictory subtle play of features. Her manner was engaging.

Robert rolled a cigarette. He smoked cigarettes because he could not afford cigars, he said. He had a cigar in his pocket which Mr. Pontellier had presented him with, and he was saving it for his after-dinner smoke.

This seemed quite proper and natural on his part. In coloring he was not unlike his companion. A clean-shaved face made the resemblance more pronounced than it would otherwise have been. There rested

no shadow of care upon his open countenance. His eyes gathered in and reflected the light and languor of the summer day.

Mrs. Pontellier reached over for a palm-leaf fan that lay on the porch and began to fan herself, while Robert sent between his lips light puffs from his cigarette. They chatted incessantly: about the things around them; their amusing adventure out in the water—it had again assumed its entertaining aspect; about the wind, the trees, the people who had gone to the *Chênière;* about the children playing croquet under the oaks, and the Farival twins, who were now performing the overture to "The Poet and the Peasant."

Robert talked a good deal about himself. He was very young, and did not know any better. Mrs. Pontellier talked a little about herself for the same reason. Each was interested in what the other said. Robert spoke of his intention to go to Mexico in the autumn, where fortune awaited him. He was always intending to go to Mexico, but some way never got there. Meanwhile he held on to his modest position in a mercantile house in New Orleans, where an equal familiarity with English, French, and Spanish gave him no small value as a clerk and correspondent.

He was spending his summer vacation, as he always did, with his mother at Grand Isle. In former times, before Robert could remember, "the house" had been a summer luxury of the Lebruns. Now, flanked by its dozen or more cottages, which were always filled with exclusive visitors from the *"Quartier Français,"* it enabled Madame Lebrun to maintain the easy and comfortable existence which appeared to be her birthright.

Mrs. Pontellier talked about her father's Mississippi plantation and her girlhood home in the old Kentucky bluegrass country. She was an American woman, with a small infusion of French which seemed to have been lost in dilution. She read a letter from her sister, who was away in the East,

and who had engaged herself to be married. Robert was interested, and wanted to know what manner of girls the sisters were, what the father was like, and how long the mother had been dead.

When Mrs. Pontellier folded the letter it was time for her to dress for the early dinner.

"I see Léonce isn't coming back," she said, with a glance in the direction whence her husband had disappeared. Robert supposed he was not, as there were a good many New Orleans club men over at Klein's.

When Mrs. Pontellier left him to enter her room, the young man descended the steps and strolled over toward the croquet players, where, during the half hour before dinner, he amused himself with the little Pontellier children, who were very fond of him.

III

It was eleven o'clock that night when Mr. Pontellier returned from Klein's hotel. He was in an excellent humor, in high spirits, and very talkative. His entrance awoke his wife, who was in bed and fast asleep when he came in. He talked to her while he undressed, telling her anecdotes and bits of news and gossip that he had gathered during the day. From his trousers pockets he took a fistful of crumpled bank notes and a good deal of silver coin, which he piled on the bureau indiscriminately with keys, knife, handkerchief, and whatever else happened to be in his pockets. She was overcome with sleep, and answered him with little half utterances.

He thought it very discouraging that his wife, who was the sole object of his existence, evinced so little interest in things which concerned him, and valued so little his conversation.

Mr. Pontellier had forgotten the bonbons and peanuts for the boys. Notwithstanding he loved them very much, and went into the adjoining room where they slept to take a look at them and make sure that they were resting comfortably. The result of his investigation was far from satisfactory. He turned and shifted the youngsters about in bed. One of them began to kick and talk about a basket full of crabs.

Mr. Pontellier returned to his wife with the information that Raoul had a high fever and needed looking after. Then he lit a cigar and went and sat near the open door to smoke it.

Mrs. Pontellier was quite sure Raoul had no fever. He had gone to bed perfectly well, she said, and nothing had ailed him all day. Mr. Pontellier was too well acquainted with fever symptoms to be mistaken. He assured her the child was consuming at that moment in the next room.

He reproached his wife with her inattention, her habitual neglect of the children. If it was not a mother's place to look after children, whose on earth was it? He himself had his hands full with his brokerage business. He could not be in two places at once; making a living for his family on the street, and staying at home to see that no harm befell them. He talked in a monotonous, insistent way.

Mrs. Pontellier sprang out of bed and went into the next room. She soon came back and sat on the edge of the bed, leaning her head down on the pillow. She said nothing, and refused to answer her husband when he questioned her. When his cigar was smoked out he went to bed, and in half a minute he was fast asleep.

Mrs. Pontellier was by that time thoroughly awake. She began to cry a little, and wiped her eyes on the sleeve of her *peignoir*. Blowing out the candle, which her husband had left burning, she slipped her bare feet into a pair of satin *mules* at the foot of the bed and went out on the porch, where she sat down in the wicker chair and began to rock gently to and fro.

It was then past midnight. The cottages were all dark. A single faint light gleamed out from the hallway of the house. There was no sound abroad except the hooting of an old owl in the top of a water oak, and the everlasting voice of the sea, that was not uplifted at that soft hour. It broke like a mournful lullaby upon the night.

The tears came so fast to Mrs. Pontellier's eyes that the damp sleeve of her *peignoir* no longer served to dry them. She was holding the back of her chair with one hand; her loose sleeve had slipped almost to the shoulder of her uplifted arm. Turning, she thrust her face, steaming and wet, into the bend of her arm, and she went on crying there, not caring any longer to dry her face, her eyes, her arms. She could not have told why she was crying. Such experiences as the foregoing were not uncommon in her married life. They seemed never before to have weighed much against the abundance of her husband's kindness and a uniform devotion which had come to be tacit and self-understood.

An indescribable oppression, which seemed to generate in some unfamiliar part of her consciousness, filled her whole being with a vague anguish. It was like a shadow, like a mist passing across her soul's summer day. It was strange and unfamiliar; it was a mood. She did not sit there inwardly upbraiding her husband, lamenting at Fate, which had directed her footsteps to the path which they had taken. She was just having a good cry all to herself. The mosquitoes made merry over her, biting her firm, round arms and nipping at her bare insteps.

The little stinging, buzzing imps succeeded in dispelling a mood which might have held her there in the darkness half a night longer.

The following morning Mr. Pontellier was up in good time to take the rockaway which was to convey him to the steamer at the wharf. He was returning to the city to his business, and they would not see him again at the Island till the coming Saturday. He had regained his composure, which seemed to have been somewhat impaired the night before. He was eager to be gone, as he looked forward to a lively week in Carondelet Street.

Mr. Pontellier gave his wife half of the money which he had brought away from Klein's hotel the evening before. She liked money as well as most women, and accepted it with no little satisfaction.

"It will buy a handsome wedding present for Sister Janet!" she exclaimed, smoothing out the bills as she counted them one by one.

"Oh! we'll treat Sister Janet better than that, my dear," he laughed, as he prepared to kiss her good-bye.

The boys were tumbling about, clinging to his legs, imploring that numerous things be brought back to them. Mr. Pontellier was a great favorite, and ladies, men, children, even nurses, were always on hand to say good-bye to him. His wife stood smiling and waving, the boys shouting, as he disappeared in the old rockaway down the sandy road.

A few days later a box arrived for Mrs. Pontellier from New Orleans. It was from her husband. It was filled with *friandises* [sweets], with luscious and toothsome bits—the finest of fruits, *patés*, a rare bottle or two, delicious syrups, and bonbons in abundance.

Mrs. Pontellier was always very generous with the contents of such a box; she was quite used to receiving them when away from home. The *patés* and fruit were brought to the dining room; the bonbons were passed around. And the ladies, selecting with dainty and discriminating fingers and a little greedily, all declared that Mr. Pontellier was the best husband in the world. Mrs. Pontellier was forced to admit that she knew of none better.

IV

It would have been a difficult matter for Mr. Pontellier to define to his own satisfaction or anyone else's wherein his wife failed in her duty toward their children. It was something which he felt rather than perceived, and he never voiced the feeling without subsequent regret and ample atonement.

If one of the little Pontellier boys took a tumble while at play, he was not apt to rush crying to his mother's arms for comfort; he would more likely pick himself up, wipe the water out of his eyes and the sand out of his mouth, and go on playing. Tots as they were, they pulled together and stood their ground in childish battles with doubled fists and uplifted voices, which usually prevailed against the other mother-tots. The quadroon nurse was looked upon as a huge encumbrance, only good to button up waists and panties and to brush and part hair; since it seemed to be a law of society that hair must be parted and brushed.

In short, Mrs. Pontellier was not a mother-woman. The mother-women seemed to prevail that summer at Grand Isle. It was easy to know them, fluttering about with extended, protecting wings when any harm, real or imaginary, threatened their precious brood. They were women who idolized their children, worshiped their husbands, and esteemed it a holy privilege to efface themselves as individuals and grow wings as ministering angels.

Many of them were delicious in the role; one of them was the embodiment of every womanly grace and charm. If her husband did not adore her, he was a brute, deserving of death by slow torture. Her name was Adèle Ratignolle. There are no words to describe her save the old ones that have served so often to picture the bygone heroine of romance and the fair lady of our dreams. There was nothing subtle or hidden about her charms; her beauty was all there, flaming and apparent: the spun-gold hair that comb nor confining pin could restrain; the blue eyes that were like nothing but sapphires; two lips that pouted, that were so red one could only think of cherries or some other delicious crimson fruit in looking at them. She was growing a little stout, but it did not seem to detract an iota from the grace of every step, pose, gesture. One would not have wanted her white neck a mite less full or her beautiful arms more slender. Never were hands more exquisite than hers, and it was a joy to look at them when she threaded her needle or adjusted her gold thimble to her taper middle finger as she sewed away on the little night-drawers or fashioned a bodice or a bib.

Madame Ratignolle was very fond of Mrs. Pontellier, and often she took her sewing and went over to sit with her in the afternoons. She was sitting there the afternoon of the day the box arrived from New Orleans. She had possession of the rocker, and she was busily engaged in sewing upon a diminutive pair of night-drawers.

She had brought the pattern of the drawers for Mrs. Pontellier to cut out—a marvel of construction, fashioned to enclose a baby's body so effectually that only two small eyes might look out from the garment, like an Eskimo's. They were designed for winter wear, when treacherous drafts came down chimneys and insidious currents of deadly cold found their way through keyholes.

Mrs. Pontellier's mind was quite at rest concerning the present material needs of her children, and she could not see the use of anticipating and making winter night garments the subject of her summer meditations. But she did not want to appear unamiable and uninterested, so she had brought forth newspapers, which she spread upon the floor of the gallery, and under Madame Ratignolle's directions she had cut a pattern of the impervious garment.

Robert was there, seated as he had been the Sunday before, and Mrs. Pontellier also occupied her former position on the upper step, leaning listlessly against the post. Beside her was a box of bonbons, which she held out at intervals to Madame Ratignolle.

That lady seemed at a loss to make a selection, but finally settled upon a stick of nougat, wondering if it were not too rich; whether it could possibly hurt her. Madame Ratignolle had been married seven years. About every two years she had a baby. At that time she had three babies, and was beginning to think of a fourth one. She was always talking about her "condition." Her "condition" was in no way apparent, and no one would have known a thing about it but for her persistence in making it the subject of conversation.

Robert started to reassure her, asserting that he had known a lady who had subsisted upon nougat during the entire—but seeing the color mount into Mrs. Pontellier's face he checked himself and changed the subject.

Mrs. Pontellier, though she had married a Creole, was not thoroughly at home in the society of Creoles; never before had she been thrown so intimately among them. There were only Creoles that summer at Lebrun's. They all knew each other, and felt like one large family, among whom existed the most amicable relations. A characteristic which distinguished them and which impressed Mrs. Pontellier most forcibly was their entire absence of prudery. Their freedom of expression was at first incomprehensible to her, though she had no difficulty in reconciling it with a lofty chastity which in the Creole woman seems to be inborn and unmistakable.

Never would Edna Pontellier forget the shock with which she heard Madame Ratignolle relating to old Monsieur Farival the harrowing story of one of her *accouchements* [confinements], withholding no intimate detail. She was growing accustomed to like shocks, but she could not keep the mounting color back from her cheeks. Oftener than once her coming had interrupted the droll story with which Robert was entertaining some amused group of married women.

A book had gone the rounds of the *pension*. When it came her turn to read it, she did so with profound astonishment. She felt moved to read the book in secret and solitude, though none of the others had done so—to hide it from view at the sound of approaching footsteps. It was openly criticized and freely discussed at table. Mrs. Pontellier gave over being astonished, and concluded that wonders would never cease.

V

They formed a congenial group sitting there that summer afternoon—Madame Ratignolle sewing away, often stopping to relate a story or incident with much expressive gesture of her perfect hands; Robert and Mrs. Pontellier sitting idle, exchanging occasional words, glances, or smiles which indicated a certain advanced stage of intimacy and *camaraderie*.

He had lived in her shadow during the past month. No one thought anything of it. Many had predicted that Robert would devote himself to Mrs. Pontellier when he arrived. Since the age of fifteen, which was eleven years before, Robert each summer at Grand Isle had constituted himself the devoted attendant of some fair dame or damsel. Sometimes it was a young girl, again a widow; but as often as not it was some interesting married woman.

For two consecutive seasons he lived in the sunlight of Mademoiselle Duvigné's presence. But she died between summers; then Robert posed as an inconsolable, prostrating himself at the feet of Madame Ratignolle for whatever crumbs of sympathy and comfort she might be pleased to vouchsafe.

Mrs. Pontellier liked to sit and gaze at her fair companion as she might look upon a faultless Madonna.

"Could anyone fathom the cruelty beneath that fair exterior?" murmured Robert. "She knew that I adored her once, and she let me adore her. It was 'Robert, come; go; stand up; sit down; do this; do that; see if the baby sleeps; my thimble, please, that I left God knows where. Come and read Daudet to me while I sew.' "

"*Par exemple!* [Upon my word!] I never

had to ask. You were always there under my feet, like a troublesome cat."

"You mean like an adoring dog. And just as soon as Ratignolle appeared on the scene, then it *was* like a dog. '*Passez! Adieu! Allez vous-en!* [Leave! Farewell! Go on!]' "

"Perhaps I feared to make Alphonse jealous," she interjoined, with excessive naïveté. That made them all laugh. The right hand jealous of the left! The heart jealous of the soul! But for that matter, the Creole husband is never jealous; with him the gangrene passion is one which has become dwarfed by disuse.

Meanwhile Robert, addressing Mrs. Pontellier, continued to tell of his one-time hopeless passion for Madame Ratignolle; of sleepless nights, of consuming flames till the very sea sizzled when he took his daily plunge. While the lady at the needle kept up a little running, contemptuous comment:

"*Blagueur—farceur—gros bête, va!* [Joker—buffoon—silly thing, go on!]"

He never assumed this seriocomic tone when alone with Mrs. Pontellier. She never knew precisely what to make of it; at that moment it was impossible for her to guess how much of it was jest and what proportion was earnest. It was understood that he had often spoken words of love to Madame Ratignolle, without any thought of being taken seriously. Mrs. Pontellier was glad he had not assumed a similar role toward herself. It would have been unacceptable and annoying.

Mrs. Pontellier had brought her sketching materials, which she sometimes dabbled with in an unprofessional way. She liked the dabbling. She felt in it satisfaction of a kind which no other employment afforded her.

She had long wished to try herself on Madame Ratignolle. Never had that lady seemed a more tempting subject than at that moment, seated there like some sensuous Madonna, with the gleam of the fading day enriching her splendid color.

Robert crossed over and seated himself upon the step below Mrs. Pontellier, that he might watch her work. She handled her brushes with a certain ease and freedom which came, not from long and close acquaintance with them, but from a natural aptitude. Robert followed her work with close attention, giving forth little ejaculatory expressions of appreciation in French, which he addressed to Madame Ratignolle.

"*Mais ce n'est pas mal! Elle s'y connait, elle a de la force, oui.* [That's not bad! She is an expert, she has passion, indeed.]"

During his oblivious attention he once quietly rested his head against Mrs. Pontellier's arm. As gently she repulsed him. Once again he repeated the offense. She could not but believe it to be thoughtlessness on his part; yet that was no reason she should submit to it. She did not remonstrate, except again to repulse him quietly but firmly. He offered no apology.

The picture completed bore no resemblance to Madame Ratignolle. She was greatly disappointed to find that it did not look like her. But it was a fair enough piece of work, and in many respects satisfying.

Mrs. Pontellier evidently did not think so. After surveying the sketch critically she drew a broad smudge of paint across its surface, and crumpled the paper between her hands.

The youngsters came tumbling up the steps, the quadroon following at the respectful distance which they required her to observe. Mrs. Pontellier made them carry her paints and things into the house. She sought to detain them for a little talk and some pleasantry. But they were greatly in earnest. They had only come to investigate the contents of the bonbon box. They accepted without murmuring what she chose to give them, each holding out two chubby hands scoop-like, in the vain hope that they might be filled; and then away they went.

The sun was low in the west, and the breeze soft and languorous that came up from the south, charged with the seductive odor of the sea. Children freshly befurbelowed were gathering for their games under the oaks. Their voices were high and penetrating.

Madame Ratignolle folded her sewing, placing thimble, scissors, and thread all neatly together in the roll, which she pinned securely. She complained of faintness. Mrs. Pontellier flew for the cologne water and a fan. She bathed Madame Ratignolle's face with cologne, while Robert plied the fan with unnecessary vigor.

The spell was soon over, and Mrs. Pontellier could not help wondering if there were not a little imagination responsible for its origin, for the rose tint had never faded from her friend's face.

She stood watching the fair woman walk down the long line of galleries with the grace and majesty which queens are sometimes supposed to possess. Her little ones ran to meet her. Two of them clung about her white skirts, the third she took from its nurse and with a thousand endearments bore it along in her own fond, encircling arms. Though, as everybody well knew, the doctor had forbidden her to lift so much as a pin!

"Are you going bathing?" asked Robert of Mrs. Pontellier. It was not so much a question as a reminder.

"Oh, no," she answered, with a tone of indecision. "I'm tired; I think not." Her glance wandered from his face away toward the Gulf, whose sonorous murmur reached her like a loving but imperative entreaty.

"Oh, come!" he insisted. "You mustn't miss your bath. Come on. The water must be delicious; it will not hurt you. Come."

He reached up for her big, rough straw hat that hung on a peg outside the door, and put it on her head. They descended the steps, and walked away together toward the beach. The sun was low in the west and the breeze was soft and warm.

VI

Edna Pontellier could not have told why, wishing to go to the beach with Robert, she should in the first place have declined, and in the second place have followed in obedience to one of the two contradictory impulses which impelled her.

A certain light was beginning to dawn dimly within her—the light which, showing the way, forbids it.

At that early period it served but to bewilder her. It moved her to dreams, to thoughtfulness, to the shadowy anguish which had overcome her the midnight when she had abandoned herself to tears.

In short, Mrs. Pontellier was beginning to realize her position in the universe as a human being, and to recognize her relations as an individual to the world within and about her. This may seem like a ponderous weight of wisdom to descend upon the soul of a young woman of twenty-eight—perhaps more wisdom than the Holy Ghost is usually pleased to vouchsafe to any woman.

But the beginning of things, of a world especially, is necessarily vague, tangled, chaotic, and exceedingly disturbing. How few of us ever emerge from such beginning! How many souls perish in its tumult!

The voice of the sea is seductive; never ceasing, whispering, clamoring, murmuring, inviting the soul to wander for a spell in abysses of solitude; to lose itself in mazes of inward contemplation.

The voice of the sea speaks to the soul. The touch of the sea is sensuous, enfolding the body in its soft, close embrace.

VII

Mrs. Pontellier was not a woman given to confidences, a characteristic hitherto contrary to her nature. Even as a child she had lived her own small life all within herself. At a very early period she had apprehended instinctively the dual life—that outward existence which conforms, the inward life which questions.

That summer at Grand Isle she began to loosen a little the mantle of reserve that had always enveloped her. There may have been—there must have been—influences, both subtle and apparent, working in their several ways to induce her to do this; but the most obvious was the influence of Adèle Ratignolle. The excessive physical charm of the Creole had first attracted her, for Edna had a sensuous susceptibility to beauty. Then the candor of the woman's whole existence, which everyone might read, and which formed so striking a contrast to her own habitual reserve—this might have furnished a link. Who can tell what metals the gods use in forging the subtle bond which we call sympathy, which we might as well call love.

The two women went away one morning to the beach together, arm in arm, under the huge white sunshade. Edna had prevailed upon Madame Ratignolle to leave the children behind, though she could not induce her to relinquish a diminutive roll of needlework, which Adèle begged to be allowed to slip into the depths of her pocket. In some unaccountable way they had escaped from Robert.

The walk to the beach was no inconsiderable one, consisting as it did of a long, sandy path, upon which a sporadic and tangled growth that bordered it on either side made frequent and unexpected inroads. There were acres of yellow chamomile reaching out on either hand. Further away still, vegetable gardens abounded, with frequent small plantations of orange or lemon trees intervening. The dark green clusters glistened from afar in the sun.

The women were both of goodly height, Madame Ratignolle possessing the more feminine and matronly figure. The charm of Edna Pontellier's physique stole insensibly upon you. The lines of her body were long, clean, and symmetrical; it was a body which occasionally fell into splendid poses; there was no suggestion of the trim, stereotyped fashion plate about it. A casual and indiscriminating observer, in passing, might not cast a second glance upon the figure. But with more feeling and discernment he would have recognized the noble beauty of its modeling, and the graceful severity of poise and movement, which made Edna Pontellier different from the crowd.

She wore a cool muslin that morning—white, with a waving vertical line of brown running through it; also a white linen collar and the big straw hat which she had taken from the peg outside the door. The hat rested any way on her yellow-brown hair, that waved a little, was heavy, and clung close to her head.

Madame Ratignolle, more careful of her complexion, had twined a gauze veil about her head. She wore dogskin gloves, with gauntlets that protected her wrists. She was dressed in pure white, with a fluffiness of ruffles that became her. The draperies and fluttering things which she wore suited her rich, luxuriant beauty as a greater severity of line could not have done.

There were a number of bathhouses along the beach, of rough but solid construction, built with small, protecting galleries facing the water. Each house consisted of two compartments, and each family at Lebrun's possessed a compartment for itself, fitted out with all the essential paraphernalia of the bath and whatever other conveniences the owners might desire. The two women had no intention of bathing; they had just strolled down to the beach for a walk and to be alone and near the water. The Pontellier and Ratignolle compartments adjoined one another under the same roof.

Mrs. Pontellier had brought down her key through force of habit. Unlocking the door of her bathroom she went inside, and soon emerged, bringing a rug, which she spread upon the floor of the gallery, and two huge hair pillows covered with crash,

which she placed against the front of the building.

The two seated themselves there in the shade of the porch, side by side, with their backs against the pillows and their feet extended. Madame Ratignolle removed her veil, wiped her face with a rather delicate handkerchief, and fanned herself with the fan which she always carried suspended somewhere about her person by a long, narrow ribbon. Edna removed her collar and opened her dress at the throat. She took the fan from Madame Ratignolle and began to fan both herself and her companion. It was very warm, and for a while they did nothing but exchange remarks about the heat, the sun, the glare. But there was a breeze blowing, a choppy, stiff wind that whipped the water into froth. It fluttered the skirts of the two women and kept them for a while engaged in adjusting, readjusting, tucking in, securing hairpins and hatpins. A few persons were sporting some distance away in the water. The beach was very still of human sound at that hour. The lady in black was reading her morning devotions on the porch of a neighboring bathhouse. Two young lovers were exchanging their hearts' yearnings beneath the children's tent, which they had found unoccupied.

Edna Pontellier, casting her eyes about, had finally kept them at rest upon the sea. The day was clear and carried the gaze out as far as the blue sky went; there were a few white clouds suspended idly over the horizon. A lateen sail was visible in the direction of Cat Island, and others to the south seemed almost motionless in the far distance.

"Of whom—of what are you thinking?" asked Adèle of her companion, whose countenance she had been watching with a little amused attention, arrested by the absorbed expression which seemed to have seized and fixed every feature into a statuesque repose.

"Nothing," returned Mrs. Pontellier,

with a start, adding at once: "How stupid! But it seems to me it is the reply we make instinctively to such a question. Let me see," she went on, throwing back her head and narrowing her fine eyes till they shone like two vivid points of light. "Let me see. I was really not conscious of thinking of anything; but perhaps I can retrace my thoughts."

"Oh! never mind!" laughed Madame Ratignolle. "I am not quite so exacting. I will let you off this time. It is really too hot to think, especially to think about thinking."

"But for the fun of it," persisted Edna. "First of all, the sight of the water stretching so far away, those motionless sails against the blue sky, made a delicious picture that I just wanted to sit and look at. The hot wind beating in my face made me think—without any connection that I can trace—of a summer day in Kentucky, of a meadow that seemed as big as the ocean to the very little girl walking through the grass, which was higher than her waist. She threw out her arms as if swimming when she walked, beating the tall grass as one strikes out in the water. Oh, I see the connection now!"

"Where were you going that day in Kentucky, walking through the grass?"

"I don't remember now. I was just walking diagonally across a big field. My sunbonnet obstructed the view. I could see only the stretch of green before me, and I felt as if I must walk on forever, without coming to the end of it. I don't remember whether I was frightened or pleased. I must have been entertained."

"Likely as not it was Sunday," she laughed; "and I was running away from prayers, from the Presbyterian service, read in a spirit of gloom by my father that chills me yet to think of."

"And have you been running away from prayers ever since, *ma chère?*" asked Madame Ratignolle, amused.

"No! oh, no!" Edna hastened to say. "I was a little unthinking child in those days,

just following a misleading impulse without question. On the contrary, during one period of my life religion took a firm hold upon me; after I was twelve and until—until—why, I suppose until now, though I never thought much about it—just driven along by habit. But do you know," she broke off, turning her quick eyes upon Madame Ratignolle and leaning forward a little so as to bring her face quite close to that of her companion, "sometimes I feel this summer as if I were walking through the green meadow again; idly, aimlessly, unthinking and unguided."

Madame Ratignolle laid her hand over that of Mrs. Pontellier, which was near her. Seeing that the hand was not withdrawn, she clasped it firmly and warmly. She even stroked it a little, fondly, with the other hand, murmuring in an undertone, "*Pauvre chérie* [Poor dear]."

The action was at first a little confusing to Edna, but she soon lent herself readily to the Creole's gentle caress. She was not accustomed to an outward and spoken expression of affection, either in herself or in others. She and her younger sister, Janet, had quarreled a good deal through force of unfortunate habit. Her older sister, Margaret, was matronly and dignified, probably from having assumed matronly and housewifely responsibilities too early in life, their mother having died when they were quite young. Margaret was not effusive; she was practical. Edna had had an occasional girlfriend, but whether accidentally or not, they seemed to have been all of one type—the self-contained. She never realized that the reserve of her own character had much, perhaps everything, to do with this. Her most intimate friend at school had been one of rather exceptional intellectual gifts, who wrote fine-sounding essays, which Edna admired and strove to imitate; and with her she talked and glowed over the English classics, and sometimes held religious and political controversies.

Edna often wondered at one propensity which sometimes had inwardly disturbed her without causing any outward show or manifestation on her part. At a very early age—perhaps it was when she traversed the ocean of waving grass—she remembered that she had been passionately enamored of a dignified and sad-eyed cavalry officer who visited her father in Kentucky. She could not leave his presence when he was there, nor remove her eyes from his face, which was something like Napoleon's, with a lock of black hair falling across the forehead. But the cavalry officer melted imperceptibly out of her existence.

At another time her affections were deeply engaged by a young gentleman who visited a lady on a neighboring plantation. It was after they went to Mississippi to live. The young man was engaged to be married to the young lady, and they sometimes called upon Margaret, driving over of afternoons in a buggy. Edna was a little miss, just merging into her teens; and the realization that she herself was nothing, nothing, nothing to the engaged young man was a bitter affliction to her. But he, too, went the way of dreams.

She was a grown young woman when she was overtaken by what she supposed to be the climax of her fate. It was when the face and figure of a great tragedian began to haunt her imagination and stir her senses. The persistence of the infatuation lent it an aspect of genuineness. The hopelessness of it colored it with the lofty tones of a great passion.

The picture of the tragedian stood enframed upon her desk. Anyone may possess the portrait of a tragedian without exciting suspicion or comment. (This was a sinister reflection which she cherished.) In the presence of others she expressed admiration for his exalted gifts, as she handed the photograph around and dwelt upon the fidelity of the likeness. When alone she sometimes picked it up and kissed the cold glass passionately.

Her marriage to Léonce Pontellier was purely an accident, in this respect resembling many other marriages which masquerade as the decrees of Fate. It was in the midst of her secret great passion that she met him. He fell in love, as men are in the habit of doing, and pressed his suit with an earnestness and an ardor which left nothing to be desired. He pleased her; his absolute devotion flattered her. She fancied there was a sympathy of thought and taste between them, in which fancy she was mistaken. Add to this the violent opposition of her father and her sister Margaret to her marriage with a Catholic, and we need seek no further for the motives which led her to accept Monsieur Pontellier for her husband.

The acme of bliss, which would have been a marriage with the tragedian, was not for her in this world. As the devoted wife of a man who worshiped her, she felt she would take her place with a certain dignity in the world of reality, closing the portals forever behind her upon the realm of romance and dreams.

But it was not long before the tragedian had gone to join the cavalry officer and the engaged young man and a few others; and Edna found herself face to face with the realities. She grew fond of her husband, realizing with some unaccountable satisfaction that no trace of passion or excessive and fictitious warmth colored her affection, thereby threatening its dissolution.

She was fond of her children in an uneven, impulsive way. She would sometimes gather them passionately to her heart; she would sometimes forget them. The year before they had spent part of the summer with their grandmother Pontellier in Iberville. Feeling secure regarding their happiness and welfare, she did not miss them except with an occasional intense longing. Their absence was a sort of relief, though she did not admit this, even to herself. It seemed to free her of a responsibility which she had blindly assumed and for which Fate had not fitted her.

Edna did not reveal so much as all this to Madame Ratignolle that summer day when they sat with faces turned to the sea. But a good part of it escaped her. She had put her head down on Madame Ratignolle's shoulder. She was flushed and felt intoxicated with the sound of her own voice and the unaccustomed taste of candor. It muddled her like wine, or like a first breath of freedom.

There was the sound of approaching voices. It was Robert, surrounded by a troop of children, searching for them. The two little Pontelliers were with him, and he carried Madame Ratignolle's little girl in his arms. There were other children beside, and two nursemaids followed, looking disagreeable and resigned.

The women at once rose and began to shake out their draperies and relax their muscles. Mrs. Pontellier threw the cushions and rug into the bathhouse. The children all scampered off to the awning, and they stood there in a line, gazing upon the intruding lovers, still exchanging their vows and sighs. The lovers got up, with only a silent protest, and walked slowly away somewhere else.

The children possessed themselves of the tent, and Mrs. Pontellier went over to join them.

Madame Ratignolle begged Robert to accompany her to the house; she complained of cramp in her limbs and stiffness of the joints. She leaned draggingly upon his arm as they walked.

VIII

"Do me a favor, Robert," spoke the pretty woman at his side, almost as soon as she and Robert had started their slow, homeward way. She looked up in his face, leaning on his arm beneath the encircling shadow of the umbrella which he had lifted.

"Granted; as many as you like," he returned, glancing down into her eyes that were full of thoughtfulness and some speculation.

"I only ask for one; let Mrs. Pontellier alone."

"*Tiens!*" he exclaimed, with a sudden, boyish laugh. "*Voilà que Madame Ratignolle est jalouse!* [Well! Madame Ratignolle is jealous!]"

"Nonsense! I'm in earnest; I mean what I say. Let Mrs. Pontellier alone."

"Why?" he asked; himself growing serious at his companion's solicitation.

"She is not one of us; she is not like us. She might make the unfortunate blunder of taking you seriously."

His face flushed with annoyance, and taking off his soft hat he began to beat it impatiently against his leg as he walked. "Why shouldn't she take me seriously?" he demanded sharply. "Am I a comedian, a clown, a jack-in-the-box? Why shouldn't she? You Creoles! I have no patience with you! Am I always to be regarded as a feature of an amusing program? I hope Mrs. Pontellier does take me seriously. I hope she has discernment enough to find in me something besides the *blagueur*. If I thought there was any doubt—"

"Oh, enough, Robert!" she broke into his heated outburst. "You are not thinking of what you are saying. You speak with about as little reflection as we might expect from one of those children down there playing in the sand. If your attentions to any married women here were ever offered with any intention of being convincing, you would not be the gentleman we all know you to be, and you would be unfit to associate with the wives and daughters of the people who trust you."

Madame Ratignolle had spoken what she believed to be the law and the gospel. The young man shrugged his shoulders impatiently.

"Oh! well! That isn't it," slamming his hat down vehemently upon his head. "You ought to feel that such things are not flattering to say to a fellow."

"Should our whole intercourse consist of an exchange of compliments? *Ma foi!* [My faith!]"

"It isn't pleasant to have a woman tell you—" he went on, unheedingly, but breaking off suddenly: "Now if I were like

Arobin—you remember Alcée Arobin and that story of the consul's wife at Biloxi?" And he related the story of Alcée Arobin and the consul's wife; and another about the tenor of the French Opera, who received letters which should never have been written; and still other stories, grave and gay, till Mrs. Pontellier and her possible propensity for taking young men seriously was apparently forgotten.

Madame Ratignolle, when they had regained her cottage, went in to take the hour's rest which she considered helpful. Before leaving her, Robert begged her pardon for the impatience—he called it rudeness—with which he had received her well-meant caution.

"You made one mistake, Adèle," he said, with a light smile; "there is no earthly possibility of Mrs. Pontellier ever taking me seriously. You should have warned me against taking myself seriously. Your advice might then have carried some weight and given me subject for some reflection. *Au revoir*. But you look tired," he added, solicitously. "Would you like a cup of bouillon? Shall I stir you a toddy? Let me mix you a toddy with a drop of Angostura."

She acceded to the suggestion of bouillon, which was grateful and acceptable. He went himself to the kitchen, which was a building apart from the cottages and lying to the rear of the house. And he himself brought her the golden-brown bouillon, in a dainty Sèvres cup, with a flaky cracker or two on the saucer.

She thrust a bare, white arm from the curtain which shielded her open door, and received the cup from his hands. She told him he was a *bon garçon* [good boy], and she meant it. Robert thanked her and turned away toward "the house."

The lovers were just entering the grounds of the *pension*. They were leaning toward each other as the water oaks bent from the sea. There was not a particle of earth beneath their feet. Their heads might have been turned upside down, so absolutely did they tread upon blue ether.

The lady in black, creeping behind them, looked a trifle paler and more jaded than usual. There was no sign of Mrs. Pontellier and the children. Robert scanned the distance for any such apparition. They would doubtless remain away till the dinner hour. The young man ascended to his mother's room. It was situated at the top of the house, made up of odd angles and a queer, sloping ceiling. Two broad dormer windows looked out toward the Gulf, and as far across it as a man's eye might reach. The furnishings of the room were light, cool, and practical.

Madame Lebrun was busily engaged at the sewing machine. A little black girl sat on the floor, and with her hands worked the treadle of the machine. The Creole woman does not take any chances which may be avoided of imperiling her health.

Robert went over and seated himself on the broad sill of one of the dormer windows. He took a book from his pocket and began energetically to read it, judging by the precision and frequency with which he turned the leaves. The sewing machine made a resounding clatter in the room; it was of a ponderous, bygone make. In the lulls, Robert and his mother exchanged bits of desultory conversation.

"Where is Mrs. Pontellier?"

"Down at the beach with the children."

"I promised to lend her the Goncourt. Don't forget to take it down when you go; it's there on the bookshelf over the small table." Clatter, clatter, clatter, bang! for the next five or eight minutes.

"Where is Victor going with the rockaway?"

"The rockaway? Victor?"

"Yes; down there in front. He seems to be getting ready to drive away somewhere."

"Call him." Clatter, clatter!

Robert uttered a shrill, piercing whistle which might have been heard back at the wharf.

"He won't look up."

Madame Lebrun flew to the window. She called "Victor!" She waved a handkerchief and called again. The young fellow below got into the vehicle and started the horse off at a gallop.

Madame Lebrun went back to the machine, crimson with annoyance. Victor was the younger son and brother—a *tête montée* [hothead], with a temper which invited violence and a will which no ax could break.

"Whenever you say the word I'm ready to thrash any amount of reason into him that he's able to hold."

"If your father had only lived!" Clatter, clatter, clatter, clatter, bang! It was a fixed belief with Madame Lebrun that the conduct of the universe and all things pertaining thereto would have been manifestly of a more intelligent and higher order had not Monsieur Lebrun been removed to other spheres during the early years of their married life.

"What do you hear from Montel?" Montel was a middle-aged gentleman whose vain ambition and desire for the past twenty years had been to fill the void which Monsieur Lebrun's taking off had left in the Lebrun household. Clatter, clatter, bang, clatter!

"I have a letter somewhere," looking in the machine drawer and finding the letter in the bottom of the workbasket. "He says to tell you he will be in Vera Cruz the beginning of next month"—clatter, clatter!—"and if you still have the intention of joining him"—bang! clatter, clatter, bang!

"Why didn't you tell me so before, mother? You know I wanted—" Clatter, clatter, clatter!

"Do you see Mrs. Pontellier starting back with the children? She will be in late to luncheon again. She never starts to get ready for luncheon till the last minute." Clatter, clatter! "Where are you going?"

"Where did you say the Goncourt was?"

IX

Every light in the hall was ablaze; every lamp turned as high as it could be without smoking the chimney or threatening explosion. The lamps were fixed at intervals against the wall, encircling the whole room. Someone had gathered orange and lemon branches, and with these fashioned graceful festoons between. The dark green of the branches stood out and glistened against the white muslin curtains which draped the windows, and which puffed, floated, and flapped at the capricious will of a stiff breeze that swept up from the Gulf.

It was Saturday night a few weeks after the intimate conversation held between Robert and Madame Ratignolle on their way from the beach. An unusual number of husbands, fathers, and friends had come down to stay over Sunday; and they were being suitably entertained by their families, with the material help of Madame Lebrun. The dining tables had all been removed to one end of the hall, and the chairs ranged about in rows and in clusters. Each little family group had had its say and exchanged its domestic gossip earlier in the evening. There was now an apparent disposition to relax; to widen the circle of confidences and give a more general tone to the conversation.

Many of the children had been permitted to sit up beyond their usual bedtime. A small band of them were lying on their stomachs on the floor looking at the colored sheets of the comic papers which Mr. Pontellier had brought down. The little Pontellier boys were permitting them to do so, and making their authority felt.

Music, dancing, and a recitation or two were the entertainments furnished, or rather, offered. But there was nothing systematic about the program, no appearance of prearrangement nor even premeditation.

At an early hour in the evening the Farival twins were prevailed upon to play the piano. They were girls of fourteen, always clad in the Virgin's colors, blue and white, having been dedicated to the Blessed Virgin at their baptism. They played a duet from "Zampa," and at the earnest solicitation of everyone present followed it with the overture to "The Poet and the Peasant."

"*Allez vous-en! Sapristi!*" shrieked the parrot outside the door. He was the only being present who possessed sufficient candor to admit that he was not listening to these gracious performances for the first time that summer. Old Monsieur Farival, grandfather of the twins, grew indignant over the interruption, and insisted upon having the bird removed and consigned to regions of darkness. Victor Lebrun objected; and his decrees were as immutable as those of Fate. The parrot fortunately offered no further interruption to the entertainment, the whole venom of his nature apparently having been cherished up and hurled against the twins in that one impetuous outburst.

Later a young brother and sister gave recitations, which everyone present had heard many times at winter evening entertainments in the city.

A little girl performed a skirt dance in the center of the floor. The mother played her accompaniments and at the same time watched her daughter with greedy admiration and nervous apprehension. She need have had no apprehension. The child was mistress of the situation. She had been properly dressed for the occasion in black tulle and black silk tights. Her little neck and arms were bare, and her hair, artificially crimped, stood out like fluffy black plumes over her head. Her poses were full of grace, and her little black-shod toes twinkled as they shot out and upward with a rapidity and suddenness which were bewildering.

But there was no reason why everyone should not dance. Madame Ratignolle could not, so it was she who gaily consented to play for the others. She played very well, keeping excellent waltz time and infusing an expression into the strains which was indeed inspiring. She was keeping up her music on account of the children, she said; because she and her husband both considered it a means of brightening the home and making it attractive.

Almost everyone danced but the twins, who could not be induced to separate during the brief period when one or the other should be whirling around the room in the arms of a man. They might have danced together, but they did not think of it.

The children were sent to bed. Some went submissively; others with shrieks and protests as they were dragged away. They had been permitted to sit up till after the ice cream, which naturally marked the limit of human indulgence.

The ice cream was passed around with cake—gold and silver cake arranged on platters in alternate slices; it had been made and frozen during the afternoon back of the kitchen by two black women, under the supervision of Victor. It was pronounced a great success—excellent if it had only contained a little less vanilla or a little more sugar, if it had been frozen a degree harder, and if the salt might have been kept out of portions of it. Victor was proud of his achievement, and went about recommending it and urging everyone to partake of it to excess.

After Mrs. Pontellier had danced twice with her husband, once with Robert, and once with Monsieur Ratignolle, who was thin and tall and swayed like a reed in the wind when he danced, she went out on the gallery and seated herself on the low windowsill, where she commanded a view of all that went on in the hall and could look out toward the Gulf. There was a soft effulgence in the east. The moon was coming up, and its mystic shimmer was casting a million lights across the distant, restless water.

"Would you like to hear Mademoiselle Reisz play?" asked Robert, coming out on the porch where she was. Of course Edna would like to hear Mademoiselle Reisz play; but she feared it would be useless to entreat her.

"I'll ask her," he said. "I'll tell her that you want to hear her. She likes you. She will come." He turned and hurried away to one of the far cottages, where Mademoiselle Reisz was shuffling away. She was dragging a chair in and out of her room, and at intervals objecting to the crying of a baby, which a nurse in the adjoining cottage was endeavoring to put to sleep. She was a disagreeable little woman, no longer young, who had quarreled with almost everyone, owing to a temper which was self-assertive and a disposition to trample upon the rights of others. Robert prevailed upon her without any too great difficulty.

She entered the hall with him during a lull in the dance. She made an awkward, imperious little bow as she went in. She was a homely woman, with a small wizened face and body and eyes that glowed. She had absolutely no taste in dress, and wore a batch of rusty black lace with a bunch of artificial violets pinned to the side of her hair.

"Ask Mrs. Pontellier what she would like to hear me play," she requested of Robert. She sat perfectly still before the piano, not touching the keys, while Robert carried her message to Edna at the window. A general air of surprise and genuine satisfaction fell upon everyone as they saw the pianist enter. There was a settling down, and a prevailing air of expectancy everywhere. Edna was a trifle embarrassed at being thus signaled out for the imperious little woman's favor. She would not dare to choose, and begged that Mademoiselle Reisz would please herself in her selections.

Edna was what she herself called very fond of music. Musical strains, well rendered, had a way of evoking pictures in her mind. She sometimes liked to sit in the room of mornings when Madame Ratignolle played or practiced. One piece which that lady played Edna had entitled "Solitude." It was a short, plaintive, minor strain. The name of the piece was something else, but she called it "Solitude." When she heard it there came before her imagination the figure of a man standing beside a desolate rock on the seashore. He

was naked. His attitude was one of hopeless resignation as he looked toward a distant bird winging its flight away from him.

Another piece called to her mind a dainty young woman clad in an Empire gown, taking mincing dancing steps as she came down a long avenue between tall hedges. Again, another reminded her of children at play, and still another of nothing on earth but a demure lady stroking a cat.

The very first chords which Mademoiselle Reisz struck upon the piano sent a keen tremor down Mrs. Pontellier's spinal column. It was not the first time she had heard an artist at the piano. Perhaps it was the first time she was ready, perhaps the first time her being was tempered to take an impress of the abiding truth.

She waited for the material pictures which she thought would gather and blaze before her imagination. She waited in vain. She saw no pictures of solitude, of hope, of longing, or of despair. But the very passions themselves were aroused within her soul, swaying it, lashing it, as the waves daily beat upon her splendid body. She trembled, she was choking, and the tears blinded her.

Mademoiselle had finished. She arose, and bowing her stiff, lofty bow, she went away, stopping for neither thanks nor applause. As she passed along the gallery she patted Edna upon the shoulder.

"Well, how did you like my music?" she asked. The young woman was unable to answer; she pressed the hand of the pianist convulsively. Mademoiselle Reisz perceived her agitation and even her tears. She patted her again upon the shoulder as she said:

"You are the only one worth playing for. Those others? Bah!" and she went shuffling and sidling on down the gallery toward her room.

But she was mistaken about "those others." Her playing had aroused a fever of enthusiasm. "What passion!" "What an artist!" "I have always said no one could

play Chopin like Mademoiselle Reisz!"
"That last prelude! Bon Dieu! It shakes a
man!"

It was growing late, and there was a
general disposition to disband. But someone, perhaps it was Robert, thought of a
bath at that mystic hour and under that
mystic moon.

X

At all events Robert proposed it, and
there was not a dissenting voice. There
was not one but was ready to follow when
he led the way. He did not lead the
way, however, he directed the way; and
he himself loitered behind with the lovers,
who had betrayed a disposition to linger
and hold themselves apart. He walked between them, whether with malicious or
mischievous intent was not wholly clear,
even to himself.

The Pontelliers and Ratignolles walked
ahead; the women leaning upon the arms of
their husbands. Edna could hear Robert's
voice behind them, and could sometimes
hear what he said. She wondered why he
did not join them. It was unlike him not
to. Of late he had sometimes held away
from her for an entire day, redoubling his
devotion upon the next and the next, as
though to make up for hours that had been
lost. She missed him the days when some
pretext served to take him away from her,
just as one misses the sun on a cloudy day
without having thought much about the
sun when it was shining.

The people walked in little groups toward the beach. They talked and laughed;
some of them sang. There was a band playing down at Klein's hotel, and the strains
reached them faintly, tempered by the
distance. There were strange, rare odors
abroad—a tangle of the sea smell and of
weeds and damp, new-plowed earth, min-
gled with the heavy perfume of a field of
white blossoms somewhere near. But the
night sat lightly upon the sea and the land.
There was no weight of darkness; there

were no shadows. The white light of the
moon had fallen upon the world like the
mystery and the softness of sleep.

Most of them walked into the water as
though into a native element. The sea was
quiet now, and swelled lazily in broad bil-
lows that melted into one another and did
not break except upon the beach in little
foamy crests that coiled back like slow,
white serpents.

Edna had attempted all summer to learn
to swim. She had received instructions
from both the men and women; in some
instances from the children. Robert had
pursued a system of lessons almost daily;
and he was nearly at the point of discour-
agement in realizing the futility of his efforts. A certain ungovernable dread hung
about her when in the water, unless there
was a hand near by that might reach out
and reassure her.

But that night she was like the little
tottering, stumbling, clutching child, who
of a sudden realizes its powers, and walks
for the first time alone, boldly and with
overconfidence. She could have shouted
for joy. She did shout for joy, as with a
sweeping stroke or two she lifted her body
to the surface of the water.

A feeling of exultation overtook her, as
if some power of significant import had
been given her to control the working of
her body and her soul. She grew daring
and reckless, overestimating her strength.
She wanted to swim far out, where no
woman had swum before.

Her unlooked-for achievement was the
subject of wonder, applause, and admiration. Each one congratulated himself that
his special teachings had accomplished this
desired end.

"How easy it is!" she thought. "It is
nothing," she said aloud; "why did I not
discover before that it was nothing. Think
of the time I have lost splashing about like
a baby!" She would not join the groups in
their sports and bouts, but intoxicated with
her newly conquered power, she swam out
alone.

371

She turned her face seaward to gather in an impression of space and solitude, which the vast expanse of water, meeting and melting with the moonlit sky, conveyed to her excited fancy. As she swam she seemed to be reaching out for the unlimited in which to lose herself.

Once she turned and looked toward the shore, toward the people she had left there. She had not gone any great distance—that is, what would have been a great distance for an experienced swimmer. But to her unaccustomed vision the stretch of water behind her assumed the aspect of a barrier which her unaided strength would never be able to overcome.

A quick vision of death smote her soul, and for a second of time appalled and enfeebled her senses. But by an effort she rallied her staggering faculties and managed to regain the land.

She made no mention of her encounter with death and her flash of terror, except to say to her husband, "I thought I should have perished out there alone."

"You were not so very far, my dear; I was watching you," he told her.

Edna went at once to the bathhouse, and she had put on her dry clothes and was ready to return home before the others had left the water. She started to walk away alone. They all called to her and shouted to her. She waved a dissenting hand, and went on, paying no further heed to their renewed cries which sought to detain her.

"Sometimes I am tempted to think that Mrs. Pontellier is capricious," said Madame Lebrun, who was amusing herself immensely and feared that Edna's abrupt departure might put an end to the pleasure.

"I know she is," assented Mr. Pontellier; "sometimes, not often."

Edna had not traversed a quarter of the distance on her way home before she was overtaken by Robert.

"Did you think I was afraid?" she asked him, without a shade of annoyance.

"No; I knew you weren't afraid."

"Then why did you come? Why didn't you stay out there with the others?"

"I never thought of it."

"Thought of what?"

"Of anything. What difference does it make?"

"I'm very tired," she uttered, complainingly.

"I know you are."

"You don't know anything about it. Why should you know? I never was so exhausted in my life. But it isn't unpleasant. A thousand emotions have swept through me tonight. I don't comprehend half of them. Don't mind what I'm saying; I am just thinking aloud. I wonder if I shall ever be stirred again as Mademoiselle Reisz's playing moved me tonight. I wonder if any night on earth will ever again be like this one. It is like a night in a dream. The people about me are like some uncanny, half-human beings. There must be spirits abroad tonight."

"There are," whispered Robert. "Didn't you know this was the twenty-eighth of August?"

"The twenty-eighth of August?"

"Yes. On the twenty-eighth of August, at the hour of midnight, and if the moon is shining—the moon must be shining—a spirit that has haunted these shores for ages rises up from the Gulf. With its own penetrating vision the spirit seeks some one mortal worthy to hold him company, worthy of being exalted for a few hours into realms of the semi-celestials. His search has always hitherto been fruitless, and he has sunk back, disheartened, into the sea. But tonight he found Mrs. Pontellier. Perhaps he will never wholly release her from the spell. Perhaps she will never again suffer a poor, unworthy earthling to walk in the shadow of her divine presence."

"Don't banter me," she said, wounded at what appeared to be his flippancy. He did not mind the entreaty, but the tone with its delicate note of pathos was like a reproach. He could not explain; he could not tell her that he had penetrated her mood and understood. He said nothing except to offer her his arm, for, by her own admission, she was exhausted. She had been walking alone with her arms hanging limp, letting her white skirts trail along the dewy path. She took his arm, but she did not lean upon it. She let her hand lie listlessly, as though her thoughts were elsewhere—somewhere in advance of her body, and she was striving to overtake them.

Robert assisted her into the hammock which swung from the post before her door out to the trunk of a tree.

"Will you stay out here and wait for Mr. Pontellier?" he asked.

"I'll stay out here. Good night."

"Shall I get you a pillow?"

"There's one here," she said, feeling about, for they were in the shadow.

"It must be soiled; the children have been tumbling it about."

"No matter." And having discovered the pillow, she adjusted it beneath her head. She extended herself in the hammock with a deep breath of relief. She was not a supercilious or an over-dainty woman. She was not much given to reclining in the hammock, and when she did so it was with no catlike suggestion of voluptuous ease, but with a beneficent repose which seemed to invade her whole body.

"Shall I stay with you till Mr. Pontellier comes?" asked Robert, seating himself on the outer edge of one of the steps and taking hold of the hammock rope which was fastened to the post.

"If you wish. Don't swing the hammock. Will you get my white shawl which I left on the windowsill over at the house?"

"Are you chilly?"

"No; but I shall be presently."

"Presently?" he laughed. "Do you know what time it is? How long are you going to stay out here?"

"I don't know. Will you get the shawl?"

"Of course I will," he said, rising. He went over to the house, walking along the grass. She watched his figure pass in and out of the strips of moonlight. It was past midnight. It was very quiet.

When he returned with the shawl she took it and kept it in her hand. She did not put it around her.

"Did you say I should stay till Mr. Pontellier came back?"

"I said you might if you wished to."

He seated himself again and rolled a cigarette, which he smoked in silence. Neither did Mrs. Pontellier speak. No multitude of words could have been more significant than those moments of silence, or more pregnant with the first-felt throbbings of desire.

When the voices of the bathers were heard approaching, Robert said good night. She did not answer him. He thought she was asleep. Again she watched his figure pass in and out of the strips of moonlight as he walked away.

XI

"What are you doing out here, Edna? I thought I should find you in bed," said her husband, when he discovered her lying there. He had walked up with Madame Lebrun and left her at the house. His wife did not reply.

"Are you asleep?" he asked, bending down close to look at her.

"No." Her eyes gleamed bright and intense, with no sleepy shadows, as they looked into his.

"Do you know it is past one o'clock? Come on," and he mounted the steps and went into their room.

"Edna!" called Mr. Pontellier from within, after a few moments had gone by.

"Don't wait for me," she answered. He thrust his head through the door.

"You will take cold out there," he said, irritably. "What folly is this? Why don't you come in?"

"It isn't cold; I have my shawl."

"The mosquitoes will devour you."

"There are no mosquitoes."

She heard him moving about the room;

every sound indicating impatience and irritation. Another time she would have gone in at his request. She would, through habit, have yielded to his desire; not with any sense of submission or obedience to his compelling wishes, but unthinkingly, as we walk, move, sit, stand, go through the daily treadmill of the life which has been portioned out to us.

"Edna, dear, are you not coming in soon?" he asked again, this time fondly, with a note of entreaty.

"No; I am going to stay out here."

"This is more than folly," he blurted out. "I can't permit you to stay out there all night. You must come in the house instantly."

With a writhing motion she settled herself more securely in the hammock. She perceived that her will had blazed up, stubborn and resistant. She could not at that moment have done other than denied and resisted. She wondered if her husband had ever spoken to her like that before, and if she had submitted to his command. Of course she had; she remembered that she had. But she could not realize why or how she should have yielded, feeling as she then did.

"Léonce, go to bed," she said. "I mean to stay out here. I don't wish to go in, and I don't intend to. Don't speak to me like that again; I shall not answer you."

Mr. Pontellier had prepared for bed, but he slipped on an extra garment. He opened a bottle of wine, of which he kept a small and select supply in a buffet of his own. He drank a glass of the wine and went out on the gallery and offered a glass to his wife. She did not wish any. He drew up the rocker, hoisted his slippered feet on the rail, and proceeded to smoke a cigar. He smoked two cigars; then he went inside and drank another glass of wine. Mrs. Pontellier again declined to accept a glass when it was offered to her. Mr. Pontellier once more seated himself with elevated feet, and after a reasonable interval of time smoked some more cigars.

Edna began to feel like one who awakens gradually out of a dream, a delicious, grotesque, impossible dream, to feel again the realities pressing into her soul. The physical need for sleep began to overtake her; the exuberance which had sustained and exalted her spirit left her helpless and yielding to the conditions which crowded her in.

The stillest hour of the night had come, the hour before dawn, when the world seems to hold its breath. The moon hung low, and had turned from silver to copper in the sleeping sky. The old owl no longer hooted, and the water oaks had ceased to moan as they bent their heads.

Edna arose, cramped from lying so long and still in the hammock. She tottered up the steps, clutching feebly at the post before passing into the house.

"Are you coming in, Léonce?" she asked, turning her face toward her husband.

"Yes, dear," he answered, with a glance following a misty puff of smoke. "Just as soon as I have finished my cigar."

XII

She slept but a few hours. They were troubled and feverish hours, disturbed with dreams that were intangible, that eluded her, leaving only an impression upon her half-awakened senses of something unattainable. She was up and dressed in the cool of the early morning. The air was invigorating and steadied somewhat her faculties. However, she was not seeking refreshment or help from any source, either external or from within. She was blindly following whatever impulse moved her, as if she had placed herself in alien hands for direction, and freed her soul of responsibility.

Most of the people at that early hour were still in bed and asleep. A few, who intended to go over to the *Chênière* for mass, were moving about. The lovers, who had laid their plans the night before, were already strolling toward the wharf. The lady

in black, with her Sunday prayer book, velvet and gold-clasped, and her Sunday silver beads, was following them at no great distance. Old Monsieur Farival was up, and was more than half inclined to do anything that suggested itself. He put on his big straw hat, and taking his umbrella from the stand in the hall, followed the lady in black, never overtaking her.

The little negro girl who worked Madame Lebrun's sewing machine was sweeping the galleries with long, absent-minded strokes of the broom. Edna sent her up into the house to awaken Robert.

"Tell him I am going to the *Chênière*. The boat is ready; tell him to hurry."

He had soon joined her. She had never sent for him before. She had never asked for him. She had never seemed to want him before. She did not appear conscious that she had done anything unusual in commanding his presence. He was apparently equally unconscious of anything extraordinary in the situation. But his face was suffused with a quiet glow when he met her.

They went together back to the kitchen to drink coffee. There was no time to wait for any nicety of service. They stood outside the window and the cook passed them their coffee and a roll, which they drank and ate from the windowsill. Edna said it tasted good. She had not thought of coffee nor of anything. He told her he had often noticed that she lacked forethought.

"Wasn't it enough to think of going to the *Chênière* and waking you up?" she laughed. "Do I have to think of everything?—as Léonce says when he's in a bad humor. I don't blame him; he'd never be in a bad humor if it weren't for me."

They took a shortcut across the sands. At a distance they could see the curious procession moving toward the wharf—the lovers, shoulder to shoulder, creeping; the lady in black, gaining steadily upon them; old Monsieur Farival, losing ground inch by inch, and a young barefooted Spanish girl, with a red kerchief on her head and a basket on her arm, bringing up the rear.

Robert knew the girl, and he talked to her a little in the boat. No one present understood what they said. Her name was Mariequita. She had a round, sly, piquant face and pretty black eyes. Her hands were small, and she kept them folded over the handle of her basket. Her feet were broad and coarse. She did not strive to hide them. Edna looked at her feet, and noticed the sand and slime between her brown toes.

Beaudelet grumbled because Mariequita was there, taking up so much room. In reality he was annoyed at having old Monsieur Farival, who considered himself the better sailor of the two. But he would not quarrel with so old a man as Monsieur Farival, so he quarreled with Mariequita. The girl was deprecatory at one moment, appealing to Robert. She was saucy the next, moving her head up and down, making "eyes" at Robert and making "mouths" at Beaudelet.

The lovers were all alone. They saw nothing, they heard nothing. The lady in black was counting her beads for the third time. Old Monsieur Farival talked incessantly of what he knew about handling a boat, and of what Beaudelet did not know on the same subject.

Edna liked it all. She looked Mariequita up and down, from her ugly brown toes to her pretty black eyes, and back again.

"Why does she look at me like that?" inquired the girl of Robert.

"Maybe she thinks you are pretty. Shall I ask her?"

"No. Is she your sweetheart?"

"She's a married lady, and has two children."

"Oh! well! Francisco ran away with Sylvano's wife, who had four children. They took all his money and one of the children and stole his boat."

"Shut up!"

"Does she understand?"

"Oh, hush!"

"Are those two married over there—leaning on each other?"

"Of course not," laughed Robert.

"Of course not," echoed Mariequita, with a serious, confirmatory bob of the head.

The sun was high up and beginning to bite. The swift breeze seemed to Edna to bury the sting of it into the pores of her face and hands. Robert held his umbrella over her.

As they went cutting sidewise through the water, the sails bellied taut, with the wind filling and overflowing them. Old Monsieur Farival laughed sardonically at something as he looked at the sails, and Beaudelet swore at the old man under his breath.

Sailing across the bay to the *Chênière Caminada,* Edna felt as if she were being borne away from some anchorage which had held her fast, whose chains had been loosening—had snapped the night before when the mystic spirit was abroad, leaving her free to drift whithersoever she chose to set her sails. Robert spoke to her incessantly; he no longer noticed Mariequita. The girl had shrimps in her bamboo basket. They were covered with Spanish moss. She beat the moss down impatiently, and muttered to herself sullenly.

"Let us go to Grande Terre tomorrow?" said Robert in a low voice.

"What shall we do there?"

"Climb up the hill to the old fort and look at the little wriggling gold snakes, and watch the lizards sun themselves."

She gazed away toward Grande Terre and thought she would like to be alone there with Robert, in the sun, listening to the ocean's roar and watching the slimy lizards writhe in and out among the ruins of the old fort.

"And the next day or the next we can sail to the Bayou Brulow," he went on.

"What shall we do there?"

"Anything—cast bait for fish."

"No; we'll go back to Grande Terre. Let the fish alone."

"We'll go wherever you like," he said. "I'll have Tonie come over and help me patch and trim my boat. We shall not need Beaudelet nor anyone. Are you afraid of the pirogue?"

"Oh, no."

"Then I'll take you some night in the pirogue when the moon shines. Maybe your Gulf spirit will whisper to you in which of these islands the treasures are hidden—direct you to the very spot, perhaps."

"And in a day we should be rich!" she laughed. "I'd give it all to you, the pirate gold and every bit of treasure we could dig up. I think you would know how to spend it. Pirate gold isn't a thing to be hoarded or utilized. It is something to squander and throw to the four winds, for the fun of seeing the golden specks fly."

"We'd share it, and scatter it together," he said. His face flushed.

They all went together up to the quaint little Gothic church of Our Lady of Lourdes, gleaming all brown and yellow with paint in the sun's glare.

Only Beaudelet remained behind, tinkering at his boat, and Mariequita walked away with her basket of shrimps, casting a look of childish ill humor and reproach at Robert from the corner of her eye.

XIII

A feeling of oppression and drowsiness overcame Edna during the service. Her head began to ache, and the lights on the altar swayed before her eyes. Another time she might have made an effort to regain her composure; but her one thought was to quit the stifling atmosphere of the church and reach the open air. She arose, climbing over Robert's feet with a muttered apology. Old Monsieur Farival, flurried, curious, stood up, but upon seeing that Robert had followed Mrs. Pontellier, he sank back into his seat. He whispered an anxious inquiry of the lady in black, who did not notice him or reply, but kept her eyes fastened upon the pages of her velvet prayer book.

"I felt giddy and almost overcome,"

Edna said, lifting her hands instinctively to her head and pushing her straw hat up from her forehead. "I couldn't have stayed through the service." They were outside in the shadow of the church. Robert was full of solicitude.

"It was folly to have thought of going in the first place, let alone staying. Come over to Madame Antoine's; you can rest there." He took her arm and led her away, looking anxiously and continuously down into her face.

How still it was, with only the voice of the sea whispering through the reeds that grew in the saltwater pools! The long line of little gray, weather-beaten houses nestled peacefully among the orange trees. It must always have been God's day on that low, drowsy island, Edna thought. They stopped, leaning over a jagged fence made of sea-drift, to ask for water. A youth, a mild-faced Acadian, was drawing water from the cistern, which was nothing more than a rusty buoy, with an opening on one side, sunk in the ground. The water which the youth handed to them in a tin pail was not cold to taste, but it was cool to her heated face, and it greatly revived and refreshed her.

Madame Antoine's cot was at the far end of the village. She welcomed them with all the native hospitality, as she would have opened her door to let the sunlight in. She was fat, and walked heavily and clumsily across the floor. She could speak no English, but when Robert made her understand that the lady who accompanied him was ill and desired to rest, she was all eagerness to make Edna feel at home and to dispose of her comfortably.

The whole place was immaculately clean, and the big, four-posted bed, snow-white, invited one to repose. It stood in a small side room which looked out across a narrow grass plot toward the shed, where there was a disabled boat lying keel upward.

Madame Antoine had not gone to mass. Her son Tonie had, but she supposed he would soon be back, and she invited Robert to be seated and wait for him. But he went and sat outside the door and smoked. Madame Antoine busied herself in the large front room preparing dinner. She was boiling mullets over a few red coals in the huge fireplace.

Edna, left alone in the little side room, loosened her clothes, removing the greater part of them. She bathed her face, her neck, and arms in the basin that stood between the windows. She took off her shoes and stockings and stretched herself in the very center of the high, white bed. How luxurious it felt to rest thus in a strange, quaint bed, with its sweet country odor of laurel lingering about the sheets and mattress! She stretched her strong limbs that ached a little. She ran her fingers through her loosened hair for a while. She looked at her round arms as she held them straight up and rubbed them one after the other, observing closely, as if it were something she saw for the first time, the fine, firm quality and texture of her flesh. She clasped her hands easily above her head, and it was thus she fell asleep.

She slept lightly at first, half awake and drowsily attentive to the things about her. She could hear Madame Antoine's heavy, scraping tread as she walked back and forth on the sanded floor. Some chickens were clucking outside the windows, scratching for bits of gravel in the grass. Later she half heard the voices of Robert and Tonie talking under the shed. She did not stir. Even her eyelids rested numb and heavily over her sleepy eyes. The voices went on—Tonie's slow, Acadian drawl, Robert's quick, soft, smooth French. She understood French imperfectly unless directly addressed, and the voices were only part of the other drowsy, muffled sounds lulling her senses.

When Edna awoke it was with the conviction that she had slept long and soundly. The voices were hushed under the shed. Madame Antoine's step was no longer to be heard in the adjoining room. Even the chickens had gone elsewhere to scratch and cluck. The mosquito bar was drawn over her; the old woman had come in while she slept and let down the bar. Edna arose quietly from the bed, and looking between the curtains of the window, she saw by the slanting rays of the sun that the afternoon was far advanced. Robert was out there under the shed, reclining in the shade against the sloping keel of the overturned boat. He was reading from a book. Tonie was no longer with him. She wondered what had become of the rest of the party. She peeped out at him two or three times as she stood washing herself in the little basin between the windows.

Madame Antoine had laid some coarse, clean towels upon a chair, and had placed a box of *poudre de riz* [rice powder] within easy reach. Edna dabbed the powder upon her nose and cheeks as she looked at herself closely in the little distorted mirror which hung on the wall above the basin. Her eyes were bright and wide awake and her face glowed.

When she had completed her toilet she walked into the adjoining room. She was very hungry. No one was there. But there was a cloth spread upon the table that stood against the wall, and a cover was laid for one, with a crusty brown loaf and a bottle of wine beside the plate. Edna bit a piece from the brown loaf, tearing it with her strong, white teeth. She poured some of the wine into the glass and drank it down. Then she went softly out of doors, and plucking an orange from the low-hanging bough of a tree, threw it at Robert, who did not know she was awake and up.

An illumination broke over his whole face when he saw her and joined her under the orange tree.

"How many years have I slept?" she inquired. "The whole island seems changed. A new race of beings must have sprung up, leaving only you and me as past relics. How many ages ago did Madame Antoine and Tonie die? and when did our people from Grand Isle disappear from the earth?"

He familiarly adjusted a ruffle upon her shoulder.

"You have slept precisely one hundred years. I was left here to guard your slumbers; and for one hundred years I have been out under the shed reading a book. The only evil I couldn't prevent was to keep a broiled fowl from drying up."

"If it has turned to stone, still will I eat it," said Edna, moving with him into the house. "But really, what has become of Monsieur Farival and the others?"

"Gone hours ago. When they found that you were sleeping they thought it best not to awake you. Anyway, I wouldn't have let them. What was I here for?"

"I wonder if Léonce will be uneasy!" she speculated, as she seated herself at table.

"Of course not; he knows you are with me," Robert replied, as he busied himself among sundry pans and covered dishes which had been left standing on the hearth.

"Where are Madame Antoine and her son?" asked Edna.

"Gone to Vespers, and to visit some friends, I believe. I am to take you back in Tonie's boat whenever you are ready to go."

He stirred the smoldering ashes till the broiled fowl began to sizzle afresh. He served her with no mean repast, dripping the coffee anew and sharing it with her. Madame Antoine had cooked little else than the mullets, but while Edna slept Robert had foraged the island. He was childishly gratified to discover her appetite, and to see the relish with which she ate the food which he had procured for her.

"Shall we go right away?" she asked, after draining her glass and brushing together the crumbs of the crusty loaf.

"The sun isn't as low as it will be in two hours," he answered.

"The sun will be gone in two hours."

"Well, let it go; who cares!"

They waited a good while under the orange trees, till Madame Antoine came back, panting, waddling, with a thousand apologies to explain her absence. Tonie did not dare to return. He was shy, and would not willingly face any woman except his mother.

It was very pleasant to stay there under the orange trees, while the sun dipped lower and lower, turning the western sky to flaming copper and gold. The shadows lengthened and crept out like stealthy, grotesque monsters across the grass.

Edna and Robert both sat upon the ground—that is, he lay upon the ground beside her, occasionally picking at the hem of her muslin gown.

Madame Antoine seated her fat body, broad and squat, upon a bench beside the door. She had been talking all the afternoon, and had wound herself up to the storytelling pitch.

And what stories she told them! But twice in her life she had left the *Chênière Caminada,* and then for the briefest span. All her years she had squatted and waddled there upon the island, gathering legends of the Baratarians and the sea. The night came on, with the moon to lighten it. Edna could hear the whispering voices of dead men and the click of muffled gold.

When she and Robert stepped into Tonie's boat, with the red lateen sail, misty spirit forms were prowling in the shadows and among the reeds, and upon the water were phantom ships, speeding to cover.

XIV

The youngest boy, Etienne, had been very naughty, Madame Ratignolle said, as she delivered him into the hands of his mother. He had been unwilling to go to bed and had made a scene; whereupon she had taken charge of him and pacified him as well as she could. Raoul had been in bed and asleep for two hours.

The youngster was in his long white nightgown, that kept tripping him up as Madame Ratignolle led him along by the hand. With the other chubby fist he rubbed his eyes, which were heavy with sleep and ill humor. Edna took him in her arms, and

seating herself in the rocker, began to coddle and caress him, calling him all manner of tender names, soothing him to sleep.

It was not more than nine o'clock. No one had yet gone to bed but the children.

Léonce had been very uneasy at first, Madame Ratignolle said, and had wanted to start at once for the *Chênière.* But Monsieur Farival had assured him that his wife was only overcome with sleep and fatigue, that Tonie would bring her safely back later in the day; and he had thus been dissuaded from crossing the bay. He had gone over to Klein's, looking up some cotton broker whom he wished to see in regard to securities, exchanges, stocks, bonds, or something of the sort, Madame Ratignolle did not remember what. He said he would not remain away late. She herself was suffering from heat and oppression, she said. She carried a bottle of salts and a large fan. She would not consent to remain with Edna, for Monsieur Ratignolle was alone, and he detested above all things to be left alone.

When Etienne had fallen asleep Edna bore him into the back room, and Robert went and lifted the mosquito bar that she might lay the child comfortably in his bed. The quadroon had vanished. When they emerged from the cottage Robert bade Edna good night.

"Do you know we have been together the whole livelong day, Robert—since early this morning?" she said at parting.

"All but the hundred years when you were sleeping. Good night."

He pressed her hand and went away in the direction of the beach. He did not join any of the others, but walked alone toward the Gulf.

Edna stayed outside, awaiting her husband's return. She had no desire to sleep or to retire; nor did she feel like going over to sit with the Ratignolles, or to join Madame Lebrun and a group whose animated voices reached her as they sat in conversation before the house. She let her mind wander back over her stay at Grand

Isle; and she tried to discover wherein this summer had been different from any and every other summer of her life. She could only realize that she herself—her present self—was in some way different from the other self. That she was seeing with different eyes and making the acquaintance of new conditions in herself that colored and changed her environment, she did not yet suspect.

She wondered why Robert had gone away and left her. It did not occur to her to think he might have grown tired of being with her the livelong day. She was not tired, and she felt that he was not. She regretted that he had gone. It was so much more natural to have him stay when he was not absolutely required to leave her.

As Edna waited for her husband she sang low a little song that Robert had sung as they crossed the bay. It began with "Ah! *si tu savais* [if you knew]," and every verse ended with "*si tu savais.*"

Robert's voice was not pretentious. It was musical and true. The voice, the notes, the whole refrain haunted her memory.

XV

When Edna entered the dining room one evening a little late, as was her habit, an unusually animated conversation seemed to be going on. Several persons were talking at once, and Victor's voice was predominating, even over that of his mother. Edna had returned late from her bath, had dressed in some haste, and her face was flushed. Her head, set off by her dainty white gown, suggested a rich, rare blossom. She took her seat at table between old Monsieur Farival and Madame Ratignolle.

As she seated herself and was about to begin to eat her soup, which had been served when she entered the room, several persons informed her simultaneously that Robert was going to Mexico. She laid her spoon down and looked about her bewildered. He had been with her, reading to her all the morning, and had never even mentioned such a place as Mexico. She had not seen him during the afternoon; she had heard someone say he was at the house, upstairs with his mother. This she had thought nothing of, though she was surprised when he did not join her later in the afternoon, when she went down to the beach.

She looked across at him, where he sat beside Madame Lebrun, who presided. Edna's face was a blank picture of bewilderment, which she never thought of disguising. He lifted his eyebrows with the pretext of a smile as he returned her glance. He looked embarrassed and uneasy.

"When is he going?" she asked of everybody in general, as if Robert were not there to answer for himself.

"Tonight!" "This very evening!" "Did you ever!" "What possesses him!" were some of the replies she gathered, uttered simultaneously in French and English.

"Impossible!" she exclaimed. "How can a person start off from Grand Isle to Mexico at a moment's notice, as if he were going over to Klein's or to the wharf or down to the beach?"

"I said all along I was going to Mexico; I've been saying so for years!" cried Robert, in an excited and irritable tone, with the air of a man defending himself against a swarm of stinging insects.

Madame Lebrun knocked on the table with her knife handle.

"Please let Robert explain why he is going, and why he is going tonight," she called out. "Really, this table is getting to be more and more like Bedlam every day, with everybody talking at once. Sometimes—I hope God will forgive me—but positively, sometimes I wish Victor would lose the power of speech."

Victor laughed sardonically as he thanked his mother for her holy wish, of which he failed to see the benefit to anybody, except that it might afford her a more ample opportunity and license to talk herself.

Monsieur Farival thought that Victor should have been taken out in mid-ocean in his earliest youth and drowned. Victor thought there would be more logic in thus disposing of old people with an established claim for making themselves universally obnoxious. Madame Lebrun grew a trifle hysterical; Robert called his brother some sharp, hard names.

"There's nothing much to explain, mother," he said; though he explained, nevertheless—looking chiefly at Edna— that he could only meet the gentleman whom he intended to join at Vera Cruz by taking such and such a steamer, which left New Orleans on such a day; that Beaudelet was going out with his lugger-load of vegetables that night, which gave him an opportunity of reaching the city and making his vessel in time.

"But when did you make up your mind to all this?" demanded Monsieur Farival.

"This afternoon," returned Robert, with a shade of annoyance.

"At what time this afternoon?" persisted the old gentleman, with nagging determination, as if he were cross-questioning a criminal in a court of justice.

"At four o'clock this afternoon, Monsieur Farival," Robert replied, in a high voice and with a lofty air, which reminded Edna of some gentleman on the stage.

She had forced herself to eat most of her soup, and now she was picking the flaky bits of a *court bouillon* [fish prepared in a wine sauce] with her fork.

The lovers were profiting by the general conversation on Mexico to speak in whispers of matters which they rightly considered were interesting to no one but themselves. The lady in black had once received a pair of prayer beads of curious workmanship from Mexico, with very special indulgence attached to them, but she had never been able to ascertain whether the indulgence extended outside the Mexican border. Father Fochel of the Cathedral had attempted to explain it; but he had not done so to her satisfaction. And she

begged that Robert would interest himself, and discover, if possible, whether she was entitled to the indulgence accompanying the remarkably curious Mexican prayer beads.

Madame Ratignolle hoped that Robert would exercise extreme caution in dealing with the Mexicans, who, she considered, were a treacherous people, unscrupulous and revengeful. She trusted she did them no injustice in thus condemning them as a race. She had known personally but one Mexican, who made and sold excellent tamales, and whom she would have trusted implicitly, so soft-spoken was he. One day he was arrested for stabbing his wife. She never knew whether he had been hanged or not.

Victor had grown hilarious, and was attempting to tell an anecdote about a Mexican girl who served chocolate one winter in a restaurant in Dauphine Street. No one would listen to him but old Monsieur Farival, who went into convulsions over the droll story.

Edna wondered if they had all gone mad, to be talking and clamoring at that rate. She herself could think of nothing to say about Mexico or the Mexicans.

"At what time do you leave?" she asked Robert.

"At ten," he told her. "Beaudelet wants to wait for the moon."

"Are you all ready to go?"

"Quite ready. I shall only take a hand-bag, and shall pack my trunk in the city."

He turned to answer some question put to him by his mother, and Edna, having finished her black coffee, left the table.

She went directly to her room. The little cottage was close and stuffy after leaving the outer air. But she did not mind; there appeared to be a hundred different things demanding her attention indoors. She began to set the toilet-stand to rights, grumbling at the negligence of the quadroon, who was in the adjoining room putting the children to bed. She gathered together stray garments that were hanging on the backs of chairs, and put each where it belonged in closet or bureau drawer. She changed her gown for a more comfortable and commodious wrapper. She rearranged her hair, combing and brushing it with unusual energy. Then she went in and assisted the quadroon in getting the boys to bed.

They were very playful and inclined to talk—to do anything but lie quiet and go to sleep. Edna sent the quadroon away to her supper and told her she need not return. Then she sat and told the children a story. Instead of soothing it excited them, and added to their wakefulness. She left them in heated argument, speculating about the conclusion of the tale which their mother promised to finish the following night.

The little black girl came in to say that Madame Lebrun would like to have Mrs. Pontellier go and sit with them over at the house till Mr. Robert went away. Edna returned answer that she had already undressed, that she did not feel quite well, but perhaps she would go over to the house later. She started to dress again, and got as far advanced as to remove her *peignoir*. But changing her mind once more she resumed the *peignoir,* and went outside and sat down before her door. She was overheated and irritable, and fanned herself energetically for a while. Madame Ratignolle came down to discover what was the matter.

"All that noise and confusion at the table must have upset me," replied Edna, "and moreover, I hate shocks and surprises. The idea of Robert starting off in such a ridiculously sudden and dramatic way! As if it were a matter of life and death! Never saying a word about it all morning when he was with me."

"Yes," agreed Madame Ratignolle. "I think it was showing us all—you especially—very little consideration. It wouldn't have surprised me in any of the others; those Lebruns are all given to heroics. But I must say I should never have expected such a thing from Robert. Are

you not coming down? Come on, dear; it doesn't look friendly."

"No," said Edna, a little sullenly. "I can't go to the trouble of dressing again; I don't feel like it."

"You needn't dress; you look all right; fasten a belt around your waist. Just look at me!"

"No," persisted Edna; "but you go on. Madame Lebrun might be offended if we both stayed away."

Madame Ratignolle kissed Edna goodnight, and went away, being in truth rather desirous of joining in the general and animated conversation which was still in progress concerning Mexico and the Mexicans.

Somewhat later Robert came up, carrying his handbag.

"Aren't you feeling well?" he asked.

"Oh, well enough. Are you going right away?"

He lit a match and looked at his watch. "In twenty minutes," he said. The sudden and brief flare of the match emphasized the darkness for a while. He sat down upon a stool which the children had left out on the porch.

"Get a chair," said Edna.

"This will do," he replied. He put on his soft hat and nervously took it off again, and wiping his face with his handkerchief, complained of the heat.

"Take the fan," said Edna, offering it to him.

"Oh, no! Thank you. It does no good; you have to stop fanning some time, and feel all the more uncomfortable afterward."

"That's one of the ridiculous things which men always say. I have never known one to speak otherwise of fanning. How long will you be gone?"

"Forever, perhaps. I don't know. It depends upon a good many things."

"Well, in case it shouldn't be forever, how long will it be?"

"I don't know."

"This seems to me perfectly preposter-

ous and uncalled for. I don't like it. I don't understand your motive for silence and mystery, never saying a word to me about it this morning." He remained silent, not offering to defend himself. He only said, after a moment:

"Don't part from me in any ill humor. I never knew you to be out of patience with me before."

"I don't want to part in any ill humor," she said. "But can't you understand? I've grown used to seeing you, to having you with me all the time, and your action seems unfriendly, even unkind. You don't even offer an excuse for it. Why, I was planning to be together, thinking of how pleasant it would be to see you in the city next winter."

"So was I," he blurted. "Perhaps that's the—" He stood up suddenly and held out his hand. "Good-bye, my dear Mrs. Pontellier; good-bye. You won't—I hope you won't completely forget me." She clung to his hand, striving to detain him.

"Write to me when you get there, won't you, Robert?" she entreated.

"I will, thank you. Good-bye."

How unlike Robert! The merest acquaintance would have said something more emphatic than "I will, thank you; good-bye," to such a request.

He had evidently already taken leave of the people over at the house, for he descended the steps and went to join Beaudelet, who was out there with an oar across his shoulder waiting for Robert. They walked away in the darkness. She could only hear Beaudelet's voice; Robert had apparently not even spoken a word of greeting to his companion.

Edna bit her handkerchief convulsively, striving to hold back and to hide, even from herself as she would have hidden from another, the emotion which was troubling—tearing—her. Her eyes were brimming with tears.

For the first time she recognized the symptoms of infatuation which she had felt incipiently as a child, as a girl in her ear-

liest teens, and later as a young woman. The recognition did not lessen the reality, the poignancy of the revelation by any suggestion or promise of instability. The past was nothing to her; offered no lesson which she was willing to heed. The future was a mystery which she never attempted to penetrate. The present alone was significant; was hers, to torture her as it was doing then with the biting conviction that she had lost that which she had held, that she had been denied that which her impassioned, newly awakened being demanded.

XVI

"Do you miss your friend greatly?" asked Mademoiselle Reisz one morning as she came creeping up behind Edna, who had just left her cottage on her way to the beach. She spent much of her time in the water since she had acquired finally the art of swimming. As their stay at Grand Isle drew near its close, she felt that she could not give too much time to a diversion which afforded her the only real pleasurable moments that she knew. When Mademoiselle Reisz came and touched her upon the shoulder and spoke to her, the woman seemed to echo the thought which was ever in Edna's mind; or, better, the feeling which constantly possessed her.

Robert's going had some way taken the brightness, the color, the meaning out of everything. The conditions of her life were in no way changed, but her whole existence was dulled, like a faded garment which seems to be no longer worth wearing. She sought him everywhere—in others whom she induced to talk about him. She went up in the mornings to Madame Lebrun's room, braving the clatter of the old sewing machine. She sat there and chatted at intervals as Robert had done. She gazed around the room at the pictures and photographs hanging upon the wall, and discovered in some corner an old family album, which she examined with the keenest interest, appealing to Madame

Lebrun for enlightenment concerning the many figures and faces which she discovered between its pages.

There was a picture of Madame Lebrun with Robert as a baby, seated in her lap, a round-faced infant with a fist in his mouth. The eyes alone in the baby suggested the man. And that was he also in kilts, at the age of five, wearing long curls and holding a whip in his hand. It made Edna laugh, and she laughed, too, at the portrait in his first long trousers; while another interested her, taken when he left for college, looking thin, long-faced, with eyes full of fire, ambition, and great intentions. But there was no recent picture, none which suggested the Robert who had gone away five days ago, leaving a void and wilderness behind him.

"Oh, Robert stopped having his pictures taken when he had to pay for them himself! He found wiser use for his money, he says," explained Madame Lebrun. She had a letter from him, written before he left New Orleans. Edna wished to see the letter, and Madame Lebrun told her to look for it either on the table or the dresser, or perhaps it was on the mantelpiece.

The letter was on the bookshelf. It possessed the greatest interest and attraction for Edna; the envelope, its size and shape, the postmark, the handwriting. She examined every detail of the outside before opening it. There were only a few lines, setting forth that he would leave the city that afternoon, that he had packed his trunk in good shape, that he was well, and sent her his love and begged to be affectionately remembered to all. There was no special message to Edna except a postscript saying that if Mrs. Pontellier desired to finish the book which he had been reading to her, his mother would find it in his room, among other books there on the table. Edna experienced a pang of jealousy because he had written to his mother rather than to her.

Everyone seemed to take for granted that she missed him. Even her husband, when he came down the Saturday following Robert's departure, expressed regret that he had gone.

"How do you get on without him, Edna?" he asked.

"It's very dull without him," she admitted. Mr. Pontellier had seen Robert in the city, and Edna asked him a dozen questions or more. Where had they met? On Carondelet Street, in the morning. They had gone "in" and had a drink and a cigar together. What had they talked about? Chiefly about his prospects in Mexico, which Mr. Pontellier thought were promising. How did he look? How did he seem—grave, or gay, or how? Quite cheerful, and wholly taken up with the idea of his trip, which Mr. Pontellier found altogether natural in a young fellow about to seek fortune and adventure in a strange, queer country.

Edna tapped her foot impatiently, and wondered why the children persisted in playing in the sun when they might be under the trees. She went down and led them out of the sun, scolding the quadroon for not being more attentive.

It did not strike her as in the least grotesque that she should be making of Robert the object of conversation and leading her husband to speak of him. The sentiment which she entertained for Robert in no way resembled that which she felt for her husband, or had ever felt, or ever expected to feel. She had all her life long been accustomed to harbor thoughts and emotions which never voiced themselves. They had never taken the form of struggles. They belonged to her and were her own, and she entertained the conviction that she had a right to them and that they concerned no one but herself. Edna had once told Madame Ratignolle that she would never sacrifice herself for her children, or for anyone. Then had followed a rather heated argument; the two women did not appear to understand each other or to be talking the same language. Edna tried to appease her friend, to explain.

"I would give up the unessential; I

would give my money, I would give my life for my children; but I wouldn't give myself. I can't make it more clear; it's only something which I am beginning to comprehend, which is revealing itself to me."

"I don't know what you would call the essential, or what you mean by the unessential," said Madame Ratignolle, cheerfully; "but a woman who would give her life for her children could do no more than that—your Bible tells you so. I'm sure I couldn't do more than that."

"Oh, yes you could!" laughed Edna.

She was not surprised at Mademoiselle Reisz's question the morning that lady, following her to the beach, tapped her on the shoulder and asked if she did not greatly miss her young friend.

"Oh, good morning, Mademoiselle; is it you? Why, of course I miss Robert. Are you going down to bathe?"

"Why should I go down to bathe at the very end of the season when I haven't been in the surf all summer," replied the woman, disagreeably.

"I beg your pardon," offered Edna, in some embarrassment, for she should have remembered that Mademoiselle Reisz's avoidance of the water had furnished a theme for much pleasantry. Some among them thought it was on account of her false hair, or the dread of getting the violets wet, while others attributed it to the natural aversion for water sometimes believed to accompany the artistic temperament. Mademoiselle offered Edna some chocolates in a paper bag, which she took from her pocket, by way of showing that she bore no ill feeling. She habitually ate chocolates for their sustaining quality; they contained much nutriment in small compass, she said. They saved her from starvation, as Madame Lebrun's table was utterly impossible; and no one save so impertinent a woman as Madame Lebrun could think of offering such food to people and requiring them to pay for it.

"She must feel very lonely without her son," said Edna, desiring to change the subject. "Her favorite son, too. It must have been quite hard to let him go."

Mademoiselle laughed maliciously.

"Her favorite son! Oh, dear! Who could have been imposing such a tale upon you? Aline Lebrun lives for Victor, and for Victor alone. She has spoiled him into the worthless creature he is. She worships him and the ground he walks on. Robert is very well in a way, to give up all the money he can earn to the family, and keep the barest pittance for himself. Favorite son, indeed! I miss the poor fellow myself, my dear. I liked to see him and to hear him about the place—the only Lebrun who is worth a pinch of salt. He comes to see me often in the city. I like to play to him. That Victor! hanging would be too good for him. It's a wonder Robert hasn't beaten him to death long ago."

"I thought he had great patience with his brother," offered Edna, glad to be talking about Robert, no matter what was said.

"Oh! he thrashed him well enough a year or two ago," said Mademoiselle. "It was about a Spanish girl, whom Victor considered that he had some sort of claim upon. He met Robert one day talking to the girl, or walking with her, or bathing with her, or carrying her basket—I don't remember what—and he became so insulting and abusive that Robert gave him a thrashing on the spot that has kept him comparatively in order for a good while. It's about time he was getting another."

"Was her name Mariequita?" asked Edna.

"Mariequita—yes, that was it; Mariequita. I had forgotten. Oh, she's a sly one, and a bad one, that Mariequita!"

Edna looked down at Mademoiselle Reisz and wondered how she could have listened to her venom so long. For some reason she felt depressed, almost unhappy. She had not intended to go into the water; but she donned her bathing suit, and left Mademoiselle alone, seated under the shade of the children's tent. The water was growing cooler as the season advanced.

Edna plunged and swam about with an abandon that thrilled and invigorated her. She remained a long time in the water, half hoping that Mademoiselle Reisz would not wait for her.

But Mademoiselle waited. She was very amiable during the walk back, and raved much over Edna's appearance in her bathing suit. She talked about music. She hoped that Edna would go to see her in the city, and wrote her address with the stub of a pencil on a piece of card which she found in her pocket.

"When do you leave?" asked Edna.

"Next Monday; and you?"

"The following week," answered Edna, adding, "It has been a pleasant summer, hasn't it, Mademoiselle?"

"Well," agreed Mademoiselle Reisz, with a shrug, "rather pleasant, if it hadn't been for the mosquitoes and the Farival twins."

XVII

The Pontelliers possessed a very charming home on Esplanade Street in New Orleans. It was a large, double cottage, with a broad front veranda, whose round, fluted columns supported the sloping roof. The house was painted a dazzling white; the outside shutters, or jalousies, were green. In the yard, which was kept scrupulously neat, were flowers and plants of every description which flourishes in South Louisiana. Within doors the appointments were perfect after the conventional type. The softest carpets and rugs covered the floors; rich and tasteful draperies hung at doors and windows. There were paintings, selected with judgment and discrimination, upon the walls. The cut glass, the silver, the heavy damask which daily appeared upon the table were the envy of many women whose husbands were less generous than Mr. Pontellier.

Mr. Pontellier was very fond of walking about his house examining its various appointments and details, to see that nothing was amiss. He greatly valued his posses-sions, chiefly because they were his, and derived genuine pleasure from contemplating a painting, a statuette, a rare lace curtain—no matter what—after he had bought it and placed it among his household gods.

On Tuesday afternoons—Tuesday being Mrs. Pontellier's reception day—there was a constant stream of callers—women who came in carriages or in the streetcars, or walked when the air was soft and distance permitted. A light-colored mulatto boy, in dress coat and bearing a diminutive silver tray for the reception of cards, admitted them. A maid, in white fluted cap, offered the callers liqueur, coffee, or chocolate, as they might desire. Mrs. Pontellier, attired in a handsome reception gown, remained in the drawing room the entire afternoon receiving her visitors. Men sometimes called in the evening with their wives.

This had been the program which Mrs. Pontellier had religiously followed since her marriage, six years before. Certain evenings during the week she and her husband attended the opera or sometimes the play.

Mr. Pontellier left his home in the mornings between nine and ten o'clock, and rarely returned before half-past six or seven in the evening—dinner being served at half-past seven.

He and his wife seated themselves at table one Tuesday evening, a few weeks after their return from Grand Isle. They were alone together. The boys were being put to bed; the patter of their bare, escaping feet could be heard occasionally, as well as the pursuing voice of the quadroon, lifted in mild protest and entreaty. Mrs. Pontellier did not wear her usual Tuesday reception gown; she was in ordinary house dress. Mr. Pontellier, who was observant about such things, noticed it, as he served the soup and handed it to the boy in waiting.

"Tired out, Edna? Whom did you have? Many callers?" he asked. He tasted his soup and began to season it with pepper, salt, vinegar, mustard—everything within reach.

"There were a good many," replied Edna, who was eating her soup with evident satisfaction. "I found their cards when I got home; I was out."

"Out!" exclaimed her husband, with something like genuine consternation in his voice as he laid down the vinegar cruet and looked at her through his glasses. "Why, what could have taken you out on Tuesday? What did you have to do?"

"Nothing. I simply felt like going out, and I went out."

"Well, I hope you left some suitable excuse," said her husband, somewhat appeased, as he added a dash of cayenne pepper to the soup.

"No, I left no excuse. I told Joe to say I was out, that was all."

"Why, my dear, I should think you'd understand by this time that people don't do such things; we've got to observe *les convenances* [social customs] if we ever expect to get on and keep up with the procession. If you felt that you had to leave home this afternoon, you should have left some suitable explanation for your absence.

"This soup is really impossible; it's strange that woman hasn't learned yet to make a decent soup. Any free-lunch stand in town serves a better one. Was Mrs. Belthrop here?"

"Bring the tray with the cards, Joe. I don't remember who was here."

The boy retired and returned after a moment, bringing the tiny silver tray, which was covered with ladies' visiting cards. He handed it to Mrs. Pontellier.

"Give it to Mr. Pontellier," she said.

Joe offered the tray to Mr. Pontellier, and removed the soup.

Mr. Pontellier scanned the names of his wife's callers, reading some of them aloud, with comments as he read.

" 'The Misses Delasidas.' I worked a big deal in futures for their father this morning; nice girls; it's time they were getting married. 'Mrs. Belthrop.' I tell you what it is, Edna; you can't afford to snub Mrs. Belthrop. Why, Belthrop could buy and sell us ten times over. His business is worth a good, round sum to me. You'd better write her a note. 'Mrs. James Highcamp.' Hugh! the less you have to do with Mrs. Highcamp, the better. 'Madame Laforcé.' Came all the way from Carrolton, too, poor old soul. 'Miss Wiggs,' 'Mrs. Eleanor Boltons.' " He pushed the cards aside.

"Mercy!" exclaimed Edna, who had been fuming. "Why are you taking the thing so seriously and making such a fuss over it?"

"I'm not making any fuss over it. But it's just such seeming trifles that we've got to take seriously; such things count."

The fish was scorched. Mr. Pontellier would not touch it. Edna said she did not mind a little scorched taste. The roast was in some way not to his fancy, and he did not like the manner in which the vegetables were served.

"It seems to me," he said, "we spend money enough in this house to procure at least one meal a day which a man could eat and retain his self-respect."

"You used to think the cook was a treasure," returned Edna, indifferently.

"Perhaps she was when she first came; but cooks are only human. They need looking after, like any other class of persons that you employ. Suppose I didn't look after the clerks in my office, just let them run things their own way; they'd soon make a nice mess of me and my business."

"Where are you going?" asked Edna, seeing that her husband arose from table without having eaten a morsel except a taste of the highly-seasoned soup.

"I'm going to get my dinner at the club. Good night." He went into the hall, took his hat and stick from the stand, and left the house.

She was somewhat familiar with such scenes. They had often made her very unhappy. On a few previous occasions she had been completely deprived of any desire to finish her dinner. Sometimes she had gone into the kitchen to administer a tardy rebuke to the cook. Once she went to her room and studied the cookbook during an entire evening, finally writing out a menu for the week, which left her harassed with a feeling that, after all, she had accomplished no good that was worth the name.

But that evening Edna finished her dinner alone, with forced deliberation. Her face was flushed and her eyes flamed with some inward fire that lighted them. After finishing her dinner she went to her room, having instructed the boy to tell any other callers that she was indisposed.

It was a large, beautiful room, rich and picturesque in the soft, dim light which the maid had turned low. She went and stood at an open window and looked out upon the deep tangle of the garden below. All the mystery and witchery of the night seemed to have gathered there amid the perfumes and the dusky and tortuous outlines of flowers and foliage. She was seeking herself and finding herself in just such sweet, half-darkness which met her moods. But the voices were not soothing that came to her from the darkness and the sky above and the stars. They jeered and sounded mournful notes without promise, devoid even of hope. She turned back into the room and began to walk to and fro down its whole length, without stopping, without resting. She carried in her hands a thin handkerchief, which she tore into ribbons, rolled into a ball, and flung from her. Once she stopped, and taking off her wedding ring, flung it upon the carpet. When she saw it lying there, she stamped her heel upon it, striving to crush it. But her small boot heel did not make an indenture, not a mark upon the little glittering circlet.

In a sweeping passion she seized a glass vase from the table and flung it upon the tiles of the hearth. She wanted to destroy something. The crash and clatter were what she wanted to hear.

A maid, alarmed at the din of breaking glass, entered the room to discover what was the matter.

"A vase fell upon the hearth," said Edna. "Never mind; leave it till morning."

"Oh! you might get some of the glass in your feet, ma'am," insisted the young woman, picking up bits of the broken vase that were scattered upon the carpet. "And here's your ring, ma'am, under the chair."

Edna held out her hand, and taking the ring, slipped it upon her finger.

XVIII

The following morning Mr. Pontellier, upon leaving for his office, asked Edna if she would not meet him in town in order to look at some new fixtures for the library.

"I hardly think we need new fixtures, Léonce. Don't let us get anything new; you are too extravagant. I don't believe you ever think of saving or putting by."

"The way to become rich is to make money, my dear Edna, not to save it," he said. He regretted that she did not feel inclined to go with him and select new fixtures. He kissed her good-bye, and told her she was not looking well and must take care of herself. She was unusually pale and very quiet.

She stood on the front veranda as he quitted the house, and absently picked a few sprays of jessamine that grew upon a trellis near by. She inhaled the odor of the blossoms and thrust them into the bosom of her white morning gown. The boys were dragging along the banquette a small "express wagon," which they had filled with blocks and sticks. The quadroon was following them with little quick steps, having assumed a fictitious animation and alacrity for the occasion. A fruit vendor was crying his wares in the street.

Edna looked straight before her with a self-absorbed expression upon her face. She felt no interest in anything about her. The street, the children, the fruit vendor, the flowers growing there under her eyes, were all part and parcel of an alien world which had suddenly become antagonistic.

She went back into the house. She had thought of speaking to the cook concerning her blunders of the previous night; but Mr. Pontellier had saved her that disagreeable mission, for which she was so poorly fitted. Mr. Pontellier's arguments were usually convincing with those whom he employed. He left home feeling quite sure that he and Edna would sit down that evening, and possibly a few subsequent evenings, to a dinner deserving of the name.

Edna spent an hour or two in looking over some of her old sketches. She could see their shortcomings and defects, which were glaring in her eyes. She tried to work a little, but found she was not in the humor. Finally she gathered together a few of the sketches—those which she considered the least discreditable; and she carried them with her when, a little later, she dressed and left the house. She looked handsome and distinguished in her street gown. The tan of the seashore had left her face, and her forehead was smooth, white, and polished beneath her heavy, yellow-brown hair. There were a few freckles on her face, and a small, dark mole near the under lip and one on the temple, half-hidden in her hair.

As Edna walked along the street she was thinking of Robert. She was still under the spell of her infatuation. She had tried to forget him, realizing the inutility of remembering. But the thought of him was like an obsession, ever pressing itself upon her. It was not that she dwelt upon details of their acquaintance, or recalled in any special or peculiar way his personality; it was his being, his existence, which dominated her thought, fading sometimes as if it would melt into the mist of the forgotten, reviving again with an intensity which filled her with an incomprehensible longing.

Edna was on her way to Madame Ratignolle's. Their intimacy, begun at Grand Isle, had not declined, and they had seen each other with some frequency since their return to the city. The Ratignolles lived at no great distance from Edna's home, on the corner of a side street, where Monsieur Ratignolle owned and conducted a drugstore which enjoyed a steady and prosperous trade. His father had been in the business before him, and Monsieur Ratignolle stood well in the community and bore an enviable reputation for integrity and clear-headedness. His family lived in commodious apartments over the store, having an entrance on the side within the *porte cochère* [carriage entrance]. There was something which Edna thought very French, very foreign, about their whole manner of living. In the large and pleasant salon which extended across the width of the house, the Ratignolles entertained their friends once a fortnight with a *soirée musicale* [musical evening], sometimes diversified by card-playing. There was a friend who played upon the cello. One brought his flute and another his violin, while there were some who sang and a number who performed upon the piano with various degrees of taste and agility. The Ratignolles' *soirées musicales* were widely known, and it was considered a privilege to be invited to them.

Edna found her friend engaged in assorting the clothes which had returned that morning from the laundry. She at once abandoned her occupation upon seeing Edna, who had been ushered without ceremony into her presence.

" 'Cité can do it as well as I; it is really her business," she explained to Edna, who apologized for interrupting her. And she summoned a young black woman, whom she instructed, in French, to be very careful in checking off the list which she handed her. She told her to notice particularly if a fine linen handkerchief of Monsieur Ratignolle's, which was missing last week, had been returned; and to be sure to set to one side such pieces as required mending and darning.

Then placing an arm around Edna's waist, she led her to the front of the house, to the salon, where it was cool and sweet with the odor of great roses that stood upon the hearth in jars.

Madame Ratignolle looked more beautiful than ever there at home, in a negligee which left her arms almost wholly bare and exposed the rich, melting curves of her white throat.

"Perhaps I shall be able to paint your picture some day," said Edna with a smile when they were seated. She produced the roll of sketches and started to unfold them. "I believe I ought to work again. I feel as if I wanted to be doing something. What do you think of them? Do you think it worthwhile to take it up again and study some more? I might study for a while with Laidpore."

She knew that Madame Ratignolle's opinion in such a matter would be next to valueless, that she herself had not alone decided, but determined; but she sought the words of praise and encouragement that would help her to put heart into her venture.

"Your talent is immense, dear!"

"Nonsense!" protested Edna, well pleased.

"Immense, I tell you," persisted Madame Ratignolle, surveying the sketches one by one, at close range, then holding them at arm's length, narrowing her eyes, and dropping her head on one side. "Surely, this Bavarian peasant is worthy of framing; and this basket of apples! never have I seen anything more lifelike. One might almost be tempted to reach out a hand and take one."

Edna could not control a feeling which bordered upon complacency at her friend's praise, even realizing, as she did, its true worth. She retained a few of the sketches, and gave all the rest to Madame Ratignolle, who appreciated the gift far beyond its value and proudly exhibited the pictures to her husband when he came up from the store a little later for his midday dinner.

Mr. Ratignolle was one of those men who are called the salt of the earth. His cheerfulness was unbounded, and it was matched by his goodness of heart, his broad charity, and common sense. He and his wife spoke English with an accent which was only discernible through its un-English emphasis and a certain carefulness and deliberation. Edna's husband spoke English with no accent whatever. The Ratignolles understood each other perfectly. If ever the fusion of two human beings into one has been accomplished on this sphere it was surely in their union.

As Edna seated herself at table with them she thought, "Better a dinner of herbs," though it did not take her long to discover that it was no dinner of herbs, but a delicious repast, simple, choice, and in every way satisfying.

Monsieur Ratignolle was delighted to see her, though he found her looking not so well as at Grand Isle, and he advised a tonic. He talked a good deal on various topics, a little politics, some city news, and neighborhood gossip. He spoke with an animation and earnestness that gave an exaggerated importance to every syllable he uttered. His wife was keenly interested in everything he said, laying down her fork the better to listen, chiming in, taking the words out of his mouth.

Edna felt depressed rather than soothed after leaving them. The little glimpse of domestic harmony which had been offered her, gave her no regret, no longing. It was not a condition of life which fitted her, and she could see in it but an appalling and hopeless ennui. She was moved by a kind of commiseration for Madame Ratignolle—a pity for that colorless existence which never uplifted its possessor beyond the region of blind contentment, in which no moment of anguish ever visited her soul, in which she would never have the taste of life's delirium. Edna vaguely wondered what she meant by "life's delirium." It had crossed her thought like some unsought, extraneous impression.

XIX

Edna could not help but think that it was very foolish, very childish, to have stamped upon her wedding ring and smashed the crystal vase upon the tiles. She was visited by no more outbursts, moving her to such futile expedients. She began to do as she liked and to feel as she liked. She completely abandoned her Tuesdays at home, and did not return the visits of those who had called upon her. She made no ineffectual efforts to conduct her household *en bonne ménagère* [as a good housewife], going and coming as it suited her fancy, and, so far as she was able, lending herself to any passing caprice.

Mr. Pontellier had been a rather courteous husband so long as he met a certain tacit submissiveness in his wife. But her new and unexpected line of conduct completely bewildered him. It shocked him. Then her absolute disregard for her duties as a wife angered him. When Mr. Pontellier became rude, Edna grew insolent. She had resolved never to take another step backward.

"It seems to me the utmost folly for a woman at the head of a household, and the mother of children, to spend in an atelier days which would be better employed contriving for the comfort of her family."

"I feel like painting," answered Edna. "Perhaps I shan't always feel like it."

"Then in God's name paint! but don't let the family go to the devil. There's Madame Ratignolle; because she keeps up her music, she doesn't let everything else go to chaos. And she's more of a musician than you are a painter."

"She isn't a musician, and I'm not a painter. It isn't on account of painting that I let things go."

"On account of what, then?"

"Oh! I don't know. Let me alone; you bother me."

It sometimes entered Mr. Pontellier's mind to wonder if his wife were not growing a little unbalanced mentally. He could see plainly that she was not herself. That is, he could not see that she was becoming herself and daily casting aside that fictitious self which we assume like a garment with which to appear before the world.

Her husband let her alone as she requested, and went away to his office. Edna went up to her atelier—a bright room in the top of the house. She was working with great energy and interest, without accomplishing anything, however, which satisfied her even in the smallest degree. For a time she had the whole household enrolled in the service of art. The boys posed for her. They thought it amusing at first, but the occupation soon lost its attractiveness when they discovered that it was not a game arranged especially for their entertainment. The quadroon sat for hours before Edna's palette, patient as a savage, while the housemaid took charge of the children, and the drawing room went undusted. But the housemaid, too, served her term as model when Edna perceived that the young woman's back and shoulders were molded on classic lines, and that her hair, loosened from its confining cap, became an inspiration. While Edna worked she sometimes sang low the little air, "*Ah! si tu savais!*"

It moved her with recollections. She could hear again the ripple of the water, the flapping sail. She could see the glint of the moon upon the bay, and could feel the soft, gusty beating of the hot south wind. A subtle current of desire passed through her body, weakening her hold upon the brushes and making her eyes burn.

There were days when she was very happy without knowing why. She was happy to be alive and breathing, when her whole being seemed to be one with the sunlight, the color, the odors, the luxuriant warmth of some perfect Southern day. She liked then to wander alone into strange and unfamiliar places. She discovered many a sunny, sleepy corner, fashioned to dream

in. And she found it good to dream and to be alone and unmolested.

There were days when she was unhappy, she did not know why—when it did not seem worthwhile to be glad or sorry, to be alive or dead; when life appeared to her like a grotesque pandemonium and humanity like worms struggling blindly toward inevitable annihilation. She could not work on such a day, nor weave fancies to stir her pulses and warm her blood.

XX

It was during such a mood that Edna hunted up Mademoiselle Reisz. She had not forgotten the rather disagreeable impression left upon her by their last interview; but she nevertheless felt a desire to see her—above all, to listen while she played upon the piano. Quite early in the afternoon she started upon her quest for the pianist. Unfortunately she had mislaid or lost Mademoiselle Reisz's card, and looking up her address in the city directory, she found that the woman lived on Bienville Street, some distance away. The directory which fell into her hands was a year or more old, however, and upon reaching the number indicated, Edna discovered that the house was occupied by a respectable family of mulattoes who had *chambres garnies* [furnished rooms] to let. They had been living there for six months, and knew absolutely nothing of a Mademoiselle Reisz. In fact, they knew nothing of any of their neighbors; their lodgers were all people of the highest distinction, they assured Edna. She did not linger to discuss class distinctions with Madame Pouponne, but hastened to a neighboring grocery store, feeling sure that Mademoiselle would have left her address with the proprietor.

He knew Mademoiselle Reisz a good deal better than he wanted to know her, he informed his questioner. In truth, he did not want to know her at all, or anything concerning her—the most disagreeable and unpopular woman who ever lived in Bienville Street. He thanked heaven she had left the neighborhood, and was equally thankful that he did not know where she had gone.

Edna's desire to see Mademoiselle Reisz had increased tenfold since these unlooked-for obstacles had arisen to thwart it. She was wondering who could give her the information she sought, when it suddenly occurred to her that Madame Lebrun would be the one most likely to do so. She knew it was useless to ask Madame Ratignolle, who was on the most distant terms with the musician, and preferred to know nothing concerning her. She had once been almost as emphatic in expressing herself upon the subject as the corner grocer.

Edna knew that Madame Lebrun had returned to the city, for it was the middle of November. And she also knew where the Lebruns lived, on Chartres Street.

Their home from the outside looked like a prison, with iron bars before the door and lower windows. The iron bars were a relic of the old *régime* [tradition], and no one had ever thought of dislodging them. At the side was a high fence enclosing the garden. A gate or door opening upon the street was locked. Edna rang the bell at this side garden gate, and stood upon the banquette, waiting to be admitted.

It was Victor who opened the gate for her. A black woman, wiping her hands upon her apron, was close at his heels. Before she saw them Edna could hear them in altercation, the woman—plainly an anomaly—claiming the right to be allowed to perform her duties, one of which was to answer the bell.

Victor was surprised and delighted to see Mrs. Pontellier, and he made no attempt to conceal either his astonishment or his delight. He was a dark-browed, good-looking youngster of nineteen, greatly resembling his mother, but with ten times her impetuosity. He instructed the black woman to go at once and inform Madame Lebrun that Mrs. Pontellier desired to see her. The woman grumbled a refusal to do part of her duty when she had not been permitted to do it all, and started back to her interrupted task of weeding the garden. Whereupon Victor administered a rebuke in the form of a volley of abuse, which, owing to its rapidity and incoherence, was all but incomprehensible to Edna. Whatever it was, the rebuke was convincing, for the woman dropped her hoe and went mumbling into the house.

Edna did not wish to enter. It was very pleasant there on the side porch, where there were chairs, a wicker lounge, and a small table. She seated herself, for she was tired from her long tramp; and she began to rock gently and smooth out the folds of her silk parasol. Victor drew up his chair beside her. He at once explained that the black woman's offensive conduct was all due to imperfect training, as he was not there to take her in hand. He had only come up from the island the morning before, and expected to return next day. He stayed all winter at the island; he lived there, and kept the place in order and got things ready for the summer visitors.

But a man needed occasional relaxation, he informed Mrs. Pontellier, and every now and again he drummed up a pretext to bring him to the city. My! but he had had a time of it the evening before! He wouldn't want his mother to know, and he began to talk in a whisper. He was scintillant with recollections. Of course, he couldn't think of telling Mrs. Pontellier all about it, she being a woman and not comprehending such things. But it all began with a girl peeping and smiling at him through the shutters as he passed by. Oh! but she was a beauty! Certainly he smiled back, and went up and talked to her. Mrs. Pontellier did not know him if she supposed he was one to let an opportunity like that escape him. Despite herself, the youngster amused her. She must have betrayed in her look some degree of interest or entertainment. The boy grew more daring, and Mrs. Pontellier might have found herself, in a little while, listening to a highly colored story but for

the timely appearance of Madame Lebrun.

That lady was still clad in white, according to her custom of the summer. Her eyes beamed an effusive welcome. Would not Mrs. Pontellier go inside? Would she partake of some refreshment? Why had she not been there before? How was that dear Mr. Pontellier and how were those sweet children? Had Mrs. Pontellier ever known such a warm November?

Victor went and reclined on the wicker lounge behind his mother's chair, where he commanded a view of Edna's face. He had taken her parasol from her hands while he spoke to her, and he now lifted it and twirled it above him as he lay on his back. When Madame Lebrun complained that it was *so* dull coming back to the city; that she saw *so* few people now; that even Victor, when he came up from the island for a day or two, had *so* much to occupy him and engage his time; then it was that the youth went into contortions on the lounge and winked mischievously at Edna. She somehow felt like a confederate in crime, and tried to look severe and disapproving.

There had been but two letters from Robert, with little in them, they told her. Victor said it was really not worthwhile to go inside for the letters, when his mother entreated him to go in search of them. He remembered the contents, which in truth he rattled off very glibly when put to the test.

One letter was written from Vera Cruz and the other from the City of Mexico. He had met Montel, who was doing everything toward his advancement. So far, the financial situation was no improvement over the one he had left in New Orleans, but of course the prospects were vastly better. He wrote of the City of Mexico, the buildings, the people and their habits, the conditions of life which he found there. He sent his love to the family. He enclosed a check to his mother, and hoped she would affectionately remember him to all his friends. That was about the substance of the two letters. Edna felt that if there had been a message for her, she would have received it. The despondent frame of mind in which she had left home began again to overtake her, and she remembered that she wished to find Mademoiselle Reisz.

Madame Lebrun knew where Mademoiselle Reisz lived. She gave Edna the address, regretting that she would not consent to stay and spend the remainder of the afternoon, and pay a visit to Mademoiselle Reisz some other day. The afternoon was already well advanced.

Victor escorted her out upon the banquette, lifted her parasol, and held it over her while he walked to the car with her. He entreated her to bear in mind that the disclosures of the afternoon were strictly confidential. She laughed and bantered him a little, remembering too late that she should have been dignified and reserved.

"How handsome Mrs. Pontellier looked!" said Madame Lebrun to her son.

"Ravishing!" he admitted. "The city atmosphere has improved her. Some way she doesn't seem like the same woman."

XXI

Some people contended that the reason Mademoiselle Reisz always chose apartments up under the roof was to discourage the approach of beggars, peddlars, and callers. There were plenty of windows in her little front room. They were for the most part dingy, but as they were nearly always open it did not make so much difference. They often admitted into the room a good deal of smoke and soot; but at the same time all the light and air that there was came through them. From her windows could be seen the crescent of the river, the masts of ships, and the big chimneys of the Mississippi steamers. A magnificent piano crowded the apartment. In the next room she slept, and in the third and last she harbored a gasoline stove on which she cooked her meals when disinclined to descend to the neighboring restaurant. It was there also that she ate, keeping her belongings in a rare old buffet, dingy and battered from a hundred years of use.

When Edna knocked at Mademoiselle Reisz's front room door and entered, she discovered that person standing beside the window, engaged in mending or patching an old prunella gaiter. The little musician laughed all over when she saw Edna. Her laugh consisted of a contortion of the face and all the muscles of the body. She seemed strikingly homely, standing there in the afternoon light. She still wore the shabby lace and the artificial bunch of violets on the side of her head.

"So you remembered me at last," said Mademoiselle. "I had said to myself, 'Ah, bah! she will never come.' "

"Did you want me to come?" asked Edna with a smile.

"I had not thought much about it," answered Mademoiselle. The two had seated themselves on a little bumpy sofa which stood against the wall. "I am glad, however, that you came. I have the water boiling back there, and was just about to make some coffee. You will drink a cup with me. And how is *la belle dame* [the beautiful lady]? Always handsome! always healthy! always contented!" She took Edna's hand between her strong wiry fingers, holding it loosely without warmth, and executing a sort of double theme upon the back and palm.

"Yes," she went on; "I sometimes thought: 'She will never come. She promised as those women in society always do, without meaning it. She will not come.' For I really don't believe you like me, Mrs. Pontellier."

"I don't know whether I like you or not," replied Edna, gazing down at the little woman with a quizzical look.

The candor of Mrs. Pontellier's admission greatly pleased Mademoiselle Reisz. She expressed her gratification by repairing forthwith to the region of the gasoline stove and rewarding her guest with the promised cup of coffee. The coffee and the biscuit accompanying it proved very acceptable to Edna, who had declined refreshment at Madame Lebrun's and was now beginning to feel hungry. Mademoiselle set the tray which she brought in upon a small table near at hand, and seated herself once again on the lumpy sofa.

"I have had a letter from your friend," she remarked, as she poured a little cream into Edna's cup and handed it to her.

"My friend?"

"Yes, your friend Robert. He wrote to me from the City of Mexico."

"Wrote to *you?*" repeated Edna in amazement, stirring her coffee absently.

"Yes, to me. Why not? Don't stir all the warmth out of your coffee; drink it. Though the letter might as well have been sent to you; it was nothing but Mrs. Pontellier from beginning to end."

"Let me see it," requested the young woman, entreatingly.

"No; a letter concerns no one but the person who writes it and the one to whom it is written."

"Haven't you just said it concerned me from beginning to end?"

"It was written about you, not to you. 'Have you seen Mrs. Pontellier? How is she looking?' he asks. 'As Mrs. Pontellier says,' or 'as Mrs. Pontellier once said.' 'If Mrs. Pontellier should call upon you, play for her that Impromptu of Chopin's, my favorite. I heard it here a day or two ago, but not as you play it. I should like to know how it affects her,' and so on, as if he supposed we were constantly in each other's society."

"Let me see the letter."

"Oh, no."

"Have you answered it?"

"No."

"Let me see the letter."

"No, and again, no."

"Then play the Impromptu for me."

"It is growing late; what time do you have to be home?"

"Time doesn't concern me. Your question seems a little rude. Play the Impromptu."

"But you have told me nothing of yourself. What are you doing?"

"Painting!" laughed Edna. "I am becoming an artist. Think of it!"

"Ah! an artist! You have pretensions, Madame."

"Why pretensions? Do you think I could not become an artist?"

"I do not know you well enough to say. I do not know your talent or your temperament. To be an artist includes much; one must possess many gifts—absolute gifts—which have not been acquired by one's own effort. And, moreover, to succeed, the artist must possess the courageous soul."

"What do you mean by the courageous soul?"

"Courageous, *ma foi!* The brave soul. The soul that dares and defies."

"Show me the letter and play for me the Impromptu. You see that I have persistence. Does that quality count for anything in art?"

"It counts with a foolish old woman whom you have captivated," replied Mademoiselle, with her wriggling laugh.

The letter was right there at hand in the drawer of the little table upon which Edna had just placed her coffee cup. Mademoiselle opened the drawer and drew forth the letter, the topmost one. She placed it in Edna's hands, and without further comment arose and went to the piano.

Mademoiselle played a soft interlude. It was an improvisation. She sat low at the instrument, and the lines of her body settled into ungraceful curves and angles that gave it an appearance of deformity. Gradually and imperceptibly the interlude melted into the soft opening minor chords of the Chopin Impromptu.

Edna did not know when the Impromptu began or ended. She sat in the sofa corner reading Robert's letter by the fading light. Mademoiselle had glided from the Chopin into the quivering love-notes of Isolde's song, and back again to the Impromptu with its soulful and poignant longing.

The shadows deepened in the little room. The music grew strange and fantastic—turbulent, insistent, plaintive and soft with entreaty. The shadows grew deeper. The music filled the room. It floated out upon the night, over the housetops, the crescent of the river, losing itself in the silence of the upper air.

Edna was sobbing, just as she had wept one midnight at Grand Isle when strange, new voices awoke in her. She arose in some agitation to take her departure. "May I come again, Mademoiselle?" she asked at the threshold.

"Come whenever you feel like it. Be careful; the stairs and landings are dark; don't stumble."

Mademoiselle reentered and lit a candle. Robert's letter was on the floor. She stooped and picked it up. It was crumpled and damp with tears. Mademoiselle smoothed the letter out, restored it to the envelope, and replaced it in the table drawer.

XXII

One morning on his way into town Mr. Pontellier stopped at the house of his old friend and family physician, Doctor Mandelet. The Doctor was a semiretired physician, resting, as the saying is, upon his laurels. He bore a reputation for wisdom rather than skill—leaving the active practice of medicine to his assistants and younger contemporaries—and was much sought for in matters of consultation. A few families, united to him by bonds of friendship, he still attended when they required the services of a physician. The Pontelliers were among these.

Mr. Pontellier found the Doctor reading at the open window of his study. His house stood rather far back from the street, in the center of a delightful garden, so that it was quiet and peaceful at the old gentleman's study window. He was a great reader. He stared up disapprovingly over his eyeglasses as Mr. Pontellier entered, wondering who had the temerity to disturb him at that hour of the morning.

"Ah, Pontellier! Not sick, I hope. Come and have a seat. What news do you bring this morning?" He was quite portly, with a profusion of gray hair, and small blue eyes which age had robbed of much of their brightness but none of their penetration.

"Oh! I'm never sick, Doctor. You know that I come of tough fiber—of that old Creole race of Pontelliers that dry up and finally blow away. I came to consult—no, not precisely to consult—to talk to you about Edna. I don't know what ails her."

"Madame Pontellier not well?" marveled the Doctor. "Why, I saw her—I think it was a week ago—walking along Canal Street, the picture of health, it seemed to me."

"Yes, yes; she seems quite well," said Mr. Pontellier, leaning forward and whirling his stick between his two hands; "but she doesn't act well. She's odd, she's not like herself. I can't make her out, and I thought perhaps you'd help me."

"How does she act?" inquired the Doctor.

"Well, it isn't easy to explain," said Mr. Pontellier, throwing himself back in his chair. "She lets the housekeeping go to the dickens."

"Well, well; women are not all alike, my dear Pontellier. We've got to consider—"

"I know that; I told you I couldn't explain. Her whole attitude—toward me and everybody and everything—has changed. You know I have a quick temper, but I don't want to quarrel or be rude to a woman, especially my wife; yet I'm driven to it, and feel like ten thousand devils after I've made a fool of myself. She's making it devilishly uncomfortable for me," he went on nervously. "She's got some sort of notion in her head concerning the eternal rights of women; and—you understand—we meet in the morning at the breakfast table."

The old gentleman lifted his shaggy eyebrows, protruded his thick nether lip, and tapped the arms of his chair with his cushioned fingertips.

"What have you been doing to her, Pontellier?"

"Doing! *Parbleu!* [By Jove!]"

"Has she," asked the Doctor, with a smile, "has she been associating of late with a circle of pseudointellectual women—super-spiritual superior beings? My wife has been telling me about them."

"That's the trouble," broke in Mr. Pontellier, "she hasn't been associating with anyone. She has abandoned her Tuesdays at home, has thrown over all her acquaintances, and goes tramping about by herself, moping in the streetcars, getting in after dark. I tell you she's peculiar. I don't like it; I feel a little worried over it."

This was a new aspect for the Doctor. "Nothing hereditary?" he asked, seriously. "Nothing peculiar about her family antecedents, is there?"

"Oh, no, indeed! She comes of sound old Presbyterian Kentucky stock. The old gentleman, her father, I have heard, used to atone for his weekday sins with his Sunday devotions. I know for a fact, that his racehorses literally ran away with the prettiest bit of Kentucky farming land I ever laid eyes upon. Margaret—you know Margaret—she has all the Presbyterianism undiluted. And the youngest is something of a vixen. By the way, she gets married in a couple of weeks from now."

"Send your wife up to the wedding," exclaimed the Doctor, foreseeing a happy solution. "Let her stay among her own people for a while; it will do her good."

"That's what I want her to do. She won't go to the marriage. She says a wedding is one of the most lamentable spectacles on earth. Nice thing for a woman to say to her husband!" exclaimed Mr. Pontellier, fuming anew at the recollection.

"Pontellier," said the Doctor, after a moment's reflection, "let your wife alone for a while. Don't bother her, and don't let her bother you. Woman, my dear friend, is a very peculiar and delicate organism—a sensitive and highly organized woman, such as I know Mrs. Pontellier to be, is especially peculiar. It would require an inspired psychologist to deal successfully with them. And when ordinary fellows like you and me attempt to cope with their idiosyncrasies the result is bungling. Most women are moody and whimsical. This is some passing whim of your wife, due to some cause or causes which you and I needn't try to fathom. But it will pass happily over, especially if you let her alone. Send her around to see me."

"Oh! I couldn't do that; there'd be no reason for it," objected Mr. Pontellier.

"Then I'll go around and see her," said the Doctor. "I'll drop in to dinner some evening *en bon ami* [as a good friend]."

"Do! by all means," urged Mr. Pontellier. "What evening will you come? Say Thursday. Will you come Thursday?" he asked, rising to take his leave.

"Very well; Thursday. My wife may possibly have some engagement for me Thursday. In case she has, I shall let you know. Otherwise, you may expect me."

Mr. Pontellier turned before leaving to say:

"I am going to New York on business very soon. I have a big scheme on hand, and want to be on the field proper to pull the ropes and handle the ribbons. We'll let you in on the inside if you say so, Doctor," he laughed.

"No, I thank you, my dear sir," returned the Doctor. "I leave such ventures to you younger men with the fever of life still in your blood."

"What I wanted to say," continued Mr. Pontellier, with his hand on the knob; "I may have to be absent a good while. Would you advise me to take Edna along?"

"By all means, if she wishes to go. If not, leave her here. Don't contradict her. The mood will pass, I assure you. It may take a month, two, three months—possibly longer, but it will pass; have patience."

"Well, good-bye, *à jeudi* [till Thursday]," said Mr. Pontellier, as he let himself out.

The Doctor would have liked during the course of conversation to ask, "Is there any man in the case?" but he knew his Creole too well to make such a blunder as that.

He did not resume his book immediately, but sat for a while meditatively looking out into the garden.

XXIII

Edna's father was in the city, and had been with them several days. She was not very warmly or deeply attached to him, but they had certain tastes in common, and when together they were companionable. His coming was in the nature of a welcome disturbance; it seemed to furnish a new direction for her emotions.

He had come to purchase a wedding gift for his daughter Janet, and an outfit for himself in which he might make a creditable appearance at her marriage. Mr. Pontellier had selected the bridal gift, as everyone immediately connected with him always deferred to his taste in such matters. And his suggestions on the question of dress—which too often assumes the nature of a problem—were of inestimable value to his father-in-law. But for the past few days the old gentleman had been upon Edna's hands, and in his society she was becoming acquainted with a new set of sensations. He had been a colonel in the Confederate army, and still maintained, with the title, the military bearing which had always accompanied it. His hair and mustache were white and silky, emphasizing the rugged bronze of his face. He was tall and thin, and wore his coats padded, which gave a fictitious breadth and depth to his shoulders and chest. Edna and her father looked very distinguished together, and excited a good deal of notice during their perambulations. Upon his arrival she began by introducing him to her atelier and making a sketch of him. He took the whole matter very seriously. If her talent

had been tenfold greater than it was, it would not have surprised him, convinced as he was that he had bequeathed to all of his daughters the germs of a masterful capability, which only depended upon their own efforts to be directed toward successful achievement.

Before her pencil he sat rigid and unflinching, as he had faced the cannon's mouth in days gone by. He resented the intrusion of the children, who gaped with wondering eyes at him, sitting so stiff up there in their mother's bright atelier. When they drew near he motioned them away with an expressive action of the foot, loath to disturb the fixed lines of his countenance, his arms, or his rigid shoulders.

Edna, anxious to entertain him, invited Mademoiselle Reisz to meet him, having promised him a treat in her piano playing; but Mademoiselle declined the invitation. So together they attended a *soirée musicale* at the Ratignolles'. Monsieur and Madame Ratignolle made much of the Colonel, installing him as the guest of honor and engaging him at once to dine with them the following Sunday, or any day which he might select. Madame coquetted with him in the most captivating and naive manner, with eyes, gestures, and a profusion of compliments, till the Colonel's old head felt thirty years younger on his padded shoulders. Edna marveled, not comprehending. She herself was almost devoid of coquetry.

There were one or two men whom she observed at the *soirée musicale;* but she would never have felt moved to any kittenish display to attract their notice—to any feline or feminine wiles to express herself toward them. Their personality attracted her in an agreeable way. Her fancy selected them, and she was glad when a lull in the music gave them an opportunity to meet her and talk with her. Often on the street the glance of strange eyes had lingered in her memory, and sometimes had disturbed her.

Mr. Pontellier did not attend these *soirées musicales.* He considered them *bour-*

geois, and found more diversion at the club. To Madame Ratignolle he said the music dispensed at her *soirées* was too "heavy," too far beyond his untrained comprehension. His excuse flattered her. But she disapproved of Mr. Pontellier's club, and she was frank enough to tell Edna so.

"It's a pity Mr. Pontellier doesn't stay home more in the evenings. I think you would be more—well, if you don't mind my saying it—more united, if he did."

"Oh! dear no!" said Edna, with a blank look in her eyes. "What should I do if he stayed home? We wouldn't have anything to say to each other."

She had not much of anything to say to her father, for that matter; but he did not antagonize her. She discovered that he interested her, though she realized that he might not interest her long; and for the first time in her life she felt as if she were thoroughly acquainted with him. He kept her busy serving him and ministering to his wants. It amused her to do so. She would not permit a servant or one of the children to do anything for him which she might do herself. Her husband noticed, and thought it was the expression of a deep filial attachment which he had never suspected.

The Colonel drank numerous "toddies" during the course of the day, which left him, however, imperturbed. He was an expert at concocting strong drinks. He had even invented some, to which he had given fantastic names, and for whose manufacture he required diverse ingredients that it devolved upon Edna to procure for him.

When Doctor Mandelet dined with the Pontelliers on Thursday he could discern in Mrs. Pontellier no trace of that morbid condition which her husband had reported to him. She was excited and in a manner radiant. She and her father had been to the racecourse, and their thoughts when they seated themselves at table were still occupied with the events of the afternoon, and their talk was still of the track. The Doctor had not kept pace with turf affairs. He had certain recollections of racing in

what he called "the good old times" when the Lecompte stables flourished, and he drew upon this fund of memories so that he might not be left out and seem wholly devoid of the modern spirit. But he failed to impose upon the Colonel, and was even far from impressing him with this trumped-up knowledge of bygone days. Edna had staked her father on his last venture, with the most gratifying results to both of them. Besides, they had met some very charming people, according to the Colonel's impressions. Mrs. Mortimer Merriman and Mrs. James Highcamp, who were there with Alcée Arobin, had joined them and had enlivened the hours in a fashion that warmed him to think of.

Mr. Pontellier himself had no particular leaning toward horse racing, and was even rather inclined to discourage it as a pastime, especially when he considered the fate of that bluegrass farm in Kentucky. He endeavored, in a general way, to express a particular disapproval, and only succeeded in arousing the ire and opposition of his father-in-law. A pretty dispute followed, in which Edna warmly espoused her father's cause and the Doctor remained neutral.

He observed his hostess attentively from under his shaggy brows, and noted a subtle change which had transformed her from the listless woman he had known into a being who, for the moment, seemed palpitant with the forces of life. Her speech was warm and energetic. There was no repression in her glance or gesture. She reminded him of some beautiful, sleek animal waking up in the sun.

The dinner was excellent. The claret was warm and the champagne was cold, and under their beneficent influence the threatened unpleasantness melted and vanished with the fumes of the wine.

Mr. Pontellier warmed up and grew reminiscent. He told some amusing plantation experiences, recollections of old Iberville and his youth, when he hunted 'possum in company with some friendly darky; thrashed the pecan trees, shot the grosbec, and roamed the woods and fields in mischievous idleness.

The Colonel, with little sense of humor and of the fitness of things, related a somber episode of those dark and bitter days, in which he had acted a conspicuous part and always formed a central figure. Nor was the Doctor happier in his selection, when he told the old, ever new and curious story of the waning of a woman's love, seeking strange, new channels, only to return to its legitimate source after days of fierce unrest. It was one of the many little human documents which had been unfolded to him during his long career as a physician. The story did not seem especially to impress Edna. She had one of her own to tell, of a woman who paddled away with her lover one night in a pirogue and never came back. They were lost amid the Baratarian Islands, and no one ever heard of them or found trace of them from that day to this. It was a pure invention. She said that Madame Antoine had related it to her. That, also, was an invention. Perhaps it was a dream she had had. But every glowing word seemed real to those who listened. They could feel the hot breath of the Southern night; they could hear the long sweep of the pirogue through the glistening moonlit water, the beating of birds' wings, rising startled from among the reeds in the saltwater pools; they could see the faces of the lovers, pale, close together, rapt in oblivious forgetfulness, drifting into the unknown.

The champagne was cold, and its subtle fumes played fantastic tricks with Edna's memory that night.

Outside, away from the glow of the fire and the soft lamplight, the night was chill and murky. The Doctor doubled his old-fashioned cloak across his breast as he strode home through the darkness. He knew his fellow creatures better than most men; knew that inner life which so seldom unfolds itself to unanointed eyes. He was sorry he had accepted Pontellier's invitation. He was growing old, and beginning

to need rest and an imperturbed spirit. He did not want the secrets of other lives thrust upon him.

"I hope it isn't Arobin," he muttered to himself as he walked. "I hope to heaven it isn't Alcée Arobin."

XXIV

Edna and her father had a warm, and almost violent dispute upon the subject of her refusal to attend her sister's wedding. Mr. Pontellier declined to interfere, to interpose either his influence or his authority. He was following Doctor Mandelet's advice, and letting her do as she liked. The Colonel reproached his daughter for her lack of filial kindness and respect, her want of sisterly affection and womanly consideration. His arguments were labored and unconvincing. He doubted if Janet would accept any excuse—forgetting that Edna had offered none. He doubted if Janet would ever speak to her again, and he was sure Margaret would not.

Edna was glad to be rid of her father when he finally took himself off with his wedding garments and his bridal gifts, with his padded shoulders, his Bible reading, his "toddies" and ponderous oaths.

Mr. Pontellier followed him closely. He meant to stop at the wedding on his way to New York and endeavor by every means which money and love could devise to atone somewhat for Edna's incomprehensible action.

"You are too lenient, too lenient by far, Léonce," asserted the Colonel. "Authority, coercion are what is needed. Put your foot down good and hard; the only way to manage a wife. Take my word for it."

The Colonel was perhaps unaware that he had coerced his own wife into her grave. Mr. Pontellier had a vague suspicion of it which he thought it needless to mention at that late day.

Edna was not so consciously gratified at her husband's leaving home as she had been over the departure of her father. As the day approached when he was to leave her for a comparatively long stay, she grew melting and affectionate, remembering his many acts of consideration and his repeated expressions of an ardent attachment. She was solicitous about her health and his welfare. She bustled around, looking after his clothing, thinking about heavy underwear, quite as Madame Ratignolle would have done under similar circumstances. She cried when he went away, calling him her dear, good friend, and she was quite certain she would grow lonely before very long and go to join him in New York.

But after all, a radiant peace settled upon her when she at last found herself alone. Even the children were gone. Old Madame Pontellier had come herself and carried them off to Iberville with their quadroon. The old madame did not venture to say she was afraid they would be neglected during Léonce's absence; she hardly ventured to think so. She was hungry for them—even a little fierce in her attachment. She did not want them to be wholly "children of the pavement," she always said when begging to have them for a space. She wished them to know the country, with its streams, its fields, its woods, its freedom, so delicious to the young. She wished them to taste something of the life their father had lived and known and loved when he, too, was a little child.

When Edna was at last alone, she breathed a big, genuine sigh of relief. A feeling that was unfamiliar but very delicious came over her. She walked all through the house, from one room to another, as if inspecting it for the first time. She tried the various chairs and lounges, as if she had never sat and reclined upon them before. And she perambulated around the outside of the house, investigating, looking to see if windows and shutters were secure and in order. The flowers were like new acquaintances; she approached them in a familiar spirit, and made herself at home among them. The garden walks were damp, and Edna called to the maid to bring out her rubber sandals. And there she stayed, and stooped, digging around the plants, trimming, picking dead, dry leaves. The children's little dog came out, interfering, getting in her way. She scolded him, laughed at him, played with him. The garden smelled so good and looked so pretty in the afternoon sunlight. Edna plucked all the bright flowers she could find, and went into the house with them, she and the little dog.

Even the kitchen assumed a sudden interesting character which she had never before perceived. She went in to give directions to the cook, to say that the butcher would have to bring much less meat, that they would require only half their usual quantity of bread, of milk and groceries. She told the cook that she herself would be greatly occupied during Mr. Pontellier's absence, and she begged her to take all thought and responsibility of the larder upon her own shoulders.

That night Edna dined alone. The candelabra, with a few candles in the center of the table, gave all the light she needed. Outside the circle of light in which she sat, the large dining room looked solemn and shadowy. The cook, placed upon her mettle, served a delicious repast—a luscious tenderloin broiled *à point* [to a turn]. The wine tasted good; the *marron glacé* [candied chestnuts] seemed to be just what she wanted. It was so pleasant, too, to dine in a comfortable *peignoir*.

She thought a little sentimentally about Léonce and the children, and wondered what they were doing. As she gave a dainty scrap or two to the doggie, she talked intimately to him about Etienne and Raoul. He was beside himself with astonishment and delight over these companionable advances, and showed his appreciation by his little quick, snappy barks and a lively agitation.

Then Edna sat in the library after dinner and read Emerson until she grew sleepy. She realized that she had neglected her reading, and determined to start anew upon a course of improving studies, now that her time was completely her own to do with as she liked.

After a refreshing bath, Edna went to bed. And as she snuggled comfortably beneath the eiderdown a sense of restfulness invaded her, such as she had not known before.

XXV

When the weather was dark and cloudy Edna could not work. She needed the sun to mellow and temper her mood to the sticking point. She had reached a stage when she seemed to be no longer feeling her way, working, when in the humor, with sureness and ease. And being devoid of ambition, and striving not toward accomplishment, she drew satisfaction from the work in itself.

On rainy or melancholy days Edna went out and sought the society of the friends she had made at Grand Isle. Or else she stayed indoors and nursed a mood with which she was becoming too familiar for her own comfort and peace of mind. It was not despair; but it seemed to her as if life were passing by, leaving its promise broken and unfulfilled. Yet there were other days when she listened, was led on and deceived by fresh promises which her youth held out to her.

She went again to the races, and again. Alcée Arobin and Mrs. Highcamp called for her one bright afternoon in Arobin's drag. Mrs. Highcamp was a worldly but unaffected, intelligent, slim, tall blond woman in the forties, with an indifferent manner and blue eyes that stared. She had a daughter who served her as a pretext for cultivating the society of young men of fashion. Alcée Arobin was one of them. He was a familiar figure at the racecourse, the opera, the fashionable clubs. There was a perpetual smile in his eyes, which seldom failed to awaken a corresponding cheerfulness in anyone who looked into them and listened to his good-humored voice. His manner was quiet, and at times a little insolent. He possessed a good figure, a pleasing face, not overburdened with depth of thought or feeling; and his dress was that of the conventional man of fashion.

He admired Edna extravagantly, after meeting her at the races with her father. He had met her before on other occasions, but she had seemed to him unapproachable until that day. It was at his instigation that Mrs. Highcamp called to ask her to go with them to the Jockey Club to witness the turf event of the season.

There were possibly a few track men out there who knew the racehorse as well as Edna, but there was certainly none who knew it better. She sat between her two companions as one having authority to speak. She laughed at Arobin's pretensions, and deplored Mrs. Highcamp's ignorance. The racehorse was a friend and intimate associate of her childhood. The atmosphere of the stables and the breath of the bluegrass paddock revived in her memory and lingered in her nostrils. She did not perceive that she was talking like her father as the sleek geldings ambled in review before them. She played for very high stakes, and fortune favored her. The fever of the game flamed in her cheeks and eyes, and it got into her blood and into her brain like an intoxicant. People turned their heads to look at her, and more than one lent an attentive ear to her utterances, hoping thereby to secure the elusive but ever-desired "tip." Arobin caught the contagion of excitement which drew him to Edna like a magnet. Mrs. Highcamp remained, as usual, unmoved, with her indifferent stare and uplifted eyebrows.

Edna stayed and dined with Mrs. Highcamp upon being urged to do so. Arobin also remained and sent away his drag.

The dinner was quiet and uninteresting, save for the cheerful efforts of Arobin to enliven things. Mrs. Highcamp deplored the absence of her daughter from the races, and tried to convey to her what she had missed by going to the "Dante reading" instead of joining them. The girl held a geranium leaf up to her nose and said nothing, but looked knowing and noncommittal. Mr. Highcamp was a plain, bald-headed man, who only talked under compulsion. He was unresponsive. Mrs. Highcamp was full of delicate courtesy and consideration toward her husband. She addressed most of her conversation to him at table. They sat in the library after dinner and read the evening papers together under the droplight; while the younger people went into the drawing room nearby and talked. Miss Highcamp played some selections from Grieg upon the piano. She seemed to have apprehended all of the composer's coldness and none of his poetry. While Edna listened she could not help wondering if she had lost her taste for music.

When the time came for her to go home, Mr. Highcamp grunted a lame offer to escort her, looking down at his slippered feet with tactless concern. It was Arobin who took her home. The car ride was long, and it was late when they reached Esplanade Street. Arobin asked permission to enter for a second to light his cigarette—his match safe was empty. He filled his match safe, but did not light his cigarette until he left her, after she had expressed her willingness to go to the races with him again.

Edna was neither tired nor sleepy. She was hungry again, for the Highcamp dinner, though of excellent quality, had lacked abundance. She rummaged in the larder and brought forth a slice of Gruyère and some crackers. She opened a bottle of beer which she found in the icebox. Edna felt extremely restless and excited. She vacantly hummed a fantastic tune as she poked at the wood embers on the hearth and munched a cracker.

She wanted something to happen—something, anything; she did not know what. She regretted that she had not made Arobin stay a half hour to talk over the horses with her. She counted the money she had won. But there was nothing else to do, so she went to bed, and tossed there for hours in a sort of monotonous agitation.

In the middle of the night she remembered that she had forgotten to write her regular letter to her husband; and she decided to do so next day and tell him about her afternoon at the Jockey Club. She lay wide awake composing a letter which was nothing like the one which she wrote next day. When the maid awoke her in the morning Edna was dreaming of Mr. Highcamp playing the piano at the entrance of a music store on Canal Street, while his wife was saying to Alcée Arobin, as they boarded an Esplanade Street car:

"What a pity that so much talent has been neglected! but I must go."

When, a few days later, Alcée Arobin again called for Edna in his drag, Mrs. Highcamp was not with him. He said they would pick her up. But as that lady had not been apprised of his intention of picking her up, she was not at home. The daughter was just leaving the house to attend the meeting of a branch Folk Lore Society, and regretted that she could not accompany them. Arobin appeared nonplussed, and asked Edna if there were anyone else she cared to ask.

She did not deem it worthwhile to go in search of any of the fashionable acquaintances from whom she had withdrawn herself. She thought of Madame Ratignolle, but knew that her fair friend did not leave the house, except to take a languid walk around the block with her husband after nightfall. Mademoiselle Reisz would have laughed at such a request from Edna. Madame Lebrun might have enjoyed the outing, but for some reason Edna did not want her. So they went alone, she and Arobin.

The afternoon was intensely interesting to her. The excitement came back upon her like a remittent fever. Her talk grew familiar and confidential. It was no labor to become intimate with Arobin. His manner invited easy confidence. The preliminary stage of becoming acquainted was one which he always endeavored to ignore when a pretty and engaging woman was concerned.

He stayed and dined with Edna. He stayed and sat beside the wood fire. They laughed and talked; and before it was time to go he was telling her how different life might have been if he had known her years before. With ingenuous frankness he spoke of what a wicked, ill-disciplined boy he had been, and impulsively drew up his cuff to exhibit upon his wrist the scar from a saber cut which he had received in a duel outside of Paris when he was nineteen. She touched his hand as she scanned the red cicatrix on the inside of his white wrist. A quick impulse that was somewhat spasmodic impelled her fingers to close in a sort of clutch upon his hand. He felt the pressure of her pointed nails in the flesh of his palm.

She arose hastily and walked toward the mantel.

"The sight of a wound or scar always agitates and sickens me," she said. "I shouldn't have looked at it."

"I beg your pardon," he entreated, following her; "it never occurred to me that it might be repulsive."

He stood close to her, and the effrontery in his eyes repelled the old, vanishing self in her, yet drew all her awakening sensuousness. He saw enough in her face to impel him to take her hand and hold it while he said his lingering good-night.

"Will you go to the races again?" he asked.

"No," she said. "I've had enough of the races. I don't want to lose all the money I've won, and I've got to work when the weather is bright, instead of—"

"Yes; work; to be sure. You promised to show me your work. What morning may I come up to your atelier? Tomorrow?"

"No!"

"Day after?"

"No, no."

"Oh, please don't refuse me! I know something of such things. I might help you with a stray suggestion or two."

"No. Good night. Why don't you go after you have said good night? I don't like you," she went on in a high, excited pitch, attempting to draw away her hand. She felt that her words lacked dignity and sincerity, and she knew that he felt it.

"I'm sorry you don't like me. I'm sorry I offended you. How have I offended you? What have I done? Can't you forgive me?" And he bent and pressed his lips upon her hand as if he wished never more to withdraw them.

"Mr. Arobin," she complained, "I'm greatly upset by the excitement of the afternoon; I'm not myself. My manner must have misled you in some way. I wish you to go, please." She spoke in a monotonous, dull tone. He took his hat from the table, and stood with eyes turned from her, looking into the dying fire. For a moment or two he kept an impressive silence.

"Your manner has not misled me, Mrs. Pontellier," he said finally. "My own emotions have done that. I couldn't help it. When I'm near you, how could I help it? Don't think anything of it, don't bother, please. You see, I go when you command me. If you wish me to stay away, I shall do so. If you let me come back, I—oh! you will let me come back?"

He cast one appealing glance at her, to which she made no response. Alcée Arobin's manner was so genuine that it often deceived even himself.

Edna did not care or think whether it were genuine or not. When she was alone she looked mechanically at the back of her hand which he had kissed so warmly. Then she leaned her head down on the mantelpiece. She felt somewhat like a woman who in a moment of passion is betrayed into an act of infidelity, and realizes the significance of the act without being wholly awakened from its glamour. The thought was passing vaguely through her mind. "What would he think?"

She did not mean her husband; she was thinking of Robert Lebrun. Her husband seemed to her now like a person whom she had married without love as an excuse.

She lit a candle and went up to her room. Alcée Arobin was absolutely nothing to her. Yet his presence, his manners, the warmth of his glances, and above all the touch of his lips upon her hand had acted like a narcotic upon her.

She slept a languorous sleep, interwoven with vanishing dreams.

XXVI

Alcée Arobin wrote Edna an elaborate note of apology, palpitant with sincerity. It embarrassed her; for in a cooler, quieter moment it appeared to her absurd that she should have taken his action so seriously, so dramatically. She felt sure that the significance of the whole occurrence had lain in her own self-consciousness. If she ignored his note it would give undue importance to a trivial affair. If she replied to it in a serious spirit it would still leave in his mind the impression that she had in a susceptible moment yielded to his influence. After all, it was no great matter to have one's hand kissed. She was provoked at his having written the apology. She answered in as light and bantering a spirit as she fancied it deserved, and said she would be glad to have him look in upon her at work whenever he felt the inclination and his business gave him the opportunity.

He responded at once by presenting himself at her home with all his disarming naïveté. And then there was scarcely a day which followed that she did not see him or was not reminded of him. He was prolific in pretexts. His attitude became one of good-humored subservience and tacit adoration. He was ready at all times to submit to her moods, which were as often kind as they were cold. She grew accustomed to him. They became intimate and friendly by imperceptible degrees, and then by leaps. He sometimes talked in a way that astonished her at first and brought the crimson into her face; in a way that pleased her at last, appealing to the animalism that stirred impatiently within her.

There was nothing which so quieted the turmoil of Edna's senses as a visit to Mademoiselle Reisz. It was then, in the presence of that personality which was offensive to her, that the woman, by her divine art, seemed to reach Edna's spirit and set it free.

It was misty, with heavy, lowering atmosphere, one afternoon, when Edna climbed the stairs to the pianist's apartments under the roof. Her clothes were dripping with moisture. She felt chilled and pinched as she entered the room. Mademoiselle was poking at a rusty stove that smoked a little and warmed the room indifferently. She was endeavoring to heat a pot of chocolate on the stove. The room looked cheerless and dingy to Edna as she entered. A bust of Beethoven, covered with a hood of dust, scowled at her from the mantelpiece.

"Ah! here comes the sunlight!" exclaimed Mademoiselle, rising from her knees before the stove. "Now it will be warm and bright enough; I can let the fire alone."

She closed the stove door with a bang, and approaching, assisted in removing Edna's dripping mackintosh.

"You are cold; you look miserable. The chocolate will soon be hot. But would you rather have a taste of brandy? I have scarcely touched the bottle which you brought me for my cold." A piece of red flannel was wrapped around Mademoiselle's throat; a stiff neck compelled her to hold her head on one side.

"I will take some brandy," said Edna, shivering as she removed her gloves and overshoes. She drank the liquor from the glass as a man would have done. Then flinging herself upon the uncomfortable sofa she said, "Mademoiselle, I am going to move away from my house on Esplanade Street."

"Ah!" ejaculated the musician, neither surprised nor especially interested. Nothing ever seemed to astonish her very much.

She was endeavoring to adjust the bunch of violets which had become loose from its fastening in her hair. Edna drew her down upon the sofa, and taking a pin from her own hair, secured the shabby artificial flowers in their accustomed place.

"Aren't you astonished?"

"Passably. Where are you going? to New York? to Iberville? to your father in Mississippi? where?"

"Just two steps away," laughed Edna, "in a little four-room house around the corner. It looks so cozy, so inviting and restful, whenever I pass by; and it's for rent. I'm tired looking after that big house. It never seemed like mine, anyway—like home. It's too much trouble. I have to keep too many servants. I am tired bothering with them."

"That is not your true reason, *ma belle* [my precious]." There is no use in telling me lies. I don't know your reason, but you have not told me the truth." Edna did not protest or endeavor to justify herself.

"The house, the money that provides for it, are not mine. Isn't that enough reason?"

"They are your husband's," returned Mademoiselle, with a shrug and a malicious elevation of the eyebrows.

"Oh! I see there is no deceiving you. Then let me tell you: It is a caprice. I have a little money of my own from my mother's estate, which my father sends me by driblets. I won a large sum this winter on the races, and I am beginning to sell my sketches. Laidpore is more and more pleased with my work; he says it grows in force and individuality. I cannot judge of that myself, but I feel that I have gained in ease and confidence. However, as I said, I have sold a good many through Laidpore. I can live in the tiny house for little or nothing, with one servant. Old Celestine, who works occasionally for me, says she will come stay with me and do my work. I know I shall like it, like the feeling of freedom and independence."

"What does your husband say?"

"I have not told him yet. I only thought of it this morning. He will think I am demented, no doubt. Perhaps you think so."

Mademoiselle shook her head slowly. "Your reason is not yet clear to me," she said.

Neither was it quite clear to Edna herself; but it unfolded itself as she sat for a while in silence. Instinct had prompted her to put away her husband's bounty in casting off her allegiance. She did not know how it would be when he returned. There would have to be an understanding, an explanation. Conditions would some way adjust themselves, she felt; but whatever came, she had resolved never again to belong to another than herself.

"I shall give a grand dinner before I leave the old house!" Edna exclaimed. "You will have to come to it, Mademoiselle. I will give you everything that you like to eat and to drink. We shall sing and laugh and be merry for once." And she uttered a sigh that came from the very depths of her being.

If Mademoiselle happened to have received a letter from Robert during the interval of Edna's visits, she would give her the letter unsolicited. And she would seat herself at the piano and play as her humor prompted her while the young woman read the letter.

The little stove was roaring; it was red-hot, and the chocolate in the tin sizzled and sputtered. Edna went forward and opened the stove door, and Mademoiselle rising, took a letter from under the bust of Beethoven and handed it to Edna.

"Another! so soon!" she exclaimed, her eyes filled with delight. "Tell me, Mademoiselle, does he know that I see his letters?"

"Never in the world! He would be angry and would never write to me again if he thought so. Does he write to you? Never a line. Does he send you a message? Never a word. It is because he loves you, poor fool, and is trying to forget you, since you are not free to listen to him or to belong to him."

"Why do you show me his letters, then?"

"Haven't you begged for them? Can I refuse you anything? Oh! you cannot deceive me," and Mademoiselle approached her beloved instrument and began to play. Edna did not at once read the letter. She sat holding it in her hand, while the music penetrated her whole being like an effulgence, warming and brightening the dark places of her soul. It prepared her for joy and exultation.

"Oh!" she exclaimed, letting the letter fall to the floor. "Why did you not tell me?" She went and grasped Mademoiselle's hands up from the keys. "Oh! unkind! malicious! Why did you not tell me?"

"That he was coming back? No great news, *ma foi*. I wonder he did not come long ago."

"But when, when?" cried Edna, impatiently. "He does not say when."

"He says 'very soon.' You know as much about it as I do; it is all in the letter."

"But why? Why is he coming? Oh, if I thought—" and she snatched the letter from the floor and turned the pages this way and that way, looking for the reason, which was left untold.

"If I were young and in love with a man," said Mademoiselle, turning on the stool and pressing her wiry hands between her knees as she looked down at Edna, who sat on the floor holding the letter, "it seems to me he would have to be some *grand esprit* [great mind]; a man with lofty aims and ability to reach them; one who stood high enough to attract the notice of his fellowmen. It seems to me if I were young and in love I should never deem a man of ordinary caliber worthy of my devotion."

"Now it is you who are telling lies and seeking to deceive me, Mademoiselle; or else you have never been in love, and know nothing about it. Why," went on Edna, clasping her knees and looking up into Mademoiselle's twisted face, "do you suppose a woman knows why she loves? Does she select? Does she say to herself: 'Go to! Here is a distinguished statesman with presidential possibilities; I shall proceed to fall in love with him.' Or, 'I shall set my heart upon this musician, whose fame is on every tongue?' Or, 'This financier, who controls the world's money markets?'"

"You are purposely misunderstanding me, *ma reine* [my queen]." Are you in love with Robert?"

"Yes," said Edna. It was the first time she had admitted it, and a glow overspread her face, blotching it with red spots.

"Why?" asked her companion. "Why do you love him when you ought not to?"

Edna, with a motion or two, dragged herself on her knees before Mademoiselle Reisz, who took the glowing face between her two hands.

"Why? Because his hair is brown and grows away from his temples; because he opens and shuts his eyes, and his nose is a little out of drawing; because he has two lips and a square chin, and a little finger which he can't straighten from having played baseball too energetically in his youth. Because—"

"Because you do, in short," laughed Mademoiselle. "What will you do when he comes back?" she asked.

"Do? Nothing, except feel glad and happy to be alive."

She was already glad and happy to be alive at the mere thought of his return. The murky, lowering sky, which had depressed her a few hours before, seemed bracing and invigorating as she splashed through the streets on her way home.

She stopped at a confectioner's and ordered a huge box of bonbons for the children in Iberville. She slipped a card in the box, on which she scribbled a tender message and sent an abundance of kisses.

Before dinner in the evening Edna wrote a charming letter to her husband, telling

him of her intention to move for a while
into the little house around the block, and
to give a farewell dinner before leaving,
regretting that he was not there to share
it, to help out with the menu and assist her
in entertaining the guests. Her letter was
brilliant and brimming with cheerfulness.

XXVII

"What is the matter with you?" asked
Arobin that evening. "I never found you
in such a happy mood." Edna was tired by
that time, and was reclining on the lounge
before the fire.

"Don't you know the weather prophet
has told us we shall see the sun pretty
soon?"

"Well, that ought to be reason enough,"
he acquiesced. "You wouldn't give me another if I sat here all night imploring you."
He sat close to her on a low taboret, and
as he spoke his fingers lightly touched the
hair that fell a little over her forehead. She
liked the touch of his fingers through her
hair, and closed her eyes sensitively.

"One of these days," she said, "I'm going to pull myself together for a while and
think—try to determine what character of
a woman I am; for, candidly, I don't know.
By all the codes which I am acquainted
with, I am a devilishly wicked specimen of
the sex. But some way I can't convince
myself that I am. I must think about it."

"Don't. What's the use? Why should you
bother thinking about it when I can tell
you what manner of woman you are." His
fingers strayed occasionally down to her
warm, smooth cheeks and firm chin, which
was growing a little full and double.

"Oh, yes! You will tell me that I am
adorable; everything that is captivating.
Spare yourself the effort."

"No; I shan't tell you anything of the
sort, though I shouldn't be lying if I did."

"Do you know Mademoiselle Reisz?" she
asked irrelevantly.

"The pianist? I know her by sight. I've
heard her play."

"She says queer things sometimes in a
bantering way that you don't notice at the
time and you find yourself thinking about
afterward."

"For instance?"

"Well, for instance, when I left her today, she put her arms around me and felt
my shoulder blades, to see if my wings
were strong, she said. 'The bird that would
soar above the level plain of tradition and
prejudice must have strong wings. It is a
sad spectacle to see the weaklings bruised,
exhausted, fluttering back to earth.' "

"Whither would you soar?"

"I'm not thinking of any extraordinary
flights. I only half comprehend her."

"I've heard she's partially demented,"
said Arobin.

"She seems to me wonderfully sane,"
Edna replied.

"I'm told she's extremely disagreeable
and unpleasant. Why have you introduced
her at a moment when I desired to talk of
you?"

"Oh! talk of me if you like," cried Edna,
clasping her hands beneath her head; "but
let me think of something else while you
do."

"I'm jealous of your thoughts tonight.
They're making you a little kinder than
usual; but some way I feel as if they were
wandering, as if they were not here with
me." She only looked at him and smiled.
His eyes were very near. He leaned upon
the lounge with an arm extended across
her, while the other hand still rested upon
her hair. They continued silently to look
into each other's eyes. When he leaned forward and kissed her, she clasped his head,
holding his lips to hers.

It was the first kiss of her life to which
her nature had really responded. It was a
flaming torch that kindled desire.

XXVIII

Edna cried a little that night after Arobin
left her. It was only one phase of the multi-
tudinous emotions which had assailed her.

There was with her an overwhelming feeling of irresponsibility. There was the shock of the unexpected and the unaccustomed. There was her husband's reproach looking at her from the external things around her which he had provided for her external existence. There was Robert's reproach making itself felt by a quicker, fiercer, more overpowering love, which had awakened within her toward him. Above all, there was understanding. She felt as if a mist had been lifted from her eyes, enabling her to look upon and comprehend the significance of life, that monster made up of beauty and brutality. But among the conflicting sensations which assailed her, there was neither shame nor remorse. There was a dull pang of regret because it was not the kiss of love which had inflamed her, because it was not love which had held this cup of life to her lips.

XXIX

Without even waiting for an answer from her husband regarding his opinion or wishes in the matter, Edna hastened her preparations for quitting her home on Esplanade Street and moving into the little house around the block. A feverish anxiety attended her every action in that direction. There was no moment of deliberation, no interval of repose between the thought and its fulfillment. Early upon the morning following those hours passed in Arobin's society, Edna set about securing her new abode and hurrying her arrangements for occupying it. Within the precincts of her home she felt like one who has entered and lingered within the portals of some forbidden temple in which a thousand muffled voices bade her begone.

Whatever was her own in the house, everything which she had acquired aside from her husband's bounty, she caused to be transported to the other house, supplying simple and meager deficiencies from her own resources.

Arobin found her with rolled sleeves, working in company with the housemaid when he looked in during the afternoon. She was splendid and robust, and had

413

never appeared handsomer than in the old blue gown, with a red silk handkerchief knotted at random around her head to protect her hair from the dust. She was mounted upon a high stepladder, unhooking a picture from the wall when he entered. He had found the front door open, and had followed his ring by walking in unceremoniously.

"Come down!" he said. "Do you want to kill yourself?" She greeted him with affected carelessness, and appeared absorbed in her occupation.

If he had expected to find her languishing, reproachful, or indulging in sentimental tears, he must have been greatly surprised.

He was no doubt prepared for any emergency, ready for any one of the foregoing attitudes, just as he bent himself easily and naturally to the situation which confronted him.

"Please come down," he insisted, holding the ladder and looking up at her.

"No," she answered; "Ellen is afraid to mount the ladder. Joe is working over at the 'pigeon house'—that's the name Ellen gives it, because it's so small and looks like a pigeon house—and someone has to do this."

Arobin pulled off his coat, and expressed himself ready and willing to tempt fate in her place. Ellen brought him one of her dust caps, and went into contortions of mirth, which she found it impossible to control, when she saw him put it on before the mirror as grotesquely as he could. Edna herself could not refrain from smiling when she fastened it at his request. So it was he who in turn mounted the ladder, unhooking pictures and curtains, and dislodging ornaments as Edna directed. When he had finished he took off his dust cap and went out to wash his hands.

Edna was sitting on the taboret, idly brushing the tips of a feather duster along the carpet when he came in again.

"Is there anything more you will let me do?" he asked.

"That is all," she answered. "Ellen can manage the rest." She kept the young woman occupied in the drawing room, unwilling to be left alone with Arobin.

"What about the dinner?" he asked; "the grand event, the *coup d'état?*"

"It will be day after tomorrow. Why do you call it the '*coup d'état?*' Oh! it will be very fine; all my best of everything—crystal, silver, and gold, Sèvres, flowers, music, and champagne to swim in. I'll let Léonce pay the bills. I wonder what he'll say when he sees the bills."

"And you ask me why I call it a *coup d'état?*" Arobin had put on his coat, and he stood before her and asked if his cravat was plumb. She told him it was, looking no higher than the tip of his collar.

"When do you go to the 'pigeon house?'—with all due acknowledgment to Ellen."

"Day after tomorrow, after the dinner. I shall sleep there."

"Ellen, will you very kindly get me a glass of water?" asked Arobin. "The dust in the curtains, if you will pardon me for hinting such a thing, has parched my throat to a crisp."

"While Ellen gets the water," said Edna, rising, "I will say good-bye and let you go. I must get rid of this grime, and I have a million things to do and think of."

"When shall I see you?" asked Arobin, seeking to detain her, the maid having left the room.

"At the dinner, of course. You are invited."

"Not before?—not tonight or tomorrow morning or tomorrow noon or night? or the day after morning or noon? Can't you see yourself, without my telling you, what an eternity it is?"

He had followed her into the hall and to the foot of the stairway, looking up at her as she mounted with her face half turned to him.

"Not an instant sooner," she said. But she laughed and looked at him with eyes that at once gave him courage to wait and made it torture to wait.

XXX

Though Edna had spoken of the dinner as a very grand affair, it was in truth a very small affair and very select, insomuch as the guests invited were few and were selected with discrimination. She had counted upon an even dozen seating themselves at her round mahogany board, forgetting for the moment that Madame Ratignolle was to the last degree *souffrante* [indisposed] and unpresentable, and not foreseeing that Madame Lebrun would send a thousand regrets at the last moment. So there were only ten, after all, which made a cozy, comfortable number.

There were Mr. and Mrs. Merriman, a pretty, vivacious little woman in the thirties; her husband, a jovial fellow, something of a shallow-pate, who laughed a good deal at other people's witticisms, and had thereby made himself extremely popular. Mrs. Highcamp had accompanied them. Of course, there was Alcée Arobin; and Mademoiselle Reisz had consented to come. Edna had sent her a fresh bunch of violets with black lace trimmings for her hair. Monsieur Ratignolle brought himself and his wife's excuses. Victor Lebrun, who happened to be in the city, bent upon relaxation, had accepted with alacrity. There was a Miss Mayblunt, no longer in her teens, who looked at the world through lorgnettes and with the keenest interest. It was thought and said that she was intellectual; it was suspected of her that she wrote under a *nom de guerre* [assumed name]. She had come with a gentleman by the name of Gouvernail, connected with one of the daily papers, of whom nothing special could be said, except that he was observant and seemed quiet and inoffensive. Edna herself made the tenth, and at half-past eight they seated themselves at table, Arobin and Monsieur Ratignolle on either side of their hostess.

Mrs. Highcamp sat between Arobin and Victor Lebrun. Then came Mrs. Merriman, Mr. Gouvernail, Miss Mayblunt, Mr. Merriman, and Mademoiselle Reisz next to Monsieur Ratignolle.

There was something extremely gorgeous about the appearance of the table, an effect of splendor conveyed by a cover of pale yellow satin under strips of lacework. There were wax candles, in massive brass candelabra, burning softly under yellow silk shades; full, fragrant roses, yellow and red, abounded. There were silver and gold, as she had said there would be, and crystal which glittered like the gems which the women wore.

The ordinary stiff dining chairs had been discarded for the occasion and replaced by the most commodious and luxurious which could be collected throughout the house. Mademoiselle Reisz, being exceedingly diminutive, was elevated upon cushions, as small children are sometimes hoisted at table upon bulky volumes.

"Something new, Edna?" exclaimed Miss Mayblunt, with lorgnette directed toward a magnificent cluster of diamonds that sparkled, that almost sputtered, in Edna's hair, just over the center of her forehead.

"Quite new; 'brand' new, in fact; a present from my husband. It arrived this morning from New York. I may as well admit that this is my birthday, and that I am twenty-nine. In good time I expect you to drink my health. Meanwhile, I shall ask you to begin with this cocktail, composed—would you say 'composed?' " with an appeal to Miss Mayblunt—"composed by my father in honor of Sister Janet's wedding."

Before each guest stood a tiny glass that looked and sparkled like a garnet gem.

"Then, all things considered," spoke Arobin, "it might not be amiss to start out by drinking the Colonel's health in the cocktail which he composed, on the birthday of the most charming of women—the daughter whom he invented."

Mr. Merriman's laugh at this sally was such a genuine outburst and so contagious that it started the dinner with an agreeable swing that never slackened.

Miss Mayblunt begged to be allowed to keep her cocktail untouched before her, just to look at. The color was marvelous! She could compare it to nothing she had ever seen, and the garnet lights which it emitted were unspeakably rare. She pronounced the Colonel an artist, and stuck to it.

Monsieur Ratignolle was prepared to take things seriously; the *mets,* the *entremets* [the main dishes; the side dishes], the service, the decorations, even the people. He looked up from his pompano and inquired of Arobin if he were related to the gentleman of that name who formed one of the firm of Laitner and Arobin, lawyers. The young man admitted that Laitner was a warm personal friend, who permitted Arobin's name to decorate the firm's letterheads and to appear upon a shingle that graced Perdido Street.

"There are so many inquisitive people and institutions abounding," said Arobin, "that one is really forced as a matter of convenience these days to assume the virtue of an occupation if he has it not."

Monsieur Ratignolle stared a little, and turned to ask Mademoiselle Reisz if she considered the symphony concerts up to the standard which had been set the previous winter. Mademoiselle Reisz answered Monsieur Ratignolle in French, which Edna thought a little rude, under the circumstances, but characteristic. Mademoiselle had only disagreeable things to say of the symphony concerts, and insulting remarks to make of all the musicians of New Orleans, singly and collectively. All her interest seemed to be centered upon the delicacies placed before her.

Mr. Merriman said that Mr. Arobin's

remark about inquisitive people reminded him of a man from Waco the other day at the St. Charles Hotel—but as Mr. Merriman's stories were always lame and lacking point, his wife seldom permitted him to complete them. She interrupted him to ask if he remembered the name of the author whose book she had bought the week before to send to a friend in Geneva. She was talking "books" with Mr. Gouvernail and trying to draw from him his opinion upon current literary topics. Her husband told the story of the Waco man privately to Miss Mayblunt, who pretended to be greatly amused and to think it extremely clever.

Mrs. Highcamp hung with languid but unaffected interest upon the warm and impetuous volubility of her left-hand neighbor, Victor Lebrun. Her attention was never for a moment withdrawn from him after seating herself at table; and when he turned to Mrs. Merriman, who was prettier and more vivacious than Mrs. Highcamp, she waited with easy indifference for an opportunity to reclaim his attention. There was the occasional sound of music, of mandolins, sufficiently removed to be an agreeable accompaniment rather than an interruption to the conversation. Outside the soft, monotonous splash of a fountain could be heard; the sound penetrated into the room with the heavy odor of jasmine that came through the open windows.

The golden shimmer of Edna's satin gown spread in rich folds on either side of her. There was a soft fall of lace encircling her shoulders. It was the color of her skin, without the glow, the myriad living tints that one may sometimes discover in vibrant flesh. There was something in her attitude, in her whole appearance when she leaned her head against the high-backed chair and spread her arms, which suggested the regal woman, the one who rules, who looks on, who stands alone.

But as she sat there amid her guests,

she felt the old ennui overtaking her; the hopelessness which so often assailed her, which came upon her like an obsession, like something extraneous, independent of volition. It was something which announced itself; a chill breath that seemed to issue from some vast cavern wherein discords wailed. There came over her the acute longing which always summoned into her spiritual vision the presence of the beloved one, overpowering her at once with a sense of the unattainable.

The moments glided on, while a feeling of good fellowship passed around the circle like a mystic cord, holding and binding these people together with jest and laughter. Monsieur Ratignolle was the first to break the pleasant charm. At ten o'clock he excused himself. Madame Ratignolle was waiting for him at home. She was *bien souffrante* [very ill], and she was filled with vague dread, which only her husband's presence could allay.

Mademoiselle Reisz arose with Monsieur Ratignolle, who offered to escort her to the car. She had eaten well; she had tasted the good, rich wines, and they must have turned her head, for she bowed pleasantly to all as she withdrew from table. She kissed Edna upon the shoulder, and whispered: "*Bonne nuit, ma reine; soyez sage.* [Good night, my queen; be prudent]." She had been a little bewildered upon rising, or rather, descending from her cushions, and Monsieur Ratignolle gallantly took her arm and led her away.

Mrs. Highcamp was weaving a garland of roses, yellow and red. When she had finished the garland, she laid it lightly upon Victor's black curls. He was reclining far back in the luxurious chair, holding a glass of champagne to the light.

As if a magician's wand had touched him, the garland of roses transformed him into a vision of Oriental beauty. His cheeks were the color of crushed grapes, and his dusky eyes glowed with a languishing fire.

"*Sapristi!*" exclaimed Arobin.

But Mrs. Highcamp had one more touch to add to the picture. She took from the back of her chair a white silken scarf, with which she had covered her shoulders in the early part of the evening. She draped it across the boy in graceful folds, and in a way to conceal his black, conventional evening dress. He did not seem to mind what she did to him, only smiled, showing a faint gleam of white teeth, while he continued to gaze with narrowing eyes at the light through his glass of champagne.

"Oh! to be able to paint in color rather than in words!" exclaimed Miss Mayblunt, losing herself in a rhapsodic dream as she looked at him.

" '*There was a graven image of Desire Painted with red blood on a ground of gold,*' "

murmured Gouvernail, under his breath.

The effect of the wine upon Victor was to change his accustomed volubility into silence. He seemed to have abandoned himself to a reverie, and to be seeing pleasing visions in the amber bead.

"Sing," entreated Mrs. Highcamp. "Won't you sing to us?"

"Let him alone," said Arobin.

"He's posing," offered Mr. Merriman; "let him have it out."

"I believe he's paralyzed," laughed Mrs. Merriman. And leaning over the youth's chair, she took the glass from his hand and held it to his lips. He sipped the wine slowly, and when he had drained the glass she laid it upon the table and wiped his lips with her little filmy handkerchief.

"Yes, I'll sing for you," he said, turning in his chair toward Mrs. Highcamp. He clasped his hands behind his head, and looking up at the ceiling began to hum a little, trying his voice like a musician tuning an instrument. Then, looking at Edna, he began to sing:

"*Ah! si tu savais!*"

"Stop!" she cried, "don't sing that. I don't want you to sing it," and she laid her glass so impetuously and blindly upon the table as to shatter it against a carafe. The wine spilled over Arobin's legs and some of it trickled down upon Mrs. Highcamp's black gauze gown. Victor had lost all idea of courtesy, or else he thought his hostess was not in earnest, for he laughed and went on:

"Ah! si tu savais
Ce que tes yeux me disent—
[Ah! If you knew/What your eyes tell me]"

"Oh! you mustn't! you mustn't," exclaimed Edna, and pushing back her chair she got up, and going behind him placed her hand over his mouth. He kissed the soft palm that pressed upon his lips.

"No, no, I won't, Mrs. Pontellier. I didn't know you meant it," looking up at her with caressing eyes. The touch of his lips was like a pleasing sting to her hand. She lifted the garland of roses from his head and flung it across the room.

"Come, Victor; you've posed long enough. Give Mrs. Highcamp her scarf."

Mrs. Highcamp undraped the scarf from about him with her own hands. Miss Mayblunt and Mr. Gouvernail suddenly conceived the notion that it was time to say good night. And Mr. and Mrs. Merriman wondered how it could be so late.

Before parting from Victor, Mrs. Highcamp invited him to call upon her daughter, who she knew would be charmed to meet him and talk French and sing French songs with him. Victor expressed his desire and intention to call upon Miss Highcamp at the first opportunity which presented itself. He asked if Arobin were going his way. Arobin was not.

The mandolin players had long since stolen away. A profound stillness had fallen upon the broad, beautiful street. The voices of Edna's disbanding guests jarred like a discordant note upon the quiet harmony of the night.

XXXI

"Well?" questioned Arobin, who had remained with Edna after the others had departed.

"Well," she reiterated, and stood up, stretching her arms, and feeling the need to relax her muscles after having been so long seated.

"What next?" he asked.

"The servants are all gone. They left when the musicians did. I have dismissed them. The house has to be closed and locked, and I shall trot around to the pigeon house, and shall send Celestine over in the morning to straighten things up."

He looked around, and began to turn out some of the lights.

"What about upstairs?" he inquired.

"I think it is all right; but there may be a window or two unlatched. We had better look; you might take a candle and see. And bring me my wrap and hat on the foot of the bed in the middle room."

He went up with the light, and Edna began closing doors and windows. She hated to shut in the smoke and the fumes of the wine. Arobin found her cape and hat, which he brought down and helped her to put on.

When everything was secured and the lights put out, they left through the front door, Arobin locking it and taking the key, which he carried for Edna. He helped her down the steps.

"Will you have a spray of jasmine?" he asked, breaking off a few blossoms as he passed.

"No; I don't want anything."

She seemed disheartened, and had nothing to say. She took his arm, which he offered her, holding up the weight of her satin train with the other hand. She looked down, noticing the black line of his leg moving in and out so close to her against the yellow shimmer of her gown. There was the whistle of a railway train somewhere in the distance, and the midnight bells were ringing. They met no one in their short walk.

The "pigeon house" stood behind a locked gate, and a shallow *parterre* [flower bed] that had been somewhat neglected. There was a small front porch, upon which a long window and the front door opened. The door opened directly into the parlor; there was no side entry. Back in the yard was a room for servants, in which old Celestine had been ensconced.

Edna had left a lamp burning low upon the table. She had succeeded in making the room look habitable and homelike. There were some books on the table and a lounge near at hand. On the floor was a fresh matting, covered with a rug or two; and on the walls hung a few tasteful pictures. But the room was filled with flowers. These were a surprise to her. Arobin had sent them, and had had Celestine distribute them during Edna's absence. Her bedroom was adjoining, and across a small passage were the dining room and kitchen.

Edna seated herself with every appearance of discomfort.

"Are you tired?" he asked.

"Yes, and chilled, and miserable. I feel as if I had been wound up to a certain pitch—too tight—and something inside of me had snapped." She rested her head against the table upon her bare arm.

"You want to rest," he said, "and to be quiet. I'll go; I'll leave you and let you rest."

"Yes," she replied.

He stood up beside her and smoothed her hair with his soft, magnetic hand. His touch conveyed to her a certain physical comfort. She could have fallen quietly asleep there if he had continued to pass his hand over her hair. He brushed the hair upward from the nape of her neck.

"I hope you will feel better and happier in the morning," he said. "You have tried to do too much in the past few days. The dinner was the last straw; you might have dispensed with it."

"Yes," she admitted; "it was stupid."

"No, it was delightful; but it has worn you out." His hand had strayed to her beautiful shoulders, and he could feel the response of her flesh to his touch. He seated himself beside her and kissed her lightly upon the shoulder.

"I thought you were going away," she said, in an uneven voice.

"I am, after I have said good night."

"Good night," she murmured.

He did not answer, except to continue to caress her. He did not say good night until she had become supple to his gentle, seductive entreaties.

XXXII

When Mr. Pontellier learned of his wife's intention to abandon her home and take up her residence elsewhere, he immediately wrote her a letter of unqualified disapproval and remonstrance. She had given reasons which he was unwilling to acknowledge as adequate. He hoped she had not acted upon her rash impulse; and he begged her to consider first, foremost, and above all else, what people would say. He was not dreaming of scandal when he uttered this warning; that was a thing which would never have entered into his mind to consider in connection with his wife's name or his own. He was simply thinking of his financial integrity. It might get noised about that the Pontelliers had met with reverses, and were forced to conduct their *ménage* [household] on a humbler scale than heretofore. It might do incalculable mischief to his business prospects.

But remembering Edna's whimsical turn of mind of late, and foreseeing that she had immediately acted upon her impetuous determination, he grasped the situation with his usual promptness and handled it with his well-known business tact and cleverness.

The same mail which brought to Edna his letter of disapproval carried instructions—the most minute instructions—to a well-known architect concerning the remodeling of his home, changes which he had long contemplated, and which he desired carried forward during his temporary absence.

Expert and reliable packers and movers were engaged to convey the furniture, carpets, pictures—everything movable, in short—to places of security. And in an incredibly short time the Pontellier house was turned over to the artisans. There was to be an addition—a small snuggery; there was to be frescoing, and hardwood flooring was to be put into such rooms as had not yet been subjected to this improvement.

Furthermore, in one of the daily papers appeared a brief notice to the effect that Mr. and Mrs. Pontellier were contemplating a summer sojourn abroad, and that their handsome residence on Esplanade Street was undergoing sumptuous alterations, and would not be ready for occupancy until their return. Mr. Pontellier had saved appearances!

Edna admired the skill of his maneuver, and avoided any occasion to balk his intentions. When the situation as set forth by Mr. Pontellier was accepted and taken for granted, she was apparently satisfied that it should be so.

The pigeon house pleased her. It at once assumed the intimate character of a home, while she herself invested it with a charm which it reflected like a warm glow. There was with her a feeling of having descended in the social scale, with a corresponding sense of having risen in the spiritual. Every step which she took toward relieving herself from obligations added to her strength and expansion as an individual. She began to look with her own eyes; to see and to apprehend the deeper undercurrents of life. No longer was she content to "feed upon opinion" when her own soul had invited her.

After a little while, a few days, in fact, Edna went up and spent a week with her children in Iberville. They were delicious February days, with all the summer's promise hovering in the air.

How glad she was to see the children!

She wept for very pleasure when she felt their little arms clasping her; their hard, ruddy cheeks pressed against her own glowing cheeks. She looked into their faces with hungry eyes that could not be satisfied with looking. And what stories they had to tell their mother! About the pigs, the cows, the mules! About riding to the mill behind Gluglu; fishing back in the lake with their Uncle Jasper; picking pecans with Lidie's little black brood, and hauling chips in their express wagon. It was a thousand times more fun to haul real chips for old lame Susie's real fire than to drag painted blocks along the banquette on Esplanade Street!

She went with them herself to see the pigs and the cows, to look at the darkies laying the cane, to thrash the pecan trees, and catch fish in the back lake. She lived with them a whole week long, giving them all of herself, and gathering and filling herself with their young existence. They listened, breathless, when she told them the house in Esplanade Street was crowded with workmen, hammering, nailing, sawing, and filling the place with clatter. They wanted to know where their bed was; what had been done with their rocking horse; and where did Joe sleep, and where had Ellen gone, and the cook? But, above all, they were fired with a desire to see the little house around the block. Was there any place to play? Were there any boys next door? Raoul, with pessimistic foreboding, was convinced that there were only girls next door. Where would they sleep, and where would papa sleep? She told them the fairies would fix it all right.

The old Madame was charmed with Edna's visit, and showered all manner of delicate attentions upon her. She was delighted to know that the Esplanade Street house was in a dismantled condition. It gave her the promise and pretext to keep the children indefinitely.

It was with a wrench and a pang that Edna left her children. She carried away with her the sound of their voices and the touch of their cheeks. All along the journey homeward their presence lingered with her like the memory of a delicious song. But by the time she had regained the city the song no longer echoed in her soul. She was again alone.

XXXIII

It happened sometimes when Edna went to see Mademoiselle Reisz that the little musician was absent, giving a lesson or making some small necessary household purchase. The key was always left in a secret hiding place in the entry, which Edna knew. If Mademoiselle happened to be away, Edna would usually enter and wait for her return.

When she knocked at Mademoiselle Reisz's door one afternoon there was no response; so unlocking the door, as usual, she entered and found the apartment deserted, as she had expected. Her day had been quite filled up, and it was for a rest, for a refuge, and to talk about Robert, that she sought out her friend.

She had worked at her canvas—a young Italian character study—all the morning, completing the work without the model; but there had been many interruptions, some incident to her modest housekeeping, and others of a social nature.

Madame Ratignolle had dragged herself over, avoiding the too public thoroughfares, she said. She complained that Edna had neglected her much of late. Besides, she was consumed with curiosity to see the little house and the manner in which it was conducted. She wanted to hear all about the dinner party; Monsieur Ratignolle had left *so* early. What had happened after he left? The champagne and grapes which Edna sent over were *too* delicious. She had so little appetite; they had refreshed and toned her stomach. Where on earth was she going to put Mr. Pontellier in that little house, and the boys? And then she made Edna promise to go to her when her hour of trial overtook her.

"At any time—any time of the day or night, dear," Edna assured her.

Before leaving Madame Ratignolle said:

"In some way you seem to me like a child, Edna. You seem to act without a certain amount of reflection which is necessary in this life. That is the reason I want to say you mustn't mind if I advise you to be a little careful while you are living here alone. Why don't you have someone come and stay with you? Wouldn't Mademoiselle Reisz come?"

"No; she wouldn't wish to come, and I shouldn't want her always with me."

"Well, the reason—you know how evil-minded the world is—someone was talking of Alcée Arobin visiting you. Of course, it wouldn't matter if Mr. Arobin had not such a dreadful reputation. Monsieur Ratignolle was telling me that his attentions alone are considered enough to ruin a woman's name."

"Does he boast of his successes?" asked Edna, indifferently, squinting at her picture.

"No, I think not. I believe he is a decent fellow as far as that goes. But his character is so well known among the men. I shan't be able to come back and see you; it was very, very imprudent today."

"Mind the step!" cried Edna.

"Don't neglect me," entreated Madame Ratignolle; "and don't mind what I said about Arobin, or having someone to stay with you."

"Of course not," Edna laughed. "You may say anything you like to me." They kissed each other good-bye. Madame Ratignolle had not far to go, and Edna stood on the porch a while watching her walk down the street.

Then in the afternoon Mrs. Merriman and Mrs. Highcamp had made their "party call." Edna felt that they might have dispensed with the formality. They had also come to invite her to play *vingt-et-un* [twenty-one; a card game] one evening at Mrs. Merriman's. She was asked to go early, to dinner, and Mr. Merriman or

Mr. Arobin would take her home. Edna accepted in a halfhearted way. She sometimes felt very tired of Mrs. Highcamp and Mrs. Merriman.

Late in the afternoon she sought refuge with Mademoiselle Reisz, and stayed there alone, waiting for her, feeling a kind of repose invade her with the very atmosphere of the shabby, unpretentious little room.

Edna sat at the window, which looked out over the housetops and across the river. The window frame was filled with pots of flowers, and she sat and picked the dry leaves from a rose geranium. The day was warm, and the breeze which blew from the river was very pleasant. She removed her hat and laid it on the piano. She went on picking the leaves and digging around the plants with her hatpin. Once she thought she heard Mademoiselle Reisz approaching. But it was a young black girl, who came in, bringing a small bundle of laundry, which she deposited in the adjoining room, and went away.

Edna seated herself at the piano, and softly picked out with one hand the bars of a piece of music which lay open before her. A half hour went by. There was the occasional sound of people going and coming in the lower hall. She was growing interested in her occupation of picking out the aria, when there was a second rap at the door. She vaguely wondered what these people did when they found Mademoiselle's door locked.

"Come in," she called, turning her face toward the door. And this time it was Robert Lebrun who presented himself. She attempted to rise; she could not have done so without betraying the agitation which mastered her at sight of him, so she fell back upon the stool, only exclaiming, "Why, Robert!"

He came and clasped her hand, seemingly without knowing what he was saying or doing.

"Mrs. Pontellier! How do you happen—oh! how well you look! Is Mademoiselle Reisz not here? I never expected to see you."

"When did you come back?" asked Edna in an unsteady voice, wiping her face with her handkerchief. She seemed ill at ease on the piano stool, and he begged her to take the chair by the window. She did so, mechanically, while he seated himself on the stool.

"I returned day before yesterday," he answered, while he leaned his arm on the keys, bringing forth a crash of discordant sound.

"Day before yesterday!" she repeated, aloud; and went on thinking to herself, "day before yesterday," in a sort of an uncomprehending way. She had pictured him seeking her at the very first hour, and he had lived under the same sky since day before yesterday; while only by accident had he stumbled upon her. Mademoiselle must have lied when she said, "Poor fool, he loves you."

"Day before yesterday," she repeated, breaking off a spray of Mademoiselle's geranium; "then if you had not met me here today you wouldn't—when—that is, didn't you mean to come and see me?"

"Of course, I should have gone to see you. There have been so many things—" he turned the leaves of Mademoiselle's music nervously. "I started in at once yesterday with the old firm. After all there is as much chance for me here as there was there—that is, I might find it profitable some day. The Mexicans were not very congenial."

So he had come back because the Mexicans were not congenial; because business was as profitable here as there; because of any reason, and not because he cared to be near her. She remembered the day she sat on the floor, turning the pages of his letter, seeking the reason which was left untold.

She had not noticed how he looked—only feeling his presence; but she turned deliberately and observed him. After all, he had been absent but a few months, and was not changed. His hair—the color of hers—waved back from his temples in the same way as before. His skin was not more burned than it had been at Grand Isle. She found in his eyes, when he looked at her for one silent moment, the same tender caress, with an added warmth and entreaty which had not been there before— the same glance which had penetrated to the sleeping places of her soul and awakened them.

A hundred times Edna had pictured Robert's return, and imagined their first meeting. It was usually at her home, whither he had sought her out at once. She always fancied him expressing or betraying in some way his love for her. And here, the reality was that they sat ten feet apart, she at the window, crushing geranium leaves in her hand and smelling them, he twirling around on the piano stool, saying:

"I was very much surprised to hear of Mr. Pontellier's absence; it's a wonder Mademoiselle Reisz did not tell me; and your moving—mother told me yesterday. I should think you would have gone to New York with him, or to Iberville with the children, rather than be bothered here with housekeeping. And you are going abroad, too, I hear. We shan't have you at Grand Isle next summer; it won't seem— do you see much of Mademoiselle Reisz? She often spoke of you in the few letters she wrote."

"Do you remember that you promised to write to me when you went away?" A flush overspread his whole face.

"I couldn't believe that my letters would be of any interest to you."

"That is an excuse; it isn't the truth." Edna reached for her hat on the piano. She adjusted it, sticking the hatpin through the heavy coil of hair with some deliberation.

"Are you not going to wait for Mademoiselle Reisz?" asked Robert.

"No; I have found when she is absent this long, she is liable not to come back till late." She drew on her gloves, and Robert picked up his hat.

"Won't you wait for her?" asked Edna.

"Not if you think she will not be back till late," adding, as if suddenly aware of some discourtesy in his speech, "and I should miss the pleasure of walking home with you." Edna locked the door and put the key back in its hiding place.

They went together, picking their way across muddy streets and sidewalks encumbered with the cheap display of small tradesmen. Part of the distance they rode in the car, and after disembarking, passed the Pontellier mansion, which looked broken and half torn asunder. Robert had never known the house, and looked at it with interest.

"I never knew you in your home," he remarked.

"I am glad you did not."

"Why?" She did not answer. They went on around the corner, and it seemed as if her dreams were coming true after all, when he followed her into the little house.

"You must stay and dine with me, Robert. You see I am all alone, and it is so long since I have seen you. There is so much I want to ask you."

She took off her hat and gloves. He stood irresolute, making some excuse about his mother who expected him; he even muttered something about an engagement. She struck a match and lit the lamp on the table; it was growing dusk. When he saw her face in the lamplight, looking pained; with all the soft lines gone out of it, he threw his hat aside and seated himself.

"Oh! you know I want to stay if you will let me!" he exclaimed. All the softness came back. She laughed, and went and put her hand on his shoulder.

"This is the first moment you have seemed like the old Robert. I'll go tell Celestine." She hurried away to tell Celestine to set an extra place. She even sent her off in search of some added delicacy which she had not thought of for herself. And she recommended great care in dripping the coffee and having the omelet done to a proper turn.

When she reentered, Robert was turning over magazines, sketches, and things that lay upon the table in great disorder. He picked up a photograph, and exclaimed:

"Alcée Arobin! What on earth is his picture doing here?"

"I tried to make a sketch of his head one day," answered Edna, "and he thought the photograph might help me. It was at the other house. I thought it had been left there. I must have packed it up with my drawing materials."

"I should think you would give it back to him if you have finished with it."

"Oh! I have a great many such photographs. I never think of returning them. They don't amount to anything." Robert kept on looking at the picture.

"It seems to me—do you think his head worth drawing? Is he a friend of Mr. Pontellier's? You never said you knew him."

"He isn't a friend of Mr. Pontellier's; he's a friend of mine. I always knew him— that is, it is only of late that I know him pretty well. But I'd rather talk about you, and know what you have been seeing and doing and feeling out there in Mexico." Robert threw aside the picture.

"I've been seeing the waves and the white beach of Grand Isle; the quiet, grassy street of the *Chênière;* the old fort at Grande Terre. I've been working like a machine, and feeling like a lost soul. There was nothing interesting."

She leaned her head upon her hand to shade her eyes from the light.

"And what have you been seeing and doing and feeling all these days?" he asked.

"I've been seeing the waves and the white beach of Grand Isle; the quiet, grassy street of the *Chênière Caminada;* the old sunny fort at Grande Terre. I've been working with a little more comprehension than a machine, and still feeling like a lost soul. There was nothing interesting."

"Mrs. Pontellier, you are cruel," he said, with feeling, closing his eyes and resting his head back in his chair. They remained in silence till old Celestine announced dinner.

XXXIV

The dining room was very small. Edna's round mahogany would have almost filled it. As it was there was but a step or two from the little table to the kitchen, to the mantel, the small buffet, and the side door that opened out on the narrow brick-paved yard.

A certain degree of ceremony settled upon them with the announcement of dinner. There was no return to personalities. Robert related incidents of his sojourn in Mexico, and Edna talked of events likely to interest him, which had occurred during his absence. The dinner was of ordinary quality, except for the few delicacies which she had sent out to purchase. Old Celestine, with a bandana *tignon* twisted about her head, hobbled in and out, taking a personal interest in everything; and she lingered occasionally to talk patois with Robert, whom she had known as a boy.

He went out to a neighboring cigar stand to purchase cigarette papers, and when he came back he found that Celestine had served the black coffee in the parlor.

"Perhaps I shouldn't have come back," he said. "When you are tired of me, tell me to go."

"You never tire me. You must have forgotten the hours and hours at Grand Isle in which we grew accustomed to each other and used to being together."

"I have forgotten nothing at Grand Isle," he said, not looking at her, but rolling a cigarette. His tobacco pouch, which he laid upon the table, was a fantastic embroidered silk affair, evidently the handiwork of a woman.

"You used to carry your tobacco in a rubber pouch," said Edna, picking up the pouch and examining the needlework.

"Yes; it was lost."

"Where did you buy this one? In Mexico?"

"It was given to me by a Vera Cruz girl; they are very generous," he replied, striking a match and lighting his cigarette.

"They are very handsome, I suppose, those Mexican women; very picturesque, with their black eyes and their lace scarfs."

"Some are; others are hideous. Just as you find women everywhere."

"What was she like—the one who gave you the pouch? You must have known her very well."

"She was very ordinary. She wasn't of the slightest importance. I knew her well enough."

"Did you visit at her house? Was it interesting? I should like to know and hear about the people you met, and the impressions they made on you."

"There are some people who leave impressions not so lasting as the imprint of an oar upon the water."

"Was she such a one?"

"It would be ungenerous for me to admit that she was of that order and kind." He thrust the pouch back in his pocket, as if to put away the subject with the trifle which had brought it up.

Arobin dropped in with a message from Mrs. Merriman, to say that the card party was postponed on account of the illness of one of her children.

"How do you do, Arobin?" said Robert, rising from the obscurity.

"Oh! Lebrun. To be sure! I heard yesterday you were back. How did they treat you down in Mexique?"

"Fairly well."

"But not well enough to keep you there. Stunning girls, though, in Mexico. I thought I should never get away from Vera Cruz when I was down there a couple of years ago."

"Did they embroider slippers and tobacco pouches and hatbands and things for you?" asked Edna.

"Oh! my! no! I didn't get so deep in their regard. I fear they made more impression on me than I made on them."

"You were less fortunate than Robert, then."

"I am always less fortunate than Robert.

Has he been imparting tender confidences?"

"I've been imposing myself long enough," said Robert, rising, and shaking hands with Edna. "Please convey my regards to Mr. Pontellier when you write."

He shook hands with Arobin and went away.

"Fine fellow, that Lebrun," said Arobin when Robert had gone. "I never heard you speak of him."

"I knew him last summer at Grand Isle," she replied. "Here is that photograph of yours. Don't you want it?"

"What do I want with it? Throw it away." She threw it back on the table.

"I'm not going to Mrs. Merriman's," she said. "If you see her, tell her so. But perhaps I had better write. I think I shall write now, and say that I am sorry her child is sick, and tell her not to count on me."

"It would be a good scheme," acquiesced Arobin. "I don't blame you; stupid lot!"

Edna opened the blotter, and having procured paper and pen, began to write the note. Arobin lit a cigar and read the evening paper, which he had in his pocket.

"What is the date?" she asked. He told her.

"Will you mail this for me when you go out?"

"Certainly." He read to her little bits out of the newspaper, while she straightened things on the table.

"What do you want to do?" he asked, throwing aside the paper. "Do you want to go out for a walk or a drive or anything? It would be a fine night to drive."

"No; I don't want to do anything but just be quiet. You go away and amuse yourself. Don't stay."

"I'll go away if I must; but I shan't amuse myself. You know that I only live when I am near you."

He stood up to bid her good night.

"Is that one of the things you always say to women?"

"I have said it before, but I don't think

I ever came so near meaning it," he answered with a smile. There were no warm lights in her eyes; only a dreamy, absent look.

"Good night. I adore you. Sleep well," he said, and he kissed her hand and went away.

She stayed alone in a kind of reverie—a sort of stupor. Step by step she lived over every instant of the time she had been with Robert after he had entered Mademoiselle Reisz's door. She recalled his words, his looks. How few and meager they had been for her hungry heart! A vision—a transcendently seductive vision of a Mexican girl arose before her. She writhed with a jealous pang. She wondered when he would come back. He had not said he would come back. She had been with him, had heard his voice and touched his hand. But some way he had seemed nearer to her off there in Mexico.

XXXV

The morning was full of sunlight and hope. Edna could see before her no denial—only the promise of excessive joy. She lay in bed awake, with bright eyes full of speculation. "He loves you, poor fool." If she could but get that conviction firmly fixed in her mind, what mattered about the rest? She felt she had been childish and unwise the night before in giving herself over to despondency. She recapitulated the motives which no doubt explained Robert's reserve. They were not insurmountable; they would not hold if he really loved her; they could not hold against her own passion, which he must come to realize in time. She pictured him going to his business that morning. She even saw how he was dressed; how he walked down one street, and turned the corner of another; saw him bending over his desk, talking to people who entered the office, going to his lunch, and perhaps watching for her on the street. He would come to her in the afternoon or evening, sit and roll his cigarette, talk a little, and go away as he had done the night before. But how delicious it would be to have him there with her! She would have no regrets, nor seek to penetrate his reserve if he still chose to wear it.

Edna ate her breakfast only half dressed. The maid brought her a delicious printed scrawl from Raoul, expressing his love, asking her to send him some bonbons, and telling her they had found that morning ten tiny white pigs all lying in a row beside Lidie's big white pig.

A letter also came from her husband, saying he hoped to be back early in March, and then they would get ready for that journey abroad which he had promised her so long, which he felt now fully able to afford; he felt able to travel as people should, without any thought of small economies—thanks to his recent speculations in Wall Street.

Much to her surprise she received a note from Arobin, written at midnight from the club. It was to say good morning to her, to hope she had slept well, to assure her of his devotion, which he trusted she in some faintest manner returned.

All these letters were pleasing to her. She answered the children in a cheerful frame of mind, promising them bonbons, and congratulating them upon their happy find of the little pigs.

She answered her husband with friendly evasiveness—not with any fixed design to mislead him, only because all sense of reality had gone out of her life; she had abandoned herself to Fate, and awaited the consequences with indifference.

To Arobin's note she made no reply. She put it under Celestine's stove lid.

Edna worked several hours with much spirit. She saw no one but a picture dealer, who asked her if it were true that she was going abroad to study in Paris.

She said possibly she might, and he negotiated with her for some Parisian studies to reach him in time for the holiday trade in December.

Robert did not come that day. She was keenly disappointed. He did not come the following day, nor the next. Each morning she awoke with hope, and each night she was a prey to despondency. She was tempted to seek him out. But far from yielding to the impulse, she avoided any occasion which might throw her in his way. She did not go to Mademoiselle Reisz's nor pass by Madame Lebrun's, as she might have done if he had still been in Mexico.

When Arobin, one night, urged her to drive with him, she went—out to the lake, on the Shell Road. His horses were full of mettle, and even a little unmanageable. She liked the rapid gait at which they spun along, and the quick, sharp sound of the horses' hoofs on the hard road. They did not stop anywhere to eat or to drink. Arobin was not needlessly imprudent. But they ate and they drank when they regained Edna's little dining room—which was comparatively early in the evening.

It was late when he left her. It was getting to be more than a passing whim with Arobin to see her and be with her. He had detected the latent sensuality, which unfolded under his delicate sense of her nature's requirements like a torpid, torrid, sensitive blossom.

There was no despondency when she fell asleep that night; nor was there hope when she awoke in the morning.

XXXVI

There was a garden out in the suburbs; a small, leafy corner, with a few green tables under the orange trees. An old cat slept all day on the stone step in the sun, and an old *mulatresse* [mulatto] slept her idle hours away in her chair at the open window, till someone happened to knock on one of the green tables. She had milk and cream cheese to sell, and bread and butter. There was no one who could make such excellent coffee or fry a chicken so golden brown as she.

The place was too modest to attract the attention of people of fashion, and so quiet as to have escaped the notice of those in search of pleasure and dissipation. Edna had discovered it accidentally one day when the high-board gate stood ajar. She caught sight of a little green table, blotched with the checkered sunlight that filtered through the quivering leaves overhead. Within she had found the slumbering *mulatresse,* the drowsy cat, and a glass of milk which reminded her of the milk she had tasted in Iberville.

She often stopped there during her perambulations; sometimes taking a book with her, and sitting an hour or two under the trees when she found the place deserted. Once or twice she took a quiet dinner there alone, having instructed Celestine beforehand to prepare no dinner at home. It was the last place in the city where she would have expected to meet anyone she knew.

Still she was not astonished when, as she was partaking of a modest dinner late in the afternoon, looking into an open book, stroking the cat, which had made friends with her—she was not greatly astonished to see Robert come in at the tall garden gate.

"I am destined to see you only by accident," she said, shoving the cat off the chair beside her. He was surprised, ill at ease, almost embarrassed at meeting her thus so unexpectedly.

"Do you come here often?" he asked.

"I almost live here," she said.

"I used to drop in very often for a cup of Catiche's good coffee. This is the first time since I came back."

"She'll bring you a plate, and you will share my dinner. There's always enough for two—even three." Edna had intended to be indifferent and as reserved as he when she met him; she had reached the determination by a laborious train of reasoning, incident to one of her despondent moods. But her resolve melted when she saw him before her, seated there beside her in the little garden, as if a designing Providence had led him into her path.

"Why have you kept away from me, Robert?" she asked, closing the book that lay open upon the table.

"Why are you so personal, Mrs. Pontellier? Why do you force me to idiotic subterfuges?" he exclaimed with sudden warmth. "I suppose there's no use telling you I've been very busy, or that I've been sick, or that I've been to see you and not found you at home. Please let me off with any one of these excuses."

"You are the embodiment of selfishness," she said. "You save yourself something—I don't know what—but there is some selfish motive, and in sparing yourself you never consider for a moment what I think, or how I feel your neglect and indifference. I suppose this is what you would call unwomanly; but I have got into a habit of expressing myself. It doesn't matter to me, and you may think me unwomanly if you like."

"No; I only think you cruel, as I said the other day. Maybe not intentionally cruel; but you seem to be forcing me into disclosures which can result in nothing; as if you would have me bare a wound for the pleasure of looking at it, without the intention or power of healing it."

"I'm spoiling your dinner, Robert; never mind what I say. You haven't eaten a morsel."

"I only came in for a cup of coffee." His sensitive face was all disfigured with excitement.

"Isn't this a delightful place?" she remarked. "I am so glad it has never actually been discovered. It is so quiet, so sweet, here. Do you notice there is scarcely a sound to be heard? It's so out of the way; and a good walk from the car. However, I don't mind walking. I always feel so sorry for women who don't like to walk; they miss so much—so many rare little glimpses of life; and we women learn so little of life on the whole.

"Catiche's coffee is always hot. I don't know how she manages it, here in the open air. Celestine's coffee gets cold bringing it from the kitchen to the dining room. Three lumps! How can you drink it so sweet? Take some of the cress with your chop; it's so biting and crisp. Then there's the advantage of being able to smoke with your coffee out here. Now, in the city— aren't you going to smoke?"

"After a while," he said, laying a cigar on the table.

"Who gave it to you?" she laughed.

"I bought it. I suppose I'm getting reckless; I bought a whole box." She was determined not to be personal again and make him uncomfortable.

The cat made friends with him, and climbed into his lap when he smoked his cigar. He stroked her silky fur, and talked a little about her. He looked at Edna's book, which he had read; and he told her the end, to save her the trouble of wading through it, he said.

Again he accompanied her back to her home; and it was after dusk when they reached the little "pigeon house." She did not ask him to remain, which he was grateful for, as it permitted him to stay without the discomfort of blundering through an excuse which he had no intention of considering. He helped her to light the lamp; then she went into her room to take off her hat and to bathe her face and hands.

When she came back Robert was not examining the pictures and magazines as before; he sat off in the shadow, leaning his head back on the chair as if in a reverie. Edna lingered a moment beside the table, arranging the books there. Then she went across the room to where he sat. She bent over the arm of his chair and called his name.

"Robert," she said, "are you asleep?"

"No," he answered, looking up at her.

She leaned over and kissed him—a soft, cool, delicate kiss, whose voluptuous sting penetrated his whole being—then she moved away from him. He followed, and took her in his arms, just holding her close to him. She put her hand up to his face and pressed his cheek against her own. The

action was full of love and tenderness. He sought her lips again. Then he drew her down upon the sofa beside him and held her hand in both of his.

"Now you know," he said, "now you know what I have been fighting against since last summer at Grand Isle; what drove me away and drove me back again."

"Why have you been fighting against it?" she asked. Her face glowed with soft lights.

"Why? Because you were not free; you were Léonce Pontellier's wife. I couldn't help loving you if you were ten times his wife; but so long as I went away from you and kept away I could help telling you so." She put her free hand up to his shoulder, and then against his cheek, rubbing it softly. He kissed her again. His face was warm and flushed.

"There in Mexico I was thinking of you all the time, and longing for you."

"But not writing to me," she interrupted.

"Something put into my head that you cared for me; and I lost my senses. I forgot everything but a wild dream of your some way becoming my wife."

"Your wife!"

"Religion, loyalty, everything would give way if only you cared."

"Then you must have forgotten that I was Léonce Pontellier's wife."

"Oh! I was demented, dreaming of wild, impossible things, recalling men who had set their wives free, we have heard of such things."

"Yes, we have heard of such things."

"I came back full of vague, mad intentions. And when I got here—"

"When you got here you never came near me!" She was still caressing his cheek.

"I realized what a cur I was to dream of such a thing, even if you had been willing."

She took his face between her hands and looked into it as if she would never withdraw her eyes more. She kissed him on the forehead, the eyes, the cheeks, and the lips.

"You have been a very, very foolish boy,

wasting your time dreaming of impossible things when you speak of Mr. Pontellier setting me free! I am no longer one of Mr. Pontellier's possessions to dispose of or not. I give myself where I choose. If he were to say, 'Here, Robert, take her and be happy; she is yours,' I should laugh at you both."

His face grew a little white. "What do you mean?" he asked.

There was a knock at the door. Old Celestine came in to say that Madame Ratignolle's servant had come around the back way with a message that Madame had been taken sick and begged Mrs. Pontellier to go to her immediately.

"Yes, yes," said Edna, rising; "I promised. Tell her yes—to wait for me. I'll go back with her."

"Let me walk over with you," offered Robert.

"No," she said; "I will go with the servant." She went into her room to put on her hat, and when she came in again she sat once more upon the sofa beside him. He had not stirred. She put her arms about his neck.

"Good-bye, my sweet Robert. Tell me good-bye." He kissed her with a degree of passion which had not before entered into his caress, and strained her to him.

"I love you," she whispered, "only you; no one but you. It was you who awoke me last summer out of a lifelong, stupid dream. Oh! you have made me so unhappy with your indifference. Oh! I have suffered, suffered! Now you are here we shall love each other, my Robert. We shall be everything to each other. Nothing else in the world is of any consequence. I must go to my friend; but you will wait for me? No matter how late; you will wait for me, Robert?"

"Don't go; don't go! Oh! Edna, stay with me," he pleaded. "Why should you go? Stay with me, stay with me."

"I shall come back as soon as I can; I shall find you here." She buried her face in his neck, and said good-bye again. Her seductive voice, together with his great love for her, had enthralled his senses, had deprived him of every impulse but the longing to hold her and keep her.

XXXVII

Edna looked in at the drugstore. Monsieur Ratignolle was putting up a mixture himself, very carefully, dropping a red liquid into a tiny glass. He was grateful to Edna for having come; her presence would be a comfort to his wife. Madame Ratignolle's sister, who had always been with her at such trying times, had not been able to come up from the plantation, and Adèle had been inconsolable until Mrs. Pontellier so kindly promised to come to her. The nurse had been with them at night for the past week, as she lived a great distance away. And Dr. Mandelet had been coming and going all the afternoon. They were then looking for him any moment.

Edna hastened upstairs by a private stairway that led from the rear of the store to the apartments above. The children were all sleeping in a back room. Madame Ratignolle was in the salon, whither she had strayed in her suffering impatience. She sat on the sofa, clad in an ample white *peignoir,* holding a handkerchief tight in her hand with a nervous clutch. Her face was drawn and pinched, her sweet blue eyes haggard and unnatural. All her beautiful hair had been drawn back and plaited. It lay in a long braid on the sofa pillow, coiled like a golden serpent. The nurse, a comfortable looking *Griffe* [mulatto] woman in white apron and cap, was urging her to return to her bedroom.

"There is no use, there is no use," she said at once to Edna. "We must get rid of Mandelet; he is getting too old and careless. He said he would be here at half-past seven; now it must be eight. See what time it is, Joséphine."

The woman was possessed of a cheerful nature, and refused to take any situation too seriously, especially a situation with which she was so familiar. She urged Madame to have courage and patience. But Madame only set her teeth hard into her under lip, and Edna saw the sweat gather in beads on her white forehead. After a moment or two she uttered a profound sigh and wiped her face with the handkerchief rolled in a ball. She appeared exhausted. The nurse gave her a fresh handkerchief, sprinkled with cologne water.

"This is too much!" she cried. "Mandelet ought to be killed! Where is Alphonse? Is it possible I am to be abandoned like this— neglected by everyone?"

"Neglected, indeed!" exclaimed the nurse. Wasn't she there? And here was Mrs. Pontellier leaving, no doubt, a pleasant evening at home to devote to her? And wasn't Monsieur Ratignolle coming that very instant through the hall? And Joséphine was quite sure she had heard Doctor Mandelet's coupé. Yes, there it was, down at the door.

Adèle consented to go back to her room. She sat on the edge of a little low couch next to her bed.

Doctor Mandelet paid no attention to Madame Ratignolle's upbraidings. He was accustomed to them at such times, and was too well convinced of her loyalty to doubt it.

He was glad to see Edna, and wanted her to go with him into the salon and entertain him. But Madame Ratignolle would not consent that Edna should leave her for an instant. Between agonizing moments, she chatted a little, and said it took her mind off her sufferings.

Edna began to feel uneasy. She was seized with a vague dread. Her own like experiences seemed far away, unreal, and only half remembered. She recalled faintly an ecstasy of pain, the heavy odor of chloroform, a stupor which had deadened sensation, and an awakening to find a little new life to which she had given being, added to the great unnumbered multitude of souls that come and go.

She began to wish she had not come;

her presence was not necessary. She might have invented a pretext for staying away; she might even invent a pretext now for going. But Edna did not go. With an inward agony, with a flaming, outspoken revolt against the ways of Nature, she witnessed the scene of torture.

She was still stunned and speechless with emotion when later she leaned over her friend to kiss her and softly say good-bye. Adèle, pressing her cheek, whispered in an exhausted voice: "Think of the children, Edna. Oh think of the children! Remember them!"

XXXVIII

Edna still felt dazed when she got outside in the open air. The Doctor's coupé had returned for him and stood before the *porte cochère*. She did not wish to enter the coupé, and told Doctor Mandelet she would walk; she was not afraid, and would go alone. He directed his carriage to meet him at Mrs. Pontellier's, and he started to walk home with her.

Up—away up, over the narrow street between the tall houses, the stars were blazing. The air was mild and caressing, but cool with the breath of spring and the night. They walked slowly, the Doctor with a heavy, measured tread and his hands behind him; Edna, in an absentminded way, as she had walked one night at Grand Isle, as if her thoughts had gone ahead of her and she was striving to overtake them.

"You shouldn't have been there, Mrs. Pontellier," he said. "That was no place for you. Adèle is full of whims at such times. There were a dozen women she might have had with her, unimpressionable women. I felt that it was cruel, cruel. You shouldn't have gone."

"Oh, well!" she answered, indifferently. "I don't know that it matters after all. One has to think of the children some time or other; the sooner the better."

"When is Léonce coming back?"

"Quite soon. Some time in March."

"And you are going abroad?"

"Perhaps—no, I am not going. I'm not going to be forced into doing things. I don't want to go abroad. I want to be let alone. Nobody has any right—except children, perhaps—and even then, it seems to me—or it did seem—" She felt that her speech was voicing the incoherency of her thoughts, and stopped abruptly.

"The trouble is," sighed the Doctor, grasping her meaning intuitively, "that youth is given up to illusions. It seems to be a provision of Nature; a decoy to secure mothers for the race. And Nature takes no account of moral consequences, of arbitrary conditions which we create, and which we feel obliged to maintain at any cost."

"Yes," she said. "The years that are gone seem like dreams—if one might go on sleeping and dreaming—but to wake up and find—oh! well! perhaps it is better to wake up after all, even to suffer, rather than to remain a dupe to illusions all one's life."

"It seems to me, my dear child," said the Doctor at parting, holding her hand, "you seem to me to be in trouble. I am not going to ask for your confidence. I will only say that if ever you feel moved to give it to me, perhaps I might help you. I know I would understand, and I tell you there are not many who would—not many, my dear."

"Some way I don't feel moved to speak of things that trouble me. Don't think I am ungrateful or that I don't appreciate your sympathy. There are periods of despondency and suffering which take possession of me. But I don't want anything but my own way. That is wanting a good deal, of course, when you have to trample upon the lives, the hearts, the prejudices of others—but no matter—still, I shouldn't want to trample upon the little lives. Oh! I don't know what I'm saying, Doctor. Good night. Don't blame me for anything."

"Yes, I will blame you if you don't come and see me soon. We will talk of things you never have dreamed of talking about before. It will do us both good. I don't want you to blame yourself, whatever comes. Good night, my child."

She let herself in at the gate, but instead of entering she sat upon the step of the porch. The night was quiet and soothing. All the tearing emotion of the last few hours seemed to fall away from her like a somber, uncomfortable garment, which she had but to loosen to be rid of. She went back to that hour before Adèle had sent for her; and her senses kindled afresh in thinking of Robert's words, the pressure of his arms, and the feeling of his lips upon her own. She could picture at that moment no greater bliss on earth than possession of the beloved one. His expression of love had already given him to her in part. When she thought that he was there at hand, waiting for her, she grew numb with the intoxication of expectancy. It was so late; he would be asleep perhaps. She would awaken him with a kiss. She hoped he would be asleep that she might arouse him with her caresses.

Still, she remembered Adèle's voice whispering, "Think of the children; think of them." She meant to think of them; that determination had driven into her soul like a death wound—but not tonight. Tomorrow would be time to think of everything.

Robert was not waiting for her in the little parlor. He was nowhere at hand. The house was empty. But he had scrawled on a piece of paper that lay in the lamplight:

"I love you. Good-bye—because I love you."

Edna grew faint when she read the words. She went and sat on the sofa. Then she stretched herself out there, never uttering a sound. She did not sleep. She did not go to bed. The lamp sputtered and went out. She was still awake in the morning, when Celestine unlocked the kitchen door and came in to light the fire.

XXXIX

Victor, with hammer and nails and scraps of scantling, was patching a corner of one of the galleries. Mariequita sat near by, dangling her legs, watching him work, and handing him nails from the toolbox. The sun was beating down upon them. The girl had covered her head with her apron folded into a square pad. They had been talking for an hour or more. She was never tired of hearing Victor describe the dinner at Mrs. Pontellier's. He exaggerated every detail, making it appear a veritable Lucullan feast. The flowers were in tubs, he said. The champagne was quaffed from huge golden goblets. Venus rising from the foam could have presented no more entrancing a spectacle than Mrs. Pontellier, blazing with beauty and diamonds at the head of the board, while the other women were all of them youthful houris, possessed of incomparable charms.

She got it into her head that Victor was in love with Mrs. Pontellier, and he gave her evasive answers, framed so as to confirm her belief. She grew sullen and cried a little, threatening to go off and leave him to his fine ladies. There were a dozen men crazy about her at the *Chênière;* and since it was the fashion to be in love with married people, why, she could run away any time she liked to New Orleans with Célina's husband.

Célina's husband was a fool, a coward, and a pig, and to prove it to her, Victor intended to hammer his head into a jelly the next time he encountered him. This assurance was very consoling to Mariequita. She dried her eyes, and grew cheerful at the prospect.

They were still talking of the dinner and the allurements of city life when Mrs. Pontellier herself slipped around the corner of the house. The two youngsters stayed dumb with amazement before what they considered to be an apparition. But it was really she in flesh and blood, looking tired and a little travel-stained.

"I walked up from the wharf," she said, "and heard the hammering. I supposed it was you, mending the porch. It's a good thing. I was always tripping over those loose planks last summer. How dreary and deserted everything looks!"

It took Victor some little time to comprehend that she had come in Beaudelet's lugger, that she had come alone, and for no purpose but to rest.

"There's nothing fixed up yet, you see. I'll give you my room; it's the only place."

"Any corner will do," she assured him.

"And if you can stand Philomel's cooking," he went on, "though I might try to get her mother while you are here. Do you think she would come?" turning to Mariequita.

Mariequita thought that perhaps Philomel's mother might come for a few days, and money enough.

Beholding Mrs. Pontellier make her appearance, the girl had at once suspected a lovers' rendezvous. But Victor's astonishment was so genuine, and Mrs. Pontellier's indifference so apparent, that the disturbing notion did not lodge long in her brain. She contemplated with the greatest interest this woman who gave the most sumptuous dinners in America, and who had all the men in New Orleans at her feet.

"What time will you have dinner?" asked Edna. "I'm very hungry; but don't get anything extra."

"I'll have it ready in little or no time," he said, bustling and packing away his tools. "You may go to my room to brush up and rest yourself. Mariequita will show you."

"Thank you," said Edna. "But, do you know, I have a notion to go down to the beach and take a good wash and even a little swim, before dinner?"

"The water is too cold!" they both exclaimed. "Don't think of it."

"Well, I might go down and try—dip my toes in. Why, it seems to me the sun is hot enough to have warmed the very depths of the ocean. Could you get me a couple of towels? I'd better go right away, so as to be back in time. It would be a little too chilly if I waited till this afternoon."

Mariequita ran over to Victor's room, and returned with some towels, which she gave to Edna.

"I hope you have fish for dinner," said Edna, as she started to walk away; "but don't do anything extra if you haven't."

"Run and find Philomel's mother," Victor instructed the girl. "I'll go to the kitchen and see what I can do. By Jiminy! Women have no consideration! She might have sent me word."

Edna walked on down to the beach rather mechanically, not noticing anything special except that the sun was hot. She was not dwelling upon any particular train of thought. She had done all the thinking which was necessary after Robert went away, when she lay awake upon the sofa till morning.

She had said over and over to herself: "Today it is Arobin; tomorrow it will be someone else. It makes no difference to me, it doesn't matter about Léonce Pontellier—but Raoul and Etienne!" She understood now clearly what she had meant long ago when she said to Adèle Ratignolle that she would give up the unessential, but she would never sacrifice herself for her children.

Despondency had come upon her there in the wakeful night, and had never lifted. There was no one thing in the world that she desired. There was no human being whom she wanted near her except Robert; and she even realized that the day would come when he, too, and the thought of him would melt out of her existence, leaving her alone. The children appeared before her like antagonists who had overcome her; who had overpowered and sought to drag her into the soul's slavery for the rest of her days. But she knew a way to elude them. She was not thinking of these things when she walked down to the beach.

The water of the Gulf stretched out before her, gleaming with the million lights of the sun. The voice of the sea is seductive, never ceasing, whispering, clamoring, murmuring, inviting the soul to wander in abysses of solitude. All along the white beach, up and down, there was no living thing in sight. A bird with a broken wing was beating the air above, reeling, fluttering, circling disabled down, down to the water.

Edna had found her old bathing suit still hanging, faded, upon its accustomed peg.

She put it on, leaving her clothing in the bathhouse. But when she was there beside the sea, absolutely alone, she cast the unpleasant, pricking garments from her, and for the first time in her life she stood naked in the open air, at the mercy of the sun, the breeze that beat upon her, and the waves that invited her.

How strange and awful it seemed to stand naked under the sky! how delicious! She felt like some newborn creature, opening its eyes in a familiar world that it had never known.

The foamy wavelets curled up to her white feet, and coiled like serpents about her ankles. She walked out. The water was chill, but she walked on. The water was deep, but she lifted her white body and reached out with a long, sweeping stroke. The touch of the sea is sensuous, enfolding the body in its soft, close embrace.

She went on and on. She remembered the night she swam far out, and recalled the terror that seized her at the fear of being unable to regain the shore. She did not look back now, but went on and on, thinking of the bluegrass meadow that she had traversed when a little child, believing that it had no beginning and no end.

Her arms and legs were growing tired.

She thought of Léonce and the children. They were a part of her life. But they need not have thought that they could possess her, body and soul. How Mademoiselle Reisz would have laughed, perhaps sneered, if she knew! "And you call yourself an artist! What pretensions, Madame! The artist must possess the courageous soul that dares and defies."

Exhaustion was pressing upon and overpowering her.

"Good-bye—because I love you." He did not know; he did not understand. He would never understand. Perhaps Doctor Mandelet would have understood if she had seen him—but it was too late; the shore was far behind her, and her strength was gone.

She looked into the distance, and the old terror flamed up for an instant, then sank again. Edna heard her father's voice and her sister Margaret's. She heard the barking of an old dog that was chained to the sycamore tree. The spurs of the cavalry officer clanged as he walked across the porch. There was the hum of bees, and the musky odor of pinks filled the air.

Rediscovering Natural Law

Scott Buchanan

Editor's Introduction

Is there in the natural order—indeed, in the cosmos—a regulative principle which entitles us to say that existence is governed by law, or laws? "God made all things according to number, weight, and measure," says the Apocrypha, and science appears to have agreed, notwithstanding that in the view of quantum physics the law is radically imprecise. But is the principle, precise or not, inherent, or is it a function of our minds, such that we cannot understand nature in any other terms? This was Kant's solution to what seemed an unanswerable question, and modern philosophy, however skeptical at times, has never got beyond it.

Supposing laws exist, are they any more than physical—do they extend as well to the moral order? A harder question still, which we are not ready as Kant was to decide in the affirmative. "The taste of good and evil depends in large part on the opinion we have of them," Montaigne says, and Hamlet's echo of this is well known. But is our thought a matter of necessity, or is it, in this regard, only an opinion, a value (or a set of values), as nowadays we tend to say? In that case, do we have any guide but what most people have accepted? "We hold these truths to be self-evident," Jefferson said, as if there were such truths, or could be, but we speak rather of tradition or consensus and make of principle a piety, a thing respectful if not right.

The political implications are serious. If no principle exists, how are we to decide whether laws are just or unjust? If we cannot do that, how can we in the United States settle claims of right under the Constitution—whether, for example, we assert an inherent right of privacy in abortion cases or deny the procedure on the ground that tradition only rules, and that no such right was recognized by those who framed the Constitution itself? What can underlie the Thirteenth, Fourteenth, and Fifteenth Amendments except a conviction that the institution of slavery was wrongly justified in 1789—that justice properly does not admit it? Shall we say only that the majority has shifted? How could it have done so on the United States Supreme Court, which having decided in 1897 that separate but equal facilities for blacks and whites were constitutional, decided in 1954 that they were not? The same Constitution governed on both occasions, and the same words. We may say, if we like, that after all, opinions vary, but we cannot say that this was on the basis of new language. We must accept that the same words had come to be differently understood, and we can reasonably account for that only if we suppose that reason somehow inheres in them.

Questions of this sort are the concern here of Scott Buchanan (1895–1968), whose discussion of them goes back to 1962, when it was published as an Occasional Paper by the Center for the Study of Democratic Institutions, where Buchanan spent the last decade of his life teaching and writing. Another paper by him on the U.S. Constitution, "The Constitution Revisited," was reprinted in *The Great Ideas Today* 1975.

The "crisis" to which these remarks were directed was what became the civil rights struggle of the 1960s, which Buchanan had foreseen as early as 1956, when he served for a year as the chairman of the Religion and Philosophy Department at Fisk University. A philosopher by training and the chief architect of the Great Books Program at St. John's College, of which he was the first dean, he had gone on to write a book-length *Essay in Politics* (1953), which he would have preferred to call "The Withering of Consent," and in which he addressed himself to what he thought of as another crisis, the failure of self-government to sustain itself in the United States of mid-century.

It is typical of Buchanan, and fundamental to his argument, that he thought natural law was something to be rediscovered—not merely described, that is to say, or advocated. Equally characteristic is the fact that he begins with Plato—the philosopher he most admired, though not for any doctrine so much as the process of Socratic questioning achieved in the Platonic Dialogues, and in which Buchanan finds the first formulation of natural law—or that the "rediscovery" he undertakes is of a tradition richly represented in *Great Books of the Western World,* on which he often wrote. See, for example, "Poetry and Mathematics," reprinted in *The Great Ideas Today* 1974. "Rediscovering Natural Law" is reprinted here with the kind permission of Douglas Buchanan, the author's son.

Rediscovering Natural Law*

A crisis in human law is the occasion for the discovery of jurisprudence. So it has been in the past; so it is at present. It is true that there have been minor crises in the life of the Supreme Court that have not led to the search for juristic reasons, as there have been political crises that have found only political solutions. In fact, the case can be made that the American government has had a happy career without need of philosophical help. This is partly because a great deal of jurisprudence was precipitated and built into the American Constitution, and because our politics has lived and flourished on its previously founded capital of wisdom. But there are signs that the present crisis in our Supreme Court and in our politics will not issue in a clarifying judgment without recourse to deeper reasonings than we have ever tried before. That is the reason that strange echoes of the great tradition of natural law are coming from the most unexpected sources.

I would like to strengthen the resonance and extend the range of these echoes by recalling the other occasions when natural law has been discovered and rediscovered in the past.

The Greeks

Plato's *Dialogues* can be read as the sustained effort to meet the crisis in Greek law when it was realized that the Peloponnesian War had been a self-inflicted wound on the city-state, not only upon Athens but upon all city-states. Plato saw the crisis epitomized in the trial of Socrates, and his record of the case, the *Apology*, became the basic text upon which all the other dialogues are extended commentaries. The many modern technical reviews of the procedure of the court that tried Socrates do not begin to compare with Plato's substantive criticism. Some of his dialogues reach into the depths of moral philosophy, some lay the foundations of political theory even to our time, still others probe the possibility of finding true science in the tangle of human opinion and observation, and they all culminate in the attempt to write a constitution founded in natural law. This reading of Plato is admittedly ex post facto, that is, seeing many complex consequences in the original; it has always been difficult to read Plato in any other way.

The Greeks were puzzled, even before Plato, by what man had made out of nature and by what he had done to himself in the process. The puzzlement had continued into the endless arguments of the Sophists about nature and convention. The arguments had continued through Plato to Aristotle's conclusion in the *Politics* that the state had been founded to meet the minimal necessities of life, but it had gone on to order artifice and convention in the good life. Plato's version had been given at greater length and detail in *The Republic*. The minimal state had arranged for the division of labor and the exchange of vital necessities. But the resulting greed and luxury had led to trade and war, which in turn infused honest labor and enjoyment with fraud, flattery, and sophistry. The

*Originally published in January 1962 as a Report to the Center for the Study of Democratic Institutions.

arts serving natural ends had been inverted so that the ends were subordinate to the means; for instance, the exchange of goods served the arts of money-making. As a consequence, vice took the place of virtue, and it was impossible in politics to tell the difference between justice and injustice. It was possible for Plato to put the strongest argument in the mouths of a series of vivid characters, such as Thrasymachus, that justice was the interest of the stronger. These were the strong characters supported by a "fevered state," a pathological polity. This account of the confusion of the arts is given in the style of fiction as a part of a utopian construction. But it is by all contemporary historical confirmation a vivid, accurate description of life in postwar Athens, and in the other Greek cities. It is not unfamiliar to us, and our nation-states.

Plato's prescription for purging the arts is to seek their roots in nature by tracing them back through the opinions and practical beliefs that they generate to their underlying sciences. He begins by showing the structure of means, ends, and skills in any art, and then goes on to show how one art serves another; for instance, how the art of flute making serves the art of flute playing. The genteel literary reading of the dialogues often attributes the frequency of the homely art theme to the earthy human qualities of Socrates's character, but the framework proposed here would make Plato the researcher in Greek technology. He is concerned to get the whole technology in a single view, and it results in the end in seeing politics, the art of government, as the master art that as end gives order to all the other arts; hence also to the classes and virtues of men.

This technology, or system of the arts, is developed, analyzed, and articulated in many places in the *Dialogues,* but most impressively in the *Gorgias,* Book I of *The Republic,* and in the *Sophist.* It is always closely associated with the running discussion of the tyrant. I think we can see why this association is made if we imagine a

similar attention to our own modern technology. If we look at all of our occupations as elementary units of a unified, highly organized industrial system, we are struck with the possibility that some dictatorial managerial bureaucracy could take over and with scientific and engineering know-how could exploit the system for almost any arbitrary purpose. It is a system of power asking for an efficient use. In fact, we are today watching with some worry a whole society or civilization devoted to just this end. In this mood we think we are wrong in attributing the diabolic force of such systems to evil men alone; the tyrannical essence of the Fascist or Communist regime belongs to the technological system as much as to the characters selected to manage it, and the rationalization of the arts that it entails is part of the secret of the satanic spectacle. It is also significant that the engineering of human beings, since they at least retain some of their rationality, involves the manufacture of an ideology to keep up morale.

*　　*　　*

The sophist was for Plato the prototype of the tyrant. With his sophisticated expertise, his claim of omniscience, his obvious hunger for power, and his hard salesmanship, he imitates and caricatures government. Our contemporary impulse is to expose and oust the tyranny and to try to democratize the system; we even fight world wars to accomplish this end. But Plato had apparently seen many vacillations between tyranny and democracy. *Demos* can also be a tyrant and will be tyrannical almost inevitably if it merely represents and organizes the will to power. Therefore, Plato in the *Sophist,* where the technical system was most completely and rationally seen, turns to a metaphysical search for the cure of the constitutional ills of technology. The search takes the form of asking for the difference between the sophist who is the technician and the statesman who must be a philosopher. Without this there is no dependable way to tell the difference between the technical rules and the political laws, between tyrannical and legitimate government. At the end of the *Sophist* there is a dark saying that the sophist technician is, like Oedipus, a patricide and a regicide: art has usurped the regulative function of knowledge or science.

There is a likely story often told in histories of science concerning the birth of Greek science. It begins by noting that the Greeks at first believed that the arts were gifts of the gods to human beings. Prometheus, Apollo, Hephaestus, Athena, Asclepius, Hermes, Aphrodite, and others taught men not only their skills but also the ends for which they were to be used. Having once delivered the doctrine and the practice, the gods continually presided over the further transmission of the arts by training and apprenticeship under human auspices. At some time, probably at the beginning of the Greek industrial revolution from subsistence to commercial agriculture, the tutelage of the gods fell into the background because somebody discovered that any free mind could initiate an art and carry it on by imitating nature. Perhaps this was celebrated in the story of Pandora's box.

But Epimetheus, Pandora's husband, made another discovery: that artistry could be detected in and extracted from nature. Nature itself was a great artist that delivered not only tricks and skills but also insights into precious secrets. Sometimes the model Artist was detected behind and above nature, sometimes it was recognized in nature itself. Thus Plato's *Demiurgos* and Galen's Nature, perhaps also the Delphic oracle, took the places of the divine inventors of the earlier period. The modern philosophical anthropologists would like to say that the Greeks first projected their arts into the Titanic and Olympian hierarchies and then shortened and simplified the projection into Nature.

A kind of sophisticated version of these myths can be seen in the vital center of Plato's *Republic*, the figure of the divided line and the allegory of the cave. The education of the philosopher-kings is a recapitulation of the mythical origin of science. Common language had attributed a kind of wisdom to the artist in recognition of his skill. This is recognized and called knowledge of the visible world in the two lower sections of Plato's divided line. Observation and practice with mirrors and instruments, which imitate nature, yield a coordination of observations that is proper to the clever artist or artisan. A kind of right opinion, born of the self-persuasion of successful practice, tempers and refines the skill and wisdom of the common man. This is the source from which modern empirical science stems. It should be recalled that it was to these men that Socrates went in his divinely assigned search for the wisest man in Hellas. If Socrates had been the sophist that Aristophanes accuses him of being, he might have educed from his survey of the arts and the artists the great composite artist that Timaeus constructs and calls the *Demiurgos*.

But obviously this is not what happened. Socrates found the artist or the technician the archetype of the foolish man; he is the man who thinks he knows when he does not know, the man who doesn't know that he does not know, the man who has no suspicion of what he does not know. And these artists may be anything from shepherds and poets to politicians; all of them are potential tyrants. These men are the prisoners in the depths of the cave who are fascinated and enslaved by the shadows that they have learned to trace and correlate and predict, even to write poems and make speeches about. Socrates had been shocked at his discovery of the learned ignorance of his fellow Athenians, and he was able to convey that shock to them. He did this through his questioning of them, but he also did it by his behavior, perhaps most effectively by his trial and death, when he defied and also obeyed the laws.

The shock marks the passage from the visible to the intelligible world in the divided line and in the cave. The shock blinds and paralyzes its victims in the visible world, and then awakes and revives them in the invisible world. The Platonic account of this shock portrays Socrates as a comic Oedipus who blinds himself in order to see. The cumulative failures of empirical observation and practice come to the crucial point of conversion and to the recognition of hypotheses and principles, the beings of the invisible world that constitute science.

For Plato the mysterious bridge from the empirical to the rational world had been provided by Pythagorean mathematics. The word *mathematics* suggests the function that it plays: it means learning. Apparently the great occasion for Pythagorean learning had been measurement of musical tones by the straight line and the numbers in the monochord, a string taken from a lyre. The tones and intervals of the musical modes, the musical appearances, were "saved" by the corresponding order of the numbers and their ratios. The same kind of correlation could be made in other material and instruments, and this led to a kind of frenzy of measurement that, carried out in the discipline of the Pythagorean order, led to the general conclusion that there were numbers in everything and that even celestial bodies played musical themes. Plato is saying that the Pythagoreans had been the mystagogues who had freed the Greek prisoners and had shown them the realities that cast the shadows on the wall of the cave. He is also saying that if the corruption of the city-state is ever to be cured, the philosopher-kings must first have become Pythagoreans and learned the sciences that will disentangle and order the arts.

But although mathematics is necessary, it is not enough. Wonderful and sweeping as it is, it is only the beginning of learning, a bridge of asses, so to speak. It substitutes objects of thought for objects of sense, but in doing this it leads on by its methods to a fourth division of the line, to objects of thought that are not mathematical. The

Dialogues themselves are the best example of this pedagogical function. Most of the arguments in the *Dialogues* are mathematical in method or in form, but mathematical subject matters are only used for illustration, and as illustrations they seem to be only paradigms of weightier matters. Not much is said about these weightier matters as the fourth division of the divided line is discussed in connection with the final stage of the education of the philosopher-king. The presumption is that the actual discussion of the whole of *The Republic* as well as the other dialogues exemplifies the subject matters, the human virtues, the nature of the city or state, the laws. But the method is clear. It is to take the hypotheses and principles that the mathematical sciences have discerned in the arts, to treat them as forms and essences in themselves, and to explore their connections; starting with ideas to move through ideas to ideas under the great categories, being and nonbeing, same and other, one and many, good and evil.* This is the dialectical method, discovered in the practice of Socratic questioning of the artists, now applied with systematic rigor exemplified in the later dialogues on the level of higher education. There is the upward dialectic that moves away from the empirical and pragmatic to the elements, causes, and principles; and there is the downward dialectic that moves from principles back through hypotheses to concrete affairs. The products of this method were to be the sciences that Aristotle founded.

The thesis that I have been following in this interpretation of the Platonic *Dialogues* is that Plato saw an epitome of the legal and political crisis of the city-state in the trial and death of Socrates. The indictment brought against Socrates was initiated by a poet and a politician, two representatives of the Athenian arts: one a practicing artist, and the other a self-styled master and

---

*See the *Syntopicon* for entries under these terms.

censor of the arts. The theme of Plato's lifelong critique of sophistry and tyranny is struck in Socrates's counterindictment and cross-questioning. The sophists are operators in opinion and power and are not concerned with wisdom and truth. Furthermore, they have no concern for the virtues of men or the common good of the state. From this scene Plato sets out to find the truth in science and the good of the state. He has Socrates accompany him as far as *The Republic,* where the arts are purged and clarified, science is established as the basis of education, and dialectic is recognized as the basic political process by which laws are made. Then Plato goes on as the Stranger through the later dialogues to the *Laws,* where he joins the Cretans in drafting a constitution.

There is no doctrinal answer to the quest, and, if we can trust the thirteenth Epistle, the default in this respect is not accidental. Plato used doctrines, even what we would call sciences, as hypotheses and starting points. He tells Dion, the Syracusan tyrant whom he tutored, that any written exposition of his teaching would be an imposture. The *Dialogues* practice what they preach, a relentless dialectical exposure of ideas masquerading in dogmas and opinions. This dialectical art was what was needed to cure the corrupt state of its ills, and it was the perpetual assignment made to the philosopher-kings who were members of the Nocturnal Council. The endless mutual persuasions in any community could result in good laws if the formal processes of government provided insights for the citizens and magistrates alike. Sciences might and would result from insights, but they are by-products, and dangerous ones at that, if they are not continually revived by criticism, revision, and relearning.

Drastic as this teaching is, and unduly skeptical as it often is in practice, as Plato remarks in warning that untempered youthful minds will misuse it, it yields, in the case of the dialogues, communicable insights. The human arts if left to themselves degenerate into a fatal confusion of sophistry and tyranny. In order to maintain their proper order and health they must be examined and reexamined for the essential knowledge that they contain and conceal. This knowledge will reveal forms, essences, and natures in which concrete affairs participate and through which concrete affairs are intelligible. Furthermore, these forms and natures are the discernible purposes of things; they must therefore be understood under the aspect of the good. These are the reported insights of Plato, which are to be found in many doctrines and sciences that the insights have generated.

It is one of the melancholy facts of history that the Greek city-state did not recover from its fatal corruption by the Peloponnesian War; that the great intellectual effort to meet the crisis, initiated by Plato and completed by Aristotle, was too late. That the effort was not too little is evidenced in the thousand-year life of the Academy, and perhaps more immediately in the planting of city-states throughout the Near and Far East by Alexander, who was Aristotle's pupil. It is in these institutions and in the Roman Empire that came heir to them that the thought bore fruit. But even with these evidences it may seem strained and overdone to read the *Dialogues* as researches in natural law. Neither Plato nor Aristotle commonly uses the phrase *natural law.* It is only in the practical and theoretical men whom they influenced that the idea of natural law comes to separate and clear formulation, and only after their thought undergoes a kind of degradation and rebirth in the minds of the Stoics during a time of troubles more extensive and acute than the period of the early decline of the city-state.

The Stoics were for the most part men of practical affairs. For them the Socrates portrayed in the *Dialogues* was a hero, and they made a doctrine out of his thought. Practical human affairs could be disentangled and straightened out by the use of reason, and for the most part reason in the dialectical style. Ethics, the science of human action, was founded on physics, the science of nature, and on logic, the rules for reasoning. The emphasis on the dialectical use of reason made physics into a cosmology rather than the empirical discipline that it is today. The great motions of the universe conformed to laws, the laws of nature, that were discoverable by reasoning or logic, or to the movements of thought among the pure forms and essences that Plato sought. For the Stoics, what Plato had described as the "community of ideas," which was only the notion of the interpenetration or mutual implication of ideas, became the *Logos,* the perhaps infinite total of all the ideas that govern the universe, or the cosmopolis. This notion is not utterly foreign to Plato's and Aristotle's thought, but it just would not have occurred to them. It would be almost inevitable to a Roman whose practical problems would drive him to a reading of the Greek philosophers.

The Romans

I do not know how the seeds of law were sown in the early Roman republic, but it is quite clear even before the republic that the characteristic Greek suspicion and hatred of tyrants was operative. The Romans were determined that they would live under a government of laws, not of men. Such a commitment did not lead to an easy political life, but there is no more enlightening theme for the interpretation of Roman history than the essential devotion of the Romans to essentially legal politics, even under the emperors. It follows from this commitment, active and practical though it may be, that the intellectual history of the Romans will concern itself with the distinction between good and bad laws. For them the laws, which at least intellectually seemed to be the solution of the problem of convention and nature for the Greeks, take the problematic place of

the arts. The right ordering of the laws takes the place of the right ordering of the arts.

By trial and error and political conflict they worked themselves through the different kinds of states that Plato and Aristotle had predicted; they passed through monarchy, oligarchy, democracy, and tyranny* and the various forms of law that are generated by them. The practices of the courts, the senate, and the tribunes and prefects invented, refined, and revised the legal corpus. Wars destroyed and renewed legal habits and understandings. The people, from tribune and emperor to slaves, increasingly became a political and a legal people. Many of the educated officials got their education from the Platonic Academy, and the vicissitudes of academic dialectic were felt and propagated throughout the Roman body politic. Repercussions from Alexandrian thinking and from the political experience of the Alexandrian city-states of the East kept the more doctrinal and scientific teachings of Aristotle alive, particularly when defense, pirating, or conquest forced changes in domestic politics.

Perhaps the great time of legal crisis came when the republic became the empire. Great affairs, commercial and military, forced revolutions, but the crucial events were met and dealt with by minds thoroughly tempered by formal legal training and by tough political experience. Cicero is only the best-known of these men because his writings have survived, but there were others who would have called themselves Stoics, some who called themselves Epicureans, and there were poets who celebrated the great events. Plutarch's *Lives* and even Shakespeare's *Julius Caesar* dramatize the intellectual character of these philosopher-kings. Plutarch makes it clear that they were imitators of the Greeks

---

*See the *Syntopicon* for entries under these terms.

intellectually and often corrupt fumblers in practice, but they are nonetheless authentic participants in Greek thought and action. They knew what it was to search for the reasons of their laws and their politics; they belong to the Hellenic world.

Virgil's *Aeneid* is an expression *de profundis* of the common Greek and Roman experience of politics. Its main structure and theme have been compared with Plato's *Statesman*. Whether Virgil had read the dialogue or not makes little difference; it would almost be better testimony if he had not read it. Plato raises the phenomenon of revolution to the status of a principle of history. Politics begins in divine government, governments of gods, not of men. Divine justice, peace, and freedom flow through channels of law throughout the community. Then, as men learn from these laws, they find themselves able to run their own common affairs; they amend the laws to meet the vicissitudes of history. As time goes on, they make new constitutions and get fresh starts out of their crises. But each new start pegs affairs on a lower level until there is the near-chaos of tyrannical democracy. Plato pictures this as the running down of a celestial clock, a kind of political entropy. But at the low point the gods again take the pilot's wheel and wind things up again. They do this through pious men. This is the principle of revolution, also the mystery of conversion, through calamity and catastrophe, in political tragedy.

The great narrative theme of *The Aeneid* recapitulates the revolutionary pattern. Pious Aeneas, carrying his even more pious father, Anchises, on his shoulders, leaves the flaming ruins of Troy. He becomes more and more like the wily Odysseus, even following the same course in the Mediterranean, falling under the charms of Dido and her imperial power, until he recalls or discovers his mission to Latium, where he repels his enemies and founds the city

of Rome under divine auspices. But Virgil is celebrating another revolution, the ignominious end of the Roman republic and the establishment of the empire under the divine Augustus. Perhaps the most impressive sign of Virgil's prophetic and magical power, for which he was famous for a thousand years and more, comes from his insinuation that the authority of law depended upon the magic of deified emperors.

Whatever the nature of the powers here invoked, the poetic facts are a monument to the depths of the crisis and the intellectual and imaginative efforts to surmount it. Many revolutions have made the same or similar appeals to divine law and government, though not all of them have founded thousand-year Reichs or empires.

But the lawyers and statesmen of Rome were more skeptical than Virgil. They did not trust the responsibility for their affairs to the gods; even some of the emperors suffered formal deification with reluctance and fear. In a more workmanlike way they paid attention to the laws, to the senate and the people, who made the laws and lived under them. But they never doubted the necessity to seek the reasons for their laws; they asked their questions of nature rather than of the gods.

It was the burdens of the empire that brought the Stoics, who had survived the corruption of the republic, into their own. Pride of wealth and power had transformed defensive wars into wars of conquest, or pacifications of the barbarians, as they were often called. The emperors, the army, and the senate came heir to responsibility for the security and order of many alien and diverse peoples. No matter how barbarous and uncivilized these people were, the Romans quickly learned that they had their own legal orders. (All Gaul is divided into three parts, each with its language, institutions, and laws.) The great debate in Julius Caesar's mind had been whether the pacified peoples should become citizens of Rome and come directly under the laws of Rome or whether Roman governors should sponsor autonomous provincial law administered by local magistrates. The debate, which continued throughout the empire, became the great political dialectic about the nature of law.

The Stoics continually made the saving distinctions. There were laws specific to a local community, civil laws, whose roots might reach far back into unique folkways and folklore, the *mores*. But among these laws and between communities, comparisons revealed a matrix of common laws, both customary and statutory, diverse in origin but identical in purpose and practice, laws of people, *ius gentium*. They revealed a body of principle upon which judges and administrators drew for reasons when they had to decide hard cases. Here the Stoic legalist saw through the artificial and conventional positive law and rediscovered what the Greeks had meant by nature. But in Stoic doctrine the principle available to reason would be selected segments of the *Logos,* which was the principle governing nature. Hence, they were called the natural law, *ius naturale*. For a judge or a prefect the Stoic slogan, return to nature, had a specific meaning; it meant return to natural law.

The distinctions between civil law, *ius gentium,* and *ius naturale* helped in the necessary task of adjusting, sorting, and codifying the bodies of law in the empire. From this process there were derived political and institutional arrangements, often invented ad hoc, to deal with that oldest of all political problems, the one and the many. But the problems that these new politics brought to light forced the more philosophical minds to a new venture in speculation. The problems of the city-state spread to the country or the region, and there seemed no end to the addition and expansion of jurisdiction. *Urs* led to *orbis,* as in the ancient days city had led to sky.

The great community was the cosmos. As civil law and the *ius gentium* dealt with the parts, so the *ius naturale* dealt with the cosmos, and Zeus, or Jupiter, was resurrected as the Great King. This has more poetry and rhetoric than it has of logic, but for a Roman it had vital reality. Both emperor and slave were helped to identify their stations and their duties in a world that rode uneasily on the surface of a chaos. The emperor was apotheosized as well as deified, and the slave, like Epictetus, could claim the dignity of cosmopolitan citizenship. Law neither before nor since has had such penetrative power.

The historic consequences of the pervasion, permeation, and penetration of this great community by law have been and still are immeasurable. That a small community could commit itself so effectively to legality, that, as it grew, it could, albeit with setbacks, invent and refine its laws to keep pace with power and dominion over ever-increasing populations and last for a thousand years—this in itself is incredible. But that the principles and the spirit, not to mention the concrete institutions and literally the same civil laws, should have expanded and permeated the civilizations of both East and West to our time, so that it is still an unfinished story—this, as history runs, is unparalleled.

It would be foolhardy to seek one cause, or any finite number of causes, to explain so much. But it would be equally foolhardy to ignore the great themes in it. The United States at its founding and also today is not ignoring some of these themes. The Roman noms de plume used by the authors of the Federalist Papers remind us that the founding fathers continually patterned their public characters on their Roman opposite numbers. We today are struggling to come to terms with the problems of our expanded power over many peoples both domestic and foreign, and we try to draw the boundaries between us and the new barbarian. The liberties under law of the American citizen are not only a slogan to be sold but a model to be loved, hated, feared, and emulated around the world. We and all the other peoples in the world are driven to think cosmopolis.

Part of the difficulty of our time is to find the boundaries of our legitimate jurisdiction, and to measure the extent of our influence and power that far outruns boundaries. There are too many people taxed by our acts without representation. Our laws reach to matters for which we do not want to take responsibility, and we have to take responsibility for matters not touched by our laws. In literal terms, we continually violate our own legitimacy. The Romans of almost any period would have been sympathetic and could with their own hindsight offer us advice. They would be familiar with the rough dynamics of legality.

If we had such a Roman delegation to consult, there would be many matters up for debate. We would undoubtedly want to tell them about their political mistakes, ask them why they did not invent better instruments of representation, why they did not federalize their empire as it grew. It would be ironic if we would want to scold them for allowing the military and the civil to become dangerously confused. They could probably tell us something about the depths of these problems that we have not plumbed.

But the most lively argument would come from a common consideration of our theory and practice of law. The delegates from the later empire would undoubtedly want to recommend the codification of our laws. We would at first demur and remind them that the codifications of their laws were early signs of death of their community; but they might in turn ask us which kind of death we prefer, swift and complete and chaotic, or slow and reasonable after a long and fruitful autumn of political service to the world. After these sober-

ing exchanges, we might be glad to weigh the costs of codification and listen to the methods and the probable discoveries that we might make. If we listened, we would be engaged in a better conversation about natural law than we pursue at present.

Pluralism is the present style in which we pose our problems to ourselves. We rather like our present illegitimacy with respect to our voluntary associations, but recently we have found it necessary to legitimize or find protections for others of our illegitimacies, and we draw our authority for doing this from the Bill of Rights. The Romans, accepting our terms, would suggest that we explore the possibilities in legal pluralism. An empire is a great school in the art of dealing with groups, minorities, and nations, whether they be inside or outside the jurisdictional boundaries. The Romans very early learned to recognize and honor the "languages, institutions, and laws" of the peoples that for one reason or another came under their aegis. They neither assimilated these heterogeneous legalities, nor did they excommunicate and ghettoize them. They undertook to enforce the living law of the group, even though this often raised serious threats to the integrities and viabilities of both the larger and the smaller communities. The discovery of common laws came to be expected, and, as they were found, they were added to the corpus of *ius gentium*. When the conflict of laws passed the bounds of literal adjudication, there was appeal to the unwritten laws of the cosmos, which were still assumed to be reasonable. The Western world has long lived under the mysterious radiations from one of the great cases that involved a Roman court and the Jewish Sanhedrin in Jerusalem. This involved not only a conflict of local and imperial laws but also an appeal through *ius gentium* and natural law to what had always been ambiguously known in the Hellenic world as divine law. What is remarkable is that this case could not have happened if there had not been an unshakable commitment to legality on the part of both communities.

In one respect the Romans governed the local communities more directly than we do in the United States: they did not recognize the so-called independent sovereignty of these subcommunities as we do our states. They sent out proconsuls, administrators, and judges to apply the laws of the senate and the Roman people. But in another respect they governed them less in that they recognized, respected, and even enforced the indigenous laws of the locality. They did not ensure to each political division a republican form of government. On the contrary, they encouraged the prior diversities in forms of government and maintained them.

The problems that this policy uncovered were lessened and moderated by the simultaneous discovery that separate peoples have some common laws, and this led to the search for the common principles behind all civil laws, and these common principles were often honored in the dealings between the empire and the surrounding barbarian peoples. Thus, the levels of plurality and unity in the empire were distinguished and correlated with the distinctions in kinds of law. The differences and similarities with our federal pattern of plurality and union are instructive. We tend to see in any empire something we now call monolithism, a heavy, enforced, coercive power. But at least in one respect the Roman laws allowed and supported more freedom, the freedom to diversify governmental and legal forms to fit local languages, institutions, and indigenous laws. The Romans thought it was in the interest of the empire to do this. Their theory of natural law enabled them to recognize and establish the diversity that resulted.

It might have been better if we had imitated this pattern in our federal Constitution, allowing the states to choose different forms of government, and it might be a good thing now if we amended the Constitution to allow it. One advantage could

have been and could still be that we would feel freer to extend law to many faltering voluntary associations without the fear that we will smother their liberties. We always have extended enforcement to private contracts; why should we not enforce as well as grant charters to corporations, schools, universities, churches, unions, which now are left to themselves to seek their legitimacies? We have enough experience to understand the principles of legal pluralism, enough also to extend it where it is needed.

But Roman law has, particularly for the Anglo-Saxon world, which does not know natural law, become identified with legalism and legal fanaticism. With regard to legalism, we are told that laws are very special instruments, that society is more than government, and there is danger of dead and unresponsive formalism in submitting social problems to legal solutions. Then there is the opposite and perhaps greater danger of legal fanaticism, which consists in imposing arbitrary legal rules on every last item and hidden corner of society. Both of these become formidable if the coercive auxiliaries of law are allowed to take the foreground, and the army or the military is allowed to back them up, as much of Roman history seems to show was the case. Because of our own recent history, we too easily associate and identify these legal diseases with one or another dictatorial totalitarianism. But the so-called totalitarian phenomenon is a quite different disease. It arises from another Roman invention, the dictatorship, whereby laws are suspended so that the power of the government can be temporarily concentrated in one person to meet an emergency. If the temporary dictatorships became permanent by stealth or by default, the result was tyranny, government without law or by the misuse of law. Formal and fanatical legalism gone to extremes may do enough damage to destroy itself, but the growth of law in itself does not lead to tyranny. The carefully framed institution of dictatorship shows that the Romans understood very well the difference between government by law and government by men.

Two treaties of Cicero, *De legibus* and *De officiis*, show the effect of paying attention to the principles of natural law in the discriminations between the kinds of law and the diverse connections they have with the structural parts of government. Too often in our sloppy ways of thinking democratically, we look upon election and appointment as the conferring of power on a representative. We picture an official as an engineer with his hands on the throttles of power. For a Roman this would have been only a secondary attribute of office. The primary attribute would have been authority and responsibility under law. These graded authorities, responsibilities, and only consequently powers were the main articulations of government. They are valid and effective only if they cut society where the natural functions and joints exist and operate. Ultimately, the specifications of office must correspond to the natural powers and faculties of individual men. The form of the state must correspond to the powers of men, as Plato had correlated them in his *Republic.* The Stoic found it easy to correlate these parts and functions with the parts and powers of the cosmopolis. The city or nation exists suspended between man, the microcosm, and the great community, the macrocosm. Nature through law penetrates and pervades all.

This is not to say that Roman law was enabled to meet all of its problems; Rome, after all, did decline and fall. Whether Gibbon is right or wrong about the primary and secondary causes of the fall, there were internal conditions continually generated by events that did not find their legitimacies. The Roman citizen, the family, the corporation, the army—these were tough and almost indestructible institutions; but there was that almost institutionalized residue known as the proletariat, part slave and part free, that had no status,

no legitimacy, no part, in the empire. That this unconquered, unpacified, unpoliticized power finally disrupted the whole legal structure is evidence of the essential place of law in a community. That the failure of law to penetrate this power was fatal is negative corroborative evidence that law was the essence of the life of the empire. It is probably true that there will be in any society a residue of rootless, unorganized, and legally unassimilated proletarians. It may be hubristic for any community to try to absorb the residue, as modern socialisms do, but the persistence of the problem probably should not yet allow us to condemn all attempts to solve it as totalitarian.

The Church

Gibbon attributes the fall of the Roman empire to barbarians without and religion within the great community. Toynbee's transformation of this formula into the generalized theme of the emergence of a religious community from the ruins of a civilization—that is, from a community that has been politicized and legalized—can be seen in still a third proposition. In order to integrate and maintain a system of civil law, the Romans had to appeal to a higher law, the natural law; but in the final crisis there was an appeal to a still higher law, divine law. This was not a new theme in Hellenic thought and experience. It is the essential theme of Greek tragedy. After human reason has been fully invested in a human enterprise, and every last glimmer of light has been collected and focused in the issues, there is a catastrophe and then a theophany. With hindsight, this is the injection by the playwright of a deus ex machina; for the victim of catastrophe, theophany is the recognition of a revelation. The Greek historians Thucydides and Herodotus saw events this way, law as the human reason of the community, full of hubris and leading inevitably to nemesis, and visited finally by divinity. The Romans were less able to use the tragic lens on themselves, but perhaps for that reason were, as a people, able to play the tragic role. If this is at all valid as a historic vision, Christianity is the climactic theophany for the series of tragic episodes in Hellenic civilization. It is the vision granted to a world disciplined and purged by a devotion to law. It allows us to see law, as it were, from above.

Of course, this is only another way of saying that Christianity was messianic. As Jewish law came to have a messianic implication, so also Roman law, even at the time of Christ, reached for salvation. Both Isaiah and Virgil, not to mention Plato, are recognized as prophets of a religious community. By the time of Constantine, church councils were quasi-constitutional conventions. From then till now, theology is continually thrashed out by dialectical methods as opinions of a supreme court. The Church is a theocracy.

The Church expanded throughout the empire, first as a proletarian organization whose sufferings and protests enriched the gospels and the sacraments, then as an illegal community strong enough to court and accept persecution, finally as a polity well-enough organized to receive the responsibilities of a faltering regime and extend its own genius to the barbarian world. It was even more penetrative and assimilative than Roman law had been in receiving and "saving" local languages, institutions, and laws. It was catholic, both in its universality and in its adaptability. It soon adopted the distinctions between kinds and levels of law from the Romans. There were local civil laws, there was the *ius gentium,* the *ius naturale,* and finally the clear acceptance of divine law, revealed, to be interpreted and adjudicated in labyrinths of local custom and hierarchies of jurisdiction.

Theology, whatever else its functions may be, was an arbitrator of law. The *logos* had had a remarkable history. First discerned and named by Heraclitus, then arithmetized by the Pythagoreans, analyzed and elaborated by Plato, applied and distributed to the sciences by Aristotle, it had identified itself in Alexandria with two great structures, the Jewish Torah and Roman natural law. The Church lifted it to a higher eminence; it became the mind of God and the exemplar of creation. It exemplified a general law of logic—the higher the eminence, the greater the scope. The Word became the Second Person of the Trinity. Plotinus and some of the Stoics had anticipated some of this transcendence, but they had not made it one of the mystical parts, a Person of the Deity. As imminent, it was providence, the government of the world; but the residue was still natural law, very much in the created world and therefore accessible to human or natural reason.

To understand this hypostasis of the *logos,* it will help to review some of the history of the dialectical process that led to it. Plato thought he had discovered an infinite process in his upward dialectic and therefore also in the downward dialectic, something like the infinites that are found in the modern mathematical continuum. It was possible to distinguish and to identify abstractions or ideas in the ascending series from particulars to the great categories of being, one, same, good, etc. Between any two members of the series there is a third to be found, and in both mathematics and logic this yields an infinity; it results in a great and refined power of calculation in mathematics and an unlimited power of speculation in logic and metaphysics. Also, Plato accepted the findings of his dialectic, wherever it went, as essences. The red in an apple, the life in a body, the justice in a community, might be encountered as accidents or properties in concrete individual things, but dialectic would show that they were also essences in their own rights, redness, the soul, and essential justice.

Aristotle found both Plato's infinities and also his hypostatization of essences indiscriminate and in the end, because of his rigorous application of the principle of contradiction, unthinkable. He found two kinds of substances in general: individual substances and God; all the rest are accidents of these substances in one mode or another. Some accidents, such as mathematical properties, can be treated as if they were substances, as quasi-substances, but they are not actually independent. This basic strategy made the founding of the Aristotelian sciences possible, and makes the basis rift between Plato and Aristotle. Free Platonic speculation continued as Neoplatonism and Stoicism, often playing havoc with the formal Aristotelian sciences, and also suffering a kind of blurred degradation in passing through the Latin language and the Roman legal mind. The results can be seen in Cicero's writings.

But the dialectical recovery came in two minds: in Plotinus, a pagan, and in Augustine, a Christian. Both were adepts in following the arguments wherever they led, to infinite series of essences. Both were mystics, and relentless in their efforts to understand what they saw by mystic vision and faith. They discovered and accepted many of the same hypostatized essences, among them, or rather as a summation of them, the *logos*. For Plotinus the passage up and down this dialectical ladder was a continuous journey demanded by his mystical vision; for Augustine, the Christian, the access to the upper part of the ladder was a gift of God's grace, a leap enabled by faith, hope, and charity within the Christian revelation. In their practice of the dialectic art there seems to be little difference. Both were guided by a divine terminus, but their visions of this differed, and it was this difference that remained to be clarified by the disputations of the schoolmen of the Middle Ages.

This difference was to become the distinction between nature and grace, in terms of human knowledge—what can be learned by the light of natural reason and what can be learned only by revelation. The revival of Aristotle helped to sharpen the argument, and the strategist of that argument was Albertus Magnus, the teacher of Thomas Aquinas. For him, Aristotle was the philosopher of nature, the mind that explored and exhausted the powers of reason for natural knowledge, physics, metaphysics, ethics, and politics. Albertus found Plato, Plotinus, Augustine, and the Augustinians the dialecticians who could probe the mysteries of the hypostases and emanations that enlightened reason found in God and the angelic hierarchy. Reason is common to the two realms, but it is put to different speculative uses and gets its medieval development from different sources. In Thomas Aquinas the line between nature and grace is sharply drawn and the consequences are precise.

To conclude this much oversimplified dialectical development, the *logos* that was understood as the essence of Roman natural law is here distinguished from it and clearly becomes divine law, the law of heaven, as it were, the exemplar of natural law. One is tempted here to recall Augustine's distinction between the city of God and the city of the world, and to say that the law of the city of God is *logos* as the law of the city of the world is natural law. Then one might go on to point out the historical consequence that the earthly church developed canon law from the *logos* as the worldly empires developed civil law from natural law. The consequence would then be the theological doctrine of the separation of church and state. But this sociological reduction, valid as it may be for understanding the civil problem of church and state, is a misunderstanding of the city of God. The earthly church, even if it were concretely catholic and universal, is only a small and distant province of the divine polity, and canon law belongs only to the local earthly community; canon law is the civil law of the city of God, as it were.

The most proper jurisdiction of divine law is heaven, where its first citizens are angels and sanctified souls. In the Thomistic doctrine the divine government rules over a perfect community in which the highest good, which is both common and individual, is immediately known and willed by intuitive intelligences. There are different degrees and modes of participation distributed according to perfect justice and love. God is the sovereign, but there is complete voluntary consent. This is the truly ideal republic in which learning and persuasion have been consummated, where the political problems of human government are already solved. It is that state toward which all human projections and strivings are directed. To use the Thomistic version of Platonic thought, the eternal law of divine government is the exemplar, "laid up in heaven," in which all human governments participate. The middle term through which the participation is mediated is natural law, as it is understood by human reason. Natural law is the human mode of understanding eternal law, or the *logos*.

The relation of divine or eternal law to natural law can be understood by analogy with the relation between the old law and the new law of the Bible. The Jewish community lived under the law of the Ten Commandments and Deuteronomy and also increasingly under the prophetic hope of a messiah. With the coming of the messiah there is a new legal dispensation that is sometimes in the Gospels called the fulfillment of the law, and sometimes in the Pauline epistles called the repeal of the law to make way for the Spirit, and again sometimes called the new law of love. The present epoch was first expected to be a thousand years of learning under the new law, a millennium at the end of which there would be the second coming of a Christ and the establishment of a divine government. The dialectical speculation of the Middle Ages did not deny the historical order, but added to it the nontemporal dialectical hierarchy of laws, positive laws of custom and statute, the *ius gentium,* the natural law, and the divine law. The dynamic strivings of history take place continually and simultaneously under these legal auspices. The levels of law provide an order of appeals from lower to higher cosmic tribunals.

The moderns

So far, I have been calling on my own meager version of the common man's history of Greece, Rome, and the Middle Ages in order to educe from primarily philosophical texts the themes that converge and coalesce in the theory of natural law. These themes seem to emerge from crucial problems that the communities tried to solve. Thus Plato, and to a lesser degree Aristotle, saw the arts or technology of the Greeks suffering from perversion and confusion and causing a fever in the political community, which Plato took to be a sign of incurable disease. The *Dialogues* are the record of the search for and partial discovery of rational science, which might provide the basis for ordering the arts including government. There is not much doubt that Aristotle brought that task to a creditable accomplishment. Though there were other purposes of this work, both Plato and Aristotle hoped and believed that such science or sciences would inform the laws by which the arts could be ordered. Neither used the phrase *natural law* in a technical legal sense to describe or name the result, but they saw an idea and a function that has ever since been designated as natural law. Because of their insights the general notion that law is a medium of knowledge and an instrument of education for the human community becomes an essential part of any natural law doctrine.

The crisis of Rome is of another kind. It arose from a conflict among a great multiplicity of laws and political communities. The Romans were driven by this problem of pluralism to search for the common features of bodies of law in order to avail themselves of principles that would guide them in articulating diverse systems and arranging workable relations between them to serve a common good that was in principle universal or catholic. Local differences forced them to construct a hierarchy of the different kinds of law, the levels of which correspond to the areas of jurisdiction. They did not stop before they identified the jurisdiction of the highest principles, the principles of natural law, with the cosmos.

The medieval philosopher of law had to deal with a community that was in principle and in dogma even more comprehensive than the Roman Stoic cosmos. The Romans conceived the gods as rulers within the natural universe. The Ruler of the Christian world transcended the universe, and the majority of His subjects were outside nature. The dialectic by which the Church interpreted the basic revelation of this supreme community was aided by grace of the theological virtues faith, hope, and charity. This makes it quite clear that natural law, whatever its transcendental derivations, is fully available to natural human reason. It is not, as often said, a matter of faith, religious commitment, or mysticism. It is a matter of knowledge if one chooses to use his natural intellectual powers in the modes of theoretical and practical reason. In fact, the seeds of natural law are embedded in every human reason, and some of its most genuine expressions come from the untutored and unsophisticated mind. If we could find some way of eliminating conventional and sophistical corruptions, we could say that the knowledge of natural law is moral common sense. Something like this elimination of corruption is in fact the aim of deliberation in legislation and due legal process in the courts. From the civil point of view, the Middle Ages are a time when law and politics squarely faced the fearsome problem of religion, the religion that Gibbon said caused the fall of the Roman empire; the outcome was the distinction between natural law and divine law. The distinction is the theoretical basis for the so-called practical agreement on the separation of church and state.

As we move into the modern period from the thirteenth century when this clarification was achieved, we encounter a series of confusions. One of these comes about from the rise of the nation-state as a transplantation and extension of the Italian city-state north of the Alps. Monarchs, pressed by the problems of size and complication, acted like the early Roman emperors; they yielded to the temptation of quasi-deification. These attempts were not successful, but they left a ragged doctrine of the divine right of kings. They leaped over natural law to divine law to root their authority in heaven, and their art of governing or reigning suffered from hubris.

Similarly, in the attempts to rebel against tyranny in the seventeenth century, the new commonwealths sanctified themselves. The Levellers, the Covenanters, the Commoners of Cromwell, thought of themselves as founders of holy communities, often recapitulating the polities that can be found in the Old Testament and in the early Christian ghettos. They took the proposition "Defiance to tyrants is obedience to God" as a constitutional principle. The conscientious withdrawal from a political community implied for them their single membership in a divine commonwealth. Most of these attempts to find the basis of political union led to short-lived polities.

But as revolutions ensued, and social contracts took the place of covenants with God, there grew up the artificial myths that parodied the biblical state of innocence. Hobbes, Locke, Rousseau, and Montesquieu substituted the state of nature for the state of innocence, and they derived individual natural rights from a variety of such "states." These accumulated and culminated in the doctrine of the rights of man of the French revolution, and the doctrines, each in its own way, led back to the puzzlement of the Greeks concerning what was natural and what was artificial and conventional in human society—consider Rousseau's prize essay on the question, Has the progress of the arts and sciences contributed more to the corruption or to the purification of morals?

These revolutionary apologies tried to return to nature, even in the Stoic sense, but it is quite clear in all of them that the nature to which they sought to return was no longer there. Something, in fact a great deal, had happened to it. Some of these things are still in stories we tell ourselves today. We see the new man of the Renaissance as a prisoner of another world released into the warm, rich, varied world of nature. He spends his time in observing and enjoying sights, sounds, smells, tastes, and feelings within himself. If he has intellectual skills, he tries to explain what he sees and hears by mathematics and experiment. He discovers for the first time what he calls the fine arts. He explores his imagination rather than his memory. He begins to invent rather than discover. As Galileo says, he reads the book of nature. He is a grammarian and an algebraist, perhaps a rhetorician, but hardly ever a dialectician or a logician. If he does venture into speculation, he thinks he has passed into the supernatural world of theology. The nature of the Greeks, the Romans, and the scholastics does not exist. The laws of nature that offer themselves for his enlightenment are mathematical and mechanical; they do not reveal their ends; they do not inform morals, to say nothing of justifying or correcting laws. The senses and the passions declare war on morals and reason, and they gradually take reason prisoner and put it to work on their side. Morals and final causes are left to poets, philosophers, and theologians, whose minds have been darkened by the dark ages and seduced by medievalism.

Nature itself is torn asunder by the battle; it is bifurcated. Part of it becomes the dark brutal motions of masses verified by measurements of primary qualities—solidity, shape, size, and motion—and part

of it becomes motions of the psyche or spirit, a stream of consciousness in which float the secondary and tertiary qualities—sense, feeling, imagination, values, and the remnants of reason that still inhabit the intellectual "soul." There are still those, like Kant, who honor, even reverence, theoretical and practical reason. But even he puts a sign over the realm of science: Let nothing enter that is not informed by mathematics; and he defines nature as "all that comes under the categories of scientific understanding." Ends are regulative but not constitutive of nature; they are ideals of reason.

Finally, nature itself reappears as an ideal person, the only half-believed mythical goddess of the poets and the idealistic philosophers. She presides over the world that has not yet been admitted to science. Natural law is the unattainable ideal of the skeptical scientist or of the positivistic and realistic legalist who has lost his way in jurisprudence. This idealized and mythical apotheosis of nature has happened before, as when the Roman poet Lucretius dedicated his poem *De Rerum Natura* to Venus, the Mother of all things that came to be and passed away in the drift of the atoms. Needless to say, Venus reigned over natural process, but did not rule. Many of the present searches for a basis of jurisprudence in natural law are reconstituting this myth.

The knowledge of nature

The way of speculation is now, as always, beset by threatening presences: on one side, religious dogma, and, on the other, empirical science. The effect so far is timidity in speculation. A part, the essential part, of natural law doctrine is speculative in both senses of that troubled word. It must be theoretical in its insistence on dealing with the facts for what they can yield in the way of knowledge, and it must dare to go beyond facts, to explore and exhaust what the always meager data indicate in the way of abstract knowledge. This is to say that we must recognize, trust, and follow reason, wherever it leads.

In one sense there has never been a time when reason was more cultivated and trusted than it is now, but this is true only when reason gives itself to mathematics and when mathematics renounces any claim to truth. Most of the other uses and levels of reason are suspect. Both the academy and the public set severe limits to the tolerance they will accord to what they call "too much discursive abstract reasoning." Abstract reasoning from hypothesis to data will pass, but the reasoning from one hypothesis to another or from hypotheses to principles is mere dialectic and leads to forbidden absolutes. This proscription eliminates one of Aristotle's intellectual skills or virtues, as well as the methods of Plato's researches in the *Dialogues*. It hides the essences that provide the clarity and structure that natural law once provided.

Another proscription of longer standing eliminates another more important intellectual skill or virtue that Aristotle and Plato depended on—intellectual intuition—the power by which the mind first seizes and contemplates an intellectual object. Kant, so far as I know, was the first to explicitly deny the possibility of intellectual intuition. More accurately, he said that it might be possible for God, but not for the human mind, which was essentially discursive and analytic. John Stuart Mill illustrates in his *Logic* the absence of intellectual intuition in modern scientific method. He sets it as a kind of puzzle for his readers to explain the fact that most of the great scientific hypotheses were established on the basis of single observations, thus raising doubts about the efficacy of his own famous "methods," in which the accumulation of many observations is necessary for verification. The still-unending attempts to validate the scientific method show that secondary inductions, those that pile up evidence and increase probability for hypotheses, follow Bacon's, Hume's, and Mill's methods, but

the primary inductions, which alone justify the secondary efforts, are still a mystery.

Aristotle, in one of his more literary paragraphs, describes the primary induction, or what he calls the intuitive induction. He says that it is as if an army is in retreat, slipping out of control into disorder, and one man, a private, decides to turn about and take a stand to face the enemy. The others note his position and posture, turn about like him, and line up on him as a pivot. This is what the single case does in the primary induction to "save the appearances" and establish the hypothesis. So the strategy of the intuitive induction may be used not only to find and verify a hypothesis but also to discover and establish a principle, which is the foundation of the science. The power of the mind that governs this strategy is the habit of intellectual intuition. The fact or the datum is the occasion, but not the source, of the insight. This is the intellectual power that Plato puts at the top of the divided line; it is also the power that is the source of Aristotle's great artistry in founding the sciences. It is that toward which the upward dialectic moves. It is the secret that the social scientist of today, lost among hypothetical values, cannot discover. It is not to be confused with hunches and emotional ecstasies, although these may contain insights needing clarification.

Trusting intellectual intuitions feels to us like betting on special experiences or falling for dogma, perhaps groping among possibilities, but, with sufficient critical strategy and dialectical discipline, it is merely recognizing what can and therefore must be thought.

I have paid this much attention to the lost powers of the intellect because these two, so-called discursive understanding and intellectual intuition, are particularly important if natural law exploration is to free itself from current epistemological tangles, most especially the tangle that is called value theory. In practical sciences, such as

455

law, the principle is the end; it is the beginning of any reasoning about the means. It must be an original starting point, as the word *principle* strictly indicates. It cannot be deduced or induced; it is a first premise. It can be reached only by intellectual intuition. Otherwise, values, subjective, relative, and apparent goods, have to be substituted for ends, or goods, that are real and known.

But the uncriticized dogmas of religion and empirical science invade and disrupt the proper work of the intellect at points that are crucial to natural-law thinking. We are shocked, romantically moved, or amused when we read Virgil's demonstration of natural love as the pivotal insight around which the *Divine Comedy* moves; when we read of the loves of the magnets in Gilbert; when Kepler attaches "intelligences" to the orbits of the planets; or when Bacon or Leibniz allows events to perceive one another. We allow the latter-day theologian to warn us off these modes of thought by telling us that these are only poetic analogies inspired by far-off divine events. Or we allow the devotees of the scientific method to tell us that such thoughts are vestiges of primitive animism and superstition. Actually, these poetic and scientific makers of the modern intellectual world were thinking in a bold and highly rational style about ends and means. They were not indulging in what we call pathetic fallacies, the imputation of psychic powers to inanimate things. It is we who are the prisoners of the pathetic fallacy; we substitute occult powers for legitimate objects of rational processes.

The result of this is that we split the natural world into two parts: one that is drained of values, and one that is haunted by errant emotions and wishes. This split is the work of about one century of the late Renaissance. The so-called rationalists were world-splitters. There was the rational world within which efficient, sometimes only mechanical, causes worked; and there was the other world in which final

causes persisted. Stones and atoms typified the former; men, the latter; and there was doubt about plants and animals. There were bold thinkers who could reduce the human world to the mechanical, and these still survive. But we are on the whole left with the moderate position in which purposes are restricted to the human world. The final causes, ends, and purposes of men, however rational they may be, must not be imputed to the natural world of science if we wish to maintain so-called objectivity.

The classical view stemming from Plato and Aristotle, and taken for granted until the late Renaissance, allowed reason to find final causes as well as efficient causes wherever it went. Long chains of reasoning in both modes comprehended nature, and ultimately the work of reason in one mode was not adequate unless it was supported by the other. Of course, there is another radical classical view, never lost in spite of the predominance of Aristotle and Plato; the view of the atomists from Leucippus and Democritus to Dalton and Newton. It is this single-minded view that has dominated the scientific method until fairly recently, when the double vision of the older view has returned to scientific respectability in the so-called principle of complementarity. It is this late and tentative revival of the full rationality that provides some of the theoretical background for the new concern about natural law.

For natural law, speculative freedom is necessary and vital. It is necessary to find some way of healing the rift that makes it necessary to warn students of one generation after another that they must not confuse the two meanings of natural law: the laws that the scientific method seeks, and the laws that underlie human law. The former are not commands of a rational creature, it is said, while the latter are. Nature is determined throughout by the laws of science, while human beings in their freedom can disobey human laws, even natural law. Both sides of the distinction are inaccurate, and the general warning is false. I shall try in the following pages to show why.

The metaphysics of natural law

Whenever and wherever ethical and legal theories have sought critical standards in natural law—in the case of the Greeks, in the case of the Romans, in the case of the medievals, even in the case of the moderns—they have sought validation for ends or values in some notion of the good, some general notion of the good that does not lie within the scope of the specific categories of their disciplines. There is that abrupt, surprising statement of Plato's at the early crisis in his search in *The Republic:* the good is the principle of all being (existence) and essence. This is a proposition in metaphysics, which is something beyond and after any science of nature, although not anywhere that is indicated in the modern term *supernatural.*

Plato and his imitator Augustine are remarkable for their addiction to dialogue and the height and speed of their ascent to metaphysics that the dialogue allows. They both are much more concerned about insight than about demonstration. Socrates or the *magister* in a dialogue begins with the ordinary judgments of his interlocutors. In expression of common sense or of conventional opinion the ordinary man makes many judgments of right and wrong, good and evil, honorable and dishonorable, fair and foul. The judgments of wrong, evil, dishonorable, and foul seem to be made with a good deal more emphasis and conviction than judgments of their opposites. The dialectician asks the reasons for these judgments, and he gets answers that reduce themselves to one hard term that comprehends a variety of synonyms. With good strategy the hard term turns out to be "evil," and it is usually asserted with a great deal of conviction. The turning point of the argument comes at this point when the questioner points out that the

interlocutor must know what good is, as otherwise he would not know the evil.

The common man at this point may feel trapped or paralyzed. Either he must go on to find out what he knows but does not think he knows, or he must stop talking. If he consents to go on, he finds he is on a very high level of abstract discourse, passing from idea to idea and increasing in altitude. With dialectical persistence and patience, seemingly very ordinary ideas take on extraordinary power and meaning. So it is with the good, and so it is with the associated so-called transcendental predicates. This discovery by the common man that he has always been involved in metaphysics with being, good, true, one, same, etc., is dazzling. As Whitehead said of Plato himself, he is in the *Dialogues* a man continually dazzled by the brilliance of his own insights. This is the intellectual intuition at work.

An apocryphal story has it that Plato once delivered a lecture on the good, and that many attended at first, but that after several hours only Aristotle remained. It has always been interesting to guess what transpired between them on that occasion. The best guess is that Aristotle talked back and that Plato joined the common search, as Socrates always did when the pupil responded. They must then have discovered something like this: anything judged to be good has an essence or form, an answer to the question, What is it? But it also has something that can be distinguished from this, its being or existence, an answer to the question, Is it? A thing is good if and insofar as its existence fulfills its essence; it is evil or bad if and insofar as its existence fails to fulfill its essence. Aristotle may have on the spot begun what he certainly went on to do later; he varied the formula to fit the different essences and their relations to their existences. Thus, a thing has a matter that more or less perfectly fits and fills the form; it has a potentiality that more or less perfectly actualizes itself; it has a contingency or dependence on circumstances that may or may not allow it to exist. A man has a desire or a will that he may not be able to realize. A form itself may have a perfection because by itself it does not need anything added to support its being. This is the good in its many contexts and relationships. It is clear that the argument could go on for a long time, perhaps after the deaths of these two men, perhaps until now and beyond.

Our first encounter with the notion of objective good based on essence and existence throws us back into a tangle of sentimental associations. If good is built into everything as other properties and accidents are, we quickly infer that the aggregate of goods adds up to a summary providence in nature or in God that justifies an ultimate optimism, the optimism made famous by Leibniz and Voltaire of the best of all possible worlds. The inference is too quick and too easy; F. H. Bradley issued a warning when he said that this is the best of all possible worlds, but everything in it is a positive evil. The best world possible is none too good.

And there is another caveat. When we infer optimistically, we are usually thinking egocentrically or anthropocentrically. If there is a massive quantum of good in the world, we think it must be a good for us. We must recall that the distribution of the transcendental good is more equable. The last discovered subatomic particle, if it exists, has its measures of essence and existence, its own proper good and evil, as do stones, plants, and animals, with no reference to men.

But the argument goes on to show that evil is also very widely distributed. Wherever there is a failure of existence to fit and fulfill an essence, there is evil, and a radical built-in evil, the so-called evil of privation. Essences can be conceived as possibilities, and there are very, very many of them, perhaps an infinite number, as Leibniz said. One can think of space and time as the narrow conditions set for their existence. The universe at any given time and place may be poor indeed in realized goods; in fact, to our minds it seems to be mainly privation and evil. But the metaphysical summary or census of goods is not our problem at this point, perhaps not possible ever for our minds.

The world presents us not only with a distributed multiplicity of goods and evils but also with a vast pattern of coexisting goods and evils. For any one good to exist, there must be a context of other goods, and they must be articulated if they do not prove to be mutually annihilating. It was this vision that lay back of modern theories of evolution. If the essences are species, then there is a struggle for existence and survival depends upon mutual adaptation. One good is the condition for the existence of another good; in fact, many other goods. One good is the means to another good considered as end. This signifies that any good is a kind of teleological center around which there exists its means of existence; and, vice versa, any good is a means to the existence of other ends. We are used to seeing ourselves, each is used to seeing himself, as ends or end, to which the universe ministers. It is a humbling and beneficial exercise to realize that all other things could validly find the center in themselves. Each entity generates a kind of individual providence for itself. It may be fortunate that not too many providences are blessed with our kind of intelligence. We have a difficult enough task to find the common good of our societies. We wonder at present whether the society of the subatomic particles in plutonium and hydrogen has a common good that can be connected with ours.

This articulation of the world as means and ends with all of its one-many and many-one relations, its versatile interchangeabilities of ends and means, its ubiquitous evils, its aspect of struggle for existence, is the teleological universe, the world under the aspect of the good. But the system of final causes is no more complicated than the systems of efficient or mechanical causes. In fact, it was possible for Bergson to make a case for thinking of mechanical causes as merely the inversion of final causes. Both, he said, are results of highly rational objective thought, the ideal objective of all scientific investigation. Science itself is fragmentary, episodic, and progressive, and therefore does not prove or demonstrate the cosmic views, either mechanical determinism or teleological order. It takes them for granted, and judges its findings by how far it fails to reach the totalities. These views are presupposed similarly by any effort to find natural law.

The sciences in natural law

Some of the answers to the questions that the Greeks were asking in their search for a rational basis for law are given in this metaphysical doctrine, the theory of the good that arises from the discovery of essences and the problems of existence that the essences pose. But the difficulties in the upward dialectic that seeks the essences are repeated in reverse in the downward dialectic that elaborates the sciences of nature. Metaphysics supplies an apparently well-grounded set of principles. Under them, Aristotle was able to establish physics, the general science of nature, within which many ingenious and elegant hypotheses ordered things by material, formal, efficient, and final causes. The strategic lines in the structure were levels in a hierarchy of beings. As corresponding to these levels he identified seven substantial forms, or essences, upon which all the other properties or accidents depended.

There were the four elements: earth, water, air, and fire. These together made up inanimate nature. We still honor them in our doctrine of phases of energy: solids, liquids, gases, and heat. Then there were plants, animals, and men. There was even room within his spheres for a fifth element, the ether, where the separated forms that later were called angels might exist.

He distinguished six kinds of motion: local motion, qualitative change, growth, decay, generation, and corruption; and these correspond to kinds of accidents inhering in the substances. There were precise definitions, rigorous methods of inference, and plenty of opportunity for empirical verification and technical application. The historical fact that many of the practitioners in these sciences did not fully avail themselves of these facilities is no refutation of their soundness. The historical fact that these sciences flourished and dominated the intellectual world for almost two thousand years, lending their rational light to two great religions, is perhaps too heavy a confirmation.

One other historical fact poses a problem for us. The period of Platonic and Aristotelian science corresponds with the period of the development of natural law. One should probably not identify natural law as exclusively Platonic or Aristotelian, but the negative evidence for this is overwhelming. Modern science, from the seventeenth century on, does not easily yield a natural-law doctrine. It is not yet time to conclude that it cannot do so. But at present we are faced with a hard choice. Either we reinstate Aristotelian science and show how it can assimilate and improve modern science, or we assume that it is dated and outmoded, abandon it, and trust our legal and moral future to the inherent regenerative powers of reason and observation. The latter alternative puts us back with the original problem of the Greeks.

One feature of the older science must be noted and emphasized again. It yielded not only rational science but also a rational method for identifying essences and ends, and these make most of the difference. Our sciences are silent or fatefully confused about value. But if we remove ourselves from the high level of pure science to technology, we find tremendous energy and courage put to the service of values. And the teleological theme in the form of utilitarianism not only informs the technological activity and theory, it projects itself back to the pure science itself. It is currently being said that the test of a hypothesis is partly, but essentially, nevertheless, the cost of its being wrong in practice. The phrase conceals a strong simplistic teleological or purposive bias. The similarly pragmatic scientific method has long used operational workability as a test for scientific validity. This may be a dialectical trope by which modern science temporarily devotes itself to the good in some technical form in order to return to a truth that can include ends and values. Perhaps we should not only be patient but view this turn of affairs with enthusiasm.

However predominant Aristotelian scientific influence was in the two thousand years in which it flourished, it was never the only style of scientific thought. It suffered from the erosions of time and habit, but it also gave ground to opposing thought. One of the resultants of the conflict is a break in its own speculative fabric. The break corresponds to a distinction that Aristotle himself made between nonrational and rational potencies. Inanimate elements, plants, and animals obey the imperatives of their natures implicitly. A stone falls and a plant grows without taking thought; it has no choice. It realizes its potency automatically, as it were. On the other hand, a man has rational potencies, and these involve thought, the entertainment of contradictions and contraries, choice between them, and the possibility of disobedience to the imperatives of his nature. The nonrational potencies therefore seem to come under the non-Aristotelian sciences of atomism and mathematical physics in which fate or determinism, but no ends, supplies the laws. It appears that man with his powers of rationality and choice escapes those kinds of necessary laws, but as the empirical and mathematical sciences progress, they bring more and more of a man's psyche under mechanical and mathematical laws. The result is that the rational potencies retreat and become isolated and imprisoned.

The defenders of the classical tradition of natural law, who should assert teleology as a parallel and coextensive interpretation with mathematical physics, actually defend teleology only in man. The reflective reason in man is clearly purposive, but the rest of nature sleeps in its mechanical and mathematical order. Technical man can impose purposes on natural objects by quasi-magical arts; he can even invent purposes and bend nature to his will. Even the Bible has authorized such control and exploitation, but in the modern style no inference is made about the implicit purposiveness in nonrational things that makes his mastery a success. The classical doctrine of human nature then exists in the modern world as a mere humanism. This, I believe, is what paralyzes the doctrine of natural law in the modern world, and prevents it from reviving its full force by penetrating the equations and the mechanisms that pervade both natural and social science. This is the reason that so-called secondary natural law seems arbitrary, dated, and dogmatic when it makes particular determinations. Science must be the mediator of natural-law thinking, and there is confusion in this area.

If I am right in finding the locus of the difficulty in the confusion of the sciences, or, to give it another name, the explosion of the notion of nature, we cannot put natural law together again without going to the center of several problems. One of these is the puzzles that modern algebra, or analysis, poses. This is very much unfinished business with both mathematicians and philosophers. Another problem comes with the great difficulty of validating the empirical scientific method. Both of these raise serious problems for natural-law theory because they are the present screen through which we think we acquire natural knowledge. They show no signs of delivering knowledge of values or ends. Natural-law theory avoids open conflict or criticism of the academic going concerns that are committed to these methods, and it seems unable to comprehend and transcend them. The writings of Lon Fuller show the frustration that results.

There are several working alternatives to the formidable task indicated above. F. S. C. Northrop boldly states the outlines of current natural knowledge based on mathematical physics, connecting it with the long mathematical tradition from the Pythagoreans to the present. Still more boldly, he allows such natural knowledge to extend itself to the human nervous system. He asserts that the latest neurology and the neurology immediately in prospect supply adequate physiological correlates of the rational human powers familiar in the humanistic tradition. At present, Northrop makes no claim that the natural law that he sees developing in his hypothetical construction yields anything but hypothetical values, and there is at present a presumption running through his thought that nothing more is needed. One must wait for developments. It is, of course, possible that such explorations will make discoveries.

As if to balance this effort, there is Jacques Ellul's description of the great technological phenomenon in *La Technique*. The technical phenomenon is the product of human art, the organization of means to human ends. From separate and isolated origins the arts as techniques have come together, have meshed and spread, and are now connected in one great system by machines, mathematical formulas, and massive organizations of men. The term *technical phenomenon* is not an accidental choice. The system as a whole is an appearance, perhaps an illusion as long as we fail to understand it, a moment in a historical dialectic that will presently negate itself. But as it stands at present, it is self-augmenting, universal in principle; increasingly interdependent in its parts, and autonomous in that its ends are intrinsic and not responsive to other ends. In these respects it is like the classical natural universe in its teleological phase.

But it is obviously artificial, an imitation of the natural universe as this was understood by the Roman Stoics. It demands and gets human acquiescence and for the most part enthusiastic obedience; in this it is like the living law of the legal realists. It has large contributions from science, but uses these for its own ends, and in turn to a great extent directs scientific investigations and sets the workable standards for scientific validity. It is as if Ellul had seen the aim of Plato's integration and criticism of the human arts and had transferred the survey to the modern situation; he also sees the sophistry and tyranny that lie potentially in technics, waiting for exploitation or for clarification. Ellul does not appeal to natural law for the latter purpose; he appeals rather to divine law, but is not very hopeful of an effective response.

Beside Fuller, Northrop, and Ellul we must put Messner's *Social Ethics: Natural Law in the Modern World*. In the first hundred pages this is a beautifully clear exposition of the classical and Catholic orthodox theory of natural law as it is derived from human nature. Then it goes on to show the presence of natural law in contemporary law, politics, and economics. In its frequent and often long passages in fine print it fights the battle of jurisprudence against its many confusers and detractors. The battle is justly and fairly fought so that clarities are exposed on both sides. But the final effect is to encapsulate a sublimity in the glass case of a museum. It does not grasp and help to reformulate the inarticulate problems of the contemporary world. When it reaches out to do so, it too often becomes an apologetic for a problematic status quo, not to say a status quo ante. Because of its restricted humanistic premises, it is not able to take on the needed critique of the natural sciences; it honors man, but it does not take into account the rest of nature and the technology in which he lives his life; it does not note the net of correlations, probabilities, and techniques in which man is already enmeshed. The following section of this paper is an attempt to state the problems that Messner leaves unresolved.

The kingdom of nature

I am persuaded at this stage that technology is the unclarified phenomenon that poses the most important problems in jurisprudence. The fates of both science and government are epitomized in its dark oracular operations. The best light I have on it comes from Kant, who thought and wrote about these matters just as the scientific and industrial revolutions were precipitating the political revolutions and innovations of the modern world. His categorical imperative is prophetic.

The categorical imperative in its first formulation provides the cardinal criterion of civil law: choose the maxims of your acts as if they were to serve as universal laws of nature. This is advice to legislators and judges. To the philosopher of law the second formulation puts it this way: all maxims ought by their own legislation to harmonize with a possible kingdom of ends as with a kingdom of nature. For the citizen the third formulation reads: treat all human beings as ends-in-themselves, not merely as means.

The habitual natural lawyer will find these formulations heavily impregnated with the terms of natural law, and this first impression will be literally accurate; but on second reading he will be disturbed by an air of the subjunctive or even optative mood. Kant seems to be saying: treat law, think about it and deal with it, *as if* the doctrine of natural law, its rational teleology, were true science. Natural law in the subjunctive or optative mood becomes then an idealistic, almost a romantic, teaching, perhaps touched with nostalgia. This also is an accurate impression, and the mood familiar in much of our contemporary jurisprudence.

In addition to Hume and Leibniz, Kant had another beloved teacher, Christian Wolff, through whom he learned an eighteenth-century version of scholastic doctrine. Much of *The Critique of Pure Reason* is a critique of Christian Wolff and his teaching, and the logic of the criticism is the logic of Newtonian mathematical physics. Kant had a great deal to do with making this logic "constitutive" of classical physics and the method of the natural sciences until fairly recently. The intellectual weight of the *Principia Mathematica* and the sharpness of Kant's critique and defense of it shifted the center of gravity away from Wolff's scholastic metaphysics and left the latter in a problematic realm that Kant called the "Ideals of Pure Reason." Kant's formulations of these ideals are unique, but they are not without context; they epitomize the scientific and philosophical thought from Nicholas of Cusa and Galileo to Newton and Leibniz. Kant might, as many of his successors did, have simply canceled out the realm of Pure Reason, but he did not do this. He emphatically and repeatedly said that the ideas of reason must be thought, they cannot be escaped; but on the other hand, they must not be allowed to invade the realm of empirical science.

But, although this separation of power is the emphatic conclusion of the critique of pure or speculative reason, it is not the final word by any means. In later works the great theme of the spontaneous legislative powers of the human mind gives a new dignity and power to the ideas of reason. These ideas are "regulative" of all the operations of the human mind; that is, they give rules for the deployment of all the constitutive concepts of science, morals, and jurisprudence. The best example of this regulative function of ideas is relevant to the theory of natural law. The idea of purpose in the universe is an idea of reason, one that should not be allowed to invade and displace the idea of mechanical cause, but it issues an imperative or rule to the investigating scientist in biology or physiology. He must conceive an organism as a system of reciprocal means and ends, and then because he has done this he must exhaustively trace the instrumental relations in the mechanisms of reciprocal efficient causes. Applied to jurisprudence, this would mean that the ideal of reason expressed in the categorical imperative demands that legislative enactments must have reasoned preambles and that judicial decisions must be reasoned opinions, both kinds of reasoning reaching to the common good and to the facts.

The notion that natural law is regulative in the Kantian sense perhaps clarifies one of the difficulties in understanding the traditional notion. It is often said that natural law is more general and abstract than civil law and never should be identified with it; it is even said that natural law is unwritten, not reducible to formula or code. And yet it is found or discovered sometimes as the principle of common law or in difficult cases where conflict or ambiguity of positive law occurs. It is further said that positive law cannot be deduced from natural law; instead, it is said that positive law is a determination of natural law by way of specification rather than deduction. Kant's natural law as a regulative ideal of reason throws these puzzles into an intelligible pattern. In part, Kant's genius lay in his skill in translating abstract concepts into rules of operation; he was an early operationalist. When an idea becomes regulative, it becomes a rule for the strategic application of other concepts. Kant revised Aristotelian logic by treating the major premise of syllogism as a rule for inferring the conclusion from the minor premise.

If we conceive natural law as a body of rules for the making, administration, and adjudication of positive laws, we have something like a solution of the preceding puzzles. Regulation by natural law then becomes the rules for referring legislation, administration, and adjudication to the rule of reason and demanding due process of law for all citizens. Natural law does not dictate positive law, but it sets the processes of law in operation and directs their activity and influence through dialectic, analogy, and example, those nobler parts of the art of rhetoric. Natural law, as reason, sits within the mind of the magistrate, lawyer, and citizen as the internal teacher.

The first formulation of the categorical imperative, cold and empty as it seems, is a good example of this function. As a legal formula it derived from the classical definition of law: a law must be universal; that is, it is rule of reason. This means that it must have equal incidence upon persons and situations; it must not be discriminatory, "a respecter of persons," or tend to be a bill of attainder or in principle be limited to a locality. But its frequent comparison with the golden rule, Do unto others as you would be done by, or, Love thy neighbor as thyself, shows that it can invoke charity as well as justice and thus qualify the common good as the intention or end of law in general. It says not only to make law itself reasonable, but to exhaust all possible reasons in the use of law. It puts law in the rich context of practical reasoning about means and ends for the sake of human action, individual and collective.

I have always been puzzled by the tortuous reasoning by which Kant ostensibly arrives at the insight that the categorical imperative expresses; the reasoning is much less revealing and convincing than the bare insight. It is as if Kant in the field of morals were surrendering to his own skill in intellectual intuition, whose validity he so fiercely denied in the first *Critique*. In the formula above, by sheer thought he grasps the rational root of the mysterious *ought* in human affairs. By apparently similar intuitions, he reaches the related content of the other two formulations. Treat all human beings as ends-in-themselves, not merely as means. Conceive nature as a kingdom of ends. Put together, these separate formulas say that all good laws must be rules of reason within a kingdom of nature, or ends in which men are masters or the ends-in-themselves.

This is good natural-law doctrine, and I have purposely omitted the phrases that in the original give it the subjunctive and romantic mood. I should like to continue in the imperative and realistic mood in order to explore the intrinsic meaning of what for Kant seems to have been a utopian ideal or vision. The metaphysical teleology that I have expounded in an earlier part of this paper is the substance of Kant's vision, but for him it is like Plato's utopian construction in *The Republic:* "a pattern laid up in heaven, beholding which, a citizen or a ruler can set his house in order." In this sense it is a regulative idea of reason.

Whatever there may be of theological overtones or presuppositions in the vision, the key phrase is "a kingdom of nature." The regulative consequences of the vision ought to appear from an examination of the constitution of this kingdom. Part of the kingdom consists of persons as rational beings whose dignity and freedom are exercised in giving to themselves universal laws in the acts of their wills. By virtue of this power of self-government, they are ends-in-themselves. The constitution of the kingdom of nature is violated if any of the kingly persons are treated merely as means. This does not mean that they are never to be treated as means. The constitutional situation is rather that the persons act reciprocally as means and ends regarding one another, or as mutual means to their common end, as the organs in an organism or as members of a free community. They may serve each other, but the royalty in each servant must also be respected. This part of the kingdom, for the sake of concreteness, can be seen in Rousseau's republic of self-governing citizens, from which Kant's vision is partly derived.

For further illustration, consider the modern business corporation. It is a rudimentary community of persons. Part of its rude state is due to its radical oligarchic polity, which is said to be unavoidable if the organization is to carry out its purpose and obligations—the running of a business. On occasion it is necessary for one oligarch to use his fellow oligarchs, with or without their permission, or to issue orders that call for sacrifice for the sake of the firm. Even if this does not actually happen, the constitution is such that it can "correctly" take place. The lines of authority from senior to junior executives and managers is more oligarchic, and to the worker employees still more so. Business being what it is, the highest imperative of the firm is to use its manpower efficiently; that is, to manage so that each member can put his full efforts to the use of the company. The ends-in-themselves in these communities are understood in law and in practice to be the stockholders; all the others consent to put themselves to the service or use of these kings.

But even at the origin of these communities there is a token recognition of each man as an end-in-himself. When an employee takes a job, he is understood to have made a free contract, to have freely consented to the service for which he is hired, and in consideration of this he is given a salary or a wage. Even in a slave system the master recognizes his obligation to feed and clothe his servants. All these devices—wages, food, and clothing—can be understood as forms of coercion, but the residue of consent can never be quite eradicated; respect for consent, no matter how small or deceptive, is nevertheless respect for man as an end-in-himself.

Latterly, the corporation has been acquiring a conscience, it is said, and the sign of this is that is makes concessions to demands or anticipates them by offering to serve the employees by supplying the means of a decent life, giving longer contracts for jobs, installing safety devices on the job and medical care for employees and their families, and establishing insurance and pensions. These services are offered for all sorts of prudential and secondary reasons, but, whatever these may be, there still remains the inescapable respect for the person as an end-in-himself and the recognition that means and ends in the corporation must operate reciprocally. Thus, the categorical imperative regulates the corporation, and there is a rising demand throughout the world that human beings shall be associated in such kingdoms of ends. The wide gap between the demand and the realization in the world as well as in the microcosm of the corporation measures the wide gap between the utopian ideal and the actual associations under its regulation.

So much for the royal class in the kingdom or cosmopolis of nature, which is not to be confused with the kingdom of heaven, with which it has some similarities. The royal or citizen class is a true natural kingdom, the kingdom of rational human nature. In fact, it is the part of the kingdom of nature upon which the traditional natural lawyer concentrates his attention. The other part of the kingdom is the rest of nature, the nonrational part of nature, anciently divided into animals, plants, earth, air, fire, and water. In spite of the fact that Kant's world no longer trusted this division or knew the essences that identified the parts, his kingdom of nature as a kingdom of ends included all those things that come under law, the laws of mechanics as well as the regulative laws of teleology. The evidence of this subsumption ought still to appeal to the modern mind: natural things are preeminently those things that welcome the imposition of human purposes in technology and industry. The ancient testimony was that God had given man dominion over all these creatures.

Although Kant did not explicitly elaborate this point, I shall not be violating his ideal and vision if I amend the third formulation of the categorical imperative to read: each natural thing, whether rational or nonrational, must be treated as an end-in-itself, not merely as a means. This follows the metaphysical teleology that I have expounded earlier. The essences and existences, the forms and matters, the potencies and the actualities of all those things that come under law, make them ends-in-themselves as well as means, and the just knowledge of them as ends is as necessary to the technician who puts them to use as his detection of their connections as means. Furthermore, they all belong to a community of reciprocal means and ends in which the condition for the human use of nature is always men's service to nature, as any farmer, craftsman, or engineer knows. To quote Plato again, a shepherd's essential business is tending sheep, let the butcher's or merchant's be what it will, and the principle so illustrated runs throughout the human arts.

Perhaps the point is worth further elucidation. We tend to understand causes, for instance, efficient causes, as falling into linear series, with action passing through them in one direction, say, from past to present and future in time. But we know on second thought that there is always a feedback, as it is called at present. There are causes that act through reaction as in Newton's third law of mechanics, where every action entails an equal and opposite reaction. For this observable schema Kant set up a separate category that he called community of causation, which is now well recognized in electrical and other energetic fields. So it is with final causes: every end that is served by means in turn serves the means in some respect. The system of final causes that we call a community is to be understood in this way.

But this lower part of the kingdom of nonrational nature, although it is made up of things that are ends-in-themselves as well as means, does not show the equality of ends that prevails in the upper rational part. Rational persons rule themselves, but they also practice a justice with respect to their nonrational subjects that takes due account of the inequality of goods that they embody. All nature is divided into species according to essential differences. Rational human beings are equal because they belong to one species by virtue of their rationality; the rest of nature is divided according to the diversity of the other essences, and among the many species there are essential inequalities, therefore different goods that arrange themselves in a hierarchy.

But this hierarchy, still taken for granted in common sense, is inherited from the scholastic tradition of natural law. In that context, the order of intrinsic natural goods-in-themselves constitutionally governs the ordering of means to ends. Since a plant had more being than inanimate nature, it had, as it were, a natural right to use earth, water, and air for its subsistence; earth, water, and air fulfilled their own ends by serving plants in what we would call their biochemical roles. Similarly, plants served natural ends by becoming food for animals, and animals in turn reached a higher level of being and goodness by serving as food and beasts of burden for men. The order of intrinsic goods, or ends-in-themselves, indicated and regulated the order of means. By contrast, in the human arts there can be inversions of the order of means and ends that violate the hierarchy of intrinsic goods. Many of the rules developed by the craftsmen in their guilds were prohibitions of these inversions, and these rules would have been recognized as just by craftsmen anywhere, even in Plato's Athens.

But there is no possibility of recovering a teleological ordering of nature in the mathematical physics of Descartes and Newton and the sciences that follow their methods and styles. The essences and species that determine goods in the hierarchy are dissolved in the variables and numbers of mathematical formulas, and these seem to offer to men many new alternative orders of means that are not subject to any regulation except human ingenuity and advantage in technology, industry, and commerce. The nonhuman things in nature are no longer judged by their intrinsic goods, but only by their unmediated subordina-

tion as means to human ends. This is the revolution in the kingdom of nature that Kant is legitimizing. The new constitution of nature is given in Newton's mathematical physics, and it is to be protected from interference by the traditional hierarchical constitution that is relegated to the realm of the Ideals of Reason. But Kant's proposed new regulative function of the old constitution is a little like the working of the regulative agencies in Washington: the regulated usurps the authority of the regulator. The new science and technology often determine the rules, whose ends only occasionally coincide with the ends of the older rules. Regulation, therefore, results only in the confusion of the hierarchy with the paradoxical vagaries of means without ends.

* * *

As a consequence of, and contributing to, the confusion there are several fashions of thought that have dominated the revolutions that have ushered in the modern world: the scientific revolution, the technical revolution, and the industrial revolution. Viewed in retrospect, this period has been marked by the unregulated exploitation of nature, both human and nonhuman. It opened with the factory system, where human beings were counted as labor power and even the pious master of the factory thought he had a vocation to recruit and direct as much human energy as possible for the manufacture of goods. Even the workers themselves at first found a new utility for their powers and consented to the conspiracy of exploitation. Later, when they realized that they were being not only used but also used up, they gradually withdrew consent. But by this time the factory and business system were recognized as the master organizations of men for the exploitation of natural resources. As natural resources became the new name for the lower orders of the kingdom of nature, so "goods" became the name for the products of the factory as they poured into the market. The only limit on the spread of exploitation of this kind was the demand of the market and the ingenuity of the producers. Both of these were objects of scientific and managerial attention, the science of economics for demand and supply, the natural sciences for the methods of natural investigation. Both kinds of science became mechanistic, ready to serve any purpose, and public, ready to serve any agent of exploitation. The accompanying styles of thought were matter-of-fact and utilitarian. Law and morals followed the fashions at decent distances.

I wish here to use the word *exploitation* in an original technical meaning. It was first applied in the mid-nineteenth century to mining. Mines and quarries were exploited; that is, their contents, minerals and chemicals, were being reduced to means and materials for the manufacturing process. It was later applied to men who were being reduced to labor power. The ends were "goods," imitations of the products that had always been the ends of the human arts. I shall not generalize too much if I mean by exploitation the reduction of natural goods to means. If I am allowed this usage, I shall be able to penetrate the dark technical phenomenon that Ellul describes. The absorption of men, machines, and materials by technology blots out the intrinsic goods, the ends-in-themselves, of the kingdom of nature, and substitutes for them the quite incommensurable and wayward series of means.

The word *machine* has an instructive history. Originally it meant a tool or instrument in a human art. Separated from the agent and its purpose and attached to a prime mover, it could operate on its own and become an automaton. Abstracted and combined with others, and the ensemble studied for itself, it seemed to take on a macabre life of its own, the Newtonian mechanical universe. Ellul, without being too explicit about it, detects a technique in a human art, abstracts it from its context, combines it with other similarly abstracted techniques, and presents the ensemble as

the technical phenomenon for our and his amazed contemplation. Ellul shows how this concatenation of means has grown, at first gradually by linkages of isolated units, latterly by an apparently built-in acceleration, until it is now unified, all but universal, self-generating, and inherently expansive over all human activity, individual and collective. His most telling observation is that in the system all ends are transformed into means; even the participating human beings are automated links, and their purposes are "values" of the variables in the technical formulas. This means that the technical phenomenon as a whole is a vast system of exploitation without a purpose. The technician who is enthusiastically building and serving the system says that society will eventually see the system and supply the purpose, but Ellul quickly answers that both the technician and society are already built into the system, and the voice of human freedom and responsibility is a programmed voice of the technical ideology.

The American humanistic critic sees this European account as an extrapolation of his own earlier warning of the gradual surrender of human affairs to the machine. He will say that we have justifiably put the nonrational parts of nature under the regime of exploitation for human welfare. This is what man's dominion or control of nature requires. But the realm of human nature must retain its ends and purposes. This is the present position of the traditional natural lawyer, also. The technician shall not pass. But this split in our culture, between material and spiritual, between the materialist and the idealist, between the technical and the cultural, has peculiar consequences. The immediate direct judgment and enjoyment of natural things, both human and nonhuman, are sharply inhibited and redirected. We all note and some of us mourn the drainage of values from work and organization. Some of us used to accept the gray neutrality of means in the lively hope that a better world was in the making. The making of means was the building of the road to a better day; the postponement and projection of ends was required by progress. We had learned the right disciplines and sentiments from theology and economics. But the better day has been coming into view, and we now see that the deferred ends have themselves become means.

In a kind of despair we have increasingly turned to the fine arts, where the bare data of nature are separated off from their sources in nature, are refined and transformed by artifice, combined and represented in theaters, museums, records, and cameras for nothing but the immediate contemplation and enjoyment of their artificial surfaces. The fine artists and the critics join, not always happily, in cults and schools that imitate, sometimes deliberately, the lower practices of pagan and orthodox religions. They also identify the painting, the dance, or the symphony with the beatific vision of an unknown god. The technicians combine these cults and build them into a technical epiphenomenon, the entertainment that eases the surrender of men to the technical system itself. The sign that signifies the takeover of technics is the appearance of massive exploitation in the entertainment or show business, the exploitation of sentiment and frustration in the audience as well as of talent and ambition in the performers.

But there are other cults that organize themselves around isolated remnants of the kingdom of nature, the apostolic lines that originated with naturalists who had literary and artistic gifts, such as Goethe and Leonardo. These original deviants from the dogmas of exploitation have more or less worthy successors, such as Ruskin, Thoreau, Fabre, Kropotkin, and Schweitzer, or even Whitman, Tagore, and Tolstoy. Schweitzer is an interesting case because he has deliberately made connection with those massive primitive and peasant cultures that survive like promontories from continents of tradition where the kingdom of nature has always been taken for granted without benefit of theoretical apology. Systems of medicine based on the Hindu, Chinese, and Malayan respect for life, which includes what we would call inanimate things, are extending our pharmacopoeia as well as our psychiatric lore of images and symbols. These cultures are now passionately responding to the magnetism of the technics of exploitation, and it may be expected that a two-way osmosis between the old and the new kingdoms of nature will take place.

But I am not recommending the cults of the fine arts and the naturalists as methods of research in natural law; they are only occasions for reminding ourselves of lost insights. We presumably have learned the hard way that human beings should not be exploited even with their consent. We have learned that the farming that becomes the quarrying and exhaustion of the soil is not true farming; that the industries that pollute air and water and turn cities into slums are not true industries; that the cities that devastate the countryside and reduce it to desert are not true cities; that the nations that destroy forests to feed smelting furnaces, or a countryside to make roads, or even wildlife to make sport, are not true polities; that even mining, the original occupation that established exploitation, if it exhausts natural resources, is not true mining. Such frustrated human arts do not belong to the kingdom of nature, no matter how well they may serve apparent human goods. The appeal to merely human ends and values does not justify or rationalize them.

We have had a rough history of learning some of these things. As long as our natural resources, so-called, were open to unlimited exploitation by free enterprise, we gradually came to realize not only that beauty was disappearing but that we were using up resources. So there was the conservation movement. Gifford Pinchot and

Theodore Roosevelt were able to isolate and establish national parks, and these have become monuments to the courage of their conviction that exploitation should be limited. But such conservation was relatively empty until it was discovered that the nursing care of national parks had high unintended uses, namely the increase in groundwater and the building of soil. Following this discovery, there now exist tree farms where industrial lumbermen have learned to care for trees and therefore to increase the lumber supply as they pursue the lumber business. This and other similar lessons have now led to long-term planning for the allocation of resources in which the aim of the prudent saving of resources for future use is always combined with the increase and enhancement of nature. Such thinking is perhaps best epitomized in the original act that established the TVA. Its stated purpose was to serve the welfare of the valley, and the purpose was carried out by planning forests, fertilizer plants, soil analysis, and flood control as well as electric power. The welfare of the valley obviously and necessarily includes concern for natural ends, nonhuman as well as human.

Out of this dialectical learning there has developed a new and somewhat mysterious science, ecology. As I understand it, ecology was originally an attempt to collate various lines of linear exploitive planning, such as an industrial firm might practice, to make an integral pattern of the side effects and unintended consequences of procurement, employment, and production. Industrial production in a complex city would present the acute problem. The result of the attempt led to another definition and posing of the problem, namely to conceive the plant as an organism with the city as the environment. Soon it was necessary to conceive the city as an organism with its environment. And so one might go on to national economies and to the world community. This is surreptitious teleological thinking, which, made explicit, would mean that everything in the situa-

tion would be viewed reciprocally with the others as means and ends. Such a conception is the aim of Patrick Geddes and Lewis Mumford when they take the organic view of the neotechnic period in technology. The purpose of the city in the valley would be the enhancement of nature, including human nature, in the valley. Human beings would no longer be exploiting nature or themselves. They would be free citizens in a constitutional kingdom of nature.

Conclusion

The foregoing reconsideration of Kant's ideal of a kingdom of nature persuades me that Jacques Ellul's somewhat puzzling account of technology is the objective description of the pathological result of an epoch of unlimited exploitation in technical development. Under the guidance of a liberal humanism in which men were allowed a teleological understanding of themselves, but nonhuman nature was not so respected, the industrial technological system progressively destroyed its ends, even its minimal human ends, which are often identical with natural ends. This system reduced itself to an automaton that has all but devoured its creators. In the face of this fait accompli, Ellul is daring us to reassert human freedom and responsibility; in other words, to conceive the artificial phenomenon as a kingdom of natural ends.

In an earlier part of this paper, I was summoning courage to answer Ellul by a head-on attack on the methods of the natural and social sciences. This would involve a critical reconsideration of analytic mathematics and some attempt to see through its opaque formulas to essences and substances or some adequate theoretical alternatives. It would in addition require a validation of an objective knowledge of goods as means and ends, perhaps the subjection of the whole technological realm to rational teleological modes of thought. I confess that I am overwhelmed not only by the fact that the current sciences are strongly entrenched in habit and going concerns but also by the enormous intellectual energy and discipline that such a critique would require.

Ellul's descriptive mosaic of the technical phenomenon shows the human arts and human doings in a massive confusion, suffering the contagions and the inversions of means and ends that recall Plato's simpler critique of the arts in Athens. Ellul is saying that we are past the point when this confusion can be brought to terms. But our system is under the test of transplanting itself part by part to undeveloped regions. As this takes place, there will be occasions when it has to be dismantled and partially reassembled, and these occasions will allow the introduction of ecological teleological planning. On these occasions, as if by flashback, we can reassess our mistakes, preeminent among them the regulative idea of unlimited exploitation of nature, the progressive fragmentation of the kingdom of nature. Where the backward peoples have not already been corrupted, there will be opportunities to observe primitive and peasant models of the arts whose ends conform with nature's ends. With proper attention and control, these could become the elements or the building blocks for a true community of means and ends.

But, of course, the chances of rapid further contagion and corruptions of the old and new systems are very great. There must be determined attention and strong control of the process if it is to provide the precious insights that are only suggested by the ecologist and the planner. Americans are afraid that the Communists have the only doctrines and controls that are needed. I am persuaded that neither we nor the Russians at present have such disciplines, and our deficiencies remind me of the Romans and their reliance on law when they came upon similar problems. As I have described them, they were able to understand their laws well enough to extend them to distant and diverse cultures, but still to give the proper measures of support to both local autonomy and total order. They were guided in this by the Stoic distinction between levels and kinds of law—civil, common, and natural. Kant is borrowing heavily from them in his exposition of the kingdom of nature as the substance of the categorical imperative.

I infer from these problems and their archetypes in Hellenic civilization that we need to rise above the clichéd issues of the cold war, that we need to delve deep into the problems that both sides have uncovered, the ordering of a runaway automatic technology, by the discoveries of new liberties under law.

Perhaps the problems can be epitomized and at the same time analyzed in the question of what corporations ought to be chartered and constitutionalized for the development of backward nations. The corporation is the elementary instrument in which technology and law are put to human use in communities that want to be kingdoms of nature. Communities on the periphery of our civilization will not only allow, they will demand the required innovation. When we have done for them we may be able to learn for ourselves. There will then be the occasion to reconsider the state of the intellectual arts that can restore the sciences that minister to rational jurisprudence.

PICTURE CREDITS

THE
GREAT IDEAS

Volumes 1 and 2